D0201941

A
Writer's
Reference

A Writer's Reference

EIGHTH EDITION

Diana Hacker

Nancy Sommers
Harvard University

Contributing ESL Specialist
Kimberli Huster
Robert Morris University

BEDFORD/ST. MARTIN'S
Boston ◆ New York

For Bedford/St. Martin's

Vice President, Editorial, Macmillan Higher Education Humanities: Edwin Hill
Editorial Director, English and Music: Karen S. Henry
Publisher for Composition: Leasa Burton
Executive Editor: Michelle M. Clark
Senior Editors: Barbara G. Flanagan and Mara Weible
Associate Editors: Kylie Paul and Alicia Young
Editorial Assistants: Amanda Legee and Stephanie Thomas
Senior Production Editor: Rosemary R. Jaffe
Production Manager: Joe Ford
Marketing Manager: Emily Rowin
Copy Editor: Linda McLatchie
Indexer: Ellen Kuhl Repetto
Photo Researcher: Sheri Blaney
Senior Art Director: Anna Palchik
Text Design: Claire Seng-Niemoeller
Cover Design: Donna Lee Dennison
Composition: Cenveo Publisher Services
Printing and Binding: RR Donnelley and Sons

Printed in China.

1   0   9   8   7
f   e   d

For information, write: Bedford/St. Martin's, 75 Arlington Street, Boston, MA 02116   (617-399-4000)

ISBN 978-1-319-08353-3 (Student Edition)
ISBN 978-1-4576-8625-2 (Instructor's Edition)

ACKNOWLEDGMENTS

Text acknowledgments and copyrights appear below. Art acknowledgments and copyrights appear on the same page as the selections they cover; these acknowledgments and copyrights constitute an extension of the copyright page. It is a violation of the law to reproduce these selections by any means whatsoever without the written permission of the copyright holder.

Stephen J. Gould, excerpt from "Were Dinosaurs Dumb?" from *Natural History*, 87(5): 9–16. Reprinted by permission of Rhonda R. Shearer.
Dorling Kindersly, excerpt from "Encyclopedia of Fishing." Copyright © Dorling Kindersley Limited, 1994. Reprinted by permission of Penguin Group, Ltd.
Anne and Jack Rudloe, excerpt from "Electric Warfare: The Fish That Kills with Thunderbolts," from *Smithsonian* 24(5): 95–105. Reprinted by permission.
Betsy Taylor, "Big Box Stores Are Bad for Main Street," from *CQ Researcher*, (November 1999). Copyright © 1999 by CQ Press, a division of Sage Publications. Reprinted with permission.
Gary Wills, excerpt from "Two Speeches on Race," originally published in the *New York Review of Books*. Copyright © 2008 by Gary Wills, used by permission of The Wiley Agency, LLC.

Preface for instructors

Dear Colleagues:

As college teachers, we have a far-reaching mission. We prepare students to write for different purposes, for different audiences, and in different genres and media. We show students how to read critically and write effectively, preparing them to join ongoing research conversations as contributors (not just as consumers) of ideas. What we teach is at the very core of students' college experience. For academic success, no skill is more critical than effective writing.

This new edition of *A Writer's Reference* grows out of my thirty years as a writing teacher and from many conversations with college faculty across disciplines. In all these conversations, I hear a similar theme: Writing is the core of a student's success, no matter the field of study. Teachers speak about ambitious assignments to teach students how to think and write clearly and precisely, how to interpret evidence and data, and how to enter research conversations with the requisite skills to manage information and avoid plagiarism. And faculty across disciplines all speak about the need for their students to have a reliable handbook to help them understand the expectations of college writing assignments and succeed as writers.

I wanted the eighth edition to capture the energy and creativity that surround conversations about student writing, wherever they take place, and to provide students with a trusted reference that supports their development as writers. I also wanted the eighth edition to align easily with course goals and program outcomes, so I spent a good deal of time reviewing such documents and talking with faculty about how *A Writer's Reference* can help them meet their goals. We all have high expectations for the writers in our courses; assigning a handbook designed specifically to meet these expectations makes possible both our mission and our students' success.

Paging through *A Writer's Reference*, you'll discover features inspired by my conversations with teachers and students. One such feature is an emphasis on the relationship between reading and writing. Turn to tabbed section A (p. 69) to see new material that helps students read critically and write insightfully, engage with print and multimodal texts, and move beyond summary to analysis. The eighth edition shows students how to read carefully to understand an author's ideas, how to read skeptically to question those ideas, and how to present their own ideas in response.

In developing the eighth edition, I wanted students to have even more tools to support the challenges they face as research writers: turning topics into questions, finding entry points in debates, and evaluating, integrating, and citing sources. In particular, I wanted to help students who are assigned to write an annotated bibliography, a core academic genre. In the eighth edition, students will find five new writing guides, helpful tools that offer step-by-step instruction for completing common college writing assignments, including writing an annotated bibliography.

A goal of the eighth edition was to develop a handbook that saves teachers' time and increases students' learning. I'm happy to say that teaching with *A Writer's Reference* has become easier than ever. The eighth edition is now available with LaunchPad—a system that includes both a print handbook and e-Pages. For the e-Pages, I've written prompts and collaborative activities called "As you write" to help students apply handbook advice to their own drafts and to offer practice with thesis statements, research questions, peer review, and more. The e-Pages also include videos and LearningCurve, game-like adaptive quizzing—all easily assignable. Turn to page xi for more about the media.

As college teachers, we help our students develop as thinkers and writers. I can't imagine work more important than this. Some years ago, a student told me that her first-year writing course encouraged her to become a person with things to say. I love these words and the hope they express that a writing course may have such a sustaining influence on one student's life. I bring certain beliefs to *A Writer's Reference*: that all students will learn to read deeply and write clearly, that they will find in their reading ideas they care about, and that they will write about these ideas with care and depth.

Nancy Sommers

What's new in this edition?

An emphasis on critical reading. Substantially revised material in tabbed section A, "Academic reading, writing, and speaking," emphasizes reading as the foundation of every college research and writing assignment. The handbook offers students a *reading process*, teaching them to read traditional and multimodal texts, research sources, their own work, and the work of their peers critically and reflectively.

Guidelines for active reading

Previewing a written text

- Who is the author? What are the author's credentials?
- What is the author's purpose: To inform? To persuade? To call to action?
- Who is the expected audience?
- When was the text written? Where was it published?
- What kind of text is it: A book? A report? A scholarly article? A policy memo?

Annotating a written text

- What surprises, puzzles, or intrigues you about the text?
- What question does the text attempt to answer?
- What is the author's thesis, or central claim?
- What type of evidence does the author provide to support the thesis? How persuasive is this evidence?

Conversing with a written text

- What are the strengths and limitations of the text?
- Has the author drawn conclusions that you question? Do you have a different interpretation of the evidence?
- Does the text raise questions that it does not answer?
- Does the author consider opposing viewpoints and treat them fairly?

Asking the "So what?" question

- Why does the author's thesis need to be argued, explained, or explored? What's at stake?
- What has the author overlooked in presenting this thesis?

Help with analyzing multimodal texts and composing in new genres. A new chapter about reading and writing about multimodal texts introduces new genres and practical strategies for analyzing these genres. Throughout the book, writing guides give tips for composing college assignments as podcasts, presentations, Web sites, and other alternatives to the traditional essay. New discussions of genre and sample papers in new genres (literacy narrative and reflective letter) align the book more closely with the goals of writing programs and the 2014 Council of Writing Program Administrators (WPA) outcomes.

Paraphrasing sources: strategies for multilingual/ESL writers. New content includes advice about paraphrasing sources effectively. This new section moves students away from the practice of word-by-word substitution and offers strategies for understanding and presenting another writer's meaning.

Practical writing guides. Five new writing guides help students compose common assignments: argument essays, analytical essays, annotated bibliographies, reflective cover letters, and literacy narratives. The guides clarify the expectations of the genre; provide a step-by-step path as students explore, draft, and revise; and lay a foundation for writing in multiple disciplines.

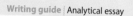

Writing guide | **Analytical essay**

An **analysis** of a text allows you to examine the parts of a text to understand *what* it means and *how* it makes its meaning. Your goal is to offer your judgment of the text and to persuade readers to see it through your analytical perspective. A sample analytical essay begins on page 80.

Key features

- **A careful and critical reading** of a text reveals what the text says, how it works, and what it means. In an analytical essay, you pay attention to the details of the text, especially its thesis and evidence.
- **A thesis that offers a clear judgment** of a text anchors your analysis. Your thesis might be the answer to a question you have posed about a text or the resolution of a problem you have identified in the text.
- **Support for the thesis** comes from evidence in the text. You summarize, paraphrase, and quote passages that support the claims you make about the text.
- **A balance of summary and analysis** helps readers who may not be familiar with the text you are analyzing. Summary answers the question of *what* a text says; an analysis looks at *how* a text makes its point.

Thinking ahead: Presenting and publishing

You may have the opportunity to present or publish your analysis in the form of a multimodal text such as a slide show presentation. Consider how adding images or sound might strengthen your analysis or help you to better reach your audience. (See section A2.)

Writing your analytical essay

○ **EXPLORE**

Generate ideas for your analysis by brainstorming responses to questions such as the following:

- What is the text about?
- What do you find most interesting, surprising, or puzzling about this text?
- What is the author's thesis or central idea? Put the author's thesis to the "So what?" test. (See p. 74.)
- What do your annotations of the text reveal about your response to it?

○ **DRAFT**

- Draft a working thesis to focus your analysis. Remember that your thesis is not the same as the author's thesis. Your thesis presents *your* judgment of the text.
- Draft a plan to organize your paragraphs. Your introductory paragraph will briefly summarize the text and offer your thesis. Your body paragraphs will support your thesis with evidence from the text. Your conclusion will pull together the major points and show the significance of your analysis. (See C1-d.)
- Identify specific words, phrases, and sentences as evidence to support your thesis.

◉ **REVISE**

Ask your reviewers to give you specific comments. You can use the following questions to guide their feedback.

- Is the introduction effective and engaging?
- Is summary balanced with analysis?
- Does the thesis offer a clear judgment of the text?
- What objections might other writers pose to your analysis?
- Is the analysis well organized? Are there clear topic sentences and transitions?
- Is there sufficient evidence? Is the evidence analyzed?
- Have you cited words, phrases, or sentences that are summarized or quoted?

Research and documentation advice fit for any college course. Substantially revised sections teach researchers to find an entry point in a debate and develop authority as a researcher. New advice on writing a research proposal gives practical help that's useful across the curriculum. And because some sources are difficult to cite, new how-to boxes address authorship and new types of sources such as course materials and reposted Web content.

R1-f Write a research proposal.

One effective way to manage your research project and focus your thinking is to write a research proposal. A proposal gives you an opportunity to look back—to remind you why you decided to enter a specific research conversation—and to look forward—to predict any difficulties or obstacles that might arise during your project. Your objective is to make a case for the question you plan to explore, the sources you plan to use, and the feasibility of the project, given the time and resources available. As you take stock of your project, you also have the valuable opportunity to receive comments from your instructor and classmates about your proposed research question and search strategy.

The following format will help you organize your proposal.

New guidelines for speaking effectively. A new section, A5, prepares students to remix, or adapt, their writing for delivery to a live audience, with emphasis on writing for the ear instead of for the eye.

Engaging new media: LaunchPad. *A Writer's Reference* is now available with LaunchPad, which includes a full e-Book that's easy to assign— as well as interactive e-Pages. The e-Pages, online at hackerhandbooks .com/writersref, engage students with writing prompts, scorable practice exercises, additional sample papers, and LearningCurve's game-like adaptive quizzes. Easy-to-spot cross-references on the print pages direct students to the e-Pages content in LaunchPad.

hackerhandbooks.com/writersref
e G5 Sentence fragments > Exercises: G5–3 to G5–7
☑ G5 Sentence fragments > LearningCurve: Sentence fragments

- ***270 practice exercises*** help students build skills and strengthen their editing. The exercises report to a gradebook so you can keep track of progress if you choose.

- *36 "As you write" prompts* encourage students to apply the lessons of the handbook to their own writing. Students complete brief writing assignments about organizing a paper, drafting thesis statements, working with peers, integrating sources, and other writing topics.

- *LearningCurve*, game-like online quizzing for 29 topics, builds confidence with sentence-level skills by adapting to students' responses and adjusting the difficulty level of the quiz items.

- *Easy access.* If you choose to package LaunchPad with the handbook, students simply use the activation code on the access card when they log in for the first time at hackerhandbooks.com /writersref.

What hasn't changed?

- The handbook speaks to everything student writers need. Even the most popular search engines can't give students the confidence that comes with a coherent, authoritative reference that covers the topics they need in a writing course. *A Writer's Reference* supports students as they compose for different purposes and audiences and in a variety of genres and as they collaborate, revise, conduct research, document sources, format their writing, and edit for clarity.

- The handbook is easy to use and easy to understand. The explanations in *A Writer's Reference* are brief, accessible, and illustrated by examples, most by student writers. The book's many charts, checklists, tabs, menus, and directories are designed to help users find what they need quickly. And the user-friendly index includes both expert (*coherence, ellipsis*) and nonexpert (*flow, dots*) terminology.

- The handbook is coherent, authoritative, and trustworthy. Writing-related resources on the Web offer *information*, but they don't offer *instruction*. With the eighth edition of *A Writer's Reference*, students have reference content that has been class-tested by literally millions of students and instructors.

Supplements and media

Visit the catalog page for *A Writer's Reference* for a complete list of instructor supplements, including *Teaching with Hacker Handbooks*, student supplements, videos, e-books (various formats), and other media: macmillanhighered.com/writersref/catalog.

Custom solutions

Many schools opt for a custom edition of *A Writer's Reference*. Some programs choose to add a section about course outcomes and policies; others choose to customize by adding student writing from the school; still others decide simply to change the cover to reflect a recognizable campus location and the school name. More and more programs are creating custom editions by including publisher-supplied content—additional tabbed sections on writing about literature, writing in the disciplines, multimodal writing, ESL support, and support for online learners. To discuss custom options for your school, contact your sales representative or visit macmillanhighered.com/catalog/other/Custom_Solutions.

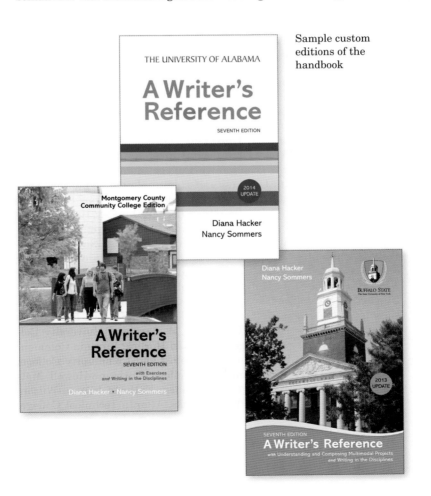

Sample custom editions of the handbook

Acknowledgments

I am grateful, as always, for the expertise, enthusiasm, and classroom experience that so many individuals—our very own handbook community—brought to the eighth edition.

Reviewers

For their participation in a focus group at the 2014 Conference on College Composition and Communication, I would like to thank Holly Bauer, University of California, San Diego; Jason DePolo, North Carolina Agricultural and Technical State University; Violet Dutcher, Eastern Mennonite University; Michael Keller, South Dakota State University; and Katherine Tirabassi, Keene State College.

I thank those instructors who offered detailed feedback on various parts of the handbook and its supplements: Marcia Allen, University of Maryland University College; Clinton Atchley, Henderson State University; Phyllis Benay, Keene State College; Wendy Brooks, Palm Beach State College; Elizabeth Browning, Virginia Western Community College; Barbara Butler, Bellevue College; Juan Calle, Broward College; Sybil Canon, Northwest Mississippi Community College; Margaret Cassidy, Adelphi University; Michele Cheung, University of Southern Maine; Vicky Chiu-Irion, University of Hawaii; Jennifer Condon, Iowa Central Community College; James Crooks, Shasta College; Jill Dahlman, University of Hawaii; Jamie Danielson, Iowa Central Community College; Tommie Delaney, Columbus State University; Susan Denning, Clark College; Larnell Dunkley, Harold Washington College; Denise Engler, American River College; Jessica Farrington, Embry-Riddle Aeronautical University; Jan Geyer, Hudson Valley Community College; Ebony Gibson, Clayton State University; Jessica Gordon, Virginia Commonwealth University; Tarez Samra Graban, Florida State University; Gwendolyn Harold, Clayton State University; Vicki Hendricks, Broward College, South Campus; Judy Hevener, Blue Ridge Community College and Stuarts Draft High School; Daniel Hirschhorn, University of Maryland University College (and Montgomery College); Christian Horlick, Virginia Commonwealth University; Barry House, Lincoln Land Community College; Susan Howard, Ivy Tech Community College; Christine Howell, Metropolitan Community College–Penn Valley; Kathryn Ingram-Wilson, Laredo Community College; Laura Jones, Atlanta Technical College; Terra Kincaid, El Paso Community College; Lola King, Trinity Valley Community College; Guy Krueger, University of Mississippi; Mildred

Landrum-Hesser, Towson University; Denise Marchionda, Middlesex Community College; Gail Marxhausens, Lone Star College CyFair; John McKinnis, Buffalo State College; Kristopher Mecholsky, University of Maryland University College; Terence Meehan, Northern Virginia Community College; Ashley Moorshead, Community College of Aurora; Joseph Nagy, University of California, Los Angeles; Luis Nazario, Pueblo Community College; Barbra Nightingale, Broward College; Shevaun Donelli O'Connell, Buffalo State College; Gary Olson, Bellevue College; MaryGrace Paden, John Tyler Community College; Jessica Parker, Metroplitan State University Denver; Michelle Paulsen, The Victoria College; Philip Peloquin, Ohio Christian University; Neil Plakcy, Broward College; Holland Prior, Azusa Pacific University; Maria Ramos, J. Sargeant Reynolds Community College; Rolando Regino, Moreno Valley College; Joanna Richter, Laredo Community College; Cortney Robbins, Indiana Tech; Sundi Rose-Holt, Columbus State University; Jay Ruzesky, Vancouver Island University; Donna Samet, Broward College; Andrea Laurencell Sheridan, SUNY Orange; Elizabeth Siler, Washington State University; Colleen Soares, University of Hawaii Leeward Community College; Neil Starr, Nova Southeastern University; Debra Stevens, Las Positats College; Patrick Tompkins, John Tyler Community College; David Wood, Northern Michigan University; Pam Wright, University of California, San Diego.

Contributors

I am grateful to the following individuals, fellow teachers of writing, for their smart revisions of important content: Kimberli Huster, ESL specialist at Robert Morris University, updated *Resources for Multilingual Writers and ESL* and wrote new material on paraphrasing sources for the Multilingual section of the handbook; and Sara McCurry, professor of English at Shasta College, revised both *Teaching with Hacker Handbooks* and *Strategies for Online Learners.*

Students

Including sample student writing in each edition of the handbook makes the resource useful for you and your students. I would like to thank the following students who have let us adapt their papers as models: Ned Bishop, Sophie Harba, Sam Jacobs, Luisa Mirano, Michelle Nguyen, Emilia Sanchez, and Ren Yoshida.

Bedford/St. Martin's

A comprehensive handbook is a collaborative writing project, and it is my pleasure to acknowledge and thank the enormously talented Bedford/St. Martin's editorial team, whose deep commitment to students informs each new feature of *A Writer's Reference*. Joan Feinberg, director of digital composition and Diana Hacker's first editor, helped shape the identity of this flagship handbook. Denise Wydra, former vice president for the humanities; Leasa Burton, publisher for composition; and Karen Henry, editorial director for English, have helped guide us with their insights about how the college handbook market is changing and how we can continue to meet the needs of the college writer in the digital age.

Michelle Clark, executive editor, is an author's dream — a treasured friend and colleague and an endless source of creativity and clarity. Michelle combines wisdom with patience, imagination with practicality, and hard work with good cheer. Barbara Flanagan, senior editor, has worked on the Hacker handbooks for more than twenty-five years and brings attention to detail, keen insights, and unrivaled expertise in documentation and media. Mara Weible, senior editor, brings to the eighth edition her teacher's sensibility and superb editorial judgment. Thanks to Kylie Paul, associate editor, for assistance with art and permissions, for managing the review process, and for developing several ancillaries, and to editorial assistants Amanda Legee and Stephanie Thomas, who helped with video content and with our student research project. Many thanks to Rosemary Jaffe, senior production editor, for keeping us on schedule and for producing both the print pages and the e-Pages with unparalleled skill and care. And I am grateful to the media team — Harriet Wald, Rebecca Merrill, Marissa Zanetti, Kimberly Hampton, and Allison Hart — for imagining and producing engaging media for the writing course. Insight from Bedford colleagues Jane Helms, Jimmy Fleming, and Nick Carbone, who, like me, spend many, many hours on the road and in faculty offices, is always treasured. Thanks to Linda McLatchie, copy editor, for her thoroughness and attention to detail; to Claire Seng-Niemoeller, text designer, who crafted another open and beautifully designed edition of the book; to Donna Dennison, art director, who has given the book a strikingly beautiful cover; and to Billy Boardman, design manager, for extending the cover design to our many versions.

Last, but never least, I offer thanks to my own students who, over many years, have shaped my teaching and helped me understand their challenges in becoming college writers. Thanks to my friends and colleagues Suzanne Lane, Maxine Rodburg, Laura Saltz, and Kerry Walk for sustaining conversations about the teaching of writing. And thanks to my family: to Joshua Alper, an attentive reader of life and literature, for his steadfastness across the drafts; to my parents, Walter and Louise Sommers, and my aunt Elsie Adler, who encouraged me to write and set me forth on a career of writing and teaching; to my extended family, Sam, Kate, Ron, Charles Mary, Devin, Demian, Liz, and Alexander, for their good humor and good cheer; and to Rachel and Curran, Alexandra and Brian, witty and wise beyond measure, always generous with their instruction and inspiration in all things that matter. And to Lailah Dragonfly, my granddaughter, thanks for the joy and sweetness you bring to life.

Nancy Sommers

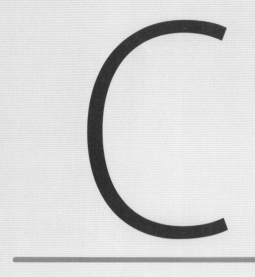

Composing
and Revising

C Composing and Revising

Writing is a process of figuring out what you think, not a matter of recording already developed thoughts. Since it's not possible to think about everything all at once, you will find the process more manageable if you handle a piece of writing in stages. You will generally move from planning to drafting to revising, but as your ideas develop, you will find yourself circling back and returning to earlier stages.

C1 Planning

C1-a Assess the writing situation.

Begin by taking a look at your writing situation. Consider your subject, your purpose, your audience, available sources of information, and any assignment requirements such as genre, length, document design, and deadlines (see the checklist on p. 5). It is likely that you will make final decisions about all of these matters later in the writing process—after a first draft, for example—but you will become a more effective writer if you think about as many of them as possible in advance.

Purpose

In many writing situations, part of your challenge will be determining your purpose, or your reason, for writing. The wording of an assignment may suggest its purpose. If no guidelines are given, you may need to ask yourself, "Why am I communicating with my readers?" or "What do I want to accomplish?" College writers most often write for the following purposes:

to inform	to analyze
to explain	to synthesize
to summarize	to propose
to persuade	to call readers to action
to evaluate	to change attitudes

Audience

Analyzing your audience can often help you determine how to accomplish your purpose—how much detail or explanation to provide, what kind of tone and language to use, and what potential objections to address. The choices you make as you write will tell readers who you think they are (novices or experts, for example) and will show respect for your readers' values and perspectives. The checklist on page 5 includes questions that will help you analyze your audience and develop an effective strategy for reaching your readers.

NOTE: When you write e-mail messages to instructors, classmates, or potential employers, respect your reader by using a concise, meaningful subject line; keeping paragraphs brief and focused; proofreading for careless errors; and paying attention to your tone. Don't write something that you wouldn't feel comfortable saying directly to your reader. Finally, avoid forwarding another person's message without permission.

Genre

Pay close attention to the genre, or type of writing assigned. Each genre is a category of writing meant for a specific purpose and audience—an essay in a writing class, a lab report in a biology class, a policy memo in a criminal justice class, or a case study for an education class. Sometimes the genre is yours to choose, and you need to decide if a particular genre—a poster presentation, an audio essay, a Web page, or a podcast, for example—will help you communicate your purpose and reach readers.

Academic English What counts as good writing varies from culture to culture. In some situations, you will need to become familiar with the writing styles—such as direct or indirect, personal or impersonal, plain or embellished—that are valued by the culture or discipline for which you are writing.

C1-b Experiment with ways to explore your subject.

Instead of plunging into a first draft, experiment with one or more techniques for exploring your subject and discovering your purpose: talking and listening, reading and annotating texts, asking questions, brainstorming, clustering, freewriting, keeping a journal, blogging. Whatever technique you turn to, the goal is the same: to generate ideas that will lead you to a question, a problem, or a topic that you want to explore further.

Talking and listening

Because writing is a process of figuring out what you think about a subject, it can be useful to try out your ideas on other people. Conversation can deepen and refine your ideas even before you begin to draft. By talking and listening to others, you can also discover what they find

hackerhandbooks.com/writersref
e C1 Planning > As you write: Thinking like a college writer
e C1 Planning > As you write: Exploring a subject

Checklist for assessing the writing situation

Subject

- Has the subject been assigned, or are you free to choose your own?
- Why is your subject worth writing about? What questions would you like to explore? How might readers benefit from reading about it?
- Do you need to narrow your subject to a more specific topic (because of length restrictions, for instance)?

Purpose and audience

- Why are you writing: To inform readers? To persuade them? To call them to action? Some combination of these?
- Who are your readers? How well informed are they about the subject?
- Will your readers resist any of your ideas? What possible objections will you need to anticipate and counter?

Genre

- What genre—type of writing—does your assignment require: A report? A proposal? An analysis of data? An essay?
- If the genre is not assigned, what genre is appropriate for your subject, purpose, and audience?
- Does the genre require a specific design format or method of organization?

Sources of information

- Where will your information come from: Reading? Research? Direct observation? Interviews? Questionnaires?
- What type of evidence suits your subject, purpose, audience, and genre?
- What documentation style is required: MLA? APA? CMS (*Chicago*)?

Length and document design

- Do you have length specifications? If not, what length seems appropriate, given your subject, purpose, audience, and genre?
- Is a particular format required? If so, do you have guidelines or examples to consult?
- How might visuals—graphs, tables, images—help you convey information?

Reviewers and deadlines

- Who will be reviewing your draft in progress: Your instructor? A writing tutor? Your classmates?
- What are your deadlines? How much time will you need for the various stages of writing, including proofreading and printing or posting the final draft?

interesting, what they are curious about, and where they disagree with you. If you are planning to develop an argument, you can try it out on listeners with other points of view.

Many writers begin a writing project by debating a point with friends or chatting with an instructor. Others prefer to record themselves talking through their own thoughts. Some writers exchange ideas by sending e-mails or texts or by posting to a blog. You may be encouraged to share ideas with your classmates in an online workshop, where you can begin to refine your thoughts before starting a draft.

Reading and annotating texts

Reading is an important way to deepen your understanding of a topic, learn from the insights and research of others, and expand your perspective. Annotating a text, written or visual, encourages you to read actively—to highlight key concepts, to note possible contradictions in an argument, or to raise questions for further research and investigation.

> **MORE HELP IN YOUR HANDBOOK**
>
> Read critically and take notes before you write.
> - Guidelines for active reading: **A2-a**
> - Taking notes: **R2-c**
> - Analyzing texts: **A1-d**

As you annotate, you record your impressions and begin a conversation with a text and its author. See A1-a for a student's annotations on an assigned article.

Asking questions

When gathering material for a story, journalists routinely ask themselves Who? What? When? Where? Why? and How? These questions help journalists get started and ensure that they will not overlook an important fact.

Whenever you are writing about ideas, events, or people, asking questions is one way to get started. One student, whose topic was the negative reaction in 1915 to D. W. Griffith's silent film *The Birth of a Nation*, began exploring her topic with this set of questions:

Who objected to the film?

What were the objections?

When were the protests first voiced?

Where were protests most strongly expressed?

Why did protesters object to the film?

How did protesters make their views known?

> **MORE HELP IN YOUR HANDBOOK**
>
> Effective college writers begin by asking questions.
> - Asking questions in academic disciplines: **A6-b**

If you are writing in a particular discipline, try to find out which questions its scholars typically explore. Look for clues in assigned readings and class discussions to understand how a discipline's questions help you grasp its concerns and conventions.

Reading an assignment

Determining the purpose of the assignment

The wording of an assignment may suggest its purpose. You might be expected to do one of the following in a college writing assignment:

- summarize information from books, lectures, or research (See A1-c.)
- analyze ideas and concepts (See A1-d.)
- take a position and defend it with evidence (See A4.)
- synthesize (combine ideas from) several sources and create an original argument (See MLA-3c and APA-3c.)

Understanding how to answer an assignment's questions

Many assignments will ask you to answer a *how* or *why* question. You cannot answer such questions using only facts; instead, you will need to take a position. For example, the question "*What* are the survival rates for leukemia patients?" can be answered by reporting facts. The question "*Why* are the survival rates for leukemia patients in one state lower than they are in a neighboring state?" must be answered with both a claim and facts.

If a list of questions appears in the assignment, be careful—instructors rarely expect you to answer all of the questions in order. Look instead for topics or themes that will help you ask your own questions.

Recognizing implied questions

When you are asked to *discuss*, *analyze*, *argue*, or *consider*, your instructor will often expect you to answer a *how or why* question.

Discuss the effects of the No Child Left Behind Act on special education programs.	=	*How* has the No Child Left Behind Act affected special education programs?
Consider the recent rise of attention deficit hyperactivity disorder diagnoses.	=	*Why* are diagnoses of attention deficit hyperactivity disorder rising?

Recognizing disciplinary expectations

When you are asked to write in a specific discipline, pay attention to the genre, or type of writing assigned. Each genre has agreed-upon expectations and disciplinary conventions. Look closely at the key terms of the assignment and know what kinds of evidence and citation style your instructor expects you to use. (See A6.)

Brainstorming

Brainstorming is a good way to figure out what you know and what questions you have. You begin by listing ideas in the order in which they occur to you. Listing ideas can help a writer narrow a subject and identify a position. An early list is often a source of ideas and a springboard to new ideas. Writers can come back to their brainstorming notes and rearrange them, delete some, or add others.

Clustering

Clustering (sometimes called *mapping*) highlights relationships among ideas. To cluster ideas, write your subject in the center of a sheet of paper, draw a circle around it, and surround the circle with related ideas connected to it with lines. If some of the satellite ideas lead to more specific clusters, write them down as well. The writer of this cluster diagram was exploring ideas for an essay on obesity in children.

CLUSTER DIAGRAM

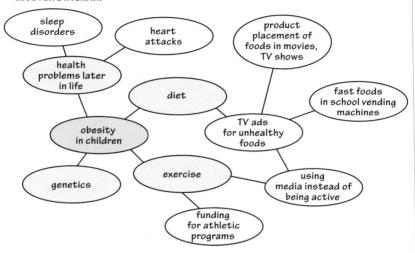

Freewriting

In its purest form, freewriting is simply nonstop writing. You set aside ten minutes or so and write whatever comes to mind, without pausing to think about word choice, spelling, or even meaning. Freewriting lets you ask questions without feeling you have to answer them. Sometimes a question that comes to mind at this stage will point you in an unexpected and productive direction.

To explore ideas on a particular topic, consider using a technique called *focused freewriting*. Again, you write quickly and freely, but this time you focus on a specific subject and pay attention to the connections among your ideas.

Keeping a journal

A journal is a collection of informal, exploratory, sometimes experimental writing. In a journal, often meant for your eyes only, you can take risks. You might freewrite, pose questions, comment on an interesting idea from one of your classes, or keep a list of questions that occur to you while reading. You might imagine a conversation between yourself and your readers or stage a debate to understand opposing positions. A journal can also serve as a sourcebook of ideas for future essays.

Blogging

Although a blog is a type of journal, it is a public writing space rather than a private one. In a blog, you might express opinions, make observations, recap events, play with language, or interpret an image. You can explore an idea for a paper by writing posts from different angles. Since most blogs have a commenting feature, you can create a conversation by inviting readers to give you feedback—ask questions, pose counterarguments, or suggest other sources on a topic.

C1-c Draft and revise a working thesis statement.

For many types of writing, you will be able to assert your central idea in a sentence or two. Such a statement, which ordinarily appears in the opening paragraph of your finished essay, is called a *thesis*.

What makes an effective thesis statement?

A successful thesis statement is a central idea that requires supporting evidence; its scope is appropriate for the assigned length of the essay; and it is focused and specific. A thesis is a promise to readers. It is often one or more of the following:

- your answer to a question you have posed
- the resolution for a problem you have identified
- a statement that announces your position on a debatable topic

Drafting a working thesis

As you explore your topic, you will begin to see possible ways to focus your material. At this point, try to settle on a *tentative* central idea, or working thesis statement. The more complex your topic, the more your focus may change. As your ideas develop, you'll need to revisit your working thesis to see if it represents the position you want to take or if it can be supported by the sources of evidence you have accumulated.

You'll find that the process of answering a question you have posed, resolving a problem you have identified, or taking a position on a debatable topic will focus your thinking and lead you to develop a working thesis. Here, for example, are one student's efforts to pose a question and draft a working thesis for an essay in his ethics course.

QUESTION

Should athletes who enhance their performance through biotechnology be banned from athletic competition?

WORKING THESIS

Athletes who boost their performance through biotechnology should be banned from athletic competition.

The working thesis offers a useful place to start writing—a way to limit the topic and focus a first draft—but it doesn't take into consideration the expectations of readers who will ask "Why?" and "So what?" The student has taken a position—athletes who boost their performance through biotechnology should be banned—but he hasn't answered *why* these athletes should be banned. To fully answer his own question and to claim something specific in his thesis, he might push his own thinking with the word *because*.

> **MORE HELP IN YOUR HANDBOOK**
>
> The thesis statement is central to many types of writing.
>
> ▶ Writing about texts: **A1**
> ▶ Constructing arguments: **A4**
> ▶ Writing research papers: **MLA-1, APA-1**, and **CMS-1**

STRONGER WORKING THESIS

Athletes who boost their performance through steroids should be banned from competition *because* biotechnology gives athletes an unfair advantage and disrupts the sense of fair play.

Revising a working thesis

As you move to a clearer and more specific position you want to take, you'll start to see ways to revise your working thesis. You may find that the evidence you collected supports a different thesis; or you may find that your position has changed as you learned more about your topic.

One effective way to revise a working thesis is to put it to the "So what?" test (see the box on p. 11). Such questions help you keep audience and purpose—and the expectations of your assignment—in mind as you revise.

Using a problem/strategy approach to revise a working thesis

Revising a working thesis is easier if you have a method or an approach. The following problem/strategy approach is an effective way to evaluate and revise a working thesis, especially if you tend to start

Putting your working thesis to the "So what?" test

Use the following questions to help you revise your working thesis.

- Why would readers want to read an essay with this thesis? How would you respond to a reader who hears your thesis and asks "So what?" or "Why does it matter?"
- Does your thesis answer a question, propose a solution to a problem, or take a position in a debate? Why will readers be interested in your answer, solution, or position?
- Will any readers disagree with this thesis? If so, what might they say?
- Is the thesis too obvious? If you cannot come up with interpretations that oppose your own, consider revising your thesis.
- Can you support your thesis with the evidence available?

out with thesis statements that are too factual, too broad, too narrow, or too vague.

A thesis should require proof or further development through facts and details; it cannot itself be a fact or a description.

WORKING THESIS The first polygraph was developed by Dr. John A. Larson in 1921.

PROBLEM The thesis is *too factual.* A reader could not disagree with it or debate it; no further development of this idea is required.

STRATEGY *Enter a debate* by posing a question about your topic that has more than one possible answer. For example: Should the polygraph be used by private employers? Your thesis should be your answer to the question.

REVISED THESIS Because the polygraph has not been proved reliable, even under controlled conditions, its use by private employers should be banned.

A thesis should be an answer to a question, not a question itself.

WORKING THESIS Would John F. Kennedy have continued to escalate the war in Vietnam if he had lived?

PROBLEM The thesis is *a question*, not an answer to a question.

STRATEGY *Take a position* on your topic by answering the question you have posed. Your thesis should be your answer to the question.

REVISED THESIS Although John F. Kennedy sent the first American troops to Vietnam before he died, an analysis of his foreign policy suggests that he would not have escalated the war had he lived.

A thesis should be of sufficient scope for your assignment; it should not be too broad.

WORKING THESIS   Mapping the human genome has many implications for health and science.

> **PROBLEM**   The thesis is *too broad*. Even in a very long research paper, you would not be able to discuss all the implications of mapping the human genome.

> **STRATEGY**   *Focus on a subtopic of your original topic.* Once you have chosen a subtopic, take a position in an ongoing debate and pose a question that has more than one answer. For example: Should people be tested for genetic diseases? Your thesis should be your answer to the question.

REVISED THESIS   Although scientists can now detect genetic predisposition for specific diseases, policymakers should establish clear guidelines about whom to test and under what circumstances.

A thesis also should not be too narrow.

WORKING THESIS   A person who carries a genetic mutation linked to a particular disease might or might not develop that disease.

> **PROBLEM**   The thesis is *too narrow*. It does not suggest any argument or debate about the topic.

> **STRATEGY**   *Identify challenging questions* that readers might ask about your topic. Then pose a question that has more than one answer. For example: Do the risks of genetic testing outweigh its usefulness? Your thesis should be your answer to this question.

REVISED THESIS   Though positive results in a genetic test do not guarantee that the disease will develop, such results can cause psychological trauma; genetic testing should therefore be avoided if possible.

A thesis should be sharply focused, not too vague. Avoid fuzzy, hard-to-define words such as *interesting*, *good*, or *disgusting*.

WORKING THESIS   The Vietnam Veterans Memorial is an interesting structure.

> **PROBLEM**   This thesis is *too fuzzy and unfocused*. It's difficult to define *interesting*, and the sentence doesn't give readers any cues about where the essay is going.

> **STRATEGY**   *Focus your thesis with concrete language and a clear plan.* Pose a question about the topic that has more than one answer. For example: How does the physical structure of the Vietnam Veterans Memorial shape the experience of visitors? Your thesis—your answer to the question—should use specific language.

REVISED THESIS   By inviting visitors to see their own reflections in the wall, the Vietnam Veterans Memorial creates a link between the present and past.

C1-d Draft a plan.

Once you have drafted a working thesis, listing and organizing your supporting ideas can help you figure out how to flesh out the thesis. Creating outlines, whether formal or informal, can help you make sure your writing is focused and logical and can help you identify any gaps in your support.

When to use an informal outline

You might want to sketch an informal outline to see how you will support your thesis and to figure out a tentative structure for your ideas. Informal outlines can take many forms. Perhaps the most common is simply the thesis followed by a list of major ideas.

> Working thesis: *Hunger Games* heroine Katniss Everdeen evolves from a character unable to connect meaningfully with others to one who leads and relies on others, and it is this change that brings about a successful revolution over the Capitol.
> - Disconnecting people from one another is part of a government plan to maintain rule.
> - Katniss remains emotionally disconnected from her own mother after her father's death.
> - Relationships with Rue and Johanna are milestones in Katniss's emotional development.
> - The Mockingjay movement succeeds not because of Katniss's charisma, but because of her ability to stir feelings of hope and connection in the Districts.

If you began by brainstorming a list of ideas, you can turn the list into a rough outline by crossing out some ideas, adding others, and putting the ideas in a logical order.

When to use a formal outline

Early in the writing process, rough outlines have certain advantages: They can be produced quickly, they are obviously tentative, and they can be revised easily. However, a formal outline may be useful later in the writing process, after you have written a rough draft, especially if your topic is complex. It can help you see whether the parts of your essay work together and whether your essay's structure is logical.

The following formal outline brought order to the research paper that appears in MLA-5b, on regulating unhealthy eating. The student's thesis is an important part of the outline. Everything else in the outline supports it, directly or indirectly.

FORMAL OUTLINE

Thesis: In the name of public health and safety, state governments have the responsibility to shape public health policies and to regulate healthy eating choices, especially since doing so offers a potentially large social benefit for a relatively small cost.

I.   Debates surrounding food regulation have a long history in the U.S.

    A.   The 1906 Pure Food and Drug Act guarantees inspection of meat and dairy products.

    B.   Such regulations are considered reasonable because consumers are protected from harm with little cost.

    C.   Consumers consider reasonable regulations to be an important government function to stop harmful items from entering the marketplace.

II.   Even though food meets safety standards, further regulation is needed.

    A.   The typical American diet—processed sugars, fats, and refined flours—is damaging over time.

    B.   Related health problems are diabetes, cancer, and heart problems.

    C.   Passing chronic-disease-related legislation is our single most important public health challenge.

III.   Legislating which foods they can eat is not a popular solution for most Americans.

    A.   A proposed New York City regulation banning the sale of soft drinks greater than twelve ounces failed in 2012, and in California a proposed soda tax failed in 2011.

    B.   Many consumers find such laws to be unreasonable restrictions on freedom of choice.

    C.   Opposition to food and beverage regulation is similar to the opposition to early tobacco legislation; the public views the issue as one of personal responsibility.

    D.   Counterpoint: Freedom of "choice" is a myth; our choices are heavily influenced by marketing.

IV.   The United States has a history of regulating unhealthy behaviors.

    A.   Tobacco-related restrictions faced opposition.

    B.   Seat belt laws are a useful analogy.

    C.   The public seems to support laws that have a good cost-benefit ratio; the cost of food/beverage regulations is low, and most people agree that the benefits would be high.

V.   Americans believe that personal choice is lost when regulations such as taxes and bans are instituted.

    A.   Regulations open up the door to excessive control and interfere with cultural and religious traditions.

B. Counterpoint: Burdens on individual liberty are a reasonable price to pay for large social health benefits.

VI. Public opposition continues to stand in the way of food regulation to promote healthier eating. We must consider whether to allow the costly trend of rising chronic disease to continue in the name of personal choice, or whether we are willing to support the legal changes and public health policies that will reverse that trend.

C2 Drafting

Generally, the introduction to a piece of writing announces the main point; the body develops it, usually in several paragraphs; and the conclusion drives it home. You can begin drafting, however, at any point. If you find it difficult to introduce a paper that you have not yet written, try drafting the body first and saving the introduction for later.

C2-a Draft an introduction.

Your introduction will usually be a paragraph of 50 to 150 words (in a longer paper, it may be more than one paragraph). Perhaps the most common strategy is to open the paragraph with a few sentences that engage the reader and establish your purpose for writing, your central idea. The statement of your main point is called a *thesis*. (See also C1-c.)

In the following introduction, the thesis is highlighted.

> As the United States industrialized in the nineteenth century, using immigrant labor, social concerns took a backseat to the task of building a prosperous nation. The government did not regulate industries and did not provide an effective safety net for the poor or for those who became sick or injured on the job. Immigrants and the poor did have a few advocates, however. Settlement houses such as Hull-House in Chicago provided information, services, and a place for reform-minded individuals to gather and work to improve the conditions of the urban poor. Alice Hamilton was one of these reformers. Her work at Hull-House spanned twenty-two years, and she later expanded her reform work throughout the nation. Hamilton's efforts helped to improve the lives of immigrants and drew attention and respect to the problems and people that until then had been ignored.

> —Laurie McDonough, student

Each sentence leading to your thesis should engage readers by drawing them into the world of the essay and showing them why your essay is worth reading.

Whether you are writing for a scholarly audience, a professional audience, or a general audience, you cannot assume your readers' interest in the topic. The hook should spark curiosity and offer readers a reason to continue.

The following chart provides strategies for drafting an introduction.

Strategies for drafting an introduction

The following strategies can provide a hook for your reader, whether you are composing a traditional essay or a multimodal work such as a slide presentation or a video.

- Offer a startling statistic or an unusual fact
- Ask a question
- Introduce a quotation or a bit of dialogue
- Provide historical background
- Define a term or concept
- Propose a problem, contradiction, or dilemma
- Use a vivid example or image
- Develop an analogy
- Relate an anecdote

Academic English If you come from a culture that prefers an indirect approach in writing, you may feel that asserting a thesis early in an essay sounds unrefined or even rude. In the United States, however, readers appreciate a direct approach; when you state your point as directly as possible, you show that you understand your topic and value your readers' time.

C2-b Draft the body.

The body of your essay develops support for your thesis, so it's important to have at least a working thesis before you start writing. What does your thesis promise readers? What question are you trying to answer? What problem are you trying to solve? What is your position on the topic? Keep these questions in mind as you draft the body of your essay.

Asking questions as you draft

You may already have written an introduction that includes your working thesis. If not, as long as you have a draft thesis, you can begin developing the body and return later to the introduction. If your working thesis suggests a plan or if you have sketched a preliminary outline, try to organize your paragraphs accordingly.

Draft the body of your essay by writing at least one paragraph about each supporting point you listed in the planning stage. As you draft the body, keep asking questions; keep anticipating what your readers may need to know.

For more detailed help with drafting and developing paragraphs, see C5.

USING SOURCES RESPONSIBLY: As you draft, keep careful notes about sources you read and consult. (See R2-c.) If you quote, paraphrase, or summarize a source, include a citation, even in your draft. You will save time and avoid plagiarism if you follow the rules of citation while drafting.

Adding visuals as you draft

As you draft, you may decide that support for your thesis could come from one or more visuals. Visuals can convey information concisely and powerfully. Graphs and tables, for example, can simplify complex numerical information. Images—including photographs and diagrams—often express an idea more vividly than words can. Keep in mind that if you download a visual or use published information to create your own visual, you must credit your source.

Always consider how a visual supports your purpose and how your audience might respond to it. A student writing about the shift from print to online news, for example, used a screen shot of a link embedded in a news article to illustrate a point (see A4-h). Another student, writing about treatments for childhood obesity, created a table to display data she discussed in her paper (see APA-5b).

As you draft, carefully choose visuals to supplement your writing, not to substitute for it. The chart on pages 18–19 describes eight types of visuals and their purposes.

Choosing visuals to suit your purpose

Pie chart

Pie charts compare a part or parts to the whole. Segments of the pie represent percentages of the whole (and always total 100 percent).

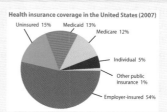

Health insurance coverage in the United States (2007)
- Uninsured 15%
- Medicaid 13%
- Medicare 12%
- Individual 5%
- Other public insurance 1%
- Employer-insured 54%

Bar graph (or line graph)

Bar graphs highlight trends over a period of time or compare numerical data. Line graphs display the same data as bar graphs; the data are graphed as points, and the points are connected with lines.

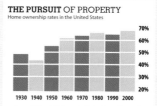

THE PURSUIT OF PROPERTY
Home ownership rates in the United States

1930 1940 1950 1960 1970 1980 1990 2000

Infographic

An infographic presents data in a visually engaging form. The data are usually numerical, as in bar graphs or line graphs, but they are represented by a graphic element instead of by bars or lines.

Just 8% of kids growing up in low-income communities graduate from college by age 24.

Table

Tables display numbers and words in columns and rows. They can be used to organize complicated numerical information into an easily understood format.

Prices of daily doses of AIDS drugs ($US)

Drug	Brazil	Uganda	Côte d'Ivoire	US
3TC (Lamuvidine)	1.56	3.26	2.95	8.70
ddC (Zalcitabine)	0.24	4.17	3.75	8.80
Didanosine	2.04	5.26	3.48	7.25
Efavirenz	6.96	n/a	6.41	13.13
Indinavir	10.32	12.79	9.07	14.93
Nelfinavir	4.14	4.45	4.39	6.47
Nevirapine	5.04	n/a	n/a	8.48
Saquinavir	6.24	7.37	5.52	6.50
Stavudine	0.56	6.19	4.10	9.07
ZDV/3TC	1.44	7.34	n/a	18.78
Zidovudine	1.08	4.34	2.43	10.12

Source: UNAIDS, 2000

Sources [top to bottom]: Kaiser Foundation; US Census Bureau; Data provided courtesy of www.postsecondary.org; UNAIDS.

Photograph

Photographs vividly depict people, scenes, or objects discussed in a text.

Diagram

Diagrams, useful in scientific and technical writing, concisely illustrate processes, structures, or interactions.

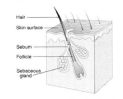

Flowchart

Flowcharts show structures (the hierarchy of employees at a company, for example) or steps in a process and their relation to one another. (See also p. 140 for another example.)

Map

Maps illustrate distances, historical information, or demographics and often use symbols for geographic features and points of interest.

Sources [top to bottom]: "Tornado Touch," photo by Fred Zwicky © 2004. Reprinted by permission of the author. Courtesy of NIAMS Image Gallery; Arizona Board of Regents; Lynn Hunt et al., *The Making of the West.* Copyright © 2005 by Bedford/St. Martin's. Reprinted by permission of Bedford/St. Martin's.

C2-c   Draft a conclusion.

A conclusion should remind readers of the essay's main idea without repeating it. Often the concluding paragraph can be relatively short. By the end of the essay, readers should already understand your main point; your conclusion drives it home and, perhaps, gives readers something more to consider.

To conclude an essay analyzing the shifting roles of women in the military services, one student discusses her topic's implications for society as a whole.

> As the military continues to train women in jobs formerly reserved for men, our understanding of women's roles in society will no doubt continue to change. As news reports of women training for and taking part in combat operations become commonplace, reports of women becoming CEOs, police chiefs, and even president of the United States will cease to surprise us. Or perhaps we have already reached this point.
>
> —Rosa Broderick, student

To make the conclusion memorable and to give a sense of completion, you might include a detail, an example, a quotation, or a statistic from the introduction to bring readers full circle.

Whatever concluding strategy you choose, keep in mind that an effective conclusion is decisive and unapologetic. Avoid introducing completely new ideas at the end of an essay. And because the conclusion is so closely tied to the rest of the essay, be prepared to rework it or replace it as you revise your draft.

Strategies for drafting a conclusion

In addition to echoing your main idea, a conclusion might do any of the following:

- Briefly summarize your essay's key points
- Propose a course of action
- Offer a recommendation
- Discuss the topic's wider significance or implications
- Redefine a key term or concept
- Pose a question for future study

C2-d Manage your files.

Keeping track of all your notes, outlines, and drafts can be challenging. Be sure to give your files distinct names that reflect the appropriate stage of your writing process, and store them in a logical place. Applying the following steps can help you explore drafting and revising possibilities with little risk.

- Create folders and subfolders for each assignment. Save notes, outlines, and drafts together.

- Label revised drafts with different file names and dates.

- Print hard copies, make backup copies, and press the Save button often.

- Always record complete bibliographic information about any sources you might use, including visuals.

- Use a comment function to make notes to yourself or to respond to the drafts of peers.

📁 **YoshidaR English 101 Portfolio**

Address 📁 C:\YoshidaR English 101 Portfolio

Name ▲
📁 Essay 1 - Literacy narrative
📁 Essay 2 - Argument paper
📁 Essay 3 - Ad analysis
📁 Essay 4 - Research paper Navajo art

Address 📁 C:\YoshidaR English 101 Portfolio\Essay 3 - Ad analysis

Name ▲
📄 YoshidaR_AdAnalysis_Draft_10-13-13.docx
📄 YoshidaR_AdAnalysis_EqualExchAd.jpg
📄 YoshidaR_AdAnalysis_FINAL_10-28-13.docx
📄 YoshidaR_AdAnalysis_PeerResponse_10-18-13.docx
📄 YoshidaR_AdAnalysis_Revision1_10-20-13.docx

C3 Reviewing, revising, and editing

Revising is rarely a one-step process. Global matters—thesis, purpose, organization, content, and overall strategy—generally receive attention first. Improvements in sentence structure, word choice, grammar, punctuation, and mechanics usually come later.

As you revise, reach out to instructors, classmates, and writing center tutors to help you review your draft to see what's working and not working. Revising is a lot easier when you seek comments from reviewers who offer suggestions and insights. Simple questions such as "Do you understand my main idea?" and "Is my draft organized?" will help you see your draft through readers' eyes. The checklist for global revision on page 29 may help you and your reviewers get started.

C3-a Develop strategies for revising with comments.

To revise is to *re-see*, and the comments you receive from your reviewers—instructors, peers, and writing center tutors—will help you re-see your draft from your readers' point of view. As you write for college courses, find reviewers and seek their feedback. When you ask readers for their comments, revision becomes a social experience, connecting you with the questions and concerns of readers who help you shape your work in progress.

Sometimes the comments you'll receive are written as shorthand commands—"Be specific!"—and sometimes as questions—"What is your main point?" Such comments don't immediately show you *how* to revise, but they do identify places where global and sentence-level revisions can improve your draft. Sort through the comments you receive with your purpose and audience in mind. And don't hesitate to ask your reviewers to explain their comments if you don't understand them.

You may also want to keep a revising and editing log, a list of the global and sentence-level concerns that come up repeatedly in your reviewers' comments. For instance, if you frequently receive comments such as "Develop more" or "Avoid run-on sentences," you can use these comments to help you learn specific lessons and to transfer your learning from one assignment to the next.

This section addresses common types of comments an instructor, a peer, or a tutor might offer and suggests specific strategies for revising.

hackerhandbooks.com/writersref

e C3 Reviewing, revising, and editing > As you write: Using reviewers' comments

e C3 Reviewing, revising, and editing > As you write: Being a peer reviewer

e C3 Reviewing, revising, and editing > Exercises: C3–1 and C3–2

THE COMMENT: *Narrow your introduction*

SIMILAR COMMENTS: *Unfocused intro • Too broad*

UNDERSTANDING THE COMMENT When readers point out that your introduction needs to be "narrowed," the comment often signals that the beginning sentences of your essay are not specific or focused.

> s even believe that rituals
>
> actions influence the outcome
>
> e fans go beyond cheering, and
>
> ssment, and chanted slurs   Narrow
> your
>
> orts.   introduction

STRATEGIES FOR REVISING

- *Reread your introduction and ask questions.* Are the sentences leading to your thesis specific enough to engage readers and communicate your purpose? Do these sentences lead logically to your thesis? Do they spark your readers' curiosity and offer them a reason to continue reading? (See C2-a.)

- *Try engaging readers with a "hook"* in your introduction—a question, a quotation, or a vivid example. (See p. 16.)

THE COMMENT: *Unclear thesis*

SIMILAR COMMENTS: *Vague thesis • State your position • What is your main point?*

UNDERSTANDING THE COMMENT When readers point out that your thesis is unclear, the comment often signals that they have a hard time identifying your essay's main point.

> the mother or other relatives.
>
> drives to dance lessons,
>
> eball team, hosts birthday
>
> omework help. Do more   Unclear
> thesis
>
> r hinder the development of

STRATEGIES FOR REVISING

- *Ask questions.* What is the thesis, position, or main point of the draft? Can you support it with the available evidence? (See C1-c and MLA-1c.)

- *Reread your entire draft.* Because ideas develop as you write, you may find that your conclusion contains a clearer statement of your main point than does your working thesis. Or you may find your thesis elsewhere in your draft. (See C2-a and C2-c.)

- *Try framing your thesis* as an answer to a question you pose, the resolution of a problem you identify, or a position you take in a debate. And put your thesis to the "So what?" test: Why would a reader be interested in this thesis? (See C1-c.)

THE COMMENT: *Develop more*

SIMILAR COMMENTS: *Undeveloped* • *Give examples* • *Explain*

UNDERSTANDING THE COMMENT   When readers suggest that you "develop more," the comment often signals that you stopped short of providing a full and detailed discussion of your idea.

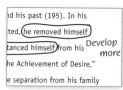

STRATEGIES FOR REVISING

- *Read your paragraph to a peer or a tutor* and ask specific questions. What's missing? Do readers need more background information or examples to understand your point? Do they need more evidence to be convinced? Is it clear what point you're making with your details? **(See A4-d.)**

- *Keep your purpose in mind.* Your assignment probably asks you to do more than summarize sources or list examples and evidence. Make sure you discuss the examples and illustrations you provide and analyze your evidence. **(See A4-e.)**

- *Think about why your main point matters to your readers.* Take another look at your points and support, and answer the "So what?" question. **(See C1-c.)**

THE COMMENT: *Be specific*

SIMILAR COMMENTS: *Need examples* • *Evidence?*

UNDERSTANDING THE COMMENT   When readers say that you need to "be specific," the comment often signals that you could strengthen your writing with additional details.

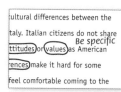

STRATEGIES FOR REVISING

- *Reread your topic sentence* to understand the focus of the paragraph. **(See C5-a.)**

- *Ask questions.* Does the paragraph contain claims that need support? Have you provided evidence—specific examples, vivid details and illustrations, statistics and facts—to help readers understand your ideas and find them persuasive? **(See A4-e.)**

- *Interpret your evidence.* Remember that details and examples don't speak for themselves. You'll need to show readers how evidence supports your claims. **(See A1-d and MLA-3c.)**

THE COMMENT: *Consider opposing viewpoints*

SIMILAR COMMENTS: *What about the other side?* • *Counterargument?*

UNDERSTANDING THE COMMENT When readers suggest that you "consider opposing viewpoints," the comment often signals that you need to recognize and respond to possible objections to your argument.

> ostile work environment
> rchers Shepard and Clifton
> es using drug-testing *Consider*
> ave lower productivity *opposing*
> ve not adopted such *viewpoints*

STRATEGIES FOR REVISING

- *Read more* to learn about the debates surrounding the topic. (See R1.)
- *Ask questions.* Are there other sides to the issue? Would a reasonable person offer an alternative explanation for the evidence or provide counterevidence? (See A3-c and A4-f.)
- *Be open-minded.* Although it might seem illogical to introduce opposing arguments, you'll show your knowledge of the topic by recognizing that not everyone draws the same conclusion. (See A4-f and A4-g.)
- *Introduce and counter objections* with phrases like these: "Some readers might point out that . . ." or "Critics of this view argue that. . . ." (See A4-f.)
- *Revise your thesis,* if necessary, to account for other points of view.

THE COMMENT: *Summarize less, analyze more*

SIMILAR COMMENTS: *Too much summary* • *Show, don't tell* • *Go deeper*

UNDERSTANDING THE COMMENT When readers point out that you need to include more analysis and less summary, the comment often signals that they are looking for your interpretation of the text.

> ages she speaks with
> or example, she speaks
> *Summarize*
> ano Texas Spanish with her *less,*
> *analyze*
> English at school (327). *more*
> r experience with speaking

STRATEGIES FOR REVISING

- *Reread your paragraph and highlight the sentences that summarize.* Then, in a different color, highlight the sentences that contain your analysis. (Summary describes what the text says; analysis offers a judgment or an interpretation of the text.) (See A1-c and A1-d.)

- *Reread the text* (or passages of the text) that you are analyzing. Pay attention to how the language and structure of the text contribute to its meaning. (See A1-a.)

- *Ask questions.* What strategies does the author use, and how do those strategies help convey the author's message? What insights about the text can you share with your readers? How can you deepen your readers' understanding of the author's main points? (See A1-a.)

THE COMMENT: More than one point in this paragraph

SIMILAR COMMENTS: *Unfocused • Lacks unity • Hard to follow*

UNDERSTANDING THE COMMENT When readers tell you that you have "more than one point in this paragraph," the comment often signals that not all sentences in your paragraph support the topic sentence.

> e he believes the social
> omic benefits. Many *More than one point*
> Most important, casino *in this paragraph*
> reas of the state that
> ecent years.

STRATEGIES FOR REVISING

- *Reread your paragraph and ask questions.* What is the main point of the paragraph? Is there a topic sentence that signals to readers what to expect in the rest of the paragraph? Have you included sentences that perhaps belong elsewhere in your draft? (See C5-a.)

- *Revisit your topic sentence.* It should serve as an important sign-post for readers. Make sure that the wording of your topic sentence is precise and that you have enough evidence to support it in the paragraph. (See C5-a.)

THE COMMENT: Cite your sources

SIMILAR COMMENTS: *Source? • Whose words? • Document*

UNDERSTANDING THE COMMENT When readers point out that you need to "cite your sources," the comment often signals that you need to acknowledge and give proper credit to the con-tributions of others.

> end, Edna Pontellier is
> a "naked . . . new-born creature"
> act of ending her own life, *Cite your sources*
> g a kind of rebirth.

STRATEGIES FOR REVISING

- *Reread your sentence and ask questions.* Have you properly acknowledged all the contributions — words, ideas, facts, or visuals—that you use as evidence? Have you given credit to the sources you quote, summarize, or paraphrase? Have you made it clear to readers how to locate the source if they want to consult it? (See MLA-2, APA-2, and CMS-2.)

- *Ask your instructor* which documentation style you are required to use—MLA, APA, or CMS.
- *Revise* by including an in-text citation for any words, ideas, facts, or visuals that you used as evidence—and by including quotation marks around any language borrowed word-for-word from a source. (See MLA-2c, APA-2c and CMS-2c.)
- *Review advice on citing sources.* (See MLA-4, APA-4, and CMS-4.)

Guidelines for peer reviewers

- View yourself as a coach, not a judge. Work with the writer to identify the strengths and limitations of the draft.
- Restate the writer's thesis and main ideas. It helps the writer to know if you understand the main point of the essay.
- Where possible, give specific compliments. Vague comments ("I liked your essay") aren't helpful. What has the writer done well?
- Ask questions about passages that you find confusing or interesting. Doing so provides clues about where to clarify and develop the draft.

Guidelines for using reviewers' comments

- Don't take criticism personally. Your reader is responding to your essay, not to you.
- Pay attention to ideas that contradict your own. Responding to readers' objections instead of dismissing them may make your essay more persuasive.
- Look for global, big-picture concerns. Focus on comments about thesis, organization, and evidence rather than commas and spelling.
- Weigh feedback carefully; sort through the comments with your goals in mind.
- Keep a revision and editing log to note the concerns that come up repeatedly in reviewers' comments.

C3-b   Approach global revision in cycles.

Revising is more effective when you approach it in cycles, rather than attempting to change everything all at once. Keep in mind these four common cycles of global revision: engage the audience, sharpen the focus, improve the organization, and strengthen the content.

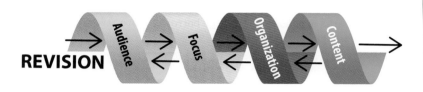

Engaging the audience

Sometimes a rough draft needs an overhaul because it is directed at no particular audience. A good question to ask yourself and your reviewers is the toughest question a reader might ask: "So what?" If your draft can't pass the "So what?" test, you may need to rethink your entire approach.

> **MORE HELP IN YOUR HANDBOOK**
>
> Seeking and using feedback are critical steps in revising a college paper.
>
> ▶ Guidelines for peer reviewers: **page 27**
>
> ▶ Revising with comments: **C3-a**

Sharpening the focus

A clearly focused draft fixes readers' attention on one central idea and does not stray from that idea. You can often sharpen the focus of a draft by clarifying the introduction (especially the thesis) and by deleting any text that is off the point.

Improving the organization

A draft is well organized when its major divisions are logical and easy to follow. To improve the organization of your draft, you may need to take one or more of the following actions: adding or sharpening topic sentences, moving blocks of text, and inserting headings.

Strengthening the content

In reviewing the content of a draft, first consider whether your argument is sound. Second, consider whether you should add or delete any text (sentences or paragraphs). If your purpose is to argue a point, consider how persuasively you have supported your point to an intelligent audience. If your purpose is to inform, be sure that you have presented your ideas clearly and with enough detail to meet your readers' expectations.

Checklist for global revision

Purpose and audience

- Does the draft address a question, a problem, or an issue that readers care about?
- Is the draft appropriate for its audience? Does it account for the audience's knowledge of and possible attitudes toward the subject?

Focus

- Is the thesis clear? Is it prominently placed?
- Does the thesis answer a reader's "So what?" question? (See p. 11.)
- If the draft has no thesis, do you have a good reason for omitting one?

Organization and paragraphing

- Is each paragraph unified around a main point?
- Does each paragraph support and develop the thesis?
- Have you provided enough organizational cues for readers (such as topic sentences or headings)?
- Have you presented ideas in a logical order?

Content

- Is the supporting material relevant and persuasive?
- Which ideas need further development? Have you left your readers with any unanswered questions?
- Are the parts proportioned sensibly? Do major ideas receive enough attention?
- Should you delete any material? Look for redundant or irrelevant information.

Point of view

- Is the dominant point of view—first person (*I* or *we*), second person (*you*), or third person (*he, she, it, one,* or *they*)—appropriate for your purpose and audience? (See S4-a.)

C3-c   Revise and edit sentences.

When you *revise* sentences, you focus on effectiveness; when you *edit*, you check for correctness. Much of this book offers advice on revising sentences for clarity and on editing them for grammar, punctuation, and mechanics.

Some writers handle sentence-level revisions directly at the computer, experimenting on-screen with a variety of possible improvements. Other writers prefer to print out a hard copy of the draft and mark it up before making changes in the file. Here is a rough-draft paragraph as one student edited it on-screen for a variety of sentence-level problems.

Although some cities have found creative ways to improve access to public transportation for passengers with physical disabilities, ~~and to fund other programs, there have been problems in~~ our city has struggled with ~~due to the need to address~~ budget constraints and competing ~~needs~~ priorities. ~~This~~ The budget crunch has led citizens to question how funds are distributed.~~?~~ For example, last year ~~when~~ city officials voted to use available funds to support ~~had to choose between allocating funds for accessible transportation or allocating funds to~~ after-school programs rather than transportation upgrades. ~~, they voted for the after-school programs.~~ It is not clear to some citizens why ~~these~~ after-school programs are more important.

The original paragraph was too wordy, a problem that can be addressed through any number of revisions.

Some of the improvements do not involve choice and must be fixed in any revision. The hyphen in *after-school programs* is necessary; a noun must be substituted for the pronoun *these* in the last sentence; and the question mark in the second sentence must be changed to a period.

Creating a personal editing log

You can use an editing log to keep a personal list of your common errors and learn the rules to correct the errors. To begin your log, review all the grammar, punctuation, and spelling errors identified in your last piece of writing—and then answer the following questions.

- What errors do you make most frequently?
- What pattern do you see in these errors?
- What rule(s) do you need to learn to correct the errors?
- Where in your handbook will you find the rules?

Sample editing log page

Original sentence

Athletes who use any type of biotechnology give themselves an unfair advantage they should be banned from competition.

Edited sentence

Athletes who use any type of biotechnology give themselves an unfair
, and
advantage they should be banned from competition.
^

Rule or pattern applied

To edit a run-on sentence, use a comma and a coordinating conjunction (*and*, *but*, *or*). A Writer's Reference, section G6-a

C3-d Proofread the final manuscript.

After revising and editing, you are ready to prepare the final copy. (See C6 for guidelines.)

Proofreading is a special kind of reading: a slow and methodical search for misspellings, typographical mistakes, and omitted words or word endings. Such errors can be difficult to spot in your own work because you may read what you intended to write, not what is actually on the page. To fight this tendency, try the following tips.

PROOFREADING TIPS

- Remove distractions and allow yourself ten to fifteen minutes of pure concentration; turn off the TV and your cell phone and find a quiet place, away from people who are talking.
- Proofread out loud, articulating each word as it is actually written.
- Proofread your sentences in reverse order.
- Proofread hard copy pages; mistakes can be difficult to catch on-screen.
- Don't rely too heavily on spell checkers and grammar checkers. Before automatically accepting their changes, consider accuracy and appropriateness.
- Ask a volunteer (a friend, roommate, or co-worker) to proofread after you. A second reader may catch something you didn't.

hackerhandbooks.com/writersref
e C3 Reviewing, revising, and editing > As you write: Proofreading your work

Although proofreading may be slow, it is crucial. Errors in an essay can be distracting and annoying. If the writer doesn't care about this piece of writing, the reader might wonder, "Why should I?" A carefully proofread essay, however, sends a positive message: It shows that you value your writing and respect your readers.

C3-e Student writing: Literacy narrative

Student writer Michelle Nguyen wrote the essay "A Place to Begin" (pp. 35–36) in response to an assignment that challenged her to think about how her experiences with writing, positive or negative, have shaped her as a writer. To get started, Nguyen listed various people who had influenced her writing and brainstormed about her experiences in ESL classes. As she reviewed her notes, she realized she wanted to focus her narrative on a single influential individual.

Here is the draft that Nguyen submitted, together with the comments she received from three of her classmates.

ROUGH DRAFT WITH PEER COMMENTS

Rough Draft

My family used to live in the heart of Hanoi, Vietnam. The neighborhood was small but swamped with crime. Drug addicts scoured the alleys and stole the most mundane things—old clothes, worn slippers, even license plates of motorbikes. Like anyone else in Vietnam in the '90s, we struggled with poverty. There was no entertainment device in our house aside from an 11" black-and-white television. Even then, electricity went off for hours on a weekly basis.

I was particularly close to a Vietnam War veteran. My parents were away a lot, so the old man became like a grandfather to me. He taught me how to ride a bicycle, how to read, how to take care of small pets. He worked sporadically from home, fixing bicycle tires and broken pedals. He was a wrinkly old man who didn't talk much. His vocal cords were damaged during the war, and it caused him pain to speak. In a neighborhood full of screaming babies and angry shop owners and slimy criminals, his home was my quiet haven. I could read and write and think and bond with someone whose worldliness came from his wordlessness.

Comment [Alex F]: Add a title to focus readers.

Comment [Brian S]: You have great details here to set the scene in Hanoi, but why does it matter that you didn't have an "entertainment device"? Choose the most interesting among all these details.

Comment [Sameera K]: I really like your introduction. It's so vivid. Think about adding a photo of your neighborhood so readers can relate. What does Hanoi look like?

Comment [Brian S]: Worldliness came from wordlessness — great phrase! Is this part of your main idea? What is your main idea?

The tiny house he lived in stood at the far end of our neighborhood. It always smelled of old clothes and forgotten memories. He was a slight man, but his piercing black eyes retained their intensity even after all these years. He must have made one fierce soldier.

> **Comment [Sameera K]:** You do a good job of showing us why this Vietnam veteran was important to you, but it seems as if this draft is more a story about him than you.

"I almost died once," he said, dusting a picture frame. It was one of those rare instances he ever mentioned his life during the war. As he talked, I perched myself on the side of an armchair, rested my head on my tiny hands, and listened intently. I didn't understand much. I just liked hearing his low, humming voice. The concept of war for me was strictly confined to the classroom, and even then, the details of combat were always murky. The teachers just needed us to know that the communist troops enjoyed a glorious victory.

"I was the only survivor of my unit. 20 guys. All dead within a year. Then they let me go," he said. His voice cracked a little and his eyes misted over as he stared at pictures from his combatant past. "We didn't even live long enough to understand what we were fighting for."

He finished the sentence with a drawn-out sigh, a small set of wrinkles gathering at the end of his eyes. Years later, as I thought about his stories, I started to wonder why he referred to his deceased comrades by the collective pronoun "we." It was as if a little bit of him died on the battlefield with them too.

> **Comment [Alex F]:** I like reading about this man, but I'm not sure what point you are making about literacy. Is the point that writing happens in quiet, not in noise?

Three years after my family left the neighborhood, I learned that the old man became stricken with cancer. When I came home the next summer, I visited his house and sat by his sickbed. His shoulder-length mop of salt and pepper hair now dwarfed his rail-thin figure. We barely exchanged a word. He just held my hands tightly until my mother called for me to leave, his skeletal fingers leaving a mark on my pale palms. Perhaps he was trying to transmit to me some of his worldliness and his wisdom. Perhaps he was telling me to go out into the world and live the free life he never had.

> **Comment [Sameera K]:** I'm curious to hear more about you and why this man was so important to you. What did he teach you about writing? What did he see in you?

> **Comment [Alex F]:** This sentence is confusing. Your draft doesn't seem to be about the selfishness or vanity of writers.

Some people say that writers are selfish and vain. The truth is, I learned to write because it gave me peace in the much too noisy world of my Vietnamese childhood. In the quiet of the old man's house, I gazed out the window, listened to my thoughts, and wrote them down. It all started with a story about a wrinkly Vietnam War veteran who didn't talk much.

> **Comment [Brian S]:** What does "it" refer to? I think you're trying to say something important here, but I'm not sure what it is.

After reading her draft and considering the feedback from her classmates, Nguyen realized that she had chosen a good direction but that she hadn't focused her draft to meet the expectations of the assignment. As her classmates pointed out, her rough draft was more a portrait of the Vietnam War veteran and not really a literacy narrative. With her classmates' questions and suggestions in mind, Nguyen developed some goals for revising her draft.

MICHELLE NGUYEN'S REVISION GOALS

- Add a title.
- Revise introduction to set the scene more dramatically. Use Sameera's idea to include a photo of my Vietnamese neighborhood.
- Make the story my story, not the man's story. What did the man see in me? Delete extra material about the old man.
- Answer Brian's question: What is my main idea?
- Follow Alex's question about the contrast between quiet and noise and Brian's suggestion about the connection between wordlessness and worldliness. Make the contrasts sharper between the noisy neighborhood and the quiet stillness of the man's house.
- Theme about literacy needs to be clearer. Figure out what main idea I'm trying to communicate. The surprise was finding writing in silence, not in the noisy exchange of voices in my neighborhood.

On the following pages is Michelle Nguyen's final draft. For a guide to writing a literacy narrative, see pages 37–38.

hackerhandbooks.com/writersref

🅴 C3 Reviewing, revising, and editing > Sample student writing
  > Nguyen, Rough Draft (literacy narrative; peer-reviewed)
  > Nguyen, "A Place to Begin" (literacy narrative)

Michelle Nguyen

Professor Wilson

English 101

22 September 2013

A Place to Begin

I grew up in the heart of Hanoi, Vietnam—Nhà Dầu—a small but busy neighborhood swamped with crime. Houses, wedged in among cafés and other local businesses (see fig. 1), measured uniformly about 200 square feet, and the walls were so thin that we could hear every heated debate and impassioned disagreement. Drug addicts scoured the vicinity and stole the most mundane things—old clothes, worn slippers, even license plates of motorbikes. It was a neighborhood where dogs howled and kids ran amok and where the earth was always moist and marked with stains. It was the 1990s Vietnam in miniature, with all the turmoil and growing pains of a newly reborn nation.

In a city perpetually inundated with screaming children and slimy criminals, I found my place in the home of a Vietnam War veteran. My parents were away a lot, so the old man became like a grandfather to me. He was a slight man who didn't talk much. His vocal cords had been damaged during the war, and it caused him pain to speak. In his quiet home, I could read and write in the presence of someone whose worldliness grew from his wordlessness.

His tiny house stood at the far end of our neighborhood and always smelled of old clothes and forgotten memories. His wall was plastered with pictures from his combatant past, pictures that told his life story when his own voice couldn't. "I almost died once," he said, dusting a picture frame. It was one of those rare instances he ever mentioned his life during the war.

I perched myself on the side of the armchair, rested my head on my tiny hands, and listened intently. I didn't understand much. I just liked hearing his low, raspy voice.

"I was the only survivor of my unit. Twenty guys. All dead within a year. Then they let me go."

He finished the sentence with a drawn-out sigh, a small set of wrinkles gathering at the corner of his eye.

I wanted to hear the details of that story yet was too afraid to ask. But the bits and pieces I did hear, I wrote down in a notebook. I wanted to

---

Vivid description and concrete details engage the reader.

Narrative is focused on one key story.

A thesis is not always required for a literacy narrative, but Nguyen uses one to capture her main idea.

Nguyen develops her narrative with dialogue.

Nguyen 2

Photograph
conveys physical
details and
provides
authenticity.

Fig. 1. Nhà Dầu neighborhood in Hanoi (personal photograph by author).

make sure that there were not only photos but also written words to bear
witness to the old veteran's existence.

Once, I caught him looking at the jumbled mess of sentences I'd
written. I ran to the table and snatched my notebook, my cheeks warmed
with a bright tinge of pink. I was embarrassed. But mostly, I was terrified
that he'd hate me for stealing his life story and turning it into a collection
of words and characters and ambivalent feelings.

"I'm sorry," I muttered, my gaze drilling a hole into the tiled floor.

Quietly, he peeled the notebook from my fingers and placed it back
on the table.

A dramatic
moment
demonstrates
the relationship
between
Nguyen and
the veteran.

In his muted way, with his mouth barely twisted in a smile, he seemed to
be granting me permission and encouraging me to keep writing. Maybe he saw a
storyteller and a writer in me, a little girl with a pencil and too much free time.

The last time I visited Nhà Dầu was for the veteran's funeral two
years ago. It was a cold November afternoon, but the weather didn't
dampen the usual tumultuous spirit of the neighborhood. I could hear the

Circling back to
the scene from
the first paragraph
gives the narrative
coherence.

jumble of shouting voices and howling dogs, yet it didn't bother me. For
a minute I closed my eyes, remembering myself as a little girl with a big
pencil, gazing out a window and scribbling words in my first notebook.

Many people think that words emerge from words and from the
exchange of voices. Perhaps this is true. But the surprising paradox of
writing for me is that I started to write in the presence of silence. It was
only in the utter stillness of a Vietnam War veteran's house that I could
hear my thoughts for the first time, appreciate language, and find the

Nguyen's main
idea gives the
story its
significance.

confidence to put words on a page. With one notebook and a pencil, and
with the encouragement of a wordless man to tell his story, I began to
write. Sometimes that's all a writer needs, a quiet place to begin.

Writing guide | Literacy narrative

A **literacy narrative** allows you to reflect on key reading or writing experiences and to ask: How have my experiences shaped who I am as a reader or writer? A sample literacy narrative begins on page 35.

Key features

- **A well-told narrative** shows readers what happened. Lively details present the sights, sounds, and smells of the world in which the story takes place. Dialogue and action add interest and energy.

- **A main idea or insight** about reading or writing gives a literacy narrative its significance and transforms it from a personal story to one with larger, universal interest.

- **A well-organized narrative**, like all essays, has a beginning, a middle, and an ending and is focused around a thesis or main idea. Narratives can be written in chronological order, in reverse chronological order, or with a series of flashbacks.

- **First-person point of view (*I*)** gives a narrative immediacy and authenticity. Your voice may be serious or humorous, but it should be appropriate for your main idea.

Thinking ahead: Presenting or publishing

You may have some flexibility in how you present or publish your literacy narrative. If you have the opportunity to submit it as a podcast, video, or another genre, leave time in your schedule for recording or filming. Also, in seeking feedback, ask reviewers to comment on your plans for using sounds or images.

Writing your literacy narrative

◌ EXPLORE

What story will you tell? You can't write about every reading or writing experience or every influential person. Find one interesting experience to focus your narrative. Generate ideas with questions such as the following:

- What challenges have you confronted as a reader or a writer?

- Who were the people who nurtured (or delayed) your reading or writing development?

- What are your best or worst childhood memories of reading or writing?

- What images do you associate with learning to read or write?

- What is significant about the story you want to tell? What larger point do you want readers to take away from your narrative? ➡

○ **DRAFT**

Figure out the best way to tell your story. A narrative isn't a list of "this happened" and then "that happened." It is a focused story with its own logic and order. You don't need to start chronologically. Experiment: What happens if you start in the middle of the story or work in reverse? Try to come up with a tentative organization, and then start to draft.

● **REVISE**

Ask reviewers for specific feedback. Here are some questions to guide their comments:

- What main idea do readers take away from your story? Ask them to summarize this idea in one sentence.
- Is the narrative focused around the main idea?
- Are the details vivid? Sufficient? Where might you convey your story more clearly? Would it help to add dialogue? Would visuals deepen the impact of your story?
- Does your introduction bring readers into the world of your story?
- Does your conclusion provide a sense of the story's importance?

C4 Preparing a portfolio; reflecting on your writing

At the end of the semester, your instructor may ask you to submit a portfolio, or collection, of your writing. A writing portfolio often consists of drafts, revisions, and reflections that demonstrate a writer's thinking and learning processes or that showcase the writer's best work. Your instructor may give you the choice of submitting your portfolio on paper or electronically.

C4-a Understand the benefits of reflection.

Reflection—the process of stepping back periodically to examine your decisions, preferences, strengths, and challenges as a writer—helps you recognize your growth as a writer and is the backbone of portfolio keeping. When you submit your portfolio for a final evaluation or reading, you may be asked to include a reflective opening statement—a cover letter, an introduction, a preface, a memo, or an essay.

Reflective writing allows you to do the following:

- show that you can identify the strengths and weaknesses of your writing
- comment on the progress you've made in the course
- understand your own writing process
- demonstrate that you've made good writing decisions
- comment on how you might use skills developed in your writing course in other courses where writing is assigned

TIP: Save your notes, drafts, and reviewers' comments for possible use in your portfolio. The more you have assembled, the more you have to choose from to represent your best work. Keep your documents organized in a paper or electronic file system for easy access. (See C2-d.)

C4-b Student writing: Reflective letter for a portfolio

Student writer Lucy Bonilla was assigned to submit a portfolio at the end of her writing course. She was asked to include three essays from the semester, with drafts, and to write a cover letter in which she reflected on her growth as a writer. On the following pages is Lucy Bonilla's reflective letter. For a guide to writing a reflective letter, see pages 42–43.

Bonilla 1

December 11, 2013

Professor Todd Andersen

Humanities Department

Johnson State College

Dear Professor Andersen,

      This semester has been more challenging than I had anticipated. I have always been a good writer, but I discovered this semester that I had to stretch myself in ways that weren't always comfortable. I learned that if I wanted to reach my readers, I needed to understand that not everyone sees the world the way I do. I needed to work with my peers and write multiple drafts to understand that a first draft is just a place to start. I have chosen three pieces of writing for my portfolio: "Negi and the Other

→

Reflective writing can take various forms. Bonilla wrote her reflection as a letter.

Reflective writing often calls for first person (I).

Bonilla 2

Bonilla lists the pieces included in her portfolio by title.

Girl: Nicknames and Identity," "School Choice Is a Bad Choice," and "Flat-footed Advertising." Each shows my growth as a writer in different ways, and the final piece was my favorite assignment of the semester.

The peer review sessions that our class held in October helped me with my analytical response paper. My group and I chose to write about "Jíbara," by Esmeralda Santiago, for the Identity unit. My first and second drafts were unfocused. I spent my first draft basically retelling the events of the essay. I think I got stuck doing that because the details of Santiago's essay are so interesting—the biting termites, the burning metal, and the *jíbara* songs on the radio—and because I didn't understand the

Bonilla comments on a specific area of growth.

differences between summary and analysis. My real progress came when I decided to focus the essay on one image—the mirror hanging in Santiago's small house, a mirror that was hung too high for her to look into. Finding a focus helped me move from listing the events of the essay to interpreting those events. I thought my peers would love my first draft, but they found it confusing. Some of their comments were hard to take, but their feedback (and all the peer feedback I received this semester) helped me see my words through a reader's eyes.

Even in the reflective document, Bonilla includes elements of good college writing, such as using transitions.

While my Identity paper shows my struggle with focus, my next paper shows my struggle with argument. For my argument essay, I wrote about charter schools. My position is that the existence of charter schools weakens the quality of public schools. In my first draft, my lines of argument were not in the best order. When I revised, I ended the paper with my most powerful argument: Because they refuse to adopt open enrollment policies and are unwilling to admit students with severe learning or behavior problems, charter schools are elitist. While revising, I also introduced a counterargument in my final draft because our class discussion showed me that many of my peers disagree with me. To persuade them, I needed to address their arguments in favor of charter schools. My essay is stronger because I acknowledged that both the proponents and opponents of abandoning charters want improved education for America's children. It took me a while to understand that including counterarguments would actually make my argument more convincing, especially to readers who don't already agree with me.

Bonilla reflects on how skills from her writing course will carry over to other courses.

Understanding the importance of counterargument helped me with other writing I did in this course, and it will help me in the writing I do for my major, political science.

Bonilla 3

Another stretch for me this semester was seeing visuals as texts that are worth more than a five-second response. The final assignment was my favorite because it involved a number of surprises. I wasn't so much surprised by the idea that ads make arguments because I understand that they are designed to persuade consumers. What was surprising was being able to see all the elements of a visual and write about how they work together to convey a clear message. For my essay "Flat-footed Advertising," I chose the EAS Performance Nutrition ad "The New Theory of Evolution for Women." In my summary of the ad, I noted that the woman who follows the EAS program for twelve weeks and "evolves" is compared to modern humans and our evolution from apes as shown in the classic 1966 *March of Progress* illustration (Howell 41). It was these familiar poses of "Nicolle," the woman in the image, that drew me to study this ad.

In my first draft, I made all of the obvious points, looking only literally at the comparison and almost congratulating the company on such a clever use of a classic scientific drawing. Your comments on my draft were a little unsettling because you asked me "So what?"—why would my ideas matter to a reader? You pushed me to consider the ad's assumptions and to question the meaning of the word *evolve*. In my revised essay, I argue that even though Nicolle is portrayed as powerful, satisfied, and "fully evolved," the EAS ad campaign rests on the assumption that performance is best measured by physical milestones. In the end, an ad that is meant to pay homage to woman's strength is in fact demeaning. My essay evolved from draft to draft because I allowed my thinking to change and develop as I revised. I've never revised as much as I did with this final assignment. I actually cared about this essay, and I wanted to show my readers why my argument mattered.

Bonilla mentions how comments on her draft helped her revise.

The expectations for college writing are different from those for high school writing. I believe that my portfolio pieces show that I finished this course as a stronger writer. I have learned to take risks in my writing and to use the feedback from you and my peers, and now I know how to acknowledge the points of view of my audience to be more persuasive. I'm glad to have had the chance to write a reflection at the end of the course. I hope you enjoy reading this portfolio and seeing the evolution of my work this semester.

In her conclusion, Bonilla summarizes her growth in the course.

Sincerely,

Lucy Bonilla

Lucy Bonilla

A **reflective letter** gives you an opportunity to introduce yourself as a writer, to show your progress and key decisions, and to introduce the contents of a portfolio. A sample reflective letter begins on page 39.

Key features

- **First-person perspective (*I*)** gives a reflective statement its individuality and authenticity. You are the writer; you are introducing your work and explaining your choices.

- **A thoughtful tone** shows you examining and learning from your experiences and evaluating your strengths and limitations as a writer. Your honest assessment of your work shows that you are a trustworthy and sincere interpreter of your progress.

- **A focused opening statement** provides readers with specific details to understand the contents and organization of your portfolio.

- **Acknowledgment** of the assistance you received shows that you are responsible to readers and reviewers.

Thinking ahead: Presenting or publishing

You may have some flexibility in how you present or publish a reflective piece for your portfolio. Some instructors require a formal essay; others may ask for a letter. Still others may invite you to submit an audio file. If you are submitting an e-portfolio, chances are that your instructor will require your reflective statement in digital form. If you're publishing for the Web, you may want to insert headings for easier navigation.

Writing your reflective letter

⬭ EXPLORE

Generate ideas by brainstorming responses to questions such as the following:

- Which piece of writing is your best entry? What does it illustrate about you as a writer, student, or researcher?

- How do the selections in your portfolio illustrate your strengths or challenges?

- What do you learn about your development when you compare your early drafts with your final drafts?

- What do your drafts reveal about your revision process? Examine in detail the revisions you made to one key piece and the changes you want readers to notice.

- How will you use the skills and experiences from your writing course in future courses?

○ **DRAFT**

Follow the guidelines given for the form of your reflective statement — an essay, a cover letter, a memo — and focus your reflections to avoid a list-like structure. Experiment with headings and various chronological or thematic groupings. Ask: What have I learned — and how?

● **REVISE**

Ask reviewers for specific feedback. Here are some questions to guide their comments:

- What major idea do readers take away from your reflective statement? Can they summarize it in one sentence?

- Where in your piece do readers want more reflection and more detailed explanations?

- Is your reflective statement focused and organized?

- Have you used specific passages from drafts, feedback, or other documents from your portfolio to illustrate your reflections?

- Have you explained how you will apply what you learned to future writing assignments?

- What added details might give readers a fuller perspective of your development and your accomplishments in the course?

C5 Writing paragraphs

Except for special-purpose paragraphs, such as introductions and conclusions (see C2-a and C2-c), paragraphs are clusters of information supporting an essay's main point (or advancing a story's action). Aim for paragraphs that are clearly focused, well developed, organized, coherent, and neither too long nor too short for easy reading.

C5-a Focus on a main point.

A paragraph should be unified around a main point. The main point should be clear to readers, and every sentence in the paragraph should relate to it.

hackerhandbooks.com/writersref

- C5 Writing paragraphs > As you write: Creating unity
- C5 Writing paragraphs > Exercises: C5–2
- ✓ C5 Writing paragraphs > LearningCurve: Topics and main ideas
- ✓ C5 Writing paragraphs > LearningCurve: Topic sentences and supporting details

Stating the main point in a topic sentence

As readers move into a paragraph, they need to know where they are—in relation to the whole essay—and what to expect in the sentences to come. A good topic sentence, a one-sentence summary of the paragraph's main point, acts as a signpost pointing in two directions: backward toward the thesis of the essay and forward toward the body of the paragraph. Usually the topic sentence (highlighted in the following example) comes first in the paragraph.

> All living creatures manage some form of communication. The dance patterns of bees in their hive help to point the way to distant flower fields or announce successful foraging. Male stickleback fish regularly swim upside-down to indicate outrage in a courtship contest. Male deer and lemurs mark territorial ownership by rubbing their own body secretions on boundary stones or trees. Everyone has seen a frightened dog put his tail between his legs and run in panic. We, too, use gestures, expressions, postures, and movement to give our words point.
>
> —Olivia Vlahos, *Human Beginnings*

In college writing, topic sentences are often necessary for advancing or clarifying the lines of an argument or reporting the research in a field. In business writing, topic sentences (along with headings) are essential because readers often scan for information and summary statements. Sometimes the topic sentence is introduced by a transitional sentence linking the paragraph to earlier material, and occasionally the topic sentence is withheld until the end of the paragraph.

> **MORE HELP IN YOUR HANDBOOK**
>
> Topic sentences let your reader know how a body paragraph relates to your essay's thesis.
>
> ▶ Effective thesis statements: **C1-c**

Sticking to the point

Sentences that do not support the topic sentence destroy the unity of a paragraph. If the paragraph is otherwise focused, such sentences can simply be deleted or perhaps moved elsewhere. In the following paragraph describing the inadequate facilities in a high school, the information about the chemistry instructor (highlighted) is clearly off the point.

> As the result of tax cuts, the educational facilities of Lincoln High School have reached an all-time low. Some of the books date back to 1990 and have long since shed their covers. The few computers in working order must share one printer. The lack of lab equipment makes it necessary for four or five students to work at one table, with most watching rather than performing experiments. Also, the chemistry instructor left to have a baby at the beginning of the semester, and most of the students don't like the substitute.

As for the furniture, many of the upright chairs have become recliners, and the desk legs are so unbalanced that they play seesaw on the floor.

Sometimes the solution for a disunified paragraph is not as simple as deleting or moving material. Writers often wander into uncharted territory because they cannot think of enough evidence to support a topic sentence. Feeling that it is too soon to break into a new paragraph, they move on to new ideas for which they have not prepared the reader. When this happens, the writer is faced with a choice: Either find more evidence to support the topic sentence or adjust the topic sentence to mesh with the evidence that is available.

C5-b Develop the main point.

Though an occasional short paragraph is fine, particularly if it functions as a transition or emphasizes a point, a series of brief paragraphs suggests inadequate development. How much development is enough? That varies, depending on the writer's purpose and audience.

For example, when health columnist Jane Brody wrote a paragraph attempting to convince readers that it is impossible to lose fat quickly, she knew that she would have to present a great deal of evidence because many dieters want to believe the opposite. She did *not* write only the following:

> When you think about it, it's impossible to lose — as many diets suggest — 10 pounds of *fat* in ten days, even on a total fast. Even a moderately active person cannot lose so much weight so fast. A less active person hasn't a prayer.

This three-sentence paragraph is too skimpy to be convincing. But the paragraph that Brody did write contains enough evidence to convince even skeptical readers.

> When you think about it, it's impossible to lose — as many . . . diets suggest — 10 pounds of *fat* in ten days, even on a total fast. A pound of body fat represents 3,500 calories. To lose 1 pound of fat, you must expend 3,500 more calories than you consume. Let's say you weigh 170 pounds and, as a moderately active person, you burn 2,500 calories a day. If your diet contains only 1,500 calories, you'd have an energy deficit of 1,000 calories a day. In a week's time that would add up to a 7,000-calorie deficit, or 2 pounds of real fat. In ten days, the accumulated deficit would represent nearly 3 pounds of lost body fat. Even if you ate nothing at all for ten days and maintained your usual level of activity, your caloric deficit would add up to 25,000 calories. . . . At 3,500 calories per pound of fat, that's still only 7 pounds of lost fat.

> —Jane Brody, *Jane Brody's Nutrition Book*

C5-c　Choose a suitable pattern of organization.

Although paragraphs (and indeed whole essays) may be patterned in any number of ways, certain patterns of organization occur frequently, either alone or in combination:

- examples and illustrations (p. 46)
- narration (p. 47)
- description (p. 47)
- process (p. 48)
- comparison and contrast (p. 48)
- analogy (p. 49)
- cause and effect (p. 49)
- classification and division (p. 50)
- definition (p. 51)

These patterns (sometimes called *methods of development*) have different uses, depending on the writer's subject and purpose.

Examples and illustrations

Providing examples, perhaps the most common method of development, is appropriate whenever the reader might be tempted to ask, "For example?"

> Normally my parents abided scrupulously by "The Budget," but several times a year Dad would dip into his battered black strongbox and splurge on some irrational, totally satisfying luxury. Once he bought over a hundred comic books at a flea market, doled out to us thereafter at the tantalizing rate of two a week. He always got a whole flat of pansies, Mom's favorite flower, for us to give her on Mother's Day. One day a boy stopped at our house selling fifty-cent raffle tickets on a sailboat, and Dad bought every ticket the boy had left—three books' worth.
>
> —Connie Hailey, student

Illustrations are extended examples, frequently presented in story form. When well selected, they can be a vivid and effective means of developing a point.

> Part of [Harriet Tubman's] strategy of conducting was, as in all battle-field operations, the knowledge of how and when to retreat. Numerous allusions have been made to her moves when she suspected that she was in danger. When she feared the party was closely pursued, she would take it for a time on a train southward

bound. No one seeing Negroes going in this direction would for an instant suppose them to be fugitives. Once on her return she was at a railroad station. She saw some men reading a poster and she heard one of them reading it aloud. It was a description of her, offering a reward for her capture. She took a southbound train to avert suspicion. At another time when Harriet heard men talking about her, she pretended to read a book which she carried. One man remarked, "This can't be the woman. The one we want can't read or write." Harriet devoutly hoped the book was right side up.

—Earl Conrad, *Harriet Tubman*

Narration

A paragraph of narration tells a story or part of a story. The following paragraph recounts one of the author's experiences in the African wild.

One evening when I was wading in the shallows of the lake to pass a rocky outcrop, I suddenly stopped dead as I saw the sinuous black body of a snake in the water. It was all of six feet long, and from the slight hood and the dark stripes at the back of the neck I knew it to be a Storm's water cobra—a deadly reptile for the bite of which there was, at that time, no serum. As I stared at it an incoming wave gently deposited part of its body on one of my feet. I remained motionless, not even breathing, until the wave rolled back into the lake, drawing the snake with it. Then I leaped out of the water as fast as I could, my heart hammering.

—Jane Goodall, *In the Shadow of Man*

Description

A descriptive paragraph sketches a portrait of a person, place, or thing by using concrete and specific details that appeal to one or more of the senses—sight, sound, smell, taste, and touch. Consider, for example, the following description of the grasshopper invasions that devastated the midwestern landscape in the late 1860s.

They came like dive bombers out of the west. They came by the millions with the rustle of their wings roaring overhead. They came in waves, like the rolls of the sea, descending with a terrifying speed, breaking now and again like a mighty surf. They came with the force of a williwaw and they formed a huge, ominous, dark brown cloud that eclipsed the sun. They dipped and touched earth, hitting objects and people like hailstones. But they were not hail. These were *live* demons. They popped, snapped, crackled, and roared. They were dark brown, an inch or longer in length, plump in the middle and tapered at the ends. They had transparent wings, slender legs, and two black eyes that flashed with a fierce intelligence.

—Eugene Boe, "Pioneers to Eternity"

Process

A process paragraph is structured in chronological order. A writer may choose this pattern either to describe how something is made or done or to explain to readers, step by step, how to do something. The following paragraph explains how to perform a "roll cast," a popular fly-fishing technique.

> Begin by taking up a suitable stance, with one foot slightly in front of the other and the rod pointing down the line. Then begin a smooth, steady draw, raising your rod hand to just above shoulder height and lifting the rod to the 10:30 or 11:00 position. This steady draw allows a loop of line to form between the rod top and the water. While the line is still moving, raise the rod slightly, then punch it rapidly forward and down. The rod is now flexed and under maximum compression, and the line follows its path, bellying out slightly behind you and coming off the water close to your feet. As you power the rod down through the 3:00 position, the belly of line will roll forward. Follow through smoothly so that the line unfolds and straightens above the water.
>
> — *The Dorling Kindersley Encyclopedia of Fishing*

Comparison and contrast

To compare two subjects is to draw attention to their similarities, although the word *compare* also has a broader meaning that includes a consideration of differences. To contrast is to focus only on differences.

Whether a paragraph stresses similarities or differences, it may be patterned in one of two ways. The two subjects may be presented one at a time, as in the following paragraph of contrast.

> So Grant and Lee were in complete contrast, representing two diametrically opposed elements in American life. Grant was the modern man emerging; beyond him, ready to come on the stage, was the great age of steel and machinery, of crowded cities and a restless, burgeoning vitality. Lee might have ridden down from the old age of chivalry, lance in hand, silken banner fluttering over his head. Each man was the perfect champion of his cause, drawing both his strengths and his weaknesses from the people he led.
>
> — Bruce Catton, "Grant and Lee: A Study in Contrasts"

Or a paragraph may proceed point by point, treating the two subjects together, one aspect at a time. The following paragraph uses the point-by-point method to contrast speeches given by Abraham Lincoln in 1860 and Barack Obama in 2008.

> Two men, two speeches. The men, both lawyers, both from Illinois, were seeking the presidency, despite what seemed their

crippling connection with extremists. Each was young by modern standards for a president. Abraham Lincoln had turned fifty-one just five days before delivering his speech. Barack Obama was forty-six when he gave his. Their political experience was mainly provincial, in the Illinois legislature for both of them, and they had received little exposure at the national level—two years in the House of Representatives for Lincoln, four years in the Senate for Obama. Yet each was seeking his party's nomination against a New York senator of longer standing and greater prior reputation—Lincoln against Senator William Seward, Obama against Senator Hillary Clinton. They were both known for having opposed an initially popular war—Lincoln against President Polk's Mexican War, raised on the basis of a fictitious provocation; Obama against President Bush's Iraq War, launched on false claims that Saddam Hussein possessed WMDs [weapons of mass destruction] and had made an alliance with Osama bin Laden.

—Garry Wills, "Two Speeches on Race"

Analogy

Analogies draw comparisons between items that appear to have little in common. Writers can use analogies to make something abstract or unfamiliar easier to grasp or to provoke fresh thoughts about a common subject. In the following paragraph, physician Lewis Thomas draws an analogy between the behavior of ants and that of humans.

Ants are so much like human beings as to be an embarrassment. They farm fungi, raise aphids as livestock, launch armies into wars, use chemical sprays to alarm and confuse enemies, capture slaves. The families of weaver ants engage in child labor, holding their larvae like shuttles to spin out the thread that sews the leaves together for their fungus gardens. They exchange information ceaselessly. They do everything but watch television.

—Lewis Thomas, "On Societies as Organisms"

Cause and effect

A paragraph may move from cause to effects or from an effect to its causes. The topic sentence in the following paragraph mentions an effect; the rest of the paragraph lists several causes.

The fantastic water clarity of the Mount Gambier sinkholes results from several factors. The holes are fed from aquifers holding rainwater that fell decades—even centuries—ago, and that has been filtered through miles of limestone. The high level of calcium that limestone adds causes the silty detritus from dead plants and animals to cling together and settle quickly to the bottom. Abundant bottom vegetation in the shallow sinkholes also helps bind the silt. And the rapid turnover of water prohibits stagnation.

—Hillary Hauser, "Exploring a Sunken Realm in Australia"

Classification and division

Classification is the grouping of items into categories according to some consistent principle. The following paragraph classifies species of electric fish.

Scientists sort electric fishes into three categories. The first comprises the strongly electric species like the marine electric rays or the freshwater African electric catfish and South American electric eel. Known since the dawn of history, these deliver a punch strong enough to stun a human. In recent years, biologists have focused on a second category: weakly electric fish in the South American and African rivers that use tiny voltages for communication and navigation. The third group contains sharks, nonelectric rays, and catfish, which do not emit a field but possess sensors that enable them to detect the minute amounts of electricity that leak out of other organisms.

— Anne and Jack Rudloe, "Electric Warfare: The Fish That Kill with Thunderbolts"

Division takes one item and divides it into parts. As with classification, division should be made according to some consistent principle. The following paragraph describes the components that make up a baseball.

Like the game itself, a baseball is composed of many layers. One of the delicious joys of childhood is to take apart a baseball and examine the wonders within. You begin by removing the red cotton thread and peeling off the leather cover—which comes from the hide of a Holstein cow and has been tanned, cut, printed, and punched with holes. Beneath the cover is a thin layer of cotton string, followed by several hundred yards of woolen yarn, which makes up the bulk of the ball. Finally, in the middle is a rubber ball, or "pill," which is a little smaller than a golf ball. Slice into the rubber and you'll find the ball's heart—a cork core. The cork is from Portugal, the rubber from southeast Asia, the covers are American, and the balls are assembled in Costa Rica.

—Dan Gutman, *The Way Baseball Works*

Definition

A definition puts a word or concept into a general class and then provides enough details to distinguish it from other members in the same class. In the following paragraph, the writer defines *envy* as a special kind of desire.

> Envy is so integral and so painful a part of what animates behavior in market societies that many people have forgotten the full meaning of the word, simplifying it into one of the synonyms of desire. It is that, which may be why it flourishes in market societies: democracies of desire, they might be called, with money for ballots, stuffing permitted. But envy is more or less than desire. It begins with an almost frantic sense of emptiness inside oneself, as if the pump of one's heart were sucking on air. One has to be blind to perceive the emptiness, of course, but that's just what envy is, a selective blindness. *Invidia*, Latin for envy, translates as "non-sight," and Dante has the envious plodding along under cloaks of lead, their eyes sewn shut with leaden wire. What they are blind to is what they have, God-given and humanly nurtured, in themselves.
>
> —Nelson W. Aldrich Jr., *Old Money*

C5-d Make paragraphs coherent.

When sentences and paragraphs flow from one to another without bumps, gaps, or shifts, they are said to be coherent. Coherence can be improved by strengthening the ties between old information and new.

Linking ideas clearly

Readers expect to learn a paragraph's main point in a topic sentence early in the paragraph. Then, as they move into the body of the paragraph, they expect to encounter specific details, facts, or examples that support the topic sentence—either directly or indirectly. In the following paragraph, all of the sentences following the topic sentence directly support it.

> A passenger list of the early years [of the Orient Express] would read like a *Who's Who of the World*, from art to politics. Sarah Bernhardt and her Italian counterpart Eleonora Duse used the train to thrill the stages of Europe. For musicians there were Toscanini and Mahler. Dancers Nijinsky and Pavlova were there, while lesser performers like Harry Houdini and the girls of the Ziegfeld Follies also rode the rails. Violinists were allowed to practice on the train, and occasionally one might see trapeze artists hanging like bats from the baggage racks.
>
> —Barnaby Conrad III, "Train of Kings"

If a sentence does not support the topic sentence directly, readers expect it to support another sentence in the paragraph and therefore to support the topic sentence indirectly. The following paragraph begins with a topic sentence. The highlighted sentences are direct supports, and the rest of the sentences are indirect supports.

> Though the open-space classroom works for many children, it is not practical for my son, David. First, David is hyperactive. When he was placed in an open-space classroom, he became distracted and confused. He was tempted to watch the movement going on around him instead of concentrating on his own work. Second, David has a tendency to transpose letters and numbers, a tendency that can be overcome only by individual attention from the instructor. In the open classroom, he was moved from teacher to teacher, with each one responsible for a different subject. No single teacher worked with David long enough to diagnose the problem, let alone help him with it. Finally, David is not a highly motivated learner. In the open classroom, he was graded "at his own level," not by criteria for a certain grade. He could receive a B in reading and still be a grade level behind, because he was doing satisfactory work "at his own level."

> — Margaret Smith, student

Repeating key words

Repetition of key words is an important technique for gaining coherence. To prevent repetitions from becoming dull, you can use variations of the key word (*hike, hiker, hiking*), pronouns referring to the word (*gamblers . . . they*), and synonyms (*run, spring, race, dash*). In the following paragraph describing plots among indentured servants in the seventeenth century, historian Richard Hofstadter binds sentences together by repeating the key word *plots* and echoing it with a variety of synonyms (which are highlighted).

> Plots hatched by several servants to run away together occurred mostly in the plantation colonies, and the few recorded servant uprisings were entirely limited to those colonies. Virginia had been forced from its very earliest years to take stringent steps against mutinous plots, and severe punishments for such behavior were recorded. Most servant plots occurred in the seventeenth century: a contemplated uprising was nipped in the bud in York County in 1661; apparently led by some left-wing offshoots of the Great Rebellion, servants plotted an insurrection in Gloucester County in 1663, and four leaders were condemned and executed; some discontented servants apparently joined Bacon's Rebellion in the 1670's. In the

1680's the planters became newly apprehensive of discontent among the servants "owing to their great necessities and want of clothes," and it was feared they would rise up and plunder the storehouses and ships; in 1682 there were plant-cutting riots in which servants and laborers, as well as some planters, took part.

—Richard Hofstadter, *America at 1750*

Using parallel structures

Parallel structures are frequently used within sentences to underscore the similarity of ideas (see S1). They may also be used to bind together a series of sentences expressing similar information. In the following passage describing folk beliefs, anthropologist Margaret Mead presents similar information in parallel grammatical form.

Actually, almost every day, even in the most sophisticated home, something is likely to happen that evokes the memory of some old folk belief. The salt spills. A knife falls to the floor. Your nose tickles. Then perhaps, with a slightly embarrassed smile, the person who spilled the salt tosses a pinch over his left shoulder. Or someone recites the old rhyme, "Knife falls, gentleman calls." Or as you rub your nose you think, That means a letter. I wonder who's writing?

—Margaret Mead, "New Superstitions for Old"

Maintaining consistency

Coherence suffers whenever a draft shifts confusingly from one point of view to another or from one verb tense to another. In addition, coherence can suffer when new information is introduced with the subject of each sentence. For advice on avoiding shifts, see S4.

Providing transitions

Transitions are bridges between what has been read and what is about to be read. Transitions help readers move from sentence to sentence; they also alert readers to more global connections of ideas—those between paragraphs or even larger blocks of text.

SENTENCE-LEVEL TRANSITIONS Certain words and phrases signal connections between (or within) sentences. Frequently used transitions are included in the chart on page 55.

---

hackerhandbooks.com/writersref

e C5 Writing paragraphs > As you write: Using transitions

e C5 Writing paragraphs > Exercises: C5–3

Skilled writers use transitional expressions with care, making sure, for example, not to use *consequently* when *also* would be more precise. They are also careful to select transitions with an appropriate tone, perhaps preferring *so* to *thus* in an informal piece, *in summary* to *in short* for a scholarly essay.

In the following paragraph, an excerpt from an argument that dinosaurs had the "'right-sized' brains for reptiles of their body size," biologist Stephen Jay Gould uses transitions (highlighted) to guide readers from one idea to the next.

> I don't wish to deny that the flattened, minuscule head of large bodied Stegosaurus houses little brain from our subjective, top-heavy perspective, but I do wish to assert that we should not expect more of the beast. First of all, large animals have relatively smaller brains than related, small animals. The correlation of brain size with body size among kindred animals (all reptiles, all mammals, for example) is remarkably regular. As we move from small to large animals, from mice to elephants or small lizards to Komodo dragons, brain size increases, but not so fast as body size. In other words, bodies grow faster than brains, and large animals have low ratios of brain weight to body weight. In fact, brains grow only about two-thirds as fast as bodies. Since we have no reason to believe that large animals are consistently stupider than their smaller relatives, we must conclude that large animals require relatively less brain to do as well as smaller animals. If we do not recognize this relationship, we are likely to underestimate the mental power of very large animals, dinosaurs in particular.
>
> —Stephen Jay Gould, "Were Dinosaurs Dumb?"

Academic English Choose transitions carefully and vary them appropriately. Each transition has a different meaning; if you use a transition with an inappropriate meaning, you might confuse your reader.

▶ **Although taking eight o'clock classes may seem unappealing, coming to school early has its advantages.** ~~Moreover,~~ *For example,* **students who arrive early typically avoid the worst traffic and find the best parking spaces.**

Common transitions

TO SHOW ADDITION	and, also, besides, further, furthermore, in addition, moreover, next, too, first, second
TO GIVE EXAMPLES	for example, for instance, to illustrate, in fact, specifically
TO COMPARE	also, similarly, likewise
TO CONTRAST	but, however, on the other hand, in contrast, nevertheless, still, even though, on the contrary, yet, although
TO SUMMARIZE OR CONCLUDE	in other words, in short, in conclusion, to sum up, therefore
TO SHOW TIME	after, as, before, next, during, later, finally, meanwhile, since, then, when, while, immediately
TO SHOW PLACE OR DIRECTION	above, below, beyond, farther on, nearby, opposite, close, to the left
TO INDICATE LOGICAL RELATIONSHIP	if, so, therefore, consequently, thus, as a result, for this reason, because, since

PARAGRAPH-LEVEL TRANSITIONS Paragraph-level transitions usually link the *first* sentence of a new paragraph with the *first* sentence of the previous paragraph. In other words, the topic sentences signal global connections.

Look for opportunities to allude to the subject of a previous paragraph (as summed up in its topic sentence) in the topic sentence of the next one. In his essay "Little Green Lies," Jonathan H. Adler uses this strategy in the topic sentences of the following paragraphs, which appear in a passage describing the benefits of plastic packaging.

> Consider aseptic packaging, the synthetic packaging for the "juice boxes" so many children bring to school with their lunch. One criticism of aseptic packaging is that it is nearly impossible to recycle, yet on almost every other count, aseptic packaging is environmentally preferable to the packaging alternatives. Not only do aseptic containers not require refrigeration to keep their contents from spoiling, but their manufacture requires less than one-10th the energy of making glass bottles.
>
> What is true for juice boxes is also true for other forms of synthetic packaging. The use of polystyrene, which is commonly (and mistakenly) referred to as "Styrofoam," can reduce food waste dramatically due to its insulating properties. (Thanks to these properties, polystyrene cups are much preferred over paper for that morning cup of coffee.) Polystyrene also requires significantly fewer resources to produce than its paper counterpart.

TRANSITIONS BETWEEN BLOCKS OF TEXT   In long essays, you will need to alert readers to connections between blocks of text that are more than one paragraph long. You can do this by inserting transitional sentences or short paragraphs at key points in the essay. Here, for example, is a transitional paragraph from a student research paper. It announces that the first part of the paper has come to a close and the second part is about to begin.

> Although the great apes have demonstrated significant language skills, one central question remains: Can they be taught to use that uniquely human language tool we call grammar, to learn the difference, for instance, between "ape bite human" and "human bite ape"? In other words, can an ape create a sentence?

C5-e   If necessary, adjust paragraph length.

Most readers feel comfortable reading paragraphs that range between one hundred and two hundred words. Shorter paragraphs can require too much starting and stopping, and longer ones can strain the reader's attention span. There are exceptions to this guideline, however. Paragraphs longer than two hundred words frequently appear in scholarly writing, where writers explore complex ideas. Paragraphs shorter than one hundred words occur in business writing and on Web sites, where readers routinely skim for main ideas; in newspapers because of narrow columns; and in informal essays to quicken the pace.

In an essay, the first and last paragraphs will ordinarily be the introduction and the conclusion. These special-purpose paragraphs are likely to be shorter than those in the body of the essay. Typically, the body paragraphs will follow the essay's outline: one paragraph per point in short essays, several paragraphs per point in longer ones. Some ideas require more development than others, however, so it is best to be flexible. If an idea stretches to a length unreasonable for a paragraph, you should divide the paragraph, even if you have presented comparable points in the essay in single paragraphs.

Paragraph breaks are not always made for strictly logical reasons. Writers use them for all of the following reasons.

REASONS FOR BEGINNING A NEW PARAGRAPH

- to mark off the introduction and the conclusion
- to signal a shift to a new idea
- to indicate an important shift in time or place
- to emphasize a point (by placing it at the beginning or the end, not in the middle, of a paragraph)

- to highlight a contrast
- to signal a change of speakers (in dialogue)
- to provide readers with a needed pause
- to break up text that looks too dense

Beware of using too many short, choppy paragraphs, however. Readers want to see how your ideas connect, and they become irritated when you break their momentum by forcing them to pause every few sentences. Here are some reasons you might have for combining some of the paragraphs in a rough draft.

REASONS FOR COMBINING PARAGRAPHS

- to clarify the essay's organization
- to connect closely related ideas
- to bind together text that looks too choppy

C6 Document design: A gallery of models

Good document design promotes readability and increases the chances that you will achieve your purpose for writing and reach your readers. How you design a document—in other words, how you format it for the printed page or for a computer screen—affects your readers' response to it. Most readers have certain expectations about how documents should be designed and formatted, usually depending on the context and the purpose of the piece of writing. This gallery features pages from both academic and business documents. The annotations on the sides of the pages point out design choices as well as important features of the writing.

Standard academic formatting

Use the manuscript format that is recommended for your academic discipline. In most English and some other humanities classes, you will be asked to use MLA (Modern Language Association) format (see MLA-5). In most social science classes, such as psychology and sociology, and in most business, education, and health-related classes, you'll be asked to use APA (American Psychological Association) format (see APA-5).

Pages 59–63 show basic formatting in MLA and APA styles. For complete student papers in MLA and APA formats, see A4-h, MLA-5b, and APA-5b.

Standard professional formatting

It helps to look at examples when you are preparing to write a professional document such as a letter, a memo, or a résumé. In general, the writing done in business and professional situations is direct, clear, and courteous—and documents are designed to be scanned easily and quickly. When writing less formal documents such as e-mail messages in academic contexts, it's just as important to craft the document for easy readability.

MLA ESSAY FORMAT

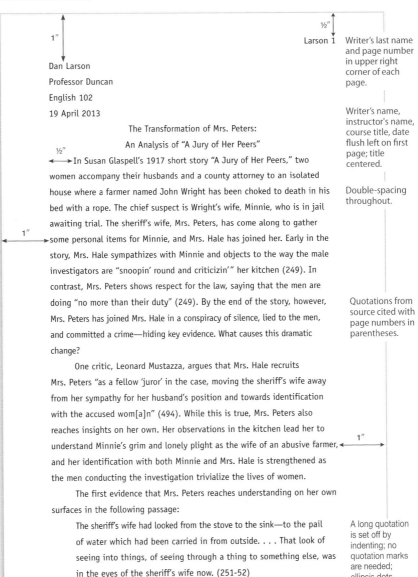

1″

½″

Larson 1

Dan Larson

Professor Duncan

English 102

19 April 2013

The Transformation of Mrs. Peters:

An Analysis of "A Jury of Her Peers"

½″

In Susan Glaspell's 1917 short story "A Jury of Her Peers," two

women accompany their husbands and a county attorney to an isolated

house where a farmer named John Wright has been choked to death in his

bed with a rope. The chief suspect is Wright's wife, Minnie, who is in jail

awaiting trial. The sheriff's wife, Mrs. Peters, has come along to gather

1″ some personal items for Minnie, and Mrs. Hale has joined her. Early in the

story, Mrs. Hale sympathizes with Minnie and objects to the way the male

investigators are "snoopin' round and criticizin'" her kitchen (249). In

contrast, Mrs. Peters shows respect for the law, saying that the men are

doing "no more than their duty" (249). By the end of the story, however,

Mrs. Peters has joined Mrs. Hale in a conspiracy of silence, lied to the men,

and committed a crime—hiding key evidence. What causes this dramatic

change?

One critic, Leonard Mustazza, argues that Mrs. Hale recruits

Mrs. Peters "as a fellow 'juror' in the case, moving the sheriff's wife away

from her sympathy for her husband's position and towards identification

with the accused wom[a]n" (494). While this is true, Mrs. Peters also

reaches insights on her own. Her observations in the kitchen lead her to

understand Minnie's grim and lonely plight as the wife of an abusive farmer,

and her identification with both Minnie and Mrs. Hale is strengthened as

the men conducting the investigation trivialize the lives of women.

The first evidence that Mrs. Peters reaches understanding on her own

surfaces in the following passage:

> The sheriff's wife had looked from the stove to the sink—to the pail
> of water which had been carried in from outside. . . . That look of
> seeing into things, of seeing through a thing to something else, was
> in the eyes of the sheriff's wife now. (251-52)

Something about the stove, the sink, and the pail of water connects

1″

1″

Writer's last name
and page number
in upper right
corner of each
page.

Writer's name,
instructor's name,
course title, date
flush left on first
page; title
centered.

Double-spacing
throughout.

Quotations from
source cited with
page numbers in
parentheses.

1″

A long quotation
is set off by
indenting; no
quotation marks
are needed;
ellipsis dots
indicate a
sentence omitted
from the source.

MLA WORKS CITED PAGE

Heading centered.

Works Cited

Ben-Zvi, Linda. " 'Murder, She Wrote': The Genesis of Susan Glaspell's
    Trifles." *Susan Glaspell: Essays on Her Theater and Fiction*, edited by
    Ben-Zvi, U of Michigan P, 1995, pp. 19-48. Originally published in
    Theatre Journal, vol. 44, no. 2, May 1992, pp. 141-62.

List alphabetized by authors' last names (or by title for works with no author).

Glaspell, Susan. "A Jury of Her Peers." *Literature and Its Writers: An
    Introduction to Fiction, Poetry, and Drama*, edited by Ann Charters
    and Samuel Charters, 6th ed., Bedford/St. Martin's, 2013, pp. 243-58.

First line of each entry at left margin; extra lines indented ½".

Hedges, Elaine. "Small Things Reconsidered: 'A Jury of Her Peers.' " *Susan
    Glaspell: Essays on Her Theater and Fiction*, edited by Linda Ben-Zvi,
    U of Michigan P, 1995, pp. 49-69.

Double-spacing throughout; no extra space between entries.

Mustazza, Leonard. "Generic Translation and Thematic Shift in Susan
    Glaspell's *Trifles* and 'A Jury of Her Peers.' " *Studies in Short Fiction*,
    vol. 26, no. 4, 1989, pp. 489-96.

APA TITLE PAGE

Header consists of shortened title (no more than 50 characters) in all capital letters at left margin and page number at right margin; on title page only, words "Running head" and colon precede shortened title.

Reaction Times for Detection of Objects
in Two Visual Search Tasks

Allison Leigh Johnson

Carthage College

Full title, writer's name, and school centered halfway down page.

Author Note

Allison Leigh Johnson, Department of Psychology, Carthage College. This research was conducted for Psychology 2300, Cognition: Theories and Application, taught by Professor Leslie Cameron.

Author's note (optional) gives writer's affiliation, information about course, and possibly acknowledgments and contact information.

APA ABSTRACT

Shortened title and page number on every page.

Abstract

Visual detection of an object can be automatic or can require attention. The reaction time varies depending on the type of search task being performed. In this visual search experiment, 3 independent variables were tested: type of search, number of distracters, and presence or absence of a target. A feature search contains distracters notably different from the target, while a conjunctive search contains distracters with features similar to the target. For this experiment, 14 Carthage College students participated in a setting of their choice. A green circle was the target. During the feature search, reaction times were similar regardless of the number of distracters and the presence or absence of the target. In the conjunctive search, the number of distracters and the presence or absence of the target affected reaction times. This visual search experiment supports the idea that feature searches are automatic and conjunctive searches require attention from the viewer.

Keywords: visual search, cognition, feature search, conjunctive search

Abstract, a 150-to-250-word overview of paper, appears on separate page. Heading centered, not boldface.

Numerals for all numbers in abstract, even numbers under 10.

Keywords (optional) help readers search for paper on the Web or in a database.

APA ESSAY FORMAT

½"

Reaction Times for Detection of Objects

in Two Visual Search Tasks

½"
Vision is one of the five senses, and it is the sense trusted most by humans (Reisberg, 2010). We use our vision for everything. We are always looking for things, whether it is where we are going or finding a friend at a party. Our vision detects the object(s) we are looking for. Some objects are easier to detect than others. Spotting your sister wearing a purple shirt in a crowd of boring white shirts is automatic and can be done with ease. However, if your sister was also wearing a white shirt, it would take much

1"
time and attention to spot her in that same crowd.

The "pop out effect" describes the quick identification of an object being searched for because of its salient features (Reeves, 2007). When you look for your sister wearing a purple shirt, for example, you use the pop out effect for quick identification. The pop out effect works when attention is drawn to a specific object that is different from the surrounding objects.

Full title, repeated and centered, not boldface.

1"

Sources cited in parentheses with author's last name and date.

APA LIST OF REFERENCES

References

Reeves, R. (2007). *The Norton psychology labs workbook*. New York, NY: Norton.

Reisberg, D. (2010). *Cognition: Exploring the science of the mind*. New York, NY: Norton.

Treisman, A. (1986). Features and objects in visual processing. *Scientific American, 255*, 114-125.

Wolfe, J. M. (1998). What do 1,000,000 trials tell us about visual search? *Psychological Science, 9*, 33-39.

ZAPS: The Norton psychology labs. (2004). Retrieved from http://wwnorton.com/ZAPS/

List of references begins on new page; heading centered, not boldface.

List alphabetized by authors' last names.

First line of each entry flush left; additional lines indented ½". Double-spacing throughout.

BUSINESS REPORT WITH A VISUAL

Report formatted in typical business style, with citations in APA style.

Employee Motivation 5

Doug Ames, manager of operations for OAISYS, noted that some of these issues keep the company from outperforming expectations: "Communication is not timely or uniform, expectations are not clear and consistent, and some employees do not contribute significantly yet nothing is done" (personal communication, February 28, 2006).

Recommendations

It appears that a combination of steps can be used to unlock greater performance for OAISYS. Most important, steps can be taken to strengthen the corporate culture in key areas such as communication, accountability, and appreciation. Employee feedback indicates that these are areas of weakness or

Visual referred to in body of report.

motivators that can be improved. This feedback is summarized in Figure 1.

A plan to use communication effectively to set expectations, share results in a timely fashion, and publicly offer appreciation to specific contributors will likely go a long way toward aligning individual motivation with corporate goals. Additionally, holding individuals accountable for results will bring parity to the workplace.

One technique that might be effective is basing compensation on specific responsibilities. Rather than tying compensation to corporate profit, tying it to individual performance will result in direct correlation between results and reward. Those who do what is necessary to achieve expected results will be rewarded. Those who miss the mark will be required to address the reasons behind their performance and either improve or take a

Figure, a bar graph, appears at bottom of page on which it is mentioned. Figure number and caption placed below figure.

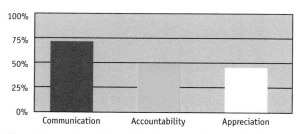

Figure 1. Areas of greatest need for improvements in motivation.

BUSINESS LETTER IN FULL BLOCK STYLE

LatinoVoice

March 16, 2013 •————————————————————— Date

Jonathan Ross
Managing Editor   Inside
Latino World Today   address
2971 East Oak Avenue
Baltimore, MD 21201

Dear Mr. Ross: •———————————————————————— Salutation

Thank you very much for taking the time yesterday to speak to the University
of Maryland's Latino Club. A number of students have told me that they enjoyed
your presentation and found your job search suggestions to be extremely
helpful.

As I mentioned to you, the club publishes a monthly newsletter, *Latino Voice*.   Paragraphs
Our purpose is to share up-to-date information and expert advice with   single-spaced,
members of the university's Latino population. Considering how much students   not indented;
benefited from your talk, I would like to publish excerpts from it in our   double-spacing
newsletter.   between
                                                                                   paragraphs.
I have transcribed parts of your presentation and organized them into
a question-and-answer format for our readers. Would you mind looking through
the enclosed article and letting me know if I may have your permission to print
it? I'm hoping to include this article in our next newsletter, so I would need
your response by April 4.

Once again, Mr. Ross, thank you for sharing your experiences with us. I would
love to be able to share your thoughts with students who couldn't hear you in
person.

Body

Sincerely, •———————————————————————————— Close

Jeffrey Richardson
                    —Signature
Jeffrey Richardson
Associate Editor   Indicates
                                                                                   something
Enc. •——————————————————————————————————— enclosed
                                                                                   with letter.

210 Student Center University of Maryland College Park MD 20742

RÉSUMÉ

Limit résumé to one page, if possible, two pages at most.

Alexis A. Smith

404 Ponce de Leon NE, #B7   404-231-1234
Atlanta, GA 30308   asmith@smith.localhost

Information organized into clear categories — Skills Summary, Education, Experience, etc. — and formatted for easy scanning.

SKILLS SUMMARY
- Writing: competent communicating to different audiences, using a range of written forms (articles, reports, flyers, pamphlets, memos, letters)
- Design: capable of creating visually appealing, audience-appropriate documents; skilled at taking and editing photographs
- Technical: proficient in Microsoft Office; comfortable with Dreamweaver, Photoshop, InDesign
- Language: fluent in spoken and written Spanish

Information presented in reverse chronological order.

EDUCATION
Bachelor of Arts, English   expected May 2014
Georgia State University, Atlanta, GA
- Emphasis areas: journalism and communication
- Study Abroad, Ecuador (Fall 2012)
- Dean's List (Fall 2012, Fall 2013, Spring 2014)

EXPERIENCE
Copyeditor   Sept. 2013-present
The Signal, Atlanta, GA

Bulleted lists organize information.

- copyedit articles for spelling, grammar, and style
- fact-check articles
- prepare copy for Web publication in Dreamweaver

Writing Tutor   Oct. 2011-present
Georgia State University Writing Studio, Atlanta, GA
- work with undergraduate and graduate students on writing projects in all subject areas
- provide technical support for multimedia projects

Present-tense verbs (*provide*) used for current activities.

OUTREACH AND ACTIVITIES
- Publicity Director, English Department Student Organization   Aug. 2013-present
- Coordinator, Georgia State University Relay for Life Student Team   April 2013, 2014

PROFESSIONAL MEMO

COMMONWEALTH PRESS
MEMORANDUM

February 26, 2013

To: Editorial assistants, Advertising Department

cc: Stephen Chapman

From: Helen Brown

Subject: Training for new database software

The new database software will be installed on your computers next week. I have scheduled a training program to help you become familiar with the software and with our new procedures for data entry and retrieval.

Training program

A member of our IT staff will teach in-house workshops on how to use the new software. If you try the software before the workshop, please be prepared to discuss any problems you encounter.

We will keep the training groups small to encourage hands-on participation and to provide individual attention. The workshops will take place in the training room on the third floor from 10:00 a.m. to 2:00 p.m.

Lunch will be provided in the cafeteria.

Sign-up

Please sign up by March 1 for one of the following dates by adding your name in the department's online calendar:

- Monday, March 4
- Wednesday, March 6
- Friday, March 8

If you will not be in the office on any of those dates, please let me know by March 1.

Date, name of recipient, name of sender on separate lines.

Subject line describes topic clearly and concisely.

Introduction states point of memo.

Headings guide readers and promote quick scanning of document.

List calls attention to important information.

E-MAIL MESSAGE

Clear, specific subject line gives purpose of message.

Introduction explains reason for writing.

Professional, straightforward tone and formal language appropriate for communicating with professor.

Message formatted to be read quickly. Bullets draw reader's eye to important details.

Desired outcome of message: request stated briefly.

Message ends with brief, friendly closing.

Send   Options... HTML

To... watterson.p@northernstate.edu

Cc... vanessatarsky@gmail.com

Subject: **Two questions about my research project**

Helvetica   10   B   I   U

Hello, Professor Watterson.

Thank you for taking the time to meet with me yesterday to talk about my research project. I am excited to start the project this week. As we discussed, I am planning to meet with a reference librarian to learn more about NSU's online resources. And I will also develop an online survey to gather my fellow nursing students' perspectives on the topic. In the meantime, I have two questions:

- Do I need approval from the college's institutional review board before I conduct my survey?

- Do I need students' approval to quote their responses in my paper?

I know this is a busy time of year, but if possible, please let me know the answers to these questions before the end of the week.

Thanks for all your help with my project.

Sincerely,

Vanessa Tarsky

A

Academic Reading, Writing, and Speaking

A Academic Reading, Writing, and Speaking

When you write in college, you pose questions, explore ideas, and engage in scholarly debates and conversations. To join in those conversations, you will read and respond to texts, evaluate other people's arguments, and put forth your own ideas.

A1 Reading and writing critically

College writing requires you to become a critical reader—questioning and conversing with the texts you read. When you read critically, you read with an open, curious, even skeptical mind to understand both what is said and why. And when you write critically, you respond to a text and its author, with thoughtful questions and insights, offering your judgment of *how* the parts of a text contribute to its overall effect.

> **MORE HELP IN YOUR HANDBOOK**
>
> Knowing the expectations for a writing assignment is a key first step in drafting.
>
> ► Understanding writing assignments: **A6-f**

A1-a Read actively.

Reading, like writing, is an active process that happens in steps. Most texts, such as the ones assigned in college, don't yield their meaning with one quick reading. Rather, they require you to read and reread to grasp the main points and to comprehend a text's many layers of meaning.

When you read actively, you pay attention to details you would miss if you just skimmed a text and let its words slip past you. First, you read to understand the main ideas. Then you pay attention to your own reactions by making note of what interests, surprises, or puzzles you. Active readers preview a text, annotate it, and then converse with it.

Previewing a text

Previewing—looking quickly through a text before you read—helps you understand its basic features and structures. A text's title, for example, may reveal an author's purpose; a text's format or design may reveal what kind of text it is—a book, a report, a policy memo, and so on. The more you know about a text before you read it, the easier it will be to dig deeper into it.

hackerhandbooks.com/writersref

🄴 A1 Reading and writing critically > As you write: Reading actively

☑ A1 Reading and writing critically > LearningCurve: Critical reading

Annotating a text

Annotating helps you record your responses to a text and answer the basic question, "What is this text about?" As you annotate, you take notes—you jot down questions and reactions in the margins of the text or on electronic or paper sticky notes. You might circle or underline the author's main points. Or you might develop your own system of annotating by placing question marks or asterisks by the text's thesis or major pieces of evidence. Your annotations will help you frame what *you* want to say about the author's ideas or questions.

The following example shows how one student, Emilia Sanchez, annotated an article from *CQ Researcher*, a newsletter about social and political issues.

ANNOTATED ARTICLE

Big Box Stores Are Bad for Main Street

BETSY TAYLOR

Opening strategy— the problem is not x, it's y.

There is plenty of reason to be concerned about the proliferation of Wal-Marts and other so-called "big box" stores. The question, however, is not whether or not these types of stores create jobs (although several studies claim they produce a net job loss in local communities) or whether they ultimately save consumers money. The real concern about having a 25-acre slab of concrete with a 100,000 square foot box of stuff land on a town is whether it's good for a community's soul.

Sentimental— what is a community's soul? I would think job security and a strong economy are better for a community's "soul" than small stores that have to lay people off or close.

Lumps all big boxes together.

The worst thing about "big boxes" is that they have a tendency to produce Ross Perot's famous "big sucking sound"—sucking the life out of cities and small towns across the country.

Assumes all small businesses are attentive.

On the other hand, small businesses are great for a community. They offer more personal service; they won't threaten to pack up and leave town if they don't get tax breaks, free roads and other blandishments; and small-business owners are much more responsive to a customer's needs. (Ever try to complain about bad service or poor quality products to the president of Home Depot?)

True?

Yet, if big boxes are so bad, why are they so successful? One glaring reason is that we've become a nation of hyper-consumers, and the big-box boys know this. Downtown shopping districts comprised of small businesses take

Logic problem? Why couldn't customer complain to store manager?

some of the efficiency out of overconsumption. There's all that hassle of having to travel from store to store, and having to pull out your credit card so many times. Occasionally, we even find ourselves chatting with the shopkeeper, wandering into a coffee shop to visit with a friend or otherwise wasting precious time that could be spent on acquiring more stuff.

Taylor wishes for a time that is long gone or never was.

Author's "either/ or" thinking isn't working. Stores like Home Depot try to encourage a community feel.

But let's face it—bustling, thriving city centers are fun. They breathe life into a community. They allow cities and towns to stand out from each other. They provide an atmosphere for people to interact with each other that just cannot be found at Target, or Wal-Mart or Home Depot.

Community vs. economy. What about prices?

Ends with emotional appeal. This appeal seems too simplistic.

Is it anti-American to be against having a retail giant set up shop in one's community? Some people would say so. On the other hand, if you board up Main Street, what's left of America?

Conversing with a text

Conversing with a text—or talking back to a text and its author—helps you move beyond your initial notes to draw conclusions about what you've read. Perhaps you ask additional questions, point out something that doesn't make sense and why, or explain how the author's points suggest wider implications. As you talk back to a text, you look more closely at how the author works through a topic, and you evaluate the author's evidence and conclusions. Conversing takes your notes to the next level. For example, student writer Emilia Sanchez noticed on a first reading that her assigned text closed with an emotional appeal to the reader. On a second reading, she started to question whether that emotional appeal worked or whether it was really too simplistic a way to look at the topic. (See A1-e.)

Many writers use a **double-entry notebook** to converse with a text and its author and to generate insights and ideas. To create one, draw a line down the center of a notebook page. On the left side, record what the author says; include quotations, sentences, and key terms from the text. On the right side, record your observations and questions.

USING SOURCES RESPONSIBLY: Put quotation marks around words you have copied, and keep an accurate record of page numbers for quotations.

Here is an excerpt from student writer Emilia Sanchez's double-entry notebook.

NOTE: To create a digital double-entry notebook, you can use a table or text boxes in a word processing program.

Ideas from the text	My responses
"The question, however, is not whether or not these types of stores create jobs (although several studies claim they produce a net job loss in local communities) or whether they ultimately save consumers money" (1011).	*Why are big-box stores bad if they create jobs or save people money? Taylor dismisses these possibilities without acknowledging their importance. My family needs to save money and needs jobs more than "chatting with the shopkeeper" (1011).*
"The real concern . . . is whether [big-box stores are] good for a community's soul" (1011). "[S]mall businesses are great for a community" (1011).	*Taylor is missing something here. Are all big-box stores bad? Are all small businesses great? Would getting rid of big-box stores save the "soul" of America? Is Main Street the "soul" of America? Taylor sounds overly sentimental. She assumes that people spend more money because they shop at big-box stores. And she assumes that small businesses are always better for consumers.*

Asking the "So what?" question

As you read and annotate a text, make sure you understand its thesis, or central idea. Ask yourself: "What is the author's thesis?" Then put the author's thesis to the "So what?" test: "Why does this thesis matter? Why does it need to be argued?" Perhaps you'll conclude that the thesis is too obvious and doesn't matter at all—or that it matters so much that you feel the author stopped short and overlooked key details. Or perhaps you'll feel that a reasonable person might draw different conclusions about the issue.

A1-b   Outline a text to identify main ideas.

You are probably familiar with using an outline as a planning tool to help you organize your ideas. An outline is a useful tool for reading, too. Outlining a text—identifying its main idea and major parts—can be an important step in your reading process.

As you outline, look closely for a text's thesis statement (main idea) and topic sentences because they serve as important signposts for readers. A thesis statement often appears in the introduction, usually in the first or second paragraph. Topic sentences can be found at the beginnings of most body paragraphs, where they announce a shift to a new topic. (See C2-a and C5-a.)

Guidelines for active reading

Previewing a written text

- Who is the author? What are the author's credentials?
- What is the author's purpose: To inform? To persuade? To call to action?
- Who is the expected audience?
- When was the text written? Where was it published?
- What kind of text is it: A book? A report? A scholarly article? A policy memo?

Annotating a written text

- What surprises, puzzles, or intrigues you about the text?
- What question does the text attempt to answer?
- What is the author's thesis, or central claim?
- What type of evidence does the author provide to support the thesis? How persuasive is this evidence?

Conversing with a written text

- What are the strengths and limitations of the text?
- Has the author drawn conclusions that you question? Do you have a different interpretation of the evidence?
- Does the text raise questions that it does not answer?
- Does the author consider opposing viewpoints and treat them fairly?

Asking the "So what?" question

- Why does the author's thesis need to be argued, explained, or explored? What's at stake?
- What has the author overlooked in presenting this thesis?

Guidelines for writing a summary

- In the first sentence, mention the title of the text, the name of the author, and the author's thesis. (See A1-c.)
- Maintain a neutral tone; be objective.
- As you present the author's ideas, use the third-person point of view and the present tense: *Taylor argues.* . . . (If you are writing in APA style, see APA-3b.)
- Keep your focus on the text. Don't state the author's ideas as if they were your own.
- Put all or most of your summary in your own words; if you borrow a phrase or a sentence from the text, put it in quotation marks and give the page number in parentheses.
- Limit yourself to presenting the text's key points.
- Be concise; make every word count.

Put the author's thesis and key points in your own words. Here, for example, are the points Emilia Sanchez identified as she prepared to write her summary and analysis of the text printed on pages 72–73. Notice that Sanchez does not simply trace the author's ideas paragraph by paragraph; instead, she sums up the article's central points.

OUTLINE OF "BIG BOX STORES ARE BAD FOR MAIN STREET"

Thesis: Whether or not they take jobs away from a community or offer low prices to consumers, we should be worried about "big-box" stores like Wal-Mart, Target, and Home Depot because they harm communities by taking the life out of downtown shopping districts.

I.   Small businesses are better for cities and towns than big-box stores are.
   A. Small businesses offer personal service, but big-box stores do not.
   B. Small businesses don't make demands on community resources as big-box stores do.
   C. Small businesses respond to customer concerns, but big-box stores do not.

II. Big-box stores are successful because they cater to consumption at the expense of benefits to the community.
   A. Buying everything in one place is convenient.
   B. Shopping at small businesses may be inefficient, but it provides opportunities for socializing.
   C. Downtown shopping districts give each city or town a special identity.

Conclusion: Although some people say that it's anti-American to oppose big-box stores, actually these stores threaten the communities that make up America by encouraging buying at the expense of the traditional interactions of Main Street.

A1-c Summarize to deepen your understanding.

Your goal in summarizing a text is to state the work's main ideas and key points simply, objectively, and accurately in your own words. Writing a summary does not require you to judge the author's ideas; it requires you to *understand* the author's ideas. Whereas in an outline you X-ray a text to see its major parts, in a summary you flesh out the parts to demonstrate your understanding of what a text says. If you have sketched a brief outline of the text (see A1-b), refer to it as you draft your summary.

MORE HELP IN YOUR HANDBOOK

Summarizing is a key research skill.

▶ Summarizing without plagiarizing: **R2-c**

▶ Putting summaries and paraphrases in your own words: **MLA-2d**, **APA-2d**, and **CMS-2d**

Reading online

For many college assignments, you will be asked to read online sources. Research has shown that readers tend to skim online texts rather than read them carefully. On the Web, it is easy to become distracted. And when you skim a text, you are less likely to remember what you have read and less inclined to reread to grasp layers of meaning.

The following strategies will help you read critically online.

Read slowly. Focus and concentration are the goals of all reading, but online readers need to work against the tendency to skim. Instead of sweeping your eyes across the page, consciously slow down the pace of your reading to focus on each sentence.

Avoid multitasking. Close other applications, especially e-mail and social media. If you follow a link for background or the definition of a term, return to the text immediately.

Annotate electronically. You can take notes and record questions on electronic texts. In a print-formatted electronic document (such as a PDF version of an article), you can use the highlighting features in your PDF reader. You might also use electronic sticky notes or the comment feature in your word processing program.

Print the text. You may want to save a text to a hard drive, USB drive, or network and then print it (making sure to record information about the source for proper citation later). Once you print it, you can easily annotate it.

Following is Emilia Sanchez's summary of the article that is printed on pages 72–73.

In her essay "Big Box Stores Are Bad for Main Street," Betsy Taylor argues that chain stores harm communities by taking the life out of downtown shopping districts. Explaining that a community's "soul" is more important than low prices or consumer convenience, she argues that small businesses are better than stores like Home Depot and Target because they emphasize personal interactions and don't place demands on a community's resources. Taylor asserts that big-box stores are successful because "we've become a nation of hyper-consumers" (1011), although the convenience of shopping in these stores comes at the expense of benefits to the community. She concludes by suggesting that it's not "anti-American" to oppose big-box stores because the damage they inflict on downtown shopping districts extends to America itself.

—Emilia Sanchez, student

A1-d   Analyze to demonstrate your critical thinking.

Whereas a summary most often answers the question of *what* a text says, an analysis looks at *how* a text conveys its main idea. As you read and reread a text—previewing, annotating, and conversing—you are forming a judgment of it. When you analyze a text, you say to readers: "Here's my reading of this text. This is what the text means and why it matters."

Balancing summary with analysis

If you have written a summary of a text, you may find it useful to refer to the main points of the summary as you write your analysis. Your readers may or may not be familiar with the text you are analyzing, so you need to summarize the text briefly to help readers understand the basis of your analysis. The following strategies will help you balance summary with analysis.

- Remember that readers are interested in your ideas about a text.
- Pose questions that lead to an interpretation or a judgment of a text rather than to a summary.
- Focus your analysis on the text's thesis and main ideas or some prominent feature of the reading.
- Pay attention to your topic sentences to make sure they signal analysis.
- Ask reviewers to give you feedback: Do you summarize too much and need to analyze more?

Here is an example of how student writer Emilia Sanchez balances summary with analysis in her essay about Betsy Taylor's article (see pp. 72–73). Before stating her thesis, Sanchez summarizes the article's purpose and central idea.

Summary
: [In her essay "Big Box Stores Are Bad for Main Street," Betsy Taylor focuses not on the economic effects of large chain stores but on the effects these stores have on the "soul" of America. She argues that stores like Home Depot, Target, and Wal-Mart are bad for America because they draw people out of downtown shopping districts and cause them to focus on consumption. In contrast, she believes that small businesses are good for America because they provide personal attention, encourage community interaction, and make each city and town unique.]

Analysis
: [But Taylor's argument is unconvincing because it is based on sentimentality—on idealized images of a quaint Main Street—rather than on the roles that businesses play in consumers' lives and communities.]

Drafting an analytical thesis statement

An effective thesis statement for analytical writing responds to a question about a text or tries to resolve a problem in the text. Remember that your thesis isn't the same as the text's thesis or main idea. Your thesis presents your judgment of the text's argument.

If student writer Emilia Sanchez had started her analysis of "Big Box Stores Are Bad for Main Street" (pp. 72–73) with this thesis statement, she merely would have repeated the main idea of the article.

INEFFECTIVE THESIS STATEMENT

Big-box stores such as Wal-Mart and Home Depot promote consumerism by offering endless goods at low prices, but they do nothing to promote community.

Sanchez wrote the following thesis statement, which offers her judgment of Taylor's argument.

EFFECTIVE THESIS STATEMENT

By ignoring the complex economic relationship between large chain stores and their communities, Taylor incorrectly assumes that simply getting rid of big-box stores would have a positive effect on America's communities.

As you draft your thesis, try asking *what*, *why*, and *how* questions to form a judgment about a text you are reading.

- What has the text's author overlooked or failed to consider? Why does this matter?
- Why might a reasonable person draw a different set of conclusions about the subject matter?
- How does the text complicate or clarify something else you've been thinking about or reading about?

> **MORE HELP IN YOUR HANDBOOK**
>
> When you analyze a text, you integrate words and ideas from the source into your own writing.
>
> ▶ Quoting or paraphrasing: **MLA-3a**, **APA-3a**, and **CMS-3a**

A1-e   Sample student essay: Analysis of an article

Following is Emilia Sanchez's analysis of the article by Betsy Taylor (see pp. 72–73). Sanchez used MLA (Modern Language Association) style to format her paper and cite the source. A guide to writing an analytical essay appears on pages 82–83.

hackerhandbooks.com/writersref

- [e] A1 Reading and writing critically > As you write: Drafting and revising an analytical thesis
- [e] A1 Reading and writing critically > As you write: Analyzing a text
- [e] A1 Reading and writing critically > As you write: Developing an analysis

Sanchez 1

Emilia Sanchez

Professor Goodwin

English 10

23 October 2013

Rethinking Big-Box Stores

Opening briefly summarizes the article's purpose and thesis.

In her essay "Big Box Stores Are Bad for Main Street," Betsy Taylor focuses not on the economic effects of large chain stores but on the effects these stores have on the "soul" of America. She argues that stores like Home Depot, Target, and Wal-Mart are bad for America because they draw people out of downtown shopping districts and cause them to focus on consumption. In contrast, she believes that small businesses are good for America because they provide personal attention, encourage community interaction, and make each city and town unique.

Sanchez begins to analyze Taylor's argument.

Thesis expresses Sanchez's judgment of Taylor's article.

But Taylor's argument is unconvincing because it is based on sentimentality—on idealized images of a quaint Main Street—rather than on the roles that businesses play in consumers' lives and communities. By ignoring the complex economic relationship between large chain stores and their communities, Taylor incorrectly assumes that simply getting rid of big-box stores would have a positive effect on America's communities.

Signal phrase introduces quotations from the source; Sanchez uses an MLA in-text citation.

Taylor's use of colorful language reveals that she has a sentimental view of American society and does not understand economic realities. In her first paragraph, Taylor refers to a big-box store as a "25-acre slab of concrete with a 100,000 square foot box of stuff" that "land[s] on a town," evoking images of a powerful monster crushing the American way of life (1011). But she oversimplifies a complex issue. Taylor does not consider that many downtown business districts failed long before chain stores moved in, when factories and mills closed and workers lost their jobs. In cities with struggling economies, big-box stores can actually provide much-needed jobs.

Sanchez identifies and challenges Taylor's assumptions.

Similarly, while Taylor blames big-box stores for harming local economies by asking for tax breaks, free roads, and other perks, she doesn't acknowledge that these stores also enter into economic partnerships with the surrounding communities by offering financial benefits to schools and hospitals.

Marginal annotations indicate MLA-style formatting and *effective writing*.

hackerhandbooks.com/writersref

🄴 A1 Reading and writing critically > Sample student writing > Sanchez, "Rethinking Big-Box Stores" (analysis of an article)

Sanchez 2

Taylor's assumption that shopping in small businesses is always better for the customer also seems driven by nostalgia for an old-fashioned Main Street rather than by the facts. While she may be right that many small businesses offer personal service and are responsive to customer complaints, she does not consider that many customers appreciate the service at big-box stores. Just as customer service is better at some small businesses than at others, it is impossible to generalize about service at all big-box stores. For example, customers depend on the lenient return policies and the wide variety of products at stores like Target and Home Depot.

Taylor blames big-box stores for encouraging American "hyper-consumerism," but she oversimplifies by equating big-box stores with bad values and small businesses with good values. Like her other points, this claim ignores the economic and social realities of American society today. Big-box stores do not force Americans to buy more. By offering lower prices in a convenient setting, however, they allow consumers to save time and purchase goods they might not be able to afford from small businesses. The existence of more small businesses would not change what most Americans can afford, nor would it reduce their desire to buy affordable merchandise.

Taylor may be right that some big-box stores have a negative impact on communities and that small businesses offer certain advantages. But she ignores the economic conditions that support big-box stores as well as the fact that Main Street was in decline before the big-box store arrived. Getting rid of big-box stores will not bring back a simpler America populated by thriving, unique Main Streets; in reality, Main Street will not survive if consumers cannot afford to shop there.

> Clear topic sentence announces a shift to a new topic.

> Sanchez refutes Taylor's claim.

> Sanchez treats the author fairly.

> Conclusion returns to the thesis and shows the wider significance of Sanchez's analysis.

Sanchez 3

Work Cited

Taylor, Betsy. "Big Box Stores Are Bad for Main Street." *CQ Researcher*, vol. 9, no. 44, 1999, p. 1011.

> Work cited page is in MLA style.

An **analysis** of a text allows you to examine the parts of a text to understand *what* it means and *how* it makes its meaning. Your goal is to offer your judgment of the text and to persuade readers to see it through your analytical perspective. A sample analytical essay begins on page 80.

Key features

- **A careful and critical reading** of a text reveals what the text says, how it works, and what it means. In an analytical essay, you pay attention to the details of the text, especially its thesis and evidence.

- **A thesis that offers a clear judgment** of a text anchors your analysis. Your thesis might be the answer to a question you have posed about a text or the resolution of a problem you have identified in the text.

- **Support for the thesis** comes from evidence in the text. You summarize, paraphrase, and quote passages that support the claims you make about the text.

- **A balance of summary and analysis** helps readers who may not be familiar with the text you are analyzing. Summary answers the question of *what* a text says; an analysis looks at *how* a text makes its point.

Thinking ahead: Presenting and publishing

You may have the opportunity to present or publish your analysis in the form of a multimodal text such as a slide show presentation. Consider how adding images or sound might strengthen your analysis or help you to better reach your audience. (See section A2.)

Writing your analytical essay

⋯ EXPLORE

Generate ideas for your analysis by brainstorming responses to questions such as the following:

- What is the text about?

- What do you find most interesting, surprising, or puzzling about this text?

- What is the author's thesis or central idea? Put the author's thesis to the "So what?" test. (See p. 74.)

- What do your annotations of the text reveal about your response to it?

○ **DRAFT**

- Draft a working thesis to focus your analysis. Remember that your thesis is not the same as the author's thesis. Your thesis presents *your* judgment of the text.

- Draft a plan to organize your paragraphs. Your introductory paragraph will briefly summarize the text and offer your thesis. Your body paragraphs will support your thesis with evidence from the text. Your conclusion will pull together the major points and show the significance of your analysis. (See C1-d.)

- Identify specific words, phrases, and sentences as evidence to support your thesis.

● **REVISE**

Ask your reviewers to give you specific comments. You can use the following questions to guide their feedback.

- Is the introduction effective and engaging?
- Is summary balanced with analysis?
- Does the thesis offer a clear judgment of the text?
- What objections might other writers pose to your analysis?
- Is the analysis well organized? Are there clear topic sentences and transitions?
- Is there sufficient evidence? Is the evidence analyzed?
- Have you cited words, phrases, or sentences that are summarized or quoted?

A2 Reading and writing about images and multimodal texts

In many of your college classes, you'll have the opportunity to read and write about images, such as photographs or paintings, as well as multimodal texts, such as advertisements, maps, videos, or Web sites. Multimodal texts combine one or more of the following modes: words, static images, moving images, and sound.

A2-a Read actively.

Any image or multimodal text can be read—that is, carefully approached and examined to understand *what* it says and *how* it communicates it purpose and reaches its audience. When you read a multimodal text, you are often reading more than words; you might also be reading a text's design

wwf.org

What will it take before we respect the planet?

Multimodal texts, such as this World Wildlife Fund (WWF) ad, combine modes. Here, words and an image work together to communicate an idea. (*Source:* Courtesy of World Wildlife Fund, WWF, www.worldwildlife.org.)

and composition, and perhaps even its pace and volume. Reading actively requires understanding the modes—words, images, and sound—separately and then analyzing how the modes work together.

When you read images or multimodal texts, it's helpful to preview, annotate, and converse with the text—just as with written texts.

MORE HELP IN YOUR HANDBOOK

Integrating visuals (images and some multimodal texts) can strengthen your writing.

▶ Adding visuals as you draft: **page 17**

▶ Choosing visuals to suit your purpose: **pages 18–19**

Previewing an image or a multimodal text

Previewing starts by looking at the basic details of an image or a multimodal text and paying attention to first impressions. You begin to ask questions about the text's subject matter and design, its context and creator, and its purpose and intended audience. The more you can gather from a first look, the easier it will be to dig deeper into the meaning of a text.

Annotating an image or a multimodal text

Annotating a text—jotting down observations and questions—helps you read actively to answer the basic question "What is this text about?" You'll often find yourself annotating, rereading, and moving back and forth between reading and writing to fully understand and analyze an image or a multimodal text. A second or third reading will raise new questions and reveal details that you didn't notice in an earlier reading.

The example on page 86 shows how one student, Ren Yoshida, annotated an advertisement.

Conversing with an image or a multimodal text

Conversing with a text—or talking back to a text and its author—helps you move beyond your early notes to form judgments about what you've read. You might choose to pose questions, point out something that is puzzling or provocative and why, or explain a disagreement you have with the text. In his annotations to the Equal Exchange ad, Ren Yoshida asks why two words, *empowering* and *farmers*, are in different fonts (see p. 86). And he further questions the meaning of the difference.

Many writers use a double-entry notebook to converse with a text and generate ideas for writing (see pp. 73–74 for guidelines on creating a double-entry notebook and for sample entries).

A2-b Outline to identify main ideas.

Outlining is a useful tool to understand a text that you've been assigned to read. One way to outline an image or a multimodal text is to try to define its main idea or purpose and sketch a list of its key elements. Because ads, Web sites, and videos may not explicitly state a purpose, you may have to puzzle it out from the details in the work.

Here is the informal outline Ren Yoshida developed as he prepared to write an analysis of the advertisement on page 86.

OUTLINE OF EQUAL EXCHANGE ADVERTISEMENT

Purpose: To persuade consumers that they can improve the lives of organic farmers and their families by purchasing Equal Exchange coffee.

Key features:
- The farmer's heart-shaped hands are outstretched, offering the viewer partnership and the product of her hard work.
- The raw coffee is surprisingly fruitlike and fresh—natural and healthy looking.
- A variety of fonts are used for emphasis, such as the elegant font for "empowering."
- Consumer support leads to a higher quality of life for the farmers and for all people, since these farmers care for the environment and plan for the future.
- The simplicity of the design reflects the simplicity of the exchange. The consumer only has to buy a cup of coffee to make a difference.

Conclusion: Equal Exchange is selling more than a product—coffee. It is selling the message that together farmers and consumers hold the future of land, environment, farms, and families in their hands.

ANNOTATED ADVERTISEMENT

What is being exchanged?

Why is "fairly traded" so hard to read?

"Empowering" — why in an elegant font? Who is empowering farmers?

"Farmers" in all capital letters — shows strength?

Straightforward design and not much text.

Outstretched hands. Is she giving a gift? Inviting partnership?

Raw coffee beans are red: earthy, natural, warm.

When you choose Equal Exchange fairly traded coffee, tea or chocolate, you join a network that empowers farmers in Latin America, Africa, and Asia to:

- **Stay on their land**
- **Care for the environment**
- **Farm organically**
- **Support their family**
- **Plan for the future**

www.equalexchange.coop

Photo: Jesus Choqueheranca de Quevero,
Coffee farmer & CEPICAFE Cooperative member, Peru

Positive verbs: consumers choose, join, empower; farmers stay, care, farm, support, plan.

Source: Equal Exchange.
Reproduced with permission.

A2-c Summarize to deepen your understanding.

Your goal in summarizing an image or a multimodal text is to state the work's central idea and key points simply, objectively, and accurately, in your own words, and usually in paragraph form. Since a summary must be fairly short, you must make judgments about what is most important. The guidelines in the chart on page 75 will help you write a summary of an image or a multimodal text.

A2-d Analyze to demonstrate your critical reading.

Whereas a summary most often answers the question of *what* a text says, an analysis looks at *how* a text conveys its main idea or message. As you read and reread an image or a multimodal text—previewing, annotating, and conversing—you are forming a judgment of it.

Balancing summary with analysis

If you have written a summary of a text, you may find it useful to refer to the main points of the summary as you write your analysis. Your readers may or may not be familiar with the visual or multimodal text you are analyzing and will need at least some summary to ground your analysis. For example, student writer Ren Yoshida summarized the Equal Exchange advertisement on page 86 by describing part of the text first, allowing readers to get their bearings, and then moving to an analytical statement about that particular part of the text.

[A farmer, her hardworking hands full of coffee beans, reaches out from an Equal Exchange advertisement. The hands, in the shape of a heart, offer to consumers the fruit of the farmer's labor. The ad's message is straightforward: in choosing Equal Exchange, consumers become global citizens, partnering with farmers to help save the planet.] Summary [Suddenly, a cup of coffee is more than just a morning ritual; a cup of coffee is a moral choice that empowers both consumers and farmers.] Analysis

Drafting an analytical thesis statement

An effective thesis statement for analytical writing about an image or a multimodal text responds to a question about the text or tries to resolve a

hackerhandbooks.com/writersref

- A2 Reading and writing (multimodal) > As you write: Reading visual texts actively
- A2 Reading and writing (multimodal) > As you write: Analyzing an image or a multimodal text
- A2 Reading and writing (multimodal) > As you write: Drafting and revising an analytical thesis (for an image or a multimodal text)

Guidelines for analyzing an image or a multimodal text

- What is your first impression of the text? What details in the text create this response?
- When and why was the text created? Where did the text appear?
- What clues suggest the text's intended audience? What assumptions are being made about the audience?
- What is the thesis, central idea, or message of the text?
- Does this text tell a story? How would you sum up the story?
- If the text is multimodal, what modes are used, and why? How do the modes work together?
- How do the arrangement of sounds or design details—images, illustrations, colors, fonts, perspective—help convey the text's meaning or serve its purpose?

problem in the text. Remember that your thesis isn't the same as the text's thesis or main idea. Your thesis presents your judgment of the text's argument. If you find that your thesis is restating the text's message, turn to your notes to see if the questions you asked earlier in the process can help you revise.

INEFFECTIVE THESIS STATEMENT

Consumers who purchase coffee from farmers in the Equal Exchange network are helping farmers stay on their land.

The thesis is ineffective because it summarizes the ad; it doesn't present an analysis. Ren Yoshida focused the thesis by questioning a single detail in the work.

QUESTIONS

The ad promises an equal exchange, but is the exchange equal between consumers and farmers? Do the words *equal exchange* and *empowering farmers* appeal to consumers' emotions?

EFFECTIVE THESIS STATEMENT

Although the ad works successfully on an emotional level, it is less successful on a logical level because of its promise for an equal exchange between consumers and farmers.

---

hackerhandbooks.com/writersref

- A2 Reading and writing (multimodal) > As you write: Learning from other writers
- A2 Reading and writing (multimodal) > Sample student writing > Yoshida, "Sometimes a Cup of Coffee Is Just a Cup of Coffee" (analysis of an advertisement)
- A2 Reading and writing (multimodal) > Sample multimodal projects > D'Amato, "Loose Leaf Teas" (Web site), and Williamson, "To the Children of America" (video essay)

A3 Reading arguments

Many of your college assignments will ask you to read and write arguments about debatable issues. The questions being debated might be matters of public policy (*Should corporations be allowed to advertise on public school property?*) or they might be scholarly issues (*What role do genes play in determining behavior?*). On such questions, reasonable people may disagree.

As you read arguments across the disciplines and enter into academic or public policy debates, pay attention to the questions being asked, the evidence being presented, and the various positions being argued. You'll find the critical reading strategies introduced in section A1—previewing, annotating, and conversing with texts—to be useful as you ask questions about an argument's logic, evidence, and use of appeals.

A3-a Distinguish between reasonable and fallacious argumentative tactics.

When you evaluate an argument, look closely at the reasoning and evidence behind it. A number of unreasonable argumentative tactics are known as *logical fallacies*. Most of the fallacies—such as hasty generalizations and false analogies—are misguided or dishonest uses of legitimate argumentative strategies. The examples in this section suggest when such strategies are reasonable and when they are not.

Generalizing (inductive reasoning)

Writers and thinkers generalize all the time. We look at a sample of data and conclude that data we have not observed will most likely conform to what we have seen. From a spoonful of soup, we conclude just how salty the whole bowl will be. After numerous unpleasant experiences with an airline, we decide to book future flights with a competitor.

When we draw a conclusion from an array of facts, we are engaged in inductive reasoning. Such reasoning deals in probability, not certainty. For a conclusion to be highly probable, it must be based on evidence that is sufficient, representative, and relevant. (See the chart on p. 91.)

hackerhandbooks.com/writersref
e A3 Reading arguments > As you write: Evaluating ads for logic and fairness

The fallacy known as *hasty generalization* is a conclusion based on insufficient or unrepresentative evidence.

HASTY GENERALIZATION

In a single year, scores on standardized tests in California's public schools rose by ten points. Therefore, more children than ever are succeeding in America's public school systems.

Data from one state do not justify a conclusion about the whole United States.

A *stereotype* is a hasty generalization about a group. Here are a few examples.

STEREOTYPES

Women are bad bosses.

Politicians are corrupt.

Children are always curious.

Stereotyping is common because of our tendency to perceive selectively. We tend to see what we want to see; we notice evidence confirming our already formed opinions and fail to notice evidence to the contrary. For example, if you have concluded that politicians are corrupt, your stereotype will be confirmed by news reports of legislators being indicted—even though every day the media describe conscientious officials serving the public honestly and well.

> **Academic English**   Many hasty generalizations contain words such as *all*, *ever*, *always*, and *never*, when qualifiers such as *most*, *many*, *usually*, and *seldom* would be more accurate.

Drawing analogies

An analogy points out a similarity between two things that are otherwise different. Analogies can be an effective means of arguing a point. It is not always easy to draw the line between a reasonable and an unreasonable analogy. At times, however, an analogy is clearly off base, in which case it is called a *false analogy*.

FALSE ANALOGY

If we can send a spacecraft to Pluto, we should be able to find a cure for the common cold.

The writer has falsely assumed that because two things are alike in one respect, they must be alike in others. Exploring the outer reaches of the solar system and finding a cure for the common cold are both scientific challenges, but the problems confronting medical researchers are quite different from those solved by space scientists.

Testing inductive reasoning

Though inductive reasoning leads to probable and not absolute truth, you can assess a conclusion's likely probability by asking three questions. This chart shows how to apply those questions to a sample conclusion based on a survey.

CONCLUSION The majority of students on our campus would volunteer at least five hours a week in a community organization if the school provided a placement service for volunteers.

EVIDENCE In a recent survey, 723 of 1,215 students questioned said they would volunteer at least five hours a week in a community organization if the school provided a placement service for volunteers.

1. Is the evidence sufficient?

   That depends. On a small campus (say, 3,000 students), the pool of students surveyed would be sufficient for market research, but on a large campus (say, 30,000), 1,215 students are only 4 percent of the population. If that 4 percent were known to be truly representative of the other 96 percent, however, even such a small sample would be sufficient (see question 2).

2. Is the evidence representative?

   The evidence is representative if those responding to the survey reflect the characteristics of the entire student population: age, sex, race, field of study, overall number of extracurricular commitments, and so on. If most of those surveyed are majors in a field like social work, however, the researchers would be wise to question the survey's conclusion.

3. Is the evidence relevant?

   Yes. The results of the survey are directly linked to the conclusion. Evidence based on a survey about the number of hours students work for pay, by contrast, would not be relevant because it would not be about *choosing to volunteer*.

Tracing causes and effects

Demonstrating a connection between causes and effects is rarely simple. For example, to explain why a chemistry course has a high failure rate, you would begin by listing possible causes: inadequate preparation of students, poor teaching, lack of qualified tutors, and so on. Next you would investigate each possible cause. Only after investigating the possible causes would you be able to weigh the relative impact of each cause and suggest appropriate remedies.

Because cause-and-effect reasoning is so complex, it is not surprising that writers frequently oversimplify it. In particular, writers sometimes assume that because one event follows another, the first is the cause of the second. This common fallacy is known as *post hoc*, from the Latin *post hoc, ergo propter hoc*, meaning "after this, therefore because of this."

POST HOC FALLACY

Since Governor Cho took office, unemployment of minorities in the state has decreased by 7 percent. Governor Cho should be applauded for reducing unemployment among minorities.

Is the governor solely responsible for the decrease? Are there other reasons? The writer must show that Governor Cho's policies are responsible for the decrease in unemployment; it is not enough to show that the decrease followed the governor's taking office.

Weighing options

Especially when reasoning about problems and solutions, writers must weigh options. To be fair, a writer should mention the full range of options, showing why one is superior to the others or might work well in combination with others.

It is unfair to suggest that only two alternatives exist when in fact there are more. Writers who set up a false choice between their preferred option and one that is clearly unsatisfactory are guilty of the *either . . . or* fallacy.

EITHER . . . OR FALLACY

Our current war against drugs has not worked. Either we should legalize drugs or we should turn the drug war over to our armed forces and let them fight it.

Are these the *only* solutions—legalizing drugs and calling out the army? Other options, such as funding for drug abuse prevention programs, are possible.

Making assumptions

An assumption is a claim that is taken to be true—without the need of proof. Most arguments are based to some extent on assumptions, since writers rarely have the time and space to prove all the conceivable claims on which an argument is based. For example, someone arguing about the best means of limiting population growth in developing countries might assume that the goal of limiting population growth is worthwhile. For most audiences, there would be no need to articulate this assumption or to defend it.

There is a danger, however, in failing to spell out and prove a claim that is clearly controversial. Consider the following short argument, in which a key claim is missing.

ARGUMENT WITH MISSING CLAIM

Violent crime is increasing. Therefore, we should vigorously enforce the death penalty.

The writer seems to be assuming that the death penalty deters violent criminals and that it is a fair punishment—and that most audiences will agree. These are not reasonable assumptions; the writer will need to state and support both claims.

When a missing claim is an assertion that few would agree with, we say that a writer is guilty of a *non sequitur* (Latin for "it does not follow").

NON SEQUITUR

Christopher gets plenty of sleep; therefore, he will be a successful student in the university's pre-med program.

Does it take more than sleep to be a successful student? Few people would agree with the missing claim—that people with good sleep habits always make successful students.

Deducing conclusions (deductive reasoning)

When we deduce a conclusion, we put things together, like any good detective. We establish that a general principle is true, that a specific case is an example of that principle, and that therefore a particular conclusion about that case is a certainty.

Deductive reasoning can often be structured in a three-step argument called a *syllogism*. The three steps are the major premise, the minor premise, and the conclusion.

1. Anything that increases radiation in the environment is dangerous to public health. (Major premise)
2. Nuclear reactors increase radiation in the environment. (Minor premise)
3. Therefore, nuclear reactors are dangerous to public health. (Conclusion)

The major premise is a generalization. The minor premise is a specific case. The conclusion follows from applying the generalization to the specific case.

Deductive arguments break down if one of the premises is not true or if the conclusion does not logically follow from the premises. In the following argument, the major premise is very likely untrue.

UNTRUE PREMISE

The police do not give speeding tickets to people driving less than five miles per hour over the limit. Dominic is driving fifty-nine miles per hour in a fifty-five-mile-per-hour zone. Therefore, the police will not give Dominic a speeding ticket.

The conclusion is true only if the premises are true. If the police sometimes give tickets for driving less than five miles per hour over the limit, Dominic cannot safely conclude that he will avoid a ticket.

In the following argument, both premises might be true, but the conclusion does not follow logically from them.

CONCLUSION DOES NOT FOLLOW

All members of our club ran in this year's Boston Marathon. Jay ran in this year's Boston Marathon. Therefore, Jay is a member of our club.

The fact that Jay ran the race is no guarantee that he is a member of the club. Presumably, many runners are nonmembers.

Assuming that both premises are true, the following argument holds up.

CONCLUSION FOLLOWS

All members of our club ran in this year's Boston Marathon. Jay is a member of our club. Therefore, Jay ran in this year's Boston Marathon.

A3-b Distinguish between legitimate and unfair emotional appeals.

There is nothing wrong with appealing to readers' emotions. After all, many issues worth arguing about have an emotional as well as a logical dimension. Even the Greek logician Aristotle lists *pathos* (emotion) as a legitimate argumentative tactic. For example, in an essay criticizing big-box stores (see pp. 72–73), writer Betsy Taylor has a good reason for tugging at readers' emotions: Her subject is the decline of city and town life. In her conclusion, Taylor appeals to readers' emotions by invoking their national pride.

LEGITIMATE EMOTIONAL APPEAL

Is it anti-American to be against having a retail giant set up shop in one's community? Some people would say so. On the other hand, if you board up Main Street, what's left of America?

Evaluating ethical, logical, and emotional appeals as a reader

Ancient Greek rhetoricians distinguished among three kinds of appeals used to influence readers—ethical, logical, and emotional. As you evaluate arguments, identify these appeals and question their effectiveness. Are they appropriate for the audience and the argument? Are they balanced and legitimate or lopsided and misleading?

Ethical appeals (*ethos*)

Ethical arguments call upon a writer's character, knowledge, and authority. Ask questions such as the following when you evaluate the ethical appeal of an argument.

- Is the writer informed and trustworthy? How does the writer establish authority?
- Is the writer fair-minded and unbiased? How does the writer establish reasonableness?
- Does the writer use sources knowledgeably and responsibly?
- How does the writer describe the views of others and deal with opposing views?

Logical appeals (*logos*)

Reasonable arguments appeal to readers' sense of logic, rely on evidence, and use inductive and deductive reasoning. Ask questions such as the following to evaluate the logical appeal of an argument.

- Is the evidence sufficient, representative, and relevant?
- Is the reasoning sound?
- Does the argument contain any logical fallacies or unjustified assumptions?
- Are there any missing or mistaken premises?

Emotional appeals (*pathos*)

Emotional arguments appeal to readers' beliefs and values. Ask questions such as the following to evaluate the emotional appeal of an argument.

- What values or beliefs does the writer address, either directly or indirectly?
- Are the emotional appeals legitimate and fair?
- Does the writer oversimplify or dramatize an issue?
- Do the emotional arguments highlight or shift attention away from the evidence?

Emotional appeals, however, are frequently misused. Many of the arguments we see in the media, for instance, strive to win our sympathy rather than our intelligent agreement. A TV commercial suggesting that you will be thin and attractive if you drink a certain diet beverage is making a pitch to emotions. So is a political speech that recommends electing a candidate because he is a devoted husband and father who serves as a volunteer firefighter.

The following passage illustrates several types of unfair emotional appeals.

UNFAIR EMOTIONAL APPEALS

This progressive proposal to build a ski resort in the state park has been carefully researched by Western Trust, the largest bank in the state; furthermore, it is favored by a majority of the local merchants. The only opposition comes from tree huggers who care more about trees than they do about people. One of their leaders was actually arrested for disturbing the peace several years ago.

Words with strong positive or negative connotations, such as *progressive* and *tree hugger*, are examples of *biased language*. Attacking the people who hold a belief (environmentalists) rather than refuting their argument is called *ad hominem*, a Latin term meaning "to the man." Associating a prestigious name (Western Trust) with the writer's side is called *transfer*. Claiming that an idea should be accepted because a large number of people (the majority of merchants) are in favor is called the *bandwagon appeal*. Bringing in irrelevant issues (the arrest) is a *red herring*, named after a trick used in fox hunts to mislead the dogs by dragging a smelly fish across the trail.

Advertising makes use of ethical, logical, and emotional appeals to persuade consumers to buy a product or embrace a brand. This Patagonia ad makes an ethical appeal with its copy that invites customers to rethink their purchasing practices. (*Source:* Property of Patagonia, Inc. Used with permission.)

A3-c Judge how fairly a writer handles opposing views.

The way in which a writer deals with opposing views is revealing. Some writers address the arguments of the opposition fairly, conceding points when necessary and countering others, all in a civil spirit. Other writers will do almost anything to win an argument: either ignoring opposing views altogether or misrepresenting such views and attacking their proponents.

Writers build credibility—*ethos*—by addressing opposing arguments fairly. As you read arguments, assess the credibility of your sources by looking at how they deal with views not in agreement with their own.

Describing the views of others

Some writers and speakers deliberately misrepresent the views of others. One way they do this is by setting up a "straw man," a character so weak that he is easily knocked down. The *straw man* fallacy consists of an oversimplification or outright distortion of opposing views. For example, in a California debate over attempts to control the mountain lion population, pro-lion groups characterized their opponents as trophy hunters bent on shooting harmless lions. In truth, such hunters were only one faction of those who saw a need to control the lion population.

During the District of Columbia's struggle for voting representation, some politicians set up a straw man, as shown in the following example.

> **STRAW MAN FALLACY**
>
> Washington, DC, residents are lobbying for statehood. Giving a city such as the District of Columbia the status of a state would be unfair.

The straw man wanted statehood. In fact, most District citizens lobbied for voting representation in any form, not necessarily through statehood.

Quoting opposing views

Writers often quote the words of writers who hold opposing views. In general, this is a good idea, for it assures some level of fairness and accuracy. At times, though, both the fairness and the accuracy are an illusion.

hackerhandbooks.com/writersref
e A3 Reading arguments > As you write: Evaluating an argument
e A3 Reading arguments > Exercise: A3–2

Checklist for reading and evaluating arguments

- What is the writer's thesis, or central claim?
- Are there gaps in reasoning? Does the argument contain any logical fallacies (see A3-a)?
- What assumptions does the argument rest on? Are there any unstated assumptions?
- What appeals — ethical, logical, or emotional — does the writer make? Are these appeals effective?
- What evidence does the writer use? Could there be alternative interpretations of the evidence?
- How does the writer handle opposing views?
- If you are not persuaded by the writer's argument, what counterarguments could you make to the writer?

A source may be misrepresented when it is quoted out of context. All quotations are to some extent taken out of context, but a fair writer will explain the context to readers. To select a provocative sentence from a source and to ignore the more moderate sentences surrounding it is both unfair and misleading. Sometimes a writer deliberately distorts a source through the device of ellipsis dots. Ellipsis dots tell readers that words have been omitted from the original source. When those words are crucial to an author's meaning, omitting them is obviously unfair. (See P6-c.)

ORIGINAL SOURCE

Johnson's *History of the American West* is riddled with inaccuracies and astonishing in its blatantly racist description of the Indian wars.   — B. R., reviewer

MISLEADING QUOTATION

According to B. R., Johnson's *History of the American West* is "astonishing in its . . . description of the Indian wars."

A4 Writing arguments

Evaluating the arguments of other writers prepares you to construct your own. When you ask questions about the logic and evidence of the arguments you read (see A3), you become more aware of such needs in your own writing. And when you pose objections to arguments, you more readily anticipate and counter objections to your own arguments.

A4-a Identify your purpose and context.

In constructing an argument, you take a stand on a debatable issue. Your purpose is to explain your understanding of the truth about a subject or to propose the best solution to a problem, reasonably and logically, without being combative. Your aim is to persuade your readers to reconsider their positions by offering new reasons to question existing viewpoints.

It is best to start by informing yourself about the debate or conversation around a subject—sometimes called its *context.* If you are planning to write about the subject of offshore drilling, you might want to read sources that shed light on the social context (the concerns of consumers, the ideas of lawmakers, the proposals of environmentalists) and sources that may inform you about the intellectual context (scientific or theoretical responses by geologists, oceanographers, or economists) in which the debate is played out. Because your readers may be aware of the social and intellectual contexts in which your issue is grounded, you will be at a disadvantage if you are not informed. Conduct some research before preparing your argument. Consulting even a few sources can help to deepen your understanding of the conversation around the issue.

Academic English   Some cultures value writers who argue with force; other cultures value writers who argue subtly or indirectly. Academic audiences in the United States will expect your writing to be assertive and confident—neither aggressive nor passive. You can create an assertive tone by acknowledging different positions and supporting your ideas with specific evidence.

TOO AGGRESSIVE	Of course only registered organ donors should be eligible for organ transplants. It's selfish and shortsighted to think otherwise.
TOO PASSIVE	I might be wrong, but I think that maybe people should have to register as organ donors if they want to be considered for a transplant.
ASSERTIVE	If only registered organ donors are eligible for transplants, more people will register as donors.

If you are uncertain about the tone of your work, ask for help at your school's writing center.

A4-b   View your audience as a panel of jurors.

Do not assume that your audience already agrees with you. Instead, envision skeptical readers who, like a panel of jurors, will make up their minds after listening to all sides of the argument. If you are arguing a public policy issue, aim your paper at readers who represent a variety of positions. In the case of the debate over offshore drilling, for example, imagine a jury that represents those who have a stake in the matter: consumers, policymakers, and environmentalists.

> **MORE HELP IN YOUR HANDBOOK**
>
> Evidence from sources can strengthen your argument.
>
> ▶ Conducting research: **R1**

Using ethical, logical, and emotional appeals as a writer

To construct a convincing argument, you must establish your credibility (*ethos*) and appeal to your readers' sense of logic and reason (*logos*) as well as to their values and beliefs (*pathos*).

Ethical appeals (*ethos*)

To accept your argument, a reader must see you as trustworthy, fair, and reasonable. When you acknowledge alternative positions, you build common ground with readers and gain their trust by showing that you are knowledgeable. And when you use sources responsibly (summarizing, paraphrasing, or quoting the views of others respectfully), you inspire readers' confidence in your judgment.

Logical appeals (*logos*)

To persuade readers, you need to appeal to their sense of logic and sound reasoning. When you provide sufficient evidence, you offer readers logical support for your argument. And when you clarify the assumptions that underlie your arguments and avoid logical fallacies, you appeal to readers' desire for reason.

Emotional appeals (*pathos*)

To establish common ground with readers, you need to appeal to their beliefs and values as well as to their minds. When you offer readers vivid examples, startling statistics, or compelling visuals, you engage readers and deepen their interest in your argument. And when you balance emotional appeals with logical appeals, you highlight the human dimension of an issue to show readers why they should care about your argument.

At times, you can deliberately narrow your audience. If you are working within a word limit, for example, you might not have the space in which to address all the concerns of all interested parties. Or you might be primarily interested in reaching one segment of a general audience, such as consumers. Once you identify a specific audience, it's helpful to think about what kinds of arguments and evidence will appeal to that audience.

A4-c In your introduction, establish credibility and state your position.

When you are constructing an argument, make sure your introduction includes a thesis statement that establishes your position on the issue you have chosen to debate (see also C2-a). In the sentences leading up to the thesis, establish your credibility (*ethos*) with readers by showing that you are knowledgeable and fair-minded. If possible, build common ground (*pathos*) with readers who may not at first agree with your views, and show them why they should consider your thesis.

In the following introduction, student Kevin Smith presents himself as someone worth listening to. Because Smith introduces both sides of the debate, readers are likely to approach his essay with an open mind.

Smith shows that he is familiar with the legal issues surrounding school prayer.

Although the Supreme Court has ruled against prayer in public schools on First Amendment grounds, many people still feel that prayer should be allowed. Such people value prayer as a practice central to their faith and believe that prayer is a way for schools to reinforce moral principles. They also compellingly point out a paradox in the First Amendment itself: at what point does the separation of church and state restrict the freedom of those who wish to practice their religion? What proponents of school prayer fail to realize, however, is that the Supreme Court's decision, although it was made on legal grounds, makes sense on religious grounds as well. Prayer is too important to be trusted to our public schools.

—Kevin Smith, student

Smith is fair-minded, presenting the views of both sides.

Thesis builds common ground.

TIP: A good way to test a thesis while drafting and revising is to imagine a counterargument to your argument (see A4-f). If you can't think of an opposing point of view, rethink your thesis and ask a classmate or writing center tutor to respond to your argument.

MORE HELP IN YOUR HANDBOOK

When you write an argument, you state your position in a thesis.

▶ Writing effective thesis statements: **C1-c**

A4-d Back up your thesis with persuasive lines of argument.

Arguments of any complexity contain lines of argument that, when taken together, might reasonably persuade readers that the thesis has merit. The following, for example, are the main lines of argument that Sam Jacobs used in his paper about the shift from print to online news (see pp. 107–11).

CENTRAL CLAIM

Thesis: The shift from print to online news provides unprecedented opportunities for readers to become more engaged with the news, to hold journalists accountable, and to participate as producers, not simply as consumers.

SUPPORTING CLAIMS

- Print news has traditionally had a one-sided relationship with its readers, delivering information for passive consumption.
- Online news invites readers to participate in a collaborative process—to question and even contribute to the content.
- Links within news stories provide transparency, allowing readers to move easily from the main story to original sources, related articles, or background materials.
- Technology has made it possible for readers to become news producer—posting text, audio, images, and video of news events.
- Citizen journalists can provide valuable information, sometimes more quickly than traditional journalists can.

If you sum up your main lines of argument, as Jacobs did, you will have a rough outline of your essay. In your paper, you will provide evidence for each of your claims.

A4-e Support your claims with specific evidence.

You will need to support your central claim and any subordinate claims with evidence: facts, statistics, examples, visuals (such as graphs or photos), expert opinion, and so on. Debatable topics require that you consult some written sources to establish your *ethos* and to persuade your audience. As you read through or view the sources, you will learn more about the arguments and counterarguments at the center of your debate.

USING SOURCES RESPONSIBLY: Remember that you must document the sources you use as evidence. Documentation gives credit to authors and shows readers how to locate a source in case they want to assess its credibility or explore the issues further.

> **MORE HELP IN YOUR HANDBOOK**
>
> Sources, when used responsibly, can support an argument.
>
> ▶ Paraphrasing, summarizing, and quoting sources: **R2-c**
> ▶ Punctuating direct quotations: **P5-a**
> ▶ Citing sources: **MLA-4b, APA-4b,** and **CMS-4b**

Using facts and statistics

A fact is something that is known with certainty because it has been objectively verified: The capital of Wyoming is Cheyenne. Carbon has an atomic weight of 12. John F. Kennedy was assassinated on November 22, 1963. Statistics are collections of numerical facts: Alcohol abuse is a factor in nearly 40 percent of traffic fatalities. More than four in ten businesses in the United States are owned by women.

Most arguments are supported at least to some extent by facts and statistics. For example, in the following passage the writer uses statistics to show that college students carry unreasonably high credit card debt.

> A 2009 study by Sallie Mae revealed that undergraduates are carrying record-high credit card balances and are relying on credit cards more than ever, especially in the economic downturn. The average credit card debt per college undergraduate is more than three thousand dollars, and three-quarters of undergraduates carry balances and incur finance charges each month (Hunter).

Writers often use statistics in selective ways to bolster their own positions. If you suspect that a writer's handling of statistics is not quite fair, track down the original sources for those statistics or read authors with opposing views, who may give you a fuller understanding of the numbers.

hackerhandbooks.com/writersref

Ⓔ A4 Writing arguments > As you write: Drafting your central claim and supporting claims

Using examples and illustrations

Examples and illustrations (extended examples, often in story form) rarely prove a point by themselves, but when used in combination with other forms of evidence they flesh out an argument with details and bring it to life. Because examples are often concrete and sometimes vivid, they can reach readers in ways that statistics and abstract ideas cannot.

In a paper arguing that online news provides opportunities for readers that print does not, Sam Jacobs describes how regular citizens using only cell phones and laptops helped save lives during Hurricane Katrina by sending important updates to the rest of the world.

Using visuals

Visuals can support your argument by providing vivid and detailed evidence and by capturing your readers' attention. Bar or line graphs, for instance, describe and organize complex statistical data; photographs can immediately and evocatively convey abstract ideas. Writers in almost every academic field use visual evidence to support their arguments or to counter opposing arguments. For example, to explain a conflict among Southeast Asian countries, a historian might choose a map to illustrate the geography. Or to refute another scholar's hypothesis about the dangers of a vegetarian diet, a nutritionist might support her claims by using a table to organize and highlight detailed numerical information. (See pp. 18–19.)

As you consider using visual evidence, ask yourself these questions:

- Is the visual accurate, credible, and relevant?
- How will the visual appeal to readers? Logically? Ethically? Emotionally?
- How will the visual evidence function? Will it provide background information? Present complex numerical information or an abstract idea? Lend authority? Refute counterarguments?

Citing expert opinion

Although they are no substitute for careful reasoning of your own, the views of an expert can contribute to the force of your argument. For example, to help him make the case that print journalism has a one-sided relationship with its readers, Sam Jacobs integrates an expert's key description.

> With the rise of the Internet, however, this model has been criticized by journalists such as Dan Gillmor, founder of the Center for Citizen Media, who argues that traditional print journalism treats "news as a lecture," whereas online news is "more of a conversation" (xxiv).

When you rely on expert opinion, make sure that your source is an expert in the field you are writing about. In some cases, you may need to provide credentials showing why your source is worth listening to, such as listing the person's position or title alongside his or her name. When including expert testimony in your paper, you can summarize or paraphrase the expert's opinion, or you can quote the expert's exact words. You will, of course, need to document the source, as Jacobs did.

A4-f Anticipate objections; counter opposing arguments.

Readers who already agree with you need no convincing, but skeptical readers may resist your arguments. To be willing to give up a position that seems reasonable, readers need to see that another position is even more reasonable. In addition to presenting your own case, therefore, you should acknowledge the opposing arguments and attempt to counter them.

It might seem at first that drawing attention to an opposing point of view or contradictory evidence would weaken your argument. But by

---

Anticipating and countering opposing arguments

To anticipate a possible objection to your argument, consider the following questions.

- Could a reasonable person draw a different conclusion from your facts or examples?
- Might a reader question any of your assumptions or offer an alternative explanation?
- Is there any evidence that might weaken your position?

The following questions may help you respond to a reader's potential objection.

- Can you concede the point to the opposition but challenge the point's importance or usefulness?
- Can you explain why readers should consider a new perspective or question a piece of evidence?
- Should you explain how your position responds to contradictory evidence?
- Can you suggest a different interpretation of the evidence?

When you write, use phrasing to signal to readers that you're about to present an objection. Often the signal phrase can go in the lead sentence of a paragraph.

Critics of this view argue that . . .
While some readers point out that . . .
Researchers challenge these claims by . . .

---

anticipating and countering objections, you show yourself as a reasonable and well-informed writer who has a thorough understanding of the significance of the issue.

There is no best place in an essay to deal with opposing views. Often it is useful to summarize the opposing position early in your essay. After stating your thesis but before developing your own arguments, you might have a paragraph that addresses the most important counterargument. Or you can anticipate objections paragraph by paragraph as you develop your case. Wherever you decide to address opposing arguments, you will enhance your credibility if you explain the arguments of others accurately and fairly.

A4-g   Build common ground.

As you counter opposing arguments, try to seek out one or two assumptions you might share with readers who do not initially agree with your views. If you can show that you share their concerns, your readers will be more likely to accept that your argument is valid. For example, to persuade people opposed to controlling the deer population with a regulated hunting season, a state wildlife commission would have to show that it too cares about preserving deer and does not want them to die needlessly. Having established these values in common, the commission might be able to persuade critics that reducing the total number of deer prevents starvation caused by overpopulation.

People believe that intelligence and decency support their side of an argument. To be persuaded, they must see these qualities in your argument. Otherwise they will persist in their opposition.

A4-h   Sample argument essay

In the paper that begins on the next page, student writer Sam Jacobs argues that the shift from print to online news benefits readers by providing them with opportunities to produce news and to think more critically as consumers of news. Notice how he appeals to his readers by presenting opposing views fairly before providing his own arguments.

In writing the paper, Jacobs consulted both print and online sources. When he quotes, summarizes, or paraphrases information from a source, he cites the source with an MLA (Modern Language Association) in-text citation. Citations in the paper refer readers to the list of works cited at the end of the paper. (For more details about citing sources, see MLA-2.)

A guide to writing an argument essay appears on pages 112–13.

hackerhandbooks.com/writersref

e A4 Writing arguments > Sample student writing > Jacobs, "From Lecture to Conversation: Redefining What's 'Fit to Print'" (argument)

Jacobs 1

Sam Jacobs

Professor Alperini

English 101

5 November 2013

From Lecture to Conversation: Redefining What's "Fit to Print"

"All the news that's fit to print," the motto of the *New York Times* since
1896, plays with the word *fit*, asserting that a news story must be newsworthy
and must not exceed the limits of the printed page. The increase in online news
consumption, however, challenges both meanings of the word *fit*, allowing
producers and consumers alike to rethink who decides which topics are worth
covering and how extensive that coverage should be. Any cultural shift usually
means that something is lost, but in this case there are clear gains. The shift
from print to online news provides unprecedented opportunities for readers to
become more engaged with the news, to hold journalists accountable, and to
participate as producers, not simply as consumers.

Guided by journalism's code of ethics—accuracy, objectivity, and
fairness—print news reporters have gathered and delivered stories according
to what editors decide is fit for their readers. Except for op-ed pages and
letters to the editor, print news has traditionally had a one-sided relationship
with its readers. The print news media's reputation for objective reporting
has been held up as "a stop sign" for readers, sending a clear message that
no further inquiry is necessary (Weinberger). With the rise of the Internet,
however, this model has been criticized by journalists such as Dan Gillmor,
founder of the Center for Citizen Media, who argues that traditional print
journalism treats "news as a lecture," whereas online news is "more of a
conversation" (xxiv). Print news arrives on the doorstep every morning
as a fully formed lecture, a product created without participation from its
readership. By contrast, online news invites readers to participate in a
collaborative process—to question and even help produce the content.

One of the most important advantages online news offers over print
news is the presence of built-in hyperlinks, which carry readers from one
electronic document to another. If readers are curious about the definition
of a term, the roots of a story, or other perspectives on a topic, links
provide a path. Links help readers become more critical consumers of
information by engaging them in a totally new way. For instance, the link

In his opening
sentences,
Jacobs provides
background for
his thesis.

Thesis states the
main point.

Jacobs does
not need a
citation for
common
knowledge.

Transition moves
from Jacobs's
main argument to
specific examples.

Marginal annotations indicate MLA-style formatting and effective writing.

Jacobs 2

embedded in the story "Credit-Shy: Younger Generation Is More Likely to
Stick to a Cash-Only Policy" (Sapin) allows readers to find out more about
the financial trends of young adults and provides statistics that confirm
the article's accuracy (see fig. 1). Other links in the article widen the
conversation. These kinds of links give readers the opportunity to conduct
their own evaluation of the evidence and verify the journalist's claims.

Links provide a kind of transparency impossible in print because they
allow readers to see through online news to the "sources, disagreements,
and the personal assumptions and values" that may have influenced a
news story (Weinberger). The International Center for Media and the
Public Agenda underscores the importance of news organizations letting
"customers in on the often tightly held little secrets of journalism." To
do so, they suggest, will lead to "accountability and accountability leads
to credibility" ("Openness"). These tools alone don't guarantee that news
producers will be responsible and trustworthy, but they encourage an open
and transparent environment that benefits news consumers.

Not only has technology allowed readers to become more critical
news consumers, but it also has helped some to become news producers.
The Web gives ordinary people the power to report on the day's events.
Anyone with an Internet connection can publish on blogs and Web
sites, engage in online discussion forums, and contribute video and
audio recordings. Citizen journalists with laptops, cell phones, and digital
camcorders have become news producers alongside large news organizations.

Not everyone embraces the spread of unregulated news reporting
online. Critics point out that citizen journalists are not necessarily
trained to be fair or ethical, for example, nor are they subject to editorial
oversight. Acknowledging that citizen reporting is more immediate
and experimental, critics also question its accuracy and accountability:
"While it has its place . . . it really isn't journalism at all, and it opens
up information flow to the strong probability of fraud and abuse. . . .
Information without journalistic standards is called gossip," writes
David Hazinski in the *Atlanta Journal-Constitution* (23A). In his book
Losing the News, media specialist Alex S. Jones argues that what passes
for news today is in fact "pseudo news" and is "far less reliable"
than traditional print news (27). Even a supporter like Gillmor is willing

---

Margin annotations:

Jacobs clarifies
key terms
(*transparency*
and
accountability).

Source is cited in
MLA style.

Jacobs develops
the thesis.

Opposing views
are presented
fairly.

Jacobs 3

to agree that citizen journalists are "nonexperts," but he argues that they are "using technology to make a profound contribution, and a real difference" (140).

> Jacobs counters opposing arguments.

Citizen reporting made a difference in the wake of Hurricane Katrina in 2005. Armed with cell phones and laptops, regular citizens relayed critical news updates in a rapidly developing crisis, often before traditional journalists were even on the scene. In 2006, the enormous contributions of citizen journalists were recognized when the New Orleans *Times-Picayune* received the Pulitzer Prize in public service for its online coverage—largely citizen-generated—of Hurricane Katrina. In recognizing the paper's "meritorious public service," the Pulitzer Prize board credited the

> A vivid example helps Jacobs make his point.

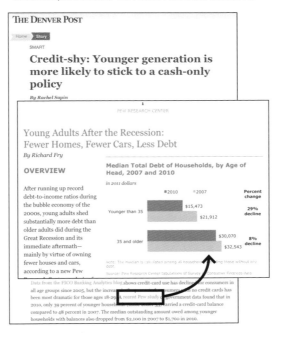

Fig. 1. Links embedded in online news articles allow readers to move from the main story to original sources, related articles, or background materials. The link in this online article (Sapin) points to a statistical report by the Pew Research Center, the original source of the author's data on young adults' spending practices.

(*Sources:* The *Denver Post;* article by Rachel Sapin, special to the *Denver Post;* graph courtesy of PEW Research Center.)

Jacobs 4

Jacobs uses specific evidence for support.

newspaper's blog for "heroic, multi-faceted coverage of [the storm] and its aftermath" ("2006"). Writing for the *Online Journalism Review*, Mark Glaser emphasizes the role that blog updates played in saving storm victims' lives. Further, he calls the *Times-Picayune*'s partnership with citizen journalists a "watershed for online journalism."

Conclusion echoes the thesis without dully repeating it.

The Internet has enabled consumers to participate in a new way in reading, questioning, interpreting, and reporting the news. Decisions about appropriate content and coverage are no longer exclusively in the hands of news editors. Ordinary citizens now have a meaningful voice in the conversation—a hand in deciding what's "fit to print." Some skeptics worry about the apparent free-for-all and loss of tradition. But the expanding definition of news provides opportunities for consumers to be more engaged with events in their communities, their nations, and the world.

Jacobs 5

Works Cited

Gillmor, Dan. *We the Media: Grassroots Journalism by the People, for the People*. O'Reilly Media, 2006.

Glaser, Mark. "NOLA.com Blogs and Forums Help Save Lives after Katrina." *OJR: The Online Journalism Review*, Knight Digital Media Center, 13 Sept. 2005, www.ojr.org/050913glaser/.

Hazinski, David. "Unfettered 'Citizen Journalism' Too Risky." *Atlanta Journal-Constitution*, 13 Dec. 2007, p. 23A. *General OneFile*, go.galegroup .com/ps/.

Jones, Alex S. *Losing the News: The Future of the News That Feeds Democracy*. Oxford UP, 2009.

"Openness and Accountability: A Study of Transparency in Global Media Outlets." *ICMPA: International Center for Media and the Public Agenda*, 2006, www.icmpa.umd.edu/pages/studies/transparency/main.html.

Sapin, Rachel. "Credit-Shy: Younger Generation Is More Likely to Stick to a Cash-Only Policy." *The Denver Post*, 26 Aug. 2013, www.denverpost .com/ci_23929523/credit-shy-younger-generation-stick-cash-only -policy.

"The 2006 Pulitzer Prize Winners: Public Service." *The Pulitzer Prizes*, Columbia U, www.pulitzer.org/prize-winners-by-year/2006. Accessed 21 Oct. 2013.

Weinberger, David. "Transparency Is the New Objectivity." *Joho the Blog*, 19 July 2009, www.hyperorg.com/blogger/2009/07/19/transparency-is -the-new-objectivity/.

Works cited page uses MLA style.

List is alphabetized by authors' last names (or by title when a work has no author).

Access date is used for a Web source that has no update date.

Writing guide | Argument essay

Composing an **argument** gives you the opportunity to propose a reasonable solution to a debatable issue. You say to your readers: "Here is my position, here is the evidence that supports the position, and here is my response to other positions on the issue." A sample argument essay begins on page 107.

Key features

- **A thesis, stated as a clear position on a debatable issue,** frames an argument essay. The issue is debatable because reasonable people disagree about it.

- **An examination of the issue's context** indicates why the issue is important, why readers should care about it, or how your position fits into the debates surrounding the topic.

- **Sufficient, representative, and relevant evidence** supports the argument's claims. Evidence needs to be specific and persuasive; quoted, summarized, or paraphrased fairly and accurately; and cited correctly.

- **Opposing positions are summarized and countered.** By anticipating and countering objections to your position, you establish common ground with readers and show yourself as a reasonable and well-informed writer.

Thinking ahead: Presenting or publishing

You may have some flexibility in how you present or publish your argument. If you submit your argument as an audio or video essay, make sure you understand the genre's conventions and think through how your voice or a combination of sounds and images can help you establish your ethos. If you are taking a position on a local issue, consider publishing your argument in the form of a newspaper op-ed or letter to the editor. The benefit? A real-world audience.

Writing your argument

⟲ EXPLORE

Generate ideas by brainstorming responses to questions such as the following.

- What is the debate around your issue? What sources will help you learn more about your issue?

- What position will you take? Why does your position need to be argued?

- What evidence supports your position? What evidence makes you question your position?

- What types of appeals—*ethos*, *logos*, *pathos*—might you use to persuade readers? How will you build common ground with your readers?

DRAFT

Try to figure out the best way to structure your argument. A typical outline might include the following steps: Capture readers' attention; state your position; give background information; outline your major claims with specific evidence; recognize and respond to opposing points of view; and end by reinforcing your point and why it matters.

As you draft, think about the best order for your claims. You could organize by strength, building to your strongest argument (instead of starting with your strongest), or by concerns your audience might have.

REVISE

Ask your reviewers for specific feedback. Here are some questions to guide their comments.

- Is the thesis clear? Is the issue debatable?
- Is the evidence persuasive? Is more needed?
- Is your argument organized logically?
- Are there any flaws in your reasoning or assumptions that weaken the argument?
- Have you presented yourself as a knowledgeable, trustworthy writer?
- Does the conclusion pull together your entire argument? How might the conclusion be more effective?

A5 Speaking confidently

Speaking and writing draw on many of the same skills. Effective speakers, like effective writers, identify their purpose, audience, and context. They project themselves as informed and reasonable, establish common ground with listeners, and use specific, memorable language and effective techniques to capture their audience's attention.

In many college classes, you'll be assigned to give an oral presentation. The more comfortable you become speaking in different settings, the easier it will be when you give a formal presentation. You can practice your speaking skills as well by contributing to class discussions, responding to the comments of fellow students, and playing an active role in team-based learning.

A5-a   Identify your purpose, audience, and context.

As you plan your presentation, be sure to strategize a bit: Identify your purpose (reason) for speaking, your audience (listeners), and the context (situation) in which you will speak.

PURPOSE
: Begin by asking: "Why am I speaking? What is my goal?" Your goal might be to inform, to persuade, to evaluate, to recommend, or to call to action.

AUDIENCE
: Effective speakers identify the needs and expectations of their audience and shape their material to meet those needs and expectations. Assess what your audience may already know and believe, what objections you might need to anticipate, and how you might engage your listeners. Ask yourself: "Who is my audience? Why have they assembled? How should I interact with them?"

CONTEXT
: Ask yourself: "What is the situation for my speech? Is it an assignment for a course? The presentation of a group project? A community meeting? And how much time do I have to speak?" The answers to these questions will help you shape your presentation for your particular speaking situation.

A5-b   Prepare a presentation.

Knowing your subject

You need to know your subject well in order to talk about it confidently. Although you should not pack too much material into a short speech, you need to speak knowledgeably to engage your audience. In preparing your speech, do some research to know what evidence — facts, statistics, visuals, expert testimony — will support your points. The more you know about your subject, the more comfortable you'll be in speaking about it.

Developing a clear structure

A good presentation is easy to follow because it has a clear beginning, middle, and end. In your introduction, preview the purpose and structure of your presentation and the question or problem you are addressing so that your audience can anticipate where you are going. Start with an opening hook: a surprising fact, a brief but vivid story, or an engaging question. For an informative speech, organize the body in a way that helps your audience remember key points of information. For a persuasive speech, organize so that you build enthusiasm for your position. And conclude your presentation by giving listeners a sense of completion. Restate the key points, and borrow an image or phrasing from your opening to make the speech come full circle.

Using signposts and repetition

As you speak, use signposts to remind the audience of your purpose and key points. Signposts guide listeners (*"The shift to online news has three important benefits for consumers."*) and help them to understand the transition from one point to the next (*"The second benefit is . . ."*). By repeating phrases, you emphasize the importance of key points and help listeners remember them. For more on transitions and repetition, see C5-d.

Writing for the ear, not the eye

Use an engaging, lively style so that the audience will enjoy listening to you. Be sure to use straightforward language that's easy on the ear, not too complicated or too abstract. Occasionally remind listeners of your main point, and keep your sentences short and direct so that listeners can easily follow your presentation. In the following example, the writer adapts a single essay sentence for a speech by breaking it into smaller chunks, engaging the audience with a question, and using plainer language.

SENTENCE FROM AN ARGUMENT ESSAY

In 2006, the enormous contributions of citizen journalists were recognized when the New Orleans *Times-Picayune* received the Pulitzer Prize in public service for its online coverage—largely citizen-generated—of Hurricane Katrina.

ESSAY MATERIAL ADAPTED FOR A SPEECH

The New Orleans *Times-Picayune* newspaper won the 2006 Pulitzer Prize in public service. Why? For its online news about Hurricane Katrina—news generated by ordinary people.

Using *ethos*, *logos*, and *pathos* as a speaker

To deliver an effective speech, you must establish your credibility (*ethos*) and appeal to your listeners' sense of logic and reason (*logos*) as well as to their values and beliefs (*pathos*).

Ethical appeals (*ethos*)

A speaker's *ethos* comes from being informed, trustworthy, and reasonable. When you speak knowledgeably about your subject, you inspire listeners' confidence.

Logical appeals (*logos*)

To engage the members of your audience, you must appeal to their need for relevant and reliable evidence. When your logic is sound and you clarify your assumptions, you gain their trust.

Emotional appeals (*pathos*)

To establish common ground with your audience, you need to appeal to their values and beliefs and show respect for their ideas. When you use vivid details and visual evidence, you deepen the interest in the human dimension of your subject.

Integrating sources with signal phrases

If you are using sources, do so responsibly. As you speak, be sure to acknowledge your sources with signal phrases ("According to *New York Times* columnist David Brooks . . ."). If you have slides, you can include signal phrases or citations on the slides. For more on integrating and citing sources, see MLA-3 and MLA-4, APA-3 and APA-4, or CMS-3 and CMS-4, depending on the required style.

Using visuals and multimedia purposefully

Well-chosen visuals, video clips, or audio clips can enhance your presentation and add variety. For example, a photograph can highlight an environmental problem, a line graph can quickly show a trend over time, and a brief video clip can capture listeners' attention.

Visuals and multimedia convey information powerfully, but you need to consider how they support your purpose and how your audience will respond. Too many visuals can be distracting, especially when they are difficult to read or don't convey a clear message, so be sure each visual serves a specific purpose. Multimedia can overwhelm a presentation and leave you without sufficient time to achieve your goals.

A5-c Focus on delivery.

Establishing a relationship

If you give your audience your full attention, they will return it. Before delivering your speech, make steady eye contact with your listeners, introduce yourself, and help your audience connect with you. If you establish a relationship with your audience, you'll start to relax into your role as a speaker and feel confident.

Starting strong and ending strong

The beginnings and endings of speeches are critical to gaining and holding an audience's attention. Just as with a written paper, your oral presentation will benefit from using effective strategies for introducing and concluding your speech. (See C2-a and C2-c.) Plan your opening strategy: Will you pose a question and ask for a show of hands? Will you tell a brief personal story? When you move confidently through your introduction, you will find your voice and connect with listeners. For a strong conclusion, look directly at your audience as you review your key points. Finish by thanking your audience and inviting questions.

Using slides and notes

Projected slides are a popular method to support your delivery. Slides offer both a sequential structure (one slide after another) and a hierarchical structure (general message with supporting bullet points). Consider what information you may need to reinforce visually in order to meet your audience's expectations. Keep slides simple and use them for a specific purpose. Don't crowd slides with text or data and don't leave listeners confused about why you are showing them.

For his presentation, student Sam Jacobs created a clear, readable slide to summarize counterarguments to his position.

 What critics say:

Citizen-journalists
- are not trained to be fair or ethical
- do not follow editorial standards
- can be unreliable and inaccurate

Listening actively and critically

Speakers have the main role in presentations, but audience members have important roles, too.

- Speakers need encouragement, so look at a speaker, make eye contact, and show your interest.
- Be ready with a question about an interesting or surprising point, and always offer a compliment on the presentation.
- In class discussions, listening is just as important as speaking. Practice being a skilled listener by focusing on the speaker—whether it's a peer or the instructor—and by paying attention to body language. Listen for *ideas* as well as words so that you can understand the speaker's point and respond.

Confident speakers rely on brief notes to remind them of the main points they wish to convey. Notes work best when you have rehearsed and know how much time to devote to each point. You might want to use notes to capture the exact wording of a quotation or the details of a research finding; or you might want to use notes as reminders to pause or to repeat key phrases.

Boosting your confidence

Effective speaking starts with good organization and a clear message. However, pay attention to additional details that will boost your confidence and strengthen your presentation:

- Dress appropriately for the occasion.
- Make eye contact; use body language and hand gestures to emphasize your points.
- Practice, practice, practice. Speak out loud in front of a mirror or a friend, and practice using visual aids. Practice is especially critical for a team presentation.
- Time your rehearsal.
- Know the setting in which you'll deliver your talk.
- Understand the room's lighting and technology; preload any necessary slides or software; check the volume for any video.

A5-d Remix an essay for a presentation.

In a college course, you may be assigned to adapt an essay you've written for delivery to a listening audience. Student writer Sam Jacobs made important adjustments as he prepared a speaking script from his argument essay. Compare the first paragraph of Jacobs's essay (p. 107) with the opening lines for his presentation below.

Good afternoon, everyone. I'm Sam Jacobs.

Friendly opening establishes a relationship with the audience.

Jacobs starts with his key question and engages the audience immediately.

Today I want to explore this question: How do consumers benefit from reading news online? But first let me have a quick show of hands: How many of you read news online? If you answered yes, you are part of the 71% of young Americans, ages 18 to 29, who read their news online, according to the Pew Center. We've grown up in a digital generation, consuming news on every possible mobile device, especially our cell phones. Most of us don't miss the newspaper arriving on the doorstep every morning. And because we expect to read news online, we take it for granted. But if we take it for granted, we might miss the benefits of participating as producers of news, not simply as consumers. The three benefits I want to explore are . . .

Establishes common ground with the audience.

Jacobs uses a source responsibly and integrates it well.

Jacobs repeats words and phrases for emphasis and uses signposts to make it easier for his listeners to follow his ideas.

A6 Writing in the disciplines

College courses expose you to the thinking of scholars in many disciplines, such as those within the humanities (literature, music, art), the social sciences (psychology, anthropology, sociology), and the sciences (biology, physics, chemistry). No matter what you study, you will be asked to write for a variety of audiences in a variety of formats and practice the methods used by the discipline's scholars and practitioners. In a criminal justice course, for example, you may be asked to write a policy memo or a legal brief; in a nursing course, you may be asked to write a case study or a practice paper. To write in these courses is to think like a criminologist or a nurse and to engage in the debates of the discipline.

hackerhandbooks.com/writersref

e A5 Speaking confidently > As you write: Remixing an essay for an oral presentation

A6-a Find commonalities across disciplines.

A good paper in any field needs to communicate a writer's purpose to an audience and to explore an engaging question about a subject. Effective writers make an argument and support their claims with evidence. Writers in most fields show readers the thesis they're developing (or, in the sciences, the hypothesis they're testing) and counter the objections of other writers. All disciplines require writers to document where they found their evidence and from whom they borrowed ideas.

A6-b Recognize the questions writers in a discipline ask.

Disciplines are characterized by the kinds of questions their scholars attempt to answer. Social scientists, for example, who analyze human behavior, might ask about the factors that cause people to act in certain ways. Historians, who seek an understanding of the past, often ask questions about the causes and effects of events and about the connections between current and past events. One way to understand how disciplines ask different questions is to look at assignments on the same topic in various fields. Many disciplines, for example, might be interested in the subject of disasters. The following are some questions that writers in different fields might ask about this subject.

EDUCATION	Should the elementary school curriculum teach students how to cope in disasters?
FILM	How has the disaster film genre changed since the advent of computer-generated imagery (CGI) in the early 1970s?
HISTORY	How did the formation of the American Red Cross change this country's approach to natural disasters?
ENGINEERING	In the wake of disastrous storm-related flooding, what recent innovations in levee design are most promising?
PSYCHOLOGY	What are the most effective ways to identify and treat post-traumatic stress (PTS) in disaster survivors?

The questions you ask in any discipline will form the basis of the thesis for your paper. The questions themselves don't communicate a central idea, but they may lead you to one. For an education paper, for example, you might begin with the question "Should the elementary school curriculum teach students how to cope in disasters?" After considering the issues involved, you might draft the following working thesis.

School systems should adopt age-appropriate curriculum units that introduce children to the risks of natural and human-made disasters and that allow children to practice coping strategies.

Whenever you write for a college course, try to determine the kinds of questions scholars in the field might ask about a topic. You can find clues in assigned readings, lecture topics, discussion groups, and the paper assignment itself.

A6-C Understand the kinds of evidence writers in a discipline use.

Regardless of the discipline in which you're writing, you must support any claims you make with evidence—facts, statistics, examples, and expert opinion.

The kinds of evidence used in different disciplines commonly overlap. Students of geography, media studies, and political science, for example, might use census data to explore different topics. The evidence that one discipline values, however, might not be sufficient to support an interpretation or a conclusion in another field. You might use anecdotes or interviews in an anthropology paper, for example, but such evidence would be irrelevant in a biology lab report. The chart on page 122 lists the kinds of evidence accepted in various disciplines.

A6-d Become familiar with a discipline's language conventions.

Every discipline has a specialized vocabulary. As you read the articles and books in a field, you'll notice certain words and phrases that come up repeatedly. Sociologists, for example, use terms such as *independent variables* and *dyads* to describe social phenomena; computer scientists might refer to *algorithm design* and *loop invariants* to describe programming methods. Practitioners in health fields use terms like *treatment plan* and *systemic assessment* to describe patient care. Use discipline-specific terms only when you are certain that you and your readers understand their meaning.

In addition to vocabulary, many fields of study have developed specialized conventions for point of view and verb tense. See the chart on page 123.

A6-e Use a discipline's preferred citation style.

In any discipline, you must give credit to those whose ideas or words you have borrowed. Avoid plagiarism by citing sources honestly and accurately.

While all disciplines emphasize careful documentation, each follows a particular system of citation that its members have agreed on.

Evidence typically used in various disciplines

Humanities: literature, art, film, music, philosophy

- Passages of text or lines of a poem
- Details from an image or a work of art
- Passages of a musical composition
- Critical essays that analyze original works

Humanities: history

- Primary sources such as photographs, letters, maps, and government documents
- Scholarly books and articles that interpret evidence

Social sciences: psychology, sociology, political science, anthropology

- Data from original experiments
- Results of field research such as interviews or surveys
- Statistics from government agencies
- Scholarly books and articles that interpret data from original experiments and from other researchers' studies
- Primary sources such as maps and government documents
- Primary sources such as artifacts

Sciences: biology, chemistry, physics

- Data from original experiments
- Scholarly articles that report findings from experiments
- Models, diagrams, or animations

Writers in the humanities usually use the system established by the Modern Language Association (MLA). Scholars in some social sciences, such as psychology and anthropology, follow the style guidelines of the American Psychological Association (APA). Scholars in history and some humanities typically follow *The Chicago Manual of Style*. For guidance on using the MLA, APA, or CMS (*Chicago*) format, see the appropriate tabbed sections in this book.

A6-f   Understand the features of writing assignments in the disciplines.

When you are asked to write in a specific discipline, or field of study, start by becoming familiar with the distinctive features of the writing in that discipline. Read the assignment carefully and try to identify its purpose and the types of evidence you are expected to use.

Point of view and verb tense in academic writing

Point of view

- Writers of analytical or research essays in the humanities usually use the third-person point of view: *Austen presents . . .* or *Castel describes the battle as. . . .*

- Scientists and most social scientists, who depend on quantitative research to present findings, tend to use the third-person point of view: *The results indicated. . . .*

- Writers in the humanities and in some social sciences occasionally use the first person in discussing their experience or in writing a personal narrative: *After spending two years interviewing families affected by the war, I began to understand that. . . .*

Present or past tense

- Literature scholars use the present tense to discuss a text: *Hughes effectively dramatizes different views of minority assertiveness.* (See MLA-3b.)

- Science and social science writers use the past tense or present perfect tense to describe experiments from source materials and the present tense to discuss the writer's own findings: *In 2003, Berkowitz released the first double-blind placebo study. . . . Rogers and Chang have found that. . . . Our results paint a murky picture.* (See APA-3b.)

- Writers in history use the present tense or the present perfect tense to discuss a text: *Shelby Foote describes the scene like this . . .* or *Shelby Foote has described the scene like this. . . .* (See CMS-3b.)

On the following pages are examples of assignments in three disciplines—psychology, biology, and nursing—along with excerpts from student papers that were written in response to the assignments.

hackerhandbooks.com/writersref

e A6 Writing in the disciplines > As you write: Examining a writing assignment from one of your courses

e A6 Writing in the disciplines > Sample student writing

  > Charat, "Always Out of Their Seats (and Fighting): Why Are Boys Diagnosed With ADHD More Often Than Girls?" (literature review)

  > Johnson/Arnold, "Distribution Pattern of Dandelion (*Taraxacum officinale*) on an Abandoned Golf Course" (lab report)

  > Riss, "Acute Lymphoblastic Leukemia and Hypertension in One Client" (nursing practice paper)

Writing in psychology

ASSIGNMENT: REVIEW OF THE LITERATURE

Write a literature review in which you report on and evaluate the published research on a behavioral disorder.

1   Key terms
2   Purpose: to report on and evaluate a body of evidence
3   Evidence: research of other psychologists

ADHD IN BOYS VS. GIRLS   3

Always Out of Their Seats (and Fighting):
Why Are Boys Diagnosed With ADHD More Often Than Girls?

Background and explanation of the writer's purpose.

Attention deficit hyperactivity disorder (ADHD) is a commonly diagnosed disorder in children that affects social, academic, or occupational functioning. As the name suggests, its hallmark characteristics are hyperactivity and lack of attention as well as impulsive behavior. For decades, studies have focused on the causes, expression, prevalence, and outcome of the disorder, but until recently very little research investigated gender differences. In fact, until the early 1990s most research focused exclusively on boys (Brown, Madan-Swain, & Baldwin, 1991), perhaps because many more boys than girls are diagnosed with ADHD. Researchers have speculated on the possible explanations for the disparity, citing reasons such as true sex differences in the manifestation of the disorder's symptoms, gender biases in those who refer children to clinicians, and possibly even the diagnostic procedures themselves (Gaub & Carlson, 1997). But the most persuasive reason is that ADHD is often a comorbid condition — that is, it coexists with other behavior disorders that are not diagnosed properly and that do exhibit gender differences.

Evidence from research the writer has reviewed.

APA citations and specialized language (ADHD, comorbid).

Thesis: writer's argument.

It has been suggested that in the United States children are often misdiagnosed as having ADHD when they actually suffer from a behavior disorder such as conduct disorder (CD) or a combination of ADHD and another behavior disorder (Disney, Elkins, McGue, & Iancono, 1999; Lilienfeld & Waldman, 1990). Conduct disorder is characterized by negative and criminal behavior in children and is highly correlated with adult diagnoses of antisocial personality disorder (ASPD). This paper first considers research that has dealt only with gender

Two sources in one parenthetical citation are separated by a semicolon.

Marginal annotations indicate appropriate formatting and effective writing.

Writing in biology

ASSIGNMENT: LAB REPORT

Write a report on an experiment you conduct on the distribution pattern of a plant species indigenous to the Northeast. Describe your methods for collecting data and interpret your experiment's results.

1   Key terms
2   Purpose: to describe the methods and interpret the results of an experiment
3   Evidence: data collected during the experiment

Distribution Pattern of Dandelion 1

CSE style, typical in sciences.

Distribution Pattern of Dandelion (*Taraxacum officinale*)
on an Abandoned Golf Course

ABSTRACT

This paper reports our study of the distribution pattern of the common dandelion (*Taraxacum officinale*) on an abandoned golf course in Hilton, NY, on 10 July 2012. An area of 6 ha was sampled with 111 randomly placed 1×1 m^2 quadrats. The dandelion count from each quadrat was used to test observed frequencies against expected frequencies based on a hypothesized random distribution.

[Abstract continues.]

Abstract: an overview of hypothesis, experiment, and results.

INTRODUCTION

Theoretically, plants of a particular species may be aggregated, random, or uniformly distributed in space.[1] The distribution type may be determined by many factors, such as availability of nutrients, competition, distance of seed dispersal, and mode of reproduction.[2]

The purpose of this study was to determine if the distribution pattern of the common dandelion (*Taraxacum officinale*) on an abandoned golf course was aggregated, random, or uniform.

Introduction: context and purpose of experiment. Instead of a thesis in the introduction, a lab report interprets the data in a later Discussion section.

METHODS

The study site was an abandoned golf course in Hilton, NY. The vegetation was predominantly grasses, along with dandelions, broad-leaf plantain (*Plantago major*), and bird's-eye speedwell (*Veronica chamaedrys*).

Scientific names for plant species.

Marginal annotations indicate appropriate formatting and effective writing.

Writing in nursing

ASSIGNMENT: NURSING PRACTICE PAPER

Write a client history, a nursing diagnosis, recommendations for care, your rationales, and expected and actual outcomes. Use interview notes, the client's health records, and relevant research findings.

1 Key terms
2 Purpose: to provide client history, diagnosis, recommendations, and outcomes
3 Evidence: interviews, health records, and research findings

---

Writer uses APA style, typical in social sciences.

ALL AND HTN IN ONE CLIENT   1

Acute Lymphoblastic Leukemia and Hypertension in One Client:

A Nursing Practice Paper

Physical History

Evidence from client's medical chart for overall assessment.

E.B. is a 16-year-old white male 5'10" tall weighing 190 lb. He was admitted to the hospital on April 14, 2012, due to decreased platelets and a need for a PRBC transfusion. He was diagnosed in October 2011 with T-cell acute lymphoblastic leukemia (ALL), after a 2-week period of decreased energy, decreased oral intake, easy bruising, and petechia. The client had experienced a 20-lb weight loss in the previous 6 months. At the time of diagnosis, his CBC showed a WBC count of 32, an H & H of 13/38, and a platelet count of 34,000. His initial chest X-ray showed an anterior mediastinal mass. Echocardiogram showed a structurally normal heart. He began induction chemotherapy on October 12, 2011, receiving vincristine, 6-mercaptopurine, doxorubicin, intrathecal methotrexate, and then high-dose methotrexate per protocol. During his hospital stay, he required packed red cells and platelets on two different occasions. He was diagnosed with hypertension (HTN) due to systolic blood pressure readings consistently ranging between 130s and 150s and was started on nifedipine. E.B. has a history of mild ADHD, migraines, and deep vein thrombosis (DVT). He has tolerated the induction and consolidation phases of chemotherapy well and is now in the maintenance phase, in which he receives a daily dose of mercaptopurine, weekly doses of methotrexate, and intermittent doses of steroids.

Specialized nursing language (*echocardiogram, chemotherapy,* and so on).

Instead of a thesis, or main claim, the writer gives a diagnosis, recommendations for care, and expected outcomes, all supported by evidence from observations and client records.

Marginal annotations indicate appropriate formatting and effective writing.

S

Sentence
Style

S Sentence Style

S1 Parallelism

If two or more ideas are parallel, they are easier to grasp when expressed in parallel grammatical form. Single words should be balanced with single words, phrases with phrases, clauses with clauses.

A kiss can be a comma, a question mark, or an exclamation point.
—Mistinguett

This novel is not to be tossed lightly aside, but to be hurled with great force.
—Dorothy Parker

In matters of principle, stand like a rock; in matters of taste, swim with the current.
—Thomas Jefferson

Writers often use parallelism to create emphasis. (See p. 153.)

S1-a Balance parallel ideas in a series.

Readers expect items in a series to appear in parallel grammatical form. When one or more of the items violate readers' expectations, a sentence will be needlessly awkward.

► **Children who study music also learn confidence, discipline,**
creativity.
and ~~they are creative.~~
The revision presents all the items in the series as nouns: *confidence*, *discipline*, and *creativity*.

► **Impressionist painters believed in focusing on ordinary**

subjects, capturing the effects of light on those subjects,
using
and ~~to use~~ short brushstrokes.
The revision uses *-ing* forms for all the items in the series: *focusing*, *capturing*, and *using*.

hackerhandbooks.com/writersref
e S1 Parallelism > Exercises: S1–2 to S1–6
✓ S1 Parallelism > LearningCurve: Parallelism

▶ **Racing to get to work on time, Sam drove down the middle**
                                          ignored
    of the road, ran one red light, and two stop signs.
                                        ^

The revision adds a verb to make the three items parallel: *drove, ran,*
and *ignored.*

In headings and lists, aim for as much parallelism as the content allows.

Headings

Headings on the same level of organization should be written in parallel form — as single words, phrases, or clauses. The following examples
show parallel headings from an environmental report and a nursing
manual, respectively.

PHRASES AS HEADINGS
Safeguarding Earth's atmosphere
Charting the path to sustainable energy
Conserving global forests

INDEPENDENT CLAUSES AS HEADINGS
Ask the patient to describe current symptoms.
Take a detailed medical history.
Record the patient's vital signs.

Lists

Lists are usually introduced with an independent clause followed by
a colon. Lists are most readable when they are presented in parallel
grammatical form. Like headings, lists might consist of words, phrases,
or clauses. The following list consists of parallel noun phrases.

Renewable energy technologies include the following: hydroelectric
power, solar power, wind energy, and geothermal energy.

S1-b Balance parallel ideas presented as pairs.

When pairing ideas, underscore their connection by expressing them in
similar grammatical form. Paired ideas are usually connected in one of
these ways:

- with a coordinating conjunction such as *and, but,* or *or*
- with a pair of correlative conjunctions such as *either . . . or* or
  not only . . . but also
- with a word introducing a comparison, usually *than* or *as*

Parallel ideas linked with coordinating conjunctions

Coordinating conjunctions (*and*, *but*, *or*, *nor*, *for*, *so*, and *yet*) link ideas of equal importance. When those ideas are closely parallel in content, they should be expressed in parallel grammatical form.

▶ **Emily Dickinson's poetry features the use of dashes and**
the capitalization of
~~**capitalizing**~~ **common words.**
^
The revision balances the nouns *use* and *capitalization*.

▶ **Many states are reducing property taxes for home owners**
extending
and ~~**extend**~~ **tax credits to renters.**
^
The revision balances the verb *reducing* with the verb *extending*.

Parallel ideas linked with correlative conjunctions

Correlative conjunctions come in pairs: *either . . . or, neither . . . nor, not only . . . but also, both . . . and, whether . . . or.* Make sure that the grammatical structure following the second half of the pair is the same as that following the first half.

▶ **Thomas Edison was not only a prolific inventor but also** ~~**was**~~

a successful entrepreneur.

The words *a prolific inventor* follow *not only,* so *a successful entrepreneur* should follow *but also.* Repeating *was* creates an unbalanced effect.

to
▶ **The clerk told me either to change my flight or take the train.**
^
To change my flight, which follows *either,* should be balanced with *to take the train,* which follows *or.*

Comparisons linked with than or as

In comparisons linked with *than* or *as,* the elements being compared should be expressed in parallel grammatical structure.

to ground
▶ **It is easier to speak in abstractions than** ~~**grounding**~~ **one's thoughts**
^
in reality.

To speak is balanced with *to ground.*

► In Pueblo culture, according to Silko, ~~to write~~ writing down the
stories of a tribe is not the same as "keeping track of all the
stories" (290).

When you are quoting from a source, parallel grammatical structure—such
as *writing . . . keeping*—helps create continuity between your sentence and
the words from the source. (See MLA-4a on citing sources in MLA style.)

Comparisons should also be logical and complete. (See S2-c.)

S1-c   Repeat function words to clarify parallels.

Function words such as prepositions (*by, to*) and subordinating conjunctions (*that, because*) signal the grammatical nature of the word groups
to follow. Although you can sometimes omit them, be sure to include
them whenever they signal parallel structures that readers might
otherwise miss.

► Our study revealed that left-handed students were more likely to
have trouble with classroom desks and *that* rearranging desks for
exam periods was useful.

A second subordinating conjunction helps readers sort out the two parallel ideas: *that* left-handed students have trouble with classroom desks
and *that* rearranging desks was useful.

S2   Needed words

Sometimes writers leave out words intentionally, and the meaning of
the sentence is not affected. But leaving out words can occasionally
cause confusion for readers or make the sentence ungrammatical. Readers need to see at a glance how the parts of a sentence are connected.

Multilingual Languages sometimes differ in the need for certain
words. In particular, be alert for missing articles, verbs, subjects, or
expletives. See M2, M3-a, and M3-b.

S2-a Add words needed to complete compound structures.

In compound structures, words are often left out for economy: *Tom is a man who means what he says and [who] says what he means.* Such omissions are acceptable as long as the omitted words are common to both parts of the compound structure.

If a sentence defies grammar or idiom because an omitted word is not common to both parts of the compound structure, the simplest solution is to put the word back in.

▶ **Advertisers target customers whom they identify through**
                            who
  demographic research or have purchased their product in
                          ^

  the past.

    The word *who* must be included because *whom . . . have purchased* is not grammatically correct.

                          accepted
▶ **Mayor Davis never has and never will accept a bribe.**
                 ^

    Has . . . accept is not grammatically correct.

                             in
▶ **Many South Pacific islanders still believe and live by ancient laws.**
                            ^

    Believe . . . by is not idiomatic in English. (For a list of common idioms, see W5-d.)

S2-b Add the word *that* if there is any danger of misreading without it.

If there is no danger of misreading, the word *that* may be omitted when it introduces a subordinate clause. *The value of a principle is the number of things [that] it will explain.* When a sentence might be misread without *that*, however, it is necessary to include the word.

▶ **In his famous obedience experiments, psychologist Stanley**
                  that
  Milgram discovered ordinary people were willing to inflict
             ^

  physical pain on strangers.

    Milgram didn't discover ordinary people; he discovered that ordinary people were willing to inflict pain on strangers. The word *that* tells readers to expect a clause, not just *ordinary people*, as the direct object of *discovered*.

S2-c   Add words needed to make comparisons logical and complete.

Comparisons should be made between items that are alike. To compare unlike items is illogical and distracting.

▶ **The forests of North America are much more extensive**
　　　　　those of
than ~~Europe.~~
　　　^

Forests must be compared with forests, not with all of Europe.

▶ **Some say that Ella Fitzgerald's renditions of Cole Porter's**
　　　　　　　　　　　　　　　　singer's.
songs are better than any other ~~singer.~~
　　　　　　　　　　　　　　^

Ella Fitzgerald's renditions cannot logically be compared with a singer. The revision uses the possessive form *singer's*, with the word *renditions* being implied.

Sometimes the word *other* must be inserted to make a comparison logical.

　　　　　　　　　　　　other
▶ **Jupiter is larger than any planet in our solar system.**
　　　　　　　　　　　　　^

Jupiter is a planet in our solar system, and it cannot be larger than itself.

Sometimes the word *as* must be inserted to make a comparison grammatically complete.

　　　　　　　　　　　as
▶ **The city of Lowell is as old, if not older than, the neighboring**
　　　　　　　　　　　　　^

city of Lawrence.

The construction *as old* is not complete without a second *as: as old as . . . the neighboring city of Lawrence.*

Comparisons should be complete enough to ensure clarity. The reader should understand what is being compared.

INCOMPLETE　　Brand X is less salty.

COMPLETE　　Brand X is less salty than Brand Y.

Finally, comparisons should leave no ambiguity for readers. If a sentence lends itself to more than one interpretation, revise the sentence to state clearly which interpretation you intend. In the following ambiguous sentence, two interpretations are possible.

AMBIGUOUS	Ken helped me more than my roommate.
CLEAR	Ken helped me more than *he helped* my roommate.
CLEAR	Ken helped me more than my roommate *did*.

S2-d Add the articles *a*, *an*, and *the* where necessary for grammatical completeness.

It is not always necessary to repeat articles with paired items: *We bought a computer and printer.* However, if one of the items requires *a* and the other requires *an*, both articles must be included.

▶ We bought a laptop and ^an^ antivirus program.

Articles are sometimes omitted in recipes and other instructions that are meant to be followed while they are being read. In nearly all other forms of writing, whether formal or informal, such omissions are inappropriate.

> **Multilingual** Choosing and using articles can be challenging for multilingual writers. See M2.

S3 Problems with modifiers

Modifiers, whether they are single words, phrases, or clauses, should point clearly to the words they modify. As a rule, related words should be kept together.

S3-a Put limiting modifiers in front of the words they modify.

Limiting modifiers such as *only, even, almost, nearly,* and *just* should appear in front of a verb only if they modify the verb: *At first, I couldn't even touch my toes, much less grasp them.* If they limit the

hackerhandbooks.com/writersref
ⓔ S3 Problems with modifiers > Exercises: S3-2 to S3-5
☑ S3 Problems with modifiers > LearningCurve: Modifiers

meaning of some other word in the sentence, they should be placed in front of that word.

▶ **The literature reveals that students learn new vocabulary**
  only
  words when they are encouraged to read.
       ^

Only limits the meaning of the *when* clause.

                    just
▶ **If you ~~just~~ interview chemistry majors, your picture of the**
                    ^
  student body's response to the new grading policies will be

  incomplete.

The adverb *just* limits the meaning of *chemistry majors*, not *interview*.

When the limiting modifier *not* is misplaced, the sentence usually suggests a meaning the writer did not intend.

                        not
▶ **In the United States in 1860, all black southerners were ~~not~~**
                        ^
  slaves.

The original sentence says that no black southerners were slaves. The revision makes the writer's real meaning clear: Some (but not all) black southerners were slaves.

S3-b   Place phrases and clauses so that readers can see at a glance what they modify.

Although phrases and clauses can appear at some distance from the words they modify, make sure your meaning is clear. When phrases or clauses are oddly placed, absurd misreadings can result.

MISPLACED	The soccer player returned to the clinic where he had undergone emergency surgery in 2012 in a limousine sent by Adidas.
REVISED	Traveling in a limousine sent by Adidas, the soccer player returned to the clinic where he had undergone emergency surgery in 2012.

The revision corrects the false impression that the soccer player underwent emergency surgery in a limousine.

    On the walls
▶ ~~There~~ **are many pictures of comedians who have performed**
    ^
  at Gavin's. ~~on the walls.~~
              ^
The comedians weren't performing on the walls; the pictures were on the walls.

Occasionally the placement of a modifier leads to an ambiguity — a squinting modifier. In such a case, two revisions will be possible, depending on the writer's intended meaning.

AMBIGUOUS	The exchange students we met for coffee occasionally questioned us about our latest slang.
CLEAR	The exchange students we occasionally met for coffee questioned us about our latest slang.
CLEAR	The exchange students we met for coffee questioned us occasionally about our latest slang.

In the original version, it was not clear whether the meeting or the questioning happened occasionally. Both revisions eliminate the ambiguity.

S3-c Move awkwardly placed modifiers.

As a rule, a sentence should flow from subject to verb to object, without lengthy detours along the way. When a long adverbial word group separates a subject from its verb, a verb from its object, or a helping verb from its main verb, the result is often awkward.

▶ ~~Hong Kong,~~ After more than 150 years of British rule, was Hong Kong

transferred back to Chinese control in 1997.

There is no reason to separate the subject, *Hong Kong*, from the verb, *was transferred*, with a long phrase.

▶ ~~Jeffrey Meyers discusses,~~ In his biography of F. Scott

Jeffrey Meyers discusses
Fitzgerald, the writer's "fascination with the superiority, the

selfishness, and the emptiness of the rich" (166).

There is no reason to separate the verb, *discusses*, from its object, *fascination*, with two prepositional phrases.

Multilingual English does not allow an adverb to appear between a verb and its object. See M3-f.

easily
▶ Yolanda lifted ~~easily~~ the fifty-pound weight.

S3-d Avoid split infinitives when they are awkward.

An infinitive consists of *to* plus the base form of a verb: *to think, to breathe, to dance.* When a modifier appears between *to* and the verb, an infinitive is said to be "split": *to carefully balance, to completely understand.*

When a long word or a phrase appears between the parts of the infinitive, the result is usually awkward.

▶ The patient should try to ~~if possible~~ avoid going up and down stairs.
   (If possible, the — inserted at beginning)

Attempts to avoid split infinitives can result in equally awkward sentences. When alternative phrasing sounds unnatural, most experts allow — and even encourage — splitting the infinitive.

AWKWARD   We decided actually to enforce the law.

BETTER   We decided to actually enforce the law.

At times, neither the split infinitive nor its alternative sounds particularly awkward. In such situations, it is usually better not to split the infinitive, especially in formal writing.

▶ Nursing students learn to ~~accurately~~ record a patient's vital
   signs/ *accurately.*

S3-e Repair dangling modifiers.

A dangling modifier fails to refer logically to any word in the sentence. Dangling modifiers are easy to repair, but they can be hard to recognize, especially in your own writing.

Recognizing dangling modifiers

Dangling modifiers are usually word groups (such as verbal phrases) that suggest but do not name an actor. When a sentence opens with such a modifier, readers expect the subject of the next clause to name the actor. If it doesn't, the modifier dangles.

▶ Understanding the need to create checks and balances on power
   the framers of
   the Constitution divided the government into three branches.

   The framers of the Constitution (not the document itself) understood the need for checks and balances.

hackerhandbooks.com/writersref

e S3 Problems with modifiers > Exercises: S3–7 to S3–10

✓ S3 Problems with modifiers > LearningCurve: Modifiers

▶ After completing seminary training, ~~women's~~ access to the
women were often denied ^

priesthood. ~~has often been denied.~~
^

Women (not their access to the priesthood) complete the training.

The following sentences illustrate four common kinds of dangling modifiers.

DANGLING   *Deciding to join the navy*, the recruiter enthusiastically pumped Joe's hand. [Participial phrase]

DANGLING   *Upon entering the doctor's office*, a skeleton caught my attention. [Preposition followed by a gerund phrase]

DANGLING   *To satisfy her mother*, the piano had to be practiced every day. [Infinitive phrase]

DANGLING   *Though not eligible for the clinical trial*, the doctor prescribed the drug for Ethan on compassionate grounds. [Elliptical clause with an understood subject and verb]

These dangling modifiers falsely suggest that the recruiter decided to join the navy, that the skeleton entered the doctor's office, that the piano intended to satisfy the mother, and that the doctor was not eligible for the clinical trial.

Although most readers will understand the writer's intended meaning in such sentences, the unintended humor can be distracting.

Repairing dangling modifiers

To repair a dangling modifier, you can revise the sentence in one of two ways:

- Name the actor in the subject of the sentence.
- Name the actor in the modifier.

Depending on your sentence, one of these revision strategies may be more appropriate than the other.

Checking for dangling modifiers

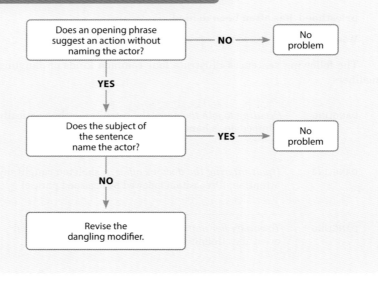

ACTOR NAMED IN SUBJECT

> Upon entering the doctor's office, a skeleton. ~~caught my~~
>   I noticed
> ~~attention.~~

> To satisfy her mother, the piano ~~had to be practiced~~
>   Jing-mei had to practice
> every day.

ACTOR NAMED IN MODIFIER

> ~~Deciding~~ to join the navy, the recruiter enthusiastically
>   When Joe decided
>   his
> pumped ~~Joe's~~ hand.

> Though not eligible for the clinical trial, the doctor
>   Ethan was
>   him
> prescribed the drug for ~~Ethan~~ on compassionate grounds.

NOTE: You cannot repair a dangling modifier just by moving it. Consider, for example, the following sentence about a skeleton. If you put the modifier at the end of the sentence (*A skeleton caught my attention upon* *entering the doctor's office*), you are still suggesting—absurdly—that the skeleton entered the office. The only way to avoid the problem is to put the word *I* in the sentence, either as the subject or in the modifier.

▶ Upon entering the doctor's office, a skeleton . ~~caught my~~
                                        I noticed
   ~~attention.~~

▶ ~~Upon entering~~ the doctor's office, a skeleton caught my attention.
   As I entered

S4 Shifts

This section can help you avoid unnecessary shifts that might distract or confuse your readers: shifts in point of view, in verb tense, in mood or voice, or from indirect to direct questions or quotations.

S4-a Make the point of view consistent in person and number.

The point of view of a piece of writing is the perspective from which it is written: first person (*I* or *we*), second person (*you*), or third person (*he, she, it, one, they*, or any noun).

The *I* (or *we*) point of view, which emphasizes the writer, is a good choice for informal letters and writing based primarily on personal experience. The *you* point of view, which emphasizes the reader, works well for giving advice or explaining how to do something. The third-person point of view, which emphasizes the subject, is appropriate in formal academic and professional writing.

Writers who have trouble settling on an appropriate point of view sometimes shift confusingly from one to another. The solution is to choose a suitable perspective and stay with it.

▶ Our class practiced rescuing a victim trapped in a wrecked car.
   We learned to dismantle the car with the essential tools. ~~You~~
                                                              We
   were graded on ~~your~~ speed and ~~your~~ skill in freeing the victim.
               our   our

   The writer should have stayed with the *we* point of view. *You* is inappropriate because the writer is not addressing readers directly. *You* should not be used in a vague sense meaning "anyone." (See p. 223.)

hackerhandbooks.com/writersref
🄴 S4 Shifts > Exercises: S4–2, S4–9 to S4–11
☑ S4 Shifts > LearningCurve: Shifts

> You need
> ▶ ~~One needs~~ a password and a credit card number to access the
>   ⌃
>   database. You will be billed at an hourly rate.

You is an appropriate choice because the writer is giving advice directly to readers.

S4-b Maintain consistent verb tenses.

Consistent verb tenses clearly establish the time of the actions being described. When a passage begins in one tense and then shifts without warning and for no reason to another, readers are distracted and confused.

> ▶ There was no way I could fight the current and win. Just as I was
>   jumped   swam
>   losing hope, a stranger ~~jumps~~ off a passing boat and ~~swims~~
>   ⌃   ⌃
>   toward me.

The writer thought that the present tense (*jumps, swims*) would convey immediacy and drama. But having begun in the past tense (*could fight, was losing*), the writer should follow through in the past tense.

Writers often encounter difficulty with verb tenses when writing about literature. Because fictional events occur outside the time frames of real life, the past tense and the present tense may seem equally appropriate. The literary convention, however, is to describe fictional events consistently in the present tense. (See p. 123.)

> ▶ The scarlet letter is a punishment sternly placed on Hester's breast
>   is
>   by the community, and yet it ~~was~~ a fanciful and imaginative
>   ⌃
>   product of Hester's own needlework.

S4-c Make verbs consistent in mood and voice.

Unnecessary shifts in the mood of a verb can be distracting and confusing to readers. There are three moods in English: the *indicative*, used for facts, opinions, and questions; the *imperative*, used for orders or advice; and the *subjunctive*, used in certain contexts to express wishes or conditions contrary to fact (see G2-g).

The following passage shifts confusingly from the indicative to the imperative mood.

▶ **The counselor advised us to spread out our core requirements**

She also suggested that we
over two or three semesters. ~~Also,~~ **pay attention to pre-**
    ^

requisites for elective courses.

The writer began by reporting the counselor's advice in the indicative mood (*counselor advised*) and switched to the imperative mood (*pay attention*); the revision puts both sentences in the indicative.

A verb may be in either the active voice (with the subject doing the action) or the passive voice (with the subject receiving the action). (See W3-a.) If a writer shifts without warning from one to the other, readers may be left wondering why.

gives it
▶ **Each student completes a self-assessment/,** ~~The self-assessment is then~~
                                              ^

exchanges
~~given~~ **to the teacher, and a copy** ~~is exchanged~~ **with a classmate.**
        ^   ^

Because the passage began in the active voice (*student completes*) and then switched to the passive (*self-assessment is given*, *copy is exchanged*), readers are left wondering who gives the self-assessment to the teacher and the classmate. The active voice, which is clearer and more direct, leaves no ambiguity.

S4-d   Avoid sudden shifts from indirect to direct questions or quotations.

An indirect question reports a question without asking it: *We asked whether we could visit Miriam.* A direct question asks directly: *Can we visit Miriam?* Sudden shifts from indirect to direct questions are awkward. In addition, sentences containing such shifts are impossible to punctuate because indirect questions must end with a period and direct questions must end with a question mark. (See p. 313.)

whether she reported
▶ **I wonder whether Karla knew of the theft and, if so,** ~~did she report~~

it to the police?.
              ^

The revision poses both questions indirectly. The writer could also ask both questions directly: *Did Karla know of the theft, and, if so, did she report it to the police?*

hackerhandbooks.com/writersref
e S4 Shifts > Exercises: S4–7 to S4–11
☑ S4 Shifts > LearningCurve: Shifts

An indirect quotation reports someone's words without quoting word-for-word: *Senator Kessel said that she wants to see evidence.* A direct quotation presents the exact words of a speaker or writer, set off with quotation marks: *Senator Kessel said, "I want to see evidence."* Unannounced shifts from indirect to direct quotations are distracting and confusing, especially when the writer fails to insert the necessary quotation marks, as in the following example.

▶ **The patient said she had been experiencing heart palpitations**

     asked me to
and ~~please~~ run as many tests as possible to find out the
       ^

problem.

The revision reports the patient's words indirectly. The writer also could quote the words directly: *The patient said, "I have been experiencing heart palpitations. Please run as many tests as possible to find out the problem."*

S5 Mixed constructions

A mixed construction contains sentence parts that do not sensibly fit together. The mismatch may be a matter of grammar or of logic.

S5-a Untangle the grammatical structure.

Once you begin a sentence, your choices are limited by the range of grammatical patterns in English. (See B2 and B3.) You cannot begin with one grammatical plan and switch without warning to another. Often you must rethink the purpose of the sentence and revise.

> MIXED   For most drivers who have a blood alcohol content of .05 percent double their risk of causing an accident.

The writer begins the sentence with a long prepositional phrase and makes it the subject of the verb *double.* But a prepositional phrase can serve only as a modifier; it cannot be the subject of a sentence.

> REVISED   For most drivers who have a blood alcohol content of .05 percent, the risk of causing an accident is doubled.

> REVISED   Most drivers who have a blood alcohol content of .05 percent double their risk of causing an accident.

In the first revision, the writer begins with the prepositional phrase and finishes the sentence with a proper subject and verb (*risk . . . is doubled*). In the second revision, the writer stays with the original verb (*double*) and begins the sentence another way, making *drivers* the subject of *double*.

► *Electing*
  ~~When the country elects~~ a president is the most important

  responsibility in a democracy.

The adverb clause *When the country elects a president* cannot serve as the subject of the verb *is*. The revision replaces the adverb clause with a gerund phrase, a word group that can function as a subject. (See B3-c and B3-b.)

► Although the United States is a wealthy nation, ~~but~~ more than

20 percent of our children live in poverty.

The coordinating conjunction *but* cannot link a subordinate clause (*Although the United States . . .*) with an independent clause (*more than 20 percent of our children live in poverty*).

Occasionally a mixed construction is so tangled that it defies grammatical analysis. When this happens, back away from the sentence, rethink what you want to say, and then rewrite the sentence.

MIXED | In the whole-word method, children learn to recognize entire words rather than by the phonics method in which they learn to sound out letters and groups of letters.

REVISED | The whole-word method teaches children to recognize entire words; the phonics method teaches them to sound out letters and groups of letters.

Multilingual English does not allow double subjects, nor does it allow an object or an adverb to be repeated in an adjective clause. Unlike some other languages, English does not allow a noun and a pronoun to be repeated in a sentence if they have the same grammatical function. See M3-c and M3-d.

► My father ~~he~~ moved to Peru before he met my mother.

S5-b Straighten out the logical connections.

The subject and the predicate (the verb and its modifiers) should make sense together; when they don't, the error is known as *faulty predication*.

▶ The court decided that ~~Tiffany's welfare~~ would not be safe living
 ^Tiffany

 with her abusive parents.

Tiffany, not her welfare, may not be safe.

▶ Under the revised plan, the elderly, ~~who now receive a double~~
 ^double personal exemption for the

 ~~personal exemption,~~ will be abolished.

The exemption, not the elderly, will be abolished.

An appositive is a noun that renames a nearby noun. When an appositive and the noun it renames are not logically equivalent, the error is known as *faulty apposition*. (See B3-c.)

▶ ~~The tax accountant,~~ a lucrative profession, requires intelligence,
 ^Tax accounting,

 patience, and attention to mathematical detail.

The tax accountant is a person, not a profession.

S5-c Avoid *is when, is where,* and *reason . . . is because* constructions.

In formal English, many readers object to *is when, is where,* and *reason . . . is because* constructions on either grammatical or logical grounds. Grammatically, the verb *is* (as well as *are, was,* and *were*) should be followed by a noun that renames the subject or by an adjective that describes the subject, not by an adverb clause beginning with *when, where,* or *because.* (See B2-b and B3-e.) Logically, the words *when, where,* and *because* suggest relations of time, place, and cause—relations that do not always make sense with *is, are, was,* or *were.*

▶ Anorexia nervosa is ~~where people~~ think they are too fat and
 ^a disorder suffered by people who

 often diet to the point of starvation.

Where refers to places. Anorexia nervosa is a disorder, not a place.

▶ The ~~reason the~~ experiment failed ~~is~~ because conditions in the

lab were not sterile.

The writer might have changed *because* to *that* (*The reason the experiment failed is that conditions in the lab were not sterile*), but the preceding revision is more concise.

S6 Sentence emphasis

Within each sentence, emphasize your point by expressing it in the subject and verb of an independent clause, the words that receive the most attention from readers (see S6-a to S6-e).

Within longer stretches of prose, you can draw attention to ideas deserving special emphasis by using a variety of techniques, often involving an unusual twist or some element of surprise (see S6-f).

S6-a Coordinate equal ideas; subordinate minor ideas.

When combining two or more ideas in one sentence, you have two choices: coordination or subordination. Choose coordination to indicate that the ideas are equal or nearly equal in importance. Choose subordination to indicate that one idea is less important than another.

Coordination

Coordination draws attention equally to two or more ideas. To coordinate single words or phrases, join them with a coordinating conjunction or with a pair of correlative conjunctions: *bananas and strawberries*; *not only a lackluster plot but also inferior acting* (see B1-g).

To coordinate independent clauses—word groups that express a complete thought and that can stand alone as a sentence—join them with a comma and a coordinating conjunction or with a semicolon:

, and	, but	, or	, nor
, for	, so	, yet	;

The semicolon is often accompanied by a conjunctive adverb such as *moreover, furthermore, therefore,* or *however* or by a transitional phrase such as *for example, in other words,* or *as a matter of fact.* (For a longer list, see p. 149.)

---

hackerhandbooks.com/writersref

🄴 S6 Sentence emphasis > Exercises: S6–3 to S6–7, S6–11 and S6–12

☑️ S6 Sentence emphasis > LearningCurve: Coordination and subordination

Assume, for example, that your intention is to draw equal attention to the following two ideas.

Social networking Web sites offer ways for people to connect in the virtual world. They do not replace face-to-face forms of social interaction.

To coordinate these ideas, you can join them with a comma and the coordinating conjunction *but* or with a semicolon and the conjunctive adverb *however*.

Social networking Web sites offer ways for people to connect in the virtual world, but they do not replace face-to-face forms of social interaction.

Social networking Web sites offer ways for people to connect in the virtual world; however, they do not replace face-to-face forms of social interaction.

It is important to choose a coordinating conjunction or conjunctive adverb appropriate to your meaning. In the preceding example, the two ideas contrast with each other, calling for *but* or *however*. (For specific coordination strategies, see the chart on p. 149.)

Subordination

To give unequal emphasis to two or more ideas, express the major idea in an independent clause and place any minor ideas in subordinate clauses or phrases. (For specific subordination strategies, see the chart on p. 150.)

Let your intended meaning determine which idea you emphasize. Consider the two ideas about social networking Web sites.

Social networking Web sites offer ways for people to connect in the virtual world. They do not replace face-to-face forms of social interaction.

If your purpose is to stress the ways that people can connect in the virtual world rather than the limitations of these connections, subordinate the idea about the limitations.

Although they do not replace face-to-face forms of social interaction, social networking Web sites offer ways for people to connect in the virtual world.

To focus on the limitations of the virtual world, subordinate the idea about the ways people connect on these Web sites.

Although social networking Web sites offer ways for people to connect in the virtual world, they do not replace face-to-face forms of social interaction.

S6-b Combine choppy sentences.

Short sentences demand attention, so you should use them primarily for emphasis. Too many short sentences, one after the other, make for a choppy style.

If an idea is not important enough to deserve its own sentence, try combining it with a sentence close by. Put any minor ideas in subordinate structures such as phrases or subordinate clauses. (See B3.)

▶ **The Parks Department keeps the use of insecticides to a**
because the
minimum/ ~~The~~ city is concerned about the environment.
   ^

The writer wanted to emphasize that the Parks Department minimizes its use of chemicals, so she put the reason in a subordinate clause beginning with *because*.

Using coordination to combine sentences of equal importance

1. Consider using a comma and a coordinating conjunction. (See P1-a.)

, and	, but	, or	, nor
, for	, so	, yet	

   ▶ **In Orthodox Jewish funeral ceremonies, the shroud is**
   and the
   a simple linen vestment/. ~~The~~ coffin is plain wood.
      ^

2. Consider using a semicolon with a conjunctive adverb or transitional phrase. (See p. 300.)

also	however	next
as a result	in addition	now
besides	in fact	of course
consequently	in other words	otherwise
finally	in the first place	still
for example	meanwhile	then
for instance	moreover	therefore
furthermore	nevertheless	thus

   in addition, she
   ▶ **Alicia scored well on the SAT/; ~~She also~~ had excellent**
      ^

   grades and a record of community service.

3. Consider using a semicolon alone. (See P3-a.)

   in
   ▶ **In youth we learn/; ~~In~~ age we understand.**
      ^

Using subordination to combine sentences of unequal importance

1. Consider putting the less important idea in a subordinate clause beginning with one of the following words. (See B3-e.)

after	before	that	which
although	even though	unless	while
as	if	until	who
as if	since	when	whom
because	so that	where	whose

     When

▶ **Elizabeth Cady Stanton proposed a convention to discuss**

    the status of women in America/, Lucretia Mott agreed.

                                                            that she

▶ **My sister owes much of her recovery to a yoga program/She**

    began ~~the program~~ three years ago.

2. Consider putting the less important idea in an appositive phrase. (See B3-c.)

▶ **Karate, ~~is~~ a discipline based on the philosophy of nonviolence/,**

    ~~It~~ teaches the art of self-defense.

3. Consider putting the less important idea in a participial phrase. (See B3-b.)

                                     E

▶ ~~American essayist Cheryl Peck was~~ Encouraged by friends to

                    American essayist Cheryl Peck
    write about her life/, ~~She~~ began combining humor and irony

    in her essays about being overweight.

Multilingual Unlike some other languages, English does not repeat objects or adverbs in adjective clauses. The relative pronoun (*that*, *which*, *whom*) or relative adverb (*where*) in the adjective clause represents the object or adverb. See M3-d.

▶ **The apartment that we rented ~~it~~ needed repairs.**

The pronoun *it* cannot repeat the relative pronoun *that*.

▶ The Chesapeake and Ohio Canal, ~~is~~ a 184-mile waterway
  ^

  constructed in the 1800s~~,~~/ ~~It~~ was a major source of
                          ^

  transportation for goods during the Civil War.

> A minor idea is now tucked into an appositive phrase (*a 184-mile water-way constructed in the 1800s*).

Although subordination is ordinarily the most effective technique for combining short, choppy sentences, coordination is appropriate when the ideas are equal in importance.

                                                    and
▶ At 3:30 p.m., Forrest displayed a flag of truce~~.~~/ ~~Forrest~~ sent in
                                                      ^

  a demand for unconditional surrender.

> Combining two short sentences by joining their predicates (*displayed . . . sent*) is an effective coordination technique.

S6-c   Avoid ineffective or excessive coordination.

Coordinate structures are appropriate only when you intend to draw readers' attention equally to two or more ideas: *Professor Sakellarios praises loudly, and she criticizes softly.* If one idea is more important than another—or if a coordinating conjunction does not clearly signal the relationship between the ideas—you should subordinate the less important idea.

INEFFECTIVE COORDINATION	Closets were taxed as rooms, and most colonists stored their clothes in chests or clothespresses.
IMPROVED WITH SUBORDINATION	Because closets were taxed as rooms, most colonists stored their clothes in chests or clothespresses.

The revision subordinates the less important idea (*closets were taxed as rooms*) by putting it in a subordinate clause. Notice that the subordinating conjunction *Because* signals the relation between the ideas more clearly than the coordinating conjunction *and*.

Because it is so easy to string ideas together with *and*, writers often rely too heavily on coordination in their rough drafts. The cure for excessive coordination is simple: Look for opportunities to tuck minor ideas into subordinate clauses or phrases.

hackerhandbooks.com/writersref

🄴 S6 Sentence emphasis > Exercises: S6–9, S6–11, and S6–12

✅ S6 Sentence emphasis > LearningCurve: Coordination and subordination

After four hours,
▶ ~~Four hours went by, and~~ a rescue truck finally arrived, but by
   ^

that time we had been evacuated in a helicopter.

Three independent clauses were excessive. The least important idea has
become a prepositional phrase.

S6-d Do not subordinate major ideas.

If a sentence buries its major idea in a subordinate construction, readers
may not give the idea enough attention. Make sure to express your major
idea in an independent clause and to subordinate any minor ideas.

                          defeated Thomas E. Dewey,
▶ Harry S. Truman, who was the unexpected winner of the 1948
                            ^

presidential election/. ~~defeated Thomas E. Dewey.~~
                   ^

The writer wanted to focus on Truman's unexpected victory, but the original sentence buried this information in an adjective clause. The revision
puts the more important idea in an independent clause and tucks the less
important idea into an adjective clause (*who defeated Thomas E. Dewey*).

As
▶ I was driving home from my new job, heading down Ranchitos
   ^

Road, ~~when~~ my car suddenly overheated.

The writer wanted to emphasize that the car overheated, not the fact of
driving home. The revision expresses the major idea in an independent
clause and places the less important idea in an adverb clause (*As I was
driving home from my new job*).

S6-e Do not subordinate excessively.

In attempting to avoid short, choppy sentences, writers sometimes go to the
opposite extreme, putting more subordinate ideas into a sentence than its
structure can bear. If a sentence collapses of its own weight, occasionally it
can be restructured. More often, however, such sentences must be divided.

▶ In *Animal Liberation*, Peter Singer argues that animals possess
                                                    H
nervous systems and can feel pain. ~~and that~~ ⱨe believes that
                                          ^   ^
"the ethical principle on which human equality rests requires

us to extend equal consideration to animals" (1).

Excessive subordination makes it difficult for the reader to focus on the quoted passage. By splitting the original sentence into two separate sentences, the writer draws attention to Peter Singer's main claim, that humans should give "equal consideration to animals." (See MLA-4a on citing sources in MLA style.)

S6-f Experiment with techniques for gaining emphasis.

By experimenting with certain techniques, usually involving some element of surprise, you can draw attention to ideas that deserve special emphasis. Use such techniques sparingly, however, or they will lose their punch. The writer who tries to emphasize everything ends up emphasizing nothing.

Using sentence endings for emphasis

You can highlight an idea simply by withholding it until the end of a sentence. The technique works something like a punch line. In the following example, the sentence's meaning is not revealed until its very last word.

> The only completely consistent people are the dead.
> —Aldous Huxley

An inverted sentence reverses the normal subject-verb order, placing the subject at the end, where it receives unusual emphasis. (Also see S7-c.)

> In golden pots are hidden the most deadly poisons.
> —Thomas Draxe

Using parallel structure for emphasis

Parallel grammatical structure draws special attention to paired ideas or to items in a series. (See S1.) When parallel ideas are paired, the emphasis falls on words that underscore comparisons or contrasts, especially when they occur at the end of a phrase or clause.

> We must *stop talking* about the *American dream* and *start listening* to the *dreams of Americans*. —Reubin Askew

In a parallel series, the emphasis falls at the end, so it is generally best to end with the most dramatic or climactic item in the series.

> Sister Charity enjoyed passing out writing punishments: translate the Ten Commandments into Latin, type a thousand-word essay on good manners, copy the New Testament with a quill pen.
> —Marie Visosky, student

Using punctuation for emphasis

Obviously the exclamation point can add emphasis, but you should not overuse it. As a rule, the exclamation point is more appropriate in dialogue than in ordinary prose.

A dash or a colon may be used to draw attention to word groups worthy of special attention. (See P3-d, P3-e, and P6-b.)

> The middle of the road is where the white line is—and that's the worst place to drive.
> —Robert Frost

> I turned to see what the anemometer read: The needle had pegged out at 106 knots. — Jonathan Shilk, student

Occasionally, a pair of dashes may be used to highlight a word or an idea.

> They carried the land itself—Vietnam, the place, the soil—a powdery orange-red dust that covered their boots and fatigues and faces.
> —Tim O'Brien

S7 Sentence variety

When a rough draft is filled with too many sentences that begin the same way or have the same structure, try injecting some variety—as long as you can do so without sacrificing clarity or ease of reading.

S7-a Vary your sentence openings.

Most sentences in English begin with the subject, move to the verb, and continue to the object, with modifiers tucked in along the way or put at the end. For the most part, such sentences are fine. Put too many of them in a row, however, and they become monotonous.

Adverbial modifiers are easily movable when they modify verbs; they can often be inserted ahead of the subject. Such modifiers might be single words, phrases, or clauses.

> ▶ Eventually a
> A few drops of sap ~~eventually~~ began to trickle into the aluminum
> ^
> bucket.

Like most adverbs, *eventually* does not need to appear close to the verb it modifies (*began*).

> Just as the sun was coming up, a
> ▶ A pair of black ducks flew over the pond. ~~just as the sun was~~
>   ^   ^
>
>   ~~coming up.~~

The adverb clause, which modifies the verb *flew*, is as clear at the beginning of the sentence as it is at the end.

Adjectives and participial phrases can frequently be moved to the beginning of a sentence without loss of clarity.

> Dejected and withdrawn,
> ▶ Edward/~~dejected and withdrawn,~~ nearly gave up his search for
>   ^
>
>   a job.

TIP: When beginning a sentence with an adjective or a participial phrase, make sure that the subject of the sentence names the person or thing described in the introductory phrase. If it doesn't, the phrase will dangle. (See S3-e.)

S7-b Use a variety of sentence structures.

A writer should not rely too heavily on simple sentences and compound sentences, for the effect tends to be both monotonous and choppy. (See S6-b and S6-c.) Too many complex or compound-complex sentences, however, can be equally monotonous. If your style tends to one extreme or the other, try to achieve a better mix of sentence types.

The major sentence types are illustrated in the following sentences, all taken from Flannery O'Connor's "The King of the Birds," an essay describing the author's pet peafowl.

SIMPLE	Frequently the cock combines the lifting of his tail with the raising of his voice.
COMPOUND	Any chicken's dusting hole is out of place in a flower bed, but the peafowl's hole, being the size of a small crater, is more so.
COMPLEX	The peacock does most of his serious strutting in the spring and summer when he has a full tail to do it with.
COMPOUND-COMPLEX	The cock's plumage requires two years to attain its pattern, and for the rest of his life, this chicken will act as though he designed it himself.

For a fuller discussion of sentence types, see B4-a.

S7-c   Try inverting sentences occasionally.

A sentence is inverted if it does not follow the normal subject-verb-object pattern. Many inversions sound artificial and should be avoided except in the most formal contexts. But if an inversion sounds natural, it can provide a welcome touch of variety.

> *Set at the top two corners of the stage were huge*
> ▸ **Huge** lavender hearts outlined in bright white lights. ~~were~~
>   ^
> ~~set at the top two corners of the stage.~~

In the revision, the subject, *hearts*, appears after the verb, *were set*. Notice that the two parts of the verb are also inverted—and separated from each other (*Set . . . were*)—without any awkwardness or loss of meaning.

Inverted sentences are used for emphasis as well as for variety (see S6-f).

S7-d   Consider adding an occasional question or quotation.

An occasional question can provide a change of pace, especially at the beginning of a paragraph, where it engages the reader's interest.

> Virginia Woolf, in her book *A Room of One's Own*, wrote that in order for a woman to write fiction she must have two things, certainly: a room of her own (with key and lock) and enough money to support herself.
>
> *What then are we to make of Phillis Wheatley, a slave, who owned not even herself?* This sickly, frail black girl who required a servant of her own at times—her health was so precarious—and who, had she been white, would have been easily considered the intellectual superior of all the women and most of the men in the society of her day. [Italics added.]
>
> —Alice Walker

Quotations can also provide variety by adding the voices of others to your own. These other voices might be quotations from written sources.

> Even when she enters the hospital on the brink of death, the anorexic will refuse help from anyone and will continue to deny needing help, especially from a doctor. At this point, reports Dr. Steven Levenkron, the anorexic is most likely "a frightened, cold, lonely, starved, and physically tortured, exhausted person—not unlike an actual concentration camp inmate" (29). In this condition she is ultimately force-fed through a tube inserted in the chest.
>
> —Jim Drew, student

Notice that the quotation from a written source is documented with a citation in parentheses. (See MLA-4a.)

Word Choice

W Word Choice

W1 Glossary of usage

This glossary includes words commonly confused (such as *accept* and *except*), words commonly misused (such as *aggravate*), and words that are nonstandard (such as *hisself*). It also lists colloquialisms and jargon. Colloquialisms are casual expressions that may be appropriate in informal speech but are inappropriate in formal writing. Jargon is needlessly technical or pretentious language that is inappropriate in most contexts. If an item is not listed here, consult the index. For irregular verbs (such as *sing, sang, sung*), see G2-a. For idiomatic use of prepositions, see W5-d.

a, an Use *an* before a vowel sound, *a* before a consonant sound: *an apple, a peach.* Problems sometimes arise with words beginning with *h* or *u*. If the *h* is silent, the word begins with a vowel sound, so use *an: an hour, an honorable deed.* If the *h* is pronounced, the word begins with a consonant sound, so use *a: a hospital, a hotel.* Words such as *university* and *union* begin with a consonant sound (a *y* sound), so use *a: a union.* Words such as *uncle* and *umbrella* begin with a vowel sound, so use *an: an underground well.* When an abbreviation or an acronym begins with a vowel sound, use *an: an EKG, an MRI, an AIDS prevention program.*

accept, except *Accept* is a verb meaning "to receive." *Except* is usually a preposition meaning "excluding." *I will accept all the packages except that one. Except* is also a verb meaning "to exclude." *Please except that item from the list.*

adapt, adopt *Adapt* means "to adjust or become accustomed"; it is usually followed by *to. Adopt* means "to take as one's own." *Our family adopted a Vietnamese child, who quickly adapted to his new life.*

adverse, averse *Adverse* means "unfavorable." *Averse* means "opposed" or "reluctant"; it is usually followed by *to. I am averse to your proposal because it could have an adverse impact on the economy.*

advice, advise *Advice* is a noun, *advise* a verb. *We advise you to follow John's advice.*

affect, effect *Affect* is usually a verb meaning "to influence." *Effect* is usually a noun meaning "result." *The drug did not affect the disease, and it had adverse side effects. Effect* can also be a verb meaning "to bring about." *Only the president can effect such a dramatic change.*

aggravate *Aggravate* means "to make worse or more troublesome." *Overgrazing aggravated the soil erosion.* In formal writing, avoid the use of *aggravate* meaning "to annoy or irritate." *Her babbling annoyed* (not *aggravated*) *me.*

agree to, agree with *Agree to* means "to give consent to." *Agree with* means "to be in accord with" or "to come to an understanding with." *He agrees with me about the need for change, but he won't agree to my plan.*

ain't *Ain't* is nonstandard. Use *am not, are not (aren't),* or *is not (isn't). I am not* (not *ain't) going home for spring break.*

all ready, already *All ready* means "completely prepared." *Already* means "previously." *Susan was all ready for the concert, but her friends had already left.*

all right *All right,* written as two words, is correct. *Alright* is nonstandard.

all together, altogether *All together* means "everyone or everything in one place." *Altogether* means "entirely." *We were not altogether certain that we could bring the family all together for the reunion.*

allude To *allude* to something is to make an indirect reference to it. Do not use *allude* to mean "to refer directly." *In his lecture, the professor referred* (not *alluded) to several pre-Socratic philosophers.*

allusion, illusion An *allusion* is an indirect reference. An *illusion* is a misconception or false impression. *Did you catch my allusion to Shakespeare? Mirrors give the room an illusion of depth.*

a lot *A lot* is two words. Do not write *alot. Sam lost a lot of weight.* See also *lots, lots of.*

among, between See *between, among.*

amongst In American English, *among* is preferred.

amoral, immoral *Amoral* means "neither moral nor immoral"; it also means "not caring about moral judgments." *Immoral* means "morally wrong." *Until recently, most business courses were taught from an amoral perspective. Murder is immoral.*

amount, number Use *amount* with quantities that cannot be counted; use *number* with those that can. *This recipe calls for a large amount of sugar. We have a large number of toads in our garden.*

an See *a, an.*

and etc. *Et cetera (etc.)* means "and so forth"; *and etc.* is redundant. See also *etc.*

and/or Avoid the awkward construction *and/or* except in technical or legal documents.

angry at, angry with Use *angry with,* not *angry at,* when referring to a person. *The coach was angry with the referee.*

ante-, anti- The prefix *ante-* means "earlier" or "in front of"; the prefix *anti-* means "against" or "opposed to." *William Lloyd Garrison was a leader of the antislavery movement during the antebellum period. Anti-* should be used with a hyphen when it is followed by a capital letter or a word beginning with *i.*

anxious *Anxious* means "worried" or "apprehensive." In formal writing, avoid using *anxious* to mean "eager." *We are eager* (not *anxious*) *to see your new house.*

anybody, anyone *Anybody* and *anyone* are singular. (See G1-e and G3-a.)

anymore Use the adverb *anymore* in a negative context to mean "any longer" or "now." *The factory isn't producing shoes anymore.* Using *anymore* in a positive context is colloquial; in formal writing, use *now* instead. *We order all our food online now* (not *anymore*).

anyone See *anybody, anyone.*

anyone, any one *Anyone*, an indefinite pronoun, means "any person at all." *Any one*, the pronoun *one* preceded by the adjective *any*, refers to a particular person or thing in a group. *Anyone from the winning team may choose any one of the prizes on display.*

anyplace In formal writing, use *anywhere*.

anyways, anywheres *Anyways* and *anywheres* are nonstandard. Use *anyway* and *anywhere*.

as Do not use *as* to mean "because" if there is any chance of ambiguity. *We canceled the picnic because* (not *as*) *it began raining. As* here could mean either "because" or "when."

as, like See *like, as.*

as to *As to* is jargon for *about. He inquired about* (not *as to*) *the job.*

averse See *adverse, averse.*

awful The adjective *awful* and the adverb *awfully* are not appropriate in formal writing.

awhile, a while *Awhile* is an adverb; it can modify a verb, but it cannot be the object of a preposition such as *for*. The two-word form *a while* is a noun preceded by an article and therefore can be the object of a preposition. *Stay awhile. Stay for a while.*

back up, backup *Back up* is a verb phrase. *Back up the car carefully. Be sure to back up your hard drive. Backup* is a noun meaning "a copy of electronically stored data." *Keep your backup in a safe place. Backup* can also be used as an adjective. *I always have a backup plan.*

bad, badly *Bad* is an adjective, *badly* an adverb. *They felt bad about ruining the surprise. Her arm hurt badly after she slid into second base.* (See G4-a, G4-b, and G4-c.)

being as, being that *Being as* and *being that* are nonstandard expressions. Write *because* instead. *Because* (not *Being as*) *I slept late, I had to skip breakfast.*

beside, besides   *Beside* is a preposition meaning "at the side of" or "next to." *Annie sleeps with a flashlight beside her bed. Besides* is a preposition meaning "except" or "in addition to." *No one besides Terrie can have that ice cream. Besides* is also an adverb meaning "in addition." *I'm not hungry; besides, I don't like ice cream.*

between, among   Ordinarily, use *among* with three or more entities, *between* with two. *The money was divided among several contestants. You have a choice between carrots and beans.*

bring, take   Use *bring* when an object is being transported toward you, *take* when it is being moved away. *Please bring me a glass of water. Please take these forms to Mr. Scott.*

burst, bursted; bust, busted   *Burst* is an irregular verb meaning "to come open or fly apart suddenly or violently." Its past tense is *burst*. The past-tense form *bursted* is nonstandard. *Bust* and *busted* are slang for *burst* and, along with *bursted*, should not be used in formal writing.

can, may   The distinction between *can* and *may* is fading, but some writers still observe it in formal writing. *Can* is traditionally reserved for ability, *may* for permission. *Can you speak French? May I help you?*

capital, capitol   *Capital* refers to a city, *capitol* to a building where lawmakers meet. *Capital* also refers to wealth or resources. *The residents of the state capital protested plans to close the streets surrounding the capitol.*

censor, censure   *Censor* means "to remove or suppress material considered objectionable." *Censure* means "to criticize severely." *The administration's policy of censoring books has been censured by the media.*

cite, site   *Cite* means "to quote as an authority or example." *Site* is usually a noun meaning "a particular place." *He cited the zoning law in his argument against the proposed site of the gas station.* Locations on the Internet are usually referred to as *sites. The library's Web site improves every week.*

climactic, climatic   *Climactic* is derived from *climax*, the point of greatest intensity in a series or progression of events. *Climatic* is derived from *climate* and refers to meteorological conditions. *The climactic period in the dinosaurs' reign was reached just before severe climatic conditions brought on an ice age.*

coarse, course   *Coarse* means "crude" or "rough in texture." *The coarse weave of the wall hanging gave it a three-dimensional quality. Course* usually refers to a path, a playing field, or a unit of study; the expression *of course* means "certainly." *I plan to take a course in car repair this summer. Of course, you are welcome to join me.*

compare to, compare with   *Compare to* means "to represent as similar." *She compared him to a wild stallion. Compare with* means "to examine similarities and differences." *The study compared the language ability of apes with that of dolphins.*

complement, compliment *Complement* is a verb meaning "to go with or complete" or a noun meaning "something that completes." As a verb, *compliment* means "to flatter"; as a noun, it means "flattering remark." *Her skill at rushing the net complements his skill at volleying. Martha's flower arrangements receive many compliments.*

conscience, conscious *Conscience* is a noun meaning "moral principles." *Conscious* is an adjective meaning "aware or alert." *Let your conscience be your guide. Were you conscious of his love for you?*

continual, continuous *Continual* means "repeated regularly and frequently." *She grew weary of the continual telephone calls. Continuous* means "extended or prolonged without interruption." *The broken siren made a continuous wail.*

could care less *Could care less* is nonstandard. Write *couldn't care less* instead. *He couldn't* (not *could*) *care less about his psychology final.*

could of *Could of* is nonstandard for *could have. We could have* (not *could of*) *taken the train.*

council, counsel A *council* is a deliberative body, and a *councilor* is a member of such a body. *Counsel* usually means "advice" and can also mean "lawyer"; a *counselor* is one who gives advice or guidance. *The councilors met to draft the council's position paper. The pastor offered wise counsel to the troubled teenager.*

criteria *Criteria* is the plural of *criterion*, which means "a standard or rule or test on which a judgment or decision can be based." *The only criterion for the scholarship is ability.*

data *Data* is a plural noun technically meaning "facts or propositions." But *data* is increasingly being accepted as a singular noun. *The new data suggest* (or *suggests*) *that our theory is correct.* (The singular *datum* is rarely used.)

different from, different than Ordinarily, write *different from. Your sense of style is different from Jim's.* However, *different than* is acceptable to avoid an awkward construction. *Please let me know if your plans are different than* (to avoid *from what*) *they were six weeks ago.*

differ from, differ with *Differ from* means "to be unlike"; *differ with* means "to disagree with." *My approach to the problem differed from hers. She differed with me about the wording of the agreement.*

disinterested, uninterested *Disinterested* means "impartial, objective"; *uninterested* means "not interested." *We sought the advice of a disinterested counselor to help us solve our problem. Mark was uninterested in anyone's opinion but his own.*

don't   *Don't* is the contraction for *do not*. *I don't want any. Don't* should not be used as the contraction for *does not*, which is *doesn't*. *He doesn't* (not *don't*) *want any.*

due to   *Due to* is an adjective phrase and should not be used as a preposition meaning "because of." *The trip was canceled because of* (not *due to*) *lack of interest. Due to* is acceptable as a subject complement and usually follows a form of the verb *be*. *His success was due to hard work.*

each   *Each* is singular. (See G1-e and G3-a.)

effect   See *affect, effect*.

e.g.   In formal writing, replace the Latin abbreviation *e.g.* with its English equivalent: *for example* or *for instance*.

either   *Either* is singular. (See G1-e and G3-a.) For *either . . . or* constructions, see G1-d and G3-a.

elicit, illicit   *Elicit* is a verb meaning "to bring out" or "to evoke." *Illicit* is an adjective meaning "unlawful." *The reporter was unable to elicit any information from the police about illicit drug traffic.*

emigrate from, immigrate to   *Emigrate* means "to leave one country or region to settle in another." *In 1903, my great-grandfather emigrated from Russia to escape the religious pogroms. Immigrate* means "to enter another country and reside there." *More than fifty thousand Bosnians immigrated to the United States in the 1990s.*

eminent, imminent   *Eminent* means "outstanding" or "distinguished." *We met an eminent professor of Greek history. Imminent* means "about to happen." *The snowstorm is imminent.*

enthused   Many people object to the use of *enthused* as an adjective. Use *enthusiastic* instead. *The children were enthusiastic* (not *enthused*) *about going to the circus.*

etc.   Avoid ending a list with *etc*. It is more emphatic to end with an example, and in most contexts readers will understand that the list is not exhaustive. When you don't wish to end with an example, *and so on* is more graceful than *etc*. (See also *and etc*.)

eventually, ultimately   Often used interchangeably, *eventually* is the better choice to mean "at an unspecified time in the future," and *ultimately* is better to mean "the furthest possible extent or greatest extreme." *He knew that eventually he would complete his degree. The existentialists considered suicide the ultimately rational act.*

everybody, everyone   *Everybody* and *everyone* are singular. (See G1-e and G3-a.)

everyone, every one   *Everyone* is an indefinite pronoun. *Every one*, the pronoun *one* preceded by the adjective *every*, means "each individual or thing in a particular group." *Every one* is usually followed by *of. Everyone wanted to go. Every one of the missing books was found.*

except See *accept, except.*

expect Avoid the informal use of *expect* meaning "to believe, think, or suppose." *I think* (not *expect*) *it will rain tonight.*

explicit, implicit *Explicit* means "expressed directly" or "clearly defined"; *implicit* means "implied, unstated." *I gave him explicit instructions not to go swimming. My mother's silence indicated her implicit approval.*

farther, further *Farther* usually describes distances. *Further* usually suggests quantity or degree. *Chicago is farther from Miami than I thought. I would be grateful for further suggestions.*

fewer, less Use *fewer* for items that can be counted; use *less* for items that cannot be counted. *Fewer people are living in the city. Please put less sugar in my tea.*

finalize *Finalize* is jargon meaning "to make final or complete." Use ordinary English instead. *The architect prepared final drawings* (not *finalized the drawings*).

firstly *Firstly* sounds pretentious, and it leads to the ungainly series *firstly, secondly, thirdly,* and so on. Write *first, second, third* instead.

further See *farther, further.*

get *Get* has many colloquial uses. In writing, avoid using *get* to mean the following: "to evoke an emotional response" (*That music always gets to me*); "to annoy" (*After a while, his sulking got to me*); "to take revenge on" (*I got back at her by leaving the room*); "to become" (*He got sick*); "to start or begin" (*Let's get going*). Avoid using *have got to* in place of *must. I must* (not *have got to*) *finish this paper tonight.*

good, well *Good* is an adjective, *well* an adverb. (See G4-a, G4-b, and G4-c.) *He hasn't felt good about his game since he sprained his wrist last season. She performed well on the uneven parallel bars.*

graduate Both of the following uses of *graduate* are standard: *My sister was graduated from UCLA last year. My sister graduated from UCLA last year.* It is nonstandard, however, to drop the word *from: My sister graduated UCLA last year.* Though this usage is common in informal English, many readers object to it.

grow Phrases such as *to grow the economy* and *to grow a business* are jargon. Usually the verb *grow* is intransitive (it does not take a direct object). *Our business has grown very quickly.* Use *grow* in a transitive sense, with a direct object, to mean "to cultivate" or "to allow to grow." *We plan to grow tomatoes this year. John is growing a beard.*

hanged, hung *Hanged* is the past-tense and past-participle form of the verb *hang* meaning "to execute." *The prisoner was hanged at dawn. Hung* is the past-tense and past-participle form of the verb *hang* meaning "to fasten or suspend." *The stockings were hung by the chimney with care.*

hardly   Avoid expressions such as *can't hardly* and *not hardly*, which are considered double negatives. *I can* (not *can't*) *hardly describe my surprise at getting the job.* (See G4-e.)

has got, have got   *Got* is unnecessary and awkward in such constructions. It should be dropped. *We have* (not *have got*) *three days to prepare for the opening.*

he   At one time *he* was commonly used to mean "he or she." Today such usage is inappropriate. (See W4-f and G3-a.)

he/she, his/her   In formal writing, use *he or she* or *his or her.* For alternatives to these wordy constructions, see W4-f and G3-a.

hisself   *Hisself* is nonstandard. Use *himself.*

hopefully   *Hopefully* means "in a hopeful manner." *We looked hopefully to the future.* Some usage experts object to the use of *hopefully* as a sentence adverb on grounds of clarity. To be safe, avoid using *hopefully* in sentences such as the following: *Hopefully, your son will recover soon.* Instead, indicate who is doing the hoping: *I hope that your son will recover soon.*

however   In the past, some writers objected to the conjunctive adverb *however* at the beginning of a sentence, but current experts allow placing the word according to the intended meaning and emphasis. All of the following sentences are correct. *Pam decided, however, to attend the lecture. However, Pam decided to attend the lecture.* (She had been considering other activities.) *Pam, however, decided to attend the lecture.* (Unlike someone else, Pam chose to attend the lecture.) (See P1-f.)

hung   See *hanged, hung.*

i.e.   In formal writing, replace the Latin abbreviation *i.e.* with its English equivalent: *that is.*

if, whether   Use *if* to express a condition and *whether* to express alternatives. *If you go on a trip, whether to Idaho or Italy, remember to bring identification.*

illusion   See *allusion, illusion.*

immigrate   See *emigrate from, immigrate to.*

imminent   See *eminent, imminent.*

immoral   See *amoral, immoral.*

implement   *Implement* is a pretentious way of saying "do," "carry out," or "accomplish." Use ordinary language instead. *We carried out* (not *implemented*) *the director's orders.*

imply, infer   *Imply* means "to suggest or state indirectly"; *infer* means "to draw a conclusion." *John implied that he knew all about computers, but the interviewer inferred that John was inexperienced.*

in, into   *In* indicates location or condition; *into* indicates movement or a change in condition. *They found the lost letters in a box after moving into the house.*

in regards to   *In regards to* confuses two different phrases: *in regard to* and *as regards*. Use one or the other. *In regard to* (or *As regards*) *the contract, ignore the first clause.*

irregardless   *Irregardless* is nonstandard. Use *regardless*.

is when, is where   These mixed constructions are often incorrectly used in definitions. *A runoff election is a second election held to break a tie* (not *is when a second election is held to break a tie*). (See S5-c.)

its, it's   *Its* is a possessive pronoun; *it's* is a contraction of *it is*. (See P4-b and P4-d.) *It's always fun to watch a dog chase its tail.*

kind(s)   *Kind* is singular and should be treated as such. Don't write *These kind of chairs are rare.* Write instead *This kind of chair is rare. Kinds* is plural and should be used only when you mean more than one kind. *These kinds of chairs are rare.*

kind of, sort of   Avoid using *kind of* or *sort of* to mean "somewhat." *The movie was somewhat* (not *sort of*) *boring.* Do not put *a* after either phrase. *That kind of* (not *kind of a*) *salesclerk annoys me.*

lay, lie   See *lie, lay.*

lead, led   *Lead* is a metallic element; it is a noun. *Led* is the past tense of the verb *lead. He led me to the treasure.*

learn, teach   *Learn* means "to gain knowledge"; *teach* means "to impart knowledge." *I must teach* (not *learn*) *my sister to read.*

leave, let   *Leave* means "to exit." Avoid using it with the nonstandard meaning "to permit." *Let* (not *Leave*) *me help you with the dishes.*

less   See *fewer, less.*

let, leave   See *leave, let.*

liable   *Liable* means "obligated" or "responsible." Do not use it to mean "likely." *You're likely* (not *liable*) *to trip if you don't tie your shoelaces.*

lie, lay   *Lie* is an intransitive verb meaning "to recline or rest on a surface." Its forms are *lie, lay, lain. Lay* is a transitive verb meaning "to put or place." Its forms are *lay, laid, laid.* (See G2-b.)

like, as   *Like* is a preposition, not a subordinating conjunction. It can be followed only by a noun or a noun phrase. *As* is a subordinating conjunction that introduces a subordinate clause. In casual speech, you may say *She looks like she hasn't slept* or *You don't know her like I do.* But in formal writing, use *as. She looks as if she hasn't slept. You don't know her as I do.* (See also B1-f and B1-g.)

loose, lose *Loose* is an adjective meaning "not securely fastened." *Lose* is a verb meaning "to misplace" or "to not win." *Did you lose your only loose pair of work pants?*

lots, lots of *Lots* and *lots of* are informal substitutes for *many, much,* or *a lot.* Avoid using them in formal writing.

mankind Avoid *mankind* whenever possible. It offends many readers because it excludes women. Use *humanity, humans, the human race,* or *humankind* instead. (See W4-f.)

may See *can, may.*

maybe, may be *Maybe* is an adverb meaning "possibly." *Maybe the sun will shine tomorrow. May be* is a verb phrase. *Tomorrow may be brighter.*

may of, might of *May of* and *might of* are nonstandard for *may have* and *might have. We might have* (not *might of*) *had too many cookies.*

media, medium *Media* is the plural of *medium. Of all the media that cover the Olympics, television is the medium that best captures the spectacle of the events.*

most *Most* is informal when used to mean "almost" and should be avoided. *Almost* (not *Most*) *everyone went to the parade.*

must of See *may of, might of. Must of* is nonstandard for *must have.*

myself *Myself* is a reflexive or intensive pronoun. Reflexive: *I cut myself.* Intensive: *I will drive you myself.* Do not use *myself* in place of *I* or *me. He gave the flowers to Melinda and me* (not *myself*). (See also G3-c.)

neither *Neither* is singular. (See G1-e and G3-a.) For *neither . . . nor* constructions, see G1-d and G3-a.

none *None* may be singular or plural. (See G1-e.)

nowheres *Nowheres* is nonstandard. Use *nowhere* instead.

number See *amount, number.*

of Use the verb *have,* not the preposition *of,* after the verbs *could, should, would, may, might,* and *must. They must have* (not *must of*) *left early.*

off of *Off* is sufficient. Omit *of. The ball rolled off* (not *off of*) *the table.*

OK, O.K., okay All three spellings are acceptable, but avoid these expressions in formal speech and writing.

parameters *Parameter* is a mathematical term that has become jargon for "fixed limit," "boundary," or "guideline." Use ordinary English instead. *The task force worked within certain guidelines* (not *parameters*).

passed, past *Passed* is the past tense of the verb *pass. Ann passed me another slice of cake. Past* usually means "belonging to a former time" or "beyond a time or place." *Our past president spoke until past midnight. The hotel is just past the next intersection.*

percent, per cent, percentage *Percent* (also spelled *per cent*) is always used with a specific number. *Percentage* is used with a descriptive term such as *large* or *small*, not with a specific number. *The candidate won 80 percent of the primary vote. A large percentage of registered voters turned out for the election.*

phenomena *Phenomena* is the plural of *phenomenon*, which means "an observable occurrence or fact." *Strange phenomena occur at all hours of the night in that house, but last night's phenomenon was the strangest of all.*

plus *Plus* should not be used to join independent clauses. *This raincoat is dirty; moreover* (not *plus*), *it has a hole in it.*

precede, proceed *Precede* means "to come before." *Proceed* means "to go forward." *As we proceeded up the mountain path, we noticed fresh tracks in the mud, evidence that a group of hikers had preceded us.*

principal, principle *Principal* is a noun meaning "the head of a school or an organization" or "a sum of money." It is also an adjective meaning "most important." *Principle* is a noun meaning "a basic truth or law." *The principal expelled her for three principal reasons. We believe in the principle of equal justice for all.*

proceed, precede See *precede, proceed*.

quote, quotation *Quote* is a verb; *quotation* is a noun. Avoid using *quote* as a shortened form of *quotation*. *Quotations* (not *Quotes*) *from his recent book are appearing in various social media channels.*

raise, rise *Raise* is a transitive verb meaning "to move or cause to move upward." It takes a direct object. *I raised the shades. Rise* is an intransitive verb meaning "to go up." *Heat rises.*

real, really *Real* is an adjective; *really* is an adverb. *Real* is sometimes used informally as an adverb, but avoid this use in formal writing. *She was really* (not *real*) *angry.* (See G4-a and G4-b.)

reason . . . is because Use *that* instead of *because*. *The reason she's cranky is that* (not *because*) *she didn't sleep last night.* (See S5-c.)

reason why The expression *reason why* is redundant. *The reason* (not *The reason why*) *Jones lost the election is clear.*

relation, relationship *Relation* describes a connection between things. *Relationship* describes a connection between people. *There is a relation between poverty and infant mortality. Our business relationship has cooled over the years.*

respectfully, respectively *Respectfully* means "showing or marked by respect." *Respectively* means "each in the order given." *He respectfully submitted his opinion to the judge. John, Tom, and Larry were a butcher, a baker, and a lawyer, respectively.*

sensual, sensuous *Sensual* means "gratifying the physical senses," especially those associated with sexual pleasure. *Sensuous* means "pleasing to the senses," especially those involved in the experience of art, music, and nature. *The sensuous music and balmy air led the dancers to more sensual movements.*

set, sit *Set* is a transitive verb meaning "to put" or "to place." Its past tense is *set*. *Sit* is an intransitive verb meaning "to be seated." Its past tense is *sat*. *She set the dough in a warm corner of the kitchen. The cat sat in the doorway.*

shall, will *Shall* was once used in place of the helping verb *will* with *I* or *we*: *I shall, we shall.* Today, however, *will* is generally accepted even when the subject is *I* or *we*. The word *shall* occurs primarily in polite questions (*Shall I find you a pillow?*) and in legalistic sentences suggesting duty or obligation (*The applicant shall file form A by December 31*).

should of *Should of* is nonstandard for *should have*. *They should have* (not *should of*) *been home an hour ago.*

since Do not use *since* to mean "because" if there is any chance of ambiguity. *Because* (not *Since*) *we won the game, we have been celebrating with pizza and dessert. Since* here could mean "because" or "from the time that."

sit See *set, sit.*

site See *cite, site.*

somebody, someone *Somebody* and *someone* are singular. (See G1-e and G3-a.)

something *Something* is singular. (See G1-e.)

sometime, some time, sometimes *Sometime* is an adverb meaning "at an indefinite time." *Some time* is the adjective *some* modifying the noun *time* and means "a period of time." *Sometimes* is an adverb meaning "at times, now and then." *I'll see you sometime soon. I haven't lived there for some time. Sometimes I see him at work.*

suppose to Write *supposed to.*

sure and Write *sure to. We were all taught to be sure to* (not *sure and*) *look both ways before crossing a street.*

take See *bring, take.*

than, then *Than* is a conjunction used in comparisons; *then* is an adverb denoting time. *That serving is more than I can eat. Tom laughed, and then we recognized him.*

that See *who, which, that.*

that, which Many writers reserve *that* for restrictive clauses, *which* for nonrestrictive clauses. (See P1-e.)

theirselves *Theirselves* is nonstandard for *themselves. The hikers pushed the fallen tree branch out of the way themselves* (not *theirselves*).

them The use of *them* in place of *those* is nonstandard. *Please take those* (not *them*) *flowers to the patient in room 220.*

then, than See *than, then*.

there, their, they're *There* is an adverb specifying place; it is also an expletive (placeholder). Adverb: *Sylvia is sitting there patiently.* Expletive: *There are two plums left. Their* is a possessive pronoun. *Fred and Jane finally washed their car. They're* is a contraction of *they are. They're later than usual today.*

they The use of *they* to indicate possession is nonstandard. Use *their* instead. *Cindy and Sam decided to sell their* (not *they*) *1975 Corvette.*

they, their The use of the plural pronouns *they* and *their* to refer to singular nouns or pronouns is nonstandard. *No one handed in his or her* (not *their*) *draft on time.* (See G3-a.)

this kind See *kind(s)*.

to, too, two *To* is a preposition; *too* is an adverb; *two* is a number. *Too many of your shots slice to the left, but the last two were just right.*

toward, towards *Toward* and *towards* are generally interchangeable, although *toward* is preferred in American English.

try and *Try and* is nonstandard for *try to. The teacher asked us all to try to* (not *try and*) *write an original haiku.*

ultimately, eventually See *eventually, ultimately*.

unique Avoid expressions such as *most unique, more straight, less perfect, very round.* Either something is unique or it isn't. It is illogical to suggest degrees of uniqueness. (See G4-d.)

usage The noun *usage* should not be substituted for *use* when the meaning is "employment of." *The use* (not *usage*) *of insulated shades has cut fuel costs dramatically.*

use to Write *used to*.

utilize *Utilize* means "to make use of." It often sounds pretentious; in most cases, *use* is sufficient. *I used* (not *utilized*) *the laser printer.*

wait for, wait on *Wait for* means "to be in readiness for" or "to await." *Wait on* means "to serve." *We're waiting for* (not *waiting on*) *Ruth to take us to the museum.*

ways *Ways* is colloquial when used to mean "distance." *The city is a long way* (not *ways*) *from here.*

weather, whether The noun *weather* refers to the state of the atmosphere. *Whether* is a conjunction referring to a choice between alternatives. *We wondered whether the weather would clear.*

well, good See *good, well*.

where Do not use *where* in place of *that. I heard that* (not *where*) *the crime rate is increasing.*

which   See *that, which* and *who, which, that.*

while   Avoid using *while* to mean "although" or "whereas" if there is any chance of ambiguity. *Although* (not *While*) *Gloria lost money in the slot machine, Tom won it at roulette.* Here *While* could mean either "although" or "at the same time that."

who, which, that   Do not use *which* to refer to persons. Use *who* instead. *That,* though generally used to refer to things, may be used to refer to a group or class of people. *The player who* (not *that* or *which*) *made the basket at the buzzer was named MVP. The team that scores the most points in this game will win the tournament.*

who, whom   *Who* is used for subjects and subject complements; *whom* is used for objects. (See G3-d.)

who's, whose   *Who's* is a contraction of *who is; whose* is a possessive pronoun. *Who's ready for more popcorn? Whose coat is this?* (See P4-b and P4-d.)

will   See *shall, will.*

would of   *Would of* is nonstandard for *would have. She would have* (not *would of*) *had a chance to play if she had arrived on time.*

you   In formal writing, avoid *you* in an indefinite sense meaning "anyone." (See G3-b.) *Any spectator* (not *You*) *could tell by the way John caught the ball that his throw would be too late.*

your, you're   *Your* is a possessive pronoun; *you're* is a contraction of *you are. Is that your new bike? You're in the finals.* (See P4-b and B1-b.)

W2   Wordy sentences

Long sentences are not necessarily wordy, nor are short sentences always concise. A sentence is wordy if it can be tightened without loss of meaning.

W2-a   Eliminate redundancies.

Writers often repeat themselves unnecessarily, thinking that expressions such as *cooperate together, yellow in color,* or *basic essentials* add emphasis to their writing. In reality, such redundancies do just the opposite. There is no need to say the same thing twice.

---

hackerhandbooks.com/writersref

e W2 Wordy sentences > Exercises : W2–3 to W2–7

✓ W2 Wordy sentences > LearningCurve: Word choice and appropriate language

> works
> ▶ Daniel ~~is now employed~~ at a private rehabilitation center
> ^
> ~~working~~ as a registered physical therapist.

Though modifiers ordinarily add meaning to the words they modify, occasionally they are redundant.

> ▶ Gabriele Muccino's film *The Pursuit of Happyness* tells the story of
>
> a single father determined ~~in his mind~~ to pull his family out of
>
> homelessness.

The word *determined* contains the idea that his resolution formed in his mind.

W2-b Avoid unnecessary repetition of words.

Though words may be repeated deliberately, for effect, repetitions will seem awkward if they are clearly unnecessary. When a more concise version is possible, choose it.

> ▶ Our fifth patient, in room six, is a̶ mentally ill.~~patient.~~
> ^
> grow
> ▶ The best teachers help each student ~~become a better student~~
> ^
> both academically and emotionally.

W2-c Cut empty or inflated phrases.

An empty phrase can be cut with little or no loss of meaning. Common examples are introductory word groups that weaken the writer's authority by apologizing or hedging: *in my opinion, I think that, it seems that, one must admit that*, and so on.

> O
> ▶ ~~In my opinion,~~ o̶ur current immigration policy is misguided.
> ^

Readers understand without being told that they are hearing the writer's opinion.

Inflated phrases can be reduced to a word or two without loss of meaning.

> now.
> ▶ We are unable to provide funding ~~at this point in time.~~
> ^

INFLATED	CONCISE
along the lines of	like
as a matter of fact	in fact
at all times	always
at the present time	now, currently
at this point in time	now, currently
because of the fact that	because
by means of	by
due to the fact that	because
for the purpose of	for
have the ability to	be able to, can
in order to	to
in spite of the fact that	although, though
in the event that	if
in the final analysis	finally

W2-d Simplify the structure.

If the structure of a sentence is needlessly indirect, try simplifying it. Look for opportunities to strengthen the verb.

▶ The analyst claimed that because of market conditions she

could not ~~make an~~ estimate ~~of~~ the company's future profits.

The verb *estimate* is more vigorous and concise than *make an estimate of.*

The colorless verbs *is*, *are*, *was*, and *were* frequently generate excess words.

▶ Investigators ~~were involved in studying~~ the effect of classical
                studied

music on unborn babies.

The revision is more direct and concise. The action (*studying*), originally appearing in a subordinate structure, has become a strong verb, *studied*.

The expletive constructions *there is* and *there are* (or *there was* and *there were*) can also lead to wordy sentences. The same is true of expletive constructions beginning with *it.*)

▶ ~~There is~~ Another module ~~that~~ tells the story of Charles Darwin
                    A

and introduces the theory of evolution.

Finally, verbs in the passive voice may be needlessly indirect. When the active voice expresses your meaning as effectively, use it. (See W3-a.)

W2-e Reduce clauses to phrases, phrases to single words.

Word groups functioning as modifiers can often be made more compact. Look for any opportunities to reduce clauses to phrases or phrases to single words.

▶ We took a side trip to Monticello, ~~which was~~ the home of

Thomas Jefferson.

▶ In ~~the~~ ^{this} essay, ~~that follows,~~ I argue against Immanuel Kant's

^{problematic} claim that we should not lie under any circumstances/. ~~which~~

~~is a problematic claim.~~

W3 Active verbs

As a rule, choose an active verb and pair it with a subject that names the person or thing doing the action. Active verbs express meaning more emphatically and vigorously than their weaker counterparts—verbs in the passive voice and forms of the verb *be*.

PASSIVE	The pumps *were destroyed* by a surge of power.
BE VERB	A surge of power *was* responsible for the destruction of the pumps.
ACTIVE	A surge of power *destroyed* the pumps.

Verbs in the passive voice lack strength because their subjects receive the action instead of doing it. Forms of the verb *be* (*be, am, is, are, was, were, being, been*) lack vigor because they convey no action.

Although passive verbs and the forms of *be* have legitimate uses, choose an active verb whenever possible.

hackerhandbooks.com/writersref
e W3 Active verbs > Exercises: W3–2 to W3–6
☑ W3 Active verbs > LearningCurve: Active and passive voice

Even among active verbs, some are more vigorous and colorful than others. Carefully selected verbs can energize a piece of writing.

▶ The goalie crouched low, ~~reached~~ out his stick, and ~~sent~~ the
⠀⠀⠀⠀⠀⠀⠀⠀⠀⠀⠀⠀⠀⠀⠀*swept*⠀⠀⠀⠀⠀⠀⠀⠀⠀⠀⠀⠀*hooked*
⠀⠀⠀⠀⠀⠀⠀⠀⠀⠀⠀⠀⠀⠀⠀⠀^⠀⠀⠀⠀⠀⠀⠀⠀⠀⠀⠀⠀⠀^

rebound away from the mouth of the net.

Academic English Although you may be tempted to avoid the passive voice completely, keep in mind that some writing situations call for it, especially scientific writing. For appropriate uses of the passive voice, see page 177; for advice about forming the passive voice, see M1-b.

W3-a Use the active voice unless you have a good reason for choosing the passive.

In the active voice, the subject does the action; in the passive voice, the subject receives the action. Although both voices are grammatically correct, the active voice is usually more effective because it is clearer and more direct.

⠀⠀⠀⠀ACTIVE⠀⠀⠀⠀Hernando *caught* the fly ball.

⠀⠀⠀⠀PASSIVE⠀⠀⠀The fly ball *was caught* by Hernando.

Passive sentences often identify the actor in a *by* phrase, as in the preceding example. Sometimes, however, that phrase is omitted, and who or what is responsible for the action becomes unclear: *The fly ball was caught*.

Most of the time, you will want to emphasize the actor, so you should use the active voice. To replace a passive verb with an active one, make the actor the subject of the sentence.

⠀⠀⠀*The settlers stripped the land of timber before realizing*
▶ ~~The land was stripped of timber before the settlers realized~~ the
⠀⠀^

consequences of their actions.

The revision emphasizes the actors (*settlers*) by naming them in the subject.

Appropriate uses of the passive

The passive voice is appropriate to emphasize the receiver of the action or to minimize the importance of the actor.

APPROPRIATE PASSIVE	Many Hawaiians *were forced* to leave their homes after the earthquake.
APPROPRIATE PASSIVE	Near harvest time, the tobacco plants *are sprayed* with a chemical to slow the growth of suckers.

The writer of the first sentence wished to emphasize the receiver of the action, *Hawaiians.* The writer of the second sentence wished to focus on the tobacco plants, not on the people spraying them.

In much scientific writing, the passive voice properly emphasizes the experiment or process being described, not the researcher. Check with your instructor for the preference in your discipline.

W3-b   Replace *be* verbs that result in dull or wordy sentences.

Not every *be* verb needs replacing. The forms of *be* (*be, am, is, are, was, were, being, been*) work well when you want to link a subject to a noun that clearly renames it or to an adjective that describes it: *Orchard House was the home of Louisa May Alcott. The harvest will be bountiful after the summer rains.*

Be verbs also are essential as helping verbs before present participles (*is flying, are disappearing*) to express ongoing action: *Derrick was fighting the fire when his wife went into labor.* (See G2-f.)

If using a *be* verb makes a sentence needlessly dull and wordy, however, consider replacing it. Often a phrase following the verb contains a noun or an adjective (such as *violation, resistant*) that suggests a more vigorous, active verb (*violate, resist*).

▶ Burying nuclear waste in Antarctica would ~~be in violation of~~ an

violate
^

international treaty.

Violate is less wordy and more vigorous than *be in violation of.*

▶ When Rosa Parks ~~was resistant to~~ giving up her seat on the bus,

resisted
^

she became a civil rights hero.

Resisted is stronger than *was resistant to.*

W3-c As a rule, choose a subject that names the person or thing doing the action.

In weak, unemphatic prose, both the actor and the action may be buried in sentence elements other than the subject and the verb. In the following weak sentence, for example, both the actor and the action appear in prepositional phrases, word groups that do not receive much attention from readers.

WEAK   The institution of the New Deal had the effect of reversing some of the economic inequalities of the Great Depression.

EMPHATIC   The New Deal reversed some of the economic inequalities of the Great Depression.

Consider the subjects and verbs of the two versions—*institution had* versus *New Deal reversed*. The latter expresses the writer's point more emphatically.

▶ ~~The use of~~ pure oxygen can ~~cause healing in~~ wounds that are otherwise untreatable.

In the original sentence, the subject and verb—*use can cause*— express the point blandly. *Oxygen can heal* makes the point more emphatically and directly.

W4 Appropriate language

Language is appropriate when it suits your subject, engages your audience, and blends naturally with your own voice.

To some extent, the conventions of the genre in which you are writing will determine your choice of language. When in doubt about the conventions of a particular genre—lab reports, informal essays, business memos, and so on—consult your instructor or look at models written by experts in the field.

W4-a Stay away from jargon.

Jargon is special language used among members of a trade, profession, or group. Use jargon only when readers will be familiar with it and when plain English will not do as well.

hackerhandbooks.com/writersref
🅔 W4 Appropriate language > Exercises: W4–2 and W4–3
✓ W4 Appropriate language > LearningCurve: Word choice and appropriate language

JARGON   We outsourced the work to an outfit in Ohio because we didn't have the bandwidth to tackle it in-house.

REVISED   We hired a company in Ohio because we had too few employees to do the work.

Broadly defined, jargon includes puffed-up language designed more to impress readers than to inform them. The following are examples from business, government, higher education, and the military, with plain English alternatives in parentheses.

ameliorate (improve)   indicator (sign)
commence (begin)   optimal (best, most favorable)
components (parts)   parameters (boundaries, limits)
endeavor (try)   peruse (read, look over)
exit (leave)   prior to (before)
facilitate (help)   utilize (use)
impact (v.) (affect)   viable (workable)

Sentences filled with jargon are hard to read, and they are often wordy as well.

▶ The CEO should ~~dialogue~~ talk with investors about ~~partnering~~ working with clients to ~~purchase~~ buy land in ~~economically deprived zones.~~ poor neighborhoods.

W4-b   Avoid pretentious language, most euphemisms, and "doublespeak."

Hoping to sound profound or poetic, some writers embroider their thoughts with large words and flowery phrases. Such pretentious language is so ornate and wordy that it obscures the writer's meaning.

▶ Taylor's ~~employment of multihued means of expression draws~~ use of colorful language reveals that she has a ~~back the curtains and lets slip the~~ nostalgic ~~vantage point from~~ view of ~~which she observes~~ American society ~~as well as her lack~~ and does not ~~of comprehension of~~ understand economic realities.

The writer of the original sentence had turned to a thesaurus (a dictionary of synonyms and antonyms) in an attempt to sound authoritative. When such a writer gains enough confidence to speak in his or her own voice, pretentious language disappears.

Euphemisms—nice-sounding words or phrases substituted for words thought to sound harsh—are sometimes appropriate. Many cultures, for example, accept euphemisms when speaking or writing about excretion (*I have to go to the bathroom*), sexual intercourse (*They did not sleep together*), and the like. We may also use euphemisms out of concern for someone's feelings. Telling parents, for example, that their daughter is "unmotivated" is more sensitive than saying she's lazy. Tact or politeness, then, can justify an occasional euphemism.

Most euphemisms, however, are needlessly evasive or even deceitful. Like pretentious language, they obscure the intended meaning.

EUPHEMISM	PLAIN ENGLISH
adult entertainment	pornography
preowned automobile	used car
economically deprived	poor
negative savings	debts
strategic withdrawal	retreat, defeat
chemical dependency	drug addiction
downsize	lay off, fire
correctional facility	prison, jail

The term *doublespeak* applies to any deliberately evasive or deceptive language, including euphemisms. Doublespeak is especially common in politics and business. A military retreat is described as *tactical redeployment*; *enhanced interrogation* is a euphemism for "torture"; and *downsizing* really means "firing employees."

W4-c   Avoid obsolete and invented words.

Although dictionaries list obsolete words such as *recomfort* and *reechy*, these words are not appropriate for current use. Invented words or expressions (called *neologisms*) are too recently created to be part of Standard English. Many fade out of use without becoming standard. *YOLO* and *MOOC* are neologisms that may not last. *Prequel* and *e-mail* are no longer neologisms; they have become Standard English. Avoid using invented words in formal writing unless they are given in the dictionary as standard or unless no other word expresses your meaning.

W4-d   In most contexts, avoid slang, regional expressions, and nonstandard English.

Slang is an informal and sometimes private vocabulary that expresses the solidarity of a group such as teenagers, rap musicians, or sports fans; it is subject to more rapid change than Standard English. For example, the slang teenagers use to express approval changes every few years; *cool*, *groovy*, *neat*, *awesome*, *phat*, and *sick* have replaced one another within the last three decades. Sometimes slang becomes so widespread that it is accepted as standard vocabulary. *Jazz*, for example, started out as slang but is now a standard term for a style of music.

Although slang has a certain vitality, it is a code that not everyone understands, and it is very informal. Therefore, it is inappropriate in most written work.

▶ When the server crashed unexpectedly, ^we lost^ three hours of unsaved data. ~~went down the tubes.~~

▶ The government's "filth" guidelines for food will ~~gross you out.~~ ^disgust you.^

Regional expressions are common to a group in a geographic area. *Let's talk with the bark off* (for *Let's speak frankly*) is an expression in the southern United States, for example. Regional expressions have the same limitations as slang and are therefore inappropriate in most writing.

▶ John was four blocks from the house before he remembered to ~~cut~~ ^turn on^ the headlights. ~~on.~~

▶ With the law enforcement budget severely cut, the city's gangs will ~~have a field day.~~ ^take advantage.^

Standard English is the language used in all academic, business, and professional fields. Nonstandard English is spoken by people with a common regional or social heritage. Although nonstandard English may be appropriate when spoken within a close group, it is out of place in most formal and informal writing.

▶ The governor said he ~~don't~~ ^doesn't^ know if he will approve the budget without the clean air provision.

If you speak a nonstandard dialect, try to identify the ways in which your dialect differs from Standard English. Look especially for the following features of nonstandard English, which commonly cause problems in writing.

Misusing verb forms such as *began* and *begun* (See G2-a.)

Leaving *-s* endings off verbs (See G2-c.)

Leaving *-ed* endings off verbs (See G2-d.)

Leaving out necessary verbs (See G2-e.)

Using double negatives (See G4-e.)

W4-e Choose an appropriate level of formality.

In deciding on a level of formality, consider both your subject and your audience. Does the subject demand a dignified treatment, or is a relaxed tone more suitable? Will readers be put off if you assume too close a relationship with them, or might you alienate them by seeming too distant?

For most college and professional writing, some degree of formality is appropriate. In a job application letter, for example, it is a mistake to sound too breezy and informal.

TOO INFORMAL	I'd like to get that sales job you've got in the paper.
MORE FORMAL	I would like to apply for the position of sales associate advertised in the *Peoria Journal Star*.

Informal writing is appropriate for private letters, personal e-mail and text messages, and business correspondence between close associates. Like spoken conversation, informal writing allows contractions (*don't*, *I'll*) and colloquial words (*kids*, *kinda*). Vocabulary and sentence structure are rarely complex.

In choosing a level of formality, above all be consistent. When a writer's voice shifts from one level of formality to another, readers receive mixed messages.

▶ Once a pitcher for the Blue Jays, Jorge shared with me the
   began
secrets of his trade. His lesson ~~commenced~~ with his famous
       thrown   ^
curveball, ~~implemented~~ by tucking the little finger behind the
       ^   revealed
ball. Next he ~~elucidated~~ the mysteries of thesucker pitch, a
       ^
slow ball coming behind a fast windup.

Words such as *commenced* and *elucidated* are inappropriate for the subject matter, and they clash with informal terms such as *sucker pitch* and *fast windup*.

W4-f Avoid sexist language.

Sexist language is language that stereotypes or demeans women or men. Using nonsexist language is a matter of courtesy—of respect for and sensitivity to the feelings of others.

Recognizing sexist language

Some sexist language is easy to recognize because it reflects genuine contempt for women: referring to a woman as a "chick," for example, or calling a lawyer a "lady lawyer."

Other forms of sexist language are less blatant. The following practices, while they may not result from conscious sexism, reflect stereotypical thinking: referring to members of one profession as exclusively male or exclusively female (teachers as women or engineers as men, for instance) or using different conventions when naming or identifying women and men.

STEREOTYPICAL LANGUAGE

After a nursing student graduates, *she* must face a difficult state board examination. [Not all nursing students are women.]

Running for city council are Boris Stotsky, an attorney, and *Mrs.* Cynthia Jones, a professor of English and *mother of three*. [The title *Mrs.* and the phrase *mother of three* are irrelevant.]

All executives' *wives* are invited to the welcome dinner. [Not all executives are men.]

Still other forms of sexist language result from outdated traditions. The pronouns *he*, *him*, and *his*, for instance, were traditionally used to refer generically to persons of either sex. Nowadays, to avoid that sexist usage, some writers use *she*, *her*, and *hers* generically or substitute the female pronouns alternately with the male pronouns.

GENERIC PRONOUNS

A journalist is motivated by *his* deadline.

A good interior designer treats *her* clients' ideas respectfully.

But both forms are sexist—for excluding one sex entirely and for making assumptions about the members of particular professions.

hackerhandbooks.com/writersref

e W4 Appropriate language > Exercises: W4–7 to W4–9
✓ W4 Appropriate language > LearningCurve: Word choice and appropriate language

Similarly, the nouns *man* and *men* were once used to refer generically to persons of either sex. Current usage demands gender-neutral terms for references to both men and women.

INAPPROPRIATE	APPROPRIATE
chairman	chairperson, moderator, chair, head
clergyman	member of the clergy, minister, rabbi, imam
congressman	member of Congress, representative, legislator
fireman	firefighter
foreman	supervisor
mailman	mail carrier, postal worker, letter carrier
to man	to operate, to staff
mankind	people, humans
manpower	personnel, staff
policeman	police officer
salesman	salesperson, sales associate, salesclerk
weatherman	forecaster, meteorologist

Revising sexist language

When revising sexist language, you may be tempted to substitute *he or she* and *his or her*. These terms are inclusive but wordy; fine in small doses, they can become awkward when repeated throughout an essay. A better revision strategy is to write in the plural; yet another strategy is to recast the sentence so that the problem does not arise.

SEXIST

A journalist is motivated by *his* deadline.

A good interior designer treats *her* clients' ideas respectfully.

ACCEPTABLE BUT WORDY

A journalist is motivated by *his or her* deadline.

A good interior designer treats *his or her* clients' ideas respectfully.

BETTER: USING THE PLURAL

Journalists are motivated by *their* deadlines.

Good interior designers treat *their* clients' ideas respectfully.

BETTER: REVISING THE SENTENCE

A journalist is motivated by *a* deadline.

A good interior designer treats clients' ideas respectfully.

For more examples of these revision strategies, see G3-a.

W4-g Revise language that may offend groups of people.

Your writing should be respectful and free of stereotypical, biased, or other offensive language. Be especially careful when describing or labeling people. Labels can become dated, and it is important to recognize when their continued use is not acceptable. When naming groups of people, choose labels that the groups currently use to describe themselves. For example, *Negro* is not an acceptable label for African Americans; instead of *Eskimo*, use *Inuit*; for other native peoples, name the specific group when possible.

▶ North Dakota takes its name from the ~~Indian~~ Lakota word meaning

"friend" or "ally."

▶ Many ~~Oriental~~ Asian immigrants have recently settled in our

town.

Negative stereotypes (such as "drives like a teenager" or "sour as a spinster") are of course offensive. But you should avoid stereotyping a person or a group even if you believe your generalization to be positive.

▶ It was no surprise that Greer, ~~a Chinese American,~~ an excellent math and science student, was

selected for the honors chemistry program in her sophomore

year.

W5 Exact language

Two reference works (or their online equivalents) will help you find words to express your meaning exactly: a good dictionary, such as *The American Heritage Dictionary* or *Merriam-Webster* online, and a collection of synonyms and antonyms, such as *Roget's International Thesaurus*.

TIP: Do not turn to a thesaurus in search of impressive words. Look instead for words that exactly express your meaning.

W5-a   Select words with appropriate connotations.

In addition to their strict dictionary meanings (or *denotations*), words have *connotations*, emotional colorings that affect how readers respond to them. The word *steel* denotes "commercial iron that contains carbon," but it also calls up a cluster of images associated with steel. These associations give the word its connotations — cold, hard, smooth, unbending.

If the connotation of a word does not seem appropriate for your purpose, your audience, or your subject matter, you should change the word. When a more appropriate synonym does not come quickly to mind, consult a dictionary or a thesaurus.

► When American soldiers returned home after World War II,
  left
  many women ~~abandoned~~ their jobs in favor of marriage.
              ^

  The word *abandoned* is too negative for the context.

                                                       sweat
► As I covered the boats with marsh grass, the ~~perspiration~~
                                                       ^
  I had worked up evaporated in the wind, and the cold

  morning air seemed even colder.

  The term *perspiration* is too dainty for the context, which suggests vigorous exercise.

W5-b   Prefer specific, concrete nouns.

Unlike general nouns, which refer to broad classes of things, specific nouns point to particular items. *Film*, for example, names a general class, *fantasy film* names a narrower class, and *The Golden Compass* is more specific still. Other examples: *team, football team, Denver Broncos; music, symphony, Beethoven's Ninth.*

Unlike abstract nouns, which refer to qualities and ideas (*justice, beauty, realism, dignity*), concrete nouns point to immediate, often sensory experiences and to physical objects (*steeple, asphalt, lilac, stone, garlic*).

Specific, concrete nouns express meaning more vividly than general or abstract ones. Although general and abstract language is sometimes necessary to convey your meaning, use specific, concrete words whenever possible.

► The senator spoke about the challenges of the future:
  pollution, dwindling resources, and terrorism.
  ~~the environment and world peace.~~
  ^

Nouns such as *thing*, *area*, *aspect*, *factor*, and *individual* are especially dull and imprecise.

▶ Toni Morrison's *Beloved* is about slavery, ~~among other things.~~

motherhood, and memory.

W5-c Do not misuse words.

If a word is not in your active vocabulary, you may find yourself misusing it, sometimes with embarrassing consequences. When in doubt, check the dictionary.

▶ The fans were ~~migrating~~ up the bleachers in search of seats.

climbing

▶ The Internet has so ~~diffused~~ our culture that it touches all

segments of society.

permeated

Also be alert for misused word forms—using a noun such as *absence* or *significance*, for example, when your meaning requires the adjective *absent* or *significant*.

▶ Most dieters are not ~~persistence~~ enough to make a permanent

change in their eating habits.

persistent

W5-d Use standard idioms.

Idioms are speech forms that follow no easily specified rules. The English say "Bernice went *to hospital*," an idiom strange to American ears, which are accustomed to hearing *the* in front of *hospital*. Native speakers of a language seldom have problems with idioms, but prepositions (such as *with*, *to*, *at*, and *of*) sometimes cause trouble, especially when they follow certain verbs and adjectives. When in doubt, consult a dictionary.

UNIDIOMATIC	IDIOMATIC
abide with (a decision)	abide by (a decision)
according with	according to
agree to (an idea)	agree with (an idea)
angry at (a person)	angry with (a person)
capable to	capable of

hackerhandbooks.com/writersref
🄴 W5 Exact language > Exercises: W5–3 and W5–4, W5–6 and W5–7
☑ W5 Exact language > LearningCurve: Word choice and appropriate language

UNIDIOMATIC	IDIOMATIC
comply to	comply with
different than (a person or thing)	different from (a person or thing)
intend on doing	intend to do
off of	off
plan on doing	plan to do
preferable than	preferable to
prior than	prior to
sure and	sure to
think on	think of, about
try and	try to
type of a	type of

> **Multilingual** Because idioms follow no particular rules, you must learn them individually. You may find it helpful to keep a list of idioms that you frequently encounter in conversation and in reading.

W5-e Do not rely heavily on clichés.

The pioneer who first announced that he had "slept like a log" no doubt amused his companions with a fresh, unlikely comparison. Today, however, that comparison is a cliché, a saying that can no longer add emphasis or surprise.

To see just how dully predictable clichés are, put your hand over the right-hand column and then finish the phrases on the left.

beat around	the bush
blind as a	bat
busy as a	bee, beaver
cool as a	cucumber
crystal	clear
dead as a	doornail
light as a	feather
like a bull	in a china shop
out of the frying pan and	into the fire
playing with	fire
selling like	hotcakes
starting out at the bottom	of the ladder
water under the	bridge
white as a	sheet, ghost
avoid clichés like the	plague

hackerhandbooks.com/writersref

e W5 Exact language > Exercises: W5–9 and W5–10

☑ W5 Exact language > LearningCurve: Word choice and appropriate language

The solution for clichés is simple: Just delete them or rewrite them.

▶ **When I received a full scholarship from my second-choice**
   felt pressured to settle for second best.
   school, I ~~found myself between a rock and a hard place.~~
               ^

Sometimes you can write around a cliché by adding an element of surprise. One student revised a cliché about butterflies in her stomach like this:

> If all of the action in my stomach is caused by butterflies, there must be a horde of them, with horseshoes on.

The image of butterflies wearing horseshoes is fresh and unlikely, not predictable like the original cliché.

W5-f Use figures of speech with care.

A figure of speech is an expression that uses words imaginatively (rather than literally) to make abstract ideas concrete. Most often, figures of speech compare two seemingly unlike things to reveal surprising similarities.

In a *simile*, the writer makes the comparison explicitly, usually by introducing it with *like* or *as*: *By the time cotton had to be picked, Grandfather's neck was as red as the clay he plowed.* In a *metaphor*, the *like* or *as* is omitted, and the comparison is implied. For example, in the Old Testament Song of Solomon, a young woman compares the man she loves to a fruit tree: *With great delight I sat in his shadow, and his fruit was sweet to my taste.*

Although figures of speech are useful devices, writers sometimes use them without thinking through the images they evoke. The result is sometimes a *mixed metaphor*, the combination of two or more images that don't make sense together.

▶ **Crossing Utah's salt flats in his new convertible, my father flew**
   at jet speed.
   ~~under a full head of steam.~~
      ^
   Flew suggests an airplane, whereas *under a full head of steam* suggests a steamboat or a train. To clarify the image, the writer should stick with one comparison or the other.

▶ **Our manager decided to put all controversial issues ~~in a~~**

   ~~holding pattern~~ on a back burner until after the annual meeting.

   Here the writer is mixing airplanes and stoves. Simply deleting one of the images corrects the problem.

W6 The dictionary and the thesaurus

W6-a The dictionary

A good dictionary, whether print or online—such as *The Random House College Dictionary* or *Merriam-Webster* online—is an indispensable writer's aid.

A sample print dictionary entry, taken from *The American Heritage Dictionary of the English Language*, appears on this page. A sample online dictionary entry, taken from *Merriam-Webster* online, appears on page 191.

PRINT DICTIONARY ENTRY

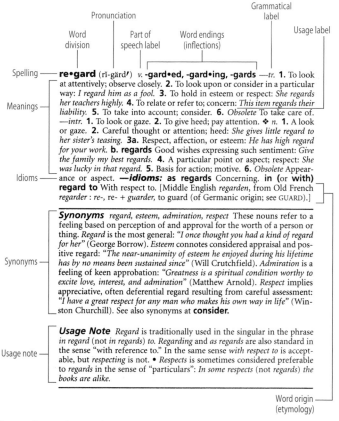

ONLINE DICTIONARY ENTRY

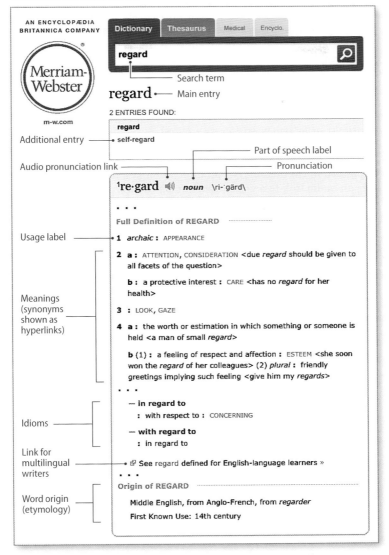

Spelling, word division, pronunciation

The main entry (*re • gard* in the sample entries) shows the correct spelling of the word. When there are two correct spellings of a word (as in *collectible, collectable*), both are given, with the preferred spelling usually appearing first.

The dot between *re* and *gard* separates the two syllables and indicates where the word should be divided if it can't fit at the end of a typed line (see P7-i). When a word is compound, the main entry shows how to write it: as one word (*crossroad*), as a hyphenated word (*cross-stitch*), or as two words (*cross section*).

The word's pronunciation is given just after the main entry. The accents indicate which syllables are stressed; the other marks are explained in the dictionary's pronunciation key. Many online entries include an audio link to a voice pronouncing the word.

Word endings and grammatical labels

When a word takes endings to indicate grammatical functions (called *inflections*), the endings are listed in boldface, as with *-garded, -garding*, and *-gards* in the sample print entry (p. 190).

Labels for the parts of speech and for other grammatical terms are sometimes abbreviated, as they are in the print entry. The most commonly used abbreviations are these:

n.	noun	adj.	adjective
pl.	plural	adv.	adverb
sing.	singular	pron.	pronoun
v.	verb	prep.	preposition
tr.	transitive verb	conj.	conjunction
intr.	intransitive verb	interj.	interjection

Meanings, word origin, synonyms, and antonyms

Sometimes a word can be used as more than one part of speech (*regard*, for instance, can be used as either a verb or a noun). In such a case, all the meanings for one part of speech are given before all the meanings for another, as in the sample entries.

The origin of the word, called its *etymology*, appears in brackets after all the meanings in the print and online versions.

Synonyms, words similar in meaning to the main entry, are frequently listed. In the sample print entry, the dictionary draws distinctions in meaning among the various synonyms. In the online entry, synonyms appear as hyperlinks. Antonyms, which do not appear in the sample entries, are words having a meaning opposite from that of the main entry.

Usage

Usage labels indicate when, where, or under what conditions a particular meaning for a word is appropriately used. Common labels are *informal* (or *colloquial*), *slang*, *archaic*, *poetic*, *nonstandard*, *dialect*, *obsolete*, and *British*. In the sample print entry, two meanings of *regard* are labeled *obsolete* because they are no longer in use. The sample online entry (p. 191) has one meaning labeled *archaic*.

Dictionaries sometimes include usage notes as well. Advice in the notes is based on the opinions of many experts and on actual usage in current publications.

W6-b The thesaurus

When you are looking for just the right word, you may want to consult a collection of synonyms and antonyms such as *Roget's International Thesaurus* or *Thesaurus.com*. Look up the adjective *still*, for example, and you will find synonyms such as *tranquil*, *quiet*, *quiescent*, *reposeful*, *calm*, *pacific*, *halcyon*, and *placid*. The list will likely contain words you've never heard of or with which you are only vaguely familiar. Whenever you are tempted to use one of these words, first look it up in the dictionary to avoid misusing it.

Do not turn to a thesaurus in search of exotic, fancy words to embellish an essay. Look instead for words that express your meaning exactly and that are familiar to both you and your readers.

G

Grammatical Sentences

G Grammatical Sentences

G1 Subject-verb agreement

In the present tense, verbs agree with their subjects in number (singular or plural) and in person (first, second, third): *I sing, you sing, she sings, we sing, they sing.* Even if your ear recognizes the standard subject-verb combinations in G1-a, you may encounter tricky situations such as those described in G1-b to G1-k.

G1-a Learn to recognize standard subject-verb combinations.

This section describes the basic guidelines for making present-tense verbs agree with their subjects. The present-tense ending *-s* (or *-es*) is used on a verb if its subject is third-person singular (*he, she, it,* and singular nouns); otherwise the verb takes no ending. Consider, for example, the present-tense forms of the verbs *love* and *try,* given at the beginning of the chart on page 198.

The verb *be* varies from this pattern; it has special forms in *both* the present and the past tense (see the end of the chart).

If you aren't sure of the standard forms, use the charts on pages 198 and 199 as you proofread your work. See also G2-c on *-s* endings of regular and irregular verbs.

G1-b Make the verb agree with its subject, not with a word that comes between.

Word groups often come between the subject and the verb. Such word groups, usually modifying the subject, may contain a noun that at first appears to be the subject. By mentally stripping away such modifiers, you can isolate the noun that is in fact the subject.

The *samples* on the tray in the lab *need* testing.

▶ **High levels of air pollution causes damage to the respiratory**

tract.

The subject is *levels,* not *pollution.* Strip away the phrase *of air pollution* to hear the correct verb: *levels cause.*

---

hackerhandbooks.com/writersref

🄴 G1 Subject-verb agreement > Exercises: G1–3 to G1–6

☑ G1 Subject-verb agreement > LearningCurve: Subject-verb agreement

Subject-verb agreement at a glance

Present-tense forms of *love* and *try* (typical verbs)

	SINGULAR		PLURAL	
FIRST PERSON	I	love	we	love
SECOND PERSON	you	love	you	love
THIRD PERSON	he/she/it*	loves	they**	love

	SINGULAR		PLURAL	
FIRST PERSON	I	try	we	try
SECOND PERSON	you	try	you	try
THIRD PERSON	he/she/it*	tries	they**	try

Present-tense forms of *have*

	SINGULAR		PLURAL	
FIRST PERSON	I	have	we	have
SECOND PERSON	you	have	you	have
THIRD PERSON	he/she/it*	has	they**	have

Present-tense forms of *do* (including negative forms)

	SINGULAR		PLURAL	
FIRST PERSON	I	do/don't	we	do/don't
SECOND PERSON	you	do/don't	you	do/don't
THIRD PERSON	he/she/it*	does/doesn't	they**	do/don't

Present-tense and past-tense forms of *be*

	SINGULAR		PLURAL	
FIRST PERSON	I	am/was	we	are/were
SECOND PERSON	you	are/were	you	are/were
THIRD PERSON	he/she/it*	is/was	they**	are/were

*And singular nouns (*child, Roger*)
**And plural nouns (*children, the Mannings*)

▶ The slaughter of pandas for their pelts ~~have~~ has caused the panda

population to decline drastically.

The subject is *slaughter*, not *pandas* or *pelts*.

NOTE: Phrases beginning with the prepositions *as well as, in addition to, accompanied by, together with,* and *along with* do not make a singular subject plural. *The governor as well as his press secretary was on the plane.* To emphasize that two people were on the plane, the writer could use *and* instead: *The governor and his press secretary were on the plane.*

When to use the -*s* (or -*es*) form of a present-tense verb

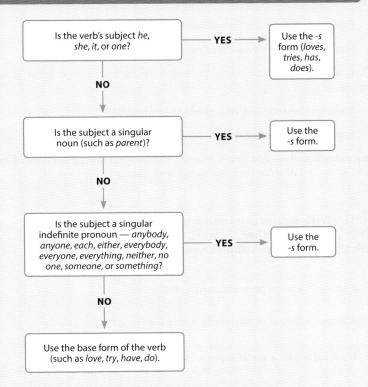

EXCEPTION: Choosing the correct present-tense form of *be* (*am*, *is*, or *are*) is not quite so simple. See the chart on the previous page for both present- and past-tense forms of *be*.

TIP: Do not use the -*s* form of a verb if it follows a modal verb such as *can*, *must*, or *should* or another helping verb. (See M1-e.)

G1-c   Treat most subjects joined with *and* as plural.

A subject with two or more parts is said to be compound. If the parts are connected with *and*, the subject is nearly always plural.

Leon and Jan often *jog* together.

► The Supreme Court's willingness to hear the case and its
                                                          have
affirmation of the original decision ~~has~~ set a new precedent.
                                       ^

EXCEPTIONS: When the parts of the subject form a single unit or when they refer to the same person or thing, treat the subject as singular.

> Fish and chips was a last-minute addition to the menu.

> Sue's friend and adviser was surprised by her decision.

When a compound subject is preceded by *each* or *every*, treat it as singular.

> Each tree, shrub, and vine needs to be sprayed.

> Every car, truck, and van is required to pass inspection.

This exception does not apply when a compound subject is followed by *each*: *Alan and Marcia each have different ideas*.

G1-d With subjects joined with *or* or *nor* (or with *either . . . or* or *neither . . . nor*), make the verb agree with the part of the subject nearer to the verb.

> A driver's *license* or credit *card is* required.

> A driver's *license* or two credit *cards are* required.

▶ If an infant or a child ~~have~~ has a high fever, call a doctor.

▶ Neither the chief financial officer nor the marketing managers ~~was~~ were able to convince the client to reconsider.

The verb must be matched with the part of the subject closer to it: *child has* in the first sentence, *managers were* in the second.

NOTE: If one part of the subject is singular and the other is plural, put the plural one last to avoid awkwardness.

G1-e Treat most indefinite pronouns as singular.

Indefinite pronouns are pronouns that do not refer to specific persons or things. The following commonly used indefinite pronouns are singular.

anybody	each	everyone	nobody	somebody
anyone	either	everything	no one	someone
anything	everybody	neither	nothing	something

Many of these words appear to have plural meanings, and they are often treated as such in casual speech. In formal written English, however, they are nearly always treated as singular.

Everyone on the team *supports* the coach.

▶ Each of the essays ~~have~~ been graded.
has

▶ Nobody who participated in the clinical trials ~~were~~ given a
was

placebo.

The subjects of these sentences are *Each* and *Nobody*. These indefinite pronouns are third-person singular, so the verbs must be *has* and *was*.

A few indefinite pronouns (*all, any, none, some*) may be singular or plural depending on the noun or pronoun they refer to.

SINGULAR   *Some* of our *luggage was* lost.

               None of his *advice makes* sense.

PLURAL   *Some* of the *rocks are* slippery.

               None of the *eggs were* broken.

NOTE: When the meaning of *none* is emphatically "not one," *none* may be treated as singular: *None* [meaning "Not one"] *of the eggs was broken.* Using *not one* is sometimes clearer: *Not one of the eggs was broken.*

G1-f Treat collective nouns as singular unless the meaning is clearly plural.

Collective nouns such as *jury, committee, audience, crowd, troop, family,* and *couple* name a class or a group. In American English, collective nouns are nearly always treated as singular: They emphasize the group as a unit. Occasionally, when there is some reason to draw attention to the individual members of the group, a collective noun may be treated as plural. (See also p. 220.)

SINGULAR   The *class respects* the teacher.

PLURAL   The *class are* debating among themselves.

To underscore the notion of individuality in the second sentence, many writers would add a clearly plural noun.

PLURAL　　　　The class *members are* debating among themselves.

▶ The board of trustees ~~meet~~ **meets** in Denver twice a year.

The board as a whole meets; there is no reason to draw attention to its individual members.

▶ A young couple ~~was~~ **were** arguing about politics while holding hands.

The meaning is clearly plural. Only separate individuals can argue and hold hands.

NOTE: The phrase *the number* is treated as singular, *a number* as plural.

SINGULAR　　　　*The number* of school-age children *is* declining.

PLURAL　　　　*A number* of children *are* attending the wedding.

NOTE: In general, when fractions or units of measurement are used with a singular noun, treat them as singular; when they are used with a plural noun, treat them as plural.

SINGULAR　　　　*Three-fourths* of the salad *has* been eaten.

SINGULAR　　　　Twenty *inches* of wallboard *was* covered with mud.

PLURAL　　　　*One-fourth* of the drivers *were* texting.

PLURAL　　　　Two *pounds* of blueberries *were* used to make the pie.

G1-g Make the verb agree with its subject even when the subject follows the verb.

Verbs ordinarily follow subjects. When this normal order is reversed, it is easy to become confused. Sentences beginning with *there is* or *there are* (or *there was* or *there were*) are inverted; the subject follows the verb.

There *are* surprisingly few *honeybees* left in southern China.

▶ There <del>was</del> ^{were} a social worker and a journalist at the meeting.

The subject, *worker and journalist*, is plural, so the verb must be *were*.

Occasionally you may decide to invert a sentence for variety or effect. When you do so, check to make sure that your subject and verb agree.

▶ Of particular concern <del>is</del> ^{are} penicillin and tetracycline, antibiotics

used to make animals more resistant to disease.

The subject, *penicillin and tetracycline*, is plural, so the verb must be *are*.

G1-h Make the verb agree with its subject, not with a subject complement.

One basic sentence pattern in English consists of a subject, a linking verb, and a subject complement: *Jack is a lawyer.* Because the subject complement (*lawyer*) names or describes the subject (*Jack*), it is sometimes mistaken for the subject. (See B2-b on subject complements.)

These *exercises are* a way to test your ability to perform under pressure.

▶ A tent and a sleeping bag <del>is</del> ^{are} the required equipment.

Tent and bag are the subject, not *equipment*.

▶ A major force in today's economy <del>are</del> ^{is} children—as consumers,

decision makers, and trend spotters.

Force is the subject, not *children*. If the corrected version seems too awkward, make *children* the subject: *Children are a major force in today's economy—as consumers, decision makers, and trend spotters.*

G1-i *Who, which,* and *that* take verbs that agree with their antecedents.

Like most pronouns, the relative pronouns *who*, *which*, and *that* have antecedents, nouns or pronouns to which they refer. Relative pronouns used as subjects of subordinate clauses take verbs that agree with their antecedents.

ANT PN V
Take a *course that prepares* you for classroom management.

One of the

Constructions such as *one of the students who* [or *one of the things that*] cause problems for writers. Do not assume that the antecedent must be *one*. Instead, consider the logic of the sentence.

▶ **Our ability to use language is one of the things that sets us**

apart from animals.

The antecedent of *that* is *things*, not *one*. Several things set us apart from animals.

Only one of the

When the word *only* comes before *one*, you are safe in assuming that *one* is the antecedent of the relative pronoun.

▶ **Veronica was the only one of the first-year Spanish students**

was
who ~~were~~ fluent enough to apply for the exchange program.
^

The antecedent of *who* is *one*, not *students*. Only one student was fluent enough.

G1-j Words such as *athletics, economics, mathematics, physics, politics, statistics, measles,* and *news* are usually singular, despite their plural form.

is
▶ **Politics ~~are~~ among my mother's favorite pastimes.**
^

EXCEPTIONS: Occasionally some of these words, especially *mathematics, economics, politics,* and *statistics,* have plural meanings: *Office politics often sway decisions about hiring and promotion. The economics of the building plan are prohibitive.*

G1-k Titles of works, company names, words mentioned as words, and gerund phrases are singular.

► *Lost Cities* ~~describe~~ ^{describes} the discoveries of fifty ancient civilizations.

► Delmonico Brothers ~~specialize~~ ^{specializes} in organic produce and additive-free meats.

► *Controlled substances* ~~are~~ ^{is} a euphemism for illegal drugs.

A gerund phrase consists of an *-ing* verb form followed by any objects, complements, or modifiers (see B3-b). Treat gerund phrases as singular.

► **Encountering long hold times ~~make~~ ^{makes} customers impatient with telephone tech support.**

G2 Verb forms, tenses, and moods

In speech, some people use verb forms and tenses that match a home dialect or variety of English. In writing, use Standard English verb forms unless you are quoting nonstandard speech or using alternative forms for literary effect. (See W4-d.)

Except for the verb *be*, all verbs in English have five forms. The following list shows the five forms and provides a sample sentence in which each might appear.

BASE FORM	Usually I (*walk*, *ride*).
PAST TENSE	Yesterday I (*walked*, *rode*).
PAST PARTICIPLE	I have (*walked*, *ridden*) many times before.
PRESENT PARTICIPLE	I am (*walking*, *riding*) right now.
-S FORM	He/she/it (*walks*, *rides*) regularly.

The verb *be* has eight forms instead of the usual five: *be, am, is, are, was, were, being, been*.

> **Multilingual** If English is not your native language, see also M1 for more help with verbs.

G2-a Choose Standard English forms of irregular verbs.

For all regular verbs, the past-tense and past-participle forms are the same (ending in -*ed* or -*d*), so there is no danger of confusion. This is not true, however, for irregular verbs, such as the following.

BASE FORM	PAST TENSE	PAST PARTICIPLE
go	went	gone
break	broke	broken
fly	flew	flown

The past-tense form always occurs alone, without a helping verb. It expresses action that occurred entirely in the past: *I rode to work yesterday. I walked to work last Tuesday*. The past participle is used with a helping verb. It forms the perfect tenses with *has, have,* or *had*; it forms the passive voice with *be, am, is, are, was, were, being,* or *been*. (See B1-c for a complete list of helping verbs and G2-f for a survey of tenses.)

PAST TENSE	Last July, we *went* to Seoul.
HELPING VERB + PAST PARTICIPLE	We *have gone* to Seoul twice.

The list of common irregular verbs beginning on page 207 will help you distinguish between the past tense and the past participle. Choose the past-participle form if the verb in your sentence requires a helping verb; choose the past-tense form if the verb does not require a helping verb. (See verb tenses in G2-f.)

> ▶ Yesterday we ~~seen~~ a documentary about Isabel Allende.
> _{saw}

The past-tense *saw* is required because there is no helping verb.

> ▶ The truck was apparently ~~stole~~ while the driver ate lunch.
> _{stolen}

> ▶ By Friday, the stock market had ~~fell~~ two hundred points.
> _{fallen}

Because of the helping verbs *was* and *had,* the past-participle forms are required: *was stolen, had fallen*.

---

hackerhandbooks.com/writersref

e G2 Verbs > Exercises: G2–2 to G2–4

✓ G2 Verbs > LearningCurve: Verbs

Common irregular verbs

BASE FORM	PAST TENSE	PAST PARTICIPLE
arise	arose	arisen
awake	awoke, awaked	awaked, awoke, awoken
be	was, were	been
beat	beat	beaten, beat
become	became	become
begin	began	begun
bend	bent	bent
bite	bit	bitten, bit
blow	blew	blown
break	broke	broken
bring	brought	brought
build	built	built
burst	burst	burst
buy	bought	bought
catch	caught	caught
choose	chose	chosen
cling	clung	clung
come	came	come
cost	cost	cost
deal	dealt	dealt
dig	dug	dug
dive	dived, dove	dived
do	did	done
draw	drew	drawn
dream	dreamed, dreamt	dreamed, dreamt
drink	drank	drunk
drive	drove	driven
eat	ate	eaten
fall	fell	fallen
fight	fought	fought
find	found	found
fly	flew	flown
forget	forgot	forgotten, forgot
freeze	froze	frozen
get	got	gotten, got
give	gave	given
go	went	gone
grow	grew	grown
hang (execute)	hanged	hanged
hang (suspend)	hung	hung
have	had	had
hear	heard	heard
hide	hid	hidden
hurt	hurt	hurt

BASE FORM	PAST TENSE	PAST PARTICIPLE
keep	kept	kept
know	knew	known
lay (put)	laid	laid
lead	led	led
lend	lent	lent
let (allow)	let	let
lie (recline)	lay	lain
lose	lost	lost
make	made	made
prove	proved	proved, proven
read	read	read
ride	rode	ridden
ring	rang	rung
rise (get up)	rose	risen
run	ran	run
say	said	said
see	saw	seen
send	sent	sent
set (place)	set	set
shake	shook	shaken
shoot	shot	shot
shrink	shrank	shrunk
sing	sang	sung
sink	sank	sunk
sit (be seated)	sat	sat
slay	slew	slain
sleep	slept	slept
speak	spoke	spoken
spin	spun	spun
spring	sprang	sprung
stand	stood	stood
steal	stole	stolen
sting	stung	stung
strike	struck	struck, stricken
swear	swore	sworn
swim	swam	swum
swing	swung	swung
take	took	taken
teach	taught	taught
throw	threw	thrown
wake	woke, waked	waked, woken
wear	wore	worn
win	won	won
wring	wrung	wrung
write	wrote	written

G2-b Distinguish among the forms of *lie* and *lay*.

Writers and speakers frequently confuse the various forms of *lie* (meaning "to recline or rest on a surface") and *lay* (meaning "to put or place something"). *Lie* is an intransitive verb; it does not take a direct object: *The tax forms lie on the table.* The verb *lay* is transitive; it takes a direct object: *Please lay the tax forms on the table.* (See B2-b.)

In addition to confusing the meaning of *lie* and *lay*, writers and speakers are often unfamiliar with the Standard English forms of these verbs.

BASE FORM	PAST TENSE	PAST PARTICIPLE	PRESENT PARTICIPLE
lie ("recline")	lay	lain	lying
lay ("put")	laid	laid	laying

▶ Sue was so exhausted that she ~~laid~~ ^{lay} down for a nap.

The past-tense form of *lie* ("to recline") is *lay.*

▶ The patient had ~~laid~~ ^{lain} in an uncomfortable position all night.

The past-participle form of *lie* ("to recline") is *lain.* If the correct English seems too stilted, recast the sentence: *The patient had been lying in an uncomfortable position all night.*

▶ The customer gently ~~lay~~ ^{laid} the iPad on the help desk counter.

The past-tense form of *lay* ("to place") is *laid.*

▶ Letters dating from 1915 were ~~laying~~ ^{lying} in a corner of the chest.

The present participle of *lie* ("to rest on a surface") is *lying.*

G2-c Use *-s* (or *-es*) endings on present-tense verbs that have third-person singular subjects.

All singular nouns (*child, tree*) and the pronouns *he, she,* and *it* are third-person singular; indefinite pronouns such as *everyone* and *neither* are also third-person singular. When the subject of a sentence is third-person singular, its verb takes an -*s* or -*es* ending in the present tense. (See also G1.)

	SINGULAR		PLURAL	
FIRST PERSON	I	know	we	know
SECOND PERSON	you	know	you	know
THIRD PERSON	he/she/it	knows	they	know
	child	knows	parents	know
	everyone	knows		

▶ My neighbor ~~drive~~ *drives* to Marco Island every weekend.

▶ Sulfur dioxide ~~turn~~ *turns* leaves yellow, ~~dissolve~~ *dissolves* marble, and ~~eat~~ *eats* away iron and steel.

The subjects *neighbor* and *sulfur dioxide* are third-person singular, so the verbs must end in -*s*.

TIP: Do not add the -*s* ending to the verb if the subject is not third-person singular. The writers of the following sentences, knowing they sometimes dropped -*s* endings from verbs, overcorrected by adding the endings where they don't belong.

▶ I prepares system specifications for every installation.

The writer mistakenly concluded that the -*s* ending belongs on present-tense verbs used with *all* singular subjects, not just *third-person* singular subjects. The pronoun *I* is first-person singular, so its verb does not require the -*s*.

▶ The wood floors requires continual sweeping.

The writer mistakenly thought that the verb needed an -*s* ending because of the plural subject. But the -*s* ending is used only on present-tense verbs with third-person *singular* subjects.

G2-d   Do not omit -*ed* endings on verbs.

Speakers who do not fully pronounce -*ed* endings sometimes omit them unintentionally in writing. Failure to pronounce -*ed* endings is common in many dialects and in informal speech even in Standard English. In the following frequently used words and phrases, for example, the -*ed* ending is not always fully pronounced.

advised	prejudiced
asked	pronounced
concerned	stereotyped
developed	supposed to
fixed	used to
frightened	

When a verb is regular, both the past tense and the past participle are formed by adding -*ed* (or -*d*) to the base form of the verb.

Past tense

Use the ending -*ed* or -*d* to express the past tense of regular verbs. The past tense is used when the action occurred entirely in the past.

▶ Over the weekend, Ed ~~fix~~ ^fixed^ his brother's skateboard and tuned up his mother's 2004 Camry.

▶ My counselor ~~advise~~ ^advised^ me to ask my graphic arts instructor for a recommendation.

Past participles

Past participles are used in three ways: (1) following *have, has,* or *had* to form one of the perfect tenses; (2) following *be, am, is, are, was, were, being,* or *been* to form the passive voice; and (3) as adjectives modifying nouns or pronouns. The perfect tenses are listed on page 213, and the passive voice is discussed in W3-a. For a discussion of participles as adjectives, see B3-b.

▶ Robin has ~~ask~~ ^asked^ the Office of Student Affairs for more housing staff for next year.

Has asked is present perfect tense (*have* or *has* followed by a past participle).

▶ Though it is not a new phenomenon, domestic violence is now ~~publicize~~ ^publicized^ more than ever.

Is publicized is a verb in the passive voice (a form of *be* followed by a past participle).

▶ All kickboxing classes end in a cool-down period to stretch ~~tighten~~ ^tightened^ muscles.

The past participle *tightened* functions as an adjective modifying the noun *muscles*.

G2-e Do not omit needed verbs.

Although Standard English allows some linking verbs and helping verbs to be contracted in informal contexts, it does not allow them to be omitted.

Linking verbs, used to link subjects to subject complements, are frequently a form of *be*: *be, am, is, are, was, were, being, been*. (See B2-b.) Some of these forms may be contracted (*I'm, she's, we're, you're, they're*), but they should not be omitted altogether.

> ▶ When we $\overset{\text{are}}{\underset{\wedge}{\text{quiet}}}$ in the evening, we can hear the crickets.

> ▶ Sherman Alexie $\overset{\text{is}}{\underset{\wedge}{\text{a}}}$ Native American author whose stories have been made into a film.

Helping verbs, used with main verbs, include forms of *be, do*, and *have* and the modal verbs *can, will, shall, could, would, should, may, might*, and *must*. (See B1-c.) Some helping verbs may be contracted (*he's leaving, we'll celebrate, they've been told*), but they should not be omitted altogether.

> ▶ We $\overset{\text{have}}{\underset{\wedge}{\text{been}}}$ in Chicago since last Thursday.

Multilingual Some languages do not require a linking verb between a subject and its complement. English, however, requires a verb in every sentence. See M3-a.

> ▶ Every night, I read a short book to my daughter. When I $\overset{\text{am}}{\underset{\wedge}{}}$ too busy, my husband reads to her.

G2-f Choose the appropriate verb tense.

Tenses indicate the time of an action in relation to the time of the speaking or writing about that action.

The most common problem with tenses—shifting confusingly from one tense to another—is discussed in section S4. Other problems with tenses are detailed in this section, after the following survey of tenses.

Survey of tenses

Tenses are classified as present, past, and future, with simple, perfect, and progressive forms for each.

SIMPLE TENSES The simple tenses indicate relatively simple time relations. The *simple present* tense is used primarily for actions occurring at the same time they are being discussed or for actions occurring regularly. The *simple past* tense is used for actions completed in the past. The *simple future* tense is used for actions that will occur in the future. In the following table, the simple tenses are given for the regular verb *walk*, the irregular verb *ride*, and the highly irregular verb *be*.

SIMPLE PRESENT

SINGULAR		PLURAL	
I	walk, ride, am	we	walk, ride, are
you	walk, ride, are	you	walk, ride, are
he/she/it	walks, rides, is	they	walk, ride, are

SIMPLE PAST

SINGULAR		PLURAL	
I	walked, rode, was	we	walked, rode, were
you	walked, rode, were	you	walked, rode, were
he/she/it	walked, rode, was	they	walked, rode, were

SIMPLE FUTURE

I, you, he/she/it, we, they	will walk, ride, be

PERFECT TENSES More complex time relations are indicated by the perfect tenses. A verb in one of the perfect tenses (a form of *have* plus the past participle) expresses an action that was or will be completed at the time of another action.

PRESENT PERFECT

I, you, we, they	have walked, ridden, been
he/she/it	has walked, ridden, been

PAST PERFECT

I, you, he/she/it, we, they	had walked, ridden, been

FUTURE PERFECT

I, you, he/she/it, we, they	will have walked, ridden, been

PROGRESSIVE FORMS The simple and perfect tenses have progressive forms that describe actions in progress. A progressive verb consists of a form of *be* followed by a present participle. The progressive forms are not normally used with certain verbs, such as *believe*, *know*, *hear*, and *seem*.

PRESENT PROGRESSIVE

I	am walking, riding, being
he/she/it	is walking, riding, being
you, we, they	are walking, riding, being

PAST PROGRESSIVE

I, he/she/it	was walking, riding, being
you, we, they	were walking, riding, being

FUTURE PROGRESSIVE

I, you, he/she/it, we, they	will be walking, riding, being

PRESENT PERFECT PROGRESSIVE

I, you, we, they	have been walking, riding, being
he/she/it	has been walking, riding, being

PAST PERFECT PROGRESSIVE

I, you, he/she/it, we, they	had been walking, riding, being

FUTURE PERFECT PROGRESSIVE

I, you, he/she/it, we, they	will have been walking, riding, being

---

Multilingual See M1-a for more specific examples of verb tenses that can be challenging for multilingual writers.

Special uses of the present tense

Use the present tense when expressing general truths, when writing about literature, and when quoting, summarizing, or paraphrasing an author's views.

General truths or scientific principles should appear in the present tense unless such principles have been disproved.

> *revolves*
> ▶ **Galileo taught that the earth ~~revolved~~ around the sun.**
> ⌃
>
> Because Galileo's teaching has not been discredited, the verb should be in the present tense. The following sentence, however, is acceptable: *Ptolemy taught that the sun revolved around the earth.*

When writing about a work of literature, you may be tempted to use the past tense. The convention in the humanities, however, is to describe fictional events in the present tense.

▶ In Masuji Ibuse's *Black Rain*, a child ~~reached~~ ^{reaches} for a pomegranate in his mother's garden, and a moment later he ~~was~~ ^{is} dead, killed by the blast of the atomic bomb.

When you are quoting, summarizing, or paraphrasing the author of a nonliterary work, use present-tense verbs such as *writes*, *reports*, *asserts*, and so on to introduce the source. This convention is usually followed even when the author is dead (unless a date or the context specifies the time of writing).

▶ Dr. Jerome Groopman ~~argued~~ ^{argues} that doctors are "susceptible to the subtle and not so subtle efforts of the pharmaceutical industry to sculpt our thinking" (9).

In MLA style, signal phrases are written in the present tense, not the past tense. (See also MLA-3b.)

APA NOTE: When you are documenting a paper with the APA (American Psychological Association) style of in-text citations, use past tense verbs such as *reported* or *demonstrated* or present perfect verbs such as *has reported* or *has demonstrated* to introduce the source. (See APA-3b.)

The past perfect tense

The past perfect tense consists of a past participle preceded by *had* (*had worked*, *had gone*). This tense is used for an action already completed by the time of another past action or for an action already completed at some specific past time.

Everyone *had spoken* by the time I arrived.

I pleaded my case, but Paula *had made up* her mind.

Writers sometimes use the simple past tense when they should use the past perfect.

▶ By the time dinner was served, the guest of honor ^{had} left.

The past perfect tense is needed because the action of leaving was already completed at a specific past time (when dinner was served).

Some writers tend to overuse the past perfect tense. Do not use the past perfect if two past actions occurred at the same time.

▶ When Ernest Hemingway lived in Cuba, he ~~had written~~ *For*

    wrote

    Whom the Bell Tolls.

Sequence of tenses with infinitives and participles

An infinitive is the base form of a verb preceded by *to*. (See B3-b.) Use the present infinitive to show action at the same time as or later than the action of the verb in the sentence.

    pay

▶ Barb had hoped to ~~have paid~~ the bill by May 1.

> The action expressed in the infinitive (*to pay*) occurred later than the action of the sentence's verb (*had hoped*).

Use the perfect form of an infinitive (*to have* followed by the past participle) for an action occurring earlier than that of the verb in the sentence.

    have joined

▶ Dan would like to ~~join~~ the navy, but he could not swim.

> The liking occurs in the present; the joining would have occurred in the past.

Like the tense of an infinitive, the tense of a participle is governed by the tense of the sentence's verb. Use the present participle (ending in *-ing*) for an action occurring at the same time as that of the sentence's verb.

> *Hiking* the Appalachian Trail, we spotted many wildflowers.

Use the past participle (such as *given* or *helped*) or the present perfect participle (*having* plus the past participle) for an action occurring before that of the verb.

> *Discovered* off the coast of Florida, the Spanish galleon yielded many treasures.

> *Having worked* her way through college, Lee graduated debt-free.

G2-g   Use the subjunctive mood in the few contexts that require it.

There are three moods in English: the *indicative*, used for facts, opinions, and questions; the *imperative*, used for orders or advice; and the *subjunctive*, used in certain contexts to express wishes, requests, or conditions contrary to fact. For many writers, the subjunctive causes the most problems.

Forms of the subjunctive

In the subjunctive mood, present-tense verbs do not change form to indicate the number and person of the subject (see G1). Instead, the subjunctive uses the base form of the verb (*be*, *drive*, *employ*) with all subjects. Also, in the subjunctive mood, there is only one past-tense form of *be*: *were* (never *was*).

It is important that you *be* [not *are*] prepared for the interview.

We asked that she *drive* [not *drives*] more slowly.

If I *were* [not *was*] you, I'd try a new strategy.

Uses of the subjunctive

The subjunctive mood appears only in a few contexts: in contrary-to-fact clauses beginning with *if* or expressing a wish; in *that* clauses following verbs such as *ask*, *insist*, *recommend*, *request*, and *suggest*; and in certain set expressions.

IN CONTRARY-TO-FACT CLAUSES BEGINNING WITH *IF* When a subordinate clause beginning with *if* expresses a condition contrary to fact, use the subjunctive *were* in place of *was*.

▶ If I ~~was~~ a member of Congress, I would vote for that bill.
    ^were^

▶ The astronomers would be able to see the moons of Jupiter tonight if the weather ~~was~~ clearer.
    ^were^

The writer is not a member of Congress, and the weather is not clear.

Do not use the subjunctive mood in *if* clauses expressing conditions that exist or may exist.

If Dana *wins* the contest, she will leave for Barcelona in June.

IN CONTRARY-TO-FACT CLAUSES EXPRESSING A WISH In formal English, use the subjunctive *were* in clauses expressing a wish or desire.

INFORMAL	I wish that Dr. Vaughn *was* my professor.
FORMAL	I wish that Dr. Vaughn *were* my professor.

IN *THAT* CLAUSES FOLLOWING VERBS SUCH AS *ASK, INSIST, REQUEST,* AND *SUGGEST*   Because requests have not yet become reality, they are expressed in the subjunctive mood.

> ▶ Professor Moore insists that her students ~~are~~ on time.
>   be

> ▶ We recommend that Lambert ~~files~~ form 1050 soon.
>   file

IN CERTAIN SET EXPRESSIONS   The subjunctive mood, once more widely used, remains in certain set expressions: *Be that as it may, as it were, far be it from me,* and so on.

G3   Pronouns

Pronouns are words that substitute for nouns (see B1-b). Pronoun errors are typically related to the four topics discussed in this section:

  a. pronoun-antecedent agreement (singular vs. plural)
  b. pronoun reference (clarity)
  c. pronoun case (personal pronouns such as *I* vs. *me, she* vs. *her*)
  d. pronoun case (*who* vs. *whom*)

For more help with pronouns, consult the glossary of usage (W1).

G3-a   Make pronouns and antecedents agree.

Many pronouns have antecedents, nouns or pronouns to which they refer. A pronoun and its antecedent agree when they are both singular or both plural.

SINGULAR   *Dr. Ava Berto* finished *her* rounds.

PLURAL   The hospital *interns* finished *their* rounds.

hackerhandbooks.com/writersref
e G3 Pronouns > Exercises: G3–3 to G3–6
✓ G3 Pronouns > LearningCurve: Pronoun agreement and pronoun reference

> **Multilingual** The pronouns *he*, *his*, *she*, *her*, *it*, and *its* must agree in gender (masculine, feminine, or neuter) with their antecedents, not with the words they modify.
>
> *Steve* visited *his* [*not her*] sister in Seattle.

Indefinite pronouns

Indefinite pronouns refer to nonspecific persons or things. Even though some of the following indefinite pronouns may seem to have plural meanings, treat them as singular in formal English.

anybody	each	everyone	nobody	somebody
anyone	either	everything	no one	someone
anything	everybody	neither	nothing	something

Everyone performs at *his or her* [*not their*] own fitness level.

When a plural pronoun refers mistakenly to a singular indefinite pronoun, you can usually choose one of three options for revision:

1. Replace the plural pronoun with *he or she* (or *his or her*).
2. Make the antecedent plural.
3. Rewrite the sentence so that no problem of agreement exists.

▶ When someone travels outside the United States for the first
        he or she needs
time, ~~they need~~ to apply for a passport.
    ^

       people travel
▶ When ~~someone travels~~ outside the United States for the first
    ^

time, they need to apply for a passport.

   Anyone who
▶ ~~When someone~~ travels outside the United States for the first
  ^   needs
time/~~they need~~ to apply for a passport.
   ^

Because the *he or she* construction is wordy, often the second or third revision strategy is more effective. Using *he* (or *his*) to refer to persons of either sex, while less wordy, is considered sexist, as is using *she* (or *her*) for all persons. Some writers alternate male and female pronouns throughout a text, but the result is often awkward. See W4-f for strategies that avoid sexist usage.

NOTE: If you change a pronoun from singular to plural (or vice versa), check to be sure that the verb agrees with the new pronoun (see G1-e).

Generic nouns

A generic noun represents a typical member of a group, such as a typical student, or any member of a group, such as any lawyer. Although generic nouns may seem to have plural meanings, they are singular.

> Every *runner* must train rigorously if *he or she wants* [not *they want*] to excel.

When a plural pronoun refers mistakenly to a generic noun, you will usually have the same three revision options as mentioned on page 219 for indefinite pronouns.

▶ A medical student must study hard if ~~they want~~ he or she wants to succeed.

▶ ~~A medical student~~ Medical students must study hard if they want to succeed.

▶ A medical student must study hard ~~if they want~~ to succeed.

Collective nouns

Collective nouns such as *jury, committee, audience, crowd, class, troop, family, team,* and *couple* name a group. Ordinarily the group functions as a unit, so the noun should be treated as singular; if the members of the group function as individuals, however, the noun should be treated as plural. (See also G1-f.)

AS A UNIT   The *committee* granted *its* permission to build.

AS INDIVIDUALS   The *committee* put *their* signatures on the document.

When treating a collective noun as plural, many writers prefer to add a clearly plural antecedent such as *members* to the sentence: *The members of the committee put their signatures on the document.*

▶ Defense attorney Clarence Darrow surprisingly urged the jury to find his client, John Scopes, guilty so that he could appeal the case to a higher court. The jury complied, returning ~~their~~ its verdict in only nine minutes.

There is no reason to draw attention to the individual members of the jury, so *jury* should be treated as singular.

Compound antecedents

In 1987, *Reagan and Gorbachev* held a summit at which *they* signed the Intermediate-Range Nuclear Forces Treaty.

With compound antecedents joined with *or* or *nor* (or with *either . . . or* or *neither . . . nor*), make the pronoun agree with the nearer antecedent.

Either *Bruce* or *Tom* should receive first prize for *his* poem.

Neither the *mouse* nor the *rats* could find *their* way through the maze.

NOTE: If one of the antecedents is singular and the other plural, as in the second example, put the plural one last to avoid awkwardness.

EXCEPTION: If one antecedent is male and the other female, do not follow the traditional rule. The sentence *Either Bruce or Elizabeth should receive first prize for her short story* makes no sense. The best solution is to recast the sentence: *The prize for best short story should go to either Bruce or Elizabeth.*

G3-b Make pronoun references clear.

In a sentence like *After Andrew intercepted the ball, he kicked it as hard as he could*, the pronouns *he* and *it* substitute for the nouns *Andrew* and *ball*. The word a pronoun refers to is called its *antecedent*.

Ambiguous reference

Ambiguous pronoun reference occurs when a pronoun could refer to two possible antecedents.

▶ ~~When Gloria set the pitcher~~ The pitcher broke when Gloria set it on the glass-topped table/. ~~it broke.~~

▶ Tom told James, "You have ~~that he had~~ won the lottery."

What broke—the pitcher or the table? Who won the lottery—Tom or James? The revisions eliminate the ambiguity.

hackerhandbooks.com/writersref

e G3 Pronouns > Exercises: G3–9 to G3–12

✓ G3 Pronouns > LearningCurve: Pronoun agreement and pronoun reference

Implied reference

A pronoun should refer to a specific antecedent, not to a word that is implied but not present in the sentence.

▶ After braiding Ann's hair, Sue decorated ~~them~~ with ribbons.
                                            the braids

The pronoun *them* referred to Ann's braids (implied by the term *braiding*), but the word *braids* did not appear in the sentence.

Modifiers, such as possessives, cannot serve as antecedents. A modifier may strongly imply the noun that a pronoun might logically refer to, but it is not itself that noun.

▶ In ~~Jamaica Kincaid's~~ "Girl," ~~she~~ describes the advice a mother
        Jamaica Kincaid

gives her daughter, including the mysterious warning not to be

"the kind of woman who the baker won't let near the bread" (454).

Using the possessive form of an author's name to introduce a source leads to a problem later in this sentence: The pronoun *she* cannot refer logically to a possessive modifier (*Jamaica Kincaid's*). The revision substitutes the noun *Jamaica Kincaid* for the pronoun *she*, thereby eliminating the problem. (For more on writing with sources in MLA style, see MLA-3.)

Broad reference of *this, that, which, and* it

For clarity, the pronouns *this, that, which,* and *it* should ordinarily refer to specific antecedents rather than to whole ideas or sentences. When a pronoun's reference is needlessly broad, either replace the pronoun with a noun or supply an antecedent to which the pronoun clearly refers.

▶ By advertising on television, pharmaceutical companies gain
                                                          the ads
exposure for their prescription drugs. Patients respond to ~~this~~

by requesting drugs they might not need.

The writer substituted the noun *ads* for the pronoun *this*, which referred broadly to the idea expressed in the preceding sentence.

▶ Romeo and Juliet were both too young to have acquired much
        a fact
wisdom, ~~and~~ that accounts for their rash actions.

The writer added an antecedent (*fact*) that the pronoun *that* clearly refers to.

Indefinite use of they, it, and you

Do not use the pronoun *they* to refer indefinitely to persons who have not been specifically mentioned. *They* should always refer to a specific antecedent.

> the school board
> ► In June, ~~they~~ voted to charge a fee for students to participate in
>   ^
> sports and music programs.

The word *it* should not be used indefinitely in constructions such as *It is said on television . . .* or *In the article, it says that. . . .*

> The
> ► ~~In the~~ article ~~it~~ states that male moths can smell female moths from
>   ^
> several miles away.

The pronoun *you* is appropriate only when the writer is addressing the reader directly: *Once you have kneaded the dough, let it rise in a warm place.* Except in informal contexts, however, *you* should not be used to mean "anyone in general." Use a noun instead.

>   a guest
> ► Ms. Pickersgill's *Guide to Etiquette* stipulates that ~~you~~ should
>   ^
> not arrive at a party too early or leave too late.

G3-c Distinguish between pronouns such as *I* and *me.*

The personal pronouns in the following chart change what is known as *case form* according to their grammatical function in a sentence. Pronouns functioning as subjects or subject complements appear in the *subjective* case; those functioning as objects appear in the *objective* case; and those showing ownership appear in the *possessive* case.

	SUBJECTIVE CASE	OBJECTIVE CASE	POSSESSIVE CASE
SINGULAR	I	me	my
	you	you	your
	he/she/it	him/her/it	his/her/its
PLURAL	we	us	our
	you	you	your
	they	them	their

hackerhandbooks.com/writersref
🄴 G3 Pronouns > Exercises: G3–15 to G3–17, G3–21 and G3–22
✅ G3 Pronouns > LearningCurve: Nouns and pronouns

Pronouns in the subjective and objective cases are frequently confused. Most of the rules in this section specify when to use one or the other of these cases (*I* or *me*, *he* or *him*, and so on). See page 226 for a special use of pronouns and nouns in the possessive case.

Subjective case (I, you, he, she, it, we, they)

When a pronoun is used as a subject complement (a word following a linking verb), your ear may mislead you, since the incorrect form is frequently heard in casual speech. (See "subject complement," B2-b.)

▶ **During the Lindbergh trial, Bruno Hauptmann repeatedly**
                                                    he.
denied that the kidnapper was him.
                                    ^

If *kidnapper was he* seems too stilted, rewrite the sentence: *During the Lindbergh trial, Bruno Hauptmann repeatedly denied that he was the kidnapper.*

Objective case (me, you, him, her, it, us, them)

When a personal pronoun is used as a direct object, an indirect object, or the object of a preposition, it must be in the objective case.

DIRECT OBJECT	Bruce found Tony and brought *him* home.
INDIRECT OBJECT	Alice gave *me* a surprise party.
OBJECT OF A PREPOSITION	Jessica wondered if the call was for *her*.

Compound word groups

When a subject or an object appears as part of a compound structure, you may occasionally become confused. To test for the correct pronoun, mentally strip away all of the compound word group except the pronoun in question.

▶ **Janice was indignant when she realized that the salesclerk was**
                                                        her.
insulting her mother and she.
                            ^

Her mother and her is the direct object of the verb *was insulting*. Strip away the words *her mother and* to hear the correct pronoun: *was insulting her* (not *was insulting she*).

When a pronoun functions as a subject or a subject complement, it must be in the subjective case.

SUBJECT   Sylvia and *he* shared the award.

SUBJECT COMPLEMENT   Greg announced that the winners were
                          Sylvia and *he*.

▶ The most traumatic experience for her father and ~~I~~ occurred
  ^me^

  long after her operation.

Her father and me is the object of the preposition *for*. Strip away the words *her father and* to test for the correct pronoun: *for me* (not *for I*).

When in doubt about the correct pronoun, some writers try to avoid making the choice by using a reflexive pronoun such as *myself*. Using a reflexive pronoun in such situations is nonstandard.

▶ **Nidra gave my cousin and ~~myself~~ some good tips on traveling in**
  ^me^

  New Delhi.

My cousin and me is the indirect object of the verb *gave*. For correct uses of *myself*, see the glossary of usage (W1).

Appositives

Appositives are noun phrases that rename nouns or pronouns. A pronoun used as an appositive has the same function (usually subject or object) as the word(s) it renames.

▶ **The managers, Dr. Bell and ~~me,~~ could not agree on a plan.**
  ^I,^

The appositive *Dr. Bell and I* renames the subject, *managers*. Test: *I could not agree* (not *me could not agree*).

▶ **The reporter found only two witnesses, the bicyclist and ~~I.~~**
  ^me.^

The appositive *the bicyclist and me* renames the direct object, *witnesses*. Test: *found me* (not *found I*).

Comparisons with *than* or *as*

When a comparison begins with *than* or *as*, your choice of a pronoun will depend on your intended meaning. To test for the correct pronoun, mentally complete the sentence: *My roommate likes football more than I [do].*

▶ **In our report on nationalized health care in the United States,**

                                   we.
we argued that Canadians are better off than ~~us.~~

We is the subject of the verb *are*, which is understood: *Canadians are better off than we [are].* If the correct English seems too formal, you can always add the verb.

                                         her.
▶ **We respected no other candidate as much as ~~she.~~**

This sentence means that we respected no other candidate as much as *we respected her. Her* is the direct object of the understood verb *respected.*

We *or* us *before a noun*

When deciding whether *we* or *us* should precede a noun, choose the pronoun that would be appropriate if the noun were omitted.

   We
▶ **~~Us~~ tenants would rather fight than move.**

                                us
▶ **Management is shortchanging ~~we~~ tenants.**

No one would say *Us would rather fight than move* or *Management is shortchanging we.*

Subjects and objects of infinitives

An infinitive is the word *to* followed by the base form of a verb. (See B3-b.) Subjects of infinitives are an exception to the rule that subjects must be in the subjective case. Whenever an infinitive has a subject, it must be in the objective case. Objects of infinitives also are in the objective case.

               me   *her*
▶ **Sue asked John and ~~I~~ to drive the mayor and ~~she~~ to the airport.**

John and me is the subject of the infinitive *to drive; mayor and her* is the direct object of the infinitive.

Possessive case to modify a gerund

A pronoun that modifies a gerund or a gerund phrase should be in the possessive case (*my, our, your, his, her, its, their*). A gerund is a verb form ending in *-ing* that functions as a noun. Gerunds frequently appear in phrases; when they do, the whole gerund phrase functions as a noun. (See B3-b.)

> ‎   your
> ► The chances of ~~you~~ being hit by lightning are about two million
>   ^
>
> **to one.**

Your modifies the gerund phrase *being hit by lightning.*

Nouns as well as pronouns may modify gerunds. To form the possessive case of a noun, use an apostrophe and an *-s* (*victim's*) or just an apostrophe (*victims'*). (See P4-a.)

> ‎   aristocracy's
> ► **The old order in France paid a high price for the** ~~aristocracy~~
>   ^
>
> **exploiting the lower classes.**

The possessive noun *aristocracy's* modifies the gerund phrase *exploiting the lower classes.*

G3-d Distinguish between *who* and *whom*.

The choice between *who* and *whom* (or *whoever* and *whomever*) occurs primarily in subordinate clauses and in questions. *Who* and *whoever*, subjective-case pronouns, are used for subjects and subject complements. *Whom* and *whomever*, objective-case pronouns, are used for objects. (See pp. 227–29.)

An exception to this general rule occurs when the pronoun functions as the subject of an infinitive (see p. 229).

Consult the chart on page 229 for a summary of the trouble spots with *who* and *whom*.

In subordinate clauses

When *who* and *whom* (or *whoever* and *whomever*) introduce subordinate clauses, their case is determined by their function *within the clause they introduce.*

In the following two examples, the pronouns *who* and *whoever* function as the subjects of the clauses they introduce.

> ‎   who
> ► **First prize goes to the runner** ~~whom~~ **earns the most points.**
>   ^
>
> The subordinate clause is *who earns the most points.* The verb of the clause is *earns,* and its subject is *who.*

hackerhandbooks.com/writersref
🄴 G3 Pronouns > Exercises: G3-19 to G3-22
☑️ G3 Pronouns > LearningCurve: Nouns and pronouns

▶ Maya Angelou's *I Know Why the Caged Bird Sings* should be read
     whoever
by ~~whomever~~ is interested in the effects of racial prejudice on
  ∧
children.

The writer selected the pronoun *whomever*, thinking that it was the object of the preposition *by*. However, the object of the preposition is the entire subordinate clause *whoever is interested in the effects of racial prejudice on children*. The verb of the clause is *is*, and the subject of the verb is *whoever*.

When functioning as an object in a subordinate clause, *whom* (or *whomever*) also appears out of order, before the subject and verb. To choose the correct pronoun, you can mentally restructure the clause.

                                      whom
▶ You will work with our senior traders, ~~who~~ you will meet later.
                                      ∧
The subordinate clause is *whom you will meet later*. The subject of the clause is *you*, and the verb is *will meet*. *Whom* is the direct object of the verb. The correct choice becomes clear if you mentally restructure the clause: *you will meet whom*.

When functioning as the object of a preposition in a subordinate clause, *whom* is often separated from its preposition.

        whom
▶ The tutor ~~who~~ I was assigned to was very supportive.
      ∧
Whom is the object of the preposition *to*. In this sentence, the writer might choose to drop *whom*: *The tutor I was assigned to was very supportive*.

NOTE: Inserted expressions such as *they know*, *I think*, and *she says* should be ignored in determining whether to use *who* or *whom*.

▶ The speech pathologist reported a particularly difficult session
                               who
with a stroke patient ~~whom~~ she knew was suffering from
                      ∧
aphasia.

Who is the subject of *was suffering*, not the object of *knew*.

In questions

When *who* and *whom* (or *whoever* and *whomever*) are used to open questions, their case is determined by their function within the question.

     Who
▶ ~~Whom~~ was responsible for creating that computer virus?
  ∧
Who is the subject of the verb *was*.

Checking for problems with *who* and *whom*

In subordinate clauses

Isolate the subordinate clause. Then read its subject, verb, and any objects, restructuring the clause if necessary. Some writers find it helpful to substitute *he* for *who* and *him* for *whom*.

> Samuels hoped to become the business partner of (whoever/whomever) found the treasure.
>
> > **TEST:** . . . *whoever* found the treasure. [. . . *he* found the treasure.]
>
> Ada always seemed to be bestowing a favor on (whoever/whomever) she worked for.
>
> > **TEST:** . . . she worked for *whomever*. [. . . she worked for *him*.]

In questions

Read the subject, verb, and any objects, rearranging the sentence structure if necessary.

> (Who/Whom) conferred with Roosevelt and Stalin at Yalta in 1945?
>
> > **TEST:** *Who* conferred . . . ?
>
> (Who/Whom) did the committee nominate?
>
> > **TEST:** The committee did nominate *whom*?

When *whom* functions as the object of a verb or the object of a preposition in a question, it appears out of normal order. To choose the correct pronoun, mentally restructure the question.

> Whom
> ▶ ~~Who~~ did the Democratic Party nominate in 1952?
>   ^

Whom is the direct object of the verb *did nominate*. This becomes clear if you restructure the question: *The Democratic Party did nominate whom in 1952?*

For subjects or objects of infinitives

An infinitive is the word *to* followed by the base form of a verb. (See B3-b.) Subjects of infinitives are an exception to the rule that subjects must be in the subjective case. The subject of an infinitive must be in the objective case. Objects of infinitives also are in the objective case.

>   whom
> ▶ When it comes to money, I know ~~who~~ to believe.
>   ^

The infinitive phrase *whom to believe* is the direct object of the verb *know*, and *whom* is the subject of the infinitive *to believe*.

G4 Adjectives and adverbs

Adjectives modify nouns or pronouns. They usually come before the word they modify; occasionally they function as complements following the word they modify. Adverbs modify verbs, adjectives, or other adverbs. (See B1-d and B1-e.)

Many adverbs are formed by adding *-ly* to adjectives (*normal, normally*; *smooth, smoothly*). But don't assume that all words ending in *-ly* are adverbs or that all adverbs end in *-ly*. Some adjectives end in *-ly* (*lovely, friendly*), and some adverbs don't (*always, here, there*). When in doubt, consult a dictionary.

> **Multilingual** Placement of adjectives and adverbs can be a tricky matter for multilingual writers. See M3-f and M4-b.

G4-a Use adjectives to modify nouns.

Adjectives ordinarily precede the nouns they modify (*tall building*). But they can also function as subject complements or object complements, following the nouns they modify.

Subject complements

A subject complement follows a linking verb and completes the meaning of the subject. (See B2-b.) When an adjective functions as a subject complement, it describes the subject.

Justice is *blind*.

Problems can arise with verbs such as *smell, taste, look,* and *feel,* which sometimes, but not always, function as linking verbs. If the word following one of these verbs describes the subject, use an adjective; if the word following the verb modifies the verb, use an adverb.

ADJECTIVE	The detective looked *cautious*.
ADVERB	The detective looked *cautiously* for fingerprints.

The adjective *cautious* describes the detective; the adverb *cautiously* modifies the verb *looked*.

hackerhandbooks.com/writersref
  G4 Adjectives and adverbs > Exercises: G4–3 to G4–5
  G4 Adjectives and adverbs > LearningCurve: Verbs, adjectives, and adverbs

Linking verbs suggest states of being, not actions. Notice, for example, the different meanings of *looked* in the preceding examples. To look cautious suggests the state of being cautious; to look cautiously is to perform an action in a cautious way.

▶ The lilacs in our yard smell especially ~~sweetly~~ *sweet* this year.

The verb *smell* suggests a state of being, not an action. Therefore, it should be followed by an adjective, not an adverb.

▶ The drawings looked ~~well~~ *good* after the architect made changes.

The verb *looked* is a linking verb suggesting a state of being, not an action. The adjective *good* is appropriate following the linking verb to describe *drawings*. (See also G4-c.)

> **Multilingual** In English, adjectives are not pluralized to agree with the words they modify: *The red* [not *reds*] *roses were a surprise.*

Object complements

An object complement follows a direct object and completes its meaning. (See B2-b.) When an adjective functions as an object complement, it describes the direct object.

Sorrow makes *us wise.*

Object complements occur with verbs such as *call, consider, create, find, keep,* and *make.* When a modifier follows the direct object of one of these verbs, use an adjective to describe the direct object; use an adverb to modify the verb.

ADJECTIVE   The referee called the plays *perfect.*

ADVERB   The referee called the plays *perfectly.*

The first sentence means that the referee considered the plays to be perfect; the second means that the referee did an excellent job of calling the plays.

G4-b Use adverbs to modify verbs, adjectives, and other adverbs.

When adverbs modify verbs (or verbals), they nearly always answer the question When? Where? How? Why? Under what conditions? How often? or To what degree? When adverbs modify adjectives or other adverbs, they usually qualify or intensify the meaning of the word they modify. (See B1-e.)

Adjectives are often used incorrectly in place of adverbs in casual or nonstandard speech.

▶ The travel arrangement worked out ~~perfect~~ ^perfectly^ for everyone.

▶ The manager must see that the office runs ~~smooth~~ ^smoothly^ and ~~efficient.~~ ^efficiently.^

The adverb *perfectly* modifies the verb *worked out*; the adverbs *smoothly* and *efficiently* modify the verb *runs*.

▶ The chance of recovering lost property looks ~~real~~ ^really^ slim.

Only adverbs can modify adjectives or other adverbs. *Really* intensifies the meaning of the adjective *slim*.

G4-c   Distinguish between *good* and *well, bad* and *badly*.

Good is an adjective (*good performance*). *Well* is an adverb when it modifies a verb (*speak well*). The use of the adjective *good* in place of the adverb *well* to modify a verb is nonstandard and especially common in casual speech.

▶ We were glad that Sanya had done ~~good~~ ^well^ on the CPA exam.

The adverb *well* modifies the verb *had done*.

Confusion can arise because *well* is an adjective when it modifies a noun or pronoun and means "healthy" or "satisfactory" (*The babies were well and warm*).

▶ Adrienne did not feel ~~good,~~ ^well,^ but she performed anyway.

As an adjective following the linking verb *did feel*, *well* describes Adrienne's health.

Bad is always an adjective and should be used to describe a noun; *badly* is always an adverb and should be used to modify a verb. The adverb *badly* is often used inappropriately to describe a noun, especially following a linking verb.

▶ The sisters felt ~~badly~~ ^bad^ when they realized they had left their brother out of the planning.

The adjective *bad* is used after the linking verb *felt* to describe the noun *sisters*.

G4-d Use comparatives and superlatives with care.

Most adjectives and adverbs have three forms: the positive, the comparative, and the superlative.

POSITIVE	COMPARATIVE	SUPERLATIVE
fast	faster	fastest
friendly	friendlier	friendliest
carefully	more carefully	most carefully
bad	worse	worst
good	better	best

Comparative versus superlative

Use the comparative to compare two things, the superlative to compare three or more.

▶ Which of these two low-carb drinks is ~~best?~~ *better?*

▶ Though Shaw and Jackson are impressive, Zhao is the ~~more~~ *most* qualified of the three candidates running for state senator.

Forming comparatives and superlatives

To form comparatives and superlatives of most one- and two-syllable adjectives, use the endings *-er* and *-est*: *smooth, smoother, smoothest*; *easy, easier, easiest*. With longer adjectives, use *more* and *most* (or *less* and *least* for downward comparisons): *exciting, more exciting, most exciting*; *helpful, less helpful, least helpful*.

Some one-syllable adverbs take the endings *-er* and *-est* (*fast, faster, fastest*), but longer adverbs and all of those ending in *-ly* form the comparative and superlative with *more* and *most* (or *less* and *least*).

The comparative and superlative forms of some adjectives and adverbs are irregular: *good, better, best; well, better, best; bad, worse, worst; badly, worse, worst.*

▶ The Kirov is the ~~talentedest~~ *most talented* ballet company we have seen.

▶ According to our projections, sales at local businesses will be ~~worser~~ *worse* than those at the chain stores this winter.

Double comparatives or superlatives

Do not use double comparatives or superlatives. When you have added
-er or -est to an adjective or adverb, do not also use *more* or *most* (or *less*
or *least*).

> ▶ Of all her family, Julia is the ~~most~~ happiest about the move.

> ▶ All the polls indicated that Gore was more ~~likelier~~ likely to win
>
> than Bush.

Absolute concepts

Avoid expressions such as *more straight*, *less perfect*, *very round*, and
most unique. Either something is unique or it isn't. It is illogical to suggest that absolute concepts come in degrees.

> ▶ That is the most ~~unique~~ unusual wedding gown I have ever seen.

> ▶ The painting is more ~~priceless~~ valuable because it is signed.

G4-e   Avoid double negatives.

Standard English allows two negatives only if a positive meaning is
intended: *The orchestra was not unhappy with its performance* (meaning that the orchestra was happy). Using a double negative to emphasize a negative meaning is nonstandard.

Negative modifiers such as *never*, *no*, and *not* should not be paired
with other negative modifiers or with negative words such as *neither*,
none, *no one*, *nobody*, and *nothing*.

> ▶ The city is not doing ~~nothing~~ anything to see that the trash is collected
>
> during the strike.

> The double negative *not . . . nothing* is nonstandard.

The modifiers *hardly*, *barely*, and *scarcely* are considered negatives
in Standard English, so they should not be used with negatives such as
not, *no one*, or *never*.

> ▶ Maxine is so weak that she ~~can't~~ can hardly climb stairs.

G5 Sentence fragments

A sentence fragment is a word group that pretends to be a sentence. Sentence fragments are easy to recognize when they appear out of context, like these:

> When the cat leaped onto the table.

> Running for the bus.

When fragments appear next to related sentences, however, they are harder to spot.

> We had just sat down to dinner. When the cat leaped onto the table.

> I tripped and twisted my ankle. Running for the bus.

Recognizing sentence fragments

To be a sentence, a word group must consist of at least one full independent clause. An independent clause includes a subject and a verb, and it either stands alone or could stand alone.

To test whether a word group is a complete sentence or a fragment, use the flowchart on page 236. By using the flowchart, you can see exactly why *When the cat leaped onto the table* is a fragment: It has a subject (*cat*) and a verb (*leaped*), but it begins with a subordinating word (*When*). *Running for the bus* is a fragment because it lacks a subject and a verb (*Running* is a verbal, not a verb). (See also B3-b and B3-e.)

Multilingual Unlike some other languages, English requires a subject and a verb in every sentence (except in commands, where the subject *you* is understood but not present: *Sit down*). See M3-a and M3-b.

> It is
> ► ~~Is~~ often hot and humid during the summer.
>   ^

> are
> ► Students usually very busy at the end of the semester.
>   ^

---

hackerhandbooks.com/writersref
e G5 Sentence fragments > Exercises: G5–3 to G5–7
✓ G5 Sentence fragments > LearningCurve: Sentence fragments

Test for fragments

*Do not mistake verbals for verbs. A verbal is a verb form (such as *walking*, *to act*) that does not function as a verb of a clause. (See B3-b.)

**The subject of a sentence may be *you*, understood but not present in the sentence. (See B2-a.)

***A sentence may open with a subordinate clause, but the sentence must also include an independent clause. (See G5-a and B4-a.)

If you find any fragments, try one of these methods of revision (see G5-a to G5-c):

1. Attach the fragment to a nearby sentence.

2. Rewrite the fragment as a complete sentence.

Repairing sentence fragments

You can repair most fragments in one of two ways:

- Pull the fragment into a nearby sentence.
- Rewrite the fragment as a complete sentence.

▶ We had just sat down to dinner/~~When~~ when the cat leaped onto the

table.

▶ Running for the bus, I tripped and twisted my ankle. ~~Running for the bus.~~

G5-a Attach fragmented subordinate clauses or turn them into sentences.

A subordinate clause is patterned like a sentence, with both a subject and a verb, but it begins with a word that marks it as subordinate. The following words commonly introduce subordinate clauses.

after	before	so that	until	while
although	even though	than	when	who
as	how	that	where	whom
as if	if	though	whether	whose
because	since	unless	which	why

Subordinate clauses function within sentences as adjectives, as adverbs, or as nouns. They cannot stand alone. (See B3-e.)

Most fragmented clauses beg to be pulled into a sentence nearby.

▶ Americans have come to fear the West Nile virus/~~Because~~ because it is

transmitted by the common mosquito.

Because introduces a subordinate clause, so it cannot stand alone. (For punctuation of subordinate clauses appearing at the end of a sentence, see P2-f.)

▶ Although psychiatrist Peter Kramer expresses concerns about Prozac/, ~~Many~~ many other doctors believe that the benefits of

antidepressants outweigh the risks.

Although introduces a subordinate clause, so it cannot stand alone. (For punctuation of subordinate clauses at the beginning of a sentence, see P1-b.)

If a fragmented clause cannot be attached to a nearby sentence or if you feel that attaching it would be awkward, try turning the clause into a sentence. The simplest way to do this is to delete the opening word or words that mark it as subordinate.

▶ **Population increases and uncontrolled development are taking a deadly toll on the environment. ~~So that across~~ the globe,** *Across*

fragile ecosystems are collapsing.

G5-b   Attach fragmented phrases or turn them into sentences.

Like subordinate clauses, phrases function within sentences as adjectives, as adverbs, or as nouns. They cannot stand alone. Fragmented phrases are often prepositional or verbal phrases; sometimes they are appositives, words or word groups that rename nouns or pronouns. (See B3-a, B3-b, and B3-c.)

Often a fragmented phrase may simply be pulled into a nearby sentence.

▶ **The archaeologists worked slowly~~,~~ ~~Examining~~ and labeling** *examining*

every pottery shard they uncovered.

The word group beginning with *Examining* is a verbal phrase.

▶ **The patient displayed symptoms of ALS~~,~~ ~~A~~neurodegenerative** *a*

disease.

A neurodegenerative disease is an appositive renaming the noun *ALS*. (For punctuation of appositives, see P1-e.)

If a fragmented phrase cannot be pulled into a nearby sentence effectively, turn the phrase into a sentence. You may need to add a subject, a verb, or both.

▶ **Jamie explained how to access our new database. ~~Also~~ how to** *She also taught us*

submit expense reports and request vendor payments.

The revision turns the fragmented phrase into a sentence by adding a subject and a verb.

G5-c Attach other fragmented word groups or turn them into sentences.

Other word groups that are commonly fragmented include parts of compound predicates, lists, and examples introduced by *for example*, *in addition*, or similar expressions.

Parts of compound predicates

A predicate consists of a verb and its objects, complements, and modifiers (see B2-b). A compound predicate includes two or more predicates joined with a coordinating conjunction such as *and*, *but*, or *or*. Because the parts of a compound predicate have the same subject, they should appear in the same sentence.

▶ **The woodpecker finch of the Galápagos Islands carefully selects**
and
a twig of a certain size and shape/And then uses this tool to pry
^
out grubs from trees.

The subject is *finch*, and the compound predicate is *selects . . . and . . . uses*. (For punctuation of compound predicates, see P2-a.)

Lists

To correct a fragmented list, often you can attach it to a nearby sentence with a colon or a dash. (See P3-d and P6-b.)

▶ **It has been said that there are only three indigenous American**
musical
art forms/: Musical comedy, jazz, and soap opera.
^

Sometimes terms like *especially*, *namely*, *like*, and *such as* introduce fragmented lists. Such fragments can usually be attached to the preceding sentence.

▶ **In the twentieth century, the South produced some great**
such
American writers/, Such as Flannery O'Connor, William
^
Faulkner, Alice Walker, and Tennessee Williams.

Examples introduced by for example, in addition, *or similar expressions*

Other expressions that introduce examples or explanations can lead to unintentional fragments. Although you may begin a sentence with some of the following words or phrases, make sure that what follows has a subject and a verb.

also	for example	mainly
and	for instance	or
but	in addition	that is

Often the easiest solution is to turn the fragment into a sentence.

▶ **In his memoir, Primo Levi describes the horrors of living in a**
  concentration camp. For example, ~~working~~ without food and
  he worked
  ^
  ~~suffering~~ **emotional abuse.**
  suffered
  ^

The writer corrected this fragment by adding a subject—*he*—and substituting verbs for the verbals *working* and *suffering*.

G5-d Exception: A fragment may be used for effect.

Writers occasionally use sentence fragments for special purposes.

FOR EMPHASIS	Following the dramatic Americanization of their children, even my parents grew more publicly confident. *Especially my mother.* — Richard Rodriguez
TO ANSWER A QUESTION	Are these new drug tests 100 percent reliable? *Not in the opinion of most experts.*
TRANSITIONS	*And now the opposing arguments.*
EXCLAMATIONS	*Not again!*
IN ADVERTISING	*Fewer carbs. Improved taste.*

Although fragments are sometimes appropriate, writers and readers do not always agree on when they are appropriate. That's why you will find it safer to write in complete sentences.

G6 Run-on sentences

Run-on sentences are independent clauses that have not been joined correctly. An independent clause is a word group that can stand alone as a sentence. (See B4-a.) When two independent clauses appear in one sentence, they must be joined in one of these ways:

- with a comma and a coordinating conjunction (*and, but, or, nor, for, so, yet*)
- with a semicolon (or occasionally with a colon or a dash)

Recognizing run-on sentences

There are two types of run-on sentences. When a writer puts no mark of punctuation and no coordinating conjunction between independent clauses, the result is called a *fused sentence*.

> | INDEPENDENT CLAUSE | | INDEPENDENT CLAUSE |
> FUSED Air pollution poses risks to all humans it can be
>
> — INDEPENDENT CLAUSE —
> deadly for asthma sufferers.

A far more common type of run-on sentence is the *comma splice* — two or more independent clauses joined with a comma but without a coordinating conjunction. In some comma splices, the comma appears alone.

> COMMA   Air pollution poses risks to all humans, it can be
> SPLICE   deadly for asthma sufferers.

In other comma splices, the comma is accompanied by a joining word that is *not* a coordinating conjunction. There are only seven coordinating conjunctions in English: *and, but, or, nor, for, so,* and *yet*.

> COMMA   Air pollution poses risks to all humans, however, it can
> SPLICE   be deadly for asthma sufferers.

However is a transitional expression, not a coordinating conjunction, and cannot be used with only a comma to join two independent clauses (see G6-b).

hackerhandbooks.com/writersref
e G6 Run-on sentences > Exercises: G6–4 to G6–9
☑ G6 Run-on sentences > LearningCurve: Run-on sentences

Recognizing run-on sentences

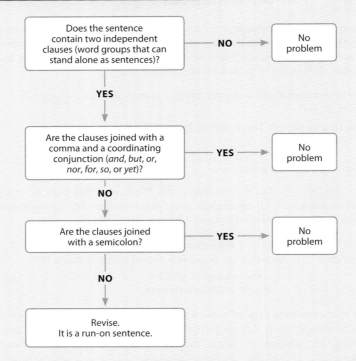

If you find an error, choose an effective method of revision. See G6-a to
G6-d for revision strategies.

Revising run-on sentences

To revise a run-on sentence, you have four choices.

1. Use a comma and a coordinating conjunction (*and, but, or, nor, for,
   so, yet*).

► Air pollution poses risks to all humans,$\overset{\text{but}}{\wedge}$ it can be deadly for

   people with asthma.

2. Use a semicolon (or, if appropriate, a colon or a dash). A semicolon may be used alone; it can also be accompanied by a transitional expression.

► Air pollution poses risks to all humans/; it can be deadly for

   people with asthma.

                                              however,
► Air pollution poses risks to all humans/; it can be deadly for

   people with asthma.

3. Make the clauses into separate sentences.

                                              It
► Air pollution poses risks to all humans/. ~~it~~ can be deadly for

   people with asthma.

4. Restructure the sentence; try subordinating a clause.

   Although air
► ~~Air~~ pollution poses risks to all humans, it can be deadly for

   people with asthma.

One of these revision techniques usually works better than the others for a particular sentence. The fourth technique, the one requiring the most extensive revision, is often the most effective.

G6-a Consider separating the clauses with a comma and a coordinating conjunction.

There are seven coordinating conjunctions in English: *and*, *but*, *or*, *nor*, *for*, *so*, and *yet*. When a coordinating conjunction joins independent clauses, it is usually preceded by a comma. (See P1-a.)

                                        but
► Some lesson plans include exercises, completing them should not

   be the focus of all class periods.

► Many government officials privately admit that the polygraph is

   yet
   unreliable, ~~however,~~ they still use it as a security measure.

   However is a transitional expression, not a coordinating conjunction, so it cannot be used with only a comma to join independent clauses. (See also G6-b.)

G6-b Consider separating the clauses with a semicolon, a colon, or a dash.

When the independent clauses are closely related and their relation is clear without a coordinating conjunction, a semicolon is an acceptable method of revision. (See P3-a.)

▶ Tragedy depicts the individual confronted with the fact of

　death⁄; comedy depicts the adaptability of human nature.
　　　　^

A semicolon is required between independent clauses that have been linked with a transitional expression (such as *however*, *therefore*, *moreover*, *in fact*, or *for example*). For a longer list, see p. 300.

▶ In his film adaptation of the short story "Killings," director

　Todd Field changed key details of the plot⁄; in fact, he added
　　　　　　　　　　　　　　　　　　　　^

　whole scenes that do not appear in the story.

A colon or a dash may be more appropriate if the first independent clause introduces the second or if the second clause summarizes or explains the first. (See P3-d and P6-b.) In formal writing, the colon is usually preferred to the dash.

　　　　　　　　　　　　　　This
▶ Nuclear waste is hazardous; ~~this~~ is an indisputable fact.
　　　　　　　　　　　　　　　^

▶ The female black widow spider is often a widow of her own

　making⁄‾she has been known to eat her partner after mating.
　　　　^

A colon is an appropriate method of revision if the first independent clause introduces a quoted sentence.

▶ Nobel Peace Prize winner Al Gore had this to say about climate

　change⁄: "The truth is that our circumstances are not only new;
　　　　^

　they are completely different than they have ever been in all of

　human history."

G6-c Consider making the clauses into separate sentences.

▶ Why should we spend money on space exploration./? ~~we~~ **We** have

enough underfunded programs here on Earth.

A question and a statement should be separate sentences.

▶ Some studies have suggested that sexual relationships set

bonobos apart from common chimpanzees./. ~~according~~ **According** to

Stanford (1998), these differences have been exaggerated.

Using a comma alone to join two independent clauses creates a comma
splice. (See also APA-4a on citing sources in APA style.)

NOTE: When two quoted independent clauses are divided by explanatory words, make each clause its own sentence.

▶ "It's always smart to learn from your mistakes," quipped my

supervisor./. ~~"it's~~ **"It's** even smarter to learn from the mistakes of

others."

G6-d Consider restructuring the sentence, perhaps by subordinating one of the clauses.

If one of the independent clauses is less important than the other, turn
the less important clause into a subordinate clause or phrase. (For more
about subordination, see S6, especially the chart on p. 150.)

▶ One of the most famous advertising slogans is Wheaties cereal's

"Breakfast of Champions," ~~it~~ **which** associated the cereal with famous

athletes.

▶ Mary McLeod Bethune, ~~was~~ the seventeenth child of former

slaves, ~~she~~ founded the National Council of Negro Women in 1935.

Minor ideas in these sentences are now expressed in subordinate clauses
or phrases.

M

Multilingual Writers and ESL Challenges

Multilingual Writers and ESL Challenges

This section of *A Writer's Reference* is primarily for multilingual writers. You may find this section helpful if you learned English as a second language (ESL) or if you speak a language other than English with your friends and family.

M1 Verbs

Both native and nonnative speakers of English encounter challenges with verbs. Section M1 focuses on specific challenges that multilingual writers sometimes face. You can find more help with verbs in other sections in the book:

making subjects and verbs agree (G1)

using irregular verb forms (G2-a, G2-b)

leaving off verb endings (G2-c, G2-d)

choosing the correct verb tense (G2-f)

avoiding inappropriate uses of the passive voice (W3-a)

M1-a Use the appropriate verb form and tense.

This section offers a brief review of English verb forms and tenses. For additional help, see G2-f and B1-c.

Basic verb forms

Every main verb in English has five forms, which are used to create all of the verb tenses in Standard English. The following chart shows these forms for the regular verb *help* and the irregular verbs *give* and *be*. See G2-a for a list of other common irregular verbs.

Basic verb forms

	REGULAR VERB *HELP*	IRREGULAR VERB *GIVE*	IRREGULAR VERB *BE**
BASE FORM	help	give	be
PAST TENSE	helped	gave	was, were
PAST PARTICIPLE	helped	given	been
PRESENT PARTICIPLE	helping	giving	being
-*S* FORM	helps	gives	is

Be also has the forms *am* and *are*, which are used in the present tense.

Verb tenses commonly used in the active voice

For descriptions and examples of all verb tenses, see G2-f. For verb tenses commonly used in the passive voice, see the chart on page 253.

Simple tenses

For general facts, states of being, habitual actions

Simple present   **Base form or -s form**

- general facts   College students often *study* late at night.
- states of being   Water *becomes* steam at 100 degrees centigrade.
- habitual, repetitive actions   We *donate* to a different charity each year.
- scheduled future events   The train *arrives* tomorrow at 6:30 p.m.

NOTE: For uses of the present tense in writing about literature, see page 215.

Simple past   **Base form + -ed or -d or irregular form**

- completed actions at a specific time in the past   The storm *destroyed* their property. She *drove* to Montana three years ago.
- facts or states of being in the past   When I *was* young, I usually *walked* to school with my sister.

Simple future   ***will* + base form**

- future actions, promises, or predictions I *will exercise* tomorrow. The snowfall *will begin* around midnight.

Simple progressive forms

For continuing actions

Present progressive   ***am, is, are* + present participle**

- actions in progress at the present time, not continuing indefinitely   The students *are taking* an exam in Room 105. The valet *is parking* the car.
- future actions (with *leave, go, come, move,* etc.)   I *am leaving* tomorrow morning.

Past progressive   ***was, were* + present participle**

- actions in progress at a specific time in the past   They *were swimming* when the storm struck.
- *was going to, were going to* for past plans that did not happen   We *were going to* drive to Florida for spring break, but the car broke down.

NOTE: Some verbs are not normally used in the progressive: *appear, believe, belong, contain, have, hear, know, like, need, see, seem, taste, understand,* and *want.*

> want
> ▶ I ~~am wanting~~ to see August Wilson's *Radio Golf.*
> ^

Perfect tenses

For actions that happened before another present or past time

Present perfect *has, have* + past participle

- repetitive or constant actions that began in the past and continue to the present

  I *have loved* cats since I was a child. Alicia *has worked* in Kenya for ten years.

- actions that happened at an unknown or unspecific time in the past

  Stephen *has visited* Wales three times.

Past perfect *had* + past participle

- actions that began or occurred before another time in the past

  She *had* just *crossed* the street when the runaway car crashed into the building.

NOTE: For more on the past perfect, see G2-f. For uses of the past perfect in conditional sentences, see M1-e.

Perfect progressive forms

For continuous past actions before another present or past time

Present perfect progressive *has, have* + *been* + present participle

- continuous actions that began in the past and continue to the present

  Yolanda *has been trying* to get a job in Boston for five years.

Past perfect progressive *had* + *been* + present participle

- actions that began and continued in the past until another past action

  By the time I moved to Georgia, I *had been supporting* myself for five years.

Verb tenses

Section G2-f describes all the verb tenses in English, showing the forms of a regular verb (*walk*), an irregular verb (*ride*), and the verb *be* in each tense. The chart on pages 250–51 provides more details about the tenses commonly used in the active voice in writing; the chart on page 253 gives details about tenses commonly used in the passive voice.

NOTE: Some of the basic verb forms (p. 249) require helping verbs in different patterns to create the English verb tenses. For example, the simple progressive in the active voice must always have a form of *be* as a helping verb: I *am* leaving tomorrow morning. You will notice in the verb tense charts on pages 250–51 and 253 that the past-participle and present-participle forms of the verb can never be used without one or more helping verbs.

M1-b **To write a verb in the passive voice, use a form of *be* with the past participle.**

When a sentence is written in the passive voice, the subject receives the action instead of doing it. (See B2-c.)

> The solution *was measured* by the lab assistant.

> Melissa *was taken* to the theater.

> The picnic *has been rescheduled* twice because of rain.

To form the passive voice, use a form of *be*—*am*, *is*, *are*, *was*, *were*, *being*, *be*, or *been*—followed by the past participle of the main verb: *was chosen*, *are remembered*. (Sometimes a form of *be* follows another helping verb: *will be considered*, *could have been broken*.)

> written
> ▶ *Dreaming in Cuban* was ~~writing~~ by Cristina García.
>
> In the passive voice, the past participle *written*, not the present participle *writing*, must follow *was* (the past tense of *be*).

> tested.
> ▶ The child is being ~~test.~~
>
> The past participle *tested*, not the base form *test*, must be used with *is being* to form the passive voice.

hackerhandbooks.com/writersref
ⓔ M1 Verbs (multilingual) > Exercises: M1–2, M1–3, and M1–13
✓ M1 Verbs (multilingual) > LearningCurve: Verbs for multilingual writers

Verb tenses commonly used in the passive voice

For details about verb tenses in the active voice, see the chart on pages 250–51.

Simple tenses (passive voice)

Simple present — *am, is, are* + past participle
- general facts — Breakfast *is served* daily.
- habitual, repetitive actions — The receipts *are counted* every night.

Simple past — *was, were* + past participle
- completed past actions — He *was punished* for being late.

Simple future — *will be* + past participle
- future actions, promises, or predictions — The decision *will be made* by the committee next week.

Simple progressive forms (passive voice)

Present progressive — *am, is, are* + *being* + past participle
- actions in progress at the present time — The new stadium *is being built* with private money.
- future actions (with *leave, go, come, move,* etc.) — Jo *is being moved* to a new class next month.

Past progressive — *was, were* + *being* + past participle
- actions in progress at a specific time in the past — We thought we *were being followed*.

Perfect tenses (passive voice)

Present perfect — *has, have* + *been* + past participle
- actions that began in the past and continue to the present — The flight *has been delayed* because of storms in the Midwest.
- actions that happened at an unknown or unspecific time in the past — Wars *have been fought* throughout history.

Past perfect — *had* + *been* + past participle
- actions that began or occurred before another time in the past — He *had been given* all the hints he needed to complete the puzzle.

NOTE: Future progressive, future perfect, and perfect progressive forms are not used in the passive voice.

For details on forming the passive voice in various tenses, consult the chart on page 253. (The active voice is generally stronger and more direct than the passive. The passive voice does have appropriate uses; see W3-a and B2-c.)

NOTE: Only transitive verbs, those that take direct objects, may be used in the passive voice. Intransitive verbs such as *occur*, *happen*, *sleep*, *die*, *become*, and *fall* are not used in the passive. (See B2-b.)

▶ The accident ~~was~~ happened suddenly.

M1-c Use the base form of the verb after a modal.

The modal verbs are *can*, *could*, *may*, *might*, *must*, *shall*, *should*, *will*, and *would*. (*Ought to* is also considered a modal verb.) The modals are used with the base form of a verb to show ability, certainty, necessity, permission, obligation, or possibility.

Modals and the verbs that follow them do not change form to indicate tense. For a summary of modals and their meanings, see the chart on pages 255–56. (See also G2-e.)

▶ The art museum will ~~launches~~ its fundraising campaign next
                                 ^launch

month.

The modal *will* must be followed by the base form *launch*, not the present tense *launches*.

▶ The translator could ~~spoke~~ many languages, so the ambassador
                       ^speak

hired her for the European tour.

The modal *could* must be followed by the base form *speak*, not the past tense *spoke*.

TIP: Do not use *to* before a main verb that follows a modal.

▶ Gina can ~~to~~ drive us home if we miss the last train.

For the use of modals in conditional sentences, see M1-e.

hackerhandbooks.com/writersref
🄴 M1 Verbs (multilingual) > Exercises: M1–5, M1–6, and M1–13
☑ M1 Verbs (multilingual) > LearningCurve: Verbs for multilingual writers

Modals and their meanings

can

- general ability (present)

  Ants *can survive* anywhere, even in space. Jorge *can run* a marathon faster than his brother.

- informal requests or permission

  Can you *tell* me where the light is? Sandy *can borrow* my calculator.

could

- general ability (past)

  Lea *could read* when she was only three years old.

- polite, informal requests or permission

  Could you *give* me that pen?

may

- formal requests or permission

  May I *see* the report? Students *may park* only in the yellow zone.

- possibility

  I *may try* to finish my homework tonight, or I *may wake up* early and *finish* it tomorrow.

might

- possibility

  Funding for the language lab *might double* by 2018.

NOTE: *Might* usually expresses a stronger possibility than *may*.

must

- necessity (present or future)

  To be effective, welfare-to-work programs *must provide* access to job training.

- strong probability

  Amy *must be* nervous. [She is probably nervous.]

- near certainty (present or past)

  I *must have left* my wallet at home. [I almost certainly left my wallet at home.]

should

- suggestions or advice

  Diabetics *should drink* plenty of water every day.

- obligations or duties

  The government *should protect* citizens' rights.

- expectations

  The books *should arrive* soon. [We expect the books to arrive soon.]

➡

Modals and their meanings, *continued*

will

- certainty
  If you don't leave now, you *will be* late for your rehearsal.

- requests
  Will you *help* me study for my psychology exam?

- promises and offers
  Jonah *will arrange* the carpool.

would

- polite requests
  Would you *help* me carry these books? I *would like* some coffee. [*Would like* is more polite than *want*.]

- habitual or repeated actions (in the past)
  Whenever Elena needed help with sewing, she *would call* her aunt.

M1-d To make negative verb forms, add *not* in the appropriate place.

If the verb is the simple present or past tense of *be* (*am, is, are, was, were*), add *not* after the verb.

Gianna is *not* a member of the club.

For simple present-tense verbs other than *be*, use *do* or *does* plus *not* before the base form of the verb. (For the correct forms of *do* and *does*, see the chart in G1-a.)

► Mariko not want more dessert.
  (does)

► Mariko does not wants more dessert.

For simple past-tense verbs other than *be*, use *did* plus *not* before the base form of the verb.

► They did not planted corn this year.
  (plant)

hackerhandbooks.com/writersref
M1 Verbs (multilingual) > Exercises: M1–8 and M1–13
M1 Verbs (multilingual) > LearningCurve: Verbs for multilingual writers

In a verb phrase consisting of one or more helping verbs and a present or past participle (*is watching*, *were living*, *has played*, *could have been driven*), use the word *not* after the first helping verb.

▶ Inna should have ~~not~~ gone dancing last night.
              ^not^

▶ Bonnie is ~~no~~ singing this weekend.
         ^not^

NOTE: English allows only one negative in an independent clause to express a negative idea; using more than one is an error known as a *double negative* (see G4-e for more on double negatives to express a positive idea).

▶ We could not find ~~no~~ books about the history of our school.
                   ^any^

M1-e In a conditional sentence, choose verb tenses according to the type of condition expressed in the sentence.

Conditional sentences contain two clauses: a subordinate clause (usually starting with *if*, *when*, or *unless*) and an independent clause. The subordinate clause (sometimes called the *if* or *unless* clause) states the condition or cause; the independent clause states the result or effect. In each example in this section, the subordinate clause (*if* clause) is marked SUB, and the independent clause is marked IND. (See B3-e on subordinate clauses.)

Factual

Factual conditional sentences express relationships based on facts. If the relationship is a scientific truth, use the present tense in both clauses.

         ┌──────── SUB ────────┐ ┌─ IND ─┐
If water *cools* to 32 degrees Fahrenheit, it *freezes*.

If the sentence describes a condition that is (or was) habitually true, use the same tense in both clauses.

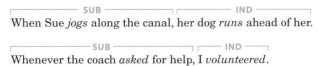

When Sue *jogs* along the canal, her dog *runs* ahead of her.

Whenever the coach *asked* for help, I *volunteered*.

Predictive

Predictive conditional sentences are used to predict the future or to express future plans or possibilities. To form a predictive sentence, use a present-tense verb in the subordinate clause; in the independent clause, use the modal *will*, *can*, *may*, *should*, or *might* plus the base form of the verb.

If you *practice* regularly, your tennis game *should improve*.

We *will lose* our remaining wetlands unless we *act* now.

TIP: In all types of conditional sentences (factual, predictive, and speculative), *if* or *unless* clauses do not use the modal verb *will*.

▸ If Liv ~~will pass~~ her history test, she will graduate this year.
  passes

Speculative

Speculative conditional sentences express unlikely, contrary-to-fact, or impossible conditions. English uses the past or past perfect tense in the *if* clause, even for conditions in the present or the future.

UNLIKELY POSSIBILITIES   If the condition is possible but unlikely in the present or the future, use the past tense in the subordinate clause; in the independent clause, use *would*, *could*, or *might* plus the base form of the verb.

If I *won* the lottery, I *would travel* to Egypt.

The writer does not expect to win the lottery. Because this is a possible but unlikely present or future situation, the past tense is used in the subordinate clause.

CONDITIONS CONTRARY TO FACT   In conditions that are currently unreal or contrary to fact, use the past-tense verb *were* (not *was*) in the *if* clause for all subjects. (See also G2-g, on the subjunctive mood.)

▶ If I ~~was~~ ^were^ president, I would make children's issues a priority.

The writer is not president, so *were* is correct in the *if* clause.

EVENTS THAT DID NOT HAPPEN   In a conditional sentence that speculates about an event that did not happen or was impossible in the past, use the past perfect tense in the *if* clause; in the independent clause, use *would have*, *could have*, or *might have* with the past participle. (See also past perfect tense, p. 251.)

┌─────── SUB ───────┐ ┌─────── IND ───────┐
If I *had saved* more money, I *would have visited* Laos last year.

The writer did not save more money and did not travel to Laos. This sentence shows a possibility that did not happen.

M1-f   Become familiar with verbs that may be followed by gerunds or infinitives.

A gerund is a verb form that ends in *-ing* and is used as a noun: *sleeping*, *dreaming*. An infinitive is the word *to* plus the base form of the verb: *to sleep*, *to dream*. The word *to* is an infinitive marker, not a preposition, in this use. (See B3-b.)

A few verbs may be followed by either a gerund or an infinitive; others may be followed by a gerund but not by an infinitive; still others may be followed by an infinitive but not by a gerund.

Verb + gerund or infinitive (no change in meaning)

The following commonly used verbs may be followed by a gerund or an infinitive, with little or no difference in meaning:

begin	like
continue	love
hate	start

I love *skiing*. I love *to ski*.

hackerhandbooks.com/writersref
🄴 M1 Verbs (multilingual) > Exercises: M1–11 to M1–13
✓ M1 Verbs (multilingual) > LearningCurve: Verbs for multilingual writers

Verb + gerund or infinitive (change in meaning)

With a few verbs, the choice of a gerund or an infinitive changes the meaning dramatically:

> forget
> remember
> stop
> try

She stopped *speaking* to Lucia. [She no longer spoke to Lucia.]

She stopped *to speak* to Lucia. [She paused so that she could speak to Lucia.]

Verb + gerund

These verbs may be followed by a gerund but not by an infinitive:

admit	finish	quit
appreciate	imagine	recall
avoid	miss	resist
deny	postpone	risk
discuss	practice	suggest
enjoy	put off	tolerate
escape		

Bill enjoys *playing* [not *to play*] the piano.

Jamie quit *smoking*.

Verb + infinitive

These verbs may be followed by an infinitive but not by a gerund:

agree	hope	promise
ask	manage	refuse
beg	mean	wait
claim	need	want
decide	offer	wish
expect	plan	would like
help	pretend	

Jill has offered *to water* [not *watering*] the plants while we are away.

Joe finally managed *to find* a parking space.

A few of these verbs may be followed either by an infinitive directly or by a noun or pronoun plus an infinitive:

ask	help	promise	would like
expect	need	want	

We asked *to speak* to the congregation.

We asked *Rabbi Abrams to speak* to our congregation.

Verb + noun or pronoun + infinitive

With certain verbs in the active voice, a noun or pronoun must come between the verb and the infinitive that follows it. The noun or pronoun usually names a person who is affected by the action of the verb.

advise	convince	order	tell
allow	encourage	persuade	urge
cause	have ("own")	remind	warn
command	instruct	require	

      V   N   ⌐INF⌐

The class encouraged Luis to tell the story of his escape.

The counselor *advised Haley to take* four courses instead of five.

Verb + noun or pronoun + unmarked infinitive

An unmarked infinitive is an infinitive without *to*. A few verbs (often called *causative verbs*) may be followed by a noun or pronoun and an unmarked infinitive.

have ("cause")	let ("allow")
help	make ("force")

▶ **Rose had the attendant ~~to~~ wash the windshield.**

▶ **Frank made me ~~to~~ carry his book for him.**

Help can be followed by a noun or pronoun and either an unmarked or a marked infinitive.

Emma *helped Brian wash* the dishes.

Emma *helped Brian to wash* the dishes.

NOTE: The infinitive is used in some typical constructions with *too* and *enough*.

> *TOO* + ADJECTIVE + INFINITIVE
> The gift is *too large to wrap*.

> *ENOUGH* + NOUN + INFINITIVE
> Our emergency pack has *enough bottled water to last* a week.

> ADJECTIVE + *ENOUGH* + INFINITIVE
> Some of the hikers felt *strong enough to climb* another thousand feet.

M2 Articles

Articles (*a*, *an*, *the*) are part of a category of words known as *noun markers* or *determiners*.

M2-a Be familiar with articles and other noun markers.

Standard English uses noun markers to help identify the nouns that follow. In addition to articles (*a*, *an*, and *the*), noun markers include the following:

- possessive nouns, such as *Elena's* (See P4-a.)
- possessive pronoun/adjectives: *my*, *your*, *his*, *her*, *its*, *our*, *their* (See B1-b.)
- demonstrative pronoun/adjectives: *this*, *that*, *these*, *those* (See B1-b.)
- quantifiers: *all*, *any*, *each*, *either*, *every*, *few*, *many*, *more*, *most*, *much*, *neither*, *several*, *some*, and so on (See M2-d.)
- numbers: *one*, *twenty-three*, and so on

Using articles and other noun markers

Articles and other noun markers always appear before nouns; sometimes other modifiers, such as adjectives and adverbs, come between a noun marker and a noun.

> ART N
> Felix is reading a book about mythology.

> ART ADJ N
> We took an exciting trip to Alaska last summer.

hackerhandbooks.com/writersref
e M2 Articles > Exercises: M2–3 to M2–6
✓ M2 Articles > LearningCurve: Articles and nouns for multilingual writers

NOUN
MARKER ADV   ADJ   N

That very delicious meal was expensive.

In most cases, do not use an article with another noun marker.

▶ ~~The~~ Natalie's older brother lives in Wisconsin.

Expressions like *a few*, *the most*, and *all the* are exceptions: *a few pota-toes*, *all the rain*. See also M2-d.

Types of articles and types of nouns

To choose an appropriate article for a noun, first determine whether the noun is *common* or *proper*, *count* or *noncount*, *singular* or *plural*, and *spe-cific* or *general*. The chart on pages 264–65 describes the types of nouns.

Articles are classified as *indefinite* and *definite*. The indefinite articles, *a* and *an*, are used with general nouns. The definite article, *the*, is used with specific nouns. (The last section of the chart on p. 265 explains general and specific nouns.)

A and *an* both mean "one" or "one among many." Use *a* before a con-sonant sound: *a banana*, *a vacation*, *a happy child*, *a united family*. Use *an* before a vowel sound: *an eggplant*, *an uncle*, *an honorable person*. (See also *a*, *an* in W1.)

The shows that a noun is specific; use *the* with one or more than one specific thing: *the newspaper*, *the soldiers*.

M2-b Use *the* with most specific common nouns.

The definite article, *the*, is used with most nouns—both count and noncount—that the reader can identify specifically. Usually the identity will be clear to the reader for one of the following reasons. (See the chart on p. 267.)

1. The noun has been previously mentioned.

                                       the
▶ A truck cut in front of our van. When truck skidded a few
                                       ^

   seconds later, we almost crashed into it.

   The article *A* is used before *truck* when the noun is first mentioned. When the noun is mentioned again, it needs the article *the* because readers can now identify which truck skidded—the one that cut in front of the van.

2. A phrase or clause following the noun restricts its identity.

                           the
▶ Bryce warned me that GPS in his car was not working.
                       ^

   The phrase *in his car* identifies the specific GPS.

Types of nouns

Common or proper

Common nouns

- name general persons, places, things, or ideas
- begin with lowercase

Examples

religion   beauty
knowledge   student
rain   country

Proper nouns

- name specific persons, places, things, or ideas
- begin with capital letter

Examples

Hinduism   President Adams
Philip   Washington Monument
New Jersey   Supreme Court
Vietnam   Renaissance

Count or noncount (common nouns only)

Count nouns

- name persons, places, things, or ideas that can be counted
- have plural forms

Examples

girl, girls
city, cities
goose, geese
philosophy, philosophies

Noncount nouns

- name things or abstract ideas that cannot be counted
- cannot be made plural

Examples

water   patience
silver   knowledge
furniture   air

NOTE: See the chart on page 268 for lists of commonly used noncount nouns.

Singular or plural (both common and proper)

Singular nouns (count and noncount)

- represent one person, place, thing, or idea

Examples

backpack   rain
country   beauty
woman   Nile River
achievement   Block Island

Plural nouns (count only)

- represent more than one person, place, thing, or idea
- must be count nouns

Examples

backpacks   Ural Mountains
countries   Falkland Islands
women   achievements

Specific (definite) or general (indefinite) (count and noncount)

Specific nouns

- name persons, places, things, or ideas that can be identified within a group of the same type

Examples

The students in Professor Martin's *class* should study.

The airplane carrying *the senator* was late.

The furniture in *the truck* was damaged.

General nouns

- name categories of persons, places, things, or ideas (often plural)

Examples

Students should study.

Books bridge *gaps* between *cultures*.

The airplane has made commuting between *cities* easy.

NOTE: Descriptive adjectives do not necessarily make a noun specific. A specific noun is one that readers can identify within a group of nouns of the same type.

▶ If I win the lottery, I will buy ~~the~~ brand-new bright red sports car.
    ^ *a*

   The reader cannot identify which specific brand-new bright red sports car the writer will buy. Even though *car* has many adjectives in front of it, it is a general noun in this sentence.

3. A superlative adjective such as *best* or *most intelligent* makes the noun's identity specific. (See also G4-d.)

▶ Our petite daughter dated tallest boy in her class.
    ^ *the*

   The superlative *tallest* makes the noun *boy* specific. Although there might be several tall boys, only one boy can be the tallest.

4. The noun describes a unique person, place, or thing.

▶ During an eclipse, one should not look directly at sun.
    ^ *the*

   There is only one sun in our solar system, so its identity is clear.

5. The context or situation makes the noun's identity clear.

▶ Please don't slam door when you leave.
    ^ *the*

   Both the speaker and the listener know which door is meant.

6. The noun is singular and refers to a scientific class or category of items (most often animals, musical instruments, and inventions).

▶ ~~Tin~~ The tin whistle is common in traditional Irish music.

The writer is referring to the tin whistle as a class of musical instruments.

M2-c Use *a* (or *an*) with common singular count nouns that refer to "one" or "any."

If a count noun refers to one unspecific item (not a whole category), use the indefinite article, *a* or *an*. *A* and *an* usually mean "one among many" but can also mean "any one." (See the chart on p. 267.)

▶ My English professor asked me to bring *a* dictionary to class.

The noun *dictionary* refers to "one unspecific dictionary" or "any dictionary."

▶ We want to rent *an* apartment close to the lake.

The noun *apartment* refers to "any apartment close to the lake," not a specific apartment.

M2-d Use a quantifier such as *some* or *more*, not *a* or *an*, with a noncount noun to express an approximate amount.

Do not use *a* or *an* with noncount nouns. Also do not use numbers or words such as *several* or *many*; they must be used with plural nouns, and noncount nouns do not have plural forms. (See the chart on p. 268 for lists of commonly used noncount nouns.)

▶ Dr. Snyder gave us ~~an~~ information about the Peace Corps.

▶ Do you have ~~many~~ money with you?

You can use quantifiers such as *enough*, *less*, and *some* to suggest approximate amounts or nonspecific quantities of noncount nouns: *a little salt*, *any homework*, *enough wood*, *less information*, *much pollution*.

Choosing articles for common nouns

Use *the*

- if the reader has enough information to identify the noun specifically

    COUNT: Please turn on *the lights*. We're going to *the zoo* tomorrow.

    NONCOUNT: *The food* throughout Italy is excellent.

Use *a* or *an*

- if the noun refers to one item *and* if the item is singular but not specific

    COUNT: Bring *a pencil* to class. Charles wrote *an essay* about his first job.

NOTE: Do not use *a* or *an* with plural or noncount nouns.

Use a quantifier (*enough, many, some*, etc.)

- if the noun represents an unspecified amount of something
- if the amount is more than one but not all items in a category

    COUNT (PLURAL): Amir showed us *some photos* of India. *Many turtles* return to the same nesting site each year.

    NONCOUNT: We didn't get *enough rain* this summer.

NOTE: Sometimes no article conveys an unspecified amount: *Amir showed us photos of India*.

Use no article

- if the noun represents all items in a category
- if the noun represents a category in general

    COUNT (PLURAL): *Students* can attend the show for free.

    NONCOUNT: *Coal* is a natural resource.

NOTE: *The* is occasionally used when a singular count noun refers to all items in a class or a specific category: *The bald eagle is no longer endangered in the United States*.

Commonly used noncount nouns

Food and drink

beef, bread, butter, candy, cereal, cheese, cream, meat, milk, pasta, rice, salt, sugar, water, wine

Nonfood substances

air, cement, coal, dirt, gasoline, gold, paper, petroleum, plastic, rain, silver, snow, soap, steel, wood, wool

Abstract nouns

advice, anger, beauty, confidence, courage, employment, fun, happiness, health, honesty, information, intelligence, knowledge, love, poverty, satisfaction, wealth

Other

biology (and other areas of study), clothing, equipment, furniture, homework, jewelry, luggage, machinery, mail, money, news, poetry, pollution, research, scenery, traffic, transportation, violence, weather, work

NOTE: A few noncount nouns (such as *love*) can also be used as count nouns: *He had two loves: music and archery.*

M2-e Do not use articles with nouns that refer to all of something or something in general.

When a noncount noun refers to all of its type or to a concept in general, it is not marked with an article.

▶ ~~The~~ kindness is a virtue.
  Kindness

The noun represents kindness in general; it does not represent a specific type of kindness, such as *the kindness he showed me after my mother's death*.

▶ In some places, ~~the~~ rice is preferred to all other grains.

The noun *rice* represents rice in general. To refer to a specific type or serving of rice, the definite article is appropriate: *The rice my husband served last night is the best I've ever tasted.*

In most cases, when you use a count noun to represent a general category, make the noun plural. Do not use unmarked singular count nouns to represent whole categories.

▶ ~~Fountain is~~ an expensive element of landscape design.
  Fountains are

Fountains is a count noun that represents fountains in general.

EXCEPTION: In some cases, *the* can be used with singular count nouns to represent a class or specific category: *The Chinese alligator is smaller than the American alligator.* See also number 6 in M2-b.

M2-f Do not use articles with most singular proper nouns. Use *the* with most plural proper nouns.

Since singular proper nouns are already specific, they typically do not need an article: *Prime Minister Cameron, Jamaica, Lake Huron, Mount Etna.*

There are, however, many exceptions. In most cases, if the proper noun consists of a common noun with modifiers (adjectives or an *of* phrase), use *the* with the proper noun.

▶ We visited ^the^ Great Wall of China last year.

▶ Rob wants to be a translator for ^the^ Central Intelligence Agency.

The is used with most plural proper nouns: *the McGregors, the Bahamas, the Finger Lakes, the United States.*

Geographic names create problems because there are so many exceptions to the rules. When in doubt, consult the chart below, check a dictionary, or ask a native speaker.

Using *the* with geographic nouns

When to omit *the*

streets, squares, parks	Ivy Street, Union Square, Denali National Park
cities, states, counties	Miami, New Mexico, Bee County
most countries, continents	Italy, China, South America, Africa
bays, single lakes	Tampa Bay, Lake Geneva
single mountains, islands	Mount Everest, Crete

When to use *the*

country names with *of* phrase	the United States (of America), the People's Republic of China
large regions, deserts	the East Coast, the Sahara
peninsulas	the Baja Peninsula, the Sinai Peninsula
oceans, seas, gulfs	the Pacific Ocean, the Dead Sea, the Persian Gulf
canals and rivers	the Panama Canal, the Amazon
mountain ranges	the Rocky Mountains, the Alps
groups of islands	the Solomon Islands

M3 Sentence structure

Although their structure can vary widely, sentences in English generally flow from subject to verb to object or complement: *Bears eat fish*. This section focuses on the major challenges that multilingual students face when writing sentences in English. For more details on the parts of speech and the elements of sentences, consult sections B1–B4.

M3-a Use a linking verb between a subject and its complement.

Some languages, such as Russian and Turkish, do not use linking verbs (*is*, *are*, *was*, *were*) between subjects and complements (nouns or adjectives that rename or describe the subject). Every English sentence, however, must include a verb. For more on linking verbs, see G2-e.

> ▶   Jim^{is} intelligent.

▶   Jim ^{is} intelligent.
        ^

▶   Many streets in San Francisco ^{are} very steep.
                                       ^

M3-b Include a subject in every sentence.

Some languages, such as Spanish and Japanese, do not require a subject in every sentence. Every English sentence, however, needs a subject.

▶   Your aunt is very energetic. ~~Seems~~ *She seems* young for her age.
                                   ^

Commands are an exception: The subject *you* is understood but not present in the sentence.

> [You] Give me the book.

The word *it* is used as the subject of a sentence describing the weather or temperature, stating the time, indicating distance, or suggesting an environmental fact.

> It is
> ~~Is~~ raining in the valley and snowing in the mountains.
> ^

> It is
> ~~Is~~ 9:15 a.m.
> ^

In most English sentences, the subject appears before the verb. Some sentences, however, are inverted: The subject comes after the verb. In these sentences, a placeholder called an *expletive* (*there* or *it*) often comes before the verb.

EXP V ┌── S ──┐
There are many people here today.

┌── S ──┐ V
(Many people are here today.)

> There is
> ~~Is~~ an apple pie in the refrigerator.
> ^

>   there are
> As you know, many religious sects in India.
>   ^

Notice that the verb agrees with the subject that follows it: *apple pie is, sects are*. (See G1-g.)

Sometimes an inverted sentence has an infinitive (*to work*) or a noun clause (*that she is intelligent*) as the subject. In such sentences, the placeholder *it* is needed before the verb. (Also see B3-b and B3-e.)

EXP V   ┌─ S ─┐
It is important to study daily.

┌─ S ─┐   V
(To study daily is important.)

>   it
> Because the road is flooded, is necessary to change our route.
>   ^

TIP: The words *here* and *there* can be used as placeholders, but they cannot be used as subjects. When they mean "in this place" (*here*) or "in that place" (*there*), they are adverbs, which are never subjects.

>   It   there.
> I just returned from Japan. ~~There~~ is very beautiful/
>   ^   ^

> This school   that school
> ~~Here~~ offers a master's degree in physical therapy; ~~there~~ has
> ^   ^
>
> only a bachelor's program.

M3-c   Do not use both a noun and a pronoun to perform the same grammatical function in a sentence.

English does not allow a subject to be repeated in its own clause.

▶   **The doctor ~~she~~ advised me to cut down on salt.**

The pronoun *she* cannot repeat the subject, *doctor.*

Do not add a pronoun even when a word group comes between the subject and the verb.

▶   **The watch that I lost on vacation ~~it~~ was in my backpack.**

The pronoun *it* cannot repeat the subject, *watch.*

Some languages allow "topic fronting," placing a word or phrase (a "topic") at the beginning of a sentence and following it with an independent clause that explains something about the topic. This form is not allowed in English because the sentence seems to start with one subject but then introduces a new subject in an independent clause.

┌─ TOPIC ┐ ┌──── IND CLAUSE ────┐
INCORRECT   The seeds I planted them last fall.

The sentence can be corrected by bringing the topic (*seeds*) into the independent clause.

the seeds

▶   **~~The seeds~~ I planted ~~them~~ last fall.**
            ^

M3-d   Do not repeat a subject, an object, or an adverb in an adjective clause.

Adjective clauses begin with relative pronouns (*who, whom, whose, which, that*) or relative adverbs (*when, where*). Relative pronouns usually serve as subjects or objects in the clauses they introduce; another word in the clause cannot serve the same function. Relative adverbs should not be repeated by other adverbs later in the clause.

┌──── ADJ CLAUSE ────┐
The cat ran under the car that was parked on the street.

▶   **The cat ran under the car that ~~it~~ was parked on the street.**

The relative pronoun *that* is the subject of the adjective clause, so the pronoun *it* cannot be added as a subject.

▶ Myrna enjoyed the investment seminars that she attended ~~them~~

last week.

The relative pronoun *that* is the object of the verb *attended*. The pronoun *them* cannot also serve as an object.

Sometimes the relative pronoun is understood but not present in the sentence. In such cases, do not add another word with the same function as the omitted pronoun.

▶ Myrna enjoyed the investment seminars she attended ~~them~~ last

week.

The relative pronoun *that* is understood after *seminars* even though it is not present in the sentence.

If the clause begins with a relative adverb, do not use another adverb with the same meaning later in the clause.

▶ The office where I work ~~there~~ is one hour from the city.

The adverb *there* cannot repeat the relative adverb *where*.

M3-e Avoid mixed constructions beginning with *although* or *because*.

A word group that begins with *although* cannot be linked to a word group that begins with *but* or *however*. The result is an error called a *mixed construction* (see also S5-a). Similarly, a word group that begins with *because* cannot be linked to a word group that begins with *so* or *therefore*.

If you want to keep *although* or *because*, drop the other linking word.

▶ Although Nikki Giovanni is best known for her poetry for adults,

~~but~~ she has written several books for children.

▶ Because German and Dutch are related languages, ~~therefore~~

tourists from Berlin can usually read a few signs in Amsterdam.

If you want to keep the other linking word, omit *although* or *because*.

▶ ~~Although~~ Nikki Giovanni is best known for her poetry for adults,

but she has written several books for children.

▶ ~~Because~~ German and Dutch are related languages**/;** therefore,
⌃ ⌃
tourists from Berlin can usually read a few signs in Amsterdam.

For advice about using commas and semicolons with linking words, see P1-a and P3-a.

M3-f Do not place an adverb between a verb and its direct object.

Adverbs modifying verbs can appear in various positions: at the beginning or end of a sentence, before or after a verb, or between a helping verb and its main verb.

Slowly, we drove along the rain-slick road.

Mia handled the teapot *very carefully*.

Martin *always* wins our tennis matches.

Christina is *rarely* late for our lunch dates.

My daughter has *often* spoken of you.

The election results were being *closely* followed by analysts.

However, an adverb cannot appear between a verb and its direct object.

carefully
▶ Mother wrapped ~~carefully~~ the gift.
⌃
The adverb *carefully* cannot appear between the verb, *wrapped*, and its direct object, *the gift*.

M4 Using adjectives

M4-a Distinguish between present participles and past participles used as adjectives.

Both present and past participles may be used as adjectives. The present participle always ends in *-ing*. Past participles usually end in *-ed*, *-d*, *-en*, *-n*, or *-t*. (See G2-a.)

PRESENT PARTICIPLES	confusing, speaking, boring
PAST PARTICIPLES	confused, spoken, bored

Like all other adjectives, participles can come before nouns; they also can follow linking verbs, in which case they describe the subject of the sentence. (See B2-b.)

Use a present participle to describe a person or thing *causing or stimulating an experience*.

The *boring lecture* put us to sleep. [The lecture caused boredom.]

Use a past participle to describe a person or thing *undergoing an experience*.

The *audience* was *bored*. [The audience experienced boredom.]

Participles that describe emotions or mental states often cause the most confusion.

annoying/annoyed	exhausting/exhausted
boring/bored	fascinating/fascinated
confusing/confused	frightening/frightened
depressing/depressed	satisfying/satisfied
exciting/excited	surprising/surprised

M4-b Place cumulative adjectives in an appropriate order.

Adjectives usually come before the nouns they modify and may also come after linking verbs. (See B1-d and B2-b.)

ADJ　　　N　　　　　　　　　V　　ADJ
Janine wore a new necklace. Janine's necklace was new.

e M4 Using adjectives > Exercises: M4–2 and M4–3, M4–5 and M4–6
✓ M4 Using adjectives > LearningCurve: Sentence structure for multilingual writers

Order of cumulative adjectives

FIRST   **ARTICLE OR OTHER NOUN MARKER**   a, an, the, her, Joe's, two, many, some

     EVALUATIVE WORD   attractive, dedicated, delicious, ugly, disgusting

     SIZE   large, enormous, small, little

     LENGTH OR SHAPE   long, short, round, square

     AGE   new, old, young, antique

     COLOR   yellow, blue, crimson

     NATIONALITY   French, Peruvian, Vietnamese

     RELIGION   Catholic, Protestant, Jewish, Muslim

     MATERIAL   silver, walnut, wool, marble

LAST   **NOUN/ADJECTIVE**   tree (as in *tree* house), kitchen (as in *kitchen* table)

THE NOUN MODIFIED   house, coat, bicycle, bread, woman, coin

My large blue wool **coat** *is in the attic.*

     my **(ARTICLE OR OTHER NOUN MARKER)**

     large **(SIZE)**

     blue **(COLOR)**

     wool **(MATERIAL)**

coat **(THE NOUN MODIFIED)**

Joe's collection includes *two small antique silver* **coins**.

     two **(ARTICLE OR OTHER NOUN MARKER)**

     small **(SIZE)**

     antique **(AGE)**

     silver **(MATERIAL)**

coins **(THE NOUN MODIFIED)**

Cumulative adjectives are adjectives that build on one another, are not joined by the word *and*, and are not separated with commas (P2-d). These adjectives must be listed in a particular order. If you use cumulative adjectives before a noun, see the chart above. The chart is only a guide; don't be surprised if you encounter exceptions.

▶ My dorm room has only a desk and a ~~plastic red stained~~ chair.
                              stained red plastic

M5 Prepositions and idiomatic expressions

M5-a Become familiar with prepositions that show time and place.

The most frequently used prepositions in English are *at*, *by*, *for*, *from*, *in*, *of*, *on*, *to*, and *with*. Prepositions can be difficult to master because the differences among them are subtle and idiomatic. The chart on page 278 is limited to three troublesome prepositions that show time and place: *at*, *on*, and *in*.

Not every possible use is listed in the chart, so don't be surprised when you encounter exceptions and idiomatic uses that you must learn one at a time. For example, in English a person rides *in* a car but *on* a bus, plane, train, or subway.

▶ My first class starts ~~on~~ 8:00 a.m.
      at

▶ The farmers go to market ~~in~~ Wednesday.
      on

M5-b Use nouns (including *-ing* forms) after prepositions.

In a prepositional phrase, use a noun (not a verb) after the preposition. Sometimes the noun will be a gerund, the *-ing* verb form that functions as a noun (see B3-b).

▶ Our student government is good at ~~save~~ money.
      saving

Distinguish between the preposition *to* and the infinitive marker *to*. If *to* is a preposition, it should be followed by a noun or a gerund.

▶ We are dedicated to ~~help~~ the poor.
      helping

If *to* is an infinitive marker, it should be followed by the base form of the verb.

▶ We want to ~~helping~~ the poor.
      help

hackerhandbooks.com/writersref
🄴 M5 Prepositions and idioms > Exercises: M5–2 and M5–3
☑ M5 Prepositions and idioms > LearningCurve: Prepositions for multilingual writers

At, on, and in to show time and place

Showing time

AT	*at* a specific time: *at* 7:20, *at* dawn, *at* dinner
ON	*on* a specific day or date: *on* Tuesday, *on* June 4
IN	*in* a part of a 24-hour period: *in* the afternoon, *in* the daytime [but *at* night]
	in a year or month: *in* 2008, *in* July
	in a period of time: finished *in* three hours

Showing place

AT	*at* a meeting place or location: *at* home, *at* the club
	at the edge of something: sitting *at* the desk
	at the corner of something: turning *at* the intersection
	at a target: throwing the snowball *at* Lucy
ON	*on* a surface: placed *on* the table, hanging *on* the wall
	on a street: the house *on* Spring Street
	on an electronic medium: *on* television, *on* the Internet
IN	*in* an enclosed space: *in* the garage, *in* an envelope
	in a geographic location: *in* San Diego, *in* Texas
	in a print medium: *in* a book, *in* a magazine

To test whether *to* is a preposition or an infinitive marker, insert a word that you know is a noun after the word *to*. If the noun makes sense in that position, *to* is a preposition. If the noun does not make sense after *to*, then *to* is an infinitive marker.

Zoe is addicted *to* _____.

They are planning *to* _____.

In the first sentence, a noun (such as *magazines*) makes sense after *to*, so *to* is a preposition and should be followed by a noun or a gerund: Zoe is addicted *to magazines*. Zoe is addicted *to running*.

In the second sentence, a noun (such as *magazines*) does not make sense after *to*, so *to* is an infinitive marker and must be followed by the base form of the verb: They are planning *to build* a new school.

M5-c Become familiar with common adjective + preposition combinations.

Some adjectives appear only with certain prepositions. These expressions are idiomatic and may be different from the combinations used in your native language.

▶ Paula is married ~~with~~ Jon.
                 to

Check an ESL dictionary for combinations that are not listed in the chart at the bottom of the page.

M5-d Become familiar with common verb + preposition combinations.

Many verbs and prepositions appear together in idiomatic phrases. Pay special attention to the combinations that are different from the combinations used in your native language.

▶ Your success depends ~~of~~ your effort.
                           on

Check an ESL dictionary for combinations that are not listed in the chart on page 280.

Adjective + preposition combinations

accustomed to	connected to	guilty of	preferable to
addicted to	covered with	interested in	proud of
afraid of	dedicated to	involved in	responsible for
angry with	devoted to	involved with	satisfied with
ashamed of	different from	known as	scared of
aware of	engaged in	known for	similar to
committed to	engaged to	made of (or made from)	tired of
concerned about	excited about	married to	worried about
concerned with	familiar with	opposed to	
	full of		

Verb + preposition combinations

agree with	compare with	forget about	speak to (*or* speak with)
apply to	concentrate on	happen to	stare at
approve of	consist of	hope for	succeed at
arrive at	count on	insist on	succeed in
arrive in	decide on	listen to	take advantage of
ask for	depend on	participate in	take care of
believe in	differ from	rely on	think about
belong to	disagree with	reply to	think of
care about	dream about	respond to	wait for
care for	dream of	result in	wait on
compare to	feel like	search for	

M6   Paraphrasing sources effectively

Effective paraphrasing is an important skill for writing in college. You will frequently paraphrase information from your textbooks to answer homework and exam questions, and you will especially need this skill when you are writing essays that incorporate information from other writers. However, learning how to paraphrase can be challenging because often the topics and the vocabulary are new and unfamiliar to multilingual writers.

The purpose of paraphrasing is to restate an author's ideas in your own words. Most writers find the following process for paraphrasing useful:

1. Read and understand the text.
2. Put the text aside.
3. Express the information in your own words.
4. Compare your paraphrase to the original text to check that you have used different words and different sentence structures but have kept the author's meaning.

This is a very effective way to paraphrase; it requires that the writer have a large vocabulary and well-developed sentence-writing abilities. Sometimes it's hard to find the right words to paraphrase a sentence or to know whether a paraphrase has the same meaning as the original source.

The following sections provide several rules of thumb that can help you develop skill with paraphrasing.

M6-a Avoid replacing a source's words with synonyms.

Learning to paraphrase will help you communicate the ideas of authors effectively and avoid plagiarism—using another person's ideas or words without giving credit to that person. However, even if you tell your reader that information comes from another author, you can still commit plagiarism if you change only the words but do not make the *presentation* of the information your own. Some writers misinterpret the instructions to "use your own words"; they simply replace words in the source with synonyms, words that have similar meanings. Such word-by-word paraphrases frequently result in awkward sentence structures and inaccuracy. Meaning in English often comes from phrases and sentences rather than from individual words. Also, synonyms have similar meanings, but they rarely have *identical* meanings. Sometimes a synonym requires a different sentence structure than the original word does.

The following examples illustrate some of the problems that can arise with word-by-word paraphrasing.

Here is a short passage from Rebecca Webber's article "Make Your Own Luck."

ORIGINAL SOURCE

People who spot and seize opportunity are different. They are more open to life's forking paths, so they see possibilities others miss. And if things don't work out the way they'd hoped, they brush off disappointment and launch themselves headlong toward the next fortunate circumstance. As a result, they're happier and more likely to achieve their goals.

—Rebecca Webber, "Make Your Own Luck," p. 64

The following is a word-by-word paraphrase of the sentences highlighted in yellow.

UNACCEPTABLE PARAPHRASE: MEANING CHANGED

Persons who see and grab chances are diverse. They are further exposed to life's dividing trails, and they view prospects others ignore.

The first problem with this paraphrase is that the student who wrote it used the same sentence structure as in the original passage. Because she did not use her own sentence structure, this paraphrase is plagiarized. Second, the words that the student substituted are not exact synonyms, so the paraphrase has lost some of the meaning of the original passage.

- The word *grab* is an informal synonym of the word *seize* and may not be acceptable in a formal paper.

- *Diverse* and *different* have similar, but not identical, meanings. The word *different* in the original passage implies that people who are open to opportunities are different from people who are not open to opportunities. Using *diverse* in this context implies that people who welcome opportunity are different from one another. Using *diverse* distorts the meaning of the sentence.

- Using *exposed* instead of *open* changes the meaning in a significant way. *Exposed* implies that something negative has happened to these people, while *open* is a positive character trait.

As you paraphrase, it might help to keep this in mind: simply substituting synonyms into the original passage does not guarantee an accurate paraphrase.

The following paraphrase of the sentence highlighted in blue demonstrates another potential problem with word-by-word paraphrases. Using synonyms often requires changing the surrounding sentence structure because in English the same word can be more than one part of speech (see p. 333). For example, *work* can be either a noun or a verb; in the following paraphrase, the student has substituted the noun *effort* for the verb *work*, but it is not an appropriate substitution.

UNACCEPTABLE PARAPHRASE: AWKWARD RESULT

And if everything don't effort out the manner they'd wanted, they rebuff disappointment and throw themselves impulsive toward the next lucky situation.

- When the student changed *things* to *everything*, she also needed to change the verb from the plural form (*don't*) to the singular form (*doesn't*).

- Using *effort* in place of *work* is inappropriate. *Effort* is a synonym for the noun *work* but not a synonym for the verb *work*. The part of speech of a word is an important consideration when choosing a synonym.

- When the student substituted *manner* for *way*, she should have used a different structure: *in the manner*.

- Although *headlong* has a similar meaning to *impulsive*, in this sentence *headlong* is an adverb modifying the verb *launch*, and *impulsive* is an adjective. An adjective cannot replace an adverb in a sentence.

M6-b Determine the meaning of the original source.

Rather than trying to paraphrase word-for-word within each sentence, a better approach is to look at an entire passage and try to understand the meaning of the passage as well as how the information is organized before you try to present it in your own words. Try to understand the meaning of each phrase or clause rather than just the meaning of each word.

ORIGINAL SOURCE

People who spot and seize opportunity are different. They are more open to life's forking paths, so they see possibilities others miss. And if things don't work out the way they'd hoped, they brush off disappointment and launch themselves headlong toward the next fortunate circumstance. As a result, they're happier and more likely to achieve their goals.

The topic sentence of a paragraph is important. The topic sentence here (the first sentence in the paragraph) tells you about a particular group of people; from the title of the article, you can tell that Webber is talking about people who create their own luck. Lucky people, according to the author, have different characteristics from people who are not lucky. The rest of the paragraph then describes how lucky people are different.

Here is the original passage as the student writer annotated it. She worked through the original passage, repeatedly asking herself, "What is the author's point here?"

ORIGINAL SOURCE WITH STUDENT ANNOTATIONS

↶Lucky people?
People who spot and seize opportunity are different. They are
↶ More willing to take risks?
more open to life's forking paths, so they see possibilities others

miss. And if things don't work out the way they'd hoped, they
↶Don't get discouraged/upset   Keep looking?↴
brush off disappointment and launch themselves headlong

toward the next fortunate circumstance. As a result, they're
↶More positive personalities overall
happier and more likely to achieve their goals.

M6-c Present the author's meaning in your own words.

If you analyze a paragraph in its entirety rather than look at each word individually, you should be able to organize your information differently from the way the original author did and write a better paraphrase. As you analyze a source, you may still need to figure out the meaning of certain words, but do not focus on word-for-word substitutions. Here is one student's paraphrase of Rebecca Webber's work using her annotations of the text (see M6-b).

> **ACCEPTABLE PARAPHRASE**
>
> Individuals notice and respond to life's chances in different ways. Some people notice opportunities that other people might not notice, they are more willing to take risks, and they do not get discouraged if their decisions do not work out. Because they do not get discouraged easily, they are able to stay positive and content and to continue to search enthusiastically for the next opportunity (Webber 64).

This paraphrase presents the student's understanding of the author's meaning—without using words or sentence structure from the original. Notice that the paraphrase includes a citation. The idea is still Webber's idea, so a citation is needed, but the student uses her own words to communicate the information from Webber's article.

P

Punctuation
and
Mechanics

P Punctuation and Mechanics

P1 The comma

The comma was invented to help readers. Without it, sentence parts can collide into one another unexpectedly, causing misreadings.

CONFUSING   If you cook Elmer will do the dishes.

CONFUSING   While we were eating a rattlesnake approached our campsite.

Add commas in the logical places (after *cook* and *eating*), and suddenly all is clear. No longer is Elmer being cooked and the rattlesnake being eaten.

Various rules have evolved to prevent such misreadings and to speed readers along through complex grammatical structures. Those rules are detailed in this section. (Section P2 explains when not to use commas.)

P1-a   Use a comma before a coordinating conjunction joining independent clauses.

When a coordinating conjunction connects two or more independent clauses — word groups that could stand alone as separate sentences — a comma must precede the conjunction. There are seven coordinating conjunctions in English: *and, but, or, nor, for, so,* and *yet.*

A comma tells readers that one independent clause has come to a close and that another is about to begin.

▶ **The department sponsored a seminar on college survival skills,**
                                                                  ^

and it also hosted a barbecue for new students.

EXCEPTION: If the two independent clauses are short and there is no danger of misreading, the comma may be omitted.

The plane took off and we were on our way.

TIP: As a rule, do *not* use a comma with a coordinating conjunction that joins only two words, phrases, or subordinate clauses. (See P2-a. See also P1-c for commas with coordinating conjunctions joining three or more elements.)

▶ **A good money manager controls expenses/and invests surplus**

dollars to meet future needs.

The word group following *and* is not an independent clause; it is the second half of a compound predicate (*controls . . . and invests*).

hackerhandbooks.com/writersref

ⓔ P1 The comma > Exercises: P1–3 and P1–4, P1–13 to P1–17 (comma review)

☑ P1 The comma > LearningCurve: Commas

P1-b Use a comma after an introductory clause or phrase.

The most common introductory word groups are clauses and phrases functioning as adverbs. Such word groups usually tell when, where, how, why, or under what conditions the main action of the sentence occurred. (See B3-a, B3-b, and B3-e.)

A comma tells readers that the introductory clause or phrase has come to a close and that the main part of the sentence is about to begin.

▶ **When Irwin was ready to iron, his cat tripped on the cord.**
         ^

Without the comma, readers may think that Irwin is ironing his cat. The comma signals that *his cat* is the subject of a new clause, not part of the introductory one.

EXCEPTION: The comma may be left out after a short adverb clause or phrase if there is no danger of misreading. *In no time we were at 2,800 feet.*

Sentences also frequently begin with participial phrases that function as adjectives, describing the noun or pronoun immediately following them. The comma tells readers that they are about to learn the identity of the person or thing described; therefore, the comma is usually required even when the phrase is short. (See B3-b.)

▶ **Buried under layers of younger rocks, the earth's oldest rocks**
                                      ^

   contain no fossils.

NOTE: Other introductory word groups include transitional expressions and absolute phrases (see P1-f).

P1-c Use a comma between all items in a series.

When three or more items are presented in a series, those items should be separated from one another with commas. Items in a series may be single words, phrases, or clauses.

▶ **Langston Hughes's poetry is concerned with racial pride, social**

   justice, and the diversity of the African American experience.
        ^

Although some writers view the last comma in a series as optional, most experts advise using the comma because its omission can result in ambiguity or misreading.

▶ **My uncle willed me all of his property, houses, and boats.**
                                                            ^

Did the uncle will his property *and* houses *and* boats—or simply his property, consisting of houses and boats? If the former meaning is intended, a comma is necessary to prevent ambiguity.

P1-d Use a comma between coordinate adjectives not joined with *and*. Do not use a comma between cumulative adjectives.

When two or more adjectives each modify a noun separately, they are coordinate.

Roberto is a *warm, gentle, affectionate* father.

If the adjectives can be joined with *and*, the adjectives are coordinate, so you should use commas: *warm* and *gentle* and *affectionate* (*warm, gentle, affectionate*).

Adjectives that do not modify the noun separately are cumulative.

Three large gray shapes moved slowly toward us.

Beginning with the adjective closest to the noun *shapes*, these modifiers lean on one another, piggyback style, with each modifying a larger word group. *Gray* modifies *shapes*, *large* modifies *gray shapes*, and *three* modifies *large gray shapes*. Cumulative adjectives cannot be joined with *and* (not *three* and *large* and *gray shapes*).

COORDINATE ADJECTIVES

▶ **Should patients with severe, irreversible brain damage be put**
                                       ^
on life support systems?

Adjectives are coordinate if they can be connected with *and*: *severe* and *irreversible*.

CUMULATIVE ADJECTIVES

▶ **Ira ordered a rich/chocolate/layer cake.**

Ira didn't order a cake that was rich and chocolate and layer. He ordered a *layer cake* that was *chocolate*, a *chocolate layer cake* that was *rich*.

hackerhandbooks.com/writersref

e   P1 The comma > Exercises: P1–7 and P1–8, P1–13 to P1–17 (comma review)
☑   P1 The comma > LearningCurve: Commas

P1-e   Use commas to set off nonrestrictive (nonessential) elements. Do not use commas to set off restrictive (essential) elements.

Certain word groups that modify nouns or pronouns can be restrictive or nonrestrictive—that is, essential or not essential to the meaning of a sentence. These word groups are usually adjective clauses, adjective phrases, or appositives.

Restrictive elements

A restrictive element defines or limits the meaning of the word it modifies; it is therefore essential to the meaning of the sentence and is not set off with commas. If you remove a restrictive modifier from a sentence, the meaning changes significantly, becoming more general than you intended.

RESTRICTIVE (NO COMMAS)

The campers need clothes *that are durable.*

Scientists *who study the earth's structure* are called geologists.

The first sentence does not mean that the campers need clothes in general. The intended meaning is more limited: The campers need durable clothes. The second sentence does not mean that scientists in general are called geologists; only those scientists who specifically study the earth's structure are called geologists. The italicized word groups are essential and are therefore not set off with commas.

Nonrestrictive elements

A nonrestrictive modifier describes a noun or pronoun whose meaning has already been clearly defined or limited. Because the modifier contains nonessential or parenthetical information, it is set off with commas. If you remove a nonrestrictive element from a sentence, the meaning does not change dramatically. Some meaning may be lost, but the defining characteristics of the person or thing described remain the same.

NONRESTRICTIVE (WITH COMMAS)

The campers need sturdy shoes, *which are expensive.*

The scientists, *who represented eight different universities*, met to review applications for the prestigious Belker Award.

hackerhandbooks.com/writersref

e P1 The comma > Exercises: P1–10, P1–13 to P1–17 (comma review)
✓ P1 The comma > LearningCurve: Commas

In the first sentence, the campers need sturdy shoes, and the shoes happen to be expensive. In the second sentence, the scientists met to review applications for the award; that they represented eight different universities is informative but not critical to the meaning of the sentence. The nonessential information in both sentences is set off with commas.

NOTE: Often it is difficult to tell whether a word group is restrictive or nonrestrictive without seeing it in context and considering the writer's meaning. Both of the following sentences are grammatically correct, but their meaning is slightly different.

> The dessert made with fresh raspberries was delicious.

> The dessert, made with fresh raspberries, was delicious.

In the first example, the phrase *made with fresh raspberries* tells readers which of two or more desserts the writer is referring to. In the example with commas, the phrase merely adds information about one dessert.

Adjective clauses

Adjective clauses are patterned like sentences, containing subjects and verbs, but they function within sentences as modifiers of nouns or pronouns. They always follow the word they modify, usually immediately. Adjective clauses begin with a relative pronoun (*who, whom, whose, which, that*) or with a relative adverb (*where, when*). (See also B3-e.)

Nonrestrictive adjective clauses are set off with commas; restrictive adjective clauses are not.

NONRESTRICTIVE CLAUSE (WITH COMMAS)

▶ **Ed's house‸ which is located on thirteen acres‸ was completely furnished with bats in the rafters and mice in the kitchen.**

The adjective clause *which is located on thirteen acres* does not restrict the meaning of *Ed's house*; the information is nonessential and is therefore set off with commas.

RESTRICTIVE CLAUSE (NO COMMAS)

▶ **The giant panda/ that was born at the San Diego Zoo in 2003/ was sent to China in 2007.**

Because the adjective clause *that was born at the San Diego Zoo in 2003* identifies one particular panda out of many, the information is essential and is therefore not set off with commas.

NOTE: Use *that* only with restrictive (essential) clauses. Many writers prefer to use *which* only with nonrestrictive (nonessential) clauses, but usage varies.

Adjective phrases

Prepositional or verbal phrases functioning as adjectives may be restrictive or nonrestrictive. Nonrestrictive phrases are set off with commas; restrictive phrases are not.

NONRESTRICTIVE PHRASE (WITH COMMAS)

▶ The helicopter, with its million-candlepower spotlight
      ^
illuminating the area, circled above.
                ^

The *with* phrase is nonessential because its purpose is not to specify which of two or more helicopters is being discussed. The phrase is not required for readers to understand the meaning of the sentence.

RESTRICTIVE PHRASE (NO COMMAS)

▶ One corner of the attic was filled with newspapers/dating

from the early 1900s.

Dating from the early 1900s restricts the meaning of *newspapers*, so the comma should be omitted.

Appositives

An appositive is a noun or noun phrase that renames a nearby noun. Nonrestrictive appositives are set off with commas; restrictive appositives are not.

NONRESTRICTIVE APPOSITIVE (WITH COMMAS)

▶ Darwin's most important book, *On the Origin of Species*, was
                                ^   ^
the result of many years of research.

Most important restricts the meaning to one book, so the appositive *On the Origin of Species* is nonrestrictive and should be set off with commas.

RESTRICTIVE APPOSITIVE (NO COMMAS)

▶ **The song/"Viva la Vida/" was blasted out of huge amplifiers at**

the concert.

Once they've read *song*, readers still don't know precisely which song the writer means. The appositive following *song* restricts its meaning, so the appositive should not be set off with commas.

P1-f Use commas to set off transitional and parenthetical expressions, absolute phrases, and word groups expressing contrast.

Transitional expressions

Transitional expressions serve as bridges between sentences or parts of sentences. They include conjunctive adverbs such as *however*, *therefore*, and *moreover* and transitional phrases such as *for example*, *as a matter of fact*, and *in other words*. (For complete lists of these expressions, see P3-a.)

When a transitional expression appears between independent clauses in a compound sentence, it is preceded by a semicolon and is usually followed by a comma. (See P3-a.)

▶ **Minh did not understand our language; moreover, he was**
                                                        ^

unfamiliar with our customs.

When a transitional expression appears at the beginning of a sentence or in the middle of an independent clause, it is usually set off with commas.

▶ **Natural foods are not always salt free; celery, for example,**
                                             ^   ^

contains more sodium than most people think.

EXCEPTION: If a transitional expression blends smoothly with the rest of the sentence, calling for little or no pause in reading, it does not need to be set off with a comma. Expressions such as *also*, *at least*, *certainly*, *consequently*, *indeed*, *of course*, *moreover*, *no doubt*, *perhaps*, *then*, and *therefore* do not always call for a pause.

Alice's bicycle is broken; *therefore* you will need to borrow Sue's.

Parenthetical expressions

Expressions that are distinctly parenthetical, providing only supplemental information, should be set off with commas. They interrupt the flow of a sentence or appear at the end as afterthoughts.

▶ Evolution, as far as we know, doesn't work this way.

Absolute phrases

An absolute phrase, which modifies the whole sentence, usually consists of a noun followed by a participle or participial phrase. (See B3-d.) Absolute phrases may appear at the beginning or at the end of a sentence and should be set off with commas.

> ─────── ABSOLUTE PHRASE ───────
>   N   PARTICIPLE

The sun appearing for the first time in a week, we were at last able to begin the archaeological dig.

▶ Elvis Presley made music industry history in the 1950s, his

records having sold more than ten million copies.

NOTE: Do not insert a comma between the noun and the participle in an absolute construction.

▶ The next contestant/being five years old, the host adjusted the

height of the microphone.

Word groups expressing contrast

Sharp contrasts beginning with words such as *not*, *never*, and *unlike* are set off with commas.

▶ Unlike Robert, Celia loves using Instagram.

P1-g Use commas to set off nouns of direct address, the words *yes* and *no*, interrogative tags, and mild interjections.

▶ Forgive me, Angela, for forgetting your birthday.

▶ The film was faithful to the book, wasn't it?

P1-h Use commas with expressions such as *he said* to set off direct quotations.

▶ In his "Letter from Birmingham Jail," Martin Luther King Jr.

wrote, "We know through painful experience that freedom
  ^
is never voluntarily given by the oppressor; it must be

demanded by the oppressed" (225).

See P5 on the use of quotation marks and pages 420–21 on citing literary sources in MLA style.

P1-i Use commas with dates, addresses, titles, and numbers.

Dates

In dates, set off the year with a pair of commas.

▶ On December 12, 1890, orders were sent out for the arrest of
                 ^   ^
Sitting Bull.

EXCEPTIONS: Commas are not needed if the date is inverted or if only the month and year are given: 15 April 2009; January 2008.

Addresses

The elements of an address or a place name are separated with commas. A zip code, however, is not preceded by a comma.

▶ Please send the package to Greg Tarvin at 708 Spring Street,
                                                            ^
Washington, IL 61571.
          ^

Titles

If a title follows a name, set off the title with a pair of commas.

▶ Ann Hall, MD, has been appointed to the board of trustees.
         ^   ^

hackerhandbooks.com/writersref

e P1 The comma > Exercises: P1–13 to P1–17 (comma review)

☑ P1 The comma > LearningCurve: Commas

Numbers

In numbers more than four digits long, use commas to separate the numbers into groups of three, starting from the right. In numbers four digits long, a comma is optional.

  3,500 [*or* 3500]   100,000   5,000,000

EXCEPTIONS: Do not use commas in street numbers, zip codes, telephone numbers, or years with four or fewer digits.

P2   Unnecessary commas

Many common misuses of the comma result from a misunderstanding of the major comma rules presented in P1.

P2-a   Do not use a comma with a coordinating conjunction that joins only two words, phrases, or subordinate clauses.

Though a comma should be used before a coordinating conjunction joining independent clauses (see P1-a) or with a series of three or more elements (see P1-c), these rules should not be extended to other compound word groups.

▶ Ron discovered a leak/and came back to fix it.

The coordinating conjunction *and* links two verbs in a compound predicate: *discovered* and *came*.

▶ We knew that she had won/but that the election was close.

The coordinating conjunction *but* links two subordinate clauses, each beginning with *that*.

P2-b   Do not use a comma to separate a verb from its subject or object.

A sentence should flow from subject to verb to object without unnecessary pauses. Commas may appear between these major sentence elements only when a specific rule calls for them.

▶ **Zoos large enough to give the animals freedom to roam/are**

becoming more popular.

The comma should not separate the subject, *Zoos*, from the verb, *are becoming*.

P2-c Do not use a comma before the first or after the last item in a series.

Though commas are required between items in a series (P1-c), do not place them either before or after the whole series.

▶ **Other causes of asthmatic attacks are/stress, change in**

temperature, and cold air.

▶ **Even novels that focus on horror, evil, and alienation/often**

have themes of spiritual renewal and redemption.

P2-d Do not use a comma between cumulative adjectives, between an adjective and a noun, or between an adverb and an adjective.

Commas are required between coordinate adjectives (those that can be joined with *and*), but they do not belong between cumulative adjectives (those that cannot be joined with *and*). (For a full discussion, see P1-d.)

▶ **In the corner of the closet, we found an old/maroon hatbox.**

A comma should never be used between an adjective and the noun that follows it.

▶ **It was a senseless, dangerous/mission.**

Nor should a comma be used between an adverb and an adjective that follows it.

▶ **Rehabilitation often helps severely/injured patients.**

P2-e   Do not use commas to set off restrictive elements.

Restrictive elements are modifiers or appositives that restrict the meaning of the nouns they follow. Because they are essential to the meaning of the sentence, they are not set off with commas. (For a full discussion of restrictive and nonrestrictive elements, see P1-e.)

▶ **Drivers/who think they own the road/make cycling a dangerous sport.**

> The modifier *who think they own the road* restricts the meaning of *Drivers* and is essential to the meaning of the sentence. Putting commas around the *who* clause falsely suggests that all drivers think they own the road.

▶ **Margaret Mead's book/*Coming of Age in Samoa*/stirred up considerable controversy when it was published in 1928.**

> Since Mead wrote more than one book, the appositive contains information essential to the meaning of the sentence.

P2-f   Do not use a comma to set off a concluding adverb clause that is essential for meaning.

When adverb clauses introduce a sentence, they are nearly always followed by a comma (see P1-b). When they conclude a sentence, however, they are not set off by commas if their content is essential to the meaning of the earlier part of the sentence. Adverb clauses beginning with *after, as soon as, because, before, if, since, unless, until,* and *when* are usually essential.

▶ **Don't visit Paris at the height of the tourist season/unless you have booked hotel reservations.**

> Without the *unless* clause, the meaning of the sentence might at first seem broader than the writer intended.

When a concluding adverb clause is nonessential, it should be preceded by a comma. Clauses beginning with *although, even though, though,* and *whereas* are usually nonessential.

▶ **The lecture seemed to last only a short time, although it had actually gone on for more than an hour.**

P2-g Do not use a comma after a phrase that begins an inverted sentence.

Though a comma belongs after most introductory phrases (see P1-b), it does not belong after phrases that begin an inverted sentence. In an inverted sentence, the subject follows the verb, and a phrase that ordinarily would follow the verb is moved to the beginning.

▶ At the bottom of the hill/sat the stubborn mule.

P2-h Avoid other common misuses of the comma.

Do not use a comma in the following situations.

AFTER A COORDINATING CONJUNCTION (*AND, BUT, OR, NOR, FOR, SO, YET*)

▶ Occasionally TV talk shows are performed live, but/more often they are recorded.

AFTER *SUCH AS* OR *LIKE*

▶ Shade-loving plants such as/begonias, impatiens, and coleus can add color to a shady garden.

AFTER *ALTHOUGH*

▶ Although/the air was balmy, the water was cold.

BEFORE A PARENTHESIS

▶ Though Sylvia's ACT score was low/(only 15), her admissions essay was superior.

TO SET OFF AN INDIRECT (REPORTED) QUOTATION

▶ Samuel Goldwyn once said/that a verbal contract isn't worth the paper it's written on.

WITH A QUESTION MARK OR AN EXCLAMATION POINT

▶ "Why don't you try it?/" she coaxed. "You can't do any worse than the rest of us."

P3 The semicolon and the colon

The semicolon is used to connect major sentence elements of equal grammatical rank.

P3-a Use a semicolon between closely related independent clauses.

Between independent clauses with no coordinating conjunction

When two independent clauses appear in one sentence, they are usually linked with a comma and a coordinating conjunction (*and, but, or, nor, for, so, yet*). If the clauses are closely related and the relation is clear without a conjunction, they may be linked with a semicolon instead.

> In film, a low-angle shot makes the subject look powerful; a high-angle shot does just the opposite.

A semicolon must be used whenever a coordinating conjunction has been omitted between independent clauses. To use merely a comma creates a type of run-on sentence known as a *comma splice*. (See G6.)

▶ In 1800, a traveler needed six weeks to get from New York to

Chicago/; in 1860, the trip by train took only two days.
  ^

Between independent clauses linked with a transitional expression

Transitional expressions include conjunctive adverbs and transitional phrases.

CONJUNCTIVE ADVERBS

accordingly	furthermore	moreover	still
also	hence	nevertheless	subsequently
anyway	however	next	then
besides	incidentally	nonetheless	therefore
certainly	indeed	now	thus
consequently	instead	otherwise	
conversely	likewise	similarly	
finally	meanwhile	specifically	

hackerhandbooks.com/writersref
e P3 The semicolon and the colon > Exercises: P3–3 to P3–6
✓ P3 The semicolon and the colon > LearningCurve: Semicolons and colons

TRANSITIONAL PHRASES

after all	at the same time	in addition	in the first place
as a matter of fact	even so	in conclusion	on the contrary
as a result	for example	in fact	on the other hand
at any rate	for instance	in other words	

When a transitional expression appears between independent clauses, it is preceded by a semicolon and usually followed by a comma.

▶ Many corals grow very gradually/; in fact, the creation of a
 ^

coral reef can take centuries.

When a transitional expression appears in the middle or at the end of the second independent clause, the semicolon goes *between the clauses*.

▶ Biologists have observed laughter in primates other than

humans/; chimpanzees, however, sound more like they are
 ^

panting than laughing.

Transitional expressions should not be confused with the coordinating conjunctions *and*, *but*, *or*, *nor*, *for*, *so*, and *yet*, which are preceded by a comma when they link independent clauses. (See P1-a.)

P3-b Use a semicolon between items in a series containing internal punctuation.

▶ Classic science fiction sagas are *Star Trek*, with Mr. Spock/;
 ^

Battlestar Galactica, with its Cylons/; and *Star Wars*, with
 ^

Han Solo, Luke Skywalker, and Darth Vader.

Without the semicolons, the reader would have to sort out the major groupings, distinguishing between important and less important pauses according to the logic of the sentence. By inserting semicolons at the major breaks, the writer does this work for the reader.

P3-c Avoid common misuses of the semicolon.

Do not use a semicolon in the following situations.

BETWEEN A SUBORDINATE CLAUSE AND THE REST OF THE SENTENCE

▶ Although children's literature was added to the National

Book Awards in 1969/, it has had its own award, the Newbery
 ^

Medal, since 1922.

BETWEEN AN APPOSITIVE AND THE WORD IT REFERS TO

▶ The scientists were fascinated by the species *Argyroneta*

aquatica̸, a spider that lives underwater.
         ^

TO INTRODUCE A LIST

▶ Some of my favorite celebrities have their own blogs̸: Ashton
                                                      ^
Kutcher, Beyoncé, and Zach Braff.

BETWEEN INDEPENDENT CLAUSES JOINED BY *AND, BUT, OR, NOR, FOR, SO,* OR *YET*

▶ Five of the applicants had worked with spreadsheets̸, but only
                                                    ^
one was familiar with database management.

EXCEPTION: If one or both of the independent clauses contain a comma, you may use a semicolon with a coordinating conjunction between the clauses.

P3-d   Use a colon after an independent clause to direct attention to a list, an appositive, a quotation, or a summary or an explanation.

A LIST

The daily exercise routine should include at least the following: ten minutes of stretching, forty abdominal crunches, and a twenty-minute run.

AN APPOSITIVE

My roommate seems to live on two things: Twizzlers and Twitter.

A QUOTATION

Consider the words of Benjamin Franklin: "There never was a good war or a bad peace."

A SUMMARY OR AN EXPLANATION

Faith is like love: It cannot be forced.

The novel is clearly autobiographical: The author even gives his own name to the main character.

---

hackerhandbooks.com/writersref

e P3 The semicolon and the colon > Exercises: P3–8 and P3–9

✓ P3 The semicolon and the colon > LearningCurve: Semicolons and colons

NOTE: For other ways of introducing quotations, see "Introducing quoted material" on pages 310–11. When an independent clause follows a colon, begin with a capital letter. Some disciplines use a lowercase letter instead. See MLA-5a, APA-5a and CMS-5a for variations.

P3-e Use a colon according to convention.

SALUTATION IN A LETTER   Dear Editor:

HOURS AND MINUTES   5:30 p.m.

PROPORTIONS   The ratio of women to men was 2:1.

TITLE AND SUBTITLE   *The Glory of Hera: Greek Mythology and the Greek Family*

BIBLIOGRAPHIC ENTRIES   Boston: Bedford, 2013

CHAPTER AND VERSE IN SACRED TEXT   Luke 2:14, Qur'an 67:3

P3-f Avoid common misuses of the colon.

A colon must be preceded by a full independent clause. Therefore, avoid using it in the following situations.

BETWEEN A VERB AND ITS OBJECT OR COMPLEMENT

▶ Some important vitamins found in vegetables are꞉ vitamin A, thiamine, niacin, and vitamin C.

BETWEEN A PREPOSITION AND ITS OBJECT

▶ The heart's two pumps each consist of꞉ an upper chamber, or atrium, and a lower chamber, or ventricle.

AFTER *SUCH AS, INCLUDING,* OR *FOR EXAMPLE*

▶ The NCAA regulates college athletic teams, including꞉ basketball, baseball, softball, and football.

P4 The apostrophe

P4-a Use an apostrophe to indicate that a noun is possessive.

Possessive nouns usually indicate ownership, as in *Tim's hat* or *the law-yer's desk*. Frequently, however, ownership is only loosely implied: *the tree's roots*, *a day's work*. If you are not sure whether a noun is posses-sive, try turning it into an *of* phrase: *the roots of the tree*, *the work of a day*. (Pronouns also have possessive forms. See p. 305 and P4-d.)

When to add -'s

1. If the noun does not end in *-s*, add *-'s*.

   Luck often propels a rock musician's career.

   The Children's Defense Fund is a nonprofit organization that supports programs for poor and minority children.

2. If the noun is singular and ends in *-s* or an *s* sound, add *-'s* to indicate possession.

   Lois's sister spent last year in India.

   Her article presents an overview of Marx's teachings.

NOTE: To avoid potentially awkward pronunciation, some writers use only the apostrophe with a singular noun ending in *-s*: *Sophocles'*.

When to add only an apostrophe

If the noun is plural and ends in *-s*, add only an apostrophe.

   Both diplomats' briefcases were searched by guards.

Joint possession

To show joint possession, use *-'s* or *(-s')* with the last noun only; to show individual possession, make all nouns possessive.

   Have you seen Joyce and Greg's new camper?

   John's and Marie's expectations of marriage couldn't have been more different.

---

hackerhandbooks.com/writersref
e P4 The apostrophe > Exercises: P4–3 to P4–5
☑ P4 The apostrophe > LearningCurve: Apostrophes

Joyce and Greg jointly own one camper. John and Marie individually have different expectations.

Compound nouns

If a noun is compound, use -'s (or -s') with the last element.

> My father-in-law's memoir about his childhood in Sri Lanka was published in October.

Indefinite pronouns

Indefinite pronouns refer to no specific person or thing: *everyone*, *someone*, *no one*, *something*. (See B1-b.)

> Someone's raincoat has been left behind.

P4-b Use an apostrophe to mark omissions in contractions and numbers.

In a contraction, the apostrophe takes the place of one or more missing letters. *It's* stands for *it is*, *can't* for *cannot*.

> It's a shame that Frank can't go on the tour.

The apostrophe is also used to mark the omission of the first two digits of a year or years.

> The reunion for the class of '12 is tonight.

> I am studying the music of the '60s generation.

P4-c Do not use an apostrophe in certain situations.

An apostrophe typically is not used to pluralize numbers, letters, abbreviations, and words mentioned as words. Note the few exceptions and be consistent throughout your paper.

Plural of numbers

Do not use an apostrophe in the plural of any numbers.

> Oksana skated nearly perfect figure 8s.

> The 1920s are known as the Jazz Age.

Plural of letters

Italicize the letter and use roman (regular) font style for the -*s* ending. (Do not italicize academic grades.)

> Two large *P*s were painted on the door.

> He received two *D*s for the first time in his life.

EXCEPTIONS: To avoid misreading, use an apostrophe to form the plural of lowercase letters and the capital letters *A* and *I*.

> Beginning readers often confuse *b*'s and *d*'s.

> Students with straight A's earn high honors.

MLA NOTE: MLA recommends using an apostrophe for the plural of single capital and lowercase letters: *H*'s, *p*'s.

Plural of abbreviations

Do not use an apostrophe to pluralize an abbreviation.

> Harriet has thirty DVDs on her desk.

> Marco earned two PhDs before his thirtieth birthday.

Plural of words mentioned as words

Generally, omit the apostrophe to form the plural of words mentioned as words. If the word is italicized, the -*s* ending appears in roman (regular) type.

> We've heard enough *maybe*s.

Words mentioned as words may also appear in quotation marks. When you choose this option, use the apostrophe.

> We've heard enough "maybe's."

P4-d Avoid common misuses of the apostrophe.

Do not use an apostrophe with nouns that are not possessive or with the possessive pronouns *its*, *whose*, *his*, *hers*, *ours*, *yours*, and *theirs*.

> outpatients
> ▶ Some ~~outpatient's~~ have special parking permits.

> its
> ▶ Each area has ~~it's~~ own conference room.
>
> *It's* means "it is." The possessive pronoun *its* contains no apostrophe despite the fact that it is possessive.

▶ We attended a reading by Junot Díaz, ~~who's~~ work focuses on

                                 whose
                                  ^

the Dominican immigration experience.

Who's means "who is." The possessive pronoun is *whose*.

P5   Quotation marks

Writers use quotation marks primarily to enclose direct quotations of another person's spoken or written words. You will also find these other uses and exceptions:

- for quotations within quotations (single quotation marks: P5-b)
- for titles of short works (P5-c)
- for words used as words (P5-d)
- with other marks of punctuation (P5-e)
- with brackets and ellipsis marks (p. 314, P6-c)
- no quotation marks for indirect quotations, paraphrases, and summaries (p. 308)
- no quotation marks for long quotations (p. 308)

P5-a   Use quotation marks to enclose direct quotations.

Direct quotations of a person's words, whether spoken or written, must be in quotation marks.

> "Twitter," according to social media researcher Jameson Brown, "is the best social network for brand to customer engagement."

In dialogue, begin a new paragraph to mark a change in speaker.

> "Mom, his name is Willie, not William. A thousand times I've told you, it's *Willie*."
> "Willie is a derivative of William, Lester. Surely his birth certificate doesn't have Willie on it, and I like calling people by their proper names."
> "Yes, it does, ma'am. My mother named me Willie K. Mason."
>   —Gloria Naylor

If a single speaker utters more than one paragraph, introduce each paragraph with a quotation mark, but do not use a closing quotation mark until the end of the speech.

Exception: indirect quotations

Do not use quotation marks around indirect quotations. An indirect quotation reports someone's ideas without using that person's exact words. In academic writing, indirect quotation is called *paraphrase* or *summary*. (See R2-c.)

> Social media researcher Jameson Brown finds Twitter the best social media tool for companies that want to reach their consumers.

Exception: long quotations

Long quotations of prose or poetry are generally set off from the text by indenting. Quotation marks are not used because the indented format tells readers that the quotation is taken word-for-word from the source.

> After making an exhaustive study of the historical record, James Horan evaluates Billy the Kid like this:
>
>> The portrait that emerges of [the Kid] from the thousands of pages of affidavits, reports, trial transcripts, his letters, and his testimony is neither the mythical Robin Hood nor the stereotyped adenoidal moron and pathological killer. Rather Billy appears as a disturbed, lonely young man, honest, loyal to his friends, dedicated to his beliefs, and betrayed by our institutions and the corrupt, ambitious, and compromising politicians in his time. (158)

The number in parentheses is a citation handled according to MLA style (see MLA-4a).

MLA, APA, and CMS have specific guidelines for what constitutes a long quotation and how it should be indented (see pp. 405, 484, and 544, respectively).

P5-b Use single quotation marks to enclose a quotation within a quotation.

> Megan Marshall notes that Elizabeth Peabody's school focused on "not merely 'teaching' but 'educating children morally and spiritually as well as intellectually from the first'" (107).

P5-c Use quotation marks around the titles of short works.

Short works include newspaper and magazine articles, poems, short stories, songs, episodes of television and radio programs, and chapters or subdivisions of books.

> James Baldwin's story "Sonny's Blues" tells the story of two brothers who come to understand each other's suffering.

NOTE: Titles of long works such as books, plays, television and radio programs, films, magazines, and so on are put in italics. (See P10-a.)

P5-d Quotation marks may be used to set off words used as words.

Although words used as words are ordinarily italicized (see p. 330), quotation marks are also acceptable. Be consistent throughout your paper.

> The words "accept" and "except" are frequently confused.

> The words *accept* and *except* are frequently confused.

P5-e Use punctuation with quotation marks according to convention.

This section describes the conventions American publishers use in placing various marks of punctuation inside or outside quotation marks. It also explains how to punctuate when introducing quoted material. (For the use of quotation marks in MLA, APA, and CMS styles, see MLA-4, APA-4a, and CMS-4, respectively. The examples in this section show MLA style.)

Periods and commas

Place periods and commas inside quotation marks.

> "I'm here as part of my service-learning project," I told the classroom teacher. "I'm hoping to become a reading specialist."

This rule applies to single quotation marks as well as double quotation marks. (See P5-b.) It also applies to all uses of quotation marks: for quoted material, for titles of works, and for words used as words.

EXCEPTION: In the MLA and APA styles of parenthetical in-text citations, the period follows the citation in parentheses.

> James M. McPherson comments, approvingly, that the Whigs "were not averse to extending the blessings of American liberty, even to Mexicans and Indians" (48).

Colons and semicolons

Put colons and semicolons outside quotation marks.

> Harold wrote, "I regret that I am unable to attend the fundraiser for diabetes research"; his letter, however, came with a substantial contribution.

Question marks and exclamation points

Put question marks and exclamation points inside quotation marks unless they apply to the whole sentence.

> Dr. Abram's first question on the first day of class was "What three goals do you have for the course?"

> Have you heard the old proverb "Do not climb the hill until you reach it"?

In the first sentence, the question mark applies only to the quoted question. In the second sentence, the question mark applies to the whole sentence.

NOTE: In MLA and APA styles for a quotation that ends with a question mark or an exclamation point, the parenthetical citation and a period should follow the entire quotation.

> Rosie Thomas asks, "Is nothing in life ever straight and clear, the way children see it?" (77).

Introducing quoted material

After a word group introducing a quotation, choose a colon, a comma, or no punctuation at all, whichever is appropriate in context.

FORMAL INTRODUCTION   If a quotation is formally introduced, a colon is appropriate. A formal introduction is a full independent clause, not just an expression such as *he writes* or *she remarked*.

> Thomas Friedman provides a challenging yet optimistic view of the future: "We need to get back to work on our country and on our planet. The hour is late, the stakes couldn't be higher, the project couldn't be harder, the payoff couldn't be greater" (25).

EXPRESSION SUCH AS *HE WRITES*   If a quotation is introduced with an expression such as *he writes* or *she remarked*—or if it is followed by such an expression—a comma is needed.

> "With regard to air travel," Stephen Ambrose notes, "Jefferson was a full century ahead of the curve" (53).

"Unless another war is prevented it is likely to bring destruction on a scale never before held possible and even now hardly conceived," Albert Einstein wrote in the aftermath of the atomic bomb (29).

BLENDED QUOTATION   When a quotation is blended into the writer's own sentence, either a comma or no punctuation is appropriate, depending on the way in which the quotation fits into the sentence structure.

The future champion could, as he put it, "float like a butterfly and sting like a bee."

Virginia Woolf wrote in 1928 that "a woman must have money and a room of her own if she is to write fiction" (4).

BEGINNING OF SENTENCE   If a quotation appears at the beginning of a sentence, use a comma after it unless the quotation ends with a question mark or an exclamation point.

"I've always thought of myself as a reporter," American poet Gwendolyn Brooks has stated (162).

"What is it?" she asked, bracing herself.

INTERRUPTED QUOTATION   If a quoted sentence is interrupted by explanatory words, use commas to set off the explanatory words. If two successive quoted sentences from the same source are interrupted by explanatory words, use a comma before the explanatory words and a period after them.

"Everyone agrees journalists must tell the truth," Bill Kovach and Tom Rosenstiel write. "Yet people are befuddled about what 'the truth' means" (37).

P5-f   Avoid common misuses of quotation marks.

Do not use quotation marks to draw attention to familiar slang, to disown trite expressions, or to justify an attempt at humor.

▶ The economist estimated that single-family home prices

would decline another 5 percent by the end of the year,

emphasizing that this was only a ⁓ballpark figure.⁓

Do not use quotation marks around the title of your own essay.

P6   Other punctuation marks

P6-a   End punctuation

The period

Use a period to end all sentences except direct questions or genuine exclamations. Also use periods in abbreviations according to convention.

TO END SENTENCES   Most sentences should end with a period. A sentence that reports a question instead of asking it directly (an indirect question) should end with a period, not a question mark.

▶   **The professor asked whether talk therapy was more beneficial**

    than antidepressants?.
                   ^

If a sentence is not a genuine exclamation, it should end with a period, not an exclamation point. (See also p. 313.)

▶   **After years of research, Dr. Low finally solved the equation!.**
                                                ^

IN ABBREVIATIONS   A period is conventionally used in abbreviations of titles and Latin words or phrases, including the time designations for morning and afternoon.

Mr.	i.e.	a.m. (or AM)
Ms.	e.g.	p.m. (or PM)
Dr.	etc.	

NOTE: If a sentence ends with a period marking an abbreviation, do not add a second period.

Do not use a period with postal abbreviations for states: MD, TX, CA.

Current usage is to omit the period in abbreviations of organization names, academic degrees, and designations for eras.

NATO	UNESCO	UCLA	BS	BC
IRS	AFL-CIO	NIH	PhD	BCE

The question mark

A direct question should be followed by a question mark.

    What is the horsepower of a 777 engine?

TIP: Do not use a question mark after an indirect question, one that is reported rather than asked directly. Use a period instead.

▶ He asked me who was teaching the math course this year~~?~~.

The exclamation point

Use an exclamation point after a word group or sentence to express exceptional feeling or to provide special emphasis. The exclamation point is rarely appropriate in academic writing.

> When Mischa entered the room, I switched on the lights, and we all yelled, "Surprise!"

TIP: Do not overuse the exclamation point.

▶ In the fisherman's memory, the fish lives on, increasing in

length and weight with each passing year, until at last it is

big enough to shade a fishing boat~~!~~.

This sentence doesn't need to be pumped up with an exclamation point. It is emphatic enough without it.

P6-b The dash, parentheses, and brackets

The dash

When typing, use two hyphens to form a dash (--). Do not put spaces before or after the dash. If your word processing program has what is known as an "em-dash" (—), you may use it instead, with no space before or after it.

Use a dash to set off parenthetical material that deserves emphasis.

> One of music's rising trends—lyrics that promote the use of synthetic drugs—is leading some artists to speak out against their peers.

Use a dash to set off appositives that contain commas. An appositive is a noun or noun phrase that renames a nearby noun. Ordinarily most appositives are set off with commas (P1-e), but when the appositive itself contains commas, a pair of dashes helps readers see the relative importance of all the pauses.

> In my hometown, people's basic needs—food, clothing, and shelter—are less costly than in a big city like Los Angeles.

A dash can also be used to introduce a list, a restatement, an amplification, or a dramatic shift in tone or thought.

> Along the wall are the bulk liquids—sesame seed oil, honey, safflower oil, and that half-liquid "peanuts only" peanut butter.

> In his last semester, Peter tried to pay more attention to his priorities—applying to graduate school and getting financial aid.

> Everywhere we looked there were little kids—a bag of Skittles in one hand and their mommy or daddy's sleeve in the other.

> Kiere took a few steps back, came running full speed, kicked a mighty kick—and missed the ball.

In the first two examples, the writer could also use a colon. (See P3-d.) The colon is more formal than the dash and not quite as dramatic.

TIP: Unless there is a specific reason for using the dash, avoid it. Unnecessary dashes create a choppy effect.

Parentheses

Use parentheses to enclose supplemental material, minor digressions, and afterthoughts.

> Nurses record patients' vital signs (temperature, pulse, and blood pressure) several times a day.

Use parentheses to enclose letters or numbers labeling items in a series.

> Regulations stipulated that only the following equipment could be used on the survival mission: (1) a knife, (2) thirty feet of parachute line, (3) a book of matches, (4) two ponchos, (5) an E tool, and (6) a signal flare.

TIP: Rough drafts are likely to contain unnecessary parentheses. As writers head into a sentence, they often think of additional details, using parentheses to work them in as best they can. Such sentences usually can be revised to add the details without parentheses.

▶ Researchers have said that seventeen million ~~(estimates run~~ ^{from} ^

~~as high as~~ twenty-three million^{to}/Americans have diabetes. ^

Brackets

Use brackets to enclose any words or phrases that you have inserted into an otherwise word-for-word quotation.

> *Audubon* reports that "if there are not enough young to balance deaths, the end of the species [California condor] is inevitable" (4).

The sentence quoted from the *Audubon* article did not contain the words *California condor* (since the context of the full article made clear what species was meant), so the writer needed to add the name in brackets.

The Latin word "sic" in brackets indicates that an error in a quoted sentence appears in the original source.

> According to the review, Nelly Furtado's performance was brilliant, "exceding [sic] the expectations of even her most loyal fans."

Do not overuse "sic," however, since calling attention to others' mistakes can appear snobbish. The preceding quotation, for example, might have been paraphrased instead: *According to the review, even Nelly Furtado's most loyal fans were surprised by the brilliance of her performance.*

NOTE: For advice on using "sic" in MLA, APA, and CMS styles, see MLA-3a, APA-3, and CMS-3, respectively.

P6-c The ellipsis mark

The ellipsis mark consists of three spaced periods. Use an ellipsis mark to indicate that you have deleted words from an otherwise word-for-word quotation.

> Shute acknowledges that treatment for autism can be expensive: "Sensory integration therapy . . . can cost up to $200 an hour" (82).

If you delete a full sentence or more in the middle of a quoted passage, use a period before the three ellipsis dots.

> "If we don't properly train, teach, or treat our growing prison population," says Luis Rodríguez, "somebody else will. . . . This may well be the safety issue of the new century" (16).

TIP: Ordinarily, do not use the ellipsis mark at the beginning or at the end of a quotation. Readers will understand that the quoted material is taken from a longer passage. (If you have cut some words from the end of the final quoted sentence, however, MLA requires an ellipsis mark.)

In quoted poetry, use a full line of ellipsis dots to indicate that you have dropped a line or more from the poem, as in this example from "To His Coy Mistress" by Andrew Marvell:

> Had we but world enough, and time,
> This coyness, lady, were no crime.
> . . . .
> But at my back I always hear
> Time's wingèd chariot hurrying near; (1-2, 21-22)

P6-d The slash

Use the slash to separate two or three lines of poetry that have been run into your text. Add a space both before and after the slash.

> In the opening lines of "Jordan," George Herbert pokes gentle fun at popular poems of his time: "Who says that fictions only and false hair / Become a verse? Is there in truth no beauty?" (1-2).

Four or more lines of poetry should be handled as an indented quotation. (See p. 308.)

The slash may occasionally be used to separate paired terms such as *pass/fail* and *producer/director*. Do not use a space before or after the slash. Be sparing in this use of the slash. In particular, avoid the use of *and/or*, *he/she*, and *his/her*. Instead of using *he/she* and *his/her* to solve sexist language problems, you can usually find more graceful alternatives. (See W4-f and G3-a.)

P7 Spelling and hyphenation

You learned to spell from repeated experience with words in both reading and writing. As you proofread, you can probably tell if a word doesn't look quite right. In such cases, the solution is simple: Look up the word in the dictionary. (See W6-a.)

P7-a Become familiar with the major spelling rules.

i *before* e *except after* c

In general, use *i* before *e* except after *c* and except when it sounds like *ay*, as in *neighbor* and *weigh*.

I BEFORE *E*	relieve, believe, sieve, niece, fierce, piece
E BEFORE *I*	receive, deceive, sleigh, freight, eight
EXCEPTIONS	seize, either, weird, height, foreign, leisure

Suffixes

FINAL SILENT -e Generally, drop a final silent -*e* when adding a suffix that begins with a vowel. Keep the final -*e* if the suffix begins with a consonant.

combine, combination	achieve, achievement
desire, desiring	care, careful
prude, prudish	entire, entirety
remove, removable	gentle, gentleness

Words such as *changeable*, *judgment*, *argument*, and *truly* are exceptions.

FINAL -y When adding -*s* or -*d* to words ending in -*y*, ordinarily change -*y* to -*ie* when the -*y* is preceded by a consonant but not when it is preceded by a vowel.

comedy, comedies	monkey, monkeys
dry, dried	play, played

With proper names ending in -*y*, however, do not change the -*y* to -*ie* even if it is preceded by a consonant: *the Doughertys.*

FINAL CONSONANTS If a final consonant is preceded by a single vowel *and* the consonant ends a one-syllable word or a stressed syllable, double the consonant when adding a suffix beginning with a vowel.

bet, betting	commit, committed	occur, occurrence

Plurals

-s OR -es Add -*s* to form the plural of most nouns; add -*es* to singular nouns ending in -*s*, -*sh*, -*ch*, and -*x*.

table, tables	church, churches
paper, papers	dish, dishes

Ordinarily add -*s* to nouns ending in -*o* when the -*o* is preceded by a vowel. Add -*es* when it is preceded by a consonant.

radio, radios	hero, heroes
video, videos	tomato, tomatoes

OTHER PLURALS To form the plural of a hyphenated compound word, add -*s* to the chief word even if it does not appear at the end.

mother-in-law, mothers-in-law

English words derived from other languages such as Latin, Greek, or French sometimes form the plural as they would in their original language.

medium, media	criterion, criteria	chateau, chateaux

Multilingual Spelling varies slightly among English-speaking countries. Variations can be confusing for some multilingual students in the United States. Following is a list of some common words with different American and British spellings. Consult a dictionary for others.

AMERICAN	BRITISH
canceled, traveled	cancelled, travelled
color, humor	colour, humour
judgment	judgement
check	cheque
realize, apologize	realise, apologise
defense	defence
anemia, anesthetic	anaemia, anaesthetic
theater, center	theatre, centre
fetus	foetus
mold, smolder	mould, smoulder
civilization	civilisation
connection, inflection	connexion, inflexion
licorice	liquorice

P7-b Discriminate between words that sound alike but have different meanings.

Words that sound alike or nearly alike but have different meanings and spellings are called *homophones*. The following sets of words are commonly confused. A careful writer will double-check their every use. (See also the glossary of usage, W1.)

affect (verb: to exert an influence)
effect (verb: to accomplish; noun: result)

its (possessive pronoun: of or belonging to it)
it's (contraction of *it is* or *it has*)

loose (adjective: free, not securely attached)
lose (verb: to fail to keep, to be deprived of)

principal (adjective: most important; noun: head of a school)
principle (noun: a fundamental guideline or truth)

their (possessive pronoun: belonging to them)
they're (contraction of *they are*)
there (adverb: that place or position)

who's (contraction of *who is* or *who has*)
whose (possessive form of *who*)

your (possessive pronoun: belonging to you)
you're (contraction of *you are*)

P7-c Be alert to commonly misspelled words.

absence	conscience	indispensable	proceed
accidentally	conscientious	inevitable	pronunciation
accommodate	conscious	intelligence	publicly
achievement	criticism	irrelevant	quiet
acknowledge	criticize	irresistible	quite
acquaintance	decision	knowledge	quizzes
acquire	definitely	library	receive
address	descendant	license	recognize
all right	desperate	lightning	referred
amateur	different	loneliness	restaurant
analyze	disastrous	maintenance	rhythm
answer	eighth	maneuver	roommate
apparently	eligible	marriage	sandwich
appearance	embarrass	mathematics	schedule
arctic	emphasize	mischievous	seize
argument	environment	necessary	separate
arithmetic	especially	noticeable	sergeant
arrangement	exaggerated	occasion	siege
ascend	exercise	occurred	similar
athlete	exhaust	occurrence	sincerely
attendance	existence	pamphlet	sophomore
basically	extraordinary	parallel	strictly
beautiful	familiar	particularly	subtly
beginning	fascinate	pastime	succeed
believe	February	permanent	surprise
benefited	foreign	permissible	thorough
bureau	forty	perseverance	tomorrow
business	fourth	phenomenon	tragedy
calendar	friend	physically	transferred
cemetery	government	practically	truly
changeable	grammar	precede	unnecessarily
column	harass	preference	usually
commitment	height	preferred	vacuum
committed	humorous	prejudice	villain
committee	incidentally	presence	weird
competitive	incredible	prevalent	whether
conceivable	independence	privilege	writing

P7-d Consult the dictionary to determine how to treat a compound word.

The dictionary indicates whether to treat a compound word as hyphenated (*water-repellent*), as one word (*waterproof*), or as two words (*water table*). If the compound word is not in the dictionary, treat it as two words.

▶ The prosecutor chose not to cross-examine any witnesses.
   ^

▶ All students are expected to record their data in a small

   note͡book.

▶ Alice walked through the looking-glass into a backward world.
   ^

P7-e Hyphenate two or more words used together as an adjective before a noun.

▶ Today's teachers depend on both traditional textbook material

   and Web-delivered content.
   ^

▶ Richa Gupta is not yet a well⁻known candidate.
   ^

   Generally, do not use a hyphen when such compounds follow the noun.

▶ After our television campaign, Richa Gupta will be well/known.

   Do not use a hyphen to connect *-ly* adverbs to the words they modify.

▶ A slowly/moving truck tied up traffic.

P7-f Hyphenate fractions and certain numbers when they are spelled out.

For numbers written as words, use a hyphen in all fractions (*two-thirds*) and in all forms of compound numbers from twenty-one to ninety-nine (*thirty-five*, *sixty-seventh*).

P7-g Use a hyphen with the prefixes *all-*, *ex-* (meaning "former"), and *self-* and with the suffix *-elect*.

▶ The private foundation is funneling more money into

self-help projects.
   ^

▶ The Student Senate bylaws require the president-elect to
                                                     ^
attend all senate meetings before the transfer of office.

P7-h Use a hyphen in certain words to avoid ambiguity.

Without the hyphen, there would be no way to distinguish between words such as *re-creation* and *recreation*.

> Bicycling in the city has always been my favorite form of recreation.

> The film was praised for its astonishing re-creation of nineteenth-century London.

Hyphens are sometimes used to separate awkward double or triple letters in compound words (*anti-intellectual*, *cross-stitch*).

P7-i Check for correct word breaks when words must be divided at the end of a line.

Some word processing programs and other computer applications automatically generate word breaks at the ends of lines. In academic writing, it's best to set your computer application not to hyphenate automatically. This setting will ensure that only words already containing a hyphen (such as *long-distance*, *pre-Roman*) will be hyphenated at the ends of lines.

E-mail addresses and URLs need special attention when they occur at the end of a line of text or in bibliographic citations. You must make a decision about hyphenation in each case.

Do not insert a hyphen to divide electronic addresses. Instead, break an e-mail address after the @ symbol or before a period. It is common practice to break a URL before most marks of punctuation. (For variations in MLA, APA, and CMS styles, see MLA-5, APA-5, and CMS-5, respectively.)

> I repeatedly e-mailed Janine at janine.r.rose@dunbaracademy .org before I gave up and called her cell phone.

> To avoid standing in line, I now order stamps online at http://www .usps.com.

P8   Capitalization

In addition to the rules in this section, a good dictionary can tell you when to use capital letters.

P8-a   Capitalize proper nouns and words derived from them; do not capitalize common nouns.

Proper nouns are the names of specific persons, places, and things. All other nouns are common nouns. The following types of words are usually capitalized: names of deities, religions, religious followers, sacred books; words of family relationship used as names; particular places; nationalities and their languages, races, tribes; educational institutions, departments, particular courses; government departments, organizations, political parties; historical movements, periods, events, documents; and trade names.

PROPER NOUNS	COMMON NOUNS
God (used as a name)	a god
Book of Common Prayer	a sacred book
Uncle Pedro	my uncle
Father (used as a name)	my father
Lake Superior	a picturesque lake
the Capital Center	a center for advanced studies
the South	a southern state
Wrigley Field	a baseball stadium
University of Wisconsin	a state university
Geology 101	geology
the Democratic Party	a political party
the Enlightenment	the eighteenth century
Advil	a painkiller

Months, holidays, and days of the week are treated as proper nouns; the seasons and numbers of the days of the month are not.

Our academic year begins on a Tuesday in early September, right after Labor Day.

Graduation is in late spring, on the second of June.

EXCEPTION: Capitalize Fourth of July (or July Fourth) when referring to the holiday.

Names of school subjects are capitalized only if they are names of languages. Names of particular courses are capitalized.

hackerhandbooks.com/writersref
e P8 Capitalization > Exercises: P8–2 and P8–3
☑ P8 Capitalization > LearningCurve: Capitalization

This semester Lee is taking math, physics, French, and English.

Professor Obembe offers Modern American Fiction 501 to graduate students.

The terms *Web* and *Internet* are typically capitalized, but related common nouns are not: *home page, operating system.* Usage varies widely, however, so check with your instructor about whether you should follow the guidelines for MLA, APA, or CMS style (MLA-5, APA-5, and CMS-5, respectively).

CAUTION: Do not capitalize common nouns to make them seem important.

P8-b Capitalize titles of persons when used as part of a proper name but usually not when used alone.

Professor Margaret Barnes; Dr. Sinyee Sein; John Scott Williams Jr.

District Attorney Marshall was reprimanded for badgering the witness.

The district attorney was elected for a two-year term.

Usage varies when the title of an important public figure is used alone: *The president* [or *President*] *vetoed the bill.*

P8-c Capitalize titles according to convention.

In both titles and subtitles of works mentioned in the text of a paper, major words such as nouns, pronouns, verbs, adjectives, and adverbs should be capitalized. Minor words such as articles, prepositions, and coordinating conjunctions are not capitalized unless they are the first or last word of a title or subtitle. (In APA style, also capitalize all words of four or more letters. See APA-5.)

Capitalize the second part of a hyphenated term in a title if it is a major word but not if it is a minor word. Capitalize chapter titles and the titles of other major divisions of a work following the same guidelines used for titles of complete works.

Seizing the Enigma: The Race to Break the German U-Boat Codes
A River Runs through It
"I Want to Hold Your Hand"
The Canadian Green Page

To see why some of the titles in the list are italicized and some are put in quotation marks, see P10-a and P5-c.

Titles of works are handled differently in the APA reference list. See "Preparing the list of references" in APA-5.

P8-d Capitalize the first word of a sentence.

The first word of a sentence should be capitalized. When a sentence appears within parentheses, capitalize its first word unless the parentheses appear within another sentence.

> Early detection of breast cancer significantly increases survival rates. (See table 2.)

> Early detection of breast cancer significantly increases survival rates (see table 2).

P8-e Capitalize the first word of a quoted sentence but not a quoted word or phrase.

> Loveless writes, "If failing schools are ever to be turned around, much more must be learned about how schools age as institutions" (25).

> Russell Baker has written that in this country, sports are "the opiate of the masses" (46).

If a quoted sentence is interrupted by explanatory words, do not capitalize the first word after the interruption. (See also P5-e.)

> "If you want to go out," he said, "tell me now."

When quoting poetry, copy the poet's capitalization exactly. Many poets capitalize the first word of every line of poetry; a few contemporary poets dismiss capitalization altogether.

> it was the week   that
> i felt the city's narrow breezes rush about
> me   —Don L. Lee

P8-f Capitalize the first word after a colon if it begins an independent clause.

If a group of words following a colon could stand on its own as a complete sentence, capitalize the first word.

> Clinical trials called into question the safety profile of the drug: A high percentage of participants reported hypertension and kidney problems.

Preferences vary among academic disciplines. See MLA-5, APA-5, and CMS-5.

Always use lowercase for a list or an appositive that follows a colon (see P3-d).

Students were divided into two groups: residents and commuters.

P9 Abbreviations and numbers

P9-a Use standard abbreviations for titles immediately before and after proper names.

TITLES BEFORE PROPER NAMES	TITLES AFTER PROPER NAMES
Mr. Rafael Zabala	William Albert Sr.
Ms. Nancy Linehan	Thomas Hines Jr.
Dr. Margaret Simmons	Robert Simkowski, MD
Rev. John Stone	Mia Chin, LLD

Do not abbreviate a title if it is not used with a proper name: *My history professor* (not *prof.*) *is an expert on race relations in South Africa.*

Avoid redundant titles such as *Dr. Amy Day, MD.* Choose one title or the other: *Dr. Amy Day* or *Amy Day, MD.*

P9-b Use abbreviations only when you are sure your readers will understand them.

Familiar abbreviations for the names of organizations, companies, countries, academic degrees, and common terms, written without periods, are generally acceptable.

CIA	FBI	MD	NAACP
NBA	CEO	PhD	DVD

Talk show host Conan O'Brien is a Harvard graduate with a BA in history.

When using an unfamiliar abbreviation (such as *NASW* for National Association of Social Workers) or a potentially ambiguous abbreviation (such as *AMA*, which can refer to either the American Medical Association or the American Management Association), write the full name followed by the abbreviation in parentheses at the first mention of the name. Then use just the abbreviation throughout the rest of the paper.

NOTE: An abbreviation that can be pronounced as a word is called an *acronym*: *NATO, MADD, OPEC*.

P9-c Use *BC, AD, a.m., p.m., No.,* and *$* only with specific dates, times, numbers, and amounts.

The abbreviation *BC* ("before Christ") follows a date, and *AD* ("*anno Domini*") precedes a date. Acceptable alternatives are *BCE* ("before the common era") and *CE* ("common era"), both of which follow a date.

40 BC (or 40 BCE)	4:00 a.m. (or AM)	No. 12 (or no. 12)
AD 44 (or 44 CE)	6:00 p.m. (or PM)	$150

Avoid using *a.m., p.m., No.,* or *$* when not accompanied by a specific numeral: *in the morning* (not *in the a.m.*).

P9-d Units of measurement

The following are typical abbreviations for units of measurement. Most social sciences and related fields use metric units (*km, mg*), but in other fields and in everyday use, US standard units (*mi, lb*) are typical. Generally, use abbreviations for units when they appear with numerals; spell out the units when they are used alone or when they are used with spelled-out numbers (see also P9-h).

METRIC UNITS	US STANDARD UNITS
m, cm, mm	yd, ft, in.
km, kph	mi, mph
kg, g, mg	lb, oz

Results were measured in pounds.

Runners in the 5-km race had to contend with a stiff headwind.

Use no periods after abbreviations for units of measurement, except the abbreviation for "inch" (*in.*), to distinguish it from the preposition *in*.

P9-e Be sparing in your use of Latin abbreviations.

Latin abbreviations are acceptable in notes and bibliographies.

> cf. (Latin *confer*, "compare")
> e.g. (Latin *exempli gratia*, "for example")
> et al. (Latin *et alia*, "and others")
> etc. (Latin *et cetera*, "and so forth")
> i.e. (Latin *id est*, "that is")
> N.B. (Latin *nota bene*, "note well")

In the text of a paper in most academic fields, use the appropriate English phrases.

P9-f Plural of abbreviations

To form the plural of most abbreviations, add -*s*, without an apostrophe: *PhDs*, *DVDs*. Do not add -*s* to indicate the plural of units of measurement: *mm* (not *mms*), *lb* (not *lbs*), *in.* (not *ins.*).

P9-g Avoid inappropriate abbreviations.

In academic writing, abbreviations for the following are not commonly accepted.

PERSONAL NAMES   Charles (not Chas.)

DAYS OF THE WEEK   Monday (not Mon.)

HOLIDAYS   Christmas (not Xmas)

MONTHS   January, February, March (not Jan., Feb., Mar.)

COURSES OF STUDY   political science (not poli. sci.)

DIVISIONS OF WRITTEN WORKS   chapter, page (not ch., p.)

STATES AND COUNTRIES   Massachusetts (not MA or Mass.)

PARTS OF A BUSINESS NAME   Adams Lighting Company (not Adams Lighting Co.); Kim and Brothers (not Kim and Bros.)

NOTE: Use abbreviations for units of measurement when they are preceded by numerals (*13 cm*). Do not abbreviate them when they are used alone. See P9-d.

EXCEPTION: Abbreviate states and provinces in complete addresses, and always abbreviate *DC* when used with *Washington*.

P9-h Follow the conventions in your discipline for spelling out or using numerals to express numbers.

In the humanities, which generally follow Modern Language Association (MLA) style, use numerals only for specific numbers larger than one hundred: *353; 1,020*. Spell out numbers one hundred and below and large round numbers: *eleven, thirty-five, fifteen million*. Treat related numbers in a passage consistently: *The survey found that 9 of the 157 students had not taken a course on alcohol use.*

The social sciences and other disciplines that follow American Psychological Association (APA) style use numerals for all but the numbers one through nine. Spell out numbers from one to nine even when they are used with related numerals in a passage: *The survey found that nine of the 157 respondents had not taken a course on alcohol use.* (An exception is the abstract of a paper, where numerals are used for all numbers. See APA-5.)

If a sentence begins with a number, spell out the number or rewrite the sentence.

> One hundred fifty
> ▶ ~~150~~ children in our program need expensive dental treatment.
>   ^

Rewriting the sentence may be less awkward if the number is long: *In our program, 150 children need expensive dental treatment.*

P9-i Use numerals according to convention in dates, addresses, and so on.

DATES   July 4, 1776; 56 BC; AD 30

ADDRESSES   77 Latches Lane, 519 West 42nd Street

PERCENTAGES   55 percent (or 55%)

FRACTIONS, DECIMALS $7/8$, 0.047

SCORES   7 to 3, 21–18

STATISTICS average age 37, average weight 180

SURVEYS 4 out of 5

EXACT AMOUNTS OF MONEY $105.37, $106,000

DIVISIONS OF BOOKS volume 3, chapter 4, page 189

DIVISIONS OF PLAYS act 3, scene 3 (or act III, scene iii)

TIME OF DAY 4:00 p.m., 1:30 a.m.

NOTE: When not using *a.m.* or *p.m.*, write out the time in words (*two o'clock in the afternoon*, *twelve noon*, *seven in the morning*).

P10 Italics

This section describes conventional uses for italics. (If your instructor prefers underlining, simply substitute underlining for italics in the examples in this section.)

Some computer and online applications do not allow for italics. To indicate words that should be italicized, you can use underscore marks or asterisks before and after the words.

I am planning to write my senior thesis on _The Book Thief_.

NOTE: Excessive use of italics to emphasize words or ideas, especially in academic writing, is distracting and should be avoided.

P10-a Italicize the titles of works according to convention.

Titles of the following types of works should be italicized.

TITLES OF BOOKS *The Color Purple*, *The Round House*

MAGAZINES *Time*, *Scientific American*, *Slate*

NEWSPAPERS the *Baltimore Sun*, the *Orlando Sentinel*

PAMPHLETS *Common Sense*, *Facts about Marijuana*

LONG POEMS *The Waste Land*, *Paradise Lost*

PLAYS *'Night Mother*, *Wicked*

FILMS *Casablanca*, *Argo*

TELEVISION PROGRAMS   *The Voice, Homeland*

RADIO PROGRAMS   *All Things Considered*

MUSICAL COMPOSITIONS   *Porgy and Bess*

CHOREOGRAPHIC WORKS   *Brief Fling*

WORKS OF VISUAL ART   *American Gothic*

VIDEO GAMES   *Everquest, Call of Duty*

DATABASES [MLA]   *ProQuest*

WEB SITES [MLA]   *Salon, Google*

COMPUTER SOFTWARE OR APPS [MLA]   *Photoshop, Instagram*

The titles of other works—including short stories, essays, episodes of radio and television programs, songs, and short poems — are enclosed in quotation marks. (See P5-c.)

NOTE: Do not use italics when referring to the Bible, titles of books in the Bible (Genesis, not *Genesis*), or titles of legal documents (the Constitution, not the *Constitution*).

P10-b   Italicize other terms according to convention.

Ships, spacecraft, and aircraft

Queen Mary 2, Endeavour, Wright Flyer

The success of the Soviets' *Sputnik* energized the US space program.

Foreign words

Shakespeare's Falstaff is a comic character known for both his excessive drinking and his general *joie de vivre.*

EXCEPTION: Do not italicize foreign words that have become a standard part of the English language—"laissez-faire," "fait accompli," "modus operandi," and "per diem," for example.

Words mentioned as words, letters mentioned as letters, and numbers mentioned as numbers

Tomás assured us that the chemicals could probably be safely mixed, but his *probably* stuck in our minds.

Some toddlers have trouble pronouncing the letters *f* and *s.*

A big *3* was painted on the stage door.

NOTE: Quotation marks may be used instead of italics to set off words mentioned as words. (See P5-d.)

B

Basic
Grammar

B Basic Grammar

B1 Parts of speech

Traditional grammar recognizes eight parts of speech: noun, pronoun, verb, adjective, adverb, preposition, conjunction, and interjection. Many words can function as more than one part of speech. For example, depending on its use in a sentence, the word *paint* can be a noun (*The paint is wet*) or a verb (*Please paint the ceiling next*).

B1-a Nouns

A noun is the name of a person, place, thing, or concept.

>   N   N   N
> The *lion* in the *cage* growled at the *zookeeper*.

Nouns sometimes function as adjectives modifying other nouns. Because of their dual roles, nouns used in this manner may be called *noun/adjectives*.

>   N/ADJ   N/ADJ
> The *leather* notebook was tucked in the *student's* backpack.

Nouns are classified in a variety of ways. *Proper* nouns are capitalized, but *common* nouns are not (see P8-a). For clarity, writers choose between *concrete* and *abstract* nouns (see W5-b). The distinction between *count* nouns and *noncount* nouns can be especially helpful to multilingual writers (see M2-a). Most nouns have singular and plural forms; *collective* nouns may be either singular or plural, depending on how they are used (see G1-f and G3-a). *Possessive* nouns require an apostrophe (see P4-a).

B1-b Pronouns

A pronoun is a word used in place of a noun. Usually the pronoun substitutes for a specific noun, known as its *antecedent*.

>   ANT   PN
> When the *battery* wears down, we recharge *it*.

hackerhandbooks.com/writersref
🄴 B1 Parts of speech > Exercises: B1–2 to B1–4, B1–6 to B1–8, B1–19 and B1–20 (all parts of speech)
☑ B1 Parts of speech > LearningCurve: Nouns and pronouns

Although most pronouns function as substitutes for nouns, some can function as adjectives modifying nouns. Such pronouns may be called *pronoun/adjectives*.

PN/ADJ
That bird was at the same window yesterday morning.

Pronouns are classified in the following ways.

PERSONAL PRONOUNS   Personal pronouns refer to specific persons or things. They always function as substitutes for nouns.

Singular: I, me, you, she, her, he, him, it

Plural: we, us, you, they, them

POSSESSIVE PRONOUNS   Possessive pronouns indicate ownership.

Singular: my, mine, your, yours, her, hers, his, its

Plural: our, ours, your, yours, their, theirs

Some of these possessive pronouns function as adjectives modifying nouns: *my, your, his, her, its, our, their*.

INTENSIVE AND REFLEXIVE PRONOUNS   Intensive pronouns emphasize a noun or another pronoun (The senator *herself* met us at the door). Reflexive pronouns name a receiver of an action identical with the doer of the action (Paula cut *herself*).

Singular: myself, yourself, himself, herself, itself

Plural: ourselves, yourselves, themselves

RELATIVE PRONOUNS   Relative pronouns introduce subordinate clauses functioning as adjectives (The writer *who won the award* refused to accept it). The relative pronoun, in this case *who*, also points back to a noun or pronoun that the clause modifies (*writer*). (See B3-e.)

who, whom, whose, which, that

The pronouns *whichever, whoever, whomever, what,* and *whatever* are sometimes considered relative pronouns, but they introduce noun clauses and do not point back to a noun or pronoun. (See "Noun clauses" in B3-e.)

INTERROGATIVE PRONOUNS   Interrogative pronouns introduce questions (*Who* is expected to win the election?).

who, whom, whose, which, what

DEMONSTRATIVE PRONOUNS   Demonstrative pronouns identify or point to nouns. Frequently they function as adjectives (*This* chair is my favorite), but they may also function as substitutes for nouns (*This* is my favorite chair).

> this, that, these, those

INDEFINITE PRONOUNS   Indefinite pronouns refer to nonspecific persons or things. Most are always singular (*everyone, each*); some are always plural (*both, many*); a few may be singular or plural (see G1-e). Most indefinite pronouns function as substitutes for nouns (*Something* is burning), but some can also function as adjectives (*All* campers must check in at the lodge).

all	anything	everyone	nobody	several
another	both	everything	none	some
any	each	few	no one	somebody
anybody	either	many	nothing	someone
anyone	everybody	neither	one	something

RECIPROCAL PRONOUNS   Reciprocal pronouns refer to individual parts of a plural antecedent (By turns, the penguins fed *one another*).

> each other, one another

NOTE: See also pronoun-antecedent agreement (G3-a), pronoun reference (G3-b), distinguishing between pronouns such as *I* and *me* (G3-c), and distinguishing between *who* and *whom* (G3-d).

B1-c Verbs

The verb of a sentence usually expresses action (*jump, think*) or being (*is, become*). It is composed of a main verb possibly preceded by one or more helping verbs.

MV
The horses *exercise* every day.

HV   MV
The task force report *was* not *completed* on schedule.

HV HV   MV
No one *has been defended* with more passion than our pastor.

Notice that words, usually adverbs, can intervene between the helping verb and the main verb (was *not* completed). (See B1-e.)

---

hackerhandbooks.com/writersref

ⓔ B1 Parts of speech > Exercises: B1–10 to B1–12, B1–19 and B1–20
  (all parts of speech)

☑ B1 Parts of speech > LearningCurve: Verbs, adjectives, and adverbs

Helping verbs

There are twenty-three helping verbs in English: forms of *have*, *do*, and *be*, which may also function as main verbs; and nine modals, which function only as helping verbs. *Have*, *do*, and *be* change form to indicate tense; the nine modals do not.

> **FORMS OF *HAVE, DO,* AND *BE***
>
> have, has, had
>
> do, does, did
>
> be, am, is, are, was, were, being, been
>
> **MODALS**
>
> can, could, may, might, must, shall, should, will, would

The verb phrase *ought to* is often classified as a modal as well.

Main verbs

The main verb of a sentence is always the kind of word that would change form if put into these test sentences:

BASE FORM	Usually I (*walk, ride*).
PAST TENSE	Yesterday I (*walked, rode*).
PAST PARTICIPLE	I have (*walked, ridden*) many times before.
PRESENT PARTICIPLE	I am (*walking, riding*) right now.
-S FORM	Usually he/she/it (*walks, rides*).

If a word doesn't change form when slipped into the test sentences, you can be certain that it is not a main verb. For example, the noun *revolution*, though it may seem to suggest an action, can never function as a main verb. Just try to make it behave like one (*Today I revolution . . . Yesterday I revolutioned . . .*) and you'll see why.

When both the past-tense and the past-participle forms of a verb end in *-ed*, the verb is regular (*walked, walked*). Otherwise, the verb is irregular (*rode, ridden*). (See G2-a.)

The verb *be* is highly irregular, having eight forms instead of the usual five: the base form *be*; the present-tense forms *am*, *is*, and *are*; the past-tense forms *was* and *were*; the present participle *being*; and the past participle *been*.

Helping verbs combine with main verbs to create tenses. See G2-f.

NOTE: Some verbs are followed by words that look like prepositions but are so closely associated with the verb that they are a part of its meaning. These words are known as *particles*. Common verb-particle combinations include *bring up*, *call off*, *drop off*, *give in*, *look up*, *run into*, and *take off*.

TIP: For more information about using verbs, see these sections of the handbook: active verbs (W3), subject-verb agreement (G1), Standard English verb forms (G2-a to G2-d), verb tense and mood (G2-f and G2-g), and multilingual/ESL challenges with verbs (M1).

B1-d Adjectives

An adjective is a word used to modify, or describe, a noun or pronoun. An adjective usually answers one of these questions: Which one? What kind of? How many?

> ADJ
> the *frisky* horse [Which horse?]

> ADJ ADJ
> *cracked old* plates [What kind of plates?]

> ADJ
> *qualified* applicants [What kind of applicants?]

> ADJ
> *nine* months [How many months?]

Adjectives usually precede the words they modify. They may also follow linking verbs, in which case they describe the subject. (See B2-b.)

> ADJ
> The decision was *unpopular*.

The definite article *the* and the indefinite articles *a* and *an* are also classified as adjectives.

> ART   ART   ART
> *A* defendant should be judged on *the* evidence provided to *the* jury, not on hearsay.

Some possessive, demonstrative, and indefinite pronouns can function as adjectives: *their*, *its*, *this*, *all* (see B1-b). And nouns can function as adjectives when they modify other nouns: *apple pie* (the noun *apple* modifies the noun *pie*; see B1-a).

TIP: You can find more details about using adjectives in G4. If you are a multilingual writer, you may find help with articles and specific uses of adjectives in M2, M4-a, and M4-b.

---

hackerhandbooks.com/writersref

e B1 Parts of speech > Exercises: B1–14 to B1–20 (all parts of speech)

☑ B1 Parts of speech > LearningCurve: Verbs, adjectives, and adverbs

B1-e Adverbs

An adverb is a word used to modify, or qualify, a verb (or verbal), an adjective, or another adverb. It usually answers one of these questions: When? Where? How? Why? Under what conditions? To what degree?

> Pull *firmly* on the emergency handle. [Pull how?]
>
> Read the text *first* and *then* complete the exercises. [Read when? Complete when?]
>
> Place the flowers *here*. [Place where?]

Adverbs modifying adjectives or other adverbs usually intensify or limit the intensity of the word they modify.

>   ADV
> Be *extremely* kind, and you will have many friends.

>   ADV
> We proceeded *very* cautiously in the dark house.

The words *not* and *never* are classified as adverbs.

Multilingual Multilingual writers can find more about the placement of adverbs in M3-f.

B1-f Prepositions

A preposition is a word placed before a noun or a pronoun to form a phrase that modifies another word in the sentence. The prepositional phrase functions as an adjective or an adverb.

>   P   P   P
> The winding road *to* the summit travels *past* craters *from* an extinct volcano.

To the summit functions as an adjective modifying the noun *road*; *past craters* functions as an adverb modifying the verb *travels*; *from an extinct volcano* functions as an adjective modifying the noun *craters*. (For more on prepositional phrases, see B3-a.)

---

hackerhandbooks.com/writersref

- **e** B1 Parts of speech > Exercises: B1–19 and B1–20 (all parts of speech)
- ☑ B1 Parts of speech > LearningCurve: Prepositions and conjunctions
- ☑ B1 Parts of speech > LearningCurve: Verbs, adjectives, and adverbs

English has a limited number of prepositions. The most common are included in the following list.

about	beside	from	outside	toward
above	besides	in	over	under
across	between	inside	past	underneath
after	beyond	into	plus	unlike
against	but	like	regarding	until
along	by	near	respecting	unto
among	concerning	next	round	up
around	considering	of	since	upon
as	despite	off	than	with
at	down	on	through	within
before	during	onto	throughout	without
behind	except	opposite	till	
below	for	out	to	

Some prepositions are more than one word long. *Along with, as well as, in addition to, next to,* and *rather than* are examples.

TIP: Prepositions are used in idioms such as *capable of* and *dig up* (see W5-d). For specific issues for multilingual writers, see M5.

B1-g Conjunctions

Conjunctions join words, phrases, or clauses, and they indicate the relation between the elements joined.

COORDINATING CONJUNCTIONS A coordinating conjunction is used to connect grammatically equal elements. (See S1-b and S6.) The coordinating conjunctions are *and, but, or, nor, for, so,* and *yet.*

The sociologist interviewed children *but* not their parents.

Write clearly, *and* your readers will appreciate your efforts.

In the first sentence, *but* connects two noun phrases; in the second, *and* connects two independent clauses.

CORRELATIVE CONJUNCTIONS Correlative conjunctions come in pairs; they connect grammatically equal elements.

either . . . or

neither . . . nor

not only . . . but also

whether . . . or

both . . . and

Either the painting was brilliant *or* it was a forgery.

SUBORDINATING CONJUNCTIONS A subordinating conjunction introduces a subordinate clause and indicates the relation of the clause to the rest of the sentence. (See B3-e.) The most common subordinating conjunctions are *after, although, as, as if, because, before, if, in order that, once, since, so that, than, that, though, unless, until, when, where, whether,* and *while.* (For a complete list, see p. 350.)

> *When* the fundraiser ends, we expect to have raised more than half a million dollars.

CONJUNCTIVE ADVERBS Conjunctive adverbs connect independent clauses and indicate the relation between the clauses. They can be used with a semicolon to join two independent clauses in one sentence, or they can be used alone with an independent clause. The most common conjunctive adverbs are *finally, furthermore, however, moreover, nevertheless, similarly, then, therefore,* and *thus.* (For a complete list, see p. 300.)

> The photographer failed to take a light reading; *therefore,* all the pictures were underexposed.

> During the day, the kitten sleeps peacefully. *However,* when night falls, the kitten is wide awake and ready to play.

Conjunctive adverbs can appear at the beginning or in the middle of a clause.

> When night falls, *however,* the kitten is wide awake and ready to play.

TIP: The ability to distinguish between conjunctive adverbs and coordinating conjunctions will help you avoid run-on sentences and make punctuation decisions (see G6, P1-a, and P1-f). The ability to recognize subordinating conjunctions will help you avoid sentence fragments (see G5).

B1-h   Interjections

An interjection is a word used to express surprise or emotion (*Oh! Hey! Wow!*).

B2   Sentence patterns

The vast majority of English sentences conform to one of five patterns:

> subject/verb/subject complement
> subject/verb/direct object
> subject/verb/indirect object/direct object
> subject/verb/direct object/object complement
> subject/verb

Adverbial modifiers (single words, phrases, or clauses) may be added to any of these patterns, and they may appear nearly anywhere—at the beginning, in the middle, or at the end.

Predicate is the grammatical term given to the verb plus its objects, complements, and adverbial modifiers.

B2-a Subjects

The subject of a sentence names whom or what the sentence is about. The simple subject is always a noun or pronoun; the complete subject consists of the simple subject and any words or word groups modifying the simple subject.

The complete subject

To find the complete subject, ask Who? or What?, insert the verb, and finish the question. The answer is the complete subject.

┌─────── COMPLETE SUBJECT ───────┐
The devastating effects of famine can last for many years.

Who or what can last for many years? *The devastating effects of famine.*

┌─────────── COMPLETE SUBJECT ───────────┐
Adventure novels that contain multiple subplots are often made into successful movies.

Who or what are often made into movies? *Adventure novels that contain multiple subplots.*

COMPLETE
┌─── SUBJECT ───┐
In our program, student teachers work full-time for ten months.

Who or what works full-time for ten months? *Student teachers.* Notice that *In our program, student teachers* is not a sensible answer to the question. (It is not safe to assume that the subject must always appear first in a sentence.)

The simple subject

To find the simple subject, strip away all modifiers in the complete subject. This includes single-word modifiers such as *the* and *devastating*, phrases such as *of famine*, and subordinate clauses such as *that contain multiple subplots*.

┌ SS ┐
The devastating effects of famine can last for many years.

┌ SS ┐
Adventure novels that contain multiple subplots are often made into successful movies.

A sentence may have a compound subject containing two or more simple subjects joined with a coordinating conjunction such as *and*, *but*, or *or*.

┌──── SS ────┐   ┌SS┐
Great commitment and a little luck make a successful actor.

Understood subjects

In imperative sentences, which give advice or issue commands, the subject is understood but not actually present in the sentence. The subject of an imperative sentence is understood to be *you*.

[*You*] Put your hands on the steering wheel.

Subject after the verb

Although the subject ordinarily comes before the verb (*The planes took off*), occasionally it does not. When a sentence begins with *There is* or *There are* (or *There was* or *There were*), the subject follows the verb. In such inverted constructions, the word *There* is an expletive, an empty word serving merely to get the sentence started.

┌ SS ┐
There are *eight planes waiting to take off*.

Occasionally a writer will invert a sentence for effect.

┌SS┐
Joyful is *the child whose school closes for snow*.

Joyful is an adjective, so it cannot be the subject. Turn this sentence around and its structure becomes obvious.

The *child* whose school closes for snow is joyful.

In questions, the subject frequently appears between the helping verb and the main verb.

HV   ⌐— SS —⌐   MV
Do *Kenyan marathoners* train year-round?

TIP: The ability to recognize the subject of a sentence will help you edit for fragments (G5), subject-verb agreement (G1), pronouns such as *I* and *me* (G3-c), missing subjects (M3-b), and repeated subjects (M3-c).

B2-b   Verbs, objects, and complements

Section B1-c explains how to find the verb of a sentence. A sentence's verb is classified as linking, transitive, or intransitive, depending on the kinds of objects or complements the verb can (or cannot) take.

Linking verbs and subject complements

Linking verbs connect the subject to a subject complement, a word or word group that completes the meaning of the subject by renaming or describing it.

If the subject complement renames the subject, it is a noun or noun equivalent (sometimes called a *predicate noun*).

⌐——————————— S ———————————⌐ ⌐ V ⌐ ⌐ SC ⌐
An e-mail message requesting personal information may be a scam.

If the subject complement describes the subject, it is an adjective or adjective equivalent (sometimes called a *predicate adjective*).

⌐——————— S ———————⌐   V   SC
Last month's temperatures were mild.

Whenever they appear as main verbs (rather than helping verbs), the forms of *be* — *be, am, is, are, was, were, being, been* — usually function as linking verbs. In the preceding examples, for instance, the main verbs are *be* and *were*.

Verbs such as *appear, become, feel, grow, look, make, seem, smell, sound,* and *taste* are linking when they are followed by a word or word group that renames or describes the subject.

⌐— S —⌐ ⌐ V —⌐   SC
As it thickens, the sauce will look unappealing.

Transitive verbs and direct objects

A transitive verb takes a direct object, a word or word group that names a receiver of the action.

$$\overbrace{\text{The hungry cat}}^{\text{S}} \overset{\text{V}}{\text{clawed}} \overbrace{\text{the bag of dry food.}}^{\text{DO}}$$

The simple direct object is always a noun or pronoun, in this case *bag*. To find it, simply strip away all modifiers.

    Transitive verbs usually appear in the active voice, with the subject doing the action and a direct object receiving the action. Active-voice sentences can be transformed into passive, with the subject receiving the action.

Transitive verbs, indirect objects, and direct objects

The direct object of a transitive verb is sometimes preceded by an indirect object, a noun or pronoun telling to whom or for whom the action of the sentence is done.

S   V   IO   —DO—   S   —V— IO —DO—
You give her some yarn, and she will knit you a scarf.

    The simple indirect object is always a noun or pronoun. To test for an indirect object, insert the word *to* or *for* before the word or word group in question. If the sentence makes sense, the word or word group is an indirect object.

    You give [to] *her* some yarn, and she will knit [for] *you* a scarf.

Transitive verbs, direct objects, and object complements

The direct object of a transitive verb is sometimes followed by an object complement, a word or word group that renames or describes the object.

S   V   DO   —OC—
People often consider chivalry a thing of the past.

—S— V   DO —OC—
The kiln makes clay firm and strong.

When the object complement renames the direct object, it is a noun or pronoun (such as *thing*). When it describes the direct object, it is an adjective (such as *firm* and *strong*).

Intransitive verbs

Intransitive verbs take no objects or complements.

```
 ┌── s ──┐   v
```
The audience laughed.

```
 ┌── s ──┐   v
```
The driver accelerated in the straightaway.

Nothing receives the actions of laughing and accelerating in these sentences, so the verbs are intransitive. Notice that such verbs may or may not be followed by adverbial modifiers. In the second sentence, *in the straightaway* is an adverbial prepositional phrase modifying *accelerated*. See B3-a.

NOTE: The dictionary will tell you whether a verb is transitive or intransitive. Some verbs can be both transitive and intransitive.

TRANSITIVE	Sandra *flew* her small plane over the canyon.
INTRANSITIVE	A flock of migrating geese *flew* overhead.

In the first example, *flew* has a direct object that receives the action: *her small plane*. In the second example, the verb is followed by an adverb (*overhead*), not by a direct object.

B3 Subordinate word groups

Subordinate word groups include phrases and clauses. Phrases are subordinate because they lack a subject and a verb; they are classified as prepositional, verbal, appositive, and absolute (see B3-a to B3-d). Subordinate clauses have a subject and a verb, but they begin with a word (such as *although*, *that*, or *when*) that marks them as subordinate (see B3-e).

B3-a Prepositional phrases

A prepositional phrase begins with a preposition such as *at, by, for, from, in, of, on, to,* or *with* (see B1-f) and usually ends with a noun or noun equivalent: *on the table, for him, by sleeping late.* The noun or noun equivalent is known as the *object of the preposition*.

Prepositional phrases function as adjectives or as adverbs. As an adjective, a prepositional phrase nearly always appears immediately following the noun or pronoun it modifies.

The hut had *walls of mud*.

Adjective phrases usually answer one or both of the questions Which one? and What kind of? If we ask Which walls? or What kind of walls? we get a sensible answer: *walls of mud*.

Adverbial prepositional phrases usually modify the verb, but they can also modify adjectives or other adverbs. When a prepositional phrase modifies the verb, it can appear nearly anywhere in a sentence.

James *walked* his dog *on a leash*.

Sabrina *will in time adjust* to life in Ecuador.

During a mudslide, the terrain *can change* drastically.

If a prepositional phrase is movable, you can be certain that it is adverbial.

In the cave, the explorers found well-preserved prehistoric drawings.

The explorers found well-preserved prehistoric drawings *in the cave*.

Adverbial word groups usually answer one of these questions: When? Where? How? Why? Under what conditions? To what degree?

James walked his dog *how*? *On a leash*.

Sabrina will adjust to life in Ecuador *when*? *In time*.

The terrain can change drastically *under what conditions*? *During a mudslide*.

In questions and subordinate clauses, a preposition may appear after its object.

What are you afraid *of*?

We avoided the bike trail *that* John had warned us *about*.

B3-b Verbal phrases

A verbal is a verb form that does not function as the verb of a clause. Verbals include infinitives (the word *to* plus the base form of the verb), present participles (the *-ing* form of the verb), and past participles (the verb form usually ending in *-d*, *-ed*, *-n*, *-en*, or *-t*). (See G2-a and B1-c.)

INFINITIVE	PRESENT PARTICIPLE	PAST PARTICIPLE
to dream	dreaming	dreamed
to choose	choosing	chosen
to build	building	built

Instead of functioning as the verb of a clause, a verbal functions as an adjective, a noun, or an adverb.

ADJECTIVE	*Broken* promises cannot be fixed.
NOUN	Constant *complaining* becomes wearisome.
ADVERB	Can you wait *to celebrate*?

Verbals with objects, complements, or modifiers form verbal phrases.

In my family, *singing loudly* is more appreciated than *singing well*.

Like verbals, verbal phrases function as adjectives, nouns, or adverbs. Verbal phrases are ordinarily classified as participial, gerund, and infinitive.

Participial phrases

Participial phrases always function as adjectives. Their verbals are either present participles (such as *dreaming*, *asking*) or past participles (such as *stolen*, *reached*).

Participial phrases frequently appear immediately following the noun or pronoun they modify.

Congress shall make no *law abridging the freedom of speech or of the press*.

Participial phrases are often movable. They can precede the word they modify.

Being a weight-bearing joint, the *knee* is among the most frequently injured.

They may also appear at some distance from the word they modify.

Last night we saw a *play* that affected us deeply, *written with profound insight into the lives of immigrants.*

Gerund phrases

Gerund phrases are built around present participles (verb forms that end in *-ing*), and they always function as nouns: usually as subjects, subject complements, direct objects, or objects of a preposition.

```
              S
```
Rationalizing a fear can eliminate it.

```
                        SC
```
The key to good sauce is browning the mushrooms.

```
                      DO
```
Lizards usually enjoy sunning themselves.

The American Heart Association has documented the benefits of
```
                    OBJ OF PREP
```
diet and exercise in reducing the risk of heart attack.

Infinitive phrases

Infinitive phrases, usually constructed around *to* plus the base form of the verb (*to call*, *to drink*), can function as nouns, as adjectives, or as adverbs. When functioning as a noun, an infinitive phrase may appear in almost any noun slot in a sentence, usually as a subject, subject complement, or direct object.

```
              S
```
To live without health insurance is risky.

Infinitive phrases functioning as adjectives usually appear immediately following the noun or pronoun they modify.

The Nineteenth Amendment gave women the *right to vote*.

The infinitive phrase modifies the noun *right*. Which right? The *right to vote*.

Adverbial infinitive phrases usually qualify the meaning of the verb, telling when, where, how, why, under what conditions, or to what degree an action occurred.

Volunteers *rolled up* their pants *to wade through the flood waters.*

NOTE: In some constructions, the infinitive is unmarked; that is, the *to* does not appear. (See M1-f.)

Graphs and charts can help researchers [*to*] *present complex data.*

B3-c Appositive phrases

Appositive phrases describe nouns or pronouns. Instead of modifying nouns or pronouns, however, appositive phrases rename them. In form they are nouns or noun equivalents.

Bloggers, *conversationalists at heart*, are the online equivalent of radio talk show hosts.

B3-d Absolute phrases

An absolute phrase modifies a whole clause or sentence, not just one word. It consists of a noun or noun equivalent usually followed by a participial phrase.

Her words reverberating in the hushed arena, the senator urged the crowd to support her former opponent.

B3-e Subordinate clauses

Subordinate clauses are patterned like sentences, having subjects and verbs and sometimes objects or complements. But they function within sentences as adjectives, adverbs, or nouns. They cannot stand alone as complete sentences.

A subordinate clause usually begins with a subordinating conjunction or a relative pronoun. The chart on page 350 classifies these words according to the kinds of clauses (adjective, adverb, or noun) they introduce.

Words that introduce subordinate clauses

Words introducing adjective clauses

RELATIVE PRONOUNS: that, which, who, whom, whose

RELATIVE ADVERBS: when, where, why

Words introducing adverb clauses

SUBORDINATING CONJUNCTIONS: after, although, as, as if, because, before, even though, if, in order that, since, so that, than, that, though, unless, until, when, where, whether, while

Words introducing noun clauses

RELATIVE PRONOUNS: which, who, whom, whose

OTHER PRONOUNS: what, whatever, whichever, whoever, whomever

OTHER SUBORDINATING WORDS: how, if, that, when, whenever, where, wherever, whether, why

---

Adjective clauses

Adjective clauses modify nouns or pronouns, usually answering the question *Which one?* or *What kind of?* Most adjective clauses begin with a relative pronoun (*who, whom, whose, which,* or *that*). In addition to introducing the clause, the relative pronoun points back to the noun that the clause modifies.

The coach chose *players who would benefit from intense drills.*

A *book that goes unread* is a writer's worst nightmare.

Relative pronouns are sometimes "understood."

The things [*that*] *we cherish most* are the things [*that*] *we might lose.*

Occasionally an adjective clause is introduced by a relative adverb, usually *when, where,* or *why.*

The aging actor returned to the *stage where he had made his debut as Hamlet half a century earlier.*

The parts of an adjective clause are often arranged as in sentences (subject/verb/object or complement).

                                        S   V   DO
Sometimes it is our closest friends who disappoint us.

Frequently, however, the object or complement appears first, out of the normal order of subject/verb/object.

> DO   S   V
> They can be the very friends whom we disappoint.

TIP: For punctuation of adjective clauses, see P1-e and P2-e. For advice about avoiding repeated words in adjective clauses, see M3-d.

Adverb clauses

Adverb clauses modify verbs, adjectives, or other adverbs, usually answering one of these questions: When? Where? Why? How? Under what conditions? To what degree? They always begin with a subordinating conjunction (such as *after*, *although*, *because*, *that*, *though*, *unless*, or *when*). (For a complete list, see the chart on p. 350.)

> *When the sun went down*, the hikers *prepared* their camp.

> Kate *would have made* the team *if she hadn't broken her ankle*.

Noun clauses

A noun clause functions just like a single-word noun, usually as a subject, a subject complement, a direct object, or an object of a preposition. It usually begins with one of the following words: *how*, *if*, *that*, *what*, *whatever*, *when*, *where*, *whether*, *which*, *who*, *whoever*, *whom*, *whomever*, *whose*, *why*. (For a complete list, see the chart on p. 350.)

>   S
> Whoever leaves the house last must double-lock the door.

>   DO
> Copernicus argued that the sun is the center of the universe.

The subordinating word introducing the clause may or may not play a significant role in the clause. In the preceding examples, *Whoever* is the subject of its clause, but *that* does not perform a function in its clause.

As with adjective clauses, the parts of a noun clause may appear in normal order (subject/verb/object or complement) or out of their normal order.

> S   V   DO
> Loyalty is what keeps a friendship strong.

> DO   S   V
> New Mexico is where we live.

B4 Sentence types

Sentences are classified in two ways: according to their structure (simple, compound, complex, and compound-complex) and according to their purpose (declarative, imperative, interrogative, and exclamatory).

B4-a Sentence structures

Depending on the number and the types of clauses they contain, sentences are classified as simple, compound, complex, or compound-complex.

Clauses come in two varieties: independent and subordinate. An independent clause contains a subject and a predicate, and it either stands alone or could stand alone as a sentence. A subordinate clause also contains a subject and a predicate, but it functions within a sentence as an adjective, an adverb, or a noun; it cannot stand alone. (See B3-e.)

Simple sentences

A simple sentence is one independent clause with no subordinate clauses.

> ———————— INDEPENDENT CLAUSE ————————
> Without a passport, Eva could not visit her grandparents in
> Hungary.

A simple sentence may contain compound elements—a compound subject, verb, or object, for example—but it does not contain more than one full sentence pattern. The following sentence is simple because its two verbs (*comes in* and *goes out*) share a subject (*Spring*).

> ———————— INDEPENDENT CLAUSE ————————
> Spring comes in like a lion and goes out like a lamb.

Compound sentences

A compound sentence is composed of two or more independent clauses with no subordinate clauses. The independent clauses are usually joined with a comma and a coordinating conjunction (*and, but, or, nor, for, so, yet*) or with a semicolon. (See P1-a and P3-a.)

INDEPENDENT

┌─── CLAUSE ───┐

INDEPENDENT

┌─── CLAUSE ───┐

The car broke down, but a rescue van arrived within minutes.

┌─── INDEPENDENT CLAUSE ───┐ ┌─ INDEPENDENT CLAUSE ─┐

A shark was spotted near shore; people left immediately.

Complex sentences

A complex sentence is composed of one independent clause with one or more subordinate clauses. (See B3-e.)

SUBORDINATE

┌─── CLAUSE ───┐

ADJECTIVE The pitcher who won the game is a rookie.

SUBORDINATE

┌─── CLAUSE ───┐

ADVERB If you leave late, take a cab home.

SUBORDINATE

┌─── CLAUSE ───┐

NOUN What matters most to us is a quick commute.

Compound-complex sentences

A compound-complex sentence contains at least two independent clauses and at least one subordinate clause. The following sentence contains two independent clauses, each of which contains a subordinate clause.

┌─ INDEPENDENT CLAUSE ─┐ ┌─ INDEPENDENT CLAUSE ─┐

┌─ SUB CL ─┐ ┌─ SUB CL ─┐

Tell the doctor how you feel, and she will decide whether you

┌──────────┐

can go home.

B4-b Sentence purposes

Writers use declarative sentences to make statements, imperative sentences to issue requests or commands, interrogative sentences to ask questions, and exclamatory sentences to make exclamations.

DECLARATIVE The echo sounded in our ears.

IMPERATIVE Love your neighbor.

INTERROGATIVE Did the better team win tonight?

EXCLAMATORY We're here to save you!

R

Researching

R Researching

A college research assignment asks you to pose questions worth exploring, to read widely in search of possible answers, to draw reasoned conclusions, and to support those conclusions with evidence. In short, it asks you to enter a research conversation by being *in* conversation with other writers and thinkers who have explored and studied your topic. As you listen to and learn from the voices already in the conversation, you'll find entry points where you can add your own insights and ideas.

R1 Thinking like a researcher; gathering sources

After you receive an assignment to write a paper that requires sources, take time to find out not only what has been written about your topic but also what's missing from the research conversation. You can stay organized by planning the search with a solid research question in mind and maintaining accurate records of the sources you consult.

R1-a Manage the project.

When you start on a research project, you need to understand the assignment, choose a direction, and quickly grasp the big picture for the topic you choose. The following tips will help you manage the beginning phase of research.

Managing time

Before beginning a research project, set a realistic schedule of deadlines for researching and for drafting, revising, and documenting the paper in the style recommended by your instructor (see the tabbed dividers marked MLA and APA/CMS). One student created a calendar to map out his tasks for a paper assigned on October 3 and due October 31, keeping in mind that some tasks might overlap or need to be repeated. See page 358.

Keeping a research log

Research is a process. As your topic evolves, you may find yourself asking new questions that require you to create a new search strategy, find additional sources, or revise your initial assumptions. A research log

SAMPLE CALENDAR FOR A RESEARCH ASSIGNMENT

2	3	4	5	6	7	8
	Receive and analyze the assignment.	Pose questions you might explore. ———→	Talk with a reference librarian; plan a ——→ search strategy.	Start research log.	Settle on a topic; narrow the focus.	Revise research questions. Locate sources. ——→
9	**10**	**11**	**12**	**13**	**14**	**15**
Read, take notes, and ———→ compile a working bibliography. ————→				Draft a working thesis and an outline.	Draft the paper. ——→	
16	**17**	**18**	**19**	**20**	**21**	**22**
——→ Draft the paper. ———→			Visit the writing center for feedback.	Do additional ————→ research if needed.		
23	**24**	**25**	**26**	**27**	**28**	**29**
Ask peers for feedback. Revise the paper; ————————→ if necessary, revise the thesis.				Prepare a list of ——→ works cited.		Proofread the final draft. ——→
30	**31**					
Proofread the final draft. ——→	Submit the final draft.					

helps you bring order to this process by keeping accurate records of the sources you read and your ideas about them. You might want to use a separate hard copy notebook for your log or create a digital file or set of files. Keeping an accurate source trail and working bibliography, and separating your own insights and ideas from those of your sources, will help you become a more efficient and effective researcher.

Getting the big picture

As you consider a possible research topic, set aside some time to learn what people are saying about it by reading sources on the Web or in library databases. Ask yourself questions such as these:

- What aspects of the topic are generating the most debate?
- Why and how are people disagreeing?
- Which arguments and approaches seem worth exploring?

Once you have an aerial view of the topic and are familiar with some of the existing research, you can zoom in closer to examine subtopics and debates that look interesting.

R1-b Pose questions worth exploring.

Every research project starts with questions. Working within the guidelines of your assignment, pose a few preliminary questions that seem worth researching—questions that you are interested in exploring, that you feel would engage your audience, and about which there is substantial debate. Here, for example, are some preliminary questions jotted down by students enrolled in a variety of courses in different disciplines.

- Why are boys diagnosed with attention deficit disorder more often than girls?
- Do nutritional food labels inform consumers or confuse them?
- How does the portrayal of family in Kathleen Grissom's *The Kitchen House* reflect the values depicted in nineteenth-century slave narratives?
- Why was amateur archaeologist Heinrich Schliemann such a controversial figure?

As you think about possible questions, choose those that are focused (not too broad), challenging (not just factual), and grounded (not too speculative) as possible entry points in a conversation.

Choosing a focused question

If your initial question is too broad, given the length of the paper you plan to write, look for ways to restrict your focus. Here, for example, is how two students narrowed their initial questions.

TOO BROAD	NARROWER
What causes depression?	How has the widespread use of antidepressant drugs affected teenage suicide rates?
What are the benefits of stricter auto emissions standards?	How will stricter auto emissions standards create new auto industry jobs and make US carmakers more competitive in the world market?

hackerhandbooks.com/writersref

e R1 Thinking like a researcher > As you write: Posing questions worth exploring

e R1 Thinking like a researcher > Exercise: R1–1

Thinking like a researcher

To develop your authority as a researcher, you need to think like a researcher—asking interesting questions, becoming well informed through reading and evaluating sources, and citing sources to acknowledge other researchers.

BE CURIOUS. What makes you angry, concerned, or perplexed? What topics and debates do you care about? What problems do you want to help solve? Explore your topic from multiple angles, and let your curiosity drive your project.

BE ENGAGED. Talk with a librarian and learn how to use your library's research tools and resources. Once you find promising sources, let one source lead you to another; follow clues (in the source's list of works cited, if one exists) to learn who else has written about your topic. Listen to the key voices in the research conversation you've joined—and then respond.

BE RESPONSIBLE. Use sources to develop and support your ideas rather than patching sources together to let them speak for you. From the start of your research project, keep careful track of sources you read or view (see R2), place quotation marks around words copied from sources, and maintain accurate records for all bibliographic information.

BE REFLECTIVE. Keep a research log, and use your log to explore various ideas you are developing and to pose counterarguments to your research argument. Research is never a straightforward path, so use your log to reflect on the evolution of your project as well as your evolution as a researcher.

Choosing a challenging question

Your research paper will engage both you and your audience if you base it on an intellectually challenging line of inquiry. Avoid factual questions that fail to provoke thought or engage readers in a debate.

TOO FACTUAL	CHALLENGING
Is autism on the rise?	Why is autism so difficult to treat?
Where is wind energy being used?	What makes wind farms economically viable?

You will need to address a factual question in the course of answering a more challenging one. For example, if you were writing about promising treatments for autism, you would no doubt answer the question "What is autism?" at some point in your paper and even analyze competing definitions of autism to help support your arguments about the challenges of treating the condition. It would be unproductive, however, to use the factual question as the focus for the whole paper.

Choosing a grounded question

You will want to make sure that your research question is grounded, not too speculative. Although speculative questions—such as those that address morality or beliefs—are worth asking in a research paper, they are unsuitable central questions. For most college courses, the central argument of a research paper should be grounded in facts and should not be based entirely on beliefs.

TOO SPECULATIVE	GROUNDED
Is it wrong to share pornographic personal photos by cell phone?	What role should the US government play in regulating mobile content?
Do medical scientists have the right to experiment on animals?	How have technical breakthroughs made medical experiments on animals increasingly unnecessary?

Finding an entry point in a research conversation

As you pose preliminary research questions, you may wonder where and how to step into a research conversation. You may need to ask:

- Who are the major writers or thinkers in the debate? What positions have they taken? What claims have they made?
- How and why do the major writers or thinkers disagree?
- What hasn't been said in this conversation and needs to be pointed out?

As you orient yourself, try using the following statements to help you find points of entry in a research conversation.

> On one side of the debate is position X, on the other side is Y, but there is a middle position, Z.
>
> The conventional view about the problem or issue needs to be challenged because . . .
>
> Key details in this debate that have been overlooked are . . .
>
> Researchers have drawn conclusion X from the evidence, but one could also draw conclusion Y.

hackerhandbooks.com/writersref
e R1 Thinking like a researcher > As you write: Entering a research conversation (with video)

Testing a research question

- Does the question allow you to enter into a research conversation that you care about?
- Is the question flexible enough to allow for many possible answers?
- Is the question clear, focused, and interesting?
- Put the question to the "So what?" test. Can you show readers why the question needs to be asked and why the answer matters? (See p. 11.)
- Is the question narrow enough, given the length of the assignment?

R1-c Map out a search strategy.

A search strategy is a systematic plan for tracking down sources. To create a search strategy appropriate for your research question, it may help to consult a reference librarian and take a look at your library's Web site, which will give you an overview of available resources.

No single search strategy works for every topic. For some topics, it may be useful to search for information in newspapers, magazines, and Web sites. For others, the best sources might be found in scholarly journals and books and specialized reference works. Still other topics might be enhanced by field research—interviews, surveys, or observation.

With the help of a reference librarian, each of the students whose research essays appear in this handbook constructed a search strategy appropriate for his or her research question.

SOPHIE HARBA Sophie Harba's topic, the role of government in legislating food choices, is the subject of lively debates in scholarly articles and in publications aimed at the general public. To find information on her topic, Harba decided to

- search the Web to locate current news, government publications, and information from organizations that focus on issues surrounding government regulation of food
- check a library database for current peer-reviewed research articles
- use the library catalog to search for a recently published book mentioned in a blog and on several well-respected Web sites

LUISA MIRANO Luisa Mirano's topic, the limitations of medications for childhood obesity, is the subject of psychological studies as well as articles in newspapers and magazines aimed at the general public.

Thinking that both scholarly and popular works would be appropriate, Mirano decided to

- search the Web to see what issues about childhood obesity might be interesting
- refine her search to focus on medications reported in newspaper and magazine articles, advocacy Web sites, and government sites
- search specialized databases related to psychology and medicine for recent scholarly and scientific articles
- track down an article that several of her sources cited as an influential study

NED BISHOP   Ned Bishop's topic, Nathan Bedford Forrest's role in the Fort Pillow massacre, has been investigated and debated by professional historians. Given the nature of his historical topic, Bishop decided to

- locate books through the library's online catalog
- locate scholarly articles by searching a database specializing in history sources
- locate newspaper articles from 1864 by searching a historical newspaper database
- use the Web to track down additional primary documents mentioned in his sources

USING SOURCES RESPONSIBLY: Use your research log to record information for every source you read or view, especially page numbers and URLs. If you gather complete publication information from the start of your project, you'll easily find it when you need to document your sources.

R1-d Search efficiently; master a few shortcuts to finding good sources.

Most students use a combination of library databases and the Web in their research. You can save yourself a lot of time by becoming an efficient searcher.

Using the library

The Web site hosted by your college library is full of useful information. In addition to dozens of databases and links to other references, many libraries offer online subject guides as well as one-on-one help from reference librarians through e-mail or chat. You can save yourself time if you get advice from your instructor, a librarian, or your library's Web site about the best place to start your search for sources.

Savvy searchers cut down on the clutter of a broad search by adding additional search terms, limiting a search to recent publications, or clicking on a database option to look at only one type of source, such as peer-reviewed articles. When looking for books, you can broaden a catalog search by asking yourself "What kind of book might contain the information I need?" After you've identified a promising book on the library shelves, looking through the books on nearby shelves can also be valuable.

Using the Web

When using a search engine, it's a good idea to use terms that are as specific as possible and to enclose search phrases in quotation marks. You can refine your search by date or by domain; for example, *autism site:.gov* will search for information about autism on government (.gov) Web sites. Use clues in what you find (such as organizations or government agencies that seem particularly informative) to refine your search.

As you examine sites, look for "about" links to learn about the site's author or sponsoring agency. Examine URLs for clues. Those that contain .k12 may be intended for young audiences; URLs ending in .gov lead to official information from US government entities. URLs may also offer clues about the country of origin: .au for Australia, .uk for United Kingdom, .in for India, and so on. If you aren't sure where a page originated, erase everything in the URL after the first slash in your address bar; the result should be the root page of the site, which may offer useful information about the site's purpose and audience (see p. 365). Avoid sites that provide information but no explanation of who the authors are or why the site was created. They may simply be advertising platforms attracting visitors with commonly sought information that is not original or substantial. For more on evaluating Web sites, see R3-c.

Using bibliographies and citations as shortcuts

Scholarly books and articles list the works the author has cited, usually at the end. These lists are useful shortcuts to additional reliable sources on your topic. For example, most of the scholarly articles that student writer Luisa Mirano consulted contained citations to related research studies, selected by experts in the field. Through these citations, she quickly located other sources

> **MORE HELP IN YOUR HANDBOOK**
>
> Freewriting, listing, and clustering can help you come up with additional search terms.
>
> ▶ Exploring your subject: **C1-b**

CHECK URLS FOR CLUES ABOUT SPONSORSHIP

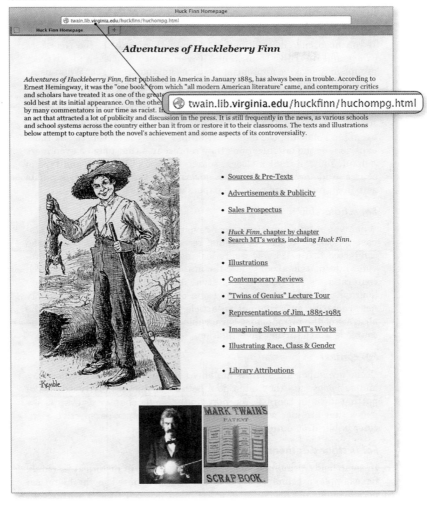

This source, from an internal page of a Web site, provides no indication of an author or a sponsor. Shortening the URL to http://twain.lib.virginia.edu/ leads to a main page that lists a university literature professor as the author and the University of Virginia Library as the sponsor.

(*Source:* Courtesy of *Mark Twain in His Times: An Electronic Archive.*)

Tips for smart searching

For currency

If you need current information, news outlets such as the *New York Times* and the BBC, think tanks, government agencies, and advocacy groups may provide appropriate sources for your research. When using Google, limit a search to the most recent year, month, week, or day.

For authority

As you search, keep an eye out for experts being cited in sources you examine. Following the citation trail may lead you to sources by those experts—or the organizations they represent—that may be even more helpful. You can limit a Google search by type of Web site and type of source. Add *site:.gov* to focus on government sources or *filetype:pdf* to zero in on reports and research papers as PDF files.

For scholarship

When you need scholarly or peer-reviewed articles, use a library database to look for reports of original research written by the people who conducted it. You'll know you're looking at a scholarly article if it provides information about where the authors work (universities, research centers), uses a formal writing style, and includes footnotes or a bibliography. Articles that are only one or two pages long are probably not scholarly. Don't rule out an article just because it's long. Read the abstract or the introductory paragraphs and the conclusion to see if the source is worth further investigation.

For context

Books are important sources in many fields such as history, philosophy, and sociology, and they often do a better job than scholarly articles of putting ideas in context. You may find a single chapter or even a few pages that are just what you need to gain a deeper perspective. Consider publication dates with your topic in mind.

For firsthand authenticity

In some fields, primary sources may be required. In historical research, for example, a primary source is one that originated in the historical period under discussion or is a firsthand account from a witness. In the sciences, a primary source (sometimes called a *primary article*) is a published report of research written by the scientist who conducted it. For more information, see page 381.

related to her topic, treatments for childhood obesity. Even popular sources such as news articles, videos, and interviews may refer to additional relevant sources that may be worth tracking down.

Using a variety of online tools and databases

You will probably find that your instructor, your librarian, or your library's Web site can be helpful in pointing you in the right direction once you have a topic and a research question. If you are still seeking some guidance about which Web sites, directories, databases, and other sources might yield useful searches, consult the e-Pages for *A Writer's Reference* (see the URL at the bottom of the page), where you will find lists of sources that might provide just the jump start you are looking for.

R1-e Conduct field research, if appropriate.

Your own field research can enhance or be the focus of a writing project. For a composition class, for example, you might want to interview a local politician about a current issue, such as the initiation of a city bike-share program. For a sociology class, you might decide to conduct a survey about campus trends in community service.

RESEARCH NOTE: Colleges and universities often require researchers to submit projects to an institutional review board (IRB) if the research involves human subjects outside a classroom setting. Before administering a survey or conducting other fieldwork, check with your instructor to see if IRB approval is required.

Interviewing

Interviews can often shed new light on a topic. Look for an expert who has firsthand knowledge of the subject, or seek out a key participant whose personal experience and expertise provide a valuable perspective.

When asking for an interview, be clear about who you are, what the purpose of the interview is, and how you would prefer to conduct it: by e-mail, over the phone, or in person. Ask questions that lead to facts, anecdotes, and opinions that will add a meaningful dimension to your paper.

USING SOURCES RESPONSIBLY: When quoting your source (the interviewee) in your paper, be accurate and fair. Do not change the meaning of your interviewee's words or take them out of context. To ensure accuracy, you might want to ask permission to record the interview or conduct it by e-mail.

Surveying opinion

For some topics, you may find it useful to survey opinions through written questionnaires, telephone or e-mail polls, or questions posted on a social media site. Many people are reluctant to fill out long questionnaires, so for a good response rate, limit your questions with your purpose in mind.

When possible, ask yes/no questions or give multiple-choice options. Surveys with such queries can be completed quickly, and the results are easy to tally. You may also want to ask a few open-ended questions to elicit more individual responses, some of which may be worth quoting in your paper.

Other field methods

Your firsthand visits to and observations of significant places, people, or events can enhance a paper in a variety of disciplines. If you aren't able to visit an organization, a company, or a historic site, you may find useful information on an official Web site or a phone number or an e-mail address to use to contact a representative.

R1-f   Write a research proposal.

One effective way to manage your research project and focus your thinking is to write a research proposal. A proposal gives you an opportunity to look back—to remind you why you decided to enter a specific research conversation—and to look forward—to predict any difficulties or obstacles that might arise during your project. Your objective is to make a case for the question you plan to explore, the sources you plan to use, and the feasibility of the project, given the time and resources available. As you take stock of your project, you also have the valuable opportunity to receive comments from your instructor and classmates about your proposed research question and search strategy.

The following format will help you organize your proposal.

- **Research question.** What question will you be exploring? Why does this question need to be asked? What do you hope to learn from the project?

- **Research conversation.** What have you learned so far about the debate or the specific research conversation you will enter? What entry point have you found to offer your own insights and ideas?

- **Search strategy.** What kinds of sources will you use to explore your question? What sources have you found most useful, and why? How will you locate a variety of sources (print and visual, primary and secondary, for example)?
- **Project challenges.** What challenges, if any, do you anticipate (locating sufficient sources, managing the project, finding a position to take)? What resources are available to help you meet these challenges?

R2 Managing information; taking notes responsibly

An effective researcher is a good record keeper. Whether you decide to keep records in your research log or in a file on your computer, you will need methods for managing information: maintaining a working bibliography (see R2-a), keeping track of source materials (see R2-b), and taking notes without plagiarizing your sources (see R2-c). (For more on avoiding plagiarism, see MLA-2 for MLA style, APA-2 for APA style, and CMS-2 for CMS style.)

R2-a Maintain a working bibliography.

Keep a record of each source you read or view. This record, called a *working bibliography*, will help you compile the list of sources that will appear at the end of your paper. The format of this list depends on the documentation style you are using (for MLA style, see MLA-4; for APA style, see APA-4; for CMS style, see CMS-4). Using the proper style in your working bibliography will ensure that you have all the information you need to correctly cite any sources you use. (See R3-e for advice on using your working bibliography as the basis for an annotated bibliography.)

Most researchers save bibliographic information from the library's catalog and databases and the Web. The information you need to collect is given in the chart on page 370. If you download a visual, you must gather the same information as for a print source.

For Web sources, some bibliographic information may not be available, but spend time looking for it before assuming that it doesn't exist. When information isn't available on the home page, you may have to follow links to interior pages. (See also pp. 366 and 383 for more details about finding bibliographic information in online sources.)

hackerhandbooks.com/writersref
e R2 Managing information > Finding research help: Choosing a documentation style

Information to collect for a working bibliography

For an entire book

- All authors; any editors or translators
- Title and subtitle
- Edition (if not the first)
- Publication information: city, publisher, and date
- Medium: print, Web, and so on
- Date you retrieved the source (for an online source)

For an article

- All authors of the article
- Title and subtitle of the article
- Title of the journal, magazine, or newspaper
- Date; volume, issue, and page numbers
- Medium: print, Web, DVD, and so on
- Date you retrieved the source (for an online source)

For an article retrieved from a database (in addition to preceding information)

- Name of the database
- Accession number or other number assigned by the database
- Digital object identifier (DOI), if there is one
- URL of the database home page or of the journal's home page if there is no DOI
- Date you retrieved the source

For a Web source (including visual, audio, and multimedia sources)

- All authors, editors, or composers of the source
- Editor or compiler of the Web source, if there is one
- Title and subtitle of the source
- Title of the longer work, if the source is contained in a longer work
- Title of the Web site
- Print publication information for the source, if available
- Online page or paragraph numbers, if the source provides them
- Date of online publication (or latest update)
- Sponsor or publisher of the site
- Date you accessed the source
- URL or permalink of the page on which the source appears

NOTE: For more details, see MLA-4b (MLA), APA-4b (APA), or CMS-4c (CMS).

USING SOURCES RESPONSIBLY: Use care when printing or saving articles in PDF files. The files themselves may not include some of the elements you need to cite the source properly, especially page numbers. You may need to record additional information from the database or Web site where you accessed the PDF file.

RESEARCH TIP: Your school may provide citation software, which automatically formats citations in any style using bibliographic information submitted by researchers. You must carefully proofread the results from these programs, however, because the citations sometimes include errors.

R2-b Keep track of source materials.

The best way to keep track of source materials is to save a copy of each potential source as you conduct your research. Many database services will allow you to e-mail, save, or print citations or full texts of articles, and you can easily download, copy, or take screen shots of information from the Web.

Working with photocopies, printouts, and electronic files—as opposed to relying on memory or hastily written notes—has several benefits. You can highlight key passages, perhaps even color-coding them to reflect topics in your outline. You can get a head start on note taking. Finally, you reduce the chances of unintentional plagiarism since you will be able to compare your use of a source in your paper with the actual source, not just with your notes.

R2-c Take notes carefully to avoid unintentional plagiarism.

When you take notes and jot down ideas, use your own words. Avoid copying passages—or cutting and pasting texts from electronic sources—without using quotation marks to indicate which words are yours and which ones you've taken from a source. Even if you half-copy the author's sentences—either by mixing the author's phrases with your own without using quotation marks, or by plugging your synonyms into the author's sentence structure—you are committing plagiarism, a serious academic offense. (For examples of this kind of plagiarism, sometimes referred to as *patchwriting*, see MLA-2, APA-2, and CMS-2.)

To take notes responsibly, make sure you understand the ideas in the source. What is the meaning of certain words? What is the argument? What is the evidence? Then, resist the temptation to look at the source as you take notes—except when you are quoting. Keep the source close by so that you can check for accuracy, but don't try to put ideas in your own words with the source's sentences in front of you. When you need to quote a source, make sure you copy the words exactly and put quotation marks around them.

For strategies for avoiding plagiarism when using sources from the Web, see pages 374–75.

USING SOURCES RESPONSIBLY: Be especially careful when using copy-and-paste functions in creating electronic files. Some researchers plagiarize their sources because they lose track of which words came from sources and which are their own. To prevent unintentional plagiarism, put quotation marks around any source text that you copy during your research.

There are three kinds of note taking: summarizing, paraphrasing, and quoting. It is good practice to keep track of exact page references for all three types of notes; you will need the page numbers later if you use the information in your paper. And it is good practice to indicate in your notes if you have summarized, paraphrased, or quoted an author's words to avoid unintentionally plagiarizing a source.

> **MORE HELP IN YOUR HANDBOOK**
>
> Annotating sources as you read them is a good way to understand the ideas of the author(s).
>
> ▶ Reading actively: **A1-a**

Summarizing without plagiarizing

A summary condenses information and captures main ideas, perhaps reducing a chapter to a short paragraph or a paragraph to a single sentence. A summary should be written in your own words; if you use phrases from the source, put them in quotation marks.

Here is a passage about marine pollution from a National Oceanic and Atmospheric Administration (NOAA) Web site. Following the passage are the student's annotations on the source—notes and questions that help him figure out the meaning—and then his summary of the passage. (The bibliographic information is recorded in MLA style.)

ORIGINAL SOURCE

A question that is often posed to the NOAA Marine Debris Program (MDP) is "How much debris is actually out there?" The MDP has recognized the need for this answer as well as the growing interest and value of citizen science. To that end, the MDP is developing and testing two types of monitoring and assessment protocols: 1) rigorous scientific survey and 2) volunteer at-sea visual survey. These types of monitoring programs are necessary in order to compare marine debris, composition, abundance, distribution, movement, and impact data on national and global scales.

—NOAA Marine Debris Program. "Efforts and Activities Related to the 'Garbage Patches.'" *Marine Debris*, 2012, pm22100.net/docs/pdf/enercoop/pollutions/noaa-plastiques.pdf.

ORIGINAL SOURCE WITH STUDENT ANNOTATIONS

A question that is often posed to the NOAA Marine Debris *⌐ by whom?* *ocean ⌐* *⌐ trash*

Program (MDP) is "How much debris is actually out there?" The

MDP has recognized the need for this answer as well as the

growing interest and value of (citizen) science. To that end, the MDP *aha*

is developing and testing two types of monitoring and assessment *ways of gathering information*

protocols: 1) rigorous scientific survey and 2) volunteer at-sea visual

survey. These types of monitoring programs are necessary in order

to compare marine debris, composition, abundance, distribution, *kinds of materials ⌐* *⌐ how much?*

movement, and impact data on national and global scales. *⌐ why it matters*

STUDENT SUMMARY

Source: NOAA Marine Debris Program. "Efforts and Activities Related to the
    'Garbage Patches.'" *Marine Debris*, 2012, pm22100.net/docs/pdf/enercoop/
    pollutions/noaa-plastiques.pdf.

Having to field citizens' questions about the size of debris fields in Earth's oceans,
the Marine Debris Program, an arm of the US National Oceanic and Atmospheric
Administration, is currently implementing methods to monitor and draw conclusions
about our oceans' patches of pollution (NOAA Marine Debris Program).

Academic English Even in the early stages of note taking, it is
important to keep in mind that in the United States written texts
are considered an author's property. (This "property" isn't a physical
object, so it is often referred to as *intellectual property*.) The author
(or the publisher) owns the language as well as any original ideas contained in the writing, whether the source is published in print or digital form. When you use another author's property in your own writing,
you are required to follow certain conventions for citing the material,
or you risk committing *plagiarism*.

Paraphrasing without plagiarizing

Like a summary, a paraphrase is written in your own words; but whereas a summary reports significant information in fewer words than the source, a paraphrase restates the information in roughly the same number of words. A successful paraphrase also uses sentence structure that's different from the original. If you retain occasional choice phrases from the source, use quotation marks so that later you will know which phrases are not your own.

USING SOURCES RESPONSIBLY: If you paraphrase a source, you must still cite the source.

As you read the following paraphrase of the original source (see p. 373), notice that the language is significantly different from that in the original.

PARAPHRASE

Source: NOAA Marine Debris Program. "Efforts and Activities Related to the 'Garbage Patches.'" *Marine Debris*, 2012, pm22100.net/docs/pdf/enercoop/pollutions/noaa-plastiques.pdf.

Citizens concerned and curious about the amount, makeup, and locations of debris patches in our oceans have been pressing NOAA's Marine Debris Program for answers. In response, the organization is preparing to implement plans and standards for expert study and nonexpert observation, both of which will yield results that will be helpful in determining the significance of the pollution problem (NOAA Marine Debris Program).

For additional practical advice on how to paraphrase, see section M6.

Using quotation marks to avoid plagiarizing

A quotation consists of the exact words from a source. In your notes, put all quoted material in quotation marks; do not assume that you will remember later which words, phrases, and passages you have quoted and which are your own. When you quote, be sure to copy the words of your source exactly, including punctuation and capitalization.

QUOTATION

Source: NOAA Marine Debris Program. "Efforts and Activities Related to the 'Garbage Patches.'" *Marine Debris*, 2012, pm22100.net/docs/pdf/enercoop/pollutions/noaa-plastiques.pdf.

The NOAA Marine Debris Program has noted that, as our oceans become increasingly polluted, surveillance is "necessary in order to compare marine debris, composition, abundance, distribution, movement, and impact data on national and global scales."

Note that because the source is from a Web site without page numbers, the in-text citation includes only the author name and not a page number.

Avoiding plagiarism from the Web

UNDERSTAND WHAT PLAGIARISM IS. When you use another author's intellectual property—language, visuals, or ideas—in your own writing without giving proper credit, you commit a kind of academic theft called *plagiarism*.

TREAT WEB SOURCES THE SAME WAY YOU TREAT PRINT SOURCES. Any language that you find on the Web must be cited, even if the material is in the public domain (which generally includes older works no longer protected by copyright law) or is publicly accessible on free sites. When you use material from Web sites sponsored by federal, state, or municipal governments (.gov sites) or by nonprofit organizations (.org sites), you must acknowledge that material, too, as intellectual property owned by those agencies.

KEEP TRACK OF WHICH WORDS COME FROM SOURCES AND WHICH ARE YOUR OWN. To prevent unintentional plagiarism when you copy and paste passages from Web sources to an electronic file, put quotation marks around any text that you have inserted into your own work. During note taking and drafting, you might use a different color font or highlighting to draw attention to text taken from sources—so that material from articles, Web sites, and other sources stands out unmistakably as someone else's words.

AVOID WEB SITES THAT BILL THEMSELVES AS "RESEARCH SERVICES" AND SELL ESSAYS. When you use Web search engines to research a topic, you will often see links to sites that appear to offer legitimate writing support but that actually sell college essays. Submitting an entire paper that you have purchased is cheating, but even using material from such a paper is considered plagiarism.

For details on avoiding plagiarism while working with sources, see MLA-2 (MLA), APA-2 (APA), and CMS-2 (CMS).

R3 Evaluating sources

You can often locate dozens or even hundreds of potential sources for your topic—far more than you will have time to read. Your challenge will be to determine what kinds of sources you need to answer your research questions and to zero in on a reasonable number of trustworthy sources. This kind of decision making is referred to as *evaluating sources*. When you evaluate a source, you make a judgment about how useful the source is to your project.

Viewing evaluation as a process

When you use sources in your writing, make a habit of evaluating, or judging the value of, those sources at each stage of your project. The following questions may help.

Evaluate as you PLAN

What kinds of sources do I need?

What do I need these sources to help me do: Define? Persuade? Inform?

Evaluate as you SEARCH

How can I find reliable sources that help me answer my research question?

Which sources will help me build my credibility as a researcher?

Evaluate as you READ

What positions do these sources take in the debate on my topic? What are their biases?

How do these sources inform my own understanding of the topic and the position I will take?

Evaluate as you WRITE

How do the sources I've chosen help me make my point?

How do my own ideas fit into the conversation on my research topic?

Evaluating sources isn't something you do in one sitting. After you do some planning, searching, and reading, for example, you may reflect on the information you have collected and conclude that you need to rethink your research question—and so you return to assessing the kinds of sources you need. You may be midway through drafting your paper when you begin to question a particular source's credibility, at which point you return to searching and reading.

R3-a Think about how sources might contribute to your writing.

How you plan to use sources will affect how you evaluate them. Not every source must directly support your thesis; sources can have other functions in a paper. They can

- provide background information or context for your topic
- explain terms or concepts that your readers might not understand

- provide evidence for your argument
- lend authority to your argument
- identify a gap or contradiction in the conversation
- offer counterarguments and alternative interpretations to your argument

As you plan your writing, you will need to think through the kinds of sources that will help you fulfill your purpose most effectively.

For examples of how student writers use sources for a variety of purposes, see MLA-1c and APA-1c.

R3-b Select sources worth your time and attention.

As you search for sources in databases, the library catalog, and search engines, you're likely to locate many more results than you can read or use. This section explains how to scan through the results for the most promising sources and how to preview them to see whether they meet your needs.

Scanning search results

As you scan through a list of search results, look for clues indicating whether a source might be useful for your purposes or not worth pursuing. You will need to use somewhat different strategies when scanning search results from a database, a library catalog, and a Web search engine.

DATABASES Most databases list at least the following information, which can help you decide if a source is relevant, current, and scholarly (see the chart on p. 380).

> The title and brief description (How relevant?)
>
> A date (How current?)
>
> The name of periodical (How scholarly?)
>
> The length (How extensive in coverage?)

> **MORE HELP IN YOUR HANDBOOK**
>
> Annotating bibliography entries can help you evaluate sources.
>
> ▶ Maintaining a working bibliography: **R2-a**
>
> ▶ Summarizing sources: **A1-c**
>
> ▶ Analyzing sources: **A1-d**
>
> ▶ Considering how sources inform your argument: **MLA-1c, APA-1c, CMS-1c**

Many databases allow you to sort your list of results by relevance or date; sorting may help you scan the information more efficiently.

LIBRARY CATALOGS The library's catalog usually lists basic information about books, periodicals, DVDs, and other material—enough to give you a first impression. As in database search results, the title and date of publication of books and other sources listed in the catalog will often be your first clues as to whether the source is worth consulting. If a title looks interesting, you can click on it for information about the subject matter and length. For books, reports, or other long sources, a table of contents may also be available.

WEB SEARCH ENGINES Reliable and unreliable sources live side-by-side online. As you scan through search results, look for the following clues about the probable relevance, currency, and reliability of a Web site.

The title, keywords, and lead-in text (How relevant?)

A date (How current?)

An indication of the site's sponsor or purpose (How reliable?)

The URL, especially the URL ending: for example, .com, .edu, .gov, or .org (How relevant? How reliable?)

Below are a few of the results that student writer Luisa Mirano retrieved after typing the keywords *childhood obesity* into a search engine; she limited her search to works with those words in the title.

Mirano found the first site, sponsored by a research-based organization, promising enough to explore for her paper. The second and fourth sites held less promise because they seemed to offer popular rather than scholarly information. In addition, the second site was full of distracting advertisements. Mirano rejected the third source not because she doubted its reliability—in fact, research from the National Institutes of Health was what she hoped to find—but because a skim of its contents revealed that the information was too general for her purposes.

EVALUATING SEARCH RESULTS: INTERNET SEARCH ENGINE

Content from a research-based organization. Promising.

> **American Obesity Association - Childhood Obesity**
> **Childhood Obesity. Obesity in children ...** Note: The term "**childhood obesity**" may refer to both **children** and adolescents. In general, we ...
> www.obesity.org/subs/childhood/ - 17k - Jan 8, 2005 - Cached - Similar pages

Popular rather than scholarly source. Not relevant.

> **Childhood Obesity**
> KS Logo, **Childhood Obesity.** advertisement. Source. ERIC Clearinghouse on Teaching and Teacher Education. Contents. ... Back to the Top Causes of **Childhood Obesity. ...**
> www.kidsource.com/kidsource/content2/obesity.html - 18k - Cached - Similar pages

Content too general. Not relevant.

> **Childhood Obesity, June 2002 Word on Health - National Institutes ...**
> **Childhood Obesity** on the Rise, an article in the June 2002 edition of The NIH Word on Health - Consumer Information Based on Research from the National ...
> www.nih.gov/news/WordonHealth/jun2002/childhoodobesity.htm - 22k - Cached - Similar pages

Popular and too general. Not relevant.

> **MayoClinic.com - Childhood obesity:** Parenting advice
> ... **Childhood obesity:** Parenting advice By Mayo Clinic staff. ... Here are some other tips to help your **obese child** — and yourself: Be a positive role model. ...
> www.mayoclinic.com/invoke.cfm?id=FL00058 - 42k - Jan 8, 2005 - Cached - Similar pages

Previewing sources

Once you have decided that a source looks promising, preview it quickly to see whether it lives up to its promise. If you can evaluate as you search, rejecting irrelevant or unreliable sources before actually reading them, you will save yourself time.

PREVIEWING AN ARTICLE

- Consider the publication in which the article is printed. Is it a scholarly journal (see the chart on p. 380)? A popular magazine? A newspaper with a national reputation?
- For a magazine or journal article, look for an abstract or a statement of purpose at the beginning; also look for a summary at the end.
- For a newspaper article, focus on the headline and the opening paragraphs for relevance.
- Scan any headings and look at any visuals—charts, graphs, diagrams, or illustrations—that might indicate the article's focus and scope.

PREVIEWING A BOOK

- Glance through the table of contents, keeping your research question in mind. Even if the entire book is not relevant, parts of it may be useful.
- Scan the preface in search of a statement of the author's purposes.
- Use the index to look up a few words related to your topic.
- If a chapter looks useful, read its opening and closing paragraphs and skim any headings.

PREVIEWING A WEB SITE

- Check to see if the sponsor is a reputable organization, a government agency, or a university. Is the group likely to look at only one side of a debatable issue?
- If you have landed on an internal page of a site and no author or sponsor is evident, try navigating to the home page, either through a link or by truncating the URL (see the tip on p. 365).
- Try to determine the purpose of the Web site. Is the site trying to sell a product? Promote an idea? Inform the public? Is the purpose consistent with your research?
- If the Web site includes statistical data (tables, graphs, charts), can you tell how and by whom the statistics were compiled? Is research cited?
- Find out when the site was created or last updated. Is it current enough for your purposes?

Determining if a source is scholarly

For many college assignments, you will be asked to use scholarly sources. These are written by experts for a knowledgeable audience and usually go into more depth than books and articles written for a general audience. (Scholarly sources are sometimes called *refereed* or *peer-reviewed* because the work is evaluated by experts in the field before publication.) To determine if a source is scholarly, look for the following:

- Formal language and presentation
- Authors who are academics or scientists
- Footnotes or a bibliography documenting the works cited by the author in the source
- Original research and interpretation (rather than a summary of other people's work)
- Quotations from and analysis of primary sources (in humanities disciplines such as literature, history, and philosophy)
- A description of research methods or a review of related research (in the sciences and social sciences)

NOTE: In some databases, searches can be limited to refereed or peer-reviewed journals.

Selecting appropriate versions of digital sources

An online source may appear as an abstract, an excerpt, or a full-text article or book. It is important to distinguish among these versions of sources and to use a complete version of a source, preferably one with page numbers, for your research.

Abstracts and excerpts are shortened versions of complete works. An abstract—a summary of a work's contents—might appear in a database record for a source and can give you clues about the usefulness of the source for your research. An excerpt is the first few sentences or paragraphs of a newspaper or magazine article and sometimes appears in a list of results from an online search. Abstracts and excerpts often provide enough information for you to determine whether the complete article would be useful for your paper. Both are brief (usually fewer than five hundred words) and generally do not contain enough information to function alone as sources in a research paper. Reading the complete article is the best way to understand the author's argument before referring to it in your own writing. A full-text work may appear online as a PDF file or as an HTML file (sometimes called a *text file*). If your source is available in both formats, choose the PDF file for your research because you will be able to cite specific page numbers.

R3-c Read with an open mind and a critical eye.

As you begin reading the sources you have chosen, keep an open mind. Do not let your personal beliefs prevent you from listening to new ideas and opposing viewpoints. Be curious about the wide range of positions in the research conversation you are entering. Your research question should guide you as you engage your sources.

When you read critically, you are examining an author's assumptions, assessing evidence, and weighing conclusions.

Reading critically means

- reading carefully (*What does the source say?*)
- reading skeptically (*Are any of the author's points or conclusions problematic?*)
- reading evaluatively (*How does this source help me make my argument?*)

To see one student's critical reading of a source text, see A1.

USING SOURCES RESPONSIBLY: Take time to read the entire source and to understand an author's arguments, assumptions, and conclusions. Try to avoid taking quotations from the first few pages of a source before you understand if the words and ideas are representative of the work as a whole.

Distinguishing between primary and secondary sources

As you begin assessing evidence in a source, determine whether you are reading a primary or a secondary source. Primary sources include original documents such as letters, diaries, films, legislative bills, laboratory studies, field research reports, and eyewitness accounts. Secondary sources are commentaries on primary sources—another writer's opinions about or interpretation of a primary source.

Although a primary source is not necessarily more reliable than a secondary source, it has the advantage of being a firsthand account. You can better evaluate what a secondary source says if you have first read any primary sources it discusses.

Being alert for signs of bias

Bias is a way of thinking, a tendency to be partial, that prevents people and publications from viewing a topic objectively. Both in print and online, some sources are more objective than others. If you are exploring the rights of organizations like WikiLeaks to distribute sensitive government documents over the Internet, for example, you may not

Evaluating all sources

Checking for signs of bias

- Does the author or publisher endorse political or religious views that could affect objectivity?
- Is the author or publisher associated with a special-interest group, such as PETA or the National Rifle Association, that might present only one side of an issue?
- Are alternative views presented and addressed? How fairly does the author treat opposing views? (See A3-c.)
- Does the author's language show signs of bias?

Assessing an argument

- What is the author's central claim or thesis?
- How does the author support this claim—with relevant and sufficient evidence or with just a few anecdotes or emotional examples?
- Are statistics consistent with those you encounter in other sources? Have they been used fairly? Does the author explain where the statistics come from?
- Are any of the author's assumptions questionable?
- Does the author consider opposing arguments and refute them persuasively? (See A4-f.)
- Does the author fall prey to any logical fallacies? (See A3-a.)

find objective, unbiased information in a US State Department report. If you are researching timber harvesting practices, you are likely to encounter bias in publications sponsored by environmental groups. As a researcher, you will need to consider any suspected bias as you assess the source. If you are uncertain about a source's special interests, seek the help of a reference librarian.

Like publishers, some authors are more objective than others. If you have reason to believe that a writer is particularly biased, you will want to assess his or her arguments with special care. For a list of questions worth asking, see the chart above.

Evaluating sources you find on the Web

Authorship

- Does the Web site or document have an author? You may need to do some hunting to find the author's name. If you have landed directly on an internal page of a site, for example, you may need to navigate to the home page or find an "about this site" link to learn the name of the author.
- If there is an author, can you tell whether he or she is knowledgeable and credible? When the author's qualifications aren't listed on the site itself, look for links to the author's home page, which may provide evidence of his or her expertise.

Sponsorship

- Who, if anyone, sponsors the site? The sponsor of a site is often named and described on the home page.
- What does the URL tell you? The URL ending often indicates the type of group hosting the site: commercial (.com), educational (.edu), nonprofit (.org), governmental (.gov), military (.mil), or network (.net). URLs may also indicate a country of origin: .uk (United Kingdom) or .jp (Japan), for instance.

Purpose and audience

- Why was the site created: To argue a position? To sell a product? To inform readers?
- Who is the site's intended audience?

Currency

- How current is the site? Check for the date of publication or the latest update, often located at the bottom of the home page or at the beginning or end of an internal page.
- How current are the site's links? If many of the links no longer work, the site may be too dated for your purposes.

Assessing the author's argument

In nearly all subjects worth writing about, there is some element of argument, so expect to encounter debates and disagreements among authors. In fact, areas of disagreement give you entry points in a research conversation. The questions in the chart on page 98 can help you weigh the strengths and weaknesses of each author's argument.

MORE HELP IN YOUR HANDBOOK

Good college writers read critically.

▶ Judging whether a source is reasonable: **A3-a**

▶ Judging whether a source is fair: **A3-c**

EVALUATING A WEB SITE: CHECKING RELIABILITY

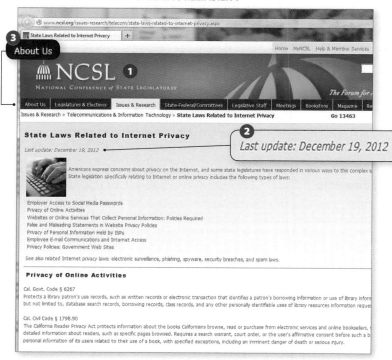

Source: Copyright © 2014 National Conference of State Legislatures.

1   This page on Internet monitoring and workplace privacy appears on a Web site sponsored by the National Conference of State Legislatures. The NCSL is a bipartisan group that functions as a clearinghouse of ideas and research of interest to state lawmakers. It is also a lobby for state issues before the US government. The URL ending .org marks this sponsor as a nonprofit organization.

2   A clear date of publication shows currency.

3   An "About Us" page confirms that this is a credible organization whose credentials can be verified.

EVALUATING A WEB SITE: CHECKING PURPOSE

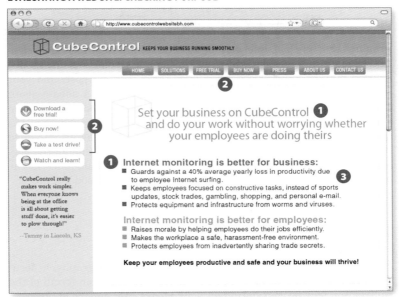

1   The site is sponsored by a company that specializes in employee-monitoring software.

2   Repeated links for trial downloads and purchase suggest the site's intended audience: consumers seeking to purchase software (probably not researchers seeking detailed information about employees' use of the Internet in the workplace).

3   The site appears to provide information and even shows statistics from studies, but ultimately the purpose of the site is to sell a product.

R3-d   Assess Web sources with special care.

Sources found on the Web can provide valuable information, but verifying their credibility may take time. Before using a Web source in your paper, make sure you know who created the material and for what purpose. Sites with reliable information can stand up to careful scrutiny. For a checklist on evaluating Web sources, see the chart on page 383.

Assessing multimodal sources with your research question in mind

You may find that, for your topic, the best sources are videos such as public service ads, interviews delivered as podcasts or blog posts, or infographics that present information as a combination of data and visuals. Though these are generally not considered scholarly sources, such sources may be appropriate given your topic, your purpose, and your audience. When student writer Sophie Harba entered a debate about the rise of chronic diseases from harmful diets, she used a graph from the US Department of Agriculture to demonstrate the dangers of the typical American diet. (Her essay begins on p. 465.) The graph added needed evidence to help answer her research question: Should the government enact laws to regulate eating choices? The guidelines in the chart on page 382 will be helpful as you evaluate multimodal sources.

R3-e Construct an annotated bibliography.

Section R2-a describes how to write a working bibliography, a document that helps you keep track of publication information for all of the sources you may be considering for your project. You may be assigned to write an annotated bibliography, a more formal document in which you summarize and evaluate those sources — at least the most promising ones. Writing brief sentences summarizing key points of a source will help you identify how the source relates to your argument and to your other sources and will help you judge whether the source is relevant and appropriate for your project. Clarifying your sources' ideas will help you separate them from your own ideas and from each other, and it will also help you move toward a draft in which you synthesize sources and present your own thesis. (See MLA-3c and APA-3c for more on synthesis.)

hackerhandbooks.com/writersref

e R3 Evaluating sources > As you write: Developing an annotated bibliography

e R3 Evaluating sources > Sample student writing

> Orlov, "Online Monitoring: A Threat to Employee Privacy in the Wired Workplace: An Annotated Bibliography" (annotated bibliography)

> Niemeyer, "Keynesian Policy: Implications for the Current U.S. Economic Crisis" (annotated bibliography)

SAMPLE ANNOTATED BIBLIOGRAPHY ENTRY (MLA STYLE)

Resnik, David. "Trans Fat Bans and Human Freedom." *American Journal of Bioethics*, vol. 10, no. 3, Mar. 2010, pp. 27-32.

Summarize the source in present tense.

Annotations should be three to seven sentences long.

In this scholarly article, bioethicist David Resnik argues that bans on unhealthy foods set a dangerous precedent to threaten our personal freedom. He claims that researchers don't have enough evidence to know whether banning trans fats will save lives or money; all we know is that such bans restrict dietary choices. Resnik explains why most Americans oppose food restrictions, noting our multiethnic heritage and regional traditions, as well as our desire for the freedom to choose our own food, even food with long-term health risks. The author acknowledges that few people would probably miss eating trans fats if they were banned entirely, but he fears that such bans would be a slippery slope and could lead to further restrictions on products such as red meat and sugary sodas, which are also known to have harmful effects. Resnik, a bioethicist, offers a well-reasoned argument, but he goes too far by insisting that all proposed food restrictions will do more harm than good. This article contributes important perspectives on why many Americans see government legislation as unreasonable and provides counterarguments to other sources that claim it would be unreasonable not to enact legislation to advance public health.

Evaluate the source for bias and relevance.

Evaluate the source for its contribution to the research project.

Writing guide | Annotated bibliography

An **annotated bibliography** gives you an opportunity to summarize, evaluate, and record publication information for your sources before drafting your research paper. You summarize each source to understand its main ideas; you evaluate each source for accuracy, quality, and relevance. Finally, you reflect, asking yourself how the source will contribute to your research project. A sample annotated bibliography entry appears on page 387.

Key features

- **A list of sources arranged in alphabetical order by author** includes complete bibliographic information for each source.

- **A brief entry for each source** is typically one hundred to two hundred words.

- **A summary** of each source states the work's main ideas and key points briefly and accurately. The summary is written in the third person and the present tense. Summarizing helps you test your understanding of a source and convey its meaning responsibly.

- **An evaluation** of the source's role and usefulness in your project includes an assessment of the source's strengths and limitations, the author's qualifications and expertise, and the function of the source in your project. Evaluating a source helps you analyze how the source fits into your project and separate the source's ideas from your own.

Thinking ahead: Presenting or publishing

You may be asked to submit your annotated bibliography electronically. If this is the case, and if any of your sources are from the Web, you may want to include links to the sources directly in your annotated bibliography.

Writing your annotated bibliography

 EXPLORE

For each source, begin by brainstorming responses to questions such as the following.

- What is the purpose of the source? Who is the author's intended audience?

- What is the author's thesis? What evidence supports the thesis?

- What qualifications and expertise does the author bring? Does the author have any biases or make any questionable assumptions?

- Why do you think this source is useful for your project?

- How does this source relate to the other sources in your bibliography?

DRAFT

- Arrange the sources in alphabetical order by author (or by title for works with no author).
- Provide consistent bibliographic information for each source. For the exact bibliographic format, see MLA-4b (MLA), APA-4b (APA), or CMS-4c (CMS).
- Start your summary by identifying the thesis and purpose of the source as well as the credentials of the source's author.
- Keep your research question in mind. How does this source contribute to your project? How does it help you take your place in the conversation?

REVISE

Ask reviewers for specific feedback. Here are some questions to guide their comments.

- Is each source summarized clearly? Have you identified the author's main idea?
- For each source, have you made a clear judgment about how and why the source is useful for your project?
- Have you used quotation marks around exact words from a source?

MLA

MLA Papers

MLA MLA Papers

Directory to MLA in-text citation models

Directory to MLA works cited models

Directory to MLA works cited models, *continued*

MLA Papers

Most English instructors and some humanities instructors will ask you to document your sources with the Modern Language Association (MLA) system of citations described in MLA-4. When writing an MLA paper that is based on sources, you face three main challenges: (1) supporting a thesis, (2) citing your sources and avoiding plagiarism, and (3) integrating quotations and other source material.

Examples in this tabbed section are drawn from one student's research about the role of government in legislating food choices. Sophie Harba's research paper, in which she argues that state governments have the responsibility to advance health policies and to regulate healthy eating choices, appears on pages 465–70.

MLA-1 | Supporting a thesis

Most research assignments ask you to form a thesis, or main idea, and to support that thesis with well-organized evidence. A working thesis will help you focus your project but remain flexible as you draft and revise your thesis. Research is an ongoing process; your ideas and your working thesis will evolve as you learn more about your topic.

MLA-1a Form a working thesis.

Once you have read a variety of sources, considered your issue from different perspectives, and chosen an entry point in the research conversation (see R1-b), you are ready to form a working thesis: a one-sentence (or occasionally a two-sentence) statement of your central idea (see also C2-a). Because it is a working, or tentative, thesis, it is flexible enough to change as your ideas develop.

In a research paper, your thesis will answer the central research question you pose (see R1-b). Here, for example, are student writer Sophie Harba's research question and working thesis.

RESEARCH QUESTION

Should the government enact laws to regulate healthy eating choices?

WORKING THESIS

Government has the responsibility to regulate healthy eating choices because of the rise of chronic diseases.

After you have written a rough draft and perhaps done more reading, you may decide to revise your thesis, as Harba did, to give it a sharper and more specific focus.

REVISED THESIS

In the name of public health and safety, state governments have the responsibility to shape health policies and to regulate healthy eating choices, especially since doing so offers a potentially large social benefit for a relatively small cost.

hackerhandbooks.com/writersref

e MLA-1 Supporting a thesis > Exercises: MLA 1–1 and MLA 1–2

The thesis usually appears at the end of the introductory paragraph. To read Sophie Harba's thesis in the context of her introduction, see page 465.

MLA-1b Organize ideas with a rough outline.

The body of your paper will consist of evidence in support of your thesis. It will be useful to sketch an informal plan that helps you begin to organize your ideas. Sophie Harba, for example, used this simple plan to outline the structure of her argument.

- Debates about the government's role in regulating food have a long history in the United States.

> **MORE HELP IN YOUR HANDBOOK**
>
> It's helpful to start off with a working thesis that answers your research question. A thesis should also stand up to the "So what?" test.
>
> ▶ Drafting a working thesis: **C1-c**

- Some experts argue that we should focus on the dangers arising from unhealthy eating habits and on preventing chronic diseases linked to diet.
- But food regulations are not a popular solution because most Americans object to any loss of personal choice.
- Laws designed to prevent chronic disease have enormous health benefits and don't ask Americans to give up their freedom; they ask Americans to see health as a matter of public good.

After you have written a rough draft, a more formal outline can be a useful way to shape the complexities of your argument. See C1-d for an example.

MLA-1c Use sources to inform and support your argument.

Used thoughtfully, the source materials you have gathered will make your argument more complex and convincing for readers. Sources can play several different roles as you develop your points.

Providing background information or context

You can use facts and statistics to support generalizations or to emphasize the importance of your topic, as student writer Sophie Harba does to demonstrate the large social benefits of laws designed to prevent chronic disease.

To give just one example, Marion Nestle, New York University professor of nutrition and public health, notes that "a 1% reduction in intake of saturated fat across the population would prevent more than 30,000 cases of coronary heart disease annually and save more than a billion dollars in health care costs" (7).

Explaining terms or concepts

If readers are unfamiliar with a word or an idea important to your topic, you must explain it for them; or if your argument depends on a key term with multiple connotations, you must explain your use of the term. Quoting or paraphrasing a source can help you define terms and concepts in accessible language. Harba defines the term *refined grains* as part of her claim that the typical American diet is getting less healthy over time.

> A diet that is low in nutritional value and high in sugars, fats, and refined grains—grains that have been processed to increase shelf life but that contain little fiber, iron, and B vitamins—can be damaging over time (United States, Dept. of Agriculture and Dept. of Health and Human Services 36).

Supporting your claims

As you draft your argument, make sure to back up your assertions with facts, examples, and other evidence from your research. (See also A4-e.) Harba, for example, uses factual evidence to make the point that the typical American diet is damaging.

> Michael Pollan, who has written extensively about Americans' unhealthy eating habits, notes that "[t]he Centers for Disease Control estimates that fully three quarters of US health care spending goes to treat chronic diseases, most of which are preventable and linked to diet: heart disease, stroke, type 2 diabetes, and at least a third of all cancers."

Lending authority to your argument

Expert opinion can give weight to your argument. (See also A4-e.) But don't rely on experts to make your argument for you. Construct your argument in your own words and, when appropriate, cite the judgment of an authority in the field to support your position.

> Debates surrounding the government's role in regulating food have a long history in the United States. According to Lorine Goodwin, a food historian, nineteenth-century reformers who sought to purify the food supply were called "fanatics" and "radicals" by critics who argued that consumers should be free to buy and eat what they want (77).

Anticipating and countering objections

Do not ignore sources that seem contrary to your position or that offer arguments different from your own. Instead, use them to give voice to opposing points of view and to state potential objections to your argument before you counter them (see A-4f). By anticipating her readers' argument that many Americans oppose laws to limit what they eat, Sophie Harba creates an opportunity to counter that objection and build common ground with her readers.

> Why is the public largely resistant to laws that would limit unhealthy choices or penalize those choices with so-called fat taxes? Many consumers and civil rights advocates find such laws to be an unreasonable restriction on individual freedom of choice. As health policy experts Mello et al. point out, opposition to food and beverage regulation is similar to the opposition to early tobacco legislation: the public views the issue as one of personal responsibility rather than one requiring government intervention (2602). In other words, if a person eats unhealthy food and becomes ill as a result, that is his or her choice. But those who favor legislation claim that freedom of choice is a myth because of the strong influence of food and beverage industry marketing on consumers' dietary habits.

MLA-2 | Citing sources; avoiding plagiarism

In a research paper, you will draw on the work of other writers, and you must document their contributions by citing your sources. Sources are cited for two reasons:

1. to tell readers where your information comes from—so that they can assess its reliability and, if interested, find and read the original source
2. to give credit to the writers from whom you have borrowed words and ideas

Borrowing another writer's language, sentence structures, or ideas without proper acknowledgment is a form of dishonesty known as *plagiarism.*

The only exception is common knowledge—information that your readers may know or could easily locate in any number of reference sources. For example, a quick search would tell you that Joel Coen directed *Fargo* in 1996 and that Emily Dickinson published only a handful of her many poems during her lifetime. As a rule, when you have seen information repeatedly in your reading, you don't need to cite it.

MLA-2a Understand how the MLA system works.

Here, briefly, is how the MLA citation system usually works. (See MLA-4 for more details and model citations.)

1. The source is introduced by a signal phrase that names its author.
2. The material being cited is followed by a page number in parentheses (unless the source is an unpaginated Web source).
3. At the end of the paper, a list of works cited (arranged alphabetically by authors' last names) gives complete publication information for the source.

IN-TEXT CITATION

Bioethicist David Resnik emphasizes that such policies, despite their potential to make our society healthier, "open the door to excessive government control over food, which could restrict dietary choices, interfere with cultural, ethnic, and religious traditions, and exacerbate socioeconomic inequalities" (31).

ENTRY IN THE LIST OF WORKS CITED

Resnik, David. "Trans Fat Bans and Human Freedom." *American Journal of Bioethics*, vol. 10, no. 3, Mar. 2010, pp. 27-32.

This basic MLA format varies for different types of sources. For a detailed discussion and other models, see MLA-4.

MLA-2b Understand what plagiarism is.

Your research paper represents your ideas in conversation with the ideas in your sources. To be fair and responsible, you must acknowledge your debt to the writers of those sources. If you don't, you commit plagiarism, a serious academic offense. (See also R2-c.)

In general, these three acts are considered plagiarism: (1) failing to cite quotations and borrowed ideas, (2) failing to enclose borrowed language in quotation marks, and (3) failing to put summaries and paraphrases in your own words. Definitions of plagiarism may vary; it's a good idea to find out how your school defines academic dishonesty.

MORE HELP IN YOUR HANDBOOK

When you use exact language from a source, you need to show that it is a quotation.

► Quotation marks for direct quotations: **P5-a**

MLA-2c Use quotation marks around borrowed language.

To indicate that you are using a source's exact phrases or sentences, you must enclose them in quotation marks unless they have been set off from the text by indenting (see p. 405). To omit the quotation marks is to claim—falsely—that the language is your own, as in the example below. Such an omission is plagiarism even if you have cited the source.

ORIGINAL SOURCE

Although these policies may have a positive impact on human health, they open the door to excessive government control over food, which could restrict dietary choices, interfere with cultural, ethnic, and religious traditions, and exacerbate socioeconomic inequalities.
— David Resnik, "Trans Fat Bans and Human Freedom," p. 31

PLAGIARISM

Bioethicist David Resnik points out that government policies to ban trans fats may have a positive impact on human health, but they open the door to excessive government control over food, which could restrict dietary choices and interfere with cultural, ethnic, and religious traditions (31).

BORROWED LANGUAGE IN QUOTATION MARKS

Bioethicist David Resnik emphasizes that government policies to ban trans fats, despite their potential to make our society healthier, "open the door to excessive government control over food, which could restrict dietary choices, interfere with cultural, ethnic, and religious traditions, and exacerbate socioeconomic inequalities" (31).

MLA-2d Put summaries and paraphrases in your own words.

Summaries and paraphrases are written in your own words. A summary condenses information from a source; a paraphrase uses roughly the same number of words as the original source to convey the information. When you summarize or paraphrase, it is not enough to name the source; you must restate the source's meaning using your own language. (See also R2-c and, if English is not your first language, M6.) You commit plagiarism if you patchwrite—half-copy the author's sentences, either by mixing the author's phrases with your own without using quotation marks or by plugging your synonyms into the author's sentence structure.

The first paraphrase of the following source is plagiarized. Even though the source is cited, too much of its language is borrowed from the original. The highlighted strings of words have been copied exactly (without quotation marks). In addition, the writer has closely echoed the sentence structure of the source, merely substituting some synonyms (*interfere with lifestyle choices* for *paternalistic intervention into lifestyle choices* and *decrease the feeling of personal responsibility* for *enfeeble the notion of personal responsibility*).

ORIGINAL SOURCE

[A]ntiobesity laws encounter strong opposition from some quarters on the grounds that they constitute paternalistic intervention into lifestyle choices and enfeeble the notion of personal responsibility. Such arguments echo those made in the early days of tobacco regulation.
— Michelle M. Mello et al., "Obesity—the New Frontier of Public Health Law," p. 2602

PLAGIARISM: UNACCEPTABLE BORROWING

Health policy experts Mello et al. argue that antiobesity laws encounter strong opposition from some people because they interfere with lifestyle choices and decrease the feeling of personal responsibility. These arguments mirror those made in the early days of tobacco regulation (2602).

To avoid plagiarizing an author's language, resist the temptation to look at the source while you are summarizing or paraphrasing. After you have read the passage you want to paraphrase, set the source aside. Ask yourself, "What is the author's meaning?" In your own words, state your understanding of the author's basic point. Return to the source and check that you haven't used the author's language or sentence structure or misrepresented the author's ideas. Following these steps will help you avoid plagiarizing the source. When you fully understand another writer's meaning, you can more easily and accurately present those ideas in your own words.

ACCEPTABLE PARAPHRASE

As health policy experts Mello et al. point out, opposition to food and beverage regulation is similar to the opposition to early tobacco legislation: the public views the issue as one of personal responsibility rather than one requiring government intervention (2602).

WHEN TO USE A PARAPHRASE

- When the ideas and information are important but the author's exact words are not necessary or expressive

- When you want to restate the source's ideas in your own words
- When you need to simplify and explain a technical or complicated source
- When you need to reorder a source's ideas

WHEN TO USE A SUMMARY

- When a passage is lengthy and you want to condense a chapter to a short paragraph or a paragraph to a single sentence
- When you want to state the source's main ideas simply and briefly in your own words
- When you want to compare or contrast arguments or ideas from various sources
- When you want to provide readers with an understanding of the source's argument before you respond to it or launch your own

MLA-3 Integrating sources

Quotations, summaries, paraphrases, and facts will help you develop your argument, but they cannot speak for you. You can use several strategies to integrate information from research sources into your paper while maintaining your own voice.

- Use sources as concisely as possible so that your own thinking and voice aren't lost (MLA-3a).
- Avoid dropping quotations into your paper without indicating the boundary between your words and the source's words (MLA-3b).
- Integrate sources to show readers how each source supports your argument and how the sources relate to one another (MLA-3c).

MLA-3a Use quotations appropriately.

In your academic writing, keep the emphasis on your ideas and your language; use your own words to summarize and to paraphrase your sources and to explain your points. Sometimes, however, quotations can be the most effective way to integrate a source's ideas.

WHEN TO USE QUOTATIONS

- When language is especially vivid or expressive
- When exact wording is needed for technical accuracy
- When it is important to let the debaters of an issue explain their positions in their own words
- When the words of an authority lend weight to an argument
- When the language of a source is the topic of your discussion (as in an analysis or interpretation)

Limiting your use of quotations

Although it is tempting to insert many quotations in your paper and to use your own words only for connecting passages, do not quote excessively.

It is not always necessary to quote full sentences from a source. To reduce your reliance on the words of others, you can often integrate language from a source into your own sentence structure. (For the use of signal phrases in integrating quotations, see MLA-3b.)

> Resnik acknowledges that his argument relies on "slippery slope" thinking, but he insists that "social and political pressures" regarding food regulations make his concerns valid (31).

Using the ellipsis mark and brackets

Two useful marks of punctuation, the ellipsis mark and brackets, allow you to keep quoted material to a minimum and to integrate it smoothly into your text.

The ellipsis mark   To condense a quoted passage, you can use the ellipsis mark (three periods, with spaces between) to indicate that you have left words out. What remains must be grammatically complete.

> And in Mississippi, legislators passed "a ban on bans—a law that forbids . . . local restrictions on food or drink" (Conly A23).

The writer has omitted the words *municipalities to place* before *local restrictions* to condense the quoted material.

On the rare occasions when you want to leave out one or more full sentences, use a period before the three ellipsis dots.

> Legal scholars Gostin and Gostin argue that "individuals have limited willpower to defer immediate gratification for longer-term health benefits. . . . A person understands that high-fat foods or a sedentary lifestyle will cause adverse health effects, or that excessive spending or gambling will cause financial hardship, but it is not always easy to refrain" (217).

Ordinarily, do not use an ellipsis mark at the beginning or at the end of a quotation. Your readers will understand that the quoted material is taken from a longer passage, so such marks are not necessary. The only exception occurs when you have dropped words at the end of the final quoted sentence. In such cases, put three ellipsis dots before the closing quotation mark and parenthetical reference.

USING SOURCES RESPONSIBLY: Make sure omissions and ellipsis marks do not distort the meaning of your source.

Brackets Brackets allow you to insert your own words into quoted material. You can insert words in brackets to clarify a confusing reference or to keep a sentence grammatical in your context. You also use brackets to indicate that you are changing a letter from capital to lowercase (or vice versa) to fit into your sentence. In the following example, the writer inserted words in brackets to clarify the meaning of *help*.

> Neergaard and Agiesta argue that "a new poll finds people are split on how much the government should do to help [find solutions to the national health crisis]— and most draw the line at attempts to force healthier eating."

To indicate an error such as a misspelling in a quotation, insert the word "sic" in brackets right after the error.

> "While Americans of every race, gender and ethnicity are affected by this disease, diabetes disproportionately effects [sic] minority populations."

Setting off long quotations

When you quote more than four typed lines of prose or more than three lines of poetry, set off the quotation by indenting it one-half inch from the left margin.

Long quotations should be introduced by an informative sentence, usually followed by a colon. Quotation marks are unnecessary because the indented format tells readers that the passage is taken word-for-word from the source.

> In response to critics who claim that laws aimed at stopping us from eating whatever we want are an assault on our freedom of choice, Conly offers a persuasive counterargument:
>
>> [L]aws aren't designed for each one of us individually. Some of us can drive safely at 90 miles per hour, but we're bound by the same laws as the people who can't, because individual speeding laws aren't practical. Giving up a little liberty is something we agree to when we agree to live in a democratic society that is governed by laws. (A23)

Notice that at the end of an indented quotation the parenthetical citation goes outside the final mark of punctuation. (When a quotation is run into your text, the opposite is true. See the sample citations on p. 404.)

MLA-3b   Use signal phrases to integrate sources.

Whenever you include a paraphrase, summary, or direct quotation of another writer's work in your paper, prepare your readers for it with introductory words called a *signal phrase*. A signal phrase usually names the author of the source and often provides some context for the source material.

When you write a signal phrase, choose a verb that is appropriate for the way you are using the source (see MLA-1c). Are you providing background, explaining a concept, supporting a claim, lending authority, or refuting a belief? See the chart below for a list of verbs commonly used in signal phrases.

Using signal phrases in MLA papers

To avoid monotony, try to vary both the language and the placement of your signal phrases.

Model signal phrases

Michael Pollan, who has written extensively about Americans' unhealthy eating habits, argues that ". . ."

As health policy experts Mello et al. point out, ". . ."

Marion Nestle, New York University professor of nutrition and public health, notes . . .

Bioethicist David Resnik acknowledges that his argument . . .

Conly offers a persuasive counterargument: ". . ."

Verbs in signal phrases

acknowledges	comments	endorses	reasons
adds	compares	grants	refutes
admits	confirms	illustrates	rejects
agrees	contends	implies	reports
argues	declares	insists	responds
asserts	denies	notes	suggests
believes	disputes	observes	thinks
claims	emphasizes	points out	writes

Note that MLA style calls for verbs in the present or present perfect tense (*argues* or *has argued*) to introduce source material unless you include a date that specifies the time of the original author's writing.

Marking boundaries

Readers need to move from your words to the words of a source without feeling a jolt. Avoid dropping quotations into the text without warning. Instead, provide clear signal phrases, including at least the author's name, to indicate the boundary between your words and the source's words. (The signal phrase is highlighted in the second example.)

DROPPED QUOTATION

Laws designed to prevent chronic disease by promoting healthier food and beverage consumption also have potentially enormous benefits. "[A] 1% reduction in intake of saturated fat across the population would prevent more than 30,000 cases of coronary heart disease annually and would save more than a billion dollars in health care costs" (Nestle 7).

QUOTATION WITH SIGNAL PHRASE

Laws designed to prevent chronic disease by promoting healthier food and beverage consumption also have potentially enormous benefits. To give just one example, Marion Nestle, New York University professor of nutrition and public health, notes that "a 1% reduction in intake of saturated fat across the population would prevent more than 30,000 cases of coronary heart disease annually and would save more than a billion dollars in health care costs" (7).

Establishing authority

Good research writers use evidence from reliable sources. The first time you mention a source, include in the signal phrase the author's title, credentials, or experience—anything that would help your readers recognize the source's authority. (Signal phrases are highlighted in the next two examples.)

SOURCE WITH NO CREDENTIALS

Michael Pollan notes that "[t]he Centers for Disease Control estimates that fully three quarters of US health care spending goes to treat chronic diseases, most of which are preventable and linked to diet: heart disease, stroke, type 2 diabetes, and at least a third of all cancers."

SOURCE WITH CREDENTIALS

Michael Pollan, who has written extensively about Americans' unhealthy eating habits, notes that "[t]he Centers for Disease Control estimates that fully three quarters of US health care spending goes to treat chronic diseases, most of which are preventable and linked to diet: heart disease, stroke, type 2 diabetes, and at least a third of all cancers."

USING SOURCES RESPONSIBLY: When you establish a source's authority, you also signal to readers your own credibility as a responsible researcher who has located trustworthy sources.

Introducing summaries and paraphrases

Introduce most summaries and paraphrases with a signal phrase that names the author and places the material in the context of your argument. Readers will then understand that everything between the signal phrase and the parenthetical citation summarizes or paraphrases the cited source.

Without the signal phrase (highlighted) in the following example, readers might think that only the quotation at the end is being cited, when in fact the whole paragraph is based on the source.

To improve public health, advocates such as Bowdoin College philosophy professor Sarah Conly contend that it is the government's duty to prevent people from making harmful choices whenever feasible and whenever public benefits outweigh the costs. In response to critics who claim that laws aimed at stopping us from eating whatever we want are an assault on our freedom of choice, Conly asserts that "laws aren't designed for each one of us individually" (A23).

There are times when a summary or a paraphrase does not require a signal phrase naming the author. When the context makes clear where the cited material begins, you may omit the signal phrase and include the author's last name in parentheses.

Using signal phrases with statistics and other facts

When you cite a statistic or another specific fact, a signal phrase is often not necessary. Readers usually will understand that the citation refers to the statistic or fact (not the whole paragraph).

Seventy-five percent of Americans are opposed to laws that restrict or put limitations on access to unhealthy foods (Neergaard and Agiesta).

There is nothing wrong, however, with using a signal phrase to introduce a statistic or another fact.

Putting source material in context

Readers should not have to guess why source material appears in your paper. A signal phrase can help you make the connection between your own ideas and those of another writer by clarifying how the source will contribute to your paper (see R3-a).

If you use another writer's words, you must explain how they relate to your argument. Since quotations don't speak for themselves, you must create a context (highlighted) for readers by embedding each quotation between sentences of your own: introduce the quotation with a signal phrase, and follow it with interpretive comments that link the quotation to your paper's argument (see also MLA-3c).

QUOTATION WITH EFFECTIVE CONTEXT

In response to critics who claim that laws aimed at stopping us from eating whatever we want are an assault on our freedom of choice, Conly offers a persuasive counterargument:

> [L]aws aren't designed for each one of us individually. Some of us can drive safely at 90 miles per hour, but we're bound by the same laws as the people who can't, because individual speeding laws aren't practical. Giving up a little liberty is something we agree to when we agree to live in a democratic society that is governed by laws. (A23)

As Conly suggests, we need to change our either/or thinking (either we have complete freedom of choice *or* we have government regulations and lose our freedom) and instead need to see health as a matter of public good, not individual liberty.

MLA-3c Synthesize sources.

When you synthesize multiple sources in a research paper, you create a conversation about your research topic. You show readers that your argument is based on your active analysis and integration of ideas, not just a series of quotations and paraphrases. Your synthesis will show how your sources relate to one another. Not every source has to "speak" to another in a research paper, but readers should be able to see how each one functions in your argument (see R3-a).

Considering how sources relate to your argument

Before you integrate sources and show readers how they relate to one another, consider how each one might contribute to your own argument. As student writer Sophie Harba became more informed about her research topic, she asked herself these questions: *What have I learned from my sources? Which sources might support my ideas or illustrate the points I want to make? What common counterarguments do I need to address to strengthen my position?* She annotated a passage from one of her sources—a nonprofit group's assertion that our choices about food are skewed by marketing messages.

STUDENT NOTES ON A SOURCE

Useful factual information ⟶
The food and beverage industry spends approximately $2 billion per year marketing to children. —"Facts on Junk Food"
Could use this to counter the personal choice point in Mello et al.

Placing sources in conversation

You can show readers how the ideas of one source relate to those of another by connecting and analyzing the ideas in your own voice. After all, you've done the research and thought through the issues, so you should control the conversation. When you effectively synthesize sources, the thread of your argument should be easy to identify and to understand, with or without your sources.

SAMPLE SYNTHESIS

Student writer Sophie Harba sets up her synthesis with a question.

> Why is the public largely resistant to laws that would limit unhealthy choices or penalize those choices with so-called fat taxes? Many consumers and civil rights advocates find such laws to be an unreasonable restriction on individual freedom of choice. As health

Student writer

Signal phrase indicates how the source contributes to Harba's argument and shows that the idea that follows is not her own.

> policy experts Mello et al. point out, opposition to food and beverage regulation is similar to the opposition to early tobacco legislation: the public views the issue as one of personal responsibility rather than one requiring government intervention (2602). In other words, if a

Source 1

Harba interprets a paraphrased source.

Harba presents a fair-minded counterposition to her argument.

> person eats unhealthy food and becomes ill as a result, that is his or her choice. But those who favor legislation claim that freedom of choice is a myth because of the strong influence of food and beverage industry marketing on consumers' dietary habits. According to one nonprofit health advocacy group, food and beverage companies spend roughly two billion dollars per year marketing directly to children. As a result, kids see nearly four

Student writer

Source 2

thousand ads per year encouraging them to eat
unhealthy food and drinks ("Facts"). As was the case
with antismoking laws passed in recent decades, taxes
and legal restrictions on junk food sales could help to
counter the strong marketing messages that promote
unhealthy products.

Student writer

Another
example
extends the
argument;
Harba follows
the source
with a closing
thought of her
own.

The United States has a history of state and local
public health laws that have successfully promoted a
particular behavior by punishing an undesirable behavior.
The decline in tobacco use as a result of antismoking taxes
and laws is perhaps the most obvious example. Another
example is legislation requiring the use of seat belts,
which have significantly reduced fatalities in car crashes.
One government agency reports that seat belt use saved
an average of more than fourteen thousand lives per year
in the United States between 2000 and 2010 (United
States, Dept. of Transportation, Natl. Highway Traffic
Safety Administration 231). Perhaps seat belt laws have
public support because the cost of wearing a seat belt is
small, especially when compared with the benefit of
saving fourteen thousand lives per year.

Source 3

Student writer

In this synthesis, Harba uses her own analysis to shape the conversation among her sources. She does not simply string quotations together or allow them to overwhelm her writing. She guides her readers through a conversation about a variety of laws that could promote and have promoted public health. She finds points of intersection among her sources, acknowledges the contributions of others in the research conversation, and shows readers, in her own voice, how the various sources support her argument.

When synthesizing sources, ask yourself the following questions:

- Which sources inform, support, or extend your argument?
- Have you varied the function of sources—to provide background, to explain concepts, to lend authority, and to anticipate counterarguments?
- Do you explain how your sources support your argument?
- Do you connect and analyze sources in your own voice?
- Is your own argument easy to identify and to understand, with or without your sources?

Reviewing an MLA paper: Use of sources

Use of quotations

- Have you used quotation marks around quoted material (unless it has been set off from the text)? (See MLA-2c.)
- Have you checked that quoted language is word-for-word accurate? If it is not, do ellipsis marks or brackets indicate the omissions or changes? (See pp. 404–05.)
- Does a clear signal phrase (usually naming the author) prepare readers for each quotation and for the purpose the quotation serves? (See MLA-3b.)
- Does a parenthetical citation follow each quotation? (See MLA-4a.)
- Is each quotation put in context? (See p. 409.)

Use of summaries and paraphrases

- Are summaries and paraphrases free of plagiarized wording—not copied or half-copied from the source? (See MLA-2d.)
- Are summaries and paraphrases documented with parenthetical citations? (See MLA-4a.)
- Do readers know where the cited material begins? In other words, does a signal phrase mark the boundary between your words and the summary or paraphrase? Or does the context alone make clear exactly what you are citing? (See MLA-3b.)
- Does a signal phrase prepare readers for the purpose the summary or paraphrase has in your argument?

Use of statistics and other facts

- Are statistics and facts (other than common knowledge) documented with parenthetical citations? (See p. 399.)
- If there is no signal phrase, will readers understand exactly which facts are being cited? (See MLA-3b.)

MLA-4 | Documenting sources

In English and other humanities classes, you may be asked to use the MLA (Modern Language Association) system for documenting sources, which is set forth in the *MLA Handbook*, 8th edition (MLA, 2016).

MLA recommends in-text citations that refer readers to a list of works cited. A typical in-text citation names the author of the source, often in a signal phrase, and gives a page number in parentheses. At the end of the paper, the list of works cited provides publication information about the source; the list is alphabetized by authors' last names (or by titles for works without authors). There is a direct connection between the in-text citation and the alphabetical listing. In the following example, that connection is highlighted in orange.

> **MORE HELP IN YOUR HANDBOOK**
>
> A works cited list includes all the sources cited in the text of a paper.
>
> ▶ MLA works cited list: **MLA-4b**
>
> ▶ Preparing the list of works cited: **MLA-5a**
>
> ▶ Sample lists of works cited: pages **60, 470**

IN-TEXT CITATION

Bioethicist David Resnik emphasizes that such policies, despite their potential to make our society healthier, "open the door to excessive government control over food, which could restrict dietary choices, interfere with cultural, ethnic, and religious traditions, and exacerbate socioeconomic inequalities" (31).

ENTRY IN THE LIST OF WORKS CITED

Resnik, David. "Trans Fat Bans and Human Freedom." *American Journal of Bioethics*, vol. 10, no. 3, Mar. 2010, pp. 27-32.

For a list of works cited that includes this entry, see page 470.

MLA-4a MLA in-text citations

MLA in-text citations are made with a combination of signal phrases and parenthetical references. A signal phrase introduces information taken from a source (a quotation, summary, paraphrase, or fact); usually the signal phrase includes the author's name. The parenthetical reference comes after the cited material, often at the end of the sentence. It includes at least a page number (except for unpaginated sources, such as those found on the Web). In the models in MLA-4a, the elements of the in-text citation are highlighted in orange.

IN-TEXT CITATION

Resnik acknowledges that his argument relies on "slippery slope" thinking, but he insists that "social and political pressures" regarding food regulation make his concerns valid (31).

Readers can look up the author's last name in the alphabetized list of works cited, where they will learn the work's title and other publication information. If readers decide to consult the source, the page number will take them straight to the passage that has been cited.

General guidelines for signal phrases and page numbers

Items 1–5 explain how the MLA system usually works for all sources—in print, on the Web, in other media, and with or without authors and page numbers. Items 6–27 give variations on the basic guidelines.

1. Author named in a signal phrase Ordinarily, introduce the material being cited with a signal phrase that includes the author's name. In addition to preparing readers for the source, the signal phrase allows you to keep the parenthetical citation brief.

> According to Lorine Goodwin, a food historian, nineteenth-century reformers
> who sought to purify the food supply were called "fanatics" and "radicals" by critics
> who argued that consumers should be free to buy and eat what they want (77).

The signal phrase—*According to Lorine Goodwin*—names the author; the parenthetical citation gives the page number of the book in which the quoted words may be found.

Notice that the period follows the parenthetical citation. When a quotation ends with a question mark or an exclamation point, leave the end punctuation inside the quotation mark and add a period at the end of your sentence.

> Burgess asks a critical question: "How can we think differently about food
> labeling?" (51).

2. Author named in parentheses If you do not give the author's name in a signal phrase, put the last name in parentheses along with the page number (if the source has one). Use no punctuation between the name and the page number: (Moran 351).

> According to a nationwide poll, 75% of Americans are opposed to laws that restrict
> or put limitations on access to unhealthy foods (Neergaard and Agiesta).

3. Author unknown If a source has no author, the works cited entry will begin with the title. In your in-text citation, either use the complete title in a signal phrase or use a short form of the title in parentheses. Titles of books and other long works are italicized; titles of articles and other short works are put in quotation marks (see also p. 463).

As a result, kids see nearly four thousand ads per year encouraging them to eat unhealthy food and drinks ("Facts").

NOTE: If the author is a corporation or a government agency, see items 8 and 17 on pages 416 and 419, respectively.

4. Page number unknown Do not include the page number if a work lacks page numbers, as is the case with many Web sources. Do not use page numbers from a printout from a Web site. (When the pages of a Web source are stable, as in PDF files, supply a page number in your in-text citation.)

Michael Pollan points out that "cheap food" actually has "significant costs—to the environment, to public health, to the public purse, even to the culture."

If a source has numbered paragraphs or sections, use "par." (or "pars.") or "sec." (or "secs.") in the parentheses: (Smith, par. 4). Notice that a comma follows the author's name.

5. One-page source If the source is one page long, MLA allows (but does not require) you to omit the page number. It's a good idea to include the page number because without it readers may not know where your citation ends or, worse, may not realize that you have provided a citation at all.

NO PAGE NUMBER IN CITATION

Sarah Conly uses John Stuart Mill's "harm principle" to argue that citizens need their government to intervene to prevent them from taking harmful actions— such as driving too fast or buying unhealthy foods—out of ignorance of the harm they can do. But government intervention may overstep in the case of food choices.

PAGE NUMBER IN CITATION

Sarah Conly uses John Stuart Mill's "harm principle" to argue that citizens need their government to intervene to prevent them from taking harmful actions—such as driving too fast or buying unhealthy foods—out of ignorance of the harm they can do (A23). But government intervention may overstep in the case of food choices.

Variations on the general guidelines

This section describes the MLA guidelines for handling a variety of situations not covered in items 1–5.

6. Two authors Name the authors in a signal phrase, as in the following example, or include their last names in the parenthetical reference: (Gostin and Gostin 214).

> As legal scholars Gostin and Gostin explain, "[I]nterventions that do not pose a truly significant burden on individual liberty" are justified if they "go a long way towards safeguarding the health and well-being of the populace" (214).

7. Three or more authors Give the first author's name followed by "et al." (Latin for "and others"). The format in your text citation will match the format in your works cited entry (see item 3 on p. 423).

> The clinical trials were extended for two years, and only after results were reviewed by an independent panel did the researchers publish their findings (Blaine et al. 35).

8. Organization as author When the author is a corporation or an organization, name that author either in the signal phrase or in the parenthetical citation. (For a government agency as author, see item 17 on p. 419.)

> The American Diabetes Association estimates that the cost of diagnosed diabetes in the United States in 2012 was $245 billion.

In the list of works cited, the American Diabetes Association is treated as the author and alphabetized under *A*. When you give the organization name in the text, spell out the name; when you use it in parentheses, abbreviate common words in the name: "Assn.," "Dept.," "Natl.," "Soc.," and so on.

> The cost of diagnosed diabetes in the United States in 2012 was estimated at $245 billion (Amer. Diabetes Assn.).

9. Authors with the same last name If your list of works cited includes works by two or more authors with the same last name, include the author's first name in the signal phrase or first initial in the parentheses.

> One approach to the problem is to introduce nutrition literacy at the K-5 level in public schools (E. Chen 15).

10. Two or more works by the same author Mention the title of the work in the signal phrase or include a short version of the title in the parentheses.

The American Diabetes Association tracks trends in diabetes across age groups. In 2012, more than 200,000 children and adolescents had diabetes ("Fast"). Because of an expected dramatic increase in diabetes in young people over the next forty years, the association encourages "strategies for implementing childhood obesity prevention programs and primary prevention programs for youth at risk of developing type 2 diabetes" ("Number").

Titles of articles and other short works are placed in quotation marks; titles of books and other long works are italicized. (See also p. 463.)

In the rare case when both the author's name and a short title must be given in parentheses, separate them with a comma.

Researchers have estimated that "the number of youth with type 2 [diabetes] could quadruple and the number with type 1 could triple" by 2050, "with an increasing proportion of youth with diabetes from minority populations" (Amer. Diabetes Assn., "Number").

11. Two or more works in one citation   To cite more than one source in the parentheses, list the authors (or titles) in alphabetical order and separate them with semicolons.

The prevalence of early-onset Type 2 diabetes has been well documented (Finn 68; Sharma 2037; Whitaker 118).

It may be less distracting to use an information note for multiple citations (see MLA-4c).

12. Repeated citations from the same source   When you are writing about a single work, you do not need to include the author's name each time you quote from or paraphrase the work. After you mention the author's name at the beginning of your paper, you may include just the page number in your parenthetical citations.

In Susan Glaspell's short story "A Jury of Her Peers," two women accompany their husbands and a county attorney to an isolated house where a farmer named John Wright has been choked to death in his bed with a rope. The chief suspect is Wright's wife, Minnie, who is in jail awaiting trial. The sheriff's wife, Mrs. Peters, has come along to gather some personal items for Minnie, and Mrs. Hale has joined her. Early in the story, Mrs. Hale sympathizes with Minnie and objects to the way the male investigators are "snoopin' round and criticizin'" her kitchen (249). In contrast, Mrs. Peters shows respect for the law, saying that the men are doing "no more than their duty" (249).

In a paper with multiple sources, if you are citing a source more than once in a paragraph, you may omit the author's name after the first mention in the paragraph as long as it is clear that you are still referring to the same source.

13. Encyclopedia or dictionary entry   When an encyclopedia or a dictionary entry does not have an author, it will be alphabetized in the list of works cited under the word or entry that you consulted (see item 28 on p. 438). Either in your text or in your parenthetical citation, mention the word or entry. No page number is required because readers can easily look up the word or entry.

> The word *crocodile* has a complex etymology ("Crocodile").

14. Multivolume work   If your paper cites more than one volume of a multivolume work, indicate in the parentheses the volume you are referring to, followed by a colon and the page number.

> In his studies of gifted children, Terman describes a pattern of accelerated
> language acquisition (2: 279).

If you cite only one volume of a multivolume work, you will include the volume number in the list of works cited and will not need to include it in the parentheses. (See the second example in item 38 on p. 443.)

15. Entire work   Use the author's name in a signal phrase or a parenthetical citation. There is no need to use a page number.

> Pollan explores the issues surrounding food production and consumption from a
> political angle.

16. Selection in an anthology or a collection   Put the name of the author of the selection (not the editor of the anthology) in the signal phrase or the parentheses.

> In "Love Is a Fallacy," the narrator's logical teachings disintegrate when Polly
> declares that she should date Petey because "[h]e's got a raccoon coat"
> (Shulman 391).

In the list of works cited, the work is alphabetized under *Shulman*, the author of the story, not under the name of the editor of the anthology. (See item 35 on p. 442.)

> Shulman, Max. "Love Is a Fallacy." *Current Issues and Enduring Questions*, edited
> by Sylvan Barnet and Hugo Bedau, 9th ed., Bedford/St. Martin's, 2011,
> pp. 383-91.

17. Government document   When a government agency is the author, you will alphabetize it in the list of works cited under the name of the government, such as United States or Great Britain (see item 70 on p. 459). For this reason, you must name the government as well as the agency in your in-text citation.

> One government agency reports that seat belt use saved an average of more than fourteen thousand lives per year in the United States between 2000 and 2010 (United States, Dept. of Transportation, Natl. Highway Traffic Safety Administration 231).

18. Historical document   For a historical document, such as the United States Constitution or the Canadian Charter of Rights and Freedoms, provide the document title, neither italicized nor in quotation marks, along with relevant article and section numbers. In parenthetical citations, use common abbreviations such as "art." and "sec." and abbreviations of well-known titles: (US Const., art. 1, sec. 2).

> While the United States Constitution provides for the formation of new states (art. 4, sec. 3), it does not explicitly allow or prohibit the secession of states.

Cite other historical documents as you would any other work, by the first element in the works cited entry (see item 72 on p. 459).

19. Legal source   For a legislative act (law) or court case, name the act or case either in a signal phrase or in parentheses. Italicize the names of cases but not the names of acts. (See also items 73 and 74 on p. 460.)

> The Jones Act of 1917 granted US citizenship to Puerto Ricans.

> In 1857, Chief Justice Roger B. Taney declared in *Dred Scott v. Sandford* that blacks, whether enslaved or free, could not be citizens of the United States.

20. Visual such as a table, a chart, or another graphic   To cite a visual that has a figure number in the source, use the abbreviation "fig." and the number in place of a page number in your parenthetical citation: (Manning, fig. 4). If you refer to the figure in your text, spell out the word "figure" in the text.

To cite a visual that does not have a figure number in a print source, use the visual's title or a description in your text and cite the author and page number as for any other source.

For a visual not in a print source, identify the visual in your text and then in parentheses use the first element in the works cited entry: the artist's or photographer's name or the title of the work. (See items 64–69 on pp. 455–58.)

Photographs such as *Woman Aircraft Worker* (Bransby) and *Women Welders* (Parks) demonstrate the US government's attempt to document the contributions of women during World War II.

21. Personal communication and social media Cite personal letters, personal interviews, e-mail messages, and social media posts by the name listed in the works cited entry, as you would for any other source. Identify the type of source in your text if you feel it is necessary for clarity. (See items 27d, 29c, and 75–79 in section MLA-4b.)

22. Web source Your in-text citation for a source from the Web should follow the same guidelines as for other sources. If the source lacks page numbers but has numbered paragraphs, sections, or divisions, use those numbers with the appropriate abbreviation in your parenthetical citation: "par.," "sec.," "ch.," "pt.," and so on. Do not add such numbers if the source itself does not use them; simply give the author or title in your in-text citation.

Julian Hawthorne points out profound differences between his father and Ralph Waldo Emerson but concludes that, in their lives and their writing, "together they met the needs of nearly all that is worthy in human nature" (ch. 4).

23. Indirect source (source quoted in another source) When a writer's or a speaker's quoted words appear in a source written by someone else, begin the parenthetical citation with the abbreviation "qtd. in." (See also item 12 on p. 429.) In the following example, Gostin and Gostin are the authors of the source given in the works cited list; the source contains a quotation by Beauchamp.

Public health researcher Dan Beauchamp has said that "public health practices are 'communal in nature, and concerned with the well-being of the community as a whole and not just the well-being of any particular person'" (qtd. in Gostin and Gostin 217).

Literary works and sacred texts

Literary works and sacred texts are usually available in a variety of editions. Your list of works cited will specify which edition you are using, and your in-text citation will usually consist of a page number from the edition you consulted (see item 24). When possible, give enough information—such as book parts, play divisions, or line numbers—so that readers can locate the cited passage in any edition of the work (see items 25–27).

24. Literary work without parts or line numbers Many literary works, such as most short stories and many novels and plays, do not have parts or line numbers. In such cases, simply cite the page number.

> At the end of Kate Chopin's "The Story of an Hour," Mrs. Mallard drops dead upon learning that her husband is alive. In the final irony of the story, doctors report that she has died of a "joy that kills" (25).

25. Verse play or poem For verse plays, give act, scene, and line numbers that can be located in any edition of the work. Use arabic numerals and separate the numbers with periods.

> In Shakespeare's *King Lear*, Gloucester, blinded for suspected treason, learns a profound lesson from his tragic experience: "A man may see how this world goes / with no eyes" (4.2.148-49).

For a poem, cite the part, stanza, and line numbers, if it has them, separated by periods.

> The Green Knight claims to approach King Arthur's court "because the praise of you, prince, is puffed so high, / And your manor and your men are considered so magnificent" (1.12.258-59).

For poems that are not divided into numbered parts or stanzas, use line numbers. For a first reference, use the word "lines": (lines 5-8). Thereafter use just the numbers: (12-13).

26. Novel with numbered divisions When a novel has numbered divisions, put the page number first, followed by a semicolon, and then the book, part, or chapter in which the passage may be found. Use abbreviations such as "bk.," "pt.," and "ch."

> One of Kingsolver's narrators, teenager Rachel, pushes her vocabulary beyond its limits. For example, Rachel complains that being forced to live in the Congo with her missionary family is "a sheer tapestry of justice" because her chances of finding a boyfriend are "dull and void" (117; bk. 2, ch. 10).

27. Sacred text When citing a sacred text such as the Bible or the Qur'an, name the edition you are using in your works cited entry (see item 39 on p. 443). In your parenthetical citation, give the book, chapter, and verse (or their equivalent), separated with periods. Common abbreviations for books of the Bible are acceptable.

> Consider the words of Solomon: "If your enemy is hungry, give him bread to eat; and if he is thirsty, give him water to drink" (*Oxford Annotated Bible*, Prov. 25.21).

The title of a sacred work is italicized when it refers to a specific edition of the work, as in the preceding example. If you refer to the book in a general sense in your text, neither italicize it nor put it in quotation marks (see also the note on p. 330 in section P10-a).

> The Bible and the Qur'an provide allegories that help readers understand how to lead a moral life.

MLA-4b MLA list of works cited

The elements you will need for the works cited list will differ slightly for some sources, but the main principles apply to all sources, whether in print or from the Web: You should identify an author, a creator, or a producer whenever possible; give a title; and provide the date on which the source was produced. Some sources will require page numbers; some will require a publisher or sponsor; and some will require other identifying information.

Section MLA-4b provides details for how to cite many of the sources you are likely to encounter. It also provides hints for what you can do when a source does not match one of the models exactly. When you cite sources, your goals are to show that your sources are reliable and relevant, to provide readers with enough information to find sources easily, and to provide that information consistently according to MLA conventions.

- ▶ Directory to MLA works cited models, page 393
- ▶ General guidelines for the works cited list, page 424

General guidelines for listing authors

The formatting of authors' names in items 1–12 applies to all sources—books, articles, Web sites—in print, on the Web, or in other media. For more models of specific source types, see items 13–79.

1. Single author

author: last
name first   title (book)   publisher   year

Bowker, Gordon. *James Joyce: A New Biography*. Farrar, Straus and Giroux, 2012.

2. Two authors

first author:
last name first

second author:
in normal order   title (book)   publisher   year

Gourevitch, Philip, and Errol Morris. *Standard Operating Procedure*. Penguin Books, 2008.

3. Three or more authors

Name the first author followed by "et al." (Latin for "and others"). In an in-text citation, use the same form for the authors' names as you use in the works cited entry. See item 7 on page 416.

first author:
last name first   "et al." for all
other authors   title (book)

Zumeta, William, et al. *Financing American Higher Education in the Era of Globalization*.

publisher   year

Harvard Education Press, 2012.

first author:
last name first   "et al." for all
other authors   title (book)

Leech, Geoffrey, et al. *Change in Contemporary English: A Grammatical Study*.

publisher   year

Cambridge UP, 2009.

4. Organization or company as author

author: organization
name, not abbreviated   title (book)   publisher   year

Human Rights Watch. *World Report of 2015: Events of 2014*. Seven Stories Press, 2015.

Your in-text citation also should treat the organization as the author (see item 8 on p. 416).

5. No author listed

a. Article or other short work

newspaper title
article title   (city in brackets)   date   page(s)

"Policing Ohio's Online Courses." *Plain Dealer* [Cleveland], 9 Oct. 2012, p. A5.

label

Editorial.

title of
Web site   publisher/
article title   sponsor

"Chapter 2: What Can Be Patented?" *Lemelson-MIT*, Massachusetts Institute of Technology,

date of access
URL   for undated site

lemelson.mit.edu/resources/chapter-2-what-can-be-patented. Accessed 4 Apr. 2016.

General guidelines for the works cited list

In the list of works cited, include only sources that you have quoted, summarized, or paraphrased in your paper. MLA's guidelines are applicable to a wide variety of sources. At times you may find that you have to adapt the guidelines and models in this section to source types you encounter in your research.

Organization of the list

The elements, or pieces of information, needed for a works cited entry are the following:

- The author (if a work has one)
- The title
- The title of the larger work in which the source is located (MLA calls this a "container")—a collection, a journal, a magazine, a Web site, and so on
- As much of the following information as is available about the source and the container:

    Editor, translator, director, performer

    Version

    Volume and issue numbers

    Publisher or sponsor

    Date of publication

    Location of the source: page numbers, URL, DOI, and so on

Not all sources will require every element. See specific models in this section for more details.

Authors

- Arrange the list alphabetically by authors' last names or by titles for works with no authors.
- For the first author, place the last name first, a comma, and the first name. Put a second author's name in normal order (first name followed by last name). For three or more authors, use "et al." after the first author's name.
- Spell out "editor," "translator," "edited by," and so on.

Titles

- In titles of works, capitalize all words except articles (*a*, *an*, *the*), prepositions, coordinating conjunctions, and the *to* in infinitives — unless the word is first or last in the title or subtitle.
- Use quotation marks for titles of articles and other short works.
- Italicize titles of books and other long works.

Publication information

- MLA no longer requires the place of publication for a book publisher.
- Use the complete version of publishers' names, except for terms such as "Inc." and "Co."; retain terms such as "Books" and "Press." For university publishers, use "U" and "P" for "University" and "Press."
- For a book, take the name of the publisher from the title page (or from the copyright page if it is not on the title page). For a Web site, the publisher might be at the bottom of a page or on the "About" page. If a work has two or more publishers, separate the names with slashes.
- If the title of a Web site and the publisher are the same or similar, use the title of the site but omit the publisher.

Dates

- For a book, give the most recent year on the title page or the copyright page. For a Web source, use the copyright date or the most recent update date. Use the complete date as listed in the source. (See item 13a.)
- Abbreviate all months except May, June, and July and give the date in inverted form: 13 Mar. 2016.
- If the source has no date, give your date of access at the end: Accessed 24 Feb. 2016.

Page numbers

- For most articles and other short works, give page numbers when they are available, preceded by "p." (or "pp." for more than one page).
- Do not use the page numbers from a printout of a Web source.
- If an article does not appear on consecutive pages, give the number of the first page followed by a plus sign: 35+.

URLs and DOIs

- Give a permalink or a DOI (digital object identifier) if a source has one. (See item 14c.)
- If a source does not have a permalink or a DOI, include a URL (omitting the protocol, such as http://).
- For a library's subscription database, such as Academic ASAP or JSTOR, include only the basic URL for the database home page. (See item 15d.)
- For open databases and archives, such as Google Books, give the complete URL for the source. (See item 30c.)

5. No author listed (cont.)

b. Television program

episode title

title of
TV show

producer   network date

"Fast Times at West Philly High." *Frontline*, produced by Debbie Morton, PBS, 2012.

c. Book, entire Web site, or other long work

title (Web site)

Women of Protest: Photographs from the Records of the National Woman's Party.

publisher/
sponsor

URL

date of access
for undated site

Library of Congress, www.loc.gov/collections/women-of-protest/. Accessed 1 May 2015.

TIP: Often the author's name is available but is not easy to find. It may appear at the end of the page, in tiny print, or on another page of the site, such as the home page. Also, an organization or a government may be the author (see items 4 and 70).

How to answer the basic question "Who is the author?"

PROBLEM: Sometimes when you need to cite a source, it's not clear who the author is. This is especially true for sources on the Web or other nonprint sources, which may have been created by one person and uploaded by a different person or an organization. Whom do you cite as the author in such a case? How do you determine who *is* the author?

EXAMPLE: The video "Surfing the Web on the Job" (see below) was uploaded to YouTube by CBSNewsOnline. Is the person or organization who uploads the video the author of the video? Not necessarily.

Surfing the Web on The Job

CBSNewsOnline · 42,491 videos

Subscribe   85,736

Uploaded on Nov 12, 2009
As the Internet continues to emerge as a critical facet of everyday life, CBS News' Daniel Sieberg reports that companies are cracking down on employees' personal Web use.

6. Two or more works by the same author   First alphabetize the works by title (ignoring the article *A*, *An*, or *The* at the beginning of a title). Use the author's name for the first entry; for subsequent entries, use three hyphens and a period. The three hyphens must stand for exactly the same name as in the first entry.

García, Cristina. *Dreams of Significant Girls*. Simon and Schuster, 2011.

---. *The Lady Matador's Hotel*. Scribner, 2010.

7. Two or more works by the same group of authors   Alphabetize the works by title. Use the authors' names in the proper form for the first entry (see items 1–4). Begin subsequent entries with three hyphens and a period. The three hyphens must stand for the same names as in the first entry.

Agha, Hussein, and Robert Malley. "The Arab Counterrevolution." *The New York Review of Books*, 29 Sept. 2011, www.nybooks.com/articles/2011/09/29/arab -counterrevolution/.

---. "This Is Not a Revolution." *The New York Review of Books*, 8 Nov. 2012, www.nybooks .com/articles/2012/11/08/not-revolution/.

STRATEGY: After you view or listen to the source a few times, ask yourself whether you can tell who is chiefly responsible for creating the content in the source. It could be an organization. It could be an identifiable individual. This video consists entirely of reporting by Daniel Sieberg, so in this case the author is Sieberg.

CITATION: To cite the source, you would use the basic MLA guidelines for a video found on the Web (item 55).

author:
last name first   title of video   Web site title   update date

Sieberg, Daniel. "Surfing the Web on the Job." *YouTube*, 12 Nov. 2009,

URL

www.youtube.com/watch?v=1wLhNwY-enY.

If you want to include the person or organization who uploaded the video, you can add it as supplementary information.

author:
last name first   title of video   Web site title   supplementary information

Sieberg, Daniel. "Surfing the Web on the Job." *YouTube*, uploaded by CBSNewsOnline,

update date   URL

12 Nov. 2009, www.youtube.com/watch?v=1wLhNwY-enY.

8. Editor or translator Begin with the editor's or translator's name. After the name(s), add "editor" (or "editors") or "translator" (or "translators").

first editor: last name first / second editor: in normal order / title (book)

Horner, Avril, and Anne Rowe, editors. *Living on Paper: Letters from Iris Murdoch.*

publisher / year

Princeton UP, 2016.

9. Author with editor or translator Begin with the name of the author. Place the editor's or translator's name after the title.

author: last name first / title (book) / translator: in normal order / publisher

Ullmann, Regina. *The Country Road: Stories.* Translated by Kurt Beals, New Directions

year

Publishing, 2015.

10. Graphic narrative or other illustrated work If a work has both an author and an illustrator, the order in your citation will depend on which of those persons you emphasize in your paper.

a. Author first If you emphasize the author's work, begin with the author's name. After the title, add "Illustrated by," followed by the illustrator's name.

Gaiman, Neil. *The Sandman: Overture.* Illustrated by J. H. William III, DC Comics, 2015.

b. Illustrator first If you emphasize the illustrator, begin your citation with the illustrator's name and the label "illustrator." After the title of the work, put the author's name, preceded by "By."

Kerascoët, illustrator. *Beautiful Darkness.* By Fabien Vehlmann, Drawn and Quarterly, 2014.

c. Author and illustrator the same person If the illustrator and the author are the same person, cite the work as you would any other work with one author (not using any labels).

Ulinich, Anya. *Lena Finkle's Magic Barrel: A Graphic Novel.* Penguin Books, 2014.

11. Author using a pseudonym (pen name) or screen name   Give the author's name as it appears in the source (the pseudonym), followed by the author's real name, if available, in parentheses. (For screen names in social media, see items 78 and 79 on pp. 460 and 461.)

Grammar Girl (Mignon Fogarty). "Lewis Carroll: He Loved to Play with Language." *QuickandDirtyTips.com*, 21 May 2015, www.quickanddirtytips.com/education/ grammar/lewis-carroll-he-loved-to-play-with-language.

Pauline. Comment on "Is This the End?" by James Atlas. *The New York Times*, 25 Nov. 2012, nyti.ms/1BRUvqQ.

12. Author quoted by another author (indirect source)   If one of your sources uses a quotation from another source and you'd like to use the quotation, provide a works cited entry for the source in which you found the quotation. In your in-text citation, indicate that the quoted words appear in the source (see item 23 on p. 420). In the following examples, Belmaker is the source in the works cited list; Townson is quoted in Belmaker.

SOURCE (BELMAKER) QUOTING ANOTHER SOURCE (TOWNSON)

Peter Townson, a journalist working with the DOHA Center for Press Freedom in Qatar, says there is one obvious reason that some countries in the Middle East have embraced social media so heartily. "It's kind of the preferred way for people to get news, because they know there's no self-censorship involved," Townson said in a phone interview.

WORKS CITED ENTRY

Belmaker, Genevieve. "Five Ways Journalists Can Use Social Media for On-the-Ground Reporting in the Middle East." *Poynter*, 19 Nov. 2012, www.poynter .org/2012/5-ways-journalists-can-use-social-media-for-on-the-ground -reporting-in-the-middle-east/195899/.

IN-TEXT CITATION

Peter Townson points out that social media in the Middle East are "kind of the preferred way for people to get news, because they know there's no self-censorship involved" (qtd. in Belmaker).

Articles and other short works

Citation at a glance: Article in a journal MLA

To cite an article in a print journal in MLA style, include the following elements:

1 Author(s) of article
2 Title and subtitle of article
3 Title of journal
4 Volume and issue numbers

5 Date of publication (including month or season, if any)
6 Page number(s) of article

JOURNAL TABLE OF CONTENTS

RHETORIC REVIEW ❸
Volume 31, Number 4, 2012
❹ ❺

Articles

FIRST PAGE OF ARTICLE

Rhetoric Review, Vol. 31, No. 4, 371–388, 2012
Copyright © Taylor & Francis Group, LLC
ISSN: 0735-0198 print / 1532-7981 online
DOI: 10.1080/07350198.2012.711196

R Routledge
Taylor & Francis Group

❶ JOSEPH TURNER

University of Delaware

❷ *Sir Gawain and the Green Knight* and the History
of Medieval Rhetoric

*During the Middle Ages, rhetoric and literature were thoroughly intertwined,
whereas current notions of disciplinarity, in which literature and rhetoric
are constructed as separate traditions, muddy our understanding of medieval*

WORKS CITED ENTRY FOR AN ARTICLE IN A PRINT JOURNAL

    1   2

Turner, Joseph. "*Sir Gawain and the Green Knight* and the History of Medieval Rhetoric."

         3   4   5   6

    Rhetoric Review, vol. 31, no. 4, 2012, pp. 371-88.

For more on citing articles in MLA style, see items 13–16.

13. Basic format for an article or other short work

a. Print

author:
last name first   article title   journal   volume,
                              title   issue

Tilman, David. "Food and Health of a Full Earth." *Daedalus*, vol. 144, no. 4,

      date   page(s)

    Fall 2015, pp. 139-53.

b. Web

author:
last name first   title of short work   title of
                                       Web site

Nelson, Libby. "How Schools Will Be Different without No Child Left Behind." *Vox*,

       date   URL

    11 Dec. 2015, www.vox.com/2015/12/11/9889350/every-student-succeeds-act-schools.

c. Database

author:
last name first   article title   journal title

Macari, Anne Marie. "Lyric Impulse in a Time of Extinction." *American Poetry Review*,

     volume,
     issue   date   page(s)   database title   database URL

    vol. 44, no. 4, July/Aug. 2015, pp. 11-14. *General OneFile*, go.galegroup.com/.

14. Article in a journal

a. Print

author: last
name first   article title   journal title

Matchie, Thomas. "Law versus Love in *The Round House*." *Midwest Quarterly*,

     volume,
     issue   date   page(s)

    vol. 56, no. 4, Summer 2015, pp. 353-64.

Citation at a glance: Article from a database MLA

To cite an article from a database in MLA style, include the following elements:

1. Author(s) of article
2. Title and subtitle of article
3. Title of journal, magazine, or newspaper
4. Volume and issue numbers (for journal)
5. Date of publication (including month or season, if any)
6. Page number(s) of article
7. Name of database
8. DOI or permalink, if available; otherwise, shortened URL of database

DATABASE RECORD

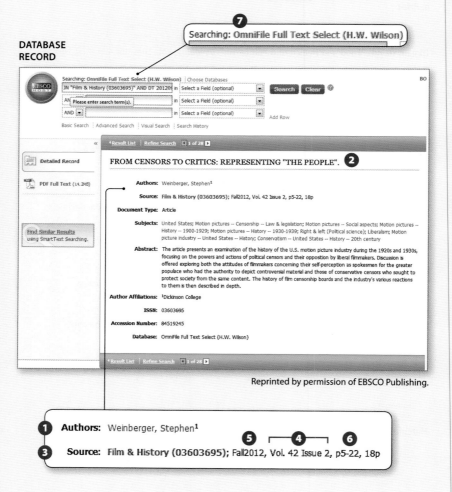

Reprinted by permission of EBSCO Publishing.

WORKS CITED ENTRY FOR AN ARTICLE FROM A DATABASE

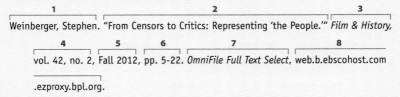

Weinberger, Stephen. "From Censors to Critics: Representing 'the People.'" *Film & History*,

vol. 42, no. 2, Fall 2012, pp. 5-22. *OmniFile Full Text Select*, web.b.ebscohost.com

.ezproxy.bpl.org.

For more on citing articles from a database in MLA style, see items 13–16.

14. Article in a journal (*cont.*)

b. Online journal

author:
last name first / article title

Cáceres, Sigfrido Burgos. "Towards Concert in Africa: Seeking Progress and Power

through Cohesion and Unity." *African Studies Quarterly*, vol. 12, no. 4, Fall 2011,
page(s) / journal title / volume, issue / date / URL

pp. 59-73, asq.africa.ufl.edu/files/Caceres-Vol12Is4.pdf.

c. Database

author:
last name first / article title / journal title

Maier, Jessica. "A 'True Likeness': The Renaissance City Portrait." *Renaissance Quarterly*,
volume, issue / date / page(s) / database title / DOI

vol. 65, no. 3, Fall 2012, pp. 711-52. *JSTOR*, doi:10.1086/668300.

15. Article in a magazine

a. Print (monthly)

author:
last name first / article title / magazine title / date / page(s)

Bryan, Christy. "Ivory Worship." *National Geographic*, Oct. 2012, pp. 28-61.

b. Print (weekly)

author:
last name first / article title / magazine title / date / page(s)

Vick, Karl. "The Stateless Statesman." *Time*, 15 Oct. 2012, pp. 32-37.

c. Web

author:
last name first / article title / Web site title / date

Leonard, Andrew. "The Surveillance State High School." *Salon*, 27 Nov. 2012,
URL

www.salon.com/2012/11/27/the_surveillance_state_high_school/.

15. Article in a magazine (*cont.*)

d. Database

author:
last name first   article title   magazine title   date   page(s)

Rosenbaum, Ron. "The Last Renaissance Man." *Smithsonian*, Nov. 2012, pp. 39-44.

database title   database URL

OmniFile Full Text Select, web.b.ebscohost.com.ezproxy.bpl.org/.

16. Article in a newspaper
If the city of publication is not obvious from the title of the newspaper, include the city in brackets after the newspaper title (see item 5a).

a. Print

author:
last name first   article title

Sherry, Allison. "Volunteers' Personal Touch Turns High-Tech Data into Votes."

newspaper title   date   page(s)

The Denver Post, 30 Oct. 2012, pp. 1A+.

Bray, Hiawatha. "As Toys Get Smarter, Privacy Issues Emerge." *The Boston Globe*, 10 Dec. 2015, p. C1.

b. Web

author:
last name first   article title

Crowell, Maddy. "How Computers Are Getting Better at Detecting Liars."

Web site title   date   URL

The Christian Science Monitor, 12 Dec. 2015, www.csmonitor.com/Science/Science-Notebook/2015/1212/How-computers-are-getting-better-at-detecting-liars.

c. Database

article title   newspaper title   date   page(s)   label

"The Road toward Peace." *The New York Times*, 15 Feb. 1945, p. 18. Editorial.

database title   database URL

ProQuest Historical Newspapers: The New York Times, search.proquest.com/hnpnewyorktimes.

17. Abstract or executive summary Include the label "Abstract" or "Executive summary," neither italicized nor in quotation marks, at the end of the entry (and before any database information).

a. Abstract of an article

Bottomore, Stephen. "The Romance of the Cinematograph." *Film History*, vol. 24, no. 3, July 2012, pp. 341-44. Abstract. *JSTOR*, doi:10.2979/filmhistory.24.3.341.

b. Abstract of a paper

Dixon, Rosemary, et al. "The Opportunities and Challenges of Virtual Library Systems: A Case Study." Paper presented at the 2011 Chicago Colloquium on Digital Humanities and Computer Science, U of Chicago, 20 Nov. 2011. Abstract.

c. Abstract of a dissertation

Moore, Courtney L. "Stress and Oppression: Identifying Possible Protective Factors for African American Men." Dissertation, Chicago School of Professional Psychology, 2016. Abstract. *ProQuest Dissertations and Theses*, search.proquest.com/docview/ 1707351557.

d. Executive summary

Pintak, Lawrence. *The Murrow Rural Information Initiative: Final Report*. Murrow College of Communication, Washington State U, 25 May 2012. Executive summary.

18. Article with a title in its title Use single quotation marks around a title of a short work or a quoted term that appears in an article title. Italicize a title or term normally italicized.

Silber, Nina. "From 'Great Emancipator' to 'Vampire Hunter': The Many Stovepipe Hats of Cinematic Lincoln." *Cognoscenti*, WBUR, 22 Nov. 2012, cognoscenti.wbur .org/2012/11/22/abraham-lincoln-nina-silber.

19. Editorial Cite as a source with no author (see item 5) and use the label "Editorial" at the end (and before any database information).

City's Blight Fight Making Difference." *The Columbus Dispatch*, 17 Nov. 2015, www.dispatch .com/content/stories/editorials/2015/11/17/1-citys-blight-fight-making -difference.html. Editorial.

20. Unsigned article Cite as a source with no author (see item 5).

"Drought and Health." *Centers for Disease Control and Prevention*, 30 July 2012, www.cdc
.gov/nceh/drought/default.htm.

21. Letter to the editor Use the label "Letter" at the end of the entry
(and before any database information). If the letter has no title, place
the label directly after the author's name.

Fahey, John A. "Recalling the Cuban Missile Crisis." *The Washington Post*, 28 Oct.
2012, p. A16. Letter. *LexisNexis Library Express*, www.lexisnexis.com/hottopics/
Inpubliclibraryexpress/.

22. Comment on an online article If the writer of the comment uses
a screen name, see item 11. After the name, include "Comment on" followed by the title of the article and the author of the article (preceded
by "by"). Continue with publication information for the article.

<small>author:
screen name</small>　　　　　　　　　　<small>article title</small>

pablosharkman. Comment on "'We Are All Implicated': Wendell Berry Laments

　　　　　　　　　　　　　　　　　<small>author of article</small>

a Disconnection from Community and the Land," by Scott Carlson.

　　　<small>Web site title</small>　　　<small>date</small>　　　<small>URL</small>

The Chronicle of Higher Education, 23 Apr. 2012, chronicle.com/article/In-Jefferson

-Lecture-Wendell/131648.

23. Paper or presentation at a conference If the paper or presentation
is included in the proceedings of a conference, cite it as a selection in an
anthology (see item 35; see also item 44 for proceedings of a conference).
If you viewed the presentation live, cite it as a lecture or public address
(see item 61).

<small>first author:　"et al." for
last name first　　others</small>　　　　<small>presentation title</small>

Zuckerman, Ethan, et al. "Big Data, Big Challenges, and Big Opportunities." Presentation

　　　　　　　　　　　　　　　　　　　<small>conference
　　　　　　　　　　　　　　　　　　　information</small>
　　　　　　<small>conference title</small>

at Wired for Change: The Power and the Pitfalls of Big Data, Ford Foundation,

　　　　<small>date</small>　　　　　　<small>URL</small>

New York, 15 Oct. 2012, www.fordfoundation.org/library/multimedia/wired-for

-change-big-data-big-challenges-and-big-opportunities/.

24. Book review Name the reviewer and the title of the review, if any,
followed by "Review of" and the title and author of the work reviewed.

Add the publication information for the publication in which the review appears. If the review has no author and no title, begin with "Review of" and alphabetize the entry by the first principal word in the title of the work reviewed.

a. Print

Flannery, Tim. "A Heroine in Defense of Nature." Review of *On a Farther Shore: The Life and Legacy of Rachel Carson*, by William Souder. *The New York Review of Books*, 22 Nov. 2012, pp. 21-23.

b. Web

Della Subin, Anna. "It Has Burned My Heart." Review of *The Lives of Muhammad*, by Kecia Ali. *London Review of Books*, 22 Oct. 2015, www.lrb.co.uk/v37/n20/anna -della-subin/it-has-burned-my-heart.

c. Database

Spychalski, John C. Review of *American Railroads—Decline and Renaissance in the Twentieth Century*, by Robert E. Gallamore and John R. Meyer. *Transportation Journal*, vol. 54, no. 4, Fall 2015, pp. 535-38. *JSTOR*, doi:10.5325/ transportationj.54.4.0535.

25. Film review or other review Name the reviewer and the title of the review, if any, followed by "Review of" and the title and writer or director of the work reviewed. Add the publication information for the publication in which the review appears. If the review has no author and no title, begin with "Review of" and alphabetize the entry by the first principal word in the title of the work reviewed.

a. Print

Lane, Anthony. "Human Bondage." Review of *Spectre*, directed by Sam Mendes. *The New Yorker*, 16 Nov. 2015, pp. 96-97.

b. Web

Savage, Phil. "*Fallout 4* Review." Review of *Fallout 4*, by Bethesda Game Studios. *PC Gamer*, Future Publishing, 8 Nov. 2015, www.pcgamer.com/fallout-4-review/.

26. Performance review Name the reviewer and the title of the review, if any, followed by "Review of" and the title and author of the work reviewed. Add the publication information for the publication in which the review appears. If the review has no author and no title, begin with

"Review of" and alphabetize the entry by the first principal word in the title of the work reviewed.

Stout, Gene. "The Ebullient Florence + the Machine Give KeyArena a Workout." Review
of *How Big How Blue How Beautiful Odyssey*. *The Seattle Times*, 28 Oct. 2015,
www.seattletimes.com/entertainment/music/the-ebullient-florence-the-machine
-give-keyarena-a-workout/.

27. Interview Begin with the person interviewed, followed by the title of the interview (if there is one). If the interview does not have a title, include the word "Interview" after the interviewee's name. If you wish to include the name of the interviewer, put it after the title of the interview.

a. Print

Weddington, Sarah. "Sarah Weddington: Still Arguing for *Roe*." Interview by Michele
Kort. *Ms.*, Winter 2013, pp. 32-35.

b. Web

Jaffrey, Madhur. "Madhur Jaffrey on How Indian Cuisine Won Western Taste Buds." Interview
by Shadrach Kabango. *Q*, CBC Radio, 29 Oct. 2015, www.cbc.ca/1.3292918.

c. Television or radio

Putin, Vladimir. Interview by Charlie Rose. *Charlie Rose: The Week*, PBS, 19 June 2015.

d. Personal To cite an interview that you conducted, begin with the name of the person interviewed. Then write "Personal interview" or "Telephone interview," followed by the date of the interview.

Akufo, Dautey. Personal interview, 11 Apr. 2016.

28. Article in a dictionary or an encyclopedia (including a wiki) List the author of the entry (if there is one), the title of the entry, the title of the reference work, the edition number (if any), the publisher, and the date of the edition. Page numbers are not necessary because the entries in the source are arranged alphabetically and are therefore easy to locate.

a. Print

Robinson, Lisa Clayton. "Harlem Writers Guild." *Africana: The Encyclopedia of the African and
African American Experience*, 2nd ed., Oxford UP, 2005.

"Ball's in Your Court, The." *The American Heritage Dictionary of Idioms*, 2nd ed., Houghton
Mifflin Harcourt, 2013.

b. Web

Durante, Amy M. "Finn Mac Cumhail." *Encyclopedia Mythica*, 17 Apr. 2011, www
.pantheon.org/articles/f/finn_mac_cumhail.html.

"House Music." *Wikipedia*, 16 Nov. 2015, en.wikipedia.org/wiki/House_music.

29. Letter

a. Print   Begin with the writer of the letter, the words "Letter to" and
the recipient, and the date of the letter. Add the title of the collection,
the editor, and publication information. Add the page range at the end.

Wharton, Edith. Letter to Henry James, 28 Feb. 1915. *Henry James and Edith Wharton:*
Letters, 1900-1915, edited by Lyall H. Powers, Scribner, 1990, pp. 323-26.

b. Web   After information about the letter writer, recipient, and date (if
known), give the name of the Web site or archive, italicized; the publisher or sponsor of the site; and the URL.

Oblinger, Maggie. Letter to Charlie Thomas, 31 Mar. 1895. *Prairie Settlement: Nebraska*
Photographs and Family Letters, 1862-1912, Library of Congress / American
Memory, memory.loc.gov/cgi-bin/query/r?ammem/ps:@field(DOCID+l306)
#l3060001.

c. Personal   To cite a letter that you received, begin with the writer's
name and add the phrase "Letter to the author," followed by the date.

Primak, Shoshana. Letter to the author, 6 May 2016.

Books and other long works

▶ Citation at a glance: Book, page 440

30. Basic format for a book

a. Print or e-book   If you have used an e-book, give the e-reader type at the
end of the entry.

author: last
name first   book title   publisher   year

Wolfe, Tom. *Back to Blood*. Little, Brown, 2012.

Beard, Mary. *SPQR: A History of Ancient Rome*. Liveright Publishing, 2015. Nook.

Citation at a glance: Book MLA

To cite a print book in MLA style, include the following elements:

1 Author(s)

2 Title and subtitle

3 Publisher

4 Year of publication (latest year)

TITLE PAGE

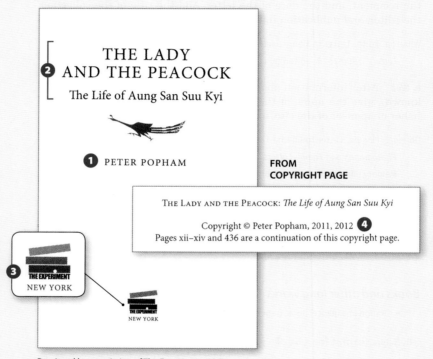

Reprinted by permission of The Experiment, LLC.

WORKS CITED ENTRY FOR A PRINT BOOK

Popham, Peter. *The Lady and the Peacock: The Life of Aung San Suu Kyi.*

The Experiment, 2012.

For more on citing books in MLA style, see items 30–41.

30. Basic format for a book (*cont.*)

b. Web Give whatever print publication information is available for the work, followed by the title of the Web site and the URL.

author: last name first   book title   translator: in normal order

Piketty, Thomas. *Capital in the Twenty-First Century*. Translated by Arthur Goldhammer,

publisher year Web site title   URL

    Harvard UP, 2014. *Google Books*, books.google.com/books?isbn=0674369556.

Saalman, Lora, editor and translator. *The China-India Nuclear Crossroads*. Carnegie

    Endowment for International Peace, 2012. *Scribd*, www.scribd.com/

    book/142083413/The-China-India-Nuclear-Crossroads.

c. Database

author: last name first   book title   city and date of original

Goldsmith, Oliver. *The Vicar of Wakefield: A Tale*. Philadelphia, 1801.

database title   URL

    America's Historical Imprints, infoweb.newsbank.com.ezproxy.bpl.org/.

31. Parts of a book

a. Foreword, introduction, preface, or afterword

author of foreword: last name first book part   book title

Bennett, Hal Zina. Foreword. *Shimmering Images: A Handy Little Guide to Writing Memoir*,

author of book: in normal order publisher year page(s)

    by Lisa Dale Norton, St. Martin's Griffin, 2008, pp. xiii-xvi.

Sullivan, John Jeremiah. "The Ill-Defined Plot." Introduction. *The Best American*

    Essays 2014, edited by Sullivan, Houghton Mifflin Harcourt, 2014,

    pp. xvii-xxvi.

b. Chapter in a book

Rizga, Kristina. "Mr. Hsu." *Mission High: One School, How Experts Tried to Fail It,*

    and the Students and Teachers Who Made It Triumph, Nation Books, 2015,

    pp. 89-114.

32. Book with a title in its title If the book title contains a title normally italicized, neither italicize the internal title nor place it in quotation marks. If the title within the title is normally put in quotation marks, retain the quotation marks and italicize the entire book title.

Shanahan, Timothy. *Philosophy and* Blade Runner. Palgrave Macmillan, 2014.

Lethem, Jonathan. *"Lucky Alan" and Other Stories*. Doubleday, 2015.

33. Book in a language other than English Capitalize the title according to the conventions of the book's language. If your readers are not familiar with the language of the book, include a translation of the title in brackets.

Vargas Llosa, Mario. *El sueño del celta [The Dream of the Celt]*. Alfaguara Ediciones, 2010.

34. Entire anthology or collection An anthology is a collection of works on a common theme, often with different authors for the selections and usually with an editor for the entire volume.

editor: title of
last name first   anthology   publisher   year

Marcus, Ben, editor. *New American Stories*. Vintage Books, 2015.

35. One selection from an anthology or a collection

▶ Citation at a glance: Selection from an anthology or a collection, page 444

author of   title of
selection   selection   title of anthology   editor(s) of
                                            anthology

Sayrafiezadeh, Saïd. "Paranoia." *New American Stories,* edited by Ben Marcus,

publisher   year   page(s)

Vintage Books, 2015, pp. 3-29.

36. Two or more selections from an anthology or a collection For two or more works from the same anthology, provide an entry for the entire anthology (see item 34) and a shortened entry for each selection. Alphabetize the entries by authors' or editors' last names.

author of selection · title of selection · editor(s) of anthology · page(s)

Eisenberg, Deborah. "Some Other, Better Otto." Marcus, pp. 94-136.

editor: last name first · title of anthology · publisher · year

Marcus, Ben, editor. *New American Stories*. Vintage Books, 2015.

author of selection · title of selection · editor(s) of anthology · page(s)

Sayrafiezadeh, Saïd. "Paranoia." Marcus, pp. 3-29.

37. Edition other than the first Include the number of the edition (2nd, 3rd, and so on). If the book has a translator or an editor in addition to the author, give the name of the translator or editor before the edition number (see item 9 for a book with an editor or translator).

Eagleton, Terry. *Literary Theory: An Introduction*. 3rd ed., U of Minnesota P, 2008.

38. Multivolume work Include the total number of volumes at the end of the entry, using the abbreviation "vols." If the volumes were published over several years, give the inclusive dates of publication.

author: last name first · book title · editor(s): in normal order · publisher · inclusive dates · total volumes

Stark, Freya. *Letters*. Edited by Lucy Moorehead, Compton Press, 1974-82. 8 vols.

If you cite only one volume in your paper, include the volume number before the publisher and give the date of publication for that volume. After the date, give the total number of volumes.

author: last name first · book title · editor(s): in normal order · volume cited · publisher · date of volume · total volumes

Stark, Freya. *Letters*. Edited by Lucy Moorehead, vol. 5, Compton Press, 1978. 8 vols.

39. Sacred text Give the title of the edition (taken from the title page), italicized; the editor's or translator's name (if any); and publication information. Add the name of the version, if there is one, before the publisher.

The Oxford Annotated Bible with the Apocrypha. Edited by Herbert G. May and Bruce M.
Metzger, Revised Standard Version, Oxford UP, 1965.

The Qur'an: Translation. Translated by Abdullah Yusuf Ali, Tahrike Tarsile Qur'an,
2001.

Citation at a glance: Selection from an anthology or a collection MLA

To cite a selection from an anthology in MLA style, include the following elements:

1 Author(s) of selection
2 Title and subtitle of selection
3 Title and subtitle of anthology
4 Editor(s) of anthology
5 Publisher
6 Year of publication
7 Page numbers of selection

FIRST PAGE OF SELECTION

TITLE PAGE OF ANTHOLOGY

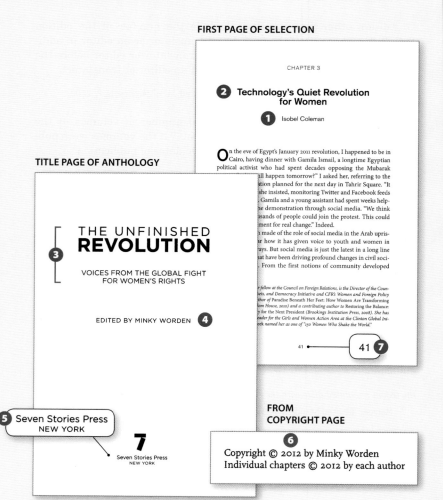

CHAPTER 3

2 **Technology's Quiet Revolution for Women**

1 Isobel Coleman

On the eve of Egypt's January 2011 revolution, I happened to be in Cairo, having dinner with Gamila Ismail, a longtime Egyptian political activist who had spent decades opposing the Mubarak [...]ll happen tomorrow?" I asked her, referring to the [...]tion planned for the next day in Tahrir Square. "It [...] she insisted, monitoring Twitter and Facebook feeds [...] Gamila and a young assistant had spent weeks help-[...]he demonstration through social media. "We think [...]sands of people could join the protest. This could [...]ment for real change." Indeed.

[...] made of the role of social media in the Arab upris-[...]r how it has given voice to youth and women in [...]ays. But social media is just the latest in a long line [...]at have been driving profound changes in civil soci-[...]. From the first notions of community developed

r fellow at the Council on Foreign Relations, is the Director of the Coun-[...]ets, and Democracy Initiative and CFR's Women and Foreign Policy [...]hor of Paradise Beneath Her Feet: How Women Are Transforming [...]om House, 2010) and a contributing author to Restoring the Balance: [...] for the Next President (Brookings Institution Press, 2008). She has [...]eader for the Girls and Women Action Area at the Clinton Global Ini-[...]ek named her as one of "150 Women Who Shake the World."

41 ● ─── 41 **7**

3 THE UNFINISHED **REVOLUTION**

VOICES FROM THE GLOBAL FIGHT FOR WOMEN'S RIGHTS

EDITED BY MINKY WORDEN **4**

FROM COPYRIGHT PAGE

6
Copyright © 2012 by Minky Worden
Individual chapters © 2012 by each author

5 Seven Stories Press
NEW YORK

7
Seven Stories Press
NEW YORK

WORKS CITED ENTRY FOR A SELECTION FROM AN ANTHOLOGY

<pre>
        1   2   3
</pre>
Coleman, Isobel. "Technology's Quiet Revolution for Women." *The Unfinished Revolution:*

<pre>
                                                            4
</pre>
Voices from the Global Fight for Women's Rights, edited by Minky Worden,

<pre>
        5   6   7
</pre>
Seven Stories Press, 2012, pp. 41-49.

For more on citing selections from anthologies in MLA style, see items 34–36.

40. Book in a series After the publication information, give the series name as it appears on the title page, followed by the series number, if any.

Denham, A. E., editor. *Plato on Art and Beauty*. Palgrave Macmillan, 2012. Philosophers
in Depth.

41. Republished book After the title of the book, give the original year of publication, followed by the current publication information. If the republished book contains new material, such as an introduction or an afterword, include information about the new material after the original date.

Trilling, Lionel. *The Liberal Imagination*. 1950. Introduction by Louis Menand, New York
Review Books, 2008.

Wilde, Oscar. *The Picture of Dorian Gray*. 1891. Barnes and Noble, 2012. Barnes and
Noble Signature Editions.

42. Pamphlet, brochure, or newsletter Cite a pamphlet, brochure, newsletter, or other small, self-contained publication as you would a book.

The Legendary Sleepy Hollow Cemetery. Friends of Sleepy Hollow Cemetery, 2008.

43. Dissertation

a. Published For dissertations that have been published in book form, italicize the title. After the title, give the label "Dissertation," the name of the institution, and the year the dissertation was accepted.

Kidd, Celeste. *Rational Approaches to Learning and Development*. Dissertation, U of
Rochester, 2013.

43. Dissertation (*cont.*)

b. Unpublished Begin with the author's name, followed by the dissertation title in quotation marks. After the title, add the label "Dissertation," the name of the institution, and the year the dissertation was accepted.

Abbas, Megan Brankley. "Knowing Islam: The Entangled History of Western Academia
and Modern Islamic Thought." Dissertation, Princeton U, 2015.

44. Proceedings of a conference Cite as you would a book, adding the name, date, and location of the conference after the title.

Sowards, Stacey K., et al., editors. *Across Borders and Environments: Communication
and Environmental Justice in International Contexts*. Proceedings of Eleventh
Biennial Conference on Communication and the Environment, 25-28 June
2011, U of Texas at El Paso, International Environmental Communication
Association, 2012.

45. Manuscript Give the author, a title or a description of the manuscript, and the date of composition (if known), followed by the location of the manuscript, including a URL if it is found on the Web.

Arendt, Hannah. *Between Past and Future*. 1st draft, Hannah Arendt Papers, Manuscript
Division, Library of Congress, pp. 108-50, memory.loc.gov/cgi-bin/ampage?collId
=mharendt&fileName=05/050030/050030page.db&recNum=0.

Web sites and parts of Web sites

46. An entire Web site

a. Web site with author or editor

author or editor: last name first	title of Web site	publisher/ sponsor	update date

Railton, Stephen. *Mark Twain in His Times*. Stephen Railton / U of Virginia Library, 2012,

URL

twain.lib.virginia.edu/.

Halsall, Paul, editor. *Internet Modern History Sourcebook*. Fordham U, 4 Nov. 2011,
legacy.fordham.edu/halsall/index.asp.

b. Web site with organization as author

organization   title of
Web site

Transparency International. *Transparency International: The Global Coalition against Corruption,*

date   URL

2015, www.transparency.org/.

c. Web site with no author
Begin with the title of the site. If the site has no title, begin with a label such as "Home page."

The Newton Project. U of Sussex, 2016, www.newtonproject.sussex.ac.uk/prism
.php?id=1.

d. Web site with no title
Use the label "Home page" or another appropriate description in place of a title.

Bae, Rebecca. Home page. Iowa State U, 2015, www.engl.iastate.edu/rebecca-bae
-directory-page/.

47. Short work from a Web site

► Citation at a glance: Short work from a Web site, page 448

a. Short work with author

author: last
name first   title of short work   title of
Web site

Gallagher, Sean. "The Last Nomads of the Tibetan Plateau." *Pulitzer Center on Crisis*

date   URL

Reporting, 25 Oct. 2012, pulitzercenter.org/reporting/china-glaciers-global
-warming-climate-change-ecosystem-tibetan-plateau-grasslands-nomads.

b. Short work with no author

title of article   title of Web site

"Social and Historical Context: Vitality." *Arapesh Grammar and Digital Language*

sponsor

Archive Project, Institute for Advanced Technology in the Humanities,

               access date
URL   for undated site

www.arapesh.org/socio_historical_context_vitality.php. Accessed 22 Mar. 2016.

Citation at a glance: Short work from a Web site MLA

To cite a short work from a Web site in MLA style, include the following elements:

1 Author(s) of short work (if any)
2 Title and subtitle of short work
3 Title and subtitle of Web site
4 Publisher or sponsor of Web site (unless it is the same as the title of site)
5 Update date
6 URL of page (or of home page of site)
7 Date of access (if no update date on site)

INTERNAL PAGE OF WEB SITE

FOOTER ON PAGE

WORKS CITED ENTRY FOR A SHORT WORK FROM A WEB SITE

        2   3   6

"Losing a Country, Finding a Home." *Amherst College,* www.amherst.edu/academiclife/

                                      7

departments/russian/acrc/lcfh. Accessed 4 Jan. 2016.

For more on citing sources from Web sites in MLA style, see items 47 and 48.

48. Long work from a Web site

author: last name first	title of long work	title of Web site	update date

Milton, John. *Paradise Lost: Book I. Poetry Foundation*, 2014,

URL

    www.poetryfoundation.org/poem/174987.

49. Entire blog   Cite a blog as you would an entire Web site (see item 46).

Ng, Amy. *Pikaland*. Pikaland Media, 2015, www.pikaland.com/.

50. Blog post or comment   Cite a blog post or comment as you would a short work from a Web site (see item 47). If the post or comment has no title, use the label "Blog post" or "Blog comment." Follow with the remaining information as for an entire blog (see item 49). (See item 11 for the use of screen names.)

author: last name first	title of blog post	title of blog	publisher/ sponsor	update date

Eakin, Emily. *"Cloud Atlas*'s Theory of Everything." *NYR Daily,* NYREV, 2 Nov. 2012,

URL

    www.nybooks.com/daily/2012/11/02/ken-wilber-cloud-atlas/.

author: screen name	label	title of blog post	author of blog post

mitchellfreedman. Comment on *"Cloud Atlas*'s Theory of Everything," by Emily Eakin.

title of blog	publisher/ sponsor	date	URL

NYR Daily, NYREV, 3 Nov. 2012, www.nybooks.com/daily/2012/11/02/ken-wilber

    -cloud-atlas/.

51. Academic course or department home page   Cite as a short work from a Web site (see item 47). For a course home page, begin with the name of the instructor and the title of the course or title of the page (use "Course home page" if there is no other title). For a department home page, begin with the name of the department and the label "Department home page." End with the URL.

Masiello, Regina. 355:101: Expository Writing. *Rutgers School of Arts and Sciences*, 2016,

    wp.rutgers.edu/courses/55-355101.

Film Studies. Department home page. *Wayne State University, College of Liberal Arts and*

    Sciences, 2016, clas.wayne.edu/FilmStudies/.

Audio, visual, and multimedia sources

52. Podcast

author:
last name first   podcast title   Web site title   publisher/sponsor

Tanner, Laura. "Virtual Reality in 9/11 Fiction." *Literature Lab*, Department of English,

URL

Brandeis U, www.brandeis.edu/departments/english/literaturelab/tanner.html. Accessed

date of access
for undated site

14 Feb. 2016.

McDougall, Christopher. "How Did Endurance Help Early Humans Survive?" *TED Radio Hour*, National Public Radio, 20 Nov. 2015, www.npr.org/2015/11/20/455904655/ how-did-endurance-help-early-humans-survive.

53. Film
Generally, begin the entry with the title, followed by the director and lead performers, as in the first example. If your paper emphasizes one or more people involved with the film, you may begin with those names, as in the second example.

film title   director

Birdman or (The Unexpected Virtue of Ignorance). Directed by Alejandro González Iñárritu,

major performers

performances by Michael Keaton, Emma Stone, Zach Galifianakis, Edward Norton,

distributor   release date

and Naomi Watts, Fox Searchlight, 2014.

director:
last name first   film title   major performers

Scott, Ridley, director. *The Martian*. Performances by Matt Damon, Jessica Chastain,

distributor   release date

Kristen Wiig, and Kate Mara, Twentieth Century Fox, 2015.

54. Supplementary material accompanying a film
Begin with the title of the supplementary material, in quotation marks, and the names of any important contributors, as for a film. End with information about the film, as in item 53, and about the location of the supplementary material.

"Sweeney's London." Produced by Eric Young. *Sweeney Todd: The Demon Barber of Fleet Street*, directed by Tim Burton, DreamWorks, 2007, disc 2.

55. Video or audio from the Web Cite video or audio that you accessed on the Web as you would a short work from a Web site (see item 47), giving information about the author before other information about the video or audio.

```
      author:                    Web site
   last name first   title of video   title      date           URL
```
Lewis, Paul. "Citizen Journalism." *YouTube*, 14 May 2011, www.youtube.com/

watch?v=9AP09_yNbcg.

```
      author:
   last name first        title of video              Web site title
```
Fletcher, Antoine. "The Ancient Art of the Atlatl." *Russell Cave National Monument*,

```
                    narrator            publisher/sponsor        date
```
narrated by Brenton Bellomy, National Park Service, 12 Feb. 2014,

```
                                  URL
```
www.nps.gov/media/video/view.htm?id=C92C0D0A-1DD8-B71C-07CBC6E8970CD73F.

```
      author:                    Web site
   last name first   title of video   title   date        URL
```
Burstein, Julie. "Four Lessons in Creativity." *TED*, Feb. 2012, www.ted.com/talks/julie

_burstein_4_lessons_in_creativity.

56. Video game List the developer or author of the game (if any); the title, italicized; the version, if there is one; and the distributor and date of publication. If the game can be played on the Web, add information as for a work from a Web site (see item 47).

Firaxis Games. *Sid Meier's Civilization Revolution*. Take-Two Interactive, 2008.

Edgeworld. Atom Entertainment, 1 May 2012, www.kabam.com/games/edgeworld.

57. Computer software or app Cite as a video game (see item 56), giving whatever information is available about the version, distributor, and date.

Words with Friends. Version 5.84. Zynga, 2013.

58. Television or radio episode or program If you are citing an episode of a program, begin with the title of the episode, in quotation marks. Then give the title of the program, italicized; relevant information about the program, such as the writer, director, performers, or narrator; the episode number (if any); the network; and the date of broadcast.

For a program you accessed on the Web, after the information about the program give the network, the original broadcast date, and the URL. If you are citing an entire program (not an episode or a segment), begin your entry with the title of the program, italicized.

a. Broadcast

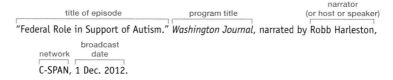

title of episode   program title   narrator (or host or speaker)

"Federal Role in Support of Autism." *Washington Journal,* narrated by Robb Harleston,

network   broadcast date

C-SPAN, 1 Dec. 2012.

The Daily Show with Trevor Noah. Comedy Central, 18 Nov. 2015.

How to cite a source reposted from another source

PROBLEM: Some sources that you find online, particularly on blogs or on video-sharing sites, did not originate with the person who uploaded or published the source online. In such a case, how do you give proper credit for the source?

EXAMPLE: Say you need to cite President John F. Kennedy's inaugural address. You have found a video on YouTube that provides footage of the address (see image). The video was uploaded by PaddyIrishMan2 on October 29, 2006. But clearly, PaddyIrishMan2 is not the author of the video or of the address.

JFK Inaugural Address 1 of 2

PaddyIrishMan2 · 12 videos

▶ Subscribe   ⟨ 403 ⟩

Uploaded on Oct 29, 2006
President John F. Kennedy's inaugural address, January 20th 1961.

Vice President Johnson, Mr. Speaker, Mr. Chief Justice, President Eisenhower, Vice President Nixon, President Truman, reverend clergy, fellow citizens, we observe today not a victory of party, but a celebration of freedom — symbolising an end, as well as a beginning — signifying renewal, as well as change. For I have sworn before you and Almighty God the same solemn oath our forebears prescribed nearly a century and three quarters ago.

b. Web

"The Cathedral." *Reply All*, narrated by Sruthi Pinnamaneni, episode 50, Gimlet Media,

7 Jan. 2016, gimletmedia.com/episode/50-the-cathedral/.

(labels above: title of episode | program title | narrator | episode | publisher/sponsor | date of posting | URL)

"Take a Giant Step." *Prairie Home Companion*, narrated by Garrison Keillor, American

Public Media, 27 Feb. 2016, prairiehome.publicradio.org/listen/full/?name=phc/

2016/02/27/phc_20160227_128.

STRATEGY: Start with what you know. The source is a video that you viewed on the Web. For this particular video, John F. Kennedy is the speaker and the author of the inaugural address. PaddyIrishMan2 is identified as the person who uploaded the source to YouTube.

CITATION: To cite the source, you can combine the basic MLA guidelines for a lecture or public address (see item 61) and for a video found on the Web (see item 55).

Kennedy, John F. "JFK Inaugural Address: 1 of 2." *YouTube*, 29 Oct. 2006,

www.youtube.com/watch?v=xE0iPY7XGBo.

(labels above: author/speaker: last name first | title of address | Web site title | update date | URL)

Because Kennedy's inauguration is a well-known historical event, you can be fairly certain that this is not the only version of the inauguration video. It is a good idea, therefore, to include information about the version you viewed as supplementary information.

Kennedy, John F. "JFK Inaugural Address: 1 of 2." *YouTube*, uploaded by PaddyIrishMan2,

29 Oct. 2006, www.youtube.com/watch?v=xE0iPY7XGBo.

(labels above: author/speaker: last name first | title of address | Web site title | supplementary information | update date | URL)

NOTE: If your work calls for a primary source, you should try to find the original source of the video; a reference librarian can help.

59. Transcript You might find a transcript related to an interview or a program on a radio or television Web site or in a transcript database. Cite the source as you would an interview (see item 27) or a radio or television program (see item 58). Add the label "Transcript" at the end of the entry.

"How Long Can Florida's Citrus Industry Survive?" *All Things Considered*, narrated
 by Greg Allen, National Public Radio, 27 Nov. 2015, www.npr.org/templates/
 transcript/transcript.php?storyId=457424528. Transcript.

"The Economics of Sleep, Part 1." *Freakonomics Radio*, narrated by Stephen J. Dubner,
 9 July 2015, freakonomics.com/2015/07/09/the-economics-of-sleep-part-1-full
 -transcript/. Transcript.

60. Performance For a live performance of a concert, a play, a ballet, or an opera, begin with the title of the work performed, italicized (unless it is named by form, number, and key). Then give the author or composer of the work; relevant information such as the director, the choreographer, the conductor, or the major performers; the theater, ballet, or opera company, if any; the theater and location; and the date of the performance.

The Draft. By Peter Snoad, directed by Diego Arciniegas, Hibernian Hall, Boston,
 10 Sept. 2015.

Symphony no. 4 in G. By Gustav Mahler, conducted by Mark Wigglesworth, performances
 by Juliane Banse and Boston Symphony Orchestra, Symphony Hall, Boston,
 17 Apr. 2009.

61. Lecture or public address Begin with the speaker's name, the title of the lecture, the sponsoring organization, location, and date. If you viewed the lecture on the Web, cite as you would a short work from a Web site (see item 47). Add the label "Address" or "Lecture" at the end if it is not clear from the title.

a. Live

Smith, Anna Deavere. "On the Road: A Search for American Character." National
 Endowment for the Humanities, John F. Kennedy Center for the Performing Arts,
 Washington, 6 Apr. 2015. Address.

b. Web

Khosla, Raj. "Precision Agriculture and Global Food Security." *US Department of State:
 Diplomacy in Action*, 26 Mar. 2013, www.state.gov/e/stas/series/212172.htm.
 Address.

62. Musical score For both print and online versions, begin with the composer's name; the title of the work, italicized (unless it is named by form, number, and key); and the date of composition. For a print source, give the publisher and date. For an online source, give the title of the Web site; the publisher or sponsor; the date; and the URL.

Beethoven, Ludwig van. Symphony no. 5 in C Minor, op. 67. 1807. *Center for Computer Assisted Research in the Humanities*, Stanford U, 2000, scores.ccarh.org/beethoven/ sym/beethoven-sym5-1.pdf.

63. Sound recording Begin with the name of the person you want to emphasize: the composer, conductor, or performer. For a long work, give the title, italicized (unless it is named by form, number, and key); the names of pertinent artists; and the orchestra and conductor. End with the manufacturer and the date.

Bizet, Georges. *Carmen*. Performances by Jennifer Larmore, Thomas Moser, Angela Gheorghiu, Samuel Ramey, and Bavarian State Orchestra and Chorus, conducted by Giuseppe Sinopoli, Warner, 1996.

Blige, Mary J. "Don't Mind." *Life II: The Journey Continues (Act 1)*, Geffen, 2011.

64. Work of art (a) For an original work of art, cite the artist's name; the title of the artwork, italicized; the date of composition; and the institution and city in which the artwork is located. (b) For artworks found on the Web, include the title of the Web site (unless it is the same as the institution) and the URL. (c) If you viewed the artwork as a reproduction in a print source, add publication information about the print source, including the page number or figure number for the artwork.

a. Original

Bradford, Mark. *Let's Walk to the Middle of the Ocean*. 2015, Museum of Modern Art, New York.

64. Work of art (*cont.*)

b. Web

Clough, Charles. *January Twenty-First*. 1988-89, Joslyn Art Museum, Omaha, www.joslyn
.org/collections-and-exhibitions/permanent-collections/modern-and-contemporary/
charles-clough-january-twenty-first/.

c. Reproduction (print)

O'Keeffe, Georgia. *Black and Purple Petunias*. 1925, private collection. *Two Lives: A
Conversation in Paintings and Photographs*, edited by Alexandra Arrowsmith and
Thomas West, HarperCollins, 1992, p. 67.

65. Photograph   (a) For an original photograph, cite the photographer's
name; the title of the photograph, italicized; the date of composition;

How to cite course materials

PROBLEM: Sometimes you will be assigned to work with materials that
an instructor has uploaded to a course Web site or has handed out in class.
Complete publication information may not always be given for such sources.
A PDF file or a hard-copy article, for instance, may have a title and
an author's name but give no other information. Or a video may
not include information about the creator or the date the video was
created. When you write a paper using such sources, how should
you cite them in your own work?

EXAMPLE: Perhaps your instructor has included a PDF
file of an article in a collection of readings on the course Web
site (see image at right). You are writing a paper in which you use
a passage from the work.

THE IMAGE OF THE RAILROAD IN *ANNA KARENINA*

Gary R. Jahn, University of Minnesota

The motif of the railroad recurs so frequently in Lev Tolstoj's *Anna
Karenina* that the conclusion that it is somehow integral to a full
understanding of the novel is inescapable. According to a recent study
the railroad is mentioned at least thirty-two times in the book,[1] and
every reader will remember that Anna and Vronskij first meet at a
railway station, that Levin intensely dislikes the railroad, and that
Anna commits suicide by leaping under a train.[2]
    M. S. Al'tman once asked why Anna, having decided to do away
with herself, should have selected such a gruesome method. The question is flippant only in its formulation, and a great deal of scholarly
effort has been devoted to answering it. A searching of the extensive
biographical data on Tolstoj has amply attested his personal aversion
for the railroad. He wrote Turgenev in 1857 that "the railroad is to
travel as a whore is to love,"[3] and it is known that he was discomfited to
the point of nausea by the swaying of railway carriages. These facts
provide a credible physiological basis for the standard, although not
unanimous,[4] Soviet view that Levin's dyspeptic attitude toward the
railroad is the correlative of Tolstoj's, that the highly autobiographical
Levin was expressing Tolstoj's belief that the railroad served only to
pander to and further inflame the already monstrous appetite of the idle
and privileged for foreign luxuries, and that this belief overlies their
mutual resentment of the forces tending to displace the landholding
nobility from its position of inherited privilege: forces which the railroad is said to symbolize. The railroad is present in the novel so that it
can be attacked, and this is precisely what Levin does in the book which
he writes about contemporary Russian life.[5] There is an indubitable
measure of truth in this understanding of the railway motif. It does
account for Levin's view of the railroad and it is also true that for him
the railroad symbolizes forces harmful to the traditional style of life of

and the institution and city in which the photograph is located. (b) For photographs found on the Web, include the title of the Web site (unless it is the same as the institution) and the URL. (c) If you viewed the photograph as a reproduction in a print source, add publication information about the print source, including the page number or figure number for the artwork. Add the label "Photograph" at the end if it is not clear from the rest of the entry.

a. Original

Feinstein, Harold. *Hangin' Out, Sharing a Public Bench, NYC.* 1948, Panopticon Gallery, Boston. Photograph.

Finotti, Leonardo. *Edificio Girón, Havana, Cuba.* 2014, Museum of Modern Art, New York. Photograph.

b. Web

Hura, Sohrab. *Old Man Lighting a Fire.* 2015, *Magnum Photos,* www.magnumphotos.com/ C.aspx?VP3=SearchResult&ALID=2K1HRG681B_Q.

STRATEGY: Look through section MLA-4b for a model that matches the type of source you're working with. Is it an article? A chapter from a book? A photograph? A video? The model or models you find will give you an idea of the information you need to gather about the source. The usual required information is (1) the author or creator, (2) the title, (3) the date the work was published or created, and (4) the URL for sources on the Web (see p. 425).

CITATION: For your citation, you can give only as much of the required information as you can find in the source. In this example, you know the source is an article with an author and a title, so you can use item 13a (basic format for an article). Because you don't have much other information about the source, it is a good idea to include the description "Course materials" and supplementary information about the course (such as its title or number and the term).

author: last name first	article title	supplementary information

Jahn, Gary R. "The Image of the Railroad in *Anna Karenina*." Course materials,

EN101, Fall 2013.

NOTE: When in doubt about how much information to include or where to find it, consult your instructor.

65. Photograph (cont.)

c. Reproduction (print)

Kertész, André. *Meudon.* 1928. *Street Photography: From Atget to Cartier-Bresson,* by
 Clive Scott, Tauris, 2011, p. 61.

66. Cartoon   Give the cartoonist's name; the title of the cartoon, if it
has one, in quotation marks; publication information; and the label
"Cartoon" at the end if it is not clear from the title. To cite an online
cartoon, cite as a short work from a Web site (item 47).

Zyglis, Adam. "City of Light." *Buffalo News,* 8 Nov. 2015, adamzyglis.buffalonews
 .com/2015/11/08/city-of-light/. Cartoon.

67. Advertisement   Name the product or company being advertised
and publication information for the source in which the advertisement
appears. Add the label "Advertisement" at the end if it is not clear from
the title.

AT&T. *National Geographic,* Dec. 2015, p. 14. Advertisement.

Toyota. *The Root.* Slate Group, 28 Nov. 2015, www.theroot.com. Advertisement.

68. Visual such as a table, a chart, or another graphic   Cite a visual as
you would a short work within a longer work.

"Brazilian Waxing and Waning: The Economy." *The Economist,* 1 Dec. 2015, www
 .economist.com/blogs/graphicdetail/2015/12/economic-backgrounder.

"Number of Measles Cases by Year since 2010." *Centers for Disease Control and
 Prevention,* 2 Jan. 2016, www.cdc.gov/measles/cases-outbreaks.html.

69. Map   Cite a map as you would a short work within a longer work.
Or, if the map is published on its own, cite it as a book or another long
work. Use the label "Map" at the end if it is not clear from the title or
source information.

"Map of Sudan." *Global Citizen,* Citizens for Global Solutions, 2011, globalsolutions.org/
 blog/bashir#.VthzNMfi_FI.

"Vote on Secession, 1861." *Perry-Castañeda Library Map Collection,* U of Texas at
 Austin, 1976, www.lib.utexas.edu/maps/atlas_texas/texas_vote_secession
 _1861.jpg.

Government and legal documents

70. Government document Treat the government agency as the author, giving the name of the government followed by the name of the department and the agency, if any. For sources found on the Web, follow the model for an entire Web site (see item 46) or for short or long works from a Web site (see items 47 and 48).

government   department   agency (or agencies)

United States, Department of Agriculture, Food and Nutrition Service, Child Nutrition

title (long work)

Programs. *Eligibility Manual for School Meals: Determining and Verifying Eligibility.*

Web site title   date   URL

National School Lunch Program, July 2015, www.fns.usda.gov/sites/default/files/

cn/SP40_CACFP18_SFSP20-2015a1.pdf.

Canada, Minister of Aboriginal Affairs and Northern Development. *2015-16 Report on Plans and Priorities*. Minister of Public Works and Government Services Canada, 2015.

71. Testimony before a legislative body

Russel, Daniel R. "Burma's Challenge: Democracy, Human Rights, Peace, and the Plight of the Rohingya." Testimony before the US House Foreign Affairs Committee, Subcommittee on East Asian and Pacific Affairs. *US Department of State: Diplomacy in Action*, 21 Oct. 2015, www.state.gov/p/eap/rls/rm/2015/10/248420.htm.

72. Historical document The titles of most historical documents, such as the US Constitution and the Canadian Charter of Rights and Freedoms, are neither italicized nor put in quotation marks. For a print version, cite as a selection in an anthology (see item 35) or as a book (with the title not italicized). For an online version, cite as a short work from a Web site (see item 47).

Jefferson, Thomas. First Inaugural Address. 1801. *The American Reader: Words That Moved a Nation*, edited by Diane Ravitch, 2nd ed., William Morrow, 2000, pp. 79-82.

Constitution of the United States. 1787. *The Charters of Freedom,* US National Archives and Records Administration, www.archives.gov/exhibits/charters/.

73. Legislative act (law) Begin with the name of the act, neither italicized nor in quotation marks. Then provide the act's Public Law number; its Statutes at Large volume and page numbers; and its date of enactment.

Electronic Freedom of Information Act Amendments of 1996. Pub. L. 104-231. 110 Stat.

    3048. 2 Oct. 1996.

74. Court case Name the first plaintiff and the first defendant. Then give the volume, name, and page number of the law report; the court name; the year of the decision; and publication information. Do not italicize the name of the case. (In the text of the paper, the name of the case is italicized; see item 19 on p. 419.)

Utah v. Evans. 536 US 452. Supreme Court of the US. 2002. *Legal Information Institute,*

    Cornell U Law School, www.law.cornell.edu/supremecourt/text/536/452.

Personal communication and social media

75. E-mail message Begin with the writer's name and the subject line. Then write "Received by," followed by the name of the recipient. End with the date of the message.

Thornbrugh, Caitlin. "Coates Lecture." Received by Rita Anderson, 20 Oct. 2015.

76. Text message

Wiley, Joanna. Message to the author, 4 Apr. 2014.

77. Posting to an online discussion list When possible, cite archived versions of postings. If you cannot locate an archived version, keep a copy of the posting for your records. Begin with the author's name, followed by the title or subject line, in quotation marks (use the label "Online posting" if the posting has no title). Then proceed as for a short work from a Web site (see item 47).

Robin, Griffith. "Write for the Reading Teacher." *Developing Digital Literacies,* NCTE,

    23 Oct. 2015, ncte.connectedcommunity.org/communities/community-home/

    digestviewer/viewthread?GroupId=1693&MID=24520&tab=digestviewer

    &CommunityKey=628d2ad6-8277-4042-a376-2b370ddceabf.

78. Facebook post or comment Cite as a short work from a Web site (see item 47), beginning with the writer's screen name, followed by the real name in parentheses, if both are known. Otherwise use whatever name is given in the source. Follow with the title of the post, if any, in quotation marks. If there is no title, use the label "Post."

Bedford English. "Stacey Cochran explores Reflective Writing in the classroom and as
   a writer: http://ow.ly/YkjVB." *Facebook*, 15 Feb. 2016, www.facebook.com/
   BedfordEnglish/posts/10153415001259607.

79. Twitter post (tweet)   Begin with the writer's screen name, followed by the real name in parentheses, if both are known. Otherwise use whatever name is given in the source. Give the text of the entire tweet in quotation marks, using the writer's capitalization and punctuation. Follow the text with the date and time noted on the tweet, and end with the URL.

Curiosity Rover. "Can you see me waving? How to spot #Mars in the night sky:
   https://youtu.be/hv8hVvJlcJQ." *Twitter*, 5 Nov. 2015, 11:00 a.m., twitter.com/
   marscuriosity/status/672859022911889408.

@grammarphobia (Patricia T. O'Conner and Steward Kellerman). "Is 'if you will,' like, a
   verbal tic? http://goo.gl/oYrTYP #English #language #grammar #etymology #usage
   #linguistics #WOTD." *Twitter*, 14 Mar. 2016, 9:12 a.m., twitter.com/grammarphobia.

MLA-4c   MLA information notes (optional)

Researchers who use the MLA system of parenthetical documentation may also use information notes for one of two purposes:

1. to provide additional material that is important but might interrupt the flow of the paper
2. to refer to several sources that support a single point or to provide comments on sources

Information notes may be either footnotes or endnotes. Footnotes appear at the foot of the page; endnotes appear on a separate page at the end of the paper, just before the list of works cited. For either style, the notes are numbered consecutively throughout the paper. The text of the paper contains a raised arabic numeral that corresponds to the number of the note.

TEXT

In the past several years, employees have filed a number of lawsuits against employers because of online monitoring practices.[1]

NOTE

    1. For a discussion of federal law applicable to electronic surveillance in the workplace, see Kesan 293.

MLA-5 | Manuscript format; sample research paper

The following guidelines are consistent with advice given in the *MLA Handbook*, 8th edition (MLA, 2016), and with typical requirements for student papers. For a sample MLA research paper, see pages 465–70.

MLA-5a MLA manuscript format

Formatting the paper

Papers written in MLA style should be formatted as follows.

Font   If your instructor does not require a specific font, choose one that is standard and easy to read (such as Times New Roman).

Title and identification   MLA does not require a title page. On the first page of your paper, place your name, your instructor's name, the course title, and the date on separate lines against the left margin. Then center your title. (See p. 465 for a sample first page.)

    If your instructor requires a title page, ask for formatting guidelines. A format similar to the one on page 526 may be acceptable.

Page numbers (running head)   Put the page number preceded by your last name in the upper right corner of each page, one-half inch below the top edge. Use arabic numerals (1, 2, 3, and so on).

Margins, line spacing, and paragraph indents   Leave margins of one inch on all sides of the page. Left-align the text.

    Double-space throughout the paper. Do not add extra space above or below the title of the paper or between paragraphs.

    Indent the first line of each paragraph one-half inch from the left margin.

Capitalization, italics, and quotation marks   In titles of works, capitalize all words except articles (*a*, *an*, *the*), prepositions (*to*, *from*, *between*, and so on), coordinating conjunctions (*and*, *but*, *or*, *nor*, *for*, *so*, *yet*), and the *to* in infinitives—unless the word is first or last in the title or subtitle. Follow these guidelines in your paper even if the title appears in all capital or all lowercase letters in the source.

In the text of an MLA paper, when a complete sentence follows a colon, lowercase the first word following the colon unless the sentence is a quotation or a well-known expression or principle.

Italicize the titles of books, journals, magazines, and other long works, such as Web sites. Use quotation marks around the titles of articles, short stories, poems, and other short works.

Long quotations   When a quotation is longer than four typed lines of prose or three lines of poetry, set it off from the text by indenting the entire quotation one-half inch from the left margin. Double-space the indented quotation and do not add extra space above or below it.

Do not use quotation marks when a quotation has been set off from the text by indenting. See page 469 for an example.

URLs   If you need to break a URL at the end of a line in the text of a paper, break it only after a slash or a double slash or before any other mark of punctuation. Do not add a hyphen. If you will post your project online or submit it electronically and you want your readers to click on your URLs, do not insert any line breaks. For MLA guidelines on dividing URLs in your list of works cited, see page 464.

Headings   MLA neither encourages nor discourages the use of headings and provides no guidelines for their use. If you would like to insert headings in a long essay or research paper, check first with your instructor.

Visuals   MLA classifies visuals as tables and figures (figures include graphs, charts, maps, photographs, and drawings). Label each table with an arabic numeral ("Table 1," "Table 2," and so on) and provide a clear caption that identifies the subject. Capitalize the caption as you would a title (see P8-c); do not italicize the label and caption or place them in quotation marks. Place the label and caption on separate lines above the table, flush with the left margin.

For a table that you have borrowed or adapted, give the source below the table in a note like the following:

Source: Boris Groysberg and Michael Slind, "Leadership Is a Conversation," *Harvard Business Review*, June 2012, p. 83.

For each figure, place the figure number (using the abbreviation "Fig.") and a caption below the figure, flush left. Capitalize the caption as you would a sentence; include source information following the caption. (When referring to the figure in your paper, use the abbreviation "fig." in parenthetical citations; otherwise spell out the word.) See page 466 for an example of a figure in a paper.

Place visuals in the text, as close as possible to the sentences that relate to them, unless your instructor prefers that visuals appear in an appendix.

Preparing the list of works cited

Begin the list of works cited on a new page at the end of the paper. Center the title "Works Cited" about one inch from the top of the page. Double-space throughout. See pages 60 and 470 for sample lists of works cited.

Alphabetizing the list   Alphabetize the list by the last names of the authors (or editors); if a work has no author or editor, alphabetize by the first word of the title other than *A*, *An*, or *The*.

If your list includes two or more works by the same author, use the author's name for the first entry only. For subsequent entries, use three hyphens followed by a period. List the titles in alphabetical order. (See items 6 and 7 on p. 427.)

Indenting   Do not indent the first line of each works cited entry, but indent any additional lines one-half inch. This technique highlights the names of the authors, making it easy for readers to scan the alphabetized list. See page 470.

URLs   If you need to include a URL in a works cited entry and it must be divided across lines, break it only after a slash or a double slash or before any other mark of punctuation. Do not add a hyphen. If you will post your project online or submit it electronically and you want your readers to click on your URLs, do not insert any line breaks.

MLA-5b   Sample MLA research paper

On the following pages is a research paper on the topic of the role of government in legislating food choices, written by Sophie Harba, a student in a composition class. Harba's paper is documented with in-text citations and a list of works cited in MLA style. Annotations in the margins of the paper draw your attention to Harba's use of MLA style and her effective writing.

---

hackerhandbooks.com/writersref
e MLA-5 Format, sample paper > Sample student writing
> Harba, "What's for Dinner? Personal Choices vs. Public Health" (research)

Harba 1

Sophie Harba

Professor Baros-Moon

Engl 1101

30 April 2013

What's for Dinner? Personal Choices vs. Public Health

Should the government enact laws to regulate healthy eating choices? Many Americans would answer an emphatic "No," arguing that what and how much we eat should be left to individual choice rather than unreasonable laws. Others might argue that it would be unreasonable for the government not to enact legislation, given the rise of chronic diseases that result from harmful diets. In this debate, both the definition of reasonable regulations and the role of government to legislate food choices are at stake. In the name of public health and safety, state governments have the responsibility to shape health policies and to regulate healthy eating choices, especially since doing so offers a potentially large social benefit for a relatively small cost.

Debates surrounding the government's role in regulating food have a long history in the United States. According to Lorine Goodwin, a food historian, nineteenth-century reformers who sought to purify the food supply were called "fanatics" and "radicals" by critics who argued that consumers should be free to buy and eat what they want (77). Thanks to regulations, though, such as the 1906 federal Pure Food and Drug Act, food, beverages, and medicine are largely free from toxins. In addition, to prevent contamination and the spread of disease, meat and dairy products are now inspected by government agents to ensure that they meet health requirements. Such regulations can be considered reasonable because they protect us from harm with little, if any, noticeable consumer cost. It is not considered an unreasonable infringement on personal choice that contaminated meat or arsenic-laced cough drops are *un*available at our local supermarket. Rather, it is an important government function to stop such harmful items from entering the marketplace.

Even though our food meets current safety standards, there is a need for further regulation. Not all food dangers, for example, arise from obvious toxins like arsenic and *E. coli*. A diet that is low in nutritional value and high in sugars, fats, and refined grains—grains that have been processed

Title is centered.

Opening research question engages readers.

Writer highlights the research conversation.

Thesis answers the research question and presents Harba's main point.

Signal phrase names the author. The parenthetical citation includes a page number.

Historical background provides context for debate.

Harba explains her use of a key term, *reasonable*.

Harba establishes common ground with the reader.

Transition helps readers move from one paragraph to the next.

Marginal annotations indicate MLA-style formatting and effective writing.

Harba 2

Harba uses a graph to illustrate Americans' poor nutritional choices.

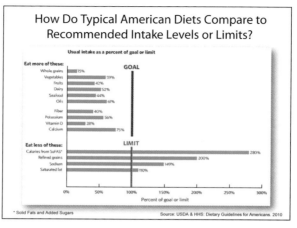

Fig. 1. This graph shows that Americans consume about three times more fats and sugars and twice as many refined grains as is recommended but only half of the recommended foods (United States, Dept. of Agriculture and Dept. of Health and Human Services, fig. 5-1).

The visual includes a figure number, descriptive caption, and source information.

to increase shelf life but that contain little fiber, iron, and B vitamins— can be damaging over time (United States, Dept. of Agriculture and Dept. of Health and Human Services 36). A graph from the government's *Dietary Guidelines for Americans, 2010* provides a visual representation of the American diet and how far off it is from the recommended nutritional standards (see fig. 1).

Michael Pollan, who has written extensively about Americans' unhealthy eating habits, notes that "[t]he Centers for Disease Control estimates that fully three quarters of US health care spending goes to treat chronic diseases, most of which are preventable and linked to diet: heart disease, stroke, type 2 diabetes, and at least a third of all cancers." In fact, the amount of money the United States spends to treat chronic illnesses is increasing so rapidly that the Centers for Disease Control has labeled chronic disease "the public health challenge of the 21st century" (United States, Dept. of Health and Human Services 1). In fighting this epidemic, the primary challenge is not the need to find a cure; the challenge is to prevent chronic diseases from striking in the first place.

No page number is available for this Web source.

Harba sets forth the urgency of her argument.

Harba 3

Legislation, however, is not a popular solution when it comes to most Americans and the food they eat. According to a nationwide poll, 75% of Americans are opposed to laws that restrict or put limitations on access to unhealthy foods (Neergaard and Agiesta). When New York mayor Michael Bloomberg proposed a regulation in 2012 banning the sale of soft drinks in servings greater than twelve ounces in restaurants and movie theaters, he was ridiculed as "Nanny Bloomberg." In California in 2011, legislators failed to pass a law that would impose a penny-per-ounce tax on soda, which would have funded obesity prevention programs. And in Mississippi, legislators passed "a ban on bans—a law that forbids . . . local restrictions on food or drink" (Conly A23).

Harba treats both sides fairly.

Why is the public largely resistant to laws that would limit unhealthy choices or penalize those choices with so-called fat taxes? Many consumers and civil rights advocates find such laws to be an unreasonable restriction on individual freedom of choice. As health policy experts Mello et al. point out, opposition to food and beverage regulation is similar to the opposition to early tobacco legislation: the public views the issue as one of personal responsibility rather than one requiring government intervention (2602). In other words, if a person eats unhealthy food and becomes ill as a result, that is his or her choice. But those who favor legislation claim that freedom of choice is a myth because of the strong influence of food and beverage industry marketing on consumers' dietary habits. According to one nonprofit health advocacy group, food and beverage companies spend roughly two billion dollars per year marketing directly to children. As a result, kids see nearly four thousand ads per year encouraging them to eat unhealthy food and drinks ("Facts"). As was the case with antismoking laws passed in recent decades, taxes and legal restrictions on junk food sales could help to counter the strong marketing messages that promote unhealthy products.

Harba anticipates objections to her idea. She counters opposing views and provides support for her argument.

The United States has a history of state and local public health laws that have successfully promoted a particular behavior by punishing an undesirable behavior. The decline in tobacco use as a result of antismoking taxes and laws is perhaps the most obvious example. Another example is legislation requiring the use of seat belts, which have significantly reduced fatalities in car crashes. One government agency reports that seat belt

An analogy extends Harba's argument.

Harba 4

use saved an average of more than fourteen thousand lives per year in the United States between 2000 and 2010 (United States, Dept. of Transportation, Natl. Highway Traffic Safety Administration 231). Perhaps seat belt laws have public support because the cost of wearing a seat belt is small, especially when compared with the benefit of saving fourteen thousand lives per year.

Laws designed to prevent chronic disease by promoting healthier food and beverage consumption also have potentially enormous benefits. To give just one example, Marion Nestle, New York University professor of nutrition and public health, notes that "a 1% reduction in intake of saturated fat across the population would prevent more than 30,000 cases of coronary heart disease annually and save more than a billion dollars in health care costs" (7). Few would argue that saving lives and dollars is not an enormous benefit. But three-quarters of Americans say they would object to the costs needed to achieve this benefit—the regulations needed to reduce saturated fat intake.

Why do so many Americans believe there is a degree of personal choice lost when regulations such as taxes, bans, or portion limits on unhealthy foods are proposed? Some critics of anti-junk-food laws believe that even if state and local laws were successful in curbing chronic diseases, they would still be unacceptable. Bioethicist David Resnik emphasizes that such policies, despite their potential to make our society healthier, "open the door to excessive government control over food, which could restrict dietary choices, interfere with cultural, ethnic, and religious traditions, and exacerbate socioeconomic inequalities" (31). Resnik acknowledges that his argument relies on "slippery slope" thinking, but he insists that "social and political pressures" regarding food regulation make his concerns valid (31). Yet the social and political pressures that Resnik cites are really just the desire to improve public health, and limiting access to unhealthy, artificial ingredients seems a small price to pay. As legal scholars L. O. Gostin and K. G. Gostin explain, "[I]nterventions that do not pose a truly significant burden on individual liberty" are justified if they "go a long way towards safeguarding the health and well-being of the populace" (214).

To improve public health, advocates such as Bowdoin College philosophy professor Sarah Conly contend that it is the government's

---

Harba introduces a direct quotation with a signal phrase and follows with a comment that shows readers why she chose to use the source.

Harba acknowledges critics and counterarguments.

Including the source's credentials makes Harba more credible.

Harba 5

duty to prevent people from making harmful choices whenever feasible
and whenever public benefits outweigh the costs. In response to critics
who claim that laws aimed at stopping us from eating whatever we
want are an assault on our freedom of choice, Conly offers a persuasive
counterargument:

> [L]aws aren't designed for each one of us individually. Some of us
> can drive safely at 90 miles per hour, but we're bound by the same
> laws as the people who can't, because individual speeding laws aren't
> practical. Giving up a little liberty is something we agree to when we
> agree to live in a democratic society that is governed by laws. (A23)

As Conly suggests, we need to change our either/or thinking (either
we have complete freedom of choice *or* we have government regulations
and lose our freedom) and instead need to see health as a matter of public
good, not individual liberty. Proposals such as Mayor Bloomberg's that seek
to limit portions of unhealthy beverages aren't about giving up liberty; they
are about asking individuals to choose substantial public health benefits at
a very small cost.

Despite arguments in favor of regulating unhealthy food as a means
to improve public health, public opposition has stood in the way of
legislation. Americans freely eat as much unhealthy food as they want, and
manufacturers and sellers of these foods have nearly unlimited freedom
to promote such products and drive increased consumption, without
any requirements to warn the public of potential hazards. Yet mounting
scientific evidence points to unhealthy food as a significant contributing
factor to chronic disease, which we know is straining our health care
system, decreasing Americans' quality of life, and leading to unnecessary
premature deaths. Americans must consider whether to allow the costly
trend of rising chronic disease to continue in the name of personal choice
or whether to support the regulatory changes and public health policies
that will reverse that trend.

Long quotation is introduced with a signal phrase naming the author.

Long quotation is set off from the text. Quotation marks are omitted.

Long quotation is followed with comments that connect the source to Harba's argument.

Conclusion sums up Harba's argument and provides closure.

Harba 6

Heading is centered.

Works Cited

Conly, Sarah. "Three Cheers for the Nanny State." *The New York Times*,
25 Mar. 2013, p. A23.

"The Facts on Junk Food Marketing and Kids." *Prevention Institute*,
www.preventioninstitute.org/focus-areas/supporting-healthy-food-a
-activity/supporting-healthy-food-and-activity-environments-advocacy/
get-involved-were-not-buying-it/735-were-not-buying-it-the-facts-on
-junk-food-marketing-and-kids.html. Accessed 21 Apr. 2013.

Goodwin, Lorine Swainston. *The Pure Food, Drink, and Drug Crusaders,
1879-1914*. McFarland, 2006.

Gostin, L. O., and K. G. Gostin. "A Broader Liberty: J. S. Mill, Paternalism,
and the Public's Health." *Public Health*, vol. 123, no. 3, 2009,
pp. 214-21, doi:10.1016/j.puhe.2008.12.024.

Mello, Michelle M., et al. "Obesity—the New Frontier of Public Health
Law." *New England Journal of Medicine*, vol. 354, no. 24, 2006,
pp. 2601-10, www.nejm.org/doi/pdf/10.1056/NEJMhpr060227.

Neergaard, Lauran, and Jennifer Agiesta. "Obesity's a Crisis but We Want
Our Junk Food, Poll Shows." *Huffington Post*, 4 Jan. 2013, www
.huffingtonpost.com/2013/01/04/obesity-junk-food-government
-intervention-poll_n_2410376.html.

Nestle, Marion. *Food Politics: How the Food Industry Influences Nutrition
and Health*. U of California P, 2013.

Pollan, Michael. "The Food Movement, Rising." *The New York Review of
Books*, 10 June 2010, www.nybooks.com/articles/2010/06/10/
food-movement-rising/.

Resnik, David. "Trans Fat Bans and Human Freedom." *American Journal of
Bioethics*, vol. 10, no. 3, Mar. 2010, pp. 27-32.

United States, Department of Agriculture and Department of Health and
Human Services. *Dietary Guidelines for Americans, 2010*, health.gov/
dietaryguidelines/dga2010/dietaryguidelines2010.pdf.

United States, Department of Health and Human Services, Centers for
Disease Control and Prevention. *The Power of Prevention*. National
Center for Chronic Disease Prevention and Health Promotion, 2009,
www.cdc.gov/chronicdisease/pdf/2009-Power-of-Prevention.pdf.

United States, Department of Transportation, National Highway Traffic
Safety Administration. *Traffic Safety Facts 2010: A Compilation of
Motor Vehicle Crash Data from the Fatality Analysis Reporting System
and the General Estimates System*. 2010, www-nrd.nhtsa.dot.gov/
Pubs/811659.pdf.

List is alphabetized by authors' last names (or by title when a work has no author).

Access date used for an online source that has no update date.

First line of each entry is at the left margin; extra lines are indented ½".

Double-spacing is used throughout.

The government agency is used as the author of a government document.

APA
CMS

APA and CMS
Papers

APA/ CMS   APA and CMS Papers

Directory to APA in-text citation models

Directory to APA reference list models

*Directory to **CMS-style notes and bibliography entries** is on page 535.*

Directory to APA reference list models, *continued*

This tabbed section shows how to document sources in APA style for the social sciences and fields such as nursing and business, and in CMS (*Chicago*) style for history and some humanities classes. It also includes discipline-specific advice on three important topics: supporting a thesis, citing sources and avoiding plagiarism, and integrating sources.

NOTE: For advice on finding and evaluating sources and on managing information in courses across the disciplines, see the tabbed section R, Researching.

APA Papers

Most instructors in the social sciences and some instructors in other disciplines will ask you to document your sources with the American Psychological Association (APA) system of in-text citations and references described in APA-4. You face three main challenges when writing a social science paper that draws on sources: (1) supporting a thesis, (2) citing your sources and avoiding plagiarism, and (3) integrating quotations and other source material.

Examples in this section are drawn from one student's research for a review of the literature on treatments for childhood obesity. Luisa Mirano's paper appears on pages 526–34.

APA-1 | Supporting a thesis

Most research assignments ask you to form a thesis, or main idea, and to support that thesis with well-organized evidence. In a paper reviewing the literature on a topic, the thesis analyzes the often competing conclusions drawn by a variety of researchers.

APA-1a Form a working thesis.

Once you have read a range of sources, considered your issue from different perspectives, and chosen an entry point in the research conversation (see R1-b), you are ready to form a working thesis: a one-sentence (or occasionally a two-sentence) statement of your central idea. (See also C1-c.) Because it is a working, or tentative, thesis, you can remain flexible and revise it as your ideas develop. Ultimately, your thesis will express not just your opinion but your informed, reasoned answer to your research question—a question about which people might disagree (see R3-c). Here, for example, is a research question posed by Luisa Mirano, a student in a psychology class, followed by her thesis in answer to that question.

RESEARCH QUESTION

Is medication the right treatment for the escalating problem of childhood obesity?

WORKING THESIS

Treating cases of childhood obesity with medication alone is too narrow an approach for this growing problem.

The thesis usually appears at the end of the introductory paragraph. To read Luisa Mirano's thesis in the context of her introduction, see page 528.

APA-1b Organize your ideas.

The American Psychological Association encourages the use of headings to help readers follow the organization of a paper. For an original research report, the major headings often follow a standard model: Method, Results, Discussion. The introduction does not have a heading; it consists of the material between the title of the paper and the first heading.

For a literature review, headings will vary. In Luisa Mirano's paper about treatments for childhood obesity, she used four questions to focus her research; the questions then became headings in her paper (see APA-5b).

> **MORE HELP IN YOUR HANDBOOK**
>
> A working thesis and rough outline can help writers get started.
> ► Drafting a working thesis: **C1-c**
> ► Sketching a plan: **C1-d**

APA-1c Use sources to inform and support your argument.

Used thoughtfully, your source materials will make your argument more complex and convincing for readers. Sources can play several different roles to support your thesis and develop your points.

Providing background information or context

You can use facts and statistics to support generalizations or to establish the importance of your topic, as student writer Luisa Mirano does in her introduction.

> In March 2004, U.S. Surgeon General Richard Carmona called attention to a health problem in the United States that, until recently, has been overlooked: childhood obesity. Carmona said that the "astounding" 15% child obesity rate constitutes an "epidemic." Since the early 1980s, that rate has "doubled in children and tripled in adolescents." Now more than nine million children are classified as obese.

Explaining terms or concepts

If readers are unlikely to be familiar with a word, a phrase, or an idea important to your topic, you must explain it for them. Quoting or paraphrasing a source can help you define terms and concepts in accessible language. Luisa Mirano uses a scholarly source to explain how one of the major obesity drugs functions.

> Sibutramine suppresses appetite by blocking the reuptake of the neurotransmitters serotonin and norepinephrine in the brain (Yanovski & Yanovski, 2002, p. 594).

Supporting your claims

As you draft, make sure to back up your assertions with facts, examples, and other evidence from your research (see also A4-e). Luisa Mirano, for example, uses one source's findings to support her central idea that the medical treatment of childhood obesity has limitations.

> As journalist Greg Critser (2003) noted in his book *Fat Land*, use of weight-loss drugs is unlikely to have an effect without the proper "support system"—one that includes doctors, facilities, time, and money (p. 3).

Lending authority to your argument

Expert opinion can add credibility to your argument (see also A4-e). But don't rely on experts to make your argument for you. Construct your argument in your own words and, when appropriate, cite the judgment of an authority in the field for support.

Both medical experts and policymakers recognize that solutions might come not only from a laboratory but also from policy, education, and advocacy. A handbook designed to educate doctors on obesity called for "major changes in some aspects of western culture" (Hoppin & Taveras, 2004, Conclusion section, para. 1).

Anticipating and countering alternative interpretations

Do not ignore sources that seem contrary to your position or that offer interpretations different from your own. Instead, use them to give voice to opposing points of view and alternative interpretations before you counter them (see A4-f). Readers often have objections in mind already, whether or not they agree with you. Mirano uses a source to acknowledge value in her opponents' position that medication alone can successfully treat childhood obesity.

As researchers Yanovski and Yanovski (2002) have explained, obesity was once considered "either a moral failing or evidence of underlying psychopathology" (p. 592). But this view has shifted: Many medical professionals now consider obesity a biomedical rather than a moral condition, influenced by both genetic and environmental factors. Yanovski and Yanovski have further noted that the development of weight-loss medications in the early 1990s showed that "obesity should be treated in the same manner as any other chronic disease . . . through the long-term use of medication" (p. 592).

APA-2 | Citing sources; avoiding plagiarism

In a research paper, you will draw on the work of other researchers and writers, and you must document their contributions by citing your sources. Sources are cited for two reasons:

1. to tell readers where your information comes from—so that they can assess its reliability and, if interested, find and read the original source
2. to give credit to the writers from whom you have borrowed words and ideas

You must cite anything you borrow from a source, including direct quotations; statistics and other specific facts; visuals such as tables, graphs, and diagrams; and any ideas you present in a summary or paraphrase.

Borrowing without proper acknowledgment is a form of dishonesty known as *plagiarism*.

The only exception is common knowledge—information that your readers may know or could easily locate in any number of reference sources.

APA-2a Understand how the APA system works.

The American Psychological Association recommends an author-date system of citations. The following is a brief description of how the author-date system usually works.

1. The source is introduced by a signal phrase that includes the last name of the author followed by the date of publication in parentheses.
2. The material being cited is followed by a page number in parentheses.
3. At the end of the paper, an alphabetized list of references gives complete publication information for the source.

IN-TEXT CITATION

As researchers Yanovski and Yanovski (2002) have explained, obesity was once considered "either a moral failing or evidence of underlying psychopathology" (p. 592).

ENTRY IN THE LIST OF REFERENCES

Yanovski, S. Z., & Yanovski, J. A. (2002). Drug therapy: Obesity. *The New England Journal of Medicine, 346*, 591-602.

This basic APA format varies for different types of sources. For a detailed discussion and other models, see APA-4.

APA-2b Understand what plagiarism is.

Your research paper represents your ideas in conversation with the ideas in your sources. To be fair and responsible, you must acknowledge your debt to the writers of those sources. When you acknowledge your sources, you avoid plagiarism, a form of academic dishonesty.

Three different acts are considered plagiarism: (1) failing to cite quotations and borrowed ideas, (2) failing to enclose borrowed language in quotation marks, and (3) failing to put summaries and

hackerhandbooks.com/writersref
APA-2 Citing sources > Exercises: APA 2–1 to APA 2–7
APA-2 Citing sources > LearningCurve: Working with sources (APA)

paraphrases in your own words. Definitions of plagiarism may vary; it's a good idea to find out how your school defines and addresses academic dishonesty.

APA-2c   Use quotation marks around borrowed language.

To indicate that you are using a source's exact phrases or sentences, you must enclose them in quotation marks unless they have been set off from the text by indenting (see p. 484). To omit the quotation marks is to claim—falsely—that the language is your own. Such an omission is plagiarism even if you have cited the source.

> **MORE HELP IN YOUR HANDBOOK**
>
> When you use exact language from a source, you need to show that it is a quotation.
>
> ▶ Quotation marks for direct quotations: **P5-a**

ORIGINAL SOURCE

In an effort to seek the causes of this disturbing trend, experts have pointed to a range of important potential contributors to the rise in childhood obesity that are unrelated to media: a reduction in physical education classes and after-school athletic programs, an increase in the availability of sodas and snacks in public schools, the growth in the number of fast-food outlets across the country, the trend toward "super-sizing" food portions in restaurants, and the increasing number of highly processed high-calorie and high-fat grocery products.

—Henry J. Kaiser Family Foundation, "The Role of Media in Childhood Obesity" (2004), p. 1

PLAGIARISM

According to the Henry J. Kaiser Family Foundation (2004), experts have pointed to a range of important potential contributors to the rise in childhood obesity that are unrelated to media (p. 1).

BORROWED LANGUAGE IN QUOTATION MARKS

According to the Henry J. Kaiser Family Foundation (2004), "experts have pointed to a range of important potential contributors to the rise in childhood obesity that are unrelated to media" (p. 1).

NOTE: Quotation marks are not used when quoted sentences are set off from the text by indenting (see p. 484).

APA-2d Put summaries and paraphrases in your own words.

Summaries and paraphrases are written in your own words. A summary condenses information; a paraphrase conveys the information using roughly the same number of words as in the original source. When you summarize or paraphrase, it is not enough to name the source; you must restate the source's meaning using your own language. (See also R2-c and, if English is not your native language, M6.) You commit plagiarism if you patchwrite — half-copy the author's sentences, either by mixing the author's phrases with your own without using quotation marks or by plugging your own synonyms into the author's sentence structure. The following paraphrases are plagiarized — even though the source is cited — because their language and sentence structure are too close to those of the source.

ORIGINAL SOURCE

In an effort to seek the causes of this disturbing trend, experts have pointed to a range of important potential contributors to the rise in childhood obesity that are unrelated to media.
— Henry J. Kaiser Family Foundation, "The Role of Media in Childhood Obesity" (2004), p. 1

UNACCEPTABLE BORROWING OF PHRASES

According to the Henry J. Kaiser Family Foundation (2004), experts have indicated a range of significant potential contributors to the rise in childhood obesity that are not linked to media (p. 1).

UNACCEPTABLE BORROWING OF STRUCTURE

According to the Henry J. Kaiser Family Foundation (2004), experts have identified a variety of key factors causing a rise in childhood obesity, factors that are not tied to media (p. 1).

To avoid plagiarizing an author's language, resist the temptation to look at the source while you are summarizing or paraphrasing. After you have read the passage you want to paraphrase, set the source aside. Ask yourself, "What is the author's meaning?" In your own words, state your understanding of the author's basic point. Return to the source and check that you haven't used the author's language or sentence structure or misrepresented the author's ideas. When you fully understand another writer's meaning, you can more easily and accurately present those ideas in your own words.

ACCEPTABLE PARAPHRASE

A report by the Henry J. Kaiser Family Foundation (2004) described causes other than media for the childhood obesity crisis (p. 1).

APA-3 Integrating sources

Quotations, summaries, paraphrases, and facts will help you support your argument, but they cannot speak for you. You can use several strategies to integrate information from sources into your paper while maintaining your own voice.

APA-3a Use quotations appropriately.

In your academic writing, keep the emphasis on your ideas; use your own words to summarize and to paraphrase your sources and to explain your points. Sometimes, however, quotations can be the most effective way to integrate a source.

WHEN TO USE QUOTATIONS

- When language is especially vivid or expressive
- When exact wording is needed for technical accuracy
- When it is important to let the debaters of an issue explain their positions in their own words
- When the words of an authority lend weight to an argument
- When the language of a source is the topic of your discussion

Limiting your use of quotations

Although it is tempting to insert many quotations in your paper and to use your own words only for connecting passages, do not quote excessively. It is almost impossible to integrate numerous long quotations smoothly into your own text.

It is not always necessary to quote full sentences from a source. To reduce your reliance on the words of others, you can often integrate language from a source into your own sentence structure.

hackerhandbooks.com/writersref

e APA-3 Integrating sources > Exercises: APA 3–1 to APA 3–7

☑ APA-3 Integrating sources > LearningCurve: Working with sources (APA)

Carmona (2004) advised the subcommittee that the situation constitutes an "epidemic" and that the skyrocketing statistics are "astounding."

As researchers continue to face a number of unknowns about obesity, it may be helpful to envision treating the disorder, as Yanovski and Yanovski (2002) suggested, "in the same manner as any other chronic disease" (p. 592).

Using the ellipsis mark

To condense a quoted passage, you can use the ellipsis mark (three periods, with spaces between) to indicate that you have omitted words. What remains must be grammatically complete.

Roman (2003) reported that "social factors are nearly as significant as individual metabolism in the formation of . . . dietary habits of adolescents" (p. 345).

The writer has omitted the words *both healthy and unhealthy* from the source.

When you want to leave out one or more full sentences, use a period before the three ellipsis dots.

According to Sothern and Gordon (2003), "Environmental factors may contribute as much as 80% to the causes of childhood obesity. . . . Research suggests that obese children demonstrate decreased levels of physical activity and increased psychosocial problems" (p. 104).

Ordinarily, do not use an ellipsis mark at the beginning or at the end of a quotation. Readers will understand that you have taken the quoted material from a longer passage. The only exception occurs when you feel it is necessary, for clarity, to indicate that your quotation begins or ends in the middle of a sentence.

USING SOURCES RESPONSIBLY: Make sure that omissions and ellipsis marks do not distort the meaning of your source.

Using brackets

Brackets allow you to insert your own words into quoted material. You can insert words in brackets to clarify a confusing reference or to keep a sentence grammatical in the context of your own writing.

The cost of treating obesity currently totals $117 billion per year—a price, according to the surgeon general, "second only to the cost of [treating] tobacco use" (Carmona, 2004).

To indicate an error such as a misspelling in a quotation, insert [*sic*], italicized and with brackets around it, right after the error. (See P6-b.)

Setting off long quotations

When you quote forty or more words from a source, set off the quotation by indenting it one-half inch from the left margin. Use the normal right margin and do not single-space the quotation.

Long quotations should be introduced by an informative sentence, usually followed by a colon. Quotation marks are unnecessary because the indented format tells readers that the passage is taken word-for-word from the source.

> Yanovski and Yanovski (2002) have described earlier treatments for obesity that
> focused on behavior modification:
>
> > With the advent of behavioral treatments for obesity in the 1960s, hope
> > arose that modification of maladaptive eating and exercise habits would
> > lead to sustained weight loss, and that time-limited programs would produce
> > permanent changes in weight. Medications for the treatment of obesity were
> > proposed as short-term adjuncts for patients, who would presumably then
> > acquire the skills necessary to continue to lose weight, reach "ideal body
> > weight," and maintain a reduced weight indefinitely. (p. 592)

Notice that at the end of an indented quotation the parenthetical citation goes outside the final mark of punctuation. (When a quotation is run into your text, the opposite is true. See the sample citations on p. 483.)

APA-3b Use signal phrases to integrate sources.

Whenever you include a paraphrase, summary, or direct quotation of another writer's work in your paper, prepare your readers for it with a signal phrase. A signal phrase usually names the author of the source, gives the publication year in parentheses, and often provides some context. It is generally acceptable in APA style to call authors by their last name only, even on a first mention. If your paper refers to two authors with the same last name, use initials as well.

When you write a signal phrase, choose a verb that is appropriate for the way you are using the source (see APA-1c). Are you providing background, explaining a concept, supporting a claim, lending authority, or refuting an argument? See the chart on page 487 for a list of verbs commonly used in signal phrases. Note that APA requires using verbs in the past tense or present perfect tense (*explained* or *has explained*) to introduce source material. Use the present tense only for discussing the applications or effects of your own results (*the data suggest*) or knowledge that has been clearly established (*researchers agree*).

Marking boundaries

Readers need to move from your words to the words of a source without feeling a jolt. Avoid dropping direct quotations into your text without warning. Instead, provide clear signal phrases, including at least the author's name and the year of publication. Signal phrases mark the boundaries between source material and your own words; they can also tell readers why a source is worth quoting. (The signal phrase is high-lighted in the second example.)

DROPPED QUOTATION

Obesity was once considered in a very different light. "For many years, obesity was approached as if it were either a moral failing or evidence of underlying psychopathology" (Yanovski & Yanovski, 2002, p. 592).

QUOTATION WITH SIGNAL PHRASE

Obesity was once considered in a very different light. As researchers Yanovski and Yanovski (2002) have explained, obesity was widely thought of as "either a moral failing or evidence of underlying psychopathology" (p. 592).

Using signal phrases with summaries and paraphrases

As with quotations, you should introduce most summaries and para-phrases with a signal phrase that mentions the author and the year and places the material in the context of your own writing. Readers will then understand where the summary or paraphrase begins.

Without the signal phrase (highlighted) in the following example, readers might think that only the last sentence is being cited, when in fact the whole paragraph is based on the source.

Carmona (2004) advised a Senate subcommittee that the problem of childhood obesity is dire and that the skyrocketing statistics—which put the child obesity rate at 15%—are cause for alarm. More than nine million children, double the number in the early 1980s, are classified as obese. Carmona warned that obesity can cause myriad physical problems that only worsen as children grow older.

There are times, however, when a summary or a paraphrase does not require a signal phrase naming the author. When the context makes clear where the cited material begins, you may omit the signal phrase and include the author's name and the year in parentheses.

Integrating statistics and other facts

When you are citing a statistic or another specific fact, a signal phrase is often not necessary. In most cases, readers will understand that the citation refers to the statistic or fact (not the whole paragraph).

> In purely financial terms, the drugs cost more than $3 a day on average (Duenwald, 2004).

There is nothing wrong, however, with using a signal phrase to introduce a statistic or another fact.

Putting source material in context

Readers should not have to guess why source material appears in your paper. If you use another writer's words, you must explain how they relate to your point. In other words, you must put the source in context. It's a good idea to embed a quotation between sentences of your own, introducing it with a signal phrase and following it up with interpretive comments that link the quotation to your paper's argument. (See also APA-3c.)

QUOTATION WITH EFFECTIVE CONTEXT

A report by the Henry J. Kaiser Family Foundation (2004) outlined trends that may have contributed to the childhood obesity crisis, including food advertising for children as well as

> a reduction in physical education classes . . . , an increase in the availability of sodas and snacks in public schools, the growth in the number of fast-food outlets . . . , and the increasing number of highly processed high-calorie and high-fat grocery products. (p. 1)

Addressing each of these areas requires more than a doctor armed with a prescription pad; it requires a broad mobilization not just of doctors and concerned parents but of educators, food industry executives, advertisers, and media representatives.

Using signal phrases in APA papers

To avoid monotony, try to vary both the language and the placement of your signal phrases.

Model signal phrases

In the words of Carmona (2004), ". . ."

As Yanovski and Yanovski (2002) have noted, ". . ."

Hoppin and Taveras (2004), medical researchers, pointed out that ". . ."

". . . ," claimed Critser (2003).

". . . ," wrote Duenwald (2004), ". . ."

Researchers McDuffie et al. (2003) have offered a compelling argument for this view: ". . ."

Hilts (2002) answered objections with the following analysis: ". . ."

Verbs in signal phrases

admitted	contended	reasoned
agreed	declared	refuted
argued	denied	rejected
asserted	emphasized	reported
believed	insisted	responded
claimed	noted	suggested
compared	observed	thought
confirmed	pointed out	wrote

APA-3c Synthesize sources.

When you synthesize multiple sources in a research paper, you create a conversation about your research topic. You show readers how the ideas of one source relate to those of another by connecting and analyzing the ideas in the context of your argument. Keep the emphasis on your own writing. The thread of your argument should be easy to identify and to understand, with or without your sources.

SAMPLE SYNTHESIS (DRAFT)

Student writer Luisa Mirano begins with a claim that needs support.

Signal phrases indicate how sources contribute to Mirano's paper and show that the ideas that follow are not her own.

Mirano interprets and connects sources. Each paragraph ends with her own thoughts.

Medical treatments have clear costs for individual patients, including unpleasant side effects, little information about long-term use, and uncertainty that they will yield significant weight loss. The financial burden is heavy as well; the drugs cost more than $3 a day on average (Duenwald, 2004). In each of the clinical trials, use of medication was accompanied by expensive behavioral therapies, including counseling, nutrition education, fitness advising, and monitoring. As Critser (2003) noted in his book *Fat Land*, use of weight-loss drugs is unlikely to have an effect without the proper "support system"—one that includes doctors, facilities, time, and money (p. 3). For many families, this level of care is prohibitively expensive.

Both medical experts and policymakers recognize that solutions might come not only from a laboratory but also from policy, education, and advocacy. A handbook designed to educate doctors on obesity called for "major changes in some aspects of western culture" (Hoppin & Taveras, 2004, Conclusion section, para. 1). Solving the childhood obesity problem will require broad mobilization of doctors and concerned parents and also of educators, food industry executives, advertisers, and media representatives.

Student writer

Source 1

Student writer

Source 2

Student writer

Source 3

Student writer

In this draft, Mirano uses her own analyses to shape the conversation among her sources. She does not simply string quotations and statistics together or allow her sources to overwhelm her writing. The final sentence, written in her own voice, gives her an opportunity to explain to readers how her sources support and extend her argument.

When synthesizing sources, ask yourself these questions:

- Which sources inform, support, or extend your argument?
- Have you varied the functions of sources — to provide background, explain concepts, lend authority, and anticipate counterarguments? Do your signal phrases indicate these functions?
- Do you explain how your sources support your argument?
- Do you connect and analyze sources in your own voice?
- Is your own argument easy to identify and to understand, with or without your sources?

| **APA-4** | Documenting sources |

In most social science classes, you will be asked to use the APA system for documenting sources, which is set forth in the *Publication Manual of the American Psychological Association*, 6th ed. (Washington, DC: APA, 2010).

APA recommends in-text citations that refer readers to a list of references. An in-text citation gives the author of the source (often in a signal phrase), the year of publication, and often a page number in parentheses. At the end of the paper, a list of references provides publication information about the source; the list is alphabetized by authors' last names (or by titles for works with no authors). The direct link between the in-text citation and the entry in the reference list is highlighted in the following example.

> **MORE HELP IN YOUR HANDBOOK**
>
> A reference list includes all the sources cited in the text of a paper.
>
> ▶ APA reference list: **APA-4b**
> ▶ Preparing the reference list: **APA-5a**
> ▶ Sample reference list: **page 534**

IN-TEXT CITATION

Yanovski and Yanovski (2002) reported that "the current state of the treatment for obesity is similar to the state of the treatment of hypertension several decades ago" (p. 600).

ENTRY IN THE LIST OF REFERENCES

Yanovski, S. Z., & Yanovski, J. A. (2002). Drug therapy: Obesity. *The New England Journal of Medicine, 346,* 591-602.

For a reference list that includes this entry, see page 534.

APA-4a   APA in-text citations

APA's in-text citations provide the author's last name and the year of publication, usually before the cited material, and a page number in parentheses directly after the cited material. In the following models, the elements of the in-text citation are highlighted.

NOTE: APA style requires the use of the past tense or the present perfect tense in signal phrases introducing cited material: *Smith (2012) reported, Smith (2012) has argued.* (See also p. 484.)

hackerhandbooks.com/writersref

🄴 APA-4 Documenting sources > Exercises: APA 4–1 to APA 4–3, APA 4–9 to APA 4–11

1. Basic format for a quotation Ordinarily, introduce the quotation with a signal phrase that includes the author's last name followed by the year of publication in parentheses. Put the page number (preceded by "p.") in parentheses after the quotation. For sources from the Web without page numbers, see item 12a on page 493.

> Critser (2003) noted that despite growing numbers of overweight Americans, many health care providers still "remain either in ignorance or outright denial about the health danger to the poor and the young" (p. 5).

If the author is not named in the signal phrase, place the author's name, the year, and the page number in parentheses after the quotation: (Critser, 2003, p. 5). (See items 6 and 12 for citing sources that lack authors; item 12 also explains how to handle sources without dates or page numbers.)

NOTE: Do not include a month in an in-text citation, even if the entry in the reference list includes the month.

2. Basic format for a summary or a paraphrase As for a quotation (see item 1), include the author's last name and the year either in a signal phrase introducing the material or in parentheses following it. Use a page number, if one is available, following the cited material. For sources from the Web without page numbers, see item 12a on page 493.

> Yanovski and Yanovski (2002) explained that sibutramine suppresses appetite by blocking the reuptake of the neurotransmitters serotonin and norepinephrine in the brain (p. 594).

> Sibutramine suppresses appetite by blocking the reuptake of the neurotransmitters serotonin and norepinephrine in the brain (Yanovski & Yanovski, 2002, p. 594).

3. Work with two authors Name both authors in the signal phrase or in parentheses each time you cite the work. In the parentheses, use "&" between the authors' names; in the signal phrase, use "and."

> According to Sothern and Gordon (2003), "Environmental factors may contribute as much as 80% to the causes of childhood obesity" (p. 104).

> Obese children often engage in limited physical activity (Sothern & Gordon, 2003, p. 104).

4. Work with three to five authors Identify all authors in the signal phrase or in parentheses the first time you cite the source.

> In 2003, Berkowitz, Wadden, Tershakovec, and Cronquist concluded, "Sibutramine
> . . . must be carefully monitored in adolescents, as in adults, to control increases
> in [blood pressure] and pulse rate" (p. 1811).

In subsequent citations, use the first author's name followed by "et al." in either the signal phrase or the parentheses.

> As Berkowitz et al. (2003) advised, "Until more extensive safety and efficacy data
> are available, . . . weight-loss medications should be used only on an experimental
> basis for adolescents" (p. 1811).

5. Work with six or more authors Use the first author's name followed by "et al." in the signal phrase or in parentheses.

> McDuffie et al. (2002) tested 20 adolescents, aged 12-16, over a three-month
> period and found that orlistat, combined with behavioral therapy, produced an
> average weight loss of 4.4 kg, or 9.7 pounds (p. 646).

6. Work with unknown author If the author is unknown, mention the work's title in the signal phrase or give the first word or two of the title in the parentheses. Titles of short works such as articles are put in quotation marks; titles of long works such as books and reports are italicized.

> Children struggling to control their weight must also struggle with the pressures of
> television advertising that, on the one hand, encourages the consumption of junk
> food and, on the other, celebrates thin celebrities ("Television," 2002).

NOTE: In the rare case when "Anonymous" is specified as the author, treat it as if it were a real name: (Anonymous, 2001). In the list of references, also use the name Anonymous as author.

7. Organization as author If the author is an organization or a government agency, name the organization in the signal phrase or in the parentheses the first time you cite the source.

> Obesity puts children at risk for a number of medical complications, including Type
> 2 diabetes, hypertension, sleep apnea, and orthopedic problems (Henry J. Kaiser
> Family Foundation, 2004, p. 1).

If the organization has a familiar abbreviation, you may include it in brackets the first time you cite the source and use the abbreviation alone in later citations.

FIRST CITATION   (Centers for Disease Control and Prevention [CDC], 2012)

LATER CITATIONS   (CDC, 2012)

8. Authors with the same last name   To avoid confusion if your reference list includes two or more authors with the same last name, use initials with the last names in your in-text citations.

Research by E. Smith (1989) revealed that. . . .

One 2012 study contradicted . . . (R. Smith, p. 234).

9. Two or more works by the same author in the same year   When your list of references includes more than one work by the same author in the same year, you will use lowercase letters ("a," "b," and so on) with the year to order the entries in the reference list. (See item 8 on p. 499.) Use those same letters with the year in the in-text citation.

Research by Durgin (2003b) has yielded new findings about the role of counseling in treating childhood obesity.

10. Two or more works in the same parentheses   Put the works in the same order that they appear in the reference list, separated with semicolons.

Researchers have indicated that studies of pharmacological treatments for childhood obesity are inconclusive (Berkowitz et al., 2003; McDuffie et al., 2002).

11. Multiple citations to the same work in one paragraph   If you give the author's name in the text of your paper (not in parentheses) and you mention that source again in the text of the same paragraph, give only the author's name, not the date, in the later citation. If any subsequent reference in the same paragraph is in parentheses, include both the author and the date in the parentheses.

Principal Jean Patrice said, "You have to be able to reach students where they are instead of making them come to you. If you don't, you'll lose them" (personal communication, April 10, 2006). Patrice expressed her desire to see all students get something out of their educational experience. This feeling is common among members of Waverly's faculty. With such a positive view of student potential, it is no wonder that 97% of Waverly High School graduates go on to a four-year university (Patrice, 2006).

12. Web source Cite sources from the Web as you would cite any other source, giving the author and the year when they are available.

> Atkinson (2001) found that children who spent at least four hours a day watching TV were less likely to engage in adequate physical activity during the week.

Usually a page number is not available; occasionally a Web source will lack an author or a date (see 12a, 12b, and 12c).

a. No page numbers When a Web source lacks stable numbered pages, you may include paragraph numbers or headings to help readers locate the passage being cited.

If the source has numbered paragraphs, use the paragraph number preceded by the abbreviation "para.": (Hall, 2012, para. 5). If the source has no numbered paragraphs but contains headings, cite the appropriate heading in parentheses; you may also indicate which paragraph under the heading you are referring to, even if the paragraphs are not numbered.

> Hoppin and Taveras (2004) pointed out that several other medications were classified by the Drug Enforcement Administration as having the "potential for abuse" ("Weight-Loss Drugs," para. 6).

NOTE: For PDF documents that have stable page numbers, give the page number in the parenthetical citation.

b. Unknown author If no author is named in the source, mention the title of the source in a signal phrase or give the first word or two of the title in parentheses (see also item 6). (If an organization serves as the author, see item 7.)

> The body's basal metabolic rate, or BMR, is a measure of its at-rest energy requirement ("Exercise," 2003).

c. Unknown date When the source does not give a date, use the abbreviation "n.d." (for "no date").

> Attempts to establish a definitive link between television programming and children's eating habits have been problematic (Magnus, n.d.).

13. An entire Web site If you are citing an entire Web site, not an internal page or a section, give the URL in the text of your paper but do not include it in the reference list.

> The U.S. Center for Nutrition Policy and Promotion website (http://www.cnpp .usda.gov/) provides useful information about diet and nutrition for children and adults.

14. Multivolume work If you have used more than one volume from a multivolume work, add the volume number in parentheses with the page number.

> Banford (2009) has demonstrated stable weight loss over time from a combination of psychological counseling, exercise, and nutritional planning (Volume 2, p. 135).

15. Personal communication Interviews that you conduct, memos, letters, e-mail messages, social media posts, and similar communications that would be difficult for your readers to retrieve should be cited in the text only, not in the reference list. (Use the first initial with the last name in parentheses.)

> One of Atkinson's colleagues, who has studied the effect of the media on children's eating habits, has contended that advertisers for snack foods will need to design ads responsibly for their younger viewers (F. Johnson, personal communication, October 20, 2013).

16. Course materials Cite lecture notes from your instructor or your own class notes as personal communication (see item 15). If your instructor distributes or posts materials that contain publication information, cite as you would the appropriate source (for instance, an article, a section in a Web document, or a video). See also item 65 on page 520.

17. Part of a source (chapter, figure) To cite a specific part of a source, such as a whole chapter or a figure or table, identify the element in parentheses. Don't abbreviate terms such as "Figure," "Chapter," and "Section"; "page" is always abbreviated "p." (or "pp." for more than one page).

> The data support the finding that weight loss stabilizes with consistent therapy and ongoing monitoring (Hanniman, 2010, Figure 8-3, p. 345).

18. Indirect source (source quoted in another source) When a writer's or a speaker's quoted words appear in a source written by someone else, begin the parenthetical citation with the words "as cited in." In the following example, Critser is the author of the source given in the reference list; that source contains a quotation by Satcher.

> Former surgeon general Dr. David Satcher described "a nation of young people seriously at risk of starting out obese and dooming themselves to the difficult task of overcoming a tough illness" (as cited in Critser, 2003, p. 4).

19. Sacred or classical text Identify the text, the version or edition you used, and the relevant part (chapter, verse, line). It is not necessary to include the source in the reference list.

> Peace activists have long cited the biblical prophet's vision of a world without war: "And they shall beat their swords into plowshares, and their spears into pruning hooks; nation shall not lift up sword against nation, neither shall they learn war any more" (Isaiah 2:4, Revised Standard Version).

APA-4b APA list of references

As you gather sources for an assignment, you will likely find sources in print, on the Web, and in other places. The information you will need for the reference list at the end of your paper will differ slightly for some sources, but the main principles apply to all sources: You should identify an author, a creator, or a producer whenever possible; give a title; and provide the date on which the source was produced. Some sources will require page numbers; some will require a publisher; and some will require retrieval information.

> ▸ General guidelines for the reference list, page 496

Section APA-4b provides specific requirements for and examples of many of the sources you are likely to encounter. When you cite sources, your goals are to show that the sources you've used are reliable and relevant to your work, to provide your readers with enough information so that they can find your sources easily, and to provide that information in a consistent way according to APA conventions.

In the list of references, include only sources that you have quoted, summarized, or paraphrased in your paper.

General guidelines for listing authors

The formatting of authors' names in items 1–12 applies to all sources in print and on the Web—books, articles, Web sites, and so on. For more models of specific source types, see items 13–69.

General guidelines for the reference list

In APA style, the alphabetical list of works cited, which appears at the end of the paper, is titled "References."

Authors and dates

- Alphabetize entries in the list of references by authors' last names; if a work has no author, alphabetize it by its title.
- For all authors' names, put the last name first, followed by a comma; use initials for the first and middle names.
- With two or more authors, use an ampersand (&) before the last author's name. Separate the names with commas. Include names for the first seven authors; if there are eight or more authors, give the first six authors, three ellipsis dots, and the last author.
- If the author is a company or an organization, give the name in normal order.
- Put the date of publication immediately after the first element of the citation. Enclose the date in parentheses, followed by a period (outside the parentheses).
- For books, give the year of publication. For magazines, newspapers, and newsletters, give the exact date as in the publication (the year plus the month or the year plus the month and the day). For sources on the Web, give the date of posting, if it is available. Use the season if the publication gives only a season and not a month.

Titles

- Italicize the titles and subtitles of books, journals, and other long works.
- Use no italics or quotation marks for the titles of articles.
- For books and articles, capitalize only the first word of the title and subtitle and all proper nouns.
- For the titles of journals, magazines, and newspapers, capitalize all words of four letters or more (and all nouns, pronouns, verbs, adjectives, and adverbs of any length).

Place of publication and publisher

- Take the information about a book from its title page and copyright page. If more than one place of publication is listed, use only the first.
- Give the city and state for all US cities. Use postal abbreviations for all states.
- Give the city and country for all non-US cities; include the province for Canadian cities. Do not abbreviate the country and province.
- Do not give a state if the publisher's name includes it (Ann Arbor: University of Michigan Press, for example).
- In publishers' names, omit terms such as "Company" (or "Co.") and "Inc." but keep "Books" and "Press." Omit first names or initials (Norton, not W. W. Norton, for example).
- If the publisher is the same as the author, use the word "Author" in the publisher position.

Volume, issue, and page numbers

- For a journal or a magazine, give only the volume number if the publication is paginated continuously through each volume; give the volume and issue numbers if each issue begins on page 1.
- Italicize the volume number and put the issue number, not italicized, in parentheses.
- For monthly magazines, give the year and the month; for weekly magazines, add the day.
- For daily and weekly newspapers, give the month, day, and year; use "p." or "pp." before page numbers (if any). For journals and magazines, do not add "p." or "pp."
- When an article appears on consecutive pages, provide the range of pages. When an article does not appear on consecutive pages, give all page numbers: A1, A17.

URLs, DOIs, and other retrieval information

- For articles and books from the Web, use the DOI (digital object identifier) if the source has one, and do not give a URL. If a source does not have a DOI, give the URL.
- Use a retrieval date for a Web source only if the content is likely to change. Most of the examples in APA-4b do not show a retrieval date because the content of the sources is stable. If you are unsure about whether to use a retrieval date, include the date or consult your instructor.

1. Single author

author: last | year
name + initial(s) (book) | title (book)

Rosenberg, T. (2011). *Join the club: How peer pressure can transform the world.*

place of
publication | publisher

New York, NY: Norton.

2. Two to seven authors

List up to seven authors by last names followed by initials. Use an ampersand (&) before the name of the last author. (See items 3–5 on pp. 490–91 for citing works with multiple authors in the text of your paper.)

all authors: | year
last name + initial(s) | (book) | title (book)

Stanford, D. J., & Bradley, B. A. (2012). *Across the Atlantic ice: The origins of America's*

place of
publication | publisher

Clovis culture. Berkeley: University of California Press.

all authors:
last name + initial(s)

Ludwig, J., Duncan, G. J., Gennetian, L. A., Katz, L. F., Kessler, R. C., Kling, J. R.,

year
(journal) | title (article)

& Sanbonmatsu, L. (2012). Neighborhood effects on the long-term well-being of

journal
title | volume | page(s) | DOI

low-income adults. *Science, 337,* 1505-1510. doi:10.1126/science.1224648

3. Eight or more authors

List the first six authors followed by three ellipsis dots and the last author's name.

Tøttrup, A. P., Klaassen, R. H. G., Kristensen, M. W., Strandberg, R., Vardanis, Y.,

Lindström, Å., . . . Thorup, K. (2012). Drought in Africa caused delayed arrival

of European songbirds. *Science, 338,* 1307. doi:10.1126/science.1227548

4. Organization as author

author:
organization name | year | title (book)

American Psychiatric Association. (2013). *Diagnostic and statistical manual of*

place | organization
edition | of publication | as author and publisher

mental disorders (5th ed.). Washington, DC: Author.

5. Unknown author   Begin the entry with the work's title.

```
                              year + month + day                    volume,
            title (article)   (weekly publication)   journal title  issue    page(s)
```
The rise of the sharing economy. (2013, March 9). *The Economist, 406*(8826), 14.

```
       title (book)        year   place of        publisher
                                  publication
```
New concise world atlas. (2010). New York, NY: Oxford University Press.

6. Author using a pseudonym (pen name) or screen name   Use the author's real name, if known, and give the pseudonym or screen name in brackets exactly as it appears in the source. If only the screen name is known, begin with that name and do not use brackets. (See also items 47 and 68 on citing screen names in social media.)

```
               year + month + day
screen name    (daily publication)                    title of original article
```
littlebigman. (2012, December 13). Re: Who's watching? Privacy concerns persist as

```
                      label           title of publication
```
smart meters roll out [Comment]. *National Geographic Daily News.* Retrieved from

```
       URL for Web publication
```
http://news.nationalgeographic.com/

7. Two or more works by the same author   Use the author's name for all entries. List the entries by year, the earliest first.

Heinrich, B. (2009). *Summer world: A season of bounty.* New York, NY: Ecco.

Heinrich, B. (2012). *Life everlasting: The animal way of death.* New York, NY: Houghton
    Mifflin Harcourt.

8. Two or more works by the same author in the same year   List the works alphabetically by title. In the parentheses, following the year add "a," "b," and so on. Use these same letters when giving the year in the in-text citation. (See also p. 525 and item 9 on p. 492.)

Bower, B. (2012a, December 15). Families in flux. *Science News, 182*(12), 16.

Bower, B. (2012b, November 3). Human-Neandertal mating gets a new date. *Science
    News, 182*(9), 8.

9. Editor   Begin with the name of the editor or editors; place the abbreviation "Ed." (or "Eds." for more than one editor) in parentheses following the name. (See item 10 for a work with both an author and an editor.)

```
           all editors:
           last name + initial(s)              year      title (book)
```
Carr, S. C., MacLachlan, M., & Furnham, A. (Eds.). (2012). *Humanitarian work psychology.*

```
     place of
     publication   publisher
```
New York, NY: Palgrave.

10. Author and editor Begin with the name of the author, followed by the name of the editor and the abbreviation "Ed." For an author with two or more editors, use the abbreviation "Ed." after each editor's name: Gray, W., & Jones, P. (Ed.), & Smith, A. (Ed.).

James, W., & Pelikan, J. (Ed.). (2009). *The varieties of religious experience.* New York, NY: Library of America. (Original work published 1902)

(labeled: author, editor, year, title (book), place of publication, publisher, original publication information)

11. Translator Begin with the name of the author. After the title, in parentheses place the name of the translator (in normal order) and the abbreviation "Trans." (for "Translator"). Add the original date of publication at the end of the entry.

Scheffer, P. (2011). *Immigrant nations* (L. Waters, Trans.). Cambridge, England: Polity Press. (Original work published 2007)

(labeled: author, year, title (book), translator, place of publication, publisher, original publication information)

12. Editor and translator If the editor and translator are the same person, the same name appears in both the editor position and the translator position.

Girard, R., & Williams, J. G. (Ed.). (2012). *Resurrection from the underground* (J. G. Williams, Trans.). East Lansing: Michigan State University Press. (Original work published 1996)

Articles and other short works

▸ Citation at a glance: Article in a journal or magazine, page 502
▸ Citation at a glance: Article from a database, page 504

13. Article in a journal If an article from the Web or a database has no DOI, include the URL for the journal's home page.

a. Print

Bippus, A. M., Dunbar, N. E., & Liu, S.-J. (2012). Humorous responses to interpersonal complaints: Effects of humor style and nonverbal expression. *The Journal of Psychology,* *146*, 437-453.

(labeled: all authors: last name + initial(s), year, article title, journal title, volume, page(s))

b. Web

all authors:
last name + initial(s) | year | article title

Vargas, N., & Schafer, M. H. (2013). Diversity in action: Interpersonal networks

volume,
journal title | issue | page(s)

and the distribution of advice. *Social Science Research, 42*(1), 46-58.

DOI

doi:10.1016/j.ssresearch.2012.08.013

author | year | article title

Brenton, S. (2011). When the personal becomes political: Mitigating damage

journal title (no volume available)

following scandals. *Current Research in Social Psychology*. Retrieved from

URL for journal home page

http://www.uiowa.edu/~grpproc/crisp/crisp.html

c. Database

year
author | (journal) | article title

Sohn, K. (2012). The social class origins of U.S. teachers, 1860-1920. *Journal of*

volume,
journal title | issue | page(s) | DOI

Social History, 45(4), 908-935. doi:10.1093/jsh/shr121

14. Article in a magazine If an article from the Web or a database has no DOI, include the URL for the magazine's home page.

a. Print

year + month | | | volume,
author | (monthly magazine) | article title | magazine title | issue | page(s)

Comstock, J. (2012, December). The underrated sense. *Psychology Today, 45*(6), 46-47.

b. Web

date of posting
author | (when available) | article title | magazine title

Burns, J. (2012, December 3). The measure of all things. *The American Prospect*. Retrieved

URL for home page

from http://prospect.org/

Citation at a glance: Article in a journal or magazine APA

To cite an article in a print journal or magazine in APA style, include the following elements:

1 Author(s)
2 Year of publication for journal; complete date for magazine
3 Title and subtitle of article
4 Name of journal or magazine
5 Volume number; issue number, if required (see p. 497)
6 Page number(s) of article

JOURNAL TABLE OF CONTENTS

FIRST PAGE OF ARTICLE

feature

School Choice Marches Forward

③

One year ago, the *Wall Street Journal* dubbed 2011 "the year of school choice," opining that "this year is shaping up as the best for reformers in a very long time." Such quotes were bound to circulate among education reformers and give traditional opponents of school choice, such as teachers unions, heartburn. Thirteen states enacted new programs that allow K–12 students to choose a public or private school instead of attending their assigned school, and similar bills were under consideration in more than two dozen states.

With so much activity, school choice moved from the margins of education reform debates and became the headline. In January 2012, *Washington Post* education reporter Michael Alison Chandler said school choice has become "a mantra of 21st-century education reform," citing policies across the country that have traditional public schools competing for students alongside charter schools and private schools.

"It took us 20 years to pass the first 20 private school–choice programs in America and in the 21st year we passed 7 new programs," says Scott Jensen with the American Federation for Children (AFC),

2011
a year of new laws and new lawsuits
By ① JONATHAN BUTCHER

a school-choice advocacy group based in Washington, D.C. "So we went from passing, on average, one each year, to seven in one fell swoop."

Programs enacted in 2011 include
• a tax-credit scholarship program in North Carolina
• Arizona's education savings account system for K–12 students
• Maine's new charter school law, which brings the total number of states, along with the District of Columbia, with charter schools to 42
• a voucher program in Indiana with broad eligibility rules.

School-choice laws also passed in Wisconsin, Washington, D.C., Oklahoma,

educationnext.org

Excerpts from *Education Next* reprinted by permission.

② ④

REFERENCE LIST ENTRY FOR AN ARTICLE IN A PRINT JOURNAL OR MAGAZINE

|1| |2| |3| |4| |5| |6|

Butcher, J. (2013). School choice marches forward. *Education Next, 13*(1), 20–27.

For more on citing articles in APA style, see items 13–15.

Citation at a glance: Article from a database APA

To cite an article from a database in APA style, include the following elements:

1 Author(s)
2 Year of publication for journal; complete date for magazine or newspaper
3 Title and subtitle of article
4 Name of periodical
5 Volume number; issue number, if required (see p. 497)
6 Page number(s)
7 DOI (digital object identifier)
8 URL for periodical's home page (if there is no DOI)

DATABASE RECORD

Reprinted by permission of EBSCO Publishing.

REFERENCE LIST ENTRY FOR AN ARTICLE FROM A DATABASE

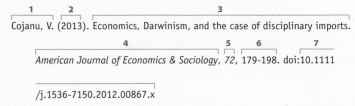

Cojanu, V. (2013). Economics, Darwinism, and the case of disciplinary imports.

American Journal of Economics & Sociology, 72, 179-198. doi:10.1111

/j.1536-7150.2012.00867.x

For more on citing articles from a database in APA style, see items 13–15.

14. Article in a magazine (*cont.*)

c. Database

Tucker, A. (2012, November). Primal instinct. *Smithsonian, 43*(7), 54-63. Retrieved from

http://www.smithsonianmag.com/

15. Article in a newspaper

a. Print

Swarns, R. L. (2012, December 9). A family, for a few days a year. *The New York Times,*

pp. 1, 20.

b. Web

Villanueva-Whitman, E. (2012, November 27). Working to stimulate memory function.

Des Moines Register. Retrieved from http://www.desmoinesregister.com/

16. Abstract   Add the label "Abstract," in brackets, after the title.

a. Abstract of a journal article

Morales, J., Calvo, A., & Bialystok, E. (2013). Working memory development in
monolingual and bilingual children [Abstract]. *Journal of Experimental Child
Psychology, 114,* 187-202. Retrieved from http://www.sciencedirect.com/

b. Abstract of a paper

Denham, B. (2012). Diffusing deviant behavior: A communication perspective on the
construction of moral panics [Abstract]. Paper presented at the AEJMC 2012
Conference, Chicago, IL. Retrieved from http://www.aejmc.org/home/2012/04
/ctm-2012-abstracts/

17. Supplemental material   If an article on the Web contains supplemental material that is not part of the main article, cite the material
as you would an article and add the label "Supplemental material" in
brackets following the title.

Reis, S., Grennfelt, P., Klimont, Z., Amann, M., ApSimon, H., Hettelingh, J.-P., . . .
Williams, M. (2012). From acid rain to climate change [Supplemental material].
Science, 338(6111), 1153-1154. doi:10.1126/science.1226514

18. Article with a title in its title   If an article title contains another
article title or a term usually placed in quotation marks, use quotation
marks around the internal title or the term.

Easterling, D., & Millesen, J. L. (2012, Summer). Diversifying civic leadership: What
it takes to move from "new faces" to adaptive problem solving. *National Civic
Review, 101*(2), 20-27. doi:10.1002/ncr.21073

19. Letter to the editor   Insert the words "Letter to the editor"
in brackets after the title of the letter. If the letter has no title, use the
bracketed words as the title (as in the following example).

Lim, C. (2012, November-December). [Letter to the editor]. *Sierra.* Retrieved from
http://www.sierraclub.org/sierra/

20. Editorial or other unsigned article

The business case for transit dollars [Editorial]. (2012, December 9). *Star Tribune.*
Retrieved from http://www.startribune.com/

21. Newsletter article   Cite as you would an article in a magazine, giving whatever publication information is available (volume, issue, page numbers, and so on).

Scrivener, L. (n.d.). Why is the minimum wage issue important for food justice

  advocates? *Food Workers—Food Justice, 15.* Retrieved from http://www

  .thedatabank.com/dpg/199/pm.asp?nav=1&ID=41429

22. Review   Give the author and title of the review (if any) and, in brackets, the type of work, the title, and the author for a book or the year for a film. If the review has no author or title, use the material in brackets as the title.

author   year
of review   (journal)   book title

Aviram, R. B. (2012). [Review of the book *What do I say? The therapist's guide to*

                         book author(s)   journal title

  answering client questions, by L. N. Edelstein & C. A. Waehler]. *Psychotherapy,*

volume,
issue   page(s)   DOI

  49(4), 570-571. doi:10.1037/a0029815

                year
   author(s)   (journal)   review title

Bradley, A., & Olufs, E. (2012). Family dynamics and school violence [Review of the

                         year   volume,
           film title   (film)   journal title   issue

  motion picture *We need to talk about Kevin*, 2011]. *PsycCRITIQUES, 57*(49).

          DOI

  doi:10.1037/a0030982

23. Published interview   Begin with the person interviewed, and put the interviewer in brackets following the title (if any).

Githongo, J. (2012, November 20). A conversation with John Githongo [Interview by

  Baobab]. *The Economist.* Retrieved from http://www.economist.com/

24. Article in a reference work (encyclopedia, dictionary, wiki)

a. Print   See also item 32 on citing a volume in a multivolume work.

Konijn, E. A. (2008). Affects and media exposure. In W. Donsbach (Ed.), *The*

  international encyclopedia of communication (Vol. 1, pp. 123-129). Malden,

  MA: Blackwell.

b. Web

Ethnomethodology. (2006). In *STS wiki*. Retrieved December 15, 2012, from http://
www.stswiki.org/index.php?title=Ethnomethodology

25. Comment on an online article   Begin with the writer's real name
or screen name. If both are given, put the real name first, followed by
the screen name in brackets. Before the title, use "Re" and a colon. Add
"Comment" in brackets following the title.

Danboy125. (2012, November 9). Re: No flowers on the psych ward [Comment]. *The
Atlantic*. Retrieved from http://www.theatlantic.com/

26. Testimony before a legislative body

Carmona, R. H. (2004, March 2). *The growing epidemic of childhood obesity*. Testimony
before the Subcommittee on Competition, Foreign Commerce, and Infrastructure
of the U.S. Senate Committee on Commerce, Science, and Transportation.
Retrieved from http://www.hhs.gov/asl/testify/t040302.html

27. Paper presented at a meeting or symposium (unpublished)

Karimi, S., Key, G., & Tat, D. (2011, April 22). *Complex predicates in focus*. Paper
presented at the West Coast Conference on Formal Linguistics, Tucson, AZ.

28. Poster session at a conference

Lacara, N. (2011, April 24). *Predicate which appositives*. Poster session presented
at the West Coast Conference on Formal Linguistics, Tucson, AZ.

Books and other long works

▶ Citation at a glance: Book, page 509

29. Basic format for a book

a. Print

author(s):
last name
+ initial(s)   year   book title

Child, B. J. (2012). *Holding our world together: Ojibwe women and the survival*

place of
publication   publisher

of community. New York, NY: Viking.

Citation at a glance: Book APA

To cite a print book in APA style, include the following elements:

1 Author(s)
2 Year of publication

3 Title and subtitle
4 Place of publication
5 Publisher

TITLE PAGE

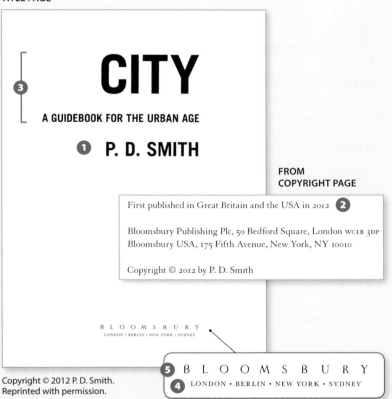

CITY

A GUIDEBOOK FOR THE URBAN AGE

1 **P. D. SMITH**

FROM COPYRIGHT PAGE

First published in Great Britain and the USA in 2012 **2**

Bloomsbury Publishing Plc, 50 Bedford Square, London WC1B 3DP
Bloomsbury USA, 175 Fifth Avenue, New York, NY 10010

Copyright © 2012 by P. D. Smith

BLOOMSBURY
LONDON · BERLIN · NEW YORK · SYDNEY

5 BLOOMSBURY
4 LONDON · BERLIN · NEW YORK · SYDNEY

Copyright © 2012 P. D. Smith.
Reprinted with permission.

REFERENCE LIST ENTRY FOR A PRINT BOOK

| 1 | 2 | 3 | 4 | 5 |

Smith, P. D. (2012). *City: A guidebook for the urban age*. London, England: Bloomsbury.

For more on citing books in APA style, see items 29–37.

29. Basic format for a book (cont.)

b. Web (or online library) Give the URL for the home page of the Web site or the online library.

author(s)   year   book title

Amponsah, N. A., & Falola, T. (2012). *Women's roles in sub-Saharan Africa*. Retrieved

URL

from http://books.google.com/

c. E-book Give the version in brackets after the title ("Kindle version," "Nook version," and so on). Include the DOI or, if a DOI is not available, the URL for the home page of the site from which you downloaded the book.

Wolf, D. A., & Folbre, N. (Eds.). (2012). *Universal coverage of long-term care in the United States* [Adobe Digital Editions version]. Retrieved from https://www .russellsage.org/

d. Database Give the URL for the database.

Beasley, M. H. (2012). *Women of the Washington press: Politics, prejudice, and persistence*. Retrieved from http://muse.jhu.edu/

30. Edition other than the first Include the edition number (abbreviated) in parentheses after the title.

Harvey, P. (2013). *An introduction to Buddhism: Teachings, history, and practices* (2nd ed.). Cambridge, England: Cambridge University Press.

31. Selection in an anthology or a collection An anthology is a collection of works on a common theme, often with different authors for the selections and usually with an editor for the entire volume.

a. Entire anthology

editor(s)   year

Warren, A. E. A., Lerner, R. M., & Phelps, E. (Eds.). (2011). *Thriving and spirituality*

place of
title of anthology   publication publisher

among youth: Research perspectives and future possibilities. Hoboken, NJ: Wiley.

b. Selection in an anthology

author of
selection   year   title of selection

Lazar, S. W. (2012). Neural correlates of positive youth development. In A. E. A. Warren,

       editors of anthology   title of anthology

    R. M. Lerner, & E. Phelps (Eds.), *Thriving and spirituality among youth: Research*

                           page numbers   place of
                           of selection publication publisher

    perspectives and future possibilities (pp. 77-90). Hoboken, NJ: Wiley.

32. Multivolume work If the volumes have been published over several years, give the span of years in parentheses. If you have used only one volume of a multivolume work, indicate the volume number after the title of the complete work; if the volume has its own title, add that title after the volume number.

a. All volumes

Khalakdina, M. (2008-2011). *Human development in the Indian context: A socio-cultural*
    focus (Vols. 1-2). New Delhi, India: Sage.

b. One volume, with title

Jensen, R. E. (Ed.). (2012). *Voices of the American West: Vol. 1. The Indian interviews*
    of Eli S. Ricker, 1903-1919. Lincoln: University of Nebraska Press.

33. Introduction, preface, foreword, or afterword

Zachary, L. J. (2012). Foreword. In L. A. Daloz, *Mentor: Guiding the journey of adult*
    learners (pp. v-vii). San Francisco, CA: Jossey-Bass.

34. Dictionary or other reference work

Leong, F. T. L. (Ed.). (2008). *Encyclopedia of counseling* (Vols. 1-4). Thousand Oaks,
    CA: Sage.

Nichols, J. D., & Nyholm, E. (2012). *A concise dictionary of Minnesota Ojibwe*.
    Minneapolis: University of Minnesota Press.

35. Republished book

Mailer, N. (2008). *Miami and the siege of Chicago: An informal history of the Republican*
    and Democratic conventions of 1968. New York, NY: New York Review Books.
    (Original work published 1968)

36. Book with a title in its title If the book title contains another book title or an article title, do not italicize the internal title and do not put quotation marks around it.

Marcus, L. (Ed.). (1999). *Sigmund Freud's* The interpretation of dreams: *New interdisciplinary essays*. Manchester, England: Manchester University Press.

37. Book in a language other than English Place the English translation, not italicized, in brackets.

Carminati, G. G., & Méndez, A. (2012). *Étapes de vie, étapes de soins* [Stages of life, stages of care]. Chêne-Bourg, Switzerland: Médecine & Hygiène.

38. Dissertation

a. Published

Hymel, K. M. (2009). *Essays in urban economics* (Doctoral dissertation). Available from ProQuest Dissertations and Theses database. (AAT 3355930)

b. Unpublished

Mitchell, R. D. (2007). *The Wesleyan Quadrilateral: Relocating the conversation* (Unpublished doctoral dissertation). Claremont School of Theology, Claremont, CA.

39. Conference proceedings

Yu, F.-Y., Hirashima, T., Supnithi, T., & Biswas, G. (2011). *Proceedings of the 19th International Conference on Computers in Education: ICCE 2011*. Retrieved from http://www.apsce.net:8080/icce2011/program/proceedings/

40. Government document If the document has a number, place the number in parentheses after the title.

U.S. Transportation Department, Pipeline and Hazardous Materials Safety Administration. (2012). *Emergency response guidebook 2012*. Washington, DC: Author.

U.S. Census Bureau, Bureau of Economic Analysis. (2012, December). *U.S. international trade in goods and services, October 2012* (Report No. CB12-232, BEA12-55, FT-900 [12-10]). Retrieved from http://www.census.gov/foreign-trade /Press-Release/2012pr/10/

41. Report from a private organization If the publisher and the author are the same, begin with the publisher. For a print source, use

"Author" as the publisher at the end of the entry (see item 4 on p. 498); for an online source, give the URL. If the report has a number, put it in parentheses following the title.

Ford Foundation. (2012, November). *Eastern Africa*. Retrieved from http://www
.fordfoundation.org/pdfs/library/Eastern-Africa-brochure-2012.pdf

Atwood, B., Beam, M., Hindman, D. B., Hindman, E. B., Pintak, L., & Shors, B. (2012,
May 25). *The Murrow Rural Information Initiative: Final report*. Pullman: Murrow
College of Communication, Washington State University.

42. Legal source The title of a court case is italicized in an in-text citation, but it is not italicized in the reference list.

Sweatt v. Painter, 339 U.S. 629 (1950). Retrieved from Cornell University Law School,
Legal Information Institute website: http://www.law.cornell.edu/supct/html
/historics/USSC_CR_0339_0629_ZS.html

43. Sacred or classical text It is not necessary to list sacred works such as the Bible or the Qur'an or classical Greek and Roman works (such as the *Odyssey*) in your reference list. See item 19 on page 495 for how to cite these sources in the text of your paper.

Web sites and parts of Web sites

▶ Citation at a glance: Section in a Web document, page 516

NOTE: In an APA paper or an APA reference list entry, the word "website" is spelled all lowercase, as one word.

44. Entire Web site Do not include an entire Web site in the reference list. Give the URL in parentheses when you mention it in the text of your paper. (See item 13 on p. 493.)

45. Document from a Web site List as many of the following elements as are available: author's name, publication date (or "n.d." if there is no date), title (in italics), publisher (if any), and URL. If the publisher is known and is not named as the author, include the publisher in your retrieval statement.

Wagner, D. A., Murphy, K. M., & De Korne, H. (2012, December). *Learning first: A*
research agenda for improving learning in low-income countries. Retrieved from
Brookings Institution website: http://www.brookings.edu/research/papers
/2012/12/learning-first-wagner-murphy-de-korne

Gerber, A. S., & Green, D. P. (2012). *Field experiments: Design, analysis, and interpretation*. Retrieved from Yale Institution for Social and Policy Studies website: http://isps.yale.edu/research/data/d081#.UUy2HFdPL5w

Centers for Disease Control and Prevention. (2012, December 10). *Concussion in winter sports*. Retrieved from http://www.cdc.gov/Features/HockeyConcussions/index .html

46. Section in a Web document   Cite as you would a chapter in a book or a selection in an anthology (see item 31b).

Pew Research Center. (2012, December 12). About the 2012 Pew global attitudes survey. In *Social networking popular across globe*. Retrieved from http://www.pewglobal .org/2012/12/12/social-networking-popular-across-globe

Chang, W.-Y., & Milan, L. M. (2012, October). Relationship between degree field and emigration. In *International mobility and employment characteristics among recent recipients of U.S. doctorates*. Retrieved from National Science Foundation website: http://www.nsf.gov/statistics/infbrief/nsf13300

47. Blog post   Begin with the writer's real name or screen name. If both are given, put the real name first, followed by the screen name in brackets. Add the date of the post (or "n.d." if the post is undated). Place the label "Blog post" in brackets following the title of the post. If there is no title, use the bracketed material as the title. End with the URL for the post.

Kerssen, T. (2012, October 5). Hunger is political: Food Sovereignty Prize honors social movements [Blog post]. Retrieved from http://www.foodfirst.org/en/node/4020

48. Blog comment   Cite as a blog post, but add "Re" and a colon before the title of the original post and the label "Blog comment" in brackets following the title.

Studebakerhawk_14611. (2012, December 5). Re: A people's history of MOOCs [Blog comment]. Retrieved from http://www.insidehighered.com/blogs/library-babel -fish/people's-history-moocs

Audio, visual, and multimedia sources

49. Podcast

Schulz, K. (2011, March). *Kathryn Schulz: On being wrong* [Video podcast]. Retrieved from TED on http://itunes.apple.com/

Taylor, A., & Parfitt, G. (2011, January 13). *Physical activity and mental health: What's the evidence?* [Audio podcast]. Retrieved from Open University on http://itunes .apple.com/

50. Video or audio on the Web

Kurzen, B. (2012, April 5). *Going beyond Muslim-Christian conflict in Nigeria* [Video file]. Retrieved from http://www.youtube.com/watch?v=JD8MIJOA050

Malone, T. W. (2012, November 21). *Collective intelligence* [Video file]. Retrieved from http://edge.org/conversation/collective-intelligence

Bever, T., Piattelli-Palmarini, M., Hammond, M., Barss, A., & Bergesen, A. (2012, February 2). *A basic introduction to Chomsky's linguistics* [Audio file]. Retrieved from University of Arizona, College of Social & Behavioral Sciences, Department of Linguistics website: http://linguistics.arizona.edu/node/711

51. Transcript of an audio or a video file

Malone, T. W. (2012, November 21). *Collective intelligence* [Transcript of video file]. Retrieved from http://edge.org/conversation/collective-intelligence

Glass, I. (2012, September 14). *Back to school* [Transcript of audio file No. 474]. In *This American life*. Retrieved from http://www.thisamericanlife.org/

52. Film (DVD, BD, or other format)   Give the director, producer, and other relevant contributors, followed by the year of the film's release and the title. In brackets, add a description of the medium. Use "Motion picture" if you viewed the film in a theater; "Video file" if you downloaded the film from the Web or through a streaming service such as Netflix; "DVD" or "BD" if you viewed the film on DVD or Blu-ray Disc. For a motion picture or a DVD or BD, add the location where the film was made and the studio. If you retrieved the film from the Web or used a streaming service, give the URL for the home page.

Affleck, B. (Director). (2012). *Argo* [Motion picture]. Burbank, CA: Warner Bros.

Ross, G. (Director and Writer), & Collins, S. (Writer). (2012). *The hunger games* [Video file]. Retrieved from http://netflix.com/

53. Television or radio program

a. Series

Hager, M. (Executive producer), & Schieffer, B. (Moderator). (2012). *Face the nation* [Television series]. Washington, DC: CBS News.

Citation at a glance: Section in a Web document APA

To cite a section in a Web document in APA style, include the following elements:

1 Author(s)

2 Date of publication or most recent update ("n.d." if there is no date)

3 Title of section

4 Title of document

5 URL of section

WEB DOCUMENT CONTENTS PAGE

3 Fertility (PDF: 14KB/2 pages)

5 🌐 http://www.health.state.mn.us/divs/chs/annsum/10annsum/Fertility2010.pdf

ON-SCREEN VIEW OF DOCUMENT

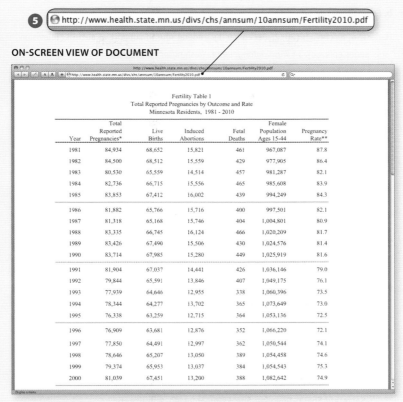

Fertility Table 1
Total Reported Pregnancies by Outcome and Rate
Minnesota Residents, 1981 - 2010

Year	Total Reported Pregnancies*	Live Births	Induced Abortions	Fetal Deaths	Female Population Ages 15-44	Pregnancy Rate**
1981	84,934	68,652	15,821	461	967,087	87.8
1982	84,500	68,512	15,559	429	977,905	86.4
1983	80,530	65,559	14,514	457	981,287	82.1
1984	82,736	66,715	15,556	465	985,608	83.9
1985	83,853	67,412	16,002	439	994,249	84.3
1986	81,882	65,766	15,716	400	997,501	82.1
1987	81,318	65,168	15,746	404	1,004,801	80.9
1988	83,335	66,745	16,124	466	1,020,209	81.7
1989	83,426	67,490	15,506	430	1,024,576	81.4
1990	83,714	67,985	15,280	449	1,025,919	81.6
1991	81,904	67,037	14,441	426	1,036,146	79.0
1992	79,844	65,591	13,846	407	1,049,175	76.1
1993	77,939	64,646	12,955	338	1,060,396	73.5
1994	78,344	64,277	13,702	365	1,073,649	73.0
1995	76,338	63,259	12,715	364	1,053,136	72.5
1996	76,909	63,681	12,876	352	1,066,220	72.1
1997	77,850	64,491	12,997	362	1,050,544	74.1
1998	78,646	65,207	13,050	389	1,054,458	74.6
1999	79,374	65,953	13,037	384	1,054,543	75.3
2000	81,039	67,451	13,200	388	1,082,642	74.9

Courtesy of the Minnesota Department of Health. Reproduced by permission.

REFERENCE LIST ENTRY FOR A SECTION IN A WEB DOCUMENT

    1   2   3   4
Minnesota Department of Health. (n.d.). Fertility. In *2010 Minnesota health statistics*

                                              5
annual summary. Retrieved from http://www.health.state.mn.us/divs/chs/annsum

/10annsum/Fertility2010.pdf

For more on citing documents from Web sites in APA style, see items 45 and 46.

53. Television or radio program (*cont.*)

b. Episode on the air

Harleston, R. (Host). (2012, December 1). Federal role in support of autism [Television series episode]. In *Washington journal*. Washington, DC: C-SPAN.

c. Episode on the Web

Morton, D. (Producer). (2012). Fast times at West Philly High [Television series episode]. In M. Hager (Executive producer), *Frontline*. Retrieved from http://www.wgbh.org/

Glass, I. (Host). (2012, November 23). Little war on the prairie (No. 479) [Radio series episode]. In *This American life*. Retrieved from http://www.thisamericanlife.org/

54. Music recording

Chibalonza, A. Jubilee. (2012). On *African voices* [CD]. Merenberg, Germany: ZYX Music.

African voices [CD]. (2012). Merenberg, Germany: ZYX Music.

55. Lecture, speech, or address

Verghese, A. (2012, December 6). *Colonialism and patterns of ethnic conflict in contemporary India*. Address at the Freeman Spogli Institute, Stanford University, Stanford, CA.

Donovan, S. (2012, June 12). *Assisted housing mobility in challenging times* [Video file]. Address at the 5th National Conference on Assisted Housing Mobility, Urban Institute, Washington, DC. Retrieved from http://www.urban.org/events/HUD -Secretary-Shaun-Donovan-Speaks-on-Housing-Mobility.cfm

56. Data set or graphic representation of data (graph, chart, table) Give information about the type of source in brackets following the title. If there is no title, give a brief description of the content of the source in brackets in place of the title. If the item is numbered in the source, indicate the number in parentheses after the title. If the graphic appears within a larger document, do not italicize the title of the graphic.

U.S. Department of Agriculture, Economic Research Service. (2011). *Daily intake of nutrients by food source: 2005-08* [Data set]. Retrieved from http://www .ers.usda.gov/data-products/food-consumption-and-nutrient-intakes.aspx

Gallup. (2012, December 5). *In U.S., more cite obesity as most urgent health problem* [Graphs]. Retrieved from http://www.gallup.com/poll/159083/cite-obesity -urgent-health-problem.aspx

57. Mobile application software (app)   Begin with the developer of the app, if known (as in the second example). Add the label "Mobile application software" in brackets after the title of the program.

MindNode Touch 2.3 [Mobile application software]. (2012). Retrieved from http://
itunes.apple.com/

Source Tree Solutions. (2012). mojoPortal [Mobile application software]. Retrieved from
http://www.microsoft.com/web/gallery/

58. Video game   Begin with the creator of the video game, if known. Add the label "Video game" in brackets after the title of the program. If the game can be played on the Web or was downloaded from the Web, give the URL instead of publication information.

Firaxis Games. (2010). Sid Meier's Civilization V [Video game]. New York, NY: Take-Two
Interactive. Xbox 360.

Atom Entertainment. (2012). Edgeworld [Video game]. Retrieved from http://www
.addictinggames.com/

59. Map

Ukraine [Map]. (2008). Retrieved from the University of Texas at Austin Perry-Castañeda
Library Map Collection website: http://www.lib.utexas.edu/maps/cia08/ukraine
_sm_2008.gif

Syrian uprising map [Map]. (2012, October). Retrieved from http://www.polgeonow
.com/2012/10/syria-uprising-map-october-2012-7.html

60. Advertisement

VMware [Advertisement]. (2012, September). *Harvard Business Review, 90*(9), 27.

61. Work of art or photograph

Olson, A. (2011). *Short story* [Painting]. Museum of Contemporary Art, Chicago, IL.

Crowner, S. (2012). *Kurtyna fragments* [Painting]. Retrieved from http://www
.walkerart.org/

Weber, J. (1992). *Toward freedom* [Outdoor mural]. Sherman Oaks, CA.

62. Brochure or fact sheet

National Council of State Boards of Nursing. (2011). *A nurse's guide to professional boundaries* [Brochure]. Retrieved from https://www.ncsbn.org/

World Health Organization. (2012, September). *Road traffic injuries* (No. 358) [Fact sheet]. Retrieved from http://www.who.int/mediacentre/factsheets/fs358 /en/index.html

63. Press release
Generally, list the organization responsible for the press release. Give the exact date.

Urban Institute. (2012, October 11). Two studies address health policy on campaign trail [Press release]. Retrieved from http://www.urban.org/publications/901537 .html

64. Presentation slides

Boeninger, C. F. (2008, August). *Web 2.0 tools for reference and instructional services* [Presentation slides]. Retrieved from http://libraryvoice.com/archives/2008 /08/04/opal-20-conference-presentation-slides

65. Lecture notes or other course materials
Cite materials that your instructor has posted on the Web as you would a Web document or a section in a Web document (see item 45 or 46). If the materials are handouts or printouts, cite whatever information is available in the source. Cite the instructor's personal notes or material that is not posted (such as slides) as personal communication in the text of your paper (see items 15 and 16 on p. 494).

Blum, R. (2011). Neurodevelopment in the first decade of life [Lecture notes and audio file]. In R. Blum & L. M. Blum, *Child health and development*. Retrieved from http://ocw.jhsph.edu/index.cfm/go/viewCourse/course/childhealth/coursePage /lectureNotes/

Personal communication and social media

66. E-mail
E-mail messages, letters, and other personal communication are not included in the list of references. (See p. 494 for citing these sources in the text of your paper.)

67. Online posting
If an online posting is not archived, cite it as a personal communication in the text of your paper and do not include it in the list of references. If the posting is archived, give the URL and the name of the discussion list if it is not part of the URL.

McKinney, J. (2006, December 19). Adult education-healthcare partnerships [Electronic
>   mailing list message]. Retrieved from http://www.nifl.gov/pipermail
>   /healthliteracy/2006/000524.html

68. Twitter post (tweet)   Use the author's real name, if it is given, and put the screen name in brackets exactly as it appears in the source (including capitalization and punctuation). If only the screen name is known, begin with that name and do not enclose it in brackets. Include the entire text of the tweet as the title, followed by the label "Tweet" in brackets; end with the URL.

CQ Researcher. (2012, December 5). Up to 80 percent of the 600,000 processed foods
>   sold in America have sugar added to their recipes. See http://bit.ly/UmfA4L
>   [Tweet]. Retrieved from https://twitter.com/cqresearcher/status
>   /276449095521038336

69. Facebook post   Use the author's name exactly as it appears in the post. In place of a title, give a few words of the post followed by the label "Facebook post" in brackets. Include the date you retrieved the source and the URL for the poster's Facebook page. If you are citing a personal Facebook page that will not be accessible to your readers, cite it as personal communication in your text, not in the reference list (see item 15 on p. 494).

U.S. Department of Education. (2012, October 9). They are resilient [Facebook post].
>   Retrieved October 15, 2012, from http://www.facebook.com/ED.gov

APA-5 | Manuscript format; sample research paper

The guidelines in this section are consistent with advice given in the *Publication Manual of the American Psychological Association*, 6th ed. (Washington, DC: APA, 2010), and with typical requirements for undergraduate papers.

APA-5a APA manuscript format

Formatting the paper

The guidelines on pages 522–24 describe APA's recommendations for formatting the text of your paper. For guidelines on preparing the reference list, see pages 524–25.

Font If your instructor does not require a specific font, choose one that is standard and easy to read (such as Times New Roman).

Title page Begin at the top left, with the words "Running head," followed by a colon and the title of your paper (shortened to no more than fifty characters) in all capital letters. Put the page number 1 flush with the right margin.

About halfway down the page, on separate lines, center the full title of your paper, your name, and your school's name. At the bottom of the page, you may add the heading "Author Note," centered, followed by a brief paragraph that lists specific information about the course or department or provides acknowledgments or contact information. See page 526 for a sample title page.

Page numbers and running head Number all pages with arabic numerals (1, 2, 3, and so on) in the upper right corner one-half inch from the top of the page. Flush with the left margin on the same line as the page number, type a running head consisting of the title of the paper (shortened to more than fifty characters) in all capital letters. On the title page only, include the words "Running head" followed by a colon before the title. See pages 526–34.

Margins, line spacing, and paragraph indents Use margins of one inch on all sides of the page. Left-align the text.

Double-space throughout the paper. Indent the first line of each paragraph one-half inch.

Capitalization, italics, and quotation marks In headings and in titles of works that appear in the text of the paper, capitalize all words of four letters or more (and all nouns, pronouns, verbs, adjectives, and adverbs of any length). Capitalize the first word following a colon if the word begins a complete sentence.

In the body of your paper, italicize the titles of books, journals, magazines, and other long works, such as Web sites. Use quotation marks around the titles of articles, short stories, and other short works.

NOTE: APA has different requirements for titles in the reference list. See page 525.

Long quotations When a quotation is forty or more words, set it off from the text by indenting it one-half inch from the left margin. Double-space the quotation. Do not use quotation marks around it. (See p. 533 for an example. See also p. 484 for more information about integrating long quotations.)

Footnotes If you insert a footnote number in the text of your paper, place the number, raised above the line, immediately following any mark of punctuation except a dash. At the bottom of the page, begin the note with a one-half-inch indent and the superscript number corresponding to the number in the text. Insert an extra double-spaced line between the last line of text on the page and the footnote. Double-space the footnote. (See p. 528 for an example.)

Abstract and keywords An abstract is a 150-to-250-word paragraph that provides readers with a quick overview of your essay. It should express your main idea and your key points; it might also briefly suggest any implications or applications of the research you discuss in the paper.

If your instructor requires one, include an abstract on a new page after the title page. Center the word "Abstract" (in regular font, not boldface) one inch from the top of the page. Double-space the abstract and do not indent the first line.

A list of keywords follows the abstract; the keywords help readers search for a published paper on the Web or in a database. Leave one line of space after the abstract and begin the next line with the word "Keywords," italicized and indented one-half inch, followed by a colon. Then list important words related to your paper. Check with your instructor for requirements in your course. (See p. 527 for an example of an abstract.)

Headings Although headings are not always necessary, their use is encouraged in the social sciences. For most undergraduate papers, one level of heading is usually sufficient. (See pp. 528–32.)

First-level headings are centered and boldface. In research papers and laboratory reports, the major headings are "Method," "Results," and "Discussion." In other types of papers, the major headings should be informative and concise, conveying the structure of the paper.

Second-level headings are flush left and boldface. Third-level headings are indented and boldface, followed by a period and the text on the same line.

In first- and second-level headings, capitalize the first and last words and all words of four or more letters (and nouns, pronouns, verbs, adjectives, and adverbs of any length). In third-level headings, capitalize only the first word, any proper nouns, and the first word after a colon.

First-Level Heading Centered

Second-Level Heading Flush Left

    Third-level heading indented. Text immediately follows.

Visuals (tables and figures) APA classifies visuals as tables and figures (figures include graphs, charts, drawings, and photographs).

Label each table with an arabic numeral (Table 1, Table 2, and so on) and provide a clear title. Place the label and title on separate lines above the table, flush left and double-spaced. Type the table number in regular font; italicize the table title.

If you have used data from an outside source or have taken or adapted the table from a source, give the source information in a note below the table. Begin with the word "Note," italicized and followed by a period. If any data in the table require an explanatory footnote, use a superscript lowercase letter in the table and in a footnote following the source note. Double-space source notes and footnotes; do not indent the first line of each note. (See p. 531.)

For each figure, place the figure number and a caption below the figure, flush left and double-spaced. Begin with the word "Figure" and an arabic numeral, both italicized, followed by a period. Place the caption, not italicized, on the same line. If you have taken or adapted the figure from an outside source, give the source information immediately following the caption. Use the term "From" or "Adapted from" before the source information.

In the text of your paper, discuss the most significant features of each visual. Place the visual as close as possible to the sentences that relate to it unless your instructor prefers that visuals appear in an appendix.

Preparing the list of references

Begin your list of references on a new page at the end of the paper. Center the title "References" one inch from the top of the page. Double-space throughout. For a sample reference list, see page 534.

Indenting entries Type the first line of each entry flush left and indent any additional lines one-half inch.

Alphabetizing the list Alphabetize the reference list by the last names of the authors (or editors) or by the first word of an organization name (if the author is an organization). When a work has no author or editor, alphabetize by the first word of the title other than *A*, *An*, or *The*.

If your list includes two or more works by the same author, arrange the entries by year, the earliest first. If your list includes two or more works by the same author in the same year, arrange the works alphabetically by title. Add the letters "a," "b," and so on within the parentheses after the year. For journal articles, use only the year and the letter: (2012a). For articles in magazines and newspapers, use the full date and the letter in the reference list: (2012a, July 7); use only the year and the letter in the in-text citation.

Authors' names Invert all authors' names and use initials instead of first names. Separate the names with commas. For two to seven authors, use an ampersand (&) before the last author's name. For eight or more authors, give the first six authors, three ellipsis dots, and the last author (see item 3 on p. 498).

Titles of books and articles In the reference list, italicize the titles and subtitles of books. Do not italicize or use quotation marks around the titles of articles. For both books and articles, capitalize only the first word of the title and subtitle (and all proper nouns). Capitalize names of journals, magazines, and newspapers as you would capitalize them normally (see P8-c).

Abbreviations for page numbers Abbreviations for "page" and "pages" ("p." and "pp.") are used before page numbers of newspaper articles and selections in anthologies (see item 15 on p. 505 and item 31 on pp. 510–11). Do not use "p." or "pp." before page numbers of articles in journals and magazines (see items 13 and 14 on pp. 500 and 501).

Breaking a URL or DOI When a URL or a DOI (digital object identifier) must be divided, break it after a double slash or before any other mark of punctuation. Do not insert a hyphen; do not add a period at the end.

APA-5b Sample APA research paper

On the following pages is a research paper on the effectiveness of treatments for childhood obesity, written by Luisa Mirano, a student in a psychology class. Mirano's assignment was to write a literature review paper documented with APA-style citations and references.

hackerhandbooks.com/writersref

APA-5 Format, sample paper > Sample student writing
> Mirano, "Can Medication Cure Obesity in Children? A Review of the Literature" (literature review)

A running head consists of a title (shortened to no more than fifty characters) in all capital letters. On the title page, it is preceded by the label "Running head." Page numbers appear in the upper right corner.

Can Medication Cure Obesity in Children?

A Review of the Literature

Luisa Mirano

Northwest-Shoals Community College

Full title, writer's name, and school name are centered halfway down the page.

An author's note lists specific information about the course or department and can provide acknowledgments and contact information.

Author Note

This paper was prepared for Psychology 108, Section B, taught by Professor Kang.

Marginal annotations indicate APA-style formatting and effective writing.

CAN MEDICATION CURE OBESITY IN CHILDREN? 2

Abstract

In recent years, policymakers and medical experts have expressed alarm about the growing problem of childhood obesity in the United States. While most agree that the issue deserves attention, consensus dissolves around how to respond to the problem. This literature review examines one approach to treating childhood obesity: medication. The paper compares the effectiveness for adolescents of the only two drugs approved by the Food and Drug Administration (FDA) for long-term treatment of obesity, sibutramine and orlistat. This examination of pharmacological treatments for obesity points out the limitations of medication and suggests the need for a comprehensive solution that combines medical, social, behavioral, and political approaches to this complex problem.

Keywords: obesity, childhood, adolescence, medication, public policy

Abstract appears on a separate page. Heading is centered and not boldface.

Keywords help readers search for a paper on the Web or in a database.

CAN MEDICATION CURE OBESITY IN CHILDREN?   3

Can Medication Cure Obesity in Children?

A Review of the Literature

In March 2004, U.S. Surgeon General Richard Carmona called attention to a health problem in the United States that, until recently, has been overlooked: childhood obesity. Carmona said that the "astounding" 15% child obesity rate constitutes an "epidemic." Since the early 1980s, that rate has "doubled in children and tripled in adolescents." Now more than nine million children are classified as obese.[1] While the traditional response to a medical epidemic is to hunt for a vaccine or a cure-all pill, childhood obesity is more elusive. The lack of success of recent initiatives suggests that medication might not be the answer for the escalating problem. This literature review considers whether the use of medication is a promising approach for solving the childhood obesity problem by responding to the following questions.

1. What are the implications of childhood obesity?

2. Is medication effective at treating childhood obesity?

3. Is medication safe for children?

4. Is medication the best solution?

Understanding the limitations of medical treatments for children highlights the complexity of the childhood obesity problem in the United States and underscores the need for physicians, advocacy groups, and policymakers to search for other solutions.

What Are the Implications of Childhood Obesity?

Obesity can be a devastating problem from both an individual and a societal perspective. Obesity puts children at risk for a number of medical complications, including Type 2 diabetes, hypertension, sleep apnea, and orthopedic problems (Henry J. Kaiser Family Foundation, 2004, p. 1). Researchers Hoppin and Taveras (2004) have noted that obesity is often associated with psychological issues such as anxiety, depression, and binge eating (Complications section, Table 4).

[1]Obesity is measured in terms of body-mass index (BMI): weight in kilograms divided by square of height in meters. A child or an adolescent with a BMI in the 95th percentile for his or her age and gender is considered obese.

Marginal annotations (left column):

Full title, centered and not boldface.

Mirano sets up her organization by posing four questions.

Mirano states her thesis.

Headings, centered and boldface, help readers follow the organization.

In a signal phrase, the word "and" links the names of two authors; the date is given in parentheses.

Mirano uses a footnote to define an essential term that would be cumbersome to define within the text.

CAN MEDICATION CURE OBESITY IN CHILDREN?   4

Obesity also poses serious problems for a society struggling to cope with rising health care costs. The cost of treating obesity currently totals $117 billion per year—a price, according to the surgeon general, "second only to the cost of [treating] tobacco use" (Carmona, 2004). And as the number of children who suffer from obesity grows, long-term costs will only increase.

Is Medication Effective at Treating Childhood Obesity?

The widening scope of the obesity problem has prompted medical professionals to rethink old conceptions of the disorder and its causes. As researchers Yanovski and Yanovski (2002) have explained, obesity was once considered "either a moral failing or evidence of underlying psychopathology" (p. 592). But this view has shifted: Many medical professionals now consider obesity a biomedical rather than a moral condition, influenced by both genetic and environmental factors. Yanovski and Yanovski have further noted that the development of weight-loss medications in the early 1990s showed that "obesity should be treated in the same manner as any other chronic disease . . . through the long-term use of medication" (p. 592).

The search for the right long-term medication has been complicated. Many of the drugs authorized by the Food and Drug Administration (FDA) in the early 1990s proved to be a disappointment. Two of the medications— fenfluramine and dexfenfluramine—were withdrawn from the market because of severe side effects (Yanovski & Yanovski, 2002, p. 592), and several others were classified by the Drug Enforcement Administration as having the "potential for abuse" (Hoppin & Taveras, 2004, Weight-Loss Drugs section, para. 6). Currently only two medications have been approved by the FDA for long-term treatment of obesity: sibutramine (marketed as Meridia) and orlistat (marketed as Xenical). This section compares studies on the effectiveness of each.

Sibutramine suppresses appetite by blocking the reuptake of the neurotransmitters serotonin and norepinephrine in the brain (Yanovski & Yanovski, 2002, p. 594). Though the drug won FDA approval in 1998, experiments to test its effectiveness for younger patients came considerably later. In 2003, University of Pennsylvania researchers Berkowitz, Wadden, Tershakovec, and Cronquist released the first double-blind placebo study testing the effect of sibutramine on adolescents, aged 13-17, over a

Because the author (Carmona) is not named in the signal phrase, his name and the date appear in parentheses.

Ellipsis mark indicates omitted words.

In a parenthetical citation, an ampersand links the names of two authors.

Mirano draws attention to an important article.

CAN MEDICATION CURE OBESITY IN CHILDREN?   5

12-month period. Their findings are summarized in Table 1. After 6 months, the group receiving medication had lost 4.6 kg (about 10 pounds) more than the control group. But during the second half of the study, when both groups received sibutramine, the results were more ambiguous. In months 6-12, the group that continued to take sibutramine gained an average of 0.8 kg, or roughly 2 pounds; the control group, which switched from placebo to sibutramine, lost 1.3 kg, or roughly 3 pounds (Berkowitz et al., 2003, p. 1808). Both groups received behavioral therapy covering diet, exercise, and mental health.

These results paint a murky picture of the effectiveness of the medication: While initial data seemed promising, the results after one year raised questions about whether medication-induced weight loss could be sustained over time. As Berkowitz et al. (2003) advised, "Until more extensive safety and efficacy data are available, . . . weight-loss medications should be used only on an experimental basis for adolescents" (p. 1811).

A study testing the effectiveness of orlistat in adolescents showed similarly ambiguous results. The FDA approved orlistat in 1999 but did not authorize it for adolescents until December 2003. Roche Laboratories (2003), maker of orlistat, released results of a one-year study testing the drug on 539 obese adolescents, aged 12-16. The drug, which promotes weight loss by blocking fat absorption in the large intestine, showed some effectiveness in adolescents: an average loss of 1.3 kg, or roughly 3 pounds, for subjects taking orlistat for one year, as opposed to an average gain of 0.67 kg, or 1.5 pounds, for the control group (pp. 8-9). See Table 1.

Short-term studies of orlistat have shown slightly more dramatic results. Researchers at the National Institute of Child Health and Human Development tested 20 adolescents, aged 12-16, over a three-month period and found that orlistat, combined with behavioral therapy, produced an average weight loss of 4.4 kg, or 9.7 pounds (McDuffie et al., 2002, p. 646). The study was not controlled against a placebo group; therefore, the relative effectiveness of orlistat in this case remains unclear.

Is Medication Safe for Children?

While modest weight loss has been documented for both medications, each carries risks of certain side effects. Sibutramine has been observed to increase

When this article was first cited, all four authors were named. In subsequent citations of a work with three to five authors, "et al." is used after the first author's name.

For a source with six or more authors, the first author's surname followed by "et al." is used for the first and subsequent references.

CAN MEDICATION CURE OBESITY IN CHILDREN?   6

Table 1

Effectiveness of Sibutramine and Orlistat in Adolescents

Mirano uses a table to summarize the findings presented in two sources.

Medication	Subjects	Treatment[a]	Side effects	Average weight loss/gain
Sibutramine	Control	0-6 mos.: placebo	Mos. 6-12: increased blood pressure; increased pulse rate	After 6 mos.: loss of 3.2 kg (7 lb)
		6-12 mos.: sibutramine		After 12 mos.: loss of 4.5 kg (9.9 lb)
	Medicated	0-12 mos.: sibutramine	Increased blood pressure; increased pulse rate	After 6 mos.: loss of 7.8 kg (17.2 lb)
				After 12 mos.: loss of 7.0 kg (15.4 lb)
Orlistat	Control	0-12 mos.: placebo	None	Gain of 0.67 kg (1.5 lb)
	Medicated	0-12 mos.: orlistat	Oily spotting; flatulence; abdominal discomfort	Loss of 1.3 kg (2.9 lb)

Note. The data on sibutramine are adapted from "Behavior Therapy and Sibutramine for the Treatment of Adolescent Obesity," by R. I. Berkowitz, T. A. Wadden, A. M. Tershakovec, & J. L. Cronquist, 2003, *Journal of the American Medical Association, 289*, pp. 1807-1809. The data on orlistat are adapted from *Xenical (Orlistat) Capsules: Complete Product Information*, by Roche Laboratories, December 2003, retrieved from http://www.rocheusa.com/products/xenical/pi.pdf

A note gives the source of the data.

[a]The medication and/or placebo were combined with behavioral therapy in all groups over all time periods.

A content note explains data common to all subjects.

blood pressure and pulse rate. In 2002, a consumer group claimed that the medication was related to the deaths of 19 people and filed a petition with the Department of Health and Human Services to ban the medication (Hilts, 2002). The sibutramine study by Berkowitz et al. (2003) noted elevated blood pressure as a side effect, and dosages had to be reduced or the medication discontinued in 19 of the 43 subjects in the first six months (p. 1809).

The main side effects associated with orlistat were abdominal discomfort, oily spotting, fecal incontinence, and nausea (Roche Laboratories, 2003, p. 13). More serious for long-term health is the concern that orlistat, being a fat-blocker, would affect absorption of fat-soluble vitamins, such as vitamin D. However, the study found that this side effect can be minimized or eliminated if patients take vitamin supplements two hours before or after administration of orlistat (p. 10). With close monitoring of patients taking the medication, many of the risks can be reduced.

Is Medication the Best Solution?

The data on the safety and efficacy of pharmacological treatments of childhood obesity raise the question of whether medication is the best solution for the problem. The treatments have clear costs for individual patients, including unpleasant side effects, little information about long-term use, and uncertainty that they will yield significant weight loss.

In purely financial terms, the drugs cost more than $3 a day on average (Duenwald, 2004). In each of the clinical trials, use of medication was accompanied by an expensive regime of behavioral therapies, including counseling, nutritional education, fitness advising, and monitoring. As journalist Greg Critser (2003) noted in his book *Fat Land*, use of weight-loss drugs is unlikely to have an effect without the proper "support system"—one that includes doctors, facilities, time, and money (p. 3). For some, this level of care is prohibitively expensive.

A third complication is that the studies focused on adolescents aged 12-16, but obesity can begin at a much younger age. Little data exist to establish the safety or efficacy of medication for treating very young children.

While the scientific data on the concrete effects of these medications in children remain somewhat unclear, medication is not the only avenue for addressing the crisis. Both medical experts and policymakers recognize that solutions might come not only from a laboratory but also from policy, education, and advocacy. A handbook designed to educate doctors on obesity called for "major changes in some aspects of western culture" (Hoppin & Taveras, 2004, Conclusion section, para. 1). Cultural change may not be the typical realm of medical professionals, but the handbook urged doctors to be proactive and

Mirano develops the paper's thesis.

CAN MEDICATION CURE OBESITY IN CHILDREN? 8

"focus [their] energy on public policies and interventions" (Conclusion section, para. 1).

> Brackets indicate Mirano's change in the quoted material.

The solutions proposed by a number of advocacy groups underscore this interest in political and cultural change. A report by the Henry J. Kaiser Family Foundation (2004) outlined trends that may have contributed to the childhood obesity crisis, including food advertising for children as well as

> a reduction in physical education classes and after-school athletic programs, an increase in the availability of sodas and snacks in public schools, the growth in the number of fast-food outlets . . . , and the increasing number of highly processed high-calorie and high-fat grocery products. (p. 1)

> A quotation longer than forty words is indented without quotation marks.

Addressing each of these areas requires more than a doctor armed with a prescription pad; it requires a broad mobilization not just of doctors and concerned parents but of educators, food industry executives, advertisers, and media representatives.

> Mirano interprets the evidence; she doesn't just report it.

The barrage of possible approaches to combating childhood obesity—from scientific research to political lobbying—indicates both the severity and the complexity of the problem. While none of the medications currently available is a miracle drug for curing the nation's nine million obese children, research has illuminated some of the underlying factors that affect obesity and has shown the need for a comprehensive approach to the problem that includes behavioral, medical, social, and political change.

> The tone of the conclusion is objective.

References

List of references begins on a new page. Heading is centered and not boldface.

Berkowitz, R. I., Wadden, T. A., Tershakovec, A. M., & Cronquist, J. L. (2003). Behavior therapy and sibutramine for the treatment of adolescent obesity. *Journal of the American Medical Association, 289,* 1805-1812.

List is alphabetized by authors' last names. All authors' names are inverted.

Carmona, R. H. (2004, March 2). *The growing epidemic of childhood obesity.* Testimony before the Subcommittee on Competition, Foreign Commerce, and Infrastructure of the U.S. Senate Committee on Commerce, Science, and Transportation. Retrieved from http://www.hhs.gov/asl/testify/t040302.html

Critser, G. (2003). *Fat land.* Boston, MA: Houghton Mifflin.

The first line of an entry is at the left margin; subsequent lines indent ½".

Duenwald, M. (2004, January 6). Slim pickings: Looking beyond ephedra. *The New York Times,* p. F1. Retrieved from http://nytimes.com/

Henry J. Kaiser Family Foundation. (2004, February). *The role of media in childhood obesity.* Retrieved from http://www.kff.org/entmedia/7030.cfm

Hilts, P. J. (2002, March 20). Petition asks for removal of diet drug from market. *The New York Times,* p. A26. Retrieved from http://nytimes.com/

Double-spacing is used throughout.

Hoppin, A. G., & Taveras, E. M. (2004, June 25). Assessment and management of childhood and adolescent obesity. *Clinical Update.* Retrieved from http://www.medscape.com/viewarticle/481633

McDuffie, J. R., Calis, K. A., Uwaifo, G. I., Sebring, N. G., Fallon, E. M., Hubbard, V. S., & Yanovski, J. A. (2002). Three-month tolerability of orlistat in adolescents with obesity-related comorbid conditions. *Obesity Research, 10,* 642-650.

Roche Laboratories. (2003, December). *Xenical (orlistat) capsules: Complete product information.* Retrieved from http://www.rocheusa.com/products/xenical/pi.pdf

Yanovski, S. Z., & Yanovski, J. A. (2002). Drug therapy: Obesity. *The New England Journal of Medicine, 346,* 591-602.

Directory to CMS-style notes and bibliography entries

CMS (*Chicago*) Papers

Most history instructors and some humanities instructors require you to document sources with footnotes or endnotes based on *The Chicago Manual of Style*, 16th ed. (Chicago: University of Chicago Press, 2010).

You face three main challenges when you write a paper that draws on sources: (1) supporting a thesis, (2) citing your sources and avoiding plagiarism, and (3) integrating quotations and other source material.

Examples in this section appear in CMS (*Chicago*) style and are drawn from one student's research on the Fort Pillow massacre, which occurred during the Civil War. Sample pages from Ned Bishop's paper are on pages 571–76.

CMS-1 | Supporting a thesis

Most assignments based on reading or research—such as those assigned in history or other humanities classes—ask you to form a thesis, or main idea, and to support that thesis with well-organized evidence.

CMS-1a Form a working thesis.

Once you have read a variety of sources, considered your issue from different perspectives, and chosen an entry point in the research conversation (see R1-b), you are ready to form a working thesis: a one-sentence (or occasionally a two-sentence) statement of your central idea. (See also C1-c.) Because it is a working, or tentative, thesis, you can remain flexible and revise it as your ideas develop. Ultimately, the thesis will express not just your opinion but your informed, reasoned answer to your research question (see R3-c). Here, for example, are student writer Ned Bishop's research question and working thesis statement.

RESEARCH QUESTION

To what extent was Confederate Major General Nathan Bedford Forrest responsible for the massacre of Union troops at Fort Pillow?

WORKING THESIS

By encouraging racism among his troops, Nathan Bedford Forrest was directly responsible for the massacre of Union troops at Fort Pillow.

Notice that the thesis expresses a view on a debatable issue—an issue about which intelligent, well-meaning people might disagree. The writer's job is to persuade such readers that this view is worth taking seriously. To read Ned Bishop's thesis in the context of his introduction, see page 572.

CMS-1b Organize your ideas.

The body of your paper will consist of evidence in support of your thesis. It will be useful to sketch an informal plan that helps you begin to organize your ideas. Ned Bishop, for example, used a simple outline to structure his ideas. In the paper, the points in the outline became headings that help readers follow his line of argument.

> **MORE HELP IN YOUR HANDBOOK**
>
> A working thesis and rough outline can help writers get started.
> ▶ Drafting a working thesis: **C1-c**
> ▶ Sketching a plan: **C1-d**

> What happened at Fort Pillow?
> Did Forrest order the massacre?
> Can Forrest be held responsible for the massacre?

CMS-1c Use sources to inform and support your argument.

Used thoughtfully, your source materials will make your argument more complex and convincing for readers. Sources can support your thesis by playing several different roles.

Providing background information or context

You can use facts and statistics to support generalizations or to establish the importance of your topic, as student writer Ned Bishop does early in his paper.

> Fort Pillow, Tennessee, which sat on a bluff overlooking the Mississippi River, had been held by the Union for two years. It was garrisoned by 580 men, 292 of them from United States Colored Heavy and Light Artillery regiments, 285 from the white Thirteenth Tennessee Cavalry. Nathan Bedford Forrest commanded about 1,500 troops.[1]

Explaining terms or concepts

If readers are unlikely to be familiar with a word, a phrase, or an idea important to your topic, you must explain it for them. Quoting or paraphrasing a source can help you define terms and concepts clearly and concisely.

> The Civil War practice of giving no quarter to an enemy—in other words, "denying [an enemy] the right of survival"—defied Lincoln's mandate for humane and merciful treatment of prisoners.[9]

Supporting your claims

As you draft, make sure to back up your assertions with facts, examples, and other evidence from your research (see also A4-e). Ned Bishop, for example, uses an eyewitness report of the racially motivated violence perpetrated by Nathan Bedford Forrest's troops.

> The slaughter at Fort Pillow was no doubt driven in large part by racial hatred. . . . A Southern reporter traveling with Forrest makes clear that the discrimination was deliberate: "Our troops maddened by the excitement, shot down the ret[r]eating Yankees, and not until they had attained t[h]e water's edge and turned to beg for mercy, did any prisoners fall in [t]o our hands—Thus the whites received quarter, but the negroes were shown no mercy."[19]

Lending authority to your argument

Expert opinion can give weight to your argument (see also A4-e). But don't rely on experts to make your argument for you. Construct your argument in your own words and, when appropriate, cite the judgment of an authority in the field for support.

> Fort Pillow is not the only instance of a massacre or threatened massacre of black soldiers by troops under Forrest's command. Biographer Brian Steel Wills points out that at Brice's Cross Roads in June 1864, "black soldiers suffered inordinately" as Forrest looked the other way and Confederate soldiers deliberately sought out those they termed "the damned negroes."[21]

Anticipating and countering alternative interpretations

Do not ignore sources that seem contrary to your position or that offer arguments different from your own. Instead, use them to give voice to opposing points of view and alternative interpretations before you counter them (see A4-f). Readers often have opposing points of view in mind already, whether or not they agree with you. Ned Bishop, for example, presents conflicting evidence to acknowledge that some readers may credit Nathan Bedford Forrest with stopping the massacre. In doing so, Bishop creates an opportunity to counter that objection and persuade those readers that Forrest can be held accountable.

Hurst suggests that the temperamental Forrest "may have ragingly ordered a massacre and even intended to carry it out—until he rode inside the fort and viewed the horrifying result" and ordered it stopped.[15] While this is an intriguing interpretation of events, even Hurst would probably admit that it is merely speculation.

CMS-2 | Citing sources; avoiding plagiarism

In a research paper, you will draw on the work of other writers, and you must document their contributions by citing your sources. Sources are cited for two reasons:

1. to tell readers where your information comes from—so that they can assess its reliability and, if interested, find and read the original source
2. to give credit to the writers from whom you have borrowed words and ideas

You must cite anything you borrow from a source, including direct quotations; statistics and other specific facts; visuals such as tables, graphs, and diagrams; and any ideas you present in a summary or paraphrase. Borrowing another writer's language, sentence structures, or ideas without proper acknowledgment is a form of dishonesty known as *plagiarism*. The only exception is common knowledge—information that your readers may know or could easily locate in any number of reference sources.

CMS-2a Use the CMS (*Chicago*) system for citing sources.

CMS citations consist of superscript numbers in the text of the paper that refer readers to notes with corresponding numbers either at the foot of the page (footnotes) or at the end of the paper (endnotes).

TEXT

Governor John Andrew was not allowed to recruit black soldiers from out of state. "Ostensibly," writes Peter Burchard, "no recruiting was done outside Massachusetts, but it was an open secret that Andrew's agents were working far and wide."[1]

NOTE

1. Peter Burchard, *One Gallant Rush: Robert Gould Shaw and His Brave Black Regiment* (New York: St. Martin's, 1965), 85.

For detailed advice on using CMS-style notes, see CMS-4. When you use footnotes or endnotes, you will usually need to provide a bibliography as well.

BIBLIOGRAPHY ENTRY

Burchard, Peter. *One Gallant Rush: Robert Gould Shaw and His Brave Black Regiment.* New York: St. Martin's, 1965.

CMS-2b   Understand what plagiarism is.

Your research paper is a collaboration between you and your sources. To be fair and ethical, you must acknowledge your debt to the writers of those sources. Failure to do so is a form of academic dishonesty known as *plagiarism*.

Three different acts are generally considered plagiarism: (1) failing to cite quotations and borrowed ideas, (2) failing to enclose borrowed language in quotation marks, and (3) failing to put summaries and paraphrases in your own words. Definitions of plagiarism may vary; it's a good idea to find out how your school defines and addresses academic dishonesty.

CMS-2c   Use quotation marks around borrowed language.

To indicate that you are using a source's exact phrases or sentences, you must enclose them in quotation marks unless they have been set off from the text by indenting (see p. 544). To omit the quotation marks is to claim—falsely—that the language is your own. Such an omission is plagiarism even if you have cited the source.

> **MORE HELP IN YOUR HANDBOOK**
>
> When you use exact language from a source, you need to show that it is a quotation.
>
> ▶ Quotation marks for direct quotations: **P5-a**

ORIGINAL SOURCE

For many Southerners it was psychologically impossible to see a black man bearing arms as anything but an incipient slave uprising complete with arson, murder, pillage, and rapine.
—Dudley Taylor Cornish, *The Sable Arm*, p. 158

PLAGIARISM

According to Civil War historian Dudley Taylor Cornish, for many Southerners it was psychologically impossible to see a black man bearing arms as anything but an incipient slave uprising complete with arson, murder, pillage, and rapine.[2]

BORROWED LANGUAGE IN QUOTATION MARKS

According to Civil War historian Dudley Taylor Cornish, "For many Southerners it was psychologically impossible to see a black man bearing arms as anything but an incipient slave uprising complete with arson, murder, pillage, and rapine."[2]

NOTE: Long quotations are set off from the text by indenting and do not need quotation marks (see the example on p. 544).

CMS-2d Put summaries and paraphrases in your own words.

Summaries and paraphrases are written in your own words. A summary condenses information; a paraphrase conveys the information using roughly the same number of words as in the original source. When you summarize or paraphrase, it is not enough to name the source; you must restate the source's meaning using your own language. (See also R2-c.) You commit plagiarism if you patchwrite—half-copy the author's sentences, either by mixing the author's phrases with your own without using quotation marks or by plugging your own synonyms into the author's sentence structure.

The first paraphrase of the following source is plagiarized—even though the source is cited—because too much of its language is borrowed from the original. The highlighted strings of words have been copied exactly (without quotation marks). In addition, the writer has closely followed the sentence structure of the original source, merely making a few substitutions (such as *Fifty percent* for *Half* and *angered and perhaps frightened* for *enraged and perhaps terrified*).

ORIGINAL SOURCE

Half of the force holding Fort Pillow were Negroes, former slaves now enrolled in the Union Army. Toward them Forrest's troops had the fierce, bitter animosity of men who had been educated to regard the colored race as inferior and who for the first time had encountered that race armed and fighting against white men. The sight enraged and perhaps terrified many of the Confederates and aroused in them the ugly spirit of a lynching mob.

—Albert Castel, "The Fort Pillow Massacre," pp. 46–47

PLAGIARISM: UNACCEPTABLE BORROWING

Albert Castel suggests that much of the brutality at Fort Pillow can be traced to racial attitudes. Fifty percent of the troops holding Fort Pillow were Negroes, former slaves who had joined the Union Army. Toward them Forrest's soldiers displayed the savage hatred of men who had been taught the inferiority of blacks and who for the first time had confronted them armed and fighting against white men. The vision angered and perhaps frightened the Confederates and aroused in them the ugly spirit of a lynching mob.[3]

To avoid plagiarizing an author's language, resist the temptation to look at the source while you are summarizing or paraphrasing. After you have read the passage you want to paraphrase, set the source aside. Ask yourself, "What is the author's meaning?" In your own words, state your understanding of the author's basic point. Return to the source and check that you haven't used the author's language or sentence structure or misrepresented the author's ideas. Following these steps will help you avoid plagiarizing the source. When you fully understand another writer's meaning, you can more easily and accurately present those ideas in your own words.

ACCEPTABLE PARAPHRASE

Albert Castel suggests that much of the brutality at Fort Pillow can be traced to racial attitudes. Nearly half of the Union troops were blacks, men whom the Confederates had been raised to consider their inferiors. The shock and perhaps fear of facing armed ex-slaves in battle for the first time may well have unleashed the fury that led to the massacre.[3]

CMS-3 | Integrating sources

Quotations, summaries, paraphrases, and facts will support your argument, but they cannot speak for you. You can use several strategies to integrate information from research sources into your paper while maintaining your own voice.

CMS-3a Use quotations appropriately.

In your academic writing, keep the emphasis on your ideas; use your own words to summarize and to paraphrase your sources and to explain your points. Sometimes, however, quotations can be the most effective way to integrate a source.

WHEN TO USE QUOTATIONS

- When language is especially vivid or expressive
- When exact wording is needed for technical accuracy
- When it is important to let the debaters of an issue explain their positions in their own words
- When the words of an authority lend weight to an argument
- When the language of a source is the topic of your discussion (as in an analysis or interpretation)

Limiting your use of quotations

Although it is tempting to insert many quotations in your paper and to use your own words only for connecting passages, do not quote excessively. It is almost impossible to integrate numerous quotations smoothly into your own text.

It is not always necessary to quote full sentences from a source. To reduce your reliance on the words of others, you can often integrate language from a source into your own sentence structure.

> As Hurst has pointed out, until "an outcry erupted in the Northern press," even the Confederates did not deny that there had been a massacre at Fort Pillow.[4]

> Union surgeon Dr. Charles Fitch testified that after he was in custody, he "saw" Confederate soldiers "kill every negro that made his appearance dressed in Federal uniform."[20]

Using the ellipsis mark

To condense a quoted passage, you can use the ellipsis mark (three periods, with spaces between) to indicate that you have left words out. What remains must be grammatically complete.

> Union surgeon Fitch's testimony that all women and children had been evacuated from Fort Pillow before the attack conflicts with Forrest's report: "We captured . . . about 40 negro women and children."[6]

The writer has omitted several words not relevant to the issue at hand: *164 Federals, 75 negro troops, and.*

When you want to leave out one or more full sentences, use a period before the three ellipsis dots. For an example, see the long quotation on page 544.

Ordinarily, do not use an ellipsis mark at the beginning or at the end of a quotation. Readers will understand that you have taken the quoted material from a longer passage, so such marks are not necessary. The only exception occurs when you have dropped words at the end of the final quoted sentence. In such cases, put three ellipsis dots before the closing quotation mark.

USING SOURCES RESPONSIBLY: Make sure omissions and ellipsis marks do not distort the meaning of your source.

Using brackets

Brackets allow you to insert your own words into quoted material to explain a confusing reference or to keep a sentence grammatical in the context of your own writing.

> According to Albert Castel, "It can be reasonably argued that he [Forrest] was justified in believing that the approaching steamships intended to aid the garrison [at Fort Pillow]."[7]

NOTE: Use the word *sic*, italicized and in brackets, to indicate that an error in a quoted sentence appears in the original source. (An example appears below.) Do not overuse *sic* to call attention to errors in a source. Sometimes paraphrasing is a better option. (See p. 314).

Setting off long quotations

CMS style allows you some flexibility in deciding whether to set off a long quotation or run it into your text. For emphasis, you may want to set off a quotation of more than four or five typed lines of text; almost certainly you should set off quotations of ten or more lines. To set off a quotation, indent it one-half inch from the left margin and use the normal right margin. Double-space the indented quotation.

Long quotations should be introduced by an informative sentence, usually followed by a colon. Quotation marks are unnecessary because the indented format tells readers that the passage is taken word-for-word from the source.

> In a letter home, Confederate officer Achilles V. Clark recounted what happened at Fort Pillow:
>
> > Words cannot describe the scene. The poor deluded negroes would run up to our men fall upon their knees and with uplifted hands scream for mercy but they were ordered to their feet and then shot down. The whitte [*sic*] men fared but little better. . . . I with several others tried to stop the butchery and at one time had partially succeeded, but Gen. Forrest ordered them shot down like dogs, and the carnage continued.[8]

CMS-3b Use signal phrases to integrate sources.

Whenever you include a paraphrase, summary, or direct quotation of another writer's work in your paper, prepare your readers for it with a *signal phrase*. A signal phrase names the author of the source and often provides some context for the source material.

When you write a signal phrase, choose a verb that is appropriate for the way you are using the source (see CMS-1c). Are you providing background, explaining a concept, supporting a claim, lending authority, or refuting an argument? By choosing an appropriate verb, you can make your source's role clear. See the chart on page 546 for a list of verbs commonly used in signal phrases.

Note that CMS style calls for verbs in the present tense or present perfect tense (*points out* or *has pointed out*) to introduce source material unless you include a date that specifies the time of the original author's writing.

The first time you mention an author, use the full name: *Shelby Foote argues. . . .* When you refer to the author again, you may use the last name only: *Foote raises an important question.*

Marking boundaries

Readers should be able to move from your own words to the words of a source without feeling a jolt. Avoid dropping quotations into your text without warning. Instead, provide clear signal phrases, usually including the author's name, to indicate the boundary between your words and the source's words. (The signal phrase is highlighted in the second example.)

DROPPED QUOTATION

Not surprisingly, those testifying on the Union and Confederate sides recalled events at Fort Pillow quite differently. Unionists claimed that their troops had abandoned their arms and were in full retreat. "The Confederates, however, all agreed that the Union troops retreated to the river with arms in their hands."[9]

QUOTATION WITH SIGNAL PHRASE

Not surprisingly, those testifying on the Union and Confederate sides recalled events at Fort Pillow quite differently. Unionists claimed that their troops had abandoned their arms and were in full retreat. "The Confederates, however," writes historian Albert Castel, "all agreed that the Union troops retreated to the river with arms in their hands."[9]

Using signal phrases in CMS papers

To avoid monotony, try to vary both the language and the placement of your signal phrases.

Model signal phrases

In the words of historian James M. McPherson, "..."[1]

As Dudley Taylor Cornish has argued, "..."[2]

In a letter to his wife, a Confederate soldier who witnessed the massacre wrote that "..."[3]

"...," claims Benjamin Quarles.[4]

"...," writes Albert Castel, "..."[5]

Shelby Foote offers an intriguing interpretation: "..."[6]

Verbs in signal phrases

admits	compares	insists	rejects
agrees	confirms	notes	reports
argues	contends	observes	responds
asserts	declares	points out	suggests
believes	denies	reasons	thinks
claims	emphasizes	refutes	writes

Using signal phrases with summaries and paraphrases

As with quotations, you should introduce most summaries and paraphrases with a signal phrase that mentions the author and places the material in the context of your own writing. Readers will then understand where the summary or paraphrase begins.

Without the signal phrase (highlighted) in the following example, readers might think that only the last sentence is being cited, when in fact the whole paragraph is based on the source.

> According to Jack Hurst, official Confederate policy was that black soldiers were to be treated as runaway slaves; in addition, the Confederate Congress decreed that white Union officers commanding black troops be killed. Confederate Lieutenant General Kirby Smith went one step further, declaring that he would kill all captured black troops. Smith's policy never met with strong opposition from the Richmond government.[10]

Integrating statistics and other facts

When you are citing a statistic or another specific fact, a signal phrase is often not necessary. In most cases, readers will understand that the citation refers to the statistic or another fact (not the whole paragraph).

> Of 295 white troops garrisoned at Fort Pillow, 168 were taken prisoner. Black troops fared worse, with only 58 of 262 captured and most of the rest presumably killed or wounded.[12]

There is nothing wrong, however, with using a signal phrase to introduce a statistic or fact.

> Shelby Foote notes that of 295 white troops garrisoned at Fort Pillow, 168 were taken prisoner but that black troops fared worse, with only 58 of 262 captured and most of the rest presumably killed or wounded.[12]

Putting source material in context

Readers should not have to guess why source material appears in your paper. A signal phrase can help you make the connection between your own ideas and those of another writer by setting up how a source will contribute to your paper (see R3).

If you use another writer's words, you must explain how they relate to your point. It's a good idea to embed a quotation between sentences of your own. In addition to introducing it with a signal phrase, follow it with interpretive comments that link the source material to your paper's argument.

QUOTATION WITH EFFECTIVE CONTEXT

> In a respected biography of Nathan Bedford Forrest, Hurst suggests that the temperamental Forrest "may have ragingly ordered a massacre and even intended to carry it out—until he rode inside the fort and viewed the horrifying result" and ordered it stopped.[11] While this is an intriguing interpretation of events, even Hurst would probably admit that it is merely speculation.

NOTE: When you bring other sources into a conversation about your research topic, you are synthesizing. For more on synthesis, see MLA-3c.

CMS-4 | Documenting sources

In history and some other humanities courses, you may be asked to use the documentation system of *The Chicago Manual of Style*, 16th ed. (Chicago: University of Chicago Press, 2010). In CMS style, superscript numbers (like this[1]) in the text of the paper refer readers to notes with corresponding numbers either at the foot of the page (footnotes) or at the end of the paper (endnotes). A bibliography is often required as well; it appears at the end of the paper and gives publication information for all the works cited in the notes.

TEXT

A Union soldier, Jacob Thompson, claimed to have seen Forrest order the killing, but when asked to describe the six-foot-two general, he called him "a little bit of a man."[12]

FOOTNOTE OR ENDNOTE

12. Brian Steel Wills, *A Battle from the Start: The Life of Nathan Bedford Forrest* (New York: HarperCollins, 1992), 187.

BIBLIOGRAPHY ENTRY

Wills, Brian Steel. *A Battle from the Start: The Life of Nathan Bedford Forrest.* New York: HarperCollins, 1992.

CMS-4a First and later notes for a source

The first time you cite a source, the note should include publication information for that work as well as the page number for the passage you are citing.

1. Peter Burchard, *One Gallant Rush: Robert Gould Shaw and His Brave Black Regiment* (New York: St. Martin's, 1965), 85.

For later references to a source you have already cited, you may simply give the author's last name, a short form of the title, and the page or pages cited. A short form of the title of a book or another long work is italicized; a short form of the title of an article or another short work is put in quotation marks.

4. Burchard, *One Gallant Rush*, 31.

When you have two notes in a row from the same source, you may use "Ibid." (meaning "in the same place") and the page number for the second note. Use "Ibid." alone if the page number is the same.

5. Jack Hurst, *Nathan Bedford Forrest: A Biography* (New York: Knopf, 1993), 8.

6. Ibid., 174.

CMS-4b CMS-style bibliography

A bibliography at the end of your paper lists the works you have cited in your notes; it may also include works you consulted but did not cite. See page 570 for how to construct the list; see page 576 for a sample bibliography.

NOTE: If you include a bibliography, *The Chicago Manual of Style* suggests that you shorten all notes, including the first reference to a source, as described at the bottom of page 548. Check with your instructor, however, to see whether using an abbreviated note for a first reference to a source is acceptable.

CMS-4c Model notes and bibliography entries

The following models are consistent with guidelines in *The Chicago Manual of Style*, 16th ed. For each type of source, a model note appears first, followed by a model bibliography entry. The note shows the format you should use when citing a source for the first time. For subsequent, or later, citations of a source, use shortened notes (see pp. 548–49).

Some sources on the Web, typically periodical articles, use a permanent locator called a digital object identifier (DOI). Use the DOI, when it is available, in place of a URL in your citations of sources from the Web.

When a URL or a DOI must break across lines, do not insert a hyphen or break at a hyphen if the URL or DOI contains one. Instead, break after a colon or a double slash or before any other mark of punctuation.

General guidelines for listing authors

1. One author

1. Salman Rushdie, *Joseph Anton: A Memoir* (New York: Random House, 2012), 135.

Rushdie, Salman. *Joseph Anton: A Memoir*. New York: Random House, 2012.

2. Two or three authors   For a work with two or three authors, give all authors' names in both the note and the bibliography entry.

2. Bill O'Reilly and Martin Dugard, *Killing Lincoln: The Shocking Assassination That Changed America Forever* (New York: Holt, 2012), 33.

O'Reilly, Bill, and Martin Dugard. *Killing Lincoln: The Shocking Assassination That Changed America Forever*. New York: Holt, 2012.

3. Four or more authors   For a work with four or more authors, in the note give the first author's name followed by "et al." (for "and others"); in the bibliography entry, list all authors' names.

3. Lynn Hunt et al., *The Making of the West: Peoples and Cultures*, 4th ed. (Boston: Bedford/St. Martin's, 2012), 541.

Hunt, Lynn, Thomas R. Martin, Barbara H. Rosenwein, R. Po-chia Hsia, and Bonnie G. Smith. *The Making of the West: Peoples and Cultures*. 4th ed. Boston: Bedford/St. Martin's, 2012.

4. Organization as author

4. Johnson Historical Society, *Images of America: Johnson* (Charleston, SC: Arcadia Publishing, 2011), 24.

Johnson Historical Society. *Images of America: Johnson*. Charleston, SC: Arcadia Publishing, 2011.

5. Unknown author

5. *The Men's League Handbook on Women's Suffrage* (London, 1912), 23.

The Men's League Handbook on Women's Suffrage. London, 1912.

6. Multiple works by the same author   In the bibliography, arrange the entries alphabetically by title. Use six hyphens in place of the author's name in the second and subsequent entries.

Winchester, Simon. *The Alice behind Wonderland*. New York: Oxford University Press, 2011.

------. *Atlantic: Great Sea Battles, Heroic Discoveries, Titanic Storms, and a Vast Ocean of a Million Stories*. New York: HarperCollins, 2010.

7. Editor

7. Teresa Carpenter, ed., *New York Diaries: 1609-2009* (New York: Modern Library, 2012), 316.

Carpenter, Teresa, ed. *New York Diaries: 1609-2009*. New York: Modern Library, 2012.

8. Editor with author

8. Susan Sontag, *As Consciousness Is Harnessed to Flesh: Journals and Notebooks, 1964-1980*, ed. David Rieff (New York: Farrar, Straus and Giroux, 2012), 265.

Sontag, Susan. *As Consciousness Is Harnessed to Flesh: Journals and Notebooks, 1964-1980*. Edited by David Rieff. New York: Farrar, Straus and Giroux, 2012.

9. Translator with author

9. Richard Bidlack and Nikita Lomagin, *The Leningrad Blockade, 1941-1944: A New Documentary from the Soviet Archives*, trans. Marian Schwartz (New Haven, CT: Yale University Press, 2012), 26.

Bidlack, Richard, and Nikita Lomagin. *The Leningrad Blockade, 1941-1944: A New Documentary from the Soviet Archives*. Translated by Marian Schwartz. New Haven, CT: Yale University Press, 2012.

Books and other long works

► Citation at a glance: Book, page 552

10. Basic format for a book

a. Print

10. Mary N. Woods, *Beyond the Architect's Eye: Photographs and the American Built Environment* (Philadelphia: University of Pennsylvania Press, 2009), 45.

Woods, Mary N. *Beyond the Architect's Eye: Photographs and the American Built Environment*. Philadelphia: University of Pennsylvania Press, 2009.

b. E-book

10. Drew Gilpin Faust, *This Republic of Suffering: Death and the American Civil War* (New York: Knopf, 2008), Nook edition, chap. 4.

Faust, Drew Gilpin. *This Republic of Suffering: Death and the American Civil War*. New York: Knopf, 2008. Nook edition.

c. Web (or online library)

10. Charles Hursthouse, *New Zealand, or Zealandia, the Britain of the South* (1857; Hathi Trust Digital Library, n.d.), 2:356, http://catalog.hathitrust.org /Record/006536666.

Hursthouse, Charles. *New Zealand, or Zealandia, the Britain of the South*. 2 vols. 1857. Hathi Trust Digital Library, n.d. http://catalog.hathitrust.org /Record/006536666.

11. Edition other than the first

11. Josephine Donovan, *Feminist Theory: The Intellectual Traditions*, 4th ed. (New York: Continuum, 2012), 86.

Donovan, Josephine. *Feminist Theory: The Intellectual Traditions*. 4th ed. New York: Continuum, 2012.

Citation at a glance: Book CMS

To cite a print book in CMS (*Chicago*) style, include the following elements:

1   Author(s)
2   Title and subtitle
3   City of publication
4   Publisher
5   Year of publication
6   Page number(s) cited (for notes)

TITLE PAGE

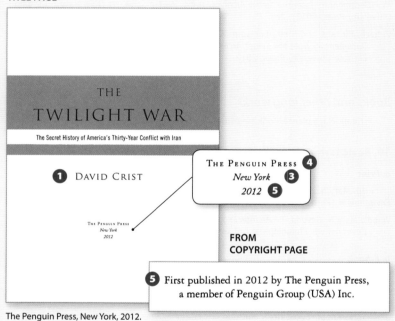

The Penguin Press, New York, 2012.

**FROM
COPYRIGHT PAGE**

5 First published in 2012 by The Penguin Press,
a member of Penguin Group (USA) Inc.

NOTE

1. David Crist, *The Twilight War: The Secret History of America's Thirty-Year Conflict with Iran* (New York: Penguin, 2012), 354.

BIBLIOGRAPHY

Crist, David. *The Twilight War: The Secret History of America's Thirty-Year Conflict with Iran.* New York: Penguin, 2012.

For more on citing books in CMS style, see items 10–18.

12. Volume in a multivolume work If each volume has its own title, give the volume title first, followed by the volume number and the title of the entire work, as in the following examples. If the volumes do not have individual titles, give the volume and page number in the note (for example, 2:356) and the total number of volumes in the bibliography entry (see item 10c).

12. Robert A. Caro, *The Passage of Power*, vol. 4 of *The Years of Lyndon Johnson* (New York: Knopf, 2012), 198.

Caro, Robert A. *The Passage of Power*. Vol. 4 of *The Years of Lyndon Johnson*. New York: Knopf, 2012.

13. Work in an anthology

13. Janet Walsh, "Unequal in Africa: How Property Rights Can Empower Women," in *The Unfinished Revolution: Voices from the Global Fight for Women's Rights*, ed. Minky Worden (New York: Seven Stories Press, 2012), 161.

Walsh, Janet. "Unequal in Africa: How Property Rights Can Empower Women." In *The Unfinished Revolution: Voices from the Global Fight for Women's Rights*, edited by Minky Worden, 159-66. New York: Seven Stories Press, 2012.

14. Introduction, preface, foreword, or afterword

14. Alice Walker, afterword to *The Indispensable Zinn: The Essential Writings of the "People's Historian,"* by Howard Zinn, ed. Timothy Patrick McCarthy (New York: New Press, 2012), 373.

Walker, Alice. Afterword to *The Indispensable Zinn: The Essential Writings of the "People's Historian,"* by Howard Zinn, 371-76. Edited by Timothy Patrick McCarthy. New York: New Press, 2012.

15. Republished book

15. W. S. Blatchley, *A Nature Wooing at Ormond by the Sea* (1902; repr., Stockbridge, MA: Hard Press, 2012), 26.

Blatchley, W. S. *A Nature Wooing at Ormond by the Sea*. 1902. Reprint, Stockbridge, MA: Hard Press, 2012.

16. Book with a title in its title Use quotation marks around any title, whether a long or a short work, within an italicized title.

16. Claudia Durst Johnson, ed., *Race in Mark Twain's "Adventures of Huckleberry Finn"* (Detroit, MI: Greenhaven Press, 2009).

Johnson, Claudia Durst, ed. *Race in Mark Twain's "Adventures of Huckleberry Finn."* Detroit, MI: Greenhaven Press, 2009.

17. Work in a series The series name follows the book title.

17. Lois E. Horton, *Harriet Tubman and the Fight for Freedom: A Brief History with Documents*, Bedford Series in History and Culture (Boston: Bedford/St. Martin's, 2013), 35.

Horton, Lois E. *Harriet Tubman and the Fight for Freedom: A Brief History with Documents*. Bedford Series in History and Culture. Boston: Bedford/St. Martin's, 2013.

18. Sacred text　Sacred texts such as the Bible are usually not included in the bibliography.

> 18. Matt. 20:4-9 (Revised Standard Version).

> 18. Qur'an 18:1-3.

19. Government document

> 19. United States Senate, Committee on Foreign Relations, *Implications of the Kyoto Protocol on Climate Change: Hearing before the Committee on Foreign Relations, United States Senate*, 105th Cong., 2nd sess. (Washington, DC: GPO, 1998).

> United States Senate. Committee on Foreign Relations. *Implications of the Kyoto Protocol on Climate Change: Hearing before the Committee on Foreign Relations, United States Senate*, 105th Cong., 2nd sess. Washington, DC: GPO, 1998.

20. Unpublished dissertation

> 20. Stephanie Lynn Budin, "The Origins of Aphrodite" (PhD diss., University of Pennsylvania, 2000), 301-2, ProQuest (AAT 9976404).

> Budin, Stephanie Lynn. "The Origins of Aphrodite." PhD diss., University of Pennsylvania, 2000. ProQuest (AAT 9976404).

For a published dissertation, italicize the title and give publication information as for a book.

21. Published proceedings of a conference　Cite as a book, adding the location and dates of the conference after the title.

> 21. Stacey K. Sowards et al., eds., *Across Borders and Environments: Communication and Environmental Justice in International Contexts*, University of Texas at El Paso, June 25-28, 2011 (Cincinnati, OH: International Environmental Communication Association, 2012), 114.

> Sowards, Stacey K., Kyle Alvarado, Diana Arrieta, and Jacob Barde, eds. *Across Borders and Environments: Communication and Environmental Justice in International Contexts*. University of Texas at El Paso, June 25-28, 2011. Cincinnati, OH: International Environmental Communication Association, 2012.

22. Source quoted in another source (a secondary source)　Sometimes you will want to use a quotation from one source that you have found in another source. In your note and bibliography entry, cite whatever information is available about the original source of the quotation, including a page number. Then add the words "quoted in" and give publication information for the source in which you found the words. In the following examples, author John Matteson quotes the words of Thomas Wentworth Higginson. Matteson's book includes a note with information about the Higginson book.

> 22. Thomas Wentworth Higginson, *Margaret Fuller Ossoli* (Boston: Houghton Mifflin, 1890), 11, quoted in John Matteson, *The Lives of Margaret Fuller* (New York: Norton, 2012), 7.

> Higginson, Thomas Wentworth. *Margaret Fuller Ossoli*. Boston: Houghton Mifflin, 1890, 11. Quoted in John Matteson, *The Lives of Margaret Fuller* (New York: Norton, 2012), 7.

Articles and other short works

▸ Citation at a glance: Article in a journal, page 556
▸ Citation at a glance: Article from a database, page 558

23. Article in a journal Include the volume and issue numbers (if the journal has them) and the date; end the bibliography entry with the page range of the article. If an article in a database or on the Web shows only a beginning page, use a plus sign after the page number instead of a page range: 212+.

a. Print

23. Catherine Foisy, "Preparing the Quebec Church for Vatican II: Missionary Lessons from Asia, Africa, and Latin America, 1945-1962," *Historical Studies* 78 (2012): 8.

Foisy, Catherine. "Preparing the Quebec Church for Vatican II: Missionary Lessons from Asia, Africa, and Latin America, 1945-1962." *Historical Studies* 78 (2012): 7-26.

b. Web Give the DOI if the article has one; if there is no DOI, give the URL for the article. For unpaginated articles on the Web, you may include in your note a locator, such as a numbered paragraph or a heading from the article.

23. Anne-Lise François, "Flower Fisting," *Postmodern Culture* 22, no. 1 (2011), doi:10.1353/pmc.2012.0004.

François, Anne-Lise. "Flower Fisting." *Postmodern Culture* 22, no. 1 (2011). doi:10.1353/pmc.2012.0004.

c. Database Give one of the following pieces of information from the database listing, in this order of preference: a DOI for the article; or the name of the database and the article number, if any; or a "stable" or "persistent" URL for the article.

23. Patrick Zuk, "Nikolay Myaskovsky and the Events of 1948," *Music and Letters* 93, no. 1 (2012): 61, Project Muse.

Zuk, Patrick. "Nikolay Myaskovsky and the Events of 1948." *Music and Letters* 93, no. 1 (2012): 61. Project Muse.

24. Article in a magazine Give the month and year for a monthly publication; give the month, day, and year for a weekly publication. End the bibliography entry with the page range of the article. If an article in a database or on the Web shows only a beginning page, use a plus sign after the page number instead of a page range: 212+.

a. Print

24. Alan Lightman, "Our Place in the Universe: Face to Face with the Infinite," *Harper's*, December 2012, 34.

Lightman, Alan. "Our Place in the Universe: Face to Face with the Infinite." *Harper's*, December 2012, 33-38.

Citation at a glance: Article in a journal CMS

To cite an article in a print journal in CMS (*Chicago*) style, include the following elements:

1 Author(s)
2 Title and subtitle of article
3 Title of journal
4 Volume and issue numbers

5 Year of publication
6 Page number(s) cited (for notes); page range of article (for bibliography)

FIRST PAGE OF ARTICLE

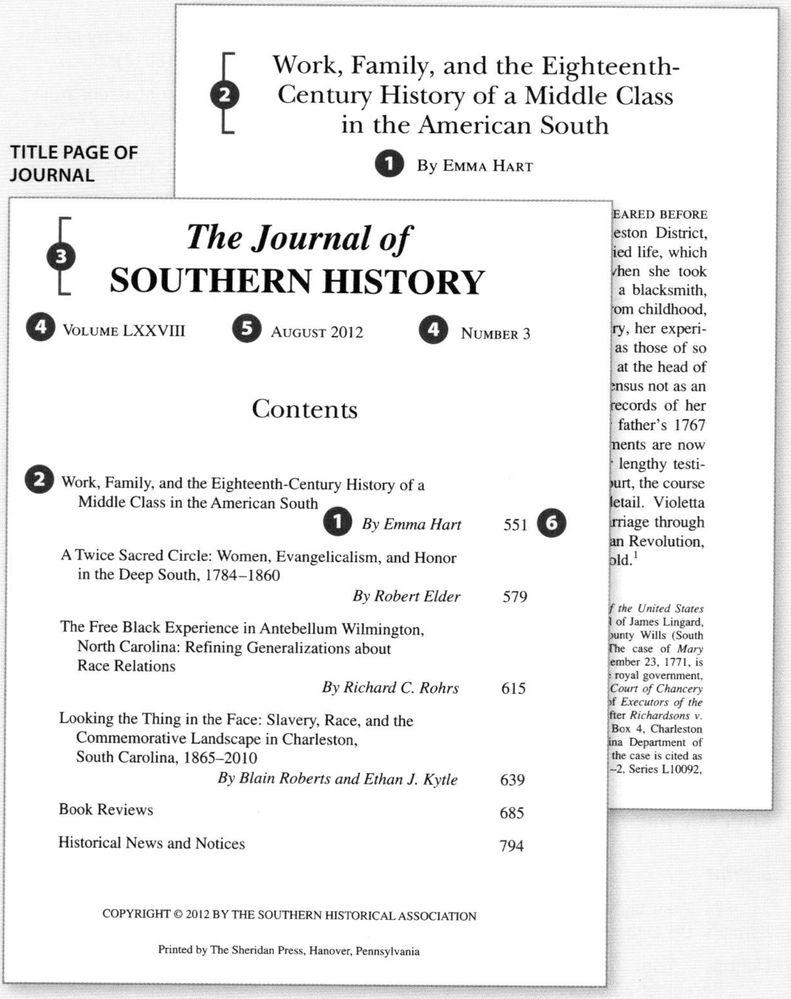

 Work, Family, and the Eighteenth-Century History of a Middle Class in the American South

1 By Emma Hart

TITLE PAGE OF JOURNAL

3 *The Journal of* **SOUTHERN HISTORY**

4 Volume LXXVIII   5 August 2012   4 Number 3

Contents

Partial text visible at right of first page:

EARED BEFORE
eston District,
ied life, which
hen she took
a blacksmith,
om childhood,
ry, her experi-
as those of so
at the head of
nsus not as an
records of her
father's 1767
nents are now
lengthy testi-
ourt, the course
letail. Violetta
rriage through
an Revolution,
old.[1]

f the United States
l of James Lingard,
ounty Wills (South
The case of *Mary
ember 23, 1771, is
royal government,
Court of Chancery
f Executors of the
fter Richardsons v.
Box 4, Charleston
na Department of
the case is cited as
–2, Series L10092,

NOTE

	1		2

1. Emma Hart, "Work, Family, and the Eighteenth-Century History of a Middle Class

	3	4	5	6

in the American South," *Journal of Southern History* 78, no. 3 (2012): 565.

BIBLIOGRAPHY

1	2

Hart, Emma. "Work, Family, and the Eighteenth-Century History of a Middle Class in the

	3	4	5	6

American South." *Journal of Southern History* 78, no. 3 (2012): 551-78.

For more on citing articles in CMS style, see items 23–25.

24. Article in a magazine (*cont.*)

b. Web   If no DOI is available, include the URL for the article.

24. James Verini, "The Tunnels of Gaza," *National Geographic*, December 2012, http://ngm.nationalgeographic.com/2012/12/gaza-tunnels/verini-text.

Verini, James. "The Tunnels of Gaza." *National Geographic*, December 2012. http://ngm .nationalgeographic.com/2012/12/gaza-tunnels/verini-text.

c. Database   Give one of the following from the database listing, in this order of preference: a DOI for the article; or the name of the database and the article number, if any; or a "stable" or "persistent" URL for the article.

24. Ron Rosenbaum, "The Last Renaissance Man," *Smithsonian*, November 2012, 40, OmniFile Full Text Select (83097302).

Rosenbaum, Ron. "The Last Renaissance Man." *Smithsonian*, November 2012, 39-44. OmniFile Full Text Select (83097302).

25. Article in a newspaper   Page numbers are not necessary; a section letter or number, if available, is sufficient.

a. Print

25. Alissa J. Rubin, "A Pristine Afghan Prison Faces a Murky Future," *New York Times*, December 18, 2012, sec. A.

Rubin, Alissa J. "A Pristine Afghan Prison Faces a Murky Future." *New York Times*, December 18, 2012, sec. A.

Citation at a glance: Article from a database CMS

To cite an article from a database in CMS (*Chicago*) style, include the following elements:

1 Author(s)
2 Title and subtitle of article
3 Title of journal
4 Volume and issue numbers
5 Year of publication

6 Page number(s) cited (for notes); page range of article (for bibliography)
7 DOI; *or* database name and article number; *or* "stable" or "persistent" URL for article

ON-SCREEN VIEW OF DATABASE RECORD

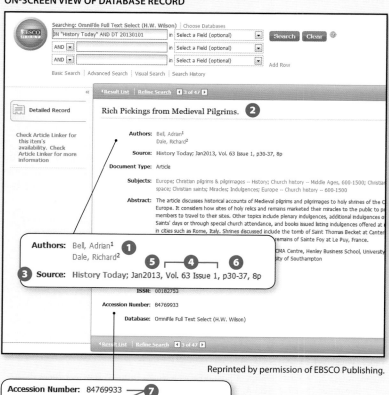

Reprinted by permission of EBSCO Publishing.

NOTE

1. Adrian Bell and Richard Dale, "Rich Pickings from Medieval Pilgrims," *History Today* 63, no. 1 (2013): 33, OmniFile Full Text Select (84769933).

(with bracket labels above: 1, 2, 3 over the first line; 4, 5, 6, 7 over the second line)

BIBLIOGRAPHY

Bell, Adrian, and Richard Dale. "Rich Pickings from Medieval Pilgrims." *History Today* 63, no. 1 (2013): 30-37. OmniFile Full Text Select (84769933).

(with bracket labels above: 1, 2, 3 over the first line; 4, 5, 6, 7 over the second line)

For more on citing articles from databases in CMS style, see items 23–25.

25. Article in a newspaper (*cont.*)

b. Web   Include the URL for the article; if the URL is very long, use the URL for the newspaper's home page. Omit page numbers, even if the source provides them.

25. David Brown, "New Burden of Disease Study Shows World's People Living Longer but with More Disability," *Washington Post*, December 13, 2012, http://www.washingtonpost.com/.

Brown, David. "New Burden of Disease Study Shows World's People Living Longer but with More Disability." *Washington Post*, December 13, 2012. http://www.washingtonpost.com/.

c. Database   Give one of the following from the database listing, in this order of preference: a DOI for the article; or the name of the database and the number assigned by the database; or a "stable" or "persistent" URL for the article.

25. "Safe in Sioux City at Last: Union Pacific Succeeds in Securing Trackage from the St. Paul Road," *Omaha Daily Herald*, May 16, 1889, America's Historical Newspapers.

"Safe in Sioux City at Last: Union Pacific Succeeds in Securing Trackage from the St. Paul Road." *Omaha Daily Herald*, May 16, 1889. America's Historical Newspapers.

26. Unsigned newspaper article   In the note, begin with the title of the article. In the bibliography entry, begin with the title of the newspaper.

26. "Rein in Charter Schools," *Chicago Sun-Times*, December 13, 2012, http://www.suntimes.com/.

Chicago Sun-Times. "Rein in Charter Schools." December 13, 2012. http://www.suntimes.com/.

27. Article with a title in its title Use italics for titles of long works such as books and for terms that are normally italicized. Use single quotation marks for titles of short works and terms that would otherwise be placed in double quotation marks.

27. Karen Garner, "Global Gender Policy in the 1990s: Incorporating the 'Vital Voices' of Women," *Journal of Women's History* 24, no. 4 (2012): 130.

Garner, Karen. "Global Gender Policy in the 1990s: Incorporating the 'Vital Voices' of Women." *Journal of Women's History* 24, no. 4 (2012): 121-48.

28. Review If the review has a title, provide it immediately following the author of the review.

28. David Denby, "Dead Reckoning," review of *Zero Dark Thirty*, directed by Kathryn Bigelow, *New Yorker*, December 24/31, 2012, 130.

Denby, David. "Dead Reckoning." Review of *Zero Dark Thirty*, directed by Kathryn Bigelow. *New Yorker*, December 24/31, 2012, 130-32.

28. David Eggleton, review of *Stalking Nabokov*, by Brian Boyd, *New Zealand Listener*, December 13, 2012, http://www.listener.co.nz/culture/books/stalking-nabokov-by-brian-boyd-review/.

Eggleton, David. Review of *Stalking Nabokov*, by Brian Boyd. *New Zealand Listener*, December 13, 2012. http://www.listener.co.nz/culture/books/stalking-nabokov-by-brian-boyd-review/.

29. Letter to the editor Do not use the letter's title, even if the publication gives one.

29. Andy Bush, letter to the editor, *Economist*, December 15, 2012, http://www.economist.com/.

Bush, Andy. Letter to the editor. *Economist*, December 15, 2012. http://www.economist.com/.

30. Article in a reference work (encyclopedia, dictionary, wiki) Reference works such as encyclopedias do not require publication information and are usually not included in the bibliography. The abbreviation "s.v." is for the Latin *sub verbo* ("under the word").

30. *Encyclopaedia Britannica*, 15th ed., s.v. "Monroe Doctrine."

30. *Wikipedia*, s.v. "James Monroe," last modified December 19, 2012, http://en.wikipedia.org/wiki/James_Monroe.

30. Bryan A. Garner, *Garner's Modern American Usage*, 3rd ed. (Oxford: Oxford University Press, 2009), s.v. "brideprice."

Garner, Bryan A. *Garner's Modern American Usage*. 3rd ed. Oxford: Oxford University Press, 2009.

31. Letter in a published collection Use the day-month-year form for the date of the letter. If the letter writer's name is part of the book title, begin the note with only the last name but begin the bibliography entry with the full name.

▶ Citation at a glance: Letter in a published collection, page 562

31. Dickens to Thomas Beard, 1 June 1840, in *The Selected Letters of Charles Dickens*, ed. Jenny Hartley (New York: Oxford University Press, 2012), 65.

Dickens, Charles. *The Selected Letters of Charles Dickens*. Edited by Jenny Hartley. New York: Oxford University Press, 2012.

Web sources

For most Web sites, include an author if a site has one, the title of the site, the sponsor, the date of publication or the modified (update) date, and the site's URL. Do not italicize a Web site title unless the site is an online book or periodical. Use quotation marks for the titles of sections or pages in a Web site. If a site does not have a date of publication or a modified date, give the date you accessed the site ("accessed January 3, 2013").

32. An entire Web site

32. Chesapeake and Ohio Canal National Historical Park, National Park Service, last modified November 25, 2012, http://www.nps.gov/choh/index.htm.

Chesapeake and Ohio Canal National Historical Park. National Park Service. Last modified November 25, 2012. http://www.nps.gov/choh/index.htm.

33. Short work from a Web site

▶ Citation at a glance: Primary source from a Web site, page 566

33. Dan Archer, "Using Illustrated Reportage to Cover Human Trafficking in Nepal's Brick Kilns," Poynter, last modified December 18, 2012, http://www.poynter.org/.

Archer, Dan. "Using Illustrated Reportage to Cover Human Trafficking in Nepal's Brick Kilns." Poynter, last modified December 18, 2012. http://www.poynter.org/.

34. Blog post   Treat as a short work from a Web site (see item 33), but italicize the name of the blog. Insert "blog" in parentheses after the name if the word *blog* is not part of the name. If the blog is part of a larger site (such as a newspaper's or an organization's site), add the title of the site after the blog title. Do not list the blog post in the bibliography; but if you cite the blog frequently in your paper, you may give a bibliography entry for the entire blog.

34. Gregory LeFever, "Skull Fraud 'Created' the Brontosaurus," *Ancient Tides* (blog), December 16, 2012, http://ancient-tides.blogspot.com/2012/12/skull-fraud-created-brontosaurus.html.

LeFever, Gregory. *Ancient Tides* (blog). http://ancient-tides.blogspot.com/.

Citation at a glance: Letter in a published collection CMS

To cite a letter in a published collection in CMS (*Chicago*) style, include the following elements:

1 Author of letter
2 Recipient of letter
3 Date of letter
4 Title of collection
5 Editor of collection
6 City of publication
7 Publisher
8 Year of publication
9 Page number(s) cited (for notes); page range of letter (for bibliography)

TITLE PAGE

4 TO HIS EXCELLENCY THOMAS JEFFERSON

......*Letters to a President*......

5 JACK McLAUGHLIN

7 AVON BOOKS **6** NEW YORK

AVON BOOKS NEW YORK

FROM COPYRIGHT PAGE

8 Copyright © 1991 by Jack McLaughlin
Cover painting by Giraudon/Art Resource, New York
Published by arrangement with W.W. Norton & Company, Inc.
Library of Congress Catalog Card Number: 90-27824
ISBN: 0-380-71964-9

Washington 30th. Oct 1805 **3**

His Excellency Ths. Jefferson **2**

SIR,

I have not the honor to be personally known to your Excellency therefore you will no doubt think it strange to receive this letter from a person of whom you have not the smallest knowledge. But in order to state to your Excellency in as few words as possible the purport of this address, I am a young man, a Roman Catholic who had been born and

partly educat
had been cor
sequence of t
that unhappy
anything in n
few years s
[m]isfortune r
[I] can attribu

Patronage   *6 1* **9**

your Excellency this very prolix letter which should it please your Excellency to give me some little Office or appointment in that extensive Country of Louisiana It should be my constant endeavour to merit the same by fidelity and an indefatigable attention to whatever business I should be assigned. May I have the satisfaction in whatsoever Country or situation [I] may be in to hear of your Excellencies long continuence of your Natural powers unempaired to conduct the Helm of this Extensive Country which are the sincere wishes of your Excellencies Mo. Obt. Hum. Servt.

1 JOHN O'NEILL

NOTE

          1   2   3   4

1. John O'Neill to Thomas Jefferson, 30 October 1805, in *To His Excellency Thomas*

                                    5   6   7   8   9

Jefferson: Letters to a President, ed. Jack McLaughlin (New York: Avon Books, 1991), 61.

BIBLIOGRAPHY

      1   1   2   3   4

O'Neill, John. John O'Neill to Thomas Jefferson, 30 October 1805. In *To His Excellency*

                                   5   9

Thomas Jefferson: Letters to a President, edited by Jack McLaughlin, 59-61.

      6   7   8

New York: Avon Books, 1991.

For another citation of a letter in CMS style, see item 31.

35. Comment on a blog post   This bibliography entry gives the blog by title only because it has many contributors, not a single author.

35. Didomyk, comment on B.C., "A New Spokesman," *Pomegranate: The Middle East* (blog), *Economist*, December 18, 2012, http://www.economist.com/blogs /pomegranate/2012/12/christians-middle-east.

Pomegranate: The Middle East (blog). *Economist*. http://www.economist.com/blogs /pomegranate/.

Audio, visual, and multimedia sources

36. Podcast   Treat as a short work from a Web site (see item 33), including the following, if available: the name of the author, speaker, or host; the title of the podcast, in quotation marks; an identifying number, if any; the title of the site on which it appears; the sponsor of the site; and the URL. Identify the type of podcast or file format; before the URL, give the date of posting or your date of access.

36. Peter Limb, "Economic and Cultural History of the Slave Trade in Western Africa," Episode 69, Africa Past and Present, African Online Digital Library, podcast audio, December 12, 2012, http://afripod.aodl.org/.

Limb, Peter. "Economic and Cultural History of the Slave Trade in Western Africa." Episode 69. Africa Past and Present. African Online Digital Library. Podcast audio. December 12, 2012. http://afripod.aodl.org/.

37. Online audio or video   Cite as a short work from a Web site (see item 33). If the source is a downloadable file, identify the file format or medium before the URL.

37. Tom Brokaw, "Global Warming: What You Need to Know," Discovery Channel, January 23, 2012, http://www.youtube.com/watch?v=xcVwLrAavyA.

Brokaw, Tom. "Global Warming: What You Need to Know." Discovery Channel, January 23, 2012. http://www.youtube.com/watch?v=xcVwLrAavyA.

38. Published or broadcast interview

38. Jane Goodall, interview by Suza Scalora, *Origin*, n.d., http://www .originmagazine.com/2012/12/07/dr-jane-goodall-interview-with-suza-scalora.

Goodall, Jane. Interview by Suza Scalora. *Origin*, n.d. http://www.originmagazine .com/2012/12/07/dr-jane-goodall-interview-with-suza-scalora.

38. Julian Castro and Joaquin Castro, interview by Charlie Rose, *Charlie Rose Show*, WGBH, Boston, December 17, 2012.

Castro, Julian, and Joaquin Castro. Interview by Charlie Rose. *Charlie Rose Show*. WGBH, Boston, December 17, 2012.

39. Film (DVD, BD, or other format)

39. *Argo*, directed by Ben Affleck (Burbank, CA: Warner Bros. Pictures, 2012).

Argo. Directed by Ben Affleck. Burbank, CA: Warner Bros. Pictures, 2012.

39. *The Dust Bowl*, directed by Ken Burns (Washington, DC: PBS, 2012), DVD.

The Dust Bowl. Directed by Ken Burns. Washington, DC: PBS, 2012. DVD.

40. Sound recording

40. Gustav Holst, *The Planets*, Royal Philharmonic Orchestra, conducted by André Previn, Telarc 80133, compact disc.

Holst, Gustav. *The Planets*. Royal Philharmonic Orchestra. Conducted by André Previn. Telarc 80133, compact disc.

41. Musical score or composition

41. Antonio Vivaldi, *L'Estro armonico*, op. 3, ed. Eleanor Selfridge-Field (Mineola, NY: Dover, 1999).

Vivaldi, Antonio. *L'Estro armonico*, op. 3. Edited by Eleanor Selfridge-Field. Mineola, NY: Dover, 1999.

42. Work of art

42. Aaron Siskind, *Untitled (The Most Crowded Block)*, gelatin silver print, 1939, Kemper Museum of Contemporary Art, Kansas City, MO.

Siskind, Aaron. *Untitled (The Most Crowded Block)*. Gelatin silver print, 1939. Kemper Museum of Contemporary Art, Kansas City, MO.

43. Performance

43. Jackie Sibblies Drury, *Social Creatures*, directed by Curt Columbus, Trinity Repertory Company, Providence, RI, March 15, 2013.

Drury, Jackie Sibblies. *Social Creatures*. Directed by Curt Columbus. Trinity Repertory Company, Providence, RI, March 15, 2013.

Personal communication and social media

44. Personal communication   Personal communications are not included in the bibliography.

44. Sara Lehman, e-mail message to author, August 13, 2012.

45. Online posting or e-mail   If an online posting has been archived, include a URL. E-mails that are not part of an online discussion are treated as personal communication (see item 44). Online postings and e-mails are not included in the bibliography.

45. Ruth E. Thaler-Carter to Copyediting-L discussion list, December 18, 2012, https://list.indiana.edu/sympa/arc/copyediting-l.

46. Facebook post   Facebook posts are not included in the bibliography.

46. US Department of Housing and Urban Development's Facebook page, accessed October 15, 2012, http://www.facebook.com/HUD.

47. Twitter post (tweet)   Tweets are not included in the bibliography.

47. National Geographic's Twitter feed, accessed December 18, 2012, https://twitter.com/NatGeo.

Citation at a glance: Primary source from a Web site CMS

To cite a primary source (or any other document) from a Web site in CMS (*Chicago*) style, include as many of the following elements as are available:

1 Author(s)
2 Title of document
3 Title of site
4 Sponsor of site

5 Publication date or modified date; date of access (if no publication date)
6 URL of document page

WEB SITE HOME PAGE

FIRST PAGE OF DOCUMENT

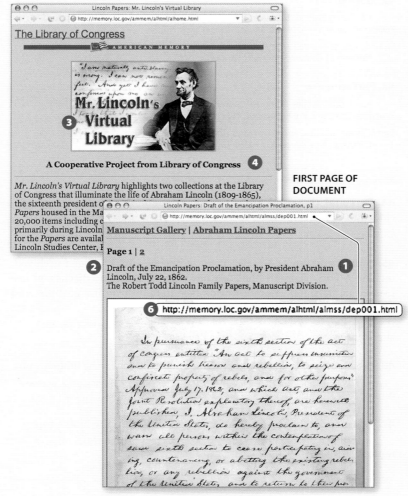

Mr. Lincoln's Virtual Library, The Library of Congress.

NOTE

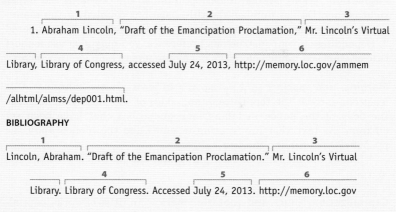

1. Abraham Lincoln, "Draft of the Emancipation Proclamation," Mr. Lincoln's Virtual Library, Library of Congress, accessed July 24, 2013, http://memory.loc.gov/ammem /alhtml/almss/dep001.html.

BIBLIOGRAPHY

Lincoln, Abraham. "Draft of the Emancipation Proclamation." Mr. Lincoln's Virtual Library. Library of Congress. Accessed July 24, 2013. http://memory.loc.gov /ammem/alhtml/almss/dep001.html.

For more on citing documents from Web sites in CMS style, see item 33.

CMS-5 | Manuscript format; sample pages

The following guidelines for formatting a CMS-style paper and preparing its endnotes and bibliography are based on *The Chicago Manual of Style*, 16th ed. (Chicago: University of Chicago Press, 2010). For pages from a sample paper, see CMS-5b.

CMS-5a CMS (*Chicago*) manuscript format

Formatting the paper

The guidelines on pages 567–69 describe recommendations for formatting the text of your paper. For guidelines on preparing the endnotes, see page 569, and for preparing the bibliography, see page 570.

Font If your instructor does not require a specific font, choose one that is standard and easy to read (such as Times New Roman).

Title page Include the full title of your paper, your name, the course title, the instructor's name, and the date. See page 571 for a sample title page.

Pagination Using arabic numerals, number the pages in the upper right corner. Do not number the title page but count it in the manuscript numbering; that is, the first page of the text will be numbered 2. Depending on your instructor's preference, you may also use a short title or your last name before the page numbers to help identify pages.

Margins, line spacing, and paragraph indents Leave margins of at least one inch at the top, bottom, and sides of the page. Double-space the body of the paper, including long quotations that have been set off from the text. (For line spacing in notes and the bibliography, see pp. 569–70.) Left-align the text.

Indent the first line of each paragraph one-half inch from the left margin.

Capitalization, italics, and quotation marks In titles of works, capitalize all words except articles (*a, an, the*), prepositions (*at, from, between,* and so on), coordinating conjunctions (*and, but, or, nor, for, so, yet*), and *to* and *as*—unless the word is first or last in the title or subtitle. Follow these guidelines in your paper even if the title is styled differently in the source.

Lowercase the first word following a colon even if the word begins a complete sentence. When the colon introduces a series of sentences or questions, capitalize the first word in all sentences in the series, including the first.

Italicize the titles of books and other long works. Use quotation marks around the titles of periodical articles, short stories, poems, and other short works.

Long quotations You can choose to set off a long quotation of five to ten typed lines by indenting the entire quotation one-half inch from the left margin. (Always set off quotations of ten or more lines.) Double-space the quotation; do not use quotation marks and do not add extra space above or below it. (See p. 572 for a long quotation in the text of a paper; see also p. 544.)

Visuals CMS classifies visuals as tables and figures (graphs, drawings, photographs, maps, and charts). Keep visuals as simple as possible.

Label each table with an arabic numeral (Table 1, Table 2, and so on) and provide a clear title that identifies the table's subject. The label and the title should appear on separate lines above the table, flush left. For a table that you have borrowed or adapted, give its source in a note like this one, below the table:

> *Source:* Edna Bonacich and Richard P. Appelbaum, *Behind the Label* (Berkeley: University of California Press, 2000), 145.

For each figure, place a label and a caption below the figure, flush left. The label and caption need not appear on separate lines. The word "Figure" may be abbreviated to "Fig."

In the text of your paper, discuss the most significant features of each visual. Place visuals as close as possible to the sentences that relate to them unless your instructor prefers that visuals appear in an appendix.

URLs and DOIs When a URL or a DOI (digital object identifier) must break across lines, do not insert a hyphen or break at a hyphen. Instead, break after a colon or a double slash or before any other mark of punctuation. If your word processing program automatically turns URLs into links (by underlining them and changing the color), turn off this feature.

Headings CMS does not provide guidelines for the use of headings in student papers. If you would like to insert headings in a long essay or research paper, check first with your instructor. See pages 572–74 for typical placement and formatting of headings in a CMS-style paper.

Preparing the endnotes

Begin the endnotes on a new page at the end of the paper. Center the title "Notes" about one inch from the top of the page, and number the pages consecutively with the rest of the paper. See page 575 for an example.

Indenting and numbering Indent the first line of each note one-half inch from the left margin; do not indent additional lines in the note. Begin the note with the arabic numeral that corresponds to the number in the text. Put a period after the number.

Line spacing Single-space each note and double-space between notes (unless your instructor prefers double-spacing throughout).

Preparing the bibliography

Typically, the notes in CMS-style papers are followed by a bibliography, an alphabetically arranged list of all the works cited or consulted. Center the title "Bibliography" about one inch from the top of the page. Number bibliography pages consecutively with the rest of the paper. See page 576 for a sample bibliography.

Alphabetizing the list   Alphabetize the bibliography by the last names of the authors (or editors); when a work has no author or editor, alphabetize it by the first word of the title other than *A*, *An*, or *The*.

If your list includes two or more works by the same author, arrange the entries alphabetically by title. Then use six hyphens instead of the author's name in all entries after the first. (See item 6 on p. 550.)

Indenting and line spacing   Begin each entry at the left margin, and indent any additional lines one-half inch. Single-space each entry and double-space between entries (unless your instructor prefers double-spacing throughout).

CMS-5b Sample pages from a CMS-style research paper

Following are pages from a research paper by Ned Bishop, a student in a history class. Bishop used CMS-style endnotes, bibliography, and manuscript format.

hackerhandbooks.com/writersref
e CMS-5 Format, sample paper > Sample student writing
> Bishop, "The Massacre at Fort Pillow: Holding Nathan Bedford Forrest Accountable" (research)

The Massacre at Fort Pillow:
Holding Nathan Bedford Forrest Accountable

Title of paper.

Ned Bishop

Writer's name.

History 214
Professor Citro
March 22, 2012

Title of course,
instructor's name,
and date.

Marginal annotations indicate CMS-style formatting **and** effective writing.

Although Northern newspapers of the time no doubt exaggerated some of the Confederate atrocities at Fort Pillow, most modern sources agree that a massacre of Union troops took place there on April 12, 1864. It seems clear that Union soldiers, particularly black soldiers, were killed after they had stopped fighting or had surrendered or were being held prisoner. Less clear is the role played by Major General Nathan Bedford Forrest in leading his troops. Although we will never know whether Forrest directly ordered the massacre, evidence suggests that he was responsible for it.

What happened at Fort Pillow?

Fort Pillow, Tennessee, which sat on a bluff overlooking the Mississippi River, had been held by the Union for two years. It was garrisoned by 580 men, 292 of them from United States Colored Heavy and Light Artillery regiments, 285 from the white Thirteenth Tennessee Cavalry. Nathan Bedford Forrest commanded about 1,500 troops.[1]

The Confederates attacked Fort Pillow on April 12, 1864, and had virtually surrounded the fort by the time Forrest arrived on the battlefield. At 3:30 p.m., Forrest demanded the surrender of the Union forces, sending in a message of the sort he had used before: "The conduct of the officers and men garrisoning Fort Pillow has been such as to entitle them to being treated as prisoners of war. . . . Should my demand be refused, I cannot be responsible for the fate of your command."[2] Union Major William Bradford, who had replaced Major Booth, killed earlier by sharpshooters, asked for an hour to consider the demand. Forrest, worried that vessels in the river were bringing in more troops, "shortened the time to twenty minutes."[3] Bradford refused to surrender, and Forrest quickly ordered the attack.

The Confederates charged to the fort, scaled the parapet, and fired on the forces within. Victory came quickly, with the Union forces running toward the river or surrendering. Shelby Foote describes the scene like this:

> Some kept going, right on into the river, where a number drowned and the swimmers became targets for marksmen on the bluff. Others, dropping their guns in terror, ran back toward the Confederates with their hands up, and of these some were spared as prisoners, while others were shot down in the act of surrender.[4]

Thesis asserts Bishop's main point.

Headings, centered, help readers follow the organization.

Statistics are cited with an endnote.

Quotation is cited with an endnote.

Long quotation is set off from text by indenting. Quotation marks are omitted.

Bishop 3

In his own official report, Forrest makes no mention of the massacre. He
does make much of the fact that the Union flag was not lowered by the Union
forces, saying that if his own men had not taken down the flag, "few, if any,
would have survived unhurt another volley."[5] However, as Jack Hurst points
out and Forrest must have known, in this twenty-minute battle, "Federals
running for their lives had little time to concern themselves with a flag."[6]

The federal congressional report on Fort Pillow, which charged
the Confederates with appalling atrocities, was strongly criticized by
Southerners. Respected writer Shelby Foote, while agreeing that
the report was "largely" fabrication, points out that the "casualty
figures . . . indicated strongly that unnecessary killing had occurred."[7] In
an important article, John Cimprich and Robert C. Mainfort Jr. argue
that the most trustworthy evidence is that written within about ten
days of the battle, before word of the congressional hearings circulated
and Southerners realized the extent of Northern outrage. The article
reprints a group of letters and newspaper sources written before April 22
and thus "untainted by the political overtones the controversy later
assumed."[8] Cimprich and Mainfort conclude that these sources "support
the case for the occurrence of a massacre" but that Forrest's role remains
"clouded" because of inconsistencies in testimony.[9]

Did Forrest order the massacre?

We will never really know whether Forrest directly ordered the
massacre, but it seems unlikely. True, Confederate soldier Achilles Clark,
who had no reason to lie, wrote to his sisters that "I with several others
tried to stop the butchery . . . but Gen. Forrest ordered them [Negro and
white Union troops] shot down like dogs, and the carnage continued."[10]
But it is not clear whether Clark heard Forrest giving the orders or was just
reporting hearsay. Many Confederates had been shouting "No quarter! No
quarter!" and, as Shelby Foote points out, these shouts were "thought by
some to be at Forrest's command."[11] A Union soldier, Jacob Thompson,
claimed to have seen Forrest order the killing, but when asked to describe
the six-foot-two general, he called him "a little bit of a man."[12]

Perhaps the most convincing evidence that Forrest did not order
the massacre is that he tried to stop it once it had begun. Historian
Albert Castel quotes several eyewitnesses on both the Union and

---

Bishop uses a primary source as well as secondary sources.

Quotation is introduced with a signal phrase.

Bishop draws attention to an article that reprints primary sources.

Topic sentence states the main idea for this section.

Writer presents a balanced view of the evidence.

Confederate sides as saying that Forrest ordered his men to stop firing.[13] In a letter to his wife three days after the battle, Confederate soldier Samuel Caldwell wrote that "if General Forrest had not run between our men & the Yanks with his pistol and sabre drawn not a man would have been spared."[14]

In a respected biography of Nathan Bedford Forrest, Hurst suggests that the temperamental Forrest "may have ragingly ordered a massacre and even intended to carry it out—until he rode inside the fort and viewed the horrifying result" and ordered it stopped.[15] While this is an intriguing interpretation of events, even Hurst would probably admit that it is merely speculation.

Can Forrest be held responsible for the massacre?

Even assuming that Forrest did not order the massacre, he can still be held accountable for it. That is because he created an atmosphere ripe for the possibility of atrocities and did nothing to ensure that it wouldn't happen. Throughout his career Forrest repeatedly threatened "no quarter," particularly with respect to black soldiers, so Confederate troops had good reason to think that in massacring the enemy they were carrying out his orders. As Hurst writes, "About all he had to do to produce a massacre was issue no order against one."[16] Dudley Taylor Cornish agrees:

> It has been asserted again and again that Forrest did not order a massacre. He did not need to. He had sought to terrify the Fort Pillow garrison by a threat of no quarter, as he had done at Union City and at Paducah in the days just before he turned on Pillow. If his men did enter the fort shouting "Give them no quarter; kill them; kill them; it is General Forrest's orders," he should not have been surprised.[17]

The slaughter at Fort Pillow was no doubt driven in large part by racial hatred. Numbers alone suggest this: Of 295 white troops, 168 were taken prisoner, but of 262 black troops, only 58 were taken into custody, with the rest either dead or too badly wounded to walk.[18] A Southern reporter traveling with Forrest makes clear that the discrimination was deliberate: "Our troops maddened by the excitement, shot down the ret[r]eating Yankees, and not until they had attained t[h]e water's edge and turned to beg for mercy, did any prisoners fall in [t]o our hands—Thus the whites received quarter, but the negroes were shown no mercy."[19]

Topic sentence for this section reinforces the thesis.

Bishop 5

Notes begin on a new page.

Notes

1. John Cimprich and Robert C. Mainfort Jr., eds., "Fort Pillow Revisited: New Evidence about an Old Controversy," *Civil War History* 28, no. 4 (1982): 293-94.

First line of each note is indented ½". Note number is followed by a period. Authors' names are not inverted.

2. Quoted in Brian Steel Wills, *A Battle from the Start: The Life of Nathan Bedford Forrest* (New York: HarperCollins, 1992), 182.

3. Ibid., 183.

4. Shelby Foote, *The Civil War, a Narrative: Red River to Appomattox* (New York: Vintage, 1986), 110.

Notes are single-spaced, with double-spacing between notes. (Some instructors may prefer double-spacing throughout.)

5. Nathan Bedford Forrest, "Report of Maj. Gen. Nathan B. Forrest, C.S. Army, Commanding Cavalry, of the Capture of Fort Pillow," Shotgun's Home of the American Civil War, accessed March 6, 2012, http://www .civilwarhome.com/forrest.htm.

6. Jack Hurst, *Nathan Bedford Forrest: A Biography* (New York: Knopf, 1993), 174.

7. Foote, *Civil War*, 111.

8. Cimprich and Mainfort, "Fort Pillow," 295.

Last names and title refer to an earlier note by the same authors.

9. Ibid., 305.

10. Ibid., 299.

11. Foote, *Civil War*, 110.

12. Quoted in Wills, *Battle from the Start*, 187.

Writer cites an indirect source: words quoted in another source.

13. Albert Castel, "The Fort Pillow Massacre: A Fresh Examination of the Evidence," *Civil War History* 4, no. 1 (1958): 44-45.

14. Cimprich and Mainfort, "Fort Pillow," 300.

15. Hurst, *Nathan Bedford Forrest*, 177.

16. Ibid.

17. Dudley Taylor Cornish, *The Sable Arm: Black Troops in the Union Army, 1861-1865* (Lawrence: University Press of Kansas, 1987), 175.

18. Foote, *Civil War*, 111.

19. Cimprich and Mainfort, "Fort Pillow," 304.

20. Quoted in Wills, *Battle from the Start,* 189.

21. Ibid., 215.

22. Quoted in Hurst, *Nathan Bedford Forrest,* 177.

23. Quoted in James M. McPherson, *Battle Cry of Freedom: The Civil War Era* (New York: Oxford University Press, 1988), 402.

Bibliography begins on a new page.

Entries are alphabetized by authors' last names.

First line of entry is at left margin; additional lines are indented ½".

Entries are single-spaced, with double-spacing between entries. (Some instructors may prefer double-spacing throughout.)

Bibliography

Castel, Albert. "The Fort Pillow Massacre: A Fresh Examination of the Evidence." *Civil War History* 4, no. 1 (1958): 37-50.

Cimprich, John, and Robert C. Mainfort Jr., eds. "Fort Pillow Revisited: New Evidence about an Old Controversy." *Civil War History* 28, no. 4 (1982): 293-306.

Cornish, Dudley Taylor. *The Sable Arm: Black Troops in the Union Army, 1861-1865*. Lawrence: University Press of Kansas, 1987.

Foote, Shelby. *The Civil War, a Narrative: Red River to Appomattox*. New York: Vintage, 1986.

Forrest, Nathan Bedford. "Report of Maj. Gen. Nathan B. Forrest, C.S. Army, Commanding Cavalry, of the Capture of Fort Pillow." Shotgun's Home of the American Civil War. Accessed March 6, 2012. http://www.civilwarhome .com/forrest.htm.

Hurst, Jack. *Nathan Bedford Forrest: A Biography*. New York: Knopf, 1993.

McPherson, James M. *Battle Cry of Freedom: The Civil War Era*. New York: Oxford University Press, 1988.

Wills, Brian Steel. *A Battle from the Start: The Life of Nathan Bedford Forrest*. New York: HarperCollins, 1992.

Index

Index

In addition to giving you page numbers, this index shows you which tabbed section to flip to. For example, the entry "*a* vs. *an*" directs you to section **W** (Word Choice), page 159, and to section **M** (Multilingual Writers and ESL Challenges), page 263. Just flip to the appropriate tabbed section and then track down the exact pages you need.

G

O

Multilingual Menu

A complete section for multilingual writers:

Multilingual and Academic English notes in other sections:

D

Writing in the Disciplines

Advice and Models

D Writing in the Disciplines

Writing in the Disciplines
Advice and Models

A Hacker Handbooks Supplement

Jonathan S. Cullick
Northern Kentucky University

Terry Myers Zawacki
George Mason University

BEDFORD/ST. MARTIN'S
Boston ◆ New York

DISCIPLINE SPECIALISTS

For their assistance and advice as discipline specialists, we thank the following: Diana Belland, Northern Kentucky University (music); Jules Benjamin, Ithaca College (history); Dorinda J. Carter, Michigan State University (education); Jennifer DeForest, University of Virginia (education); Susan Durham, George Mason University (nursing); C. Dale Elifrits, Northern Kentucky University (geology/engineering); Aimee Frame, University of Cincinnati (engineering); Devon Johnson, George Mason University (criminal justice); Victoria McMillan, Colgate University (biology); James Morris, Harvard University (biology); Kirsten Olson, Wheaton College (education); Shannon Portillo, George Mason University (criminal justice); Sherry Robertson, Arizona State University (business); and Beth Schneider, George Mason University (business).

Printed in China.

1 0 9 8 7
f e d c b

For information, write: Bedford/St. Martin's, 75 Arlington Street, Boston, MA 02116   (617-399-4000)

ISBN 978-1-319-08354-0

ACKNOWLEDGMENTS

Jules Benjamin, "Wage Slavery or True Independence? Women Workers in the Lowell, Massachusetts, Textile Mills, 1820–1850," excerpt from *A Student's Guide to History*, Eleventh Edition. Copyright © 2010 by Bedford/St. Martin's. Reprinted with permission.

Valerie Charat, "Always Out of Their Seats (and Fighting): Why Are Boys Diagnosed with ADHD More Often Than Girls?" (December 15, 2006). Reprinted with permission.

Onnalee L. Gibson, "A Reflection on Service Learning: Working with Eric" (April 25, 2006). Reprinted with permission.

Tom Houston, "Concert Review" (February 27, 2008). Reprinted with permission.

Marin Johnson and Laura Arnold, "Distribution Pattern of Dandelion (*Taraxacum officinale*) on an Abandoned Golf Course" (September 13, 2005). Reprinted with permission.

Victoria McMillan, excerpt from *Writing Papers in the Biological Sciences*, Fourth Edition. Copyright © 2006 by Bedford/St. Martin's. Reprinted with permission.

Alice O'Bryan, "Site Stabilization Plan for Erosion Control" (May 5, 2008). Reprinted with permission.

Kelly Ratajczak, "Proposal to Add a Wellness Program" (April 21, 2006). Reprinted with permission.

Julie Riss, "Acute Lymphoblastic Leukemia and Hypertension in One Client: A Nursing Practice Paper" (May 18, 2006). Reprinted with permission.

Brian Spencer, "Positively Affecting Employee Motivation" (March 9, 2006). Reprinted with permission.

Chris Thompson, "Crime in Leesburg, Virginia." Reprinted with permission.

Writing in the Disciplines

Advice and Models

D Writing in the Disciplines

D1 Introduction: Writing in different disciplines

Succeeding in college requires performing well in different kinds of courses and on various kinds of assignments. You know you will be assigned writing in your college writing courses, but it may surprise you to know that other college courses require writing—courses you might not expect, like nursing and psychology. The strategies you develop in your first-year composition course will help you write well in other academic courses.

The academic community is divided into broad subject areas called *disciplines*. The disciplines are generally grouped into five major fields of study, which are further broken down into more specific subjects. The five disciplines and a few representative subjects are social sciences (psychology, sociology, criminology); natural sciences (biology, physics, chemistry); mathematics and engineering; humanities and the arts (history, literature, music); and professions and applied sciences (business, education, nursing).

Each discipline has its own set of expectations and conventions for both reading and writing. Some of the expectations and conventions—writing with a clear main idea, for instance—are common across disciplines; those are covered in your handbook. Other expectations and conventions are unique to each discipline. These include the following:

- purpose for writing
- audience
- questions asked by scholars and practitioners
- types of evidence used
- language and writing conventions
- citation style

When you are asked to write in a specific discipline, start by becoming familiar with the distinctive features of writing in that discipline. For example, if you are asked to write a lab report for a biology class, your purpose might be to present results of an experiment. Your evidence would be the data you collected while conducting your experiment, and you would use scientific terms in your report. You would also use the CSE (Council of Science Editors) guidelines for citation of your sources. If you are asked to write a case study for an education class, your purpose might be to analyze student-teacher interactions in a classroom. Your evidence might be data on a combination of personal observations and interviews. You would use terms from the field in your case study and cite your sources using the guidelines of the American Psychological Association (APA).

The following sections provide guidelines for writing in nine disciplines: biology, business, criminal justice/criminology, education, engineering, history, music, nursing, and psychology. Each section begins with advice about the expectations for writing in that discipline and closes with a model or two of student writing.

D2 Writing in the biological sciences

Biologists use writing in many ways. They write reports analyzing the data they collect from their experiments as well as reviews of other scientists' research or proposed research. They write proposals to convince funding agencies to award grants for their research. If they teach, biologists also write lectures. Some biologists may communicate with a general audience by writing newspaper and magazine articles. In addition, they may lend their expertise to public-policy decision making by government officials, weighing in on, say, the issue of global warming or stem cell research.

When you write in biology courses, your goal will generally be to convince readers of the validity of the conclusions you draw from observations, from experimental data, or from your evaluations of previously published or proposed research. For most assignments, you will need to use a scientific style of writing, conveying your information to readers as succinctly and accurately as possible.

D2-a Determine your audience and their needs in the biological sciences.

When you write in biology, your audience may consist of researchers, professors, other students, and sometimes members of the government or business communities and the general public. Researchers or teachers may read to find out the results of an experiment, an analysis of new data, or information supporting or critiquing a theory. They may need this information to guide their own research projects or improve their assignments and classroom materials. Students read to learn about major concepts and discoveries as well as methods for conducting laboratory experiments. Researchers, teachers, and students expect detailed, specific presentation of data and findings in words and in graphic form, such as diagrams and graphs. Members of the general public want to understand how concepts affect personal decisions they must make about issues such as medical care or nutritional choices. People working in government or business may have to make decisions about funding for research proposals. For more general audiences, you may not need to provide the same level of detail. For example, the public or businesspeople may not need species names to be written in Latin. In all cases, however, your readers expect you to be completely objective and to present information as clearly as possible.

D2-b Recognize the forms of writing in the biological sciences.

When you take courses in biology, you may be asked to write any of the following:

- laboratory notebooks
- research papers
- laboratory reports
- literature reviews
- research proposals
- poster presentations

Laboratory notebooks

If you are required to complete laboratory exercises, you will need to carefully record your experiments in a notebook. A laboratory notebook should be detailed and accurate so that anyone who wishes to repeat your experiment can do so. The laboratory notebook also provides crucial material for any report or article you may write later about your experiment. Researchers take notebooks seriously, never removing a page or erasing entries. That practice keeps them from misrepresenting results.

Your notebook will typically have the following components:

- table of contents
- date of each experiment
- title
- purpose (the objective of the experiment)
- materials (a list of equipment, specimens, and chemicals you used in the experiment)

- procedures (the method you planned to follow as well as any alterations you made to that procedure while conducting the experiment)
- results (the data gathered from the experiment)
- data analysis (calculations based on your data)
- discussion (your assessment of whether the experiment was successful, your interpretation of your results, your accounting for any surprising results, and your conclusions about what you learned from the experiment)
- acknowledgments (those who helped you with the experiment)

Research papers and laboratory reports

When instructors refer to *research papers*, they may have different assignments in mind. One assignment might ask you to present your synthesis of many sources of information about, for instance, a genetic syndrome to demonstrate your understanding of the characteristics of the disorder and other researchers' investigations of the causes of the syndrome.

Another assignment might require you to report on the results of an experiment you conducted and to interpret your results; this document is typically called a *laboratory report*. Unlike the laboratory notebook, a lab report may relate your interpretations to what others in the field have concluded from their own experiments. Biologists publish research papers and reports in journals after the papers have undergone rigorous and impartial review by other biologists, called a *peer review*, to make sure that the scientific process used by the researchers is sound.

Whether published in a journal or written for a college course, research papers and reports based on original experiments follow a standard format and include the following sections:

- abstract (a 100-to-125-word summary of your report)
- introduction (the context for your experiment, such as what has been published on the topic in the field, as well as the purpose of the experiment)
- materials and methods (details of how you conducted the experiment so that other researchers can repeat the experiment to try to reproduce your results; your description of the methodology you used so that readers can determine if your interpretations are supported by the data)
- results (a presentation of what you observed in the experiment)
- figures and tables

- discussion (your interpretation of the results as well as a comparison of your interpretation and that of other researchers in the field)
- references (a list of the sources cited in your paper)

Literature reviews

Literature reviews can have different objectives, such as comparing or contrasting approaches to a problem or examining the literature in the field to propose an alternative theory. Another purpose is to inform biologists about the latest advances in the field. In a review, you will consider the findings of a number of research papers and evaluate those papers' conclusions and perhaps suggest a direction for future research. A critical review analyzes the methods and interpretations of data from one or more journal articles. You may be asked to write a literature review as an introduction to a larger piece of writing, such as a report of a study you conducted. In that case, the review will survey previously published findings relevant to the question that your study investigates.

A literature review assignment is an opportunity to learn about an area in the field and to see what old or new questions may benefit from research.

While the format of reviews varies with their purpose, reviews typically have an abstract, an introduction, a discussion of the research being reviewed, a conclusion, and a references section.

Research proposals

In a research proposal, the biologist poses a significant question and a hypothesis (or hypotheses) and suggests one or more experiments to test the hypothesis. The project can have specific practical applications; for example, one Arctic biologist submitted to the United States Geological Survey a proposal for an ecological monitoring program at a national park. Research proposals that seek funding for an experiment must include detailed budgets.

Whether written by scholars requesting support from an agency or by students in a course, research proposals are evaluated for how well they justify their project with a carefully conceived experiment design.

Poster presentations

At professional gatherings such as annual conventions in the field, biologists have the opportunity to present their work in the form of a poster rather than as a formal talk. Conference attendees approach presenters in an exhibit area to talk about their research, which the posters concisely summarize. A poster features a brief introduction to the presenter's research project, a description of the method, information about the experiment's subjects, the experiment's results, and the presenter's conclusions. Poster presentations also feature graphs and tables since it is important to convey information to attendees quickly and concisely as they walk through the exhibit area. An effective poster presentation will encourage the audience to ask questions and carry on an informal conversation with the presenter.

Your instructor may ask you to create a poster presentation about an experiment you or other researchers have conducted both to help you understand complex concepts and to practice your communication skills.

NOTE: Some presenters use presentation software to create a slide show that they can click through for a small audience or project on a screen for a larger group. Presenters generally include the same kinds of information in slide presentations as they do in poster presentations.

D2-c   Know the questions biologists ask.

Biologists, like other scientists, ask questions about the natural world. Their questions are either *why* questions or *how* questions, such as the following:

- Why don't newborns see well?
- Why does body size of species skew to the right on a distribution curve? That is, why are there so many small animals?
- How does cellular senescence prevent cancer?
- How do island plants self-pollinate?

As they attempt to answer such questions, biologists first offer a tentative explanation, or hypothesis, for something they have observed. They perform an experiment to test their hypothesis. If the results from the experiment match the original predictions, then they consider the hypothesis supported, but not proved, since biologists cannot account for all conditions. Other biologists will continue to formulate new hypotheses and offer new findings.

D2-d   Understand the kinds of evidence biologists use.

Biologists use many kinds of evidence:

- data from site studies or site surveys
- observations of specimens with the aid of special equipment, such as a microscope

- observations and measurements made in experimental settings
- data taken from reports that other biologists have published

Data in biology, which are either quantitative (that which can be counted) or qualitative (that which can be described without numbers), can take various forms, depending on the nature of the site, the type of experiment, or the specialized field in which the research is performed. Following are some examples.

- For a study of the mating choices of female swordfish, biologists might record and analyze responses from females placed in tanks with males.
- In forensic biology, researchers might interpret the data they collect from tests on criminal suspects' DNA samples.
- Plant biologists might analyze the rates of survival of native tree seedlings affected by chemicals released by invasive plant species.

Because evidence can have more than one plausible interpretation, biologists offer alternative explanations for the results obtained in experiments. For example, the authors of one article suggested that differences in the type and availability of prey could account for why Atlantic blue marlin larvae grew faster in one body of water than in another, but they also recognized that other possible causes related to differences in spawning populations.

D2-e Become familiar with writing conventions in the biological sciences.

Biologists agree on several conventions when they write.

- Scientific writing often uses the passive voice to describe how a researcher has performed an experiment (*Blue marlin larvae were collected*). The passive voice can be useful for drawing attention to the action itself, not to who has performed the action. But biologists use the active voice whenever possible to convey information clearly and efficiently (*Researchers collected blue marlin larvae*). With the use of the active voice, the first-person pronouns *I* and *we* are acceptable, even preferred, if the passive voice creates awkward-sounding sentences and adds unnecessary words.
- Direct quotation of sources is rare; instead, biologists paraphrase to demonstrate their understanding of the source material and to convey information economically.

- Biologists use the past tense to describe the materials and methods and the results of their own experiments.
- Biologists use the present tense to describe the published findings of other studies.
- Biologists often include specific scientific names for species (*Canis latrans* for the coyote, for instance).

D2-f Use the CSE system for citing sources.

Biologists typically use the style recommended by the Council of Science Editors (CSE) to format their paper, to cite sources in the text of the paper, and to list the sources at the end. The CSE describes three citation systems in *Scientific Style and Format: The CSE Manual for Authors, Editors, and Publishers*, 8th ed. (Chicago: CSE, 2014). In the *name-year* system, the author's last name and the date of publication are cited in the text. In the *citation-sequence* system, each source is assigned a number the first time it is used in the text, and the same number identifies the source each time it appears. In the *citation-name* system, each source is assigned a number in the order in which it appears in the alphabetical list at the end of the paper. That number is used each time the source is cited in the text.

With all three systems, biologists place bibliographic information for each source at the end of the paper in a section called References or Cited References.

D2-g Sample student paper: Laboratory report

Conducting an experiment gives you practice in collecting and interpreting data. Writing a laboratory report allows you to describe an experiment and its results. The following laboratory report was written for a botany course. The writers used the style guidelines of the Council of Science Editors (CSE) for formatting their paper and citing and listing sources in the citation-sequence system.

Distribution Pattern of Dandelion

(*Taraxacum officinale*)

on an Abandoned Golf Course

Title page consists of a descriptive title and the writers' names in the center of the page and the course, instructor, and date centered at the bottom of the page.

Marin Johnson

Laura Arnold

Lab 4

Botany 100A

Professor Ketchum

September 13, XXXX

Marginal annotations indicate CSE-style formatting and effective writing.

Distribution Pattern of Dandelion 2

ABSTRACT

This paper reports our study of the distribution pattern of the common dandelion (*Taraxacum officinale*) at an abandoned golf course in Hilton, NY, on 10 July 2005. An area of 6 ha was sampled with 111 randomly placed $1 \times 1 \text{ m}^2$ quadrats. The dandelion count from each quadrat was used to test observed frequencies against expected frequencies based on a hypothesized random distribution. We concluded that the distribution of dandelions was not random. We next calculated the coefficient of dispersion to test whether the distribution was aggregated (clumped) or uniform. The calculated value of this coefficient was greater than 1.0, suggesting that the distribution was aggregated. Such aggregated distributions are the most commonly observed types in natural populations.

INTRODUCTION

Theoretically, plants of a particular species may be aggregated (clumped), random, or uniformly distributed in space.[1] The distribution type may be determined by many factors, such as availability of nutrients, competition, distance of seed dispersal, and mode of reproduction.[2]

The purpose of this study was to determine if the distribution pattern of the common dandelion (*Taraxacum officinale*) on an abandoned golf course was aggregated, random, or uniform.

METHODS

The study site was an abandoned golf course in Hilton, NY. The vegetation was predominantly grasses, along with dandelions, broad-leaf plantain (*Plantago major*), and bird's-eye speedwell (*Veronica chamaedrys*). We sampled an area of approximately 6 ha on 10 July 2005, approximately two weeks after the golf course had been mowed.

To ensure random sampling, we threw a tennis ball high in the air over the study area. At the spot where the tennis ball came to rest, we placed one corner of a $1 \times 1 \text{ m}^2$ metal frame (quadrat). We then counted the number of dandelion plants within this quadrat. We repeated this procedure for a total of 111 randomly placed quadrats.

We used a two-step procedure.[2] We first tested whether the distribution of dandelion was random or nonrandom. From the counts of the number of dandelions in our 111 quadrats, we used a log-likelihood ratio

---

Side notes (left margin):

An abstract summarizes the report in about 100–125 words. You may or may not be required to include an abstract with a brief lab report.

Introduction states the purpose of the experiment.

Citations are numbered in the order in which they appear in the text (citation-sequence system).

The writers use scientific names for plant species.

Detailed description of researchers' methods.

Distribution Pattern of Dandelion 3

(*G*) test to examine the goodness of fit between our observed frequencies and those expected based on the Poisson series $e^{-\mu}$, $\mu e^{-\mu}$, $\mu^2/2!e^{-\mu}$, $\mu^3/3!e^{-\mu}$, . . . , where μ is the mean density of plants per quadrat. In carrying out this test, we grouped observed and expected frequencies so that no group had an expected frequency less than 1.0.[3] We then determined whether the distribution was aggregated or uniform by calculating the coefficient of dispersion (ratio of the variance to the mean). A coefficient > 1 indicates an aggregated distribution whereas a coefficient < 1 indicates a more uniform distribution. Finally, we tested the significance of any departure of the ratio from a value of 1 by means of a *t*-test.

Specialized language of the field.

RESULTS

Headings organize the report into major sections.

Table 1 shows the number of quadrats containing 0, 1, 2, . . . , 17 dandelion plants. More than two-thirds (67.6%) of the 111 quadrats contained no dandelion plants; almost 90% (89.2%) of the quadrats contained fewer than 3 dandelion plants. We observed a highly significant lack of fit between our observed frequencies and expected frequencies based on the Poisson distribution ($G = 78.4$, df $= 3$, $P < 0.001$). Thus, our data indicated that the distribution pattern of dandelion plants on the abandoned golf course was not random. The mean number of dandelion plants per quadrat was 1.05 (SD $= 2.50$), and the coefficient of dispersion was 5.95. A *t*-test showed that this value is significantly greater than 1.0 ($t = 36.7$, df $= 110$, $P < 0.001$), which strongly supports an aggregated distribution of the dandelion plants.

DISCUSSION

Writers interpret their results and compare them with results of other researchers.

An aggregated (clumped) distribution is the most commonly observed distribution type in natural populations.[4] Among plants, aggregated distributions often arise in species that have poorly dispersed seeds or vegetative reproduction.[2] In the dandelion, the seeds are contained in light, parachute-bearing fruits that are widely dispersed by the wind. This method of seed dispersal would tend to produce a random distribution. However, dandelion plants also reproduce vegetatively by producing new shoots from existing taproots, and what we considered as groups of closely spaced separate individuals probably represented

Distribution Pattern of Dandelion 4

Table presents the data collected by the researchers in an accessible format.

Table 1 Frequency distribution of dandelion (*Taraxacum officinale*) plants in 1×1 m^2 quadrats positioned randomly over 6 ha on an abandoned golf course

Nr per quadrat	Observed frequency (f_i)	Expected frequency $(f_i)^a$
0	75	38.68594
1	12	40.77707
2	12	21.49062
3	2	7.550757
4	3	1.989727
5	2	0.419456
6	0	0.073688
7	2	0.011096
8	0	0.001462
9	1	0.000171
10	0	1.8×10^{-5}
11	0	1.73×10^{-6}
12	0	1.52×10^{-7}
13	1	1.23×10^{-8}
14	0	9.27×10^{-10}
15	0	6.52×10^{-11}
16	0	4.29×10^{-12}
17	1	2.66×10^{-13}
	Total 111	

[a] Expected frequencies were calculated from the successive terms of the Poisson distribution (see Methods).

shoots originating from the same plant. Thus, vegetative reproduction probably accounted for the observed aggregated distribution in this species.

REFERENCES

Sources are listed and numbered in the order in which they appear in the text.

1. Ketchum J. Lab manual for Botany 100; 2005.

2. Kershaw KA, Looney JHH. Quantitative and dynamic plant ecology. 3rd ed. London: Edward Arnold; 1985.

3. Zar JH. Biostatistical analysis. 5th ed. Englewood Cliffs (NJ): Prentice Hall; 2005.

4. Begon M, Harper JL, Townsend CR. Ecology: individuals, populations and communities. Oxford: Blackwell Science Limited; 1996.

D3 Writing in business

Communication, especially writing, is central to the business world. Because business writers generally aim to persuade or inform their audiences, they place a premium on clarity, brevity, and focus. When you write in business courses, your goal will be to communicate in a straightforward manner and with a clear purpose.

D3-a Determine your audience and their needs in business.

When you write in business, your audience may be varied. One type of audience might be executives, managers, and employees in various departments of a company—accounting, research and development, sales, and clerical support. Another audience might consist of stockholders, clients, and potential customers. Audiences within a business organization read to consider proposals for revising existing products, services, projects, policies, or procedures or for creating new ones. Business owners and executives may read to gather information to help them evaluate projects in progress, to assess sales, and to make decisions about changing product designs or adopting new marketing strategies. They read to understand whether a course of action would be feasible and profitable for the business. Managers, salespeople, and other employees read memos, e-mail, and other documents to help them conduct the daily transactions and activities of the organization, solve daily problems, and respond to customers. Customers read the publications of a business to learn about products and services and to determine whether it would benefit them to do business with a particular company.

For all of your readers, present empirical data such as sales figures or cost structures in easily readable formats such as tables, charts, and graphs. It might also be appropriate to give your readers opinions from questionnaires or surveys. A business owner deciding whether to adopt a marketing strategy might want to read feedback from potential customers, and a potential customer might want to read testimonials from satisfied customers. Respect your readers' time. Make sure your writing is clear, straightforward, focused, attractively presented on paper or a Web site, and as brief as possible. Because trust is essential in business transactions, maintain a respectful tone and project a credible image. Business writing should make personal connections and use inclusive language.

D3-b   Recognize the forms of writing in business.

In business courses, you will be asked to create documents that mirror the ones written in professional settings. The different forms of business writing covered in this section are used for varied purposes, such as informing and persuading. Assignments in business courses may include the following:

- reports
- proposals
- executive summaries
- memos and correspondence
- presentations
- brochures, newsletters, and Web sites

Reports

Reports present factual information for a variety of purposes. If your company is considering the development of a new product, you may be asked to write a feasibility report that lays out the pros and cons. If you are asked to determine how your sales compare with those of a competitor, you will need to write an investigative report. A progress report updates a client or supervisor about the status of a project. A formal report details a major project and generally requires research.

Proposals

Proposals are written with the goal of convincing a specific audience to adopt a plan. A solicited proposal is directed to an audience that has requested it. An unsolicited proposal is written for an audience that has not indicated interest. An internal proposal is directed at others within an organization. An external proposal is directed at clients or potential clients. The length of a proposal will vary depending on your goals and your intended audience.

Executive summaries

An executive summary provides a concise summary of the key points in a longer document, such as a proposal or a report, with the goal of drawing the reader's attention to the longer document.

Memos and correspondence

In business, communication often takes place via letter, memo, or e-mail. Letters and e-mail are written to clients, customers, and colleagues. Memos convey information to others in the same organization for a variety of purposes. A memo might summarize the results of a study or project, describe policies or standards, put forth a plan, or assign tasks.

Presentations

Presentations are usually done orally, in front of a group, to instruct, persuade, or inform. Presenters often use presentation software or tools such as whiteboards to prepare and display visuals—graphs, tables, charts, transparencies, and so on.

Brochures, newsletters, and Web sites

Brochures generally convey information about products or services to clients, donors, or consumers. Newsletters generally provide information about an organization to clients, members, or subscribers. Web sites may either advertise products or provide information about an organization.

D3-c Know the questions business writers ask.

In business, your purpose and your understanding of your audience will determine the questions you ask.

- If you are writing a proposal to persuade a client to adopt a product, you will ask, "How will this product benefit my client?" and "What does my client need?"
- If you are asked to write a report informing your supervisor of your progress on a project, you will ask, "What does my supervisor need to know to authorize me to proceed?" You will also want to ask, "What does my supervisor already know?" and "How can I target this report to address my supervisor's specific concerns?"
- If you are applying for a job, you will ask, "What qualifications do I have for this job?"

D3-d Understand the kinds of evidence business writers use.

In business, your purpose for writing, your audience, and the questions you ask will determine the type of evidence you use. The following are some examples of the way you might use evidence in business writing.

- If you are writing a report or a proposal, you may need to gather data through interviews, direct observation, surveys, or questionnaires. The sources of data you choose will be determined by your audience. For example, if you are studying the patterns of customer traffic at a supermarket to recommend a new layout, you might go to the supermarket and observe customers or you might ask them to fill out surveys as they leave the store. If your audience is the store manager, you might focus on surveys at one store. If your audience is the owner of a large grocery chain, you would probably need to use data from several stores.

- If you are writing an investigative report in which you consider how to entice users to a health club, your evidence might include facts and statistics about the health benefits of exercise that you have drawn from published materials such as books, articles, and reports. You might also conduct research about the facilities of a competitor. In a long proposal or report, your evidence will probably come from a variety of sources rather than just one source.

- If you are applying for a job, your evidence will be your past experience and qualifications. For example, you might explain that you have worked in the industry for six years and held three management positions. You might also discuss how the skills you learned in those jobs will be transferable to the new position.

- If you are writing a brochure to promote a service, your evidence might be testimonials from satisfied users of the service. For example, a brochure advertising nanny services might quote a customer who says, "We found a full-time nanny who is both experienced and energetic—a perfect fit for our family."

D3-e   Become familiar with writing conventions in business.

In business, writing should be straightforward and professional, but not too formal.

- Buzzwords (*value-added, win-win, no-brainer*) and clichés (*The early bird catches the worm*) should be used sparingly. This kind of vocabulary is imprecise and can sound phony or insincere.

- Use personal pronouns such as *you* and *I*. Where appropriate (in letters, e-mail, proposals), you can use the pronoun *you* to emphasize the interests of your readers. When you are addressing multiple readers, you might want to avoid using *you* unless it is clear that you are referring to all readers. When you are expressing your opinion, you should use the pronoun *I*. When you are speaking on behalf of your company, you should use the pronoun *we*.

- It is important to avoid language that could offend someone on the grounds of race, gender, sexual orientation, or disability. Use terms like *chair* or *chairperson* instead of *chairman* or *chairwoman*. Unless it is relevant to your point, avoid describing people by race or ethnicity. If you are describing someone with a disability, use phrases like *client with a disability* rather than *disabled client* to show that you recognize the disability as one trait rather than as a defining characteristic of the person. (Also see "appropriate language" in your handbook.)

- Business writing should always be concise. Avoid using words that are not essential to your point. Instead of writing *at this point in time*, just write *now*. Also avoid words that make a simple idea unnecessarily complicated. Using the passive voice often creates such complications. Instead of writing *This report was prepared to inform our customers*, write *We prepared this report to inform our customers*.

D3-f Use the APA or CMS (*Chicago*) system in business writing.

Business students typically use the style guidelines of the American Psychological Association (APA) or *The Chicago Manual of Style* (CMS) for formatting their paper, for citing sources in the text of their paper, and for listing sources at the end. The APA system is set forth in the *Publication Manual of the American Psychological Association*, 6th ed. (Washington, DC: APA, 2010). CMS style is found in *The Chicago Manual of Style*, 16th ed. (Chicago: University of Chicago Press, 2010). (For more details, see the documentation sections in your handbook.) In business courses, instructors will usually indicate which style they prefer.

D3-g Sample student papers: An investigative report and a proposal

Sample report

Different business situations require different types of reports. Formal reports are comprehensive discussions of a topic from multiple angles, while investigative reports often focus on a specific issue. If you are asked to write a report, you should always be sure that you understand the expectations of your audience.

The investigative report beginning on page D-21 was written for an introductory course in business writing. The student, Brian Spencer, was asked to research the problem of employee motivation at a small company. He used the style guidelines of the American Psychological Association (APA) to format the paper and to cite and list sources.

Sample proposal

Proposals are written to convince a specific audience to adopt a plan. If you are asked to write a proposal, you might start by identifying the purpose and the audience for the document.

The internal proposal beginning on page D-28 was written for a course in business writing. The student, Kelly Ratajczak, wrote her proposal in the form of a memorandum to the senior vice president of human resources at the medium-size company where she completed an internship. Her goal was to convince the vice president to adopt a wellness program for employees.

SAMPLE REPORT

Positively Affecting Employee Motivation

Prepared by Brian Spencer

Report Distributed March 9, XXXX

Prepared for OAISYS

The title page of a business report is counted in the numbering, although a header and page number do not appear.

Title, writer's name, and date, centered on page; company name, centered at bottom.

Marginal annotations indicate business-style formatting and effective writing.

In a typical business report, the page header contains an abbreviated title and the page number.

Abstract

Corporate goals, such as sales quotas or increases in market share, do not always take into account employee motivation. Motivating employees is thus a challenge and an opportunity for firms that want to outperform their competitors. For a firm to achieve its goals, its employees must be motivated to perform effectively.

Abstract, on a separate page, provides a brief summary of the report.

Empirical research conducted with employees of a subject firm, OAISYS, echoed theories published by leading authorities in journals, books, and online reports. These theories argue that monetary incentives are not the primary drivers for employee motivation. Clear expectations, communication of progress toward goals, accountability, and public appreciation are common primary drivers. A firm aiming to achieve superior performance should focus on these activities.

While not strictly APA style, the formatting of the business report is consistent with the style typically used in business. Headings are flush with the left margin and boldface. Paragraphs are separated by an extra line of space, and the first line of each paragraph is not indented.

Employee Motivation 3

Introduction

All firms strive to maximize performance. Such performance is typically
defined by one or more tangible measurements such as total sales, earnings
per share, return on assets, and so on. The performance of a firm is created
and delivered by its employees. Employees, however, are not necessarily
motivated to do their part to maximize a firm's performance. Factors that
motivate employees can be much more complex than corporate goals. This
report will define the problem of employee motivation in one company and
examine potential solutions.

OAISYS is a small business based in Tempe, Arizona, that manufactures
business call recording products. Currently OAISYS employs 27 people. The
business has been notably successful, generating annual compound sales
growth of over 20% during the last three years. The company's management
and board of directors expect revenue growth to accelerate over the coming
three years to an annual compound rate of over 35%. This ambitious
corporate goal will require maximum productivity and effectiveness from all
employees, both current and prospective. OAISYS's management requested
an analysis of its current personnel structure focused on the alignment of
individual employee motivation with its corporate goal.

Background on Current Human Resources Program

OAISYS is currently structured departmentally by function. It has teams
for research and development, sales, marketing, operations, and
administration. Every employee has access to the same employment
benefits, consisting of medical insurance, a 401(k) plan, flexible spending
accounts, short- and long-term disability insurance, and the like.

Members of the sales team receive a yearly salary, quarterly commissions
tied to sales quotas, and quarterly bonuses tied to the performance of
specific tasks. These tasks can change quarterly to maintain alignment with
strategic initiatives.

All employees not in the sales department receive a yearly salary and
profit sharing at the end of the year. The formula for profit sharing is not

Introduction clearly presents the problem to be discussed and sets forth the scope of the report.

Heading announces the purpose of each section.

Employee Motivation 4

known by the employees, and specific information about profits is infrequently communicated. When profitability is discussed, it is only in general terms. Key employees, as determined by the management, are given stock option grants periodically. This process is informal and very confidential.

Disconnect Between Company and Employees

One common assumption is that a human resources program such as OAISYS's should be the platform for motivation. But monetary compensation is not the only driver of employee motivation (Dickson, 1973). In fact, studies have found that other factors are actually the primary drivers of employee motivation. Security, career advancement, the type of work, and pride in one's company are actually the highest-rated factors in employee satisfaction (Accel TEAM, 2005).

Spencer presents evidence from research studies.

These conclusions drawn from the empirical research of others are supported by interviews conducted with current OAISYS employees. Justin Crandall, a current design engineer, stated that his primary motivation is the opportunity to work with leading-edge development tools to pursue results of the highest quality (personal communication, March 1, 2006). Crandall's strongest sense of frustration comes from a cluttered organizational structure because it restricts his ability to pursue innovative, high-quality results.

Spencer provides evidence from interviews with current employees.

Interviews are considered personal communication in APA style; they are cited in the text of the paper but not given in the reference list.

Todd Lindburg, the most senior design engineer on staff, had similar sentiments. His greatest motivator is the opportunity to create something lasting and important to the long-term success of the business (personal communication, March 2, 2006). Jack Wikselaar, vice president of sales, said he receives his strongest motivation from providing fulfilling job opportunities for others (personal communication, March 3, 2006).

These findings of what motivates employees tell only half the story. Other research (*Motivating*, 2006) suggests that businesses can actually demotivate employees through certain behaviors, such as the following:

Employee Motivation 5

- company politics
- unclear expectations
- unnecessary rules and procedures
- unproductive meetings
- poor communication
- toleration of poor performance

Doug Ames, manager of operations for OAISYS, noted that some of these issues keep the company from outperforming expectations: "Communication is not timely or uniform, expectations are not clear and consistent, and some employees do not contribute significantly yet nothing is done" (personal communication, February 28, 2006).

Recommendations

It appears that a combination of steps can be used to unlock greater performance for OAISYS. Most important, steps can be taken to strengthen the corporate culture in key areas such as communication, accountability, and appreciation. Employee feedback indicates that these are areas of weakness or motivators that can be improved. This feedback is summarized in Figure 1.

A plan to use communication effectively to set expectations, share results in a timely fashion, and publicly offer appreciation to specific contributors will likely go a long way toward aligning individual motivation with corporate goals. Additionally, holding individuals accountable for results will bring parity to the workplace.

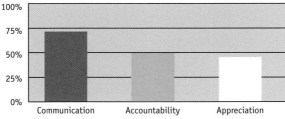

Figure 1. Areas of greatest need for improvements in motivation.

A list draws readers' attention to important information.

The author lays out recommendations for action. Some reports also include a Conclusions section.

Graphic illustrates support for the report's key recommendation.

One technique that might be effective is basing compensation on specific responsibilities. Rather than tying compensation to corporate profit, tying it to individual performance will result in direct correlation between results and reward. Those who do what is necessary to achieve expected results will be rewarded. Those who miss the mark will be required to address the reasons behind their performance and either improve or take a different role. Professor of organizational behavior Jesper Sorenson (2002) has noted that "quantitative analyses have shown that firms with strong cultures outperform firms with weak cultures" (p. 70). Taking steps to strengthen the corporate culture is critical to the company's success.

Employee Motivation 7

References

Accel TEAM. (2005). *Employee motivation in the workplace*. Retrieved from
      http://www.accel-team.com/motivation

Dickson, W. J. (1973). Hawthorne experiments. In C. Heyel (Ed.), *The
      encyclopedia of management* (2nd ed., pp. 298-302). New York, NY:
      Van Nostrand Reinhold.

Motivating employees without money. (2006). Retrieved from http://www
      .employer-employee.com/howtomot.htm

Sorenson, J. B. (2002). The strength of corporate culture and the reliability
      of firm performance. *Administrative Science Quarterly*, *47*(1), 70-71.

Spencer provides a
list of sources using
APA style.

SAMPLE PROPOSAL

MEMORANDUM

Internal proposal is structured in memo format; subject is identified in the header.

To: Jay Crosson, Senior Vice President, Human Resources

From: Kelly Ratajczak, Intern, Purchasing Department

Subject: Proposal to Add a Wellness Program

Date: April 24, XXXX

Ratajczak opens with a clear, concise statement of her main point.

Health care costs are rising. In the long run, implementing a wellness program in our corporate culture will decrease the company's health care costs.

Introductory section provides supporting background information.

Research indicates that nearly 70% of health care costs are from common illnesses related to high blood pressure, overweight, lack of exercise, high cholesterol, stress, poor nutrition, and other preventable health issues (Hall, 2006). Health care costs are a major expense for most businesses, and they do not reflect costs due to the loss of productivity or absenteeism. A wellness program would address most, if not all, of these health care issues and related costs.

Headings clearly define the sections of the proposal.

Benefits of Healthier Employees

A wellness program would substantially reduce costs associated with employee health care, and in addition our company would prosper through many other benefits. Businesses that have wellness programs show a lower cost in production, fewer sick days, and healthier employees ("Workplace Health," 2006). Our healthier employees will help to cut not only our production and absenteeism costs but also potential costs such as higher turnover because of low employee morale.

While not strictly APA style, the memo format for a proposal is consistent with the style typically used in business. A header at the top of each page contains an abbreviated title and an arabic page number (the first page is counted in the numbering, although a number does not appear). Headings are flush with the left margin and boldface. Paragraphs are separated by an extra line of space, and the first line of each paragraph is not indented.

Implementing the Program

Implementing a good wellness program means making small changes to the work environment, starting with a series of information sessions. Simple changes to our work environment should include healthier food selections in vending machines and in the employee cafeteria. A smoke-free environment, inside and outside the building, could be a new company policy. An important step is to educate our employees through information seminars and provide health care guides and pamphlets for work and home. In addition, the human resources department could expand the current employee assistance program by developing online materials

Marginal annotations indicate business-style formatting and effective writing.

Wellness Program Proposal 2

that help employees and their families to assess their individual health goals.

Each health program is different in its own way, and there are a number of programs that can be designed to meet the needs of our individual employees. Some programs that are becoming increasingly popular in the workplace are the following ("Workplace Health," 2006):

- health promotion programs
- subsidized health club membership
- return-to-work programs
- health-risk appraisals and screenings

Obstacles: Individual and Financial

The largest barrier in a wellness program is changing the habits and behaviors of our employees. Various incentives such as monetary bonuses, vacation days, merchandise rewards, recognition, and appreciation help to instill new habits and attitudes. Providing a healthy environment and including family in certain programs also help to encourage healthier choices and behaviors (Hall, 2006).

In the long run, the costs of incorporating a wellness program will be far less than rising costs associated with health care. An employee's sense of recognition, appreciation, or accomplishment is an incentive that has relatively low or no costs. The owner of Natural Ovens Bakery, Paul Sitt, has stated that his company gained financially after providing programs including free healthy lunches for employees (Springer, 2005). Sitt said he believes that higher morale and keeping valuable employees have helped his business tremendously.

It is important that our company be healthy in every way possible. Research shows that 41% of businesses already have some type of wellness program in progress and that 32% will incorporate programs within the next year ("Workplace Health," 2006). Our company should always be ahead of our competitors. I want to thank you for your time, and I look forward to discussing this proposal with you further next week.

> Ratajczak identifies and responds to potential concerns.

> The concluding paragraph summarizes the main point, provides support for being competitive, and indicates a willingness to discuss the proposal.

References

Ratajczak provides a list of sources, formatted in APA style.

Hall, B. (2006). Good health pays off! Fundamentals of health promotion

incentives. *Journal of Deferred Compensation 11*(2), 16-26. Retrieved

from http://www.aspenpublishers.com/

Springer, D. (2005, October 28). Key to business success? *La Crosse

Tribune*. Retrieved from http://lacrossetribune.com/

Workplace health and productivity programs lower absenteeism,

costs. (2006). *Managing Benefit Plans 6*(2), 1-4. Retrieved

from http://www.ioma.com/

D4 Writing in criminal justice and criminology

Criminal justice and criminology are part of the same broad field. Criminal justice refers to the application of policing practices and policies, and criminology is chiefly concerned with the theories that explain those practices and policies. The field of criminal justice and criminology draws from a diverse range of disciplines, including sociology, political science, public administration, psychology, history, and law. Holding this multidisciplinary field together is its fundamental focus on justice. Whatever your specialization as a student—policing, law enforcement management, juvenile justice, corrections, law and the courts, or homeland security—you may be asked to write papers on topics such as policing practices and policies, the administration of justice, legal decision making, and the theories criminologists use to explain and analyze crime. Your instructors may also ask you to imagine different audiences and purposes to prepare you for the wide range of readers and writing tasks you'll encounter in various workplaces.

D4-a Determine your audience and their needs in criminal justice and criminology.

Criminal justice professionals write for diverse audiences, including peers and supervisors in an organization or members of other, related organizations, readers of professional and academic publications, and the general public. When you write in a criminal justice course, you might be asked to imagine that you are writing a memo to a new police chief explaining local crime trends and demographics. Or you might write a memo to the head of a law enforcement organization describing a policing practice or policy and making recommendations for change. You might write about the same practice or policy for an audience of public defenders or for public resources officers who must make sure that citizens understand what the policy means to them. You might be asked to write an article about the practice or policy for a magazine such as *Police Chief*, whose audience consists of many different kinds of practitioners in the field. Given these multiple and often overlapping audiences, you must analyze your readers' needs carefully.

D4-b Recognize the forms of writing in criminal justice and criminology.

When you take courses in criminal justice and criminology, you may be asked to write in a variety of forms for diverse audiences and purposes. These forms include the following:

- research papers
- analytical papers
- argument or position papers
- investigative and administrative reports
- policy memos
- case briefs and legal briefs
- case plans (or case notes)

Research papers

A research paper in a criminal justice course requires you to identify an issue or a topic and then to research or explore the data that have been compiled about the topic (called *secondary sources*). You might also be expected to use *primary sources*—interviews or surveys that you conduct. In most cases, you'll be expected to find your own angle on the topic and to make an argument about it. You might also be required to apply a theory you've studied to your research findings. In a policing course, you might investigate whether police officers from different racial and ethnic backgrounds make decisions differently. To obtain information, you might conduct interviews and read published studies. In a social inequality and justice class, you might investigate whether the focus of racial profiling shifted from African Americans to Muslims after September 11, 2001, and what scholars are saying about possible trends. In a course on corrections, you might examine the punitive practice of solitary confinement and consider what this prison practice indicates about US law and society.

Analytical papers

Often you'll be given assignments that ask you to apply the theories you've studied to a situation, a legal case, or a personal account written by someone in the criminal justice system. For assignments like these, you will generally be expected to describe the theory and its main components and to use the theory to explain specific situations and people's behaviors and life choices. For example, you might be asked to analyze how discretionary theory applies to street-level policing or to critique a theory by comparing it with other theories that attempt to explain the same behaviors and choices. Sometimes analytical papers conclude with program or policy recommendations based on the usefulness or persuasiveness of the theory.

Argument or position papers

In argument or position papers, you are expected to present both sides of an issue in a balanced way and then to take a position. Your position will be based on your analysis of the course readings and lectures or on research you've conducted, not on your personal opinion. You might also be asked to compare or contrast relevant theories and cases to support your position. For example, an assignment might ask you to argue for more or less discretionary power for street-level policing, using as evidence cases in which that power has been used or abused. Or, after investigating trends in racial profiling, you might take a position supporting or opposing changes in the current policies. Or you might argue that the practice of long-term solitary confinement is or is not justified as a crime control approach in US penal policy.

Investigative and administrative reports

Law enforcement professionals and criminologists write both investigative and administrative reports. Some common investigative reports are crime and arrest reports, incident and accident reports, and presentencing reports. A typical crime or arrest report includes a clear timeline of events, for both the crime and the investigation, such as when the defendant was taken into custody, read his or her Miranda rights, and interviewed. The report should also include other details about the criminal investigation—for example, where the interview with the defendant took place, who else was present, and whether any other witnesses were interviewed. Administrative reports typically include a description of a problem, supported by research and statistical data, and recommendations based on an analysis of the data. A consultant's administrative report to a new police chief, for example, may include a briefing about the demographics and crime problems in the local area, an analysis of official crime statistics using the FBI's Uniform Crime Reports, a summary of the findings, and recommendations based on the findings.

Both investigative and administrative reports may be formatted as memos and written to specific audiences who need the information to make decisions, formulate policy, and implement recommendations. In all cases, accuracy, completeness, and objectivity are key to an effective report.

Policy memos

Policy memos are written for many purposes—to inform, to explain, to document, to persuade, or to make a request. The format and style will vary from organization to organization, so you must be aware of the audience's expectations and the conventions set by the organization you're writing for. Typically, the purpose of a policy memo is to help the audience understand the issue and interpret the policy to make practical judgments. You might be asked to write a policy memo to the head of a criminal justice organization, such as the Transportation Security Administration, about the effects of racial profiling on a particular group. Your memo might include a description of the policies being used to address the problem; an argument, based on research, for changing the policies; and recommendations for policies or programs that would benefit the group about which you're concerned.

Case briefs and legal briefs

A brief is a document presented to interested members of a court of law. Briefs are addressed to a specific audience and typically include a short description of a legal case, highlighting key issues, relevant facts, and, if applicable, a history of related court decisions; an analysis and interpretation of how the case applies to a particular organization; and the legal principles and jurisdictional issues related to the desired outcome. For a case brief assignment, you might be asked to write to a public defender or a future judge on how to interpret issues involved in a specific case. A legal brief assignment might ask you to analyze documents submitted for a moot court exercise and to argue for one side.

Your instructor may ask you to follow the IRAC model when you write case and legal briefs. IRAC is an organizational approach used in legal writing as a method for problem solving and structuring an analysis. The acronym IRAC stands for the following steps:

Issue: State the legal issue of relevance.

Rules: List all the statutes and case law relevant to your brief.

Analysis or Application: Provide arguments in favor of and against the decision in this case.

Conclusion: Provide an answer to the legal issue raised.

Another organizational approach is based on the acronym PEAR:

Position: State a position.

Explanation: Explain the position.

Alternatives: Examine the alternative positions.

Response: Respond to potential objections.

NOTE: The explanations of the IRAC and PEAR models are adapted from the *Criminology, Law, and Society Writing Guide* from George Mason University at http://wac.gmu.edu/supporting/guides/CLS/.

Case plans (or case notes)

Case plans, or case notes, may be written as memos or as part of presentencing and postsentencing reports. They might be addressed to courtroom work groups, such as public defenders, prosecutors, judges, and probation officers. Case notes may be addressed to social workers and treatment providers in problem-solving courts such as drug and mental health courts. As the number of work groups expands, audience analysis becomes more complicated because each group may have different goals for its clients and constituencies. For example, a social worker might be interested in resources and treatment; lawyers, in justice; and judges, in the legal aspects of the case. Given the complexity of this writing task, there is no template to guide you. You will typically learn on the job or from models your instructor provides. In general, case notes and plans must be straightforward, clear, and well organized, with the goals and purpose carefully laid out in the introduction along with a preview of the main topics that you will cover. Be sure to include subheadings so that the various audiences can skim through the notes to identify information related to their concerns.

D4-c Know the questions criminal justice professionals and criminologists ask.

Generally, the questions that criminal justice professionals and criminologists ask can be divided into two broad areas of inquiry, one focused on legal systems, the other focused on justice organizations. Within these two broad areas are big-issue questions about crime, law enforcement, society, ethics, and social justice.

- What is deviance, and what is crime?
- What are the causes of crime?
- What is the difference between the law on the books and the law in action?
- What is effective policing?
- What are the theories and laws related to discretionary decision making for practitioners in the field?
- What policing, corrections, and court system policies and practices work to reduce crime and its social effects?

While most of your courses will take up these broad questions in one way or another, each course will have its own focusing questions. A course on policing in the United States, for example, will focus on the role of police in protecting the public against crime and disorder, influences on the decisions police make, the moral and ethical issues they confront, what good policing looks like, and the trends, innovations, and reforms that affect the policing profession. In a corrections course, the focus will be on postsentencing and postrelease issues, with questions about jail and prison management, probation and parole, and compliance with supervision and treatment follow-up requirements.

D4-d   Understand the kinds of evidence criminal justice professionals and criminologists use.

Criminal justice professionals and criminologists use many different kinds of evidence—quantitative, qualitative, historical, and legal—to answer the questions they pose. Most practitioners rely on methods derived from the social sciences to gather evidence: interviews, direct observation, surveys, narrative analysis, natural setting experiments, and analysis of demographic, statistical, legal, geographic, and historical data. Criminologists also use theory-based evidence or the history of a theory or law enforcement policy.

As a student, you will probably be required to use both primary and secondary sources as evidence and to gather and analyze both quantitative and qualitative data. Quantitative data may include crime statistics, incarceration rates, racial profiling data from police stops, ticketing rates, and data on crime statistics linked to geographic areas. Qualitative data may include your own observations, others' responses to interviews and surveys, and the stories people tell about their encounters with crime and the criminal justice system.

Your instructors will also expect you to consult relevant secondary sources, including articles in scholarly and popular periodicals (such as *Police Chief*), news media, government and legal documents, statistical reports, and organizational Web sites, reports, and studies.

D4-e   Become familiar with writing conventions in criminal justice and criminology.

Scholars and practitioners in the criminal justice field value independent thought; the ability to gather, synthesize, and analyze evidence from diverse sources; and the ability to interpret theory and to apply theory to practice and practice to theory. Beyond these broad goals, practitioners agree that writing in the field must be clear, concise, accurate, objective, and well organized, with a clear statement of the writer's purpose and main points. Writers must convey knowledge of the topic in a voice, tone, and format appropriate to the purpose and audience. They must present facts and evidence in an objective, balanced way to allow readers to draw their own conclusions.

To be objective, writers must strive for factual description. For example, in a crime report they should note the date, time, and location of a crime or suspected criminal behavior; they should also describe people and their actions as factually as possible, including identifying characteristics such as gender, race or ethnicity, age, height, weight, and distinctive features like facial hair, tattoos, scars, or physical mannerisms. Subjective descriptions such as "the perpetrator looked suspicious" are meaningless and unfair if not backed up with factual details. It is also important to avoid language that could be construed as offensive or that reveals biases toward gender, race, ethnicity, disabilities, and socioeconomic class.

In the criminal justice field, accuracy is crucial, whether in an arrest report, a briefing memo, a case plan, a researched report, or the application of a theory to an issue, a practice, or a policy. Errors and inaccuracies can cause readers to misinterpret a report, disregard a memo, or throw a case out of court.

First-person pronouns are rarely used in research papers, reports, policy memos, briefings, or analytical papers, in part because writers must present their views objectively, logically, and factually. While the writer of a memo or briefing report may use *I* on occasion, the content and the recommendations being made must be based on the writer's analysis of the evidence, not on personal opinions or biases. The diverse audiences for these documents also expect clear, concise writing, so writers typically use the active voice and paraphrases rather than extensive quotations from their research. In some circumstances, however, it is important to include direct quotations as this information might be critical to an accurate interpretation of the problem, issue, or policy.

D4-f Use the APA or CMS (*Chicago*) system in writing in criminal justice and criminology.

While professionals in the field generally use the documentation style prescribed by the organization or academic journal for which they are writing, instructors typically ask students to use the style guidelines of the American Psychological Association (APA) or the name-year system of *The Chicago Manual of Style* (CMS) to format their paper, to document sources in the text of their paper, and to list sources at the end. Both systems call for in-text, parenthetical citations rather than footnotes or endnotes. The APA system is set forth in the *Publication Manual of the American Psychological Association*, 6th ed. (Washington, DC: APA, 2010). CMS style is found in *The Chicago Manual of Style*, 16th ed. (Chicago: University of Chicago Press, 2010). (For more details, see the documentation sections in your handbook.)

Sometimes students are asked to use *Bluebook* style (or, as it's sometimes called, modified Bluebooking) when they cite sources in case briefs and legal briefs. *Bluebook* format is used by courts, attorneys, and law schools; however, most instructors do not require students to learn this specialized style.

D4-g Sample student paper: Administrative report

Administrative reports are written for specific audiences, typically supervisors, to provide information about an issue or a problem of concern to an organization. When you are asked to write a report, you will be expected to identify the issue or problem, find and analyze relevant statistics and other research, and make recommendations for future actions.

The following administrative report was written for an introductory course on crime and crime policy. Students were asked to imagine that they had been hired as a consultant by the new police chief in their hometown. They were asked to brief the chief about crime in the area, to explain how crime statistics for their town compare with the national average using the FBI's Uniform Crime Reports, and to interpret the statistics so that the chief could decide how best to use the department's resources. The student writer, Chris Thompson, analyzed crime statistics for his hometown of Leesburg, Virginia. He used APA guidelines to format his paper and to cite and list his sources.

Running head: CRIME IN LEESBURG, VIRGINIA   1

The header consists of a shortened title in all capital letters at the left margin and the page number at the right margin; on the title page only, the shortened title is preceded by the words "Running head" and a colon.

Crime in Leesburg, Virginia

Chris Thompson

George Mason University

Full title, writer's name, and school, halfway down the page.

An author's note lists specific information about the course or department and can provide acknowledgments and contact information.

Author Note

This paper was prepared for Administration of Justice 305: Crime Policy, taught by Professor Devon Johnson.

Marginal annotations indicate APA-style formatting and effective writing.

Full title, repeated.

Introduction establishes the purpose of the report and acknowledges the audience.

Centered headings define the major sections of the report.

Thompson provides demographic information relevant to the crime statistics he will analyze.

In-text citation from a Web site is in APA style.

Thompson points to the data tables, explaining their purpose and sources.

Thompson uses a major section of the report to analyze details from the tables.

Crime in Leesburg, Virginia

This report reviews crime statistics in Leesburg, Virginia, to familiarize the new police chief with the town and offer some suggestions about where to focus law enforcement resources. It analyzes local and national statistics from the FBI's Uniform Crime Reports (UCR) for the United States and for Leesburg and offers a basic assessment of the town's needs to provide a useful snapshot for the chief of police.

Description of Leesburg, Virginia

Leesburg, Virginia, is a suburb of Washington, DC, 40 miles to the northwest. In 2008, its population was 39,899 (U.S. Department of Justice, 2009, Table 8). Like many northern Virginia and southern Maryland communities, it serves as a suburban bedroom community to those employed in the nation's capital. The town has grown significantly in the last three decades.

Leesburg's population is predominantly middle and upper middle class, with a median household income 75% higher than the national average (Town of Leesburg, Virginia, 2009a). Leesburg is populated by young (median age 32.3), well-educated (about 50% with a bachelor's degree, about 17% with an advanced degree) citizens; half are white-collar professionals (Town of Leesburg, Virginia, 2009a).

The Leesburg Police Department has 77 sworn officers, operates 24 hours a day, and uses numerous special teams and modern law enforcement techniques. The department has divided the city into three patrol areas to address the specific needs of each zone (Town of Leesburg, Virginia, 2009b).

Nature and Extent of Crime in Leesburg, Virginia

Tables 1 and 2 show the FBI's UCR statistics for 2008. Table 1 contains statistics for Leesburg and the United States, and Table 2 presents the crime rate in Leesburg as a percentage of the national average. A discussion of the accuracy of the UCR is on page 5.

Crime Rates in Leesburg Compared With the National Average

The following list of index crimes compares their rates in Leesburg, Virginia (first value), with the national average (second value). In general, the crime rate in Leesburg is lower than it is across the country. This may be due in part to the demographics of the town's residents and the commuter-oriented suburban nature of the community.

CRIME IN LEESBURG, VIRGINIA   3

Table 1

Crime Rates, by Crime, in Leesburg, Virginia, and in the United States, 2008

	Leesburg		United States	
Offense type	No. reported offenses	Rate per 100,000 inhabitants	No. reported offenses	Rate per 100,000 inhabitants
Violent crime				
Forcible rape	7	17.5	89,000	29.3
Murder and nonnegligent manslaughter	1	2.5	16,272	5.4
Robbery	22	55.1	441,855	145.3
Aggravated assault	29	72.7	834,885	274.6
Total violent crime	59	147.8	1,382,012	454.5
Property crime				
Larceny theft	715	1,792	6,588,873	2,167
Burglary	62	155.4	2,222,196	730.8
Vehicle theft	25	62.7	956,846	314.7
Total property crime	802	2,010	9,767,915	3,212.5

Note. The data for Leesburg, Virginia, are from U.S. Department of Justice (2009), Table 8. The data for the United States are from U.S. Department of Justice (2009), Table 1.

Larceny Theft: 1,792 vs. 2,167 per 100,000

Larceny theft is one of the few index crimes found close to the same level in Leesburg as in the entire nation and thus represents an area of interest for the Leesburg police.

Forcible Rape: 17.5 vs. 29.3 per 100,000

The incidence of forcible rape is slightly more than half the national average. Rape crimes may be an area of concern in Leesburg.

Murder and Nonnegligent Manslaughter: 2.5 vs. 5.4 per 100,000

The most serious crimes, those involving the loss of a human life, are approximately half as prevalent in Leesburg as in the United States as a whole. Murder is typically not a crime that can be countered through patrol.

Robbery: 55.1 vs. 145.3 per 100,000

Robbery (a direct, personal theft from an individual) in Leesburg

---

The data tables are presented in APA style. The columns are clearly labeled, and the data categories reinforce the writer's purpose.

Thompson organizes his discussion of the crimes in Leesburg by most to least concerning.

Subheadings are flush left and boldface.

CRIME IN LEESBURG, VIRGINIA   4

Table 2

Crime Rates in Leesburg, Virginia, Compared With the National Average, 2008

Offense type	Crime rate in Leesburg per 100,000 inhabitants	Crime rate in the United States per 100,000 inhabitants	Crime rate in Leesburg compared with national average (%)
Violent crime			
Forcible rape	17.5	29.3	59.7
Murder and nonnegligent manslaughter	2.5	5.4	46.2
Robbery	55.1	145.3	37.9
Aggravated assault	72.7	274.6	26.4
Total violent crime	147.8	454.5	32.5
Property crime			
Larceny theft	1,792	2,167	82.6
Burglary	155.4	730.8	21.2
Vehicle theft	62.7	314.7	19.9
Total property crime	2,010	3,212.5	62.5

Note. The data for Leesburg, Virginia, are from U.S. Department of Justice (2009), Table 8. The data for the United States are from U.S. Department of Justice (2009), Table 1.

is approximately one-third the national average. Leesburg is not prone to the frequency of robberies found in urban areas, perhaps because most robberies are committed by residents of the same community, and the community of Leesburg is fairly homogeneous in terms of income levels.

Aggravated Assault: 72.7 vs. 274.6 per 100,000

The rate of felony assaults (attempts to commit or acts resulting in serious bodily harm) in Leesburg is roughly one-quarter that in the nation as a whole.

Burglary: 155.4 vs. 730.8 per 100,000

The incidence of burglary (breaking into the home of another person with the intent to commit a felony) in Leesburg is one-fifth the national average. The suburban nature of Leesburg may contribute to this low level.

CRIME IN LEESBURG, VIRGINIA   5

Vehicle Theft: 62.7 vs. 314.7 per 100,000

Motor vehicle theft is uncommon in Leesburg, about one-fifth as likely as in the nation as a whole.

Areas of Interest for a New Police Chief

Overall, forcible rape and larceny theft are the two crimes of most interest to the Leesburg police because their frequency is closer to the national average than the frequency of other crimes. While overall crime is low in Leesburg, these two crimes stand out based solely on the FBI UCR statistics. The police may want to pay particular attention to these crimes for reasons not apparent in the UCR.

Forcible rape is typically an underreported crime because of victim-related factors such as shame and distrust of the system. This crime is of particular concern because even the UCR statistics may not reflect an accurate crime rate (Mosher, Miethe, & Phillips, 2002). The actual instances of rape may be significantly higher than those reported in the UCR. Policy implications may include an increased community policing focus on rape prevention as well as targeted police patrolling of areas where reported rapes occur.

The desire to file an insurance claim for larceny theft (which often requires a police report) may cause more citizens to come forward when they are victims of this particular crime. For this reason, the actual instances of larceny theft are likely closer to those captured in the UCR. Increased patrolling of residential neighborhoods during work hours may reduce burglary rates because most burglaries occur during the day when the occupants are at work.

Accuracy of UCR Statistics

The FBI's UCR, while useful in showing crime trends, is not without its faults. The UCR contains only crimes reported to or observed by law enforcement officers; therefore, it does not provide a complete portrait of crime. The National Crime Victimization Survey (NCVS) revealed that, in many cases, roughly half of the total crimes committed in the United States go unreported (Mosher et al., 2002). The reasons vary but include distrust or lack of faith in the police and the judicial system, shame about or apathy toward the crime, fear of reprisals, inability to recognize the perpetrator, and victim participation in illegal activities at the time of

Thompson interprets the crime statistics and makes recommendations for allocating department resources.

Thompson discusses issues related to the reporting of crime and the accuracy of the UCR. To analyze the strengths and weaknesses of the UCR, he draws on secondary sources.

CRIME IN LEESBURG, VIRGINIA   6

In APA style for a work with three to five authors, all authors are given the first time the source is cited; in subsequent citations, the first author is followed by "et al."

victimization (Mosher et al., 2002). The new police chief should keep these limitations in mind when evaluating UCR statistics.

In addition, classifying crimes is often subjective. Mosher et al. (2002) pointed out that "political manipulation and fabrication of these data by police departments" can easily distort statistics related to an individual incident or a whole reporting agency (p. 84). Some of these distortions are a product of police officer discretion stemming from the "legal seriousness of the crime," "the complainant's preferences," any relationship between the police officer and the offender, the level of respect shown by the complainant, and the financial or social status of the complainant (p. 85).

Conclusion

Thompson summarizes the findings in the report and provides a recommendation. He ends by explaining the importance of crime data analysis for policymaking and assessment.

The town of Leesburg, Virginia, is, in general, a safe place to live. Overall, it experiences a rate of crime considerably lower than the national average. The incidence of property crime is 62.5% of the national average, and the incidence of violent crime is 32.5% of the national average. Leesburg does, however, have two potential problem areas: forcible rape and larceny theft.

This report's initial examination of the data from the UCR is of limited value because of the UCR's lack of depth and breadth in exploring local crime. To obtain a better picture of crime in Leesburg, the new police chief should request a report that compares local, regional, and national crime statistics over several years using the FBI's UCR combined with NCVS data to develop an accurate picture of overall crime. Carefully weighing that information and evaluating it to reveal the big picture are both a means and an end in the law enforcement world: They allow policymakers to make decisions that may reduce the crime rate.

CRIME IN LEESBURG, VIRGINIA   7

References

Mosher, C. J., Miethe, T. D., & Phillips, D. M. (2002). *The mismeasure of crime*. Thousand Oaks, CA: Sage.

Town of Leesburg, Virginia. (2009a). *Demographics*. Retrieved from http://www.leesburgva.gov/index.aspx?page=210

Town of Leesburg, Virginia. (2009b). *Field operations division*. Retrieved from http://www.leesburgva.gov/index.aspx?page=955

U.S. Department of Justice, Federal Bureau of Investigation. (2009). *Crime in the United States 2008*. Retrieved from http://www2.fbi.gov/ucr/cius2008/index.html

List of references is in APA style.

List of references begins on a new page. The first line of each entry is at the left margin; subsequent lines indent ½".

D5   Writing in education

The field of education draws on the knowledge and the methods of a variety of disciplines. As you study to become a teacher, you will take courses that focus on such diverse topics as the history of education, the psychology of teaching and learning, the development of curriculum, and instructional methods. You will also learn how to navigate classrooms and schools through both course work and field placements. Depending on what you plan to teach, you may also take courses in a specific content area (such as history or mathematics) or courses that focus on children with special needs. The writing you do in education courses will be designed to help you become a successful teacher.

D5-a   Determine your audience and their needs in education.

Audiences in the field of education may be school administrators, teachers, students, parents, or policymakers. Administrators read documents to evaluate faculty and assess programs, to revise or develop new programs and curricula, to create policy, to solve problems, to resolve student issues, and to communicate with parents. Teachers read scholarship in their fields to learn about new theoretical findings and methods. Because assessment is a major topic in academic institutions, teachers read reports on student and program assessment as well as informational documents that help them participate in making school policy for testing and placement. Students and parents read publications from their schools and school districts to learn about student performance and school policy. Policymakers such as school board members and state legislators expect information, assessment reports, and proposals about schools, curricula, and programs to be presented with numerical data in the form of graphs and tables.

When you write in education courses, be sure to give your readers empirical data, such as test scores, presented in an easily understandable format. You may need to provide direct observations of student performance as well. Always maintain student confidentiality. Because student groups are so diverse and because positive community relations are essential to every school, be sensitive to student backgrounds and respectful toward students and parents.

D5-b Recognize the forms of writing in education.

Although there are many paths you can take as you train to become a teacher, you will encounter similar writing assignments in different courses. These may include the following:

- reflective essays, journals, and field notes
- curriculum designs and lesson plans
- reviews of instructional materials
- case studies
- research papers
- self-evaluations
- portfolios

Reflective essays, journals, and field notes

Much of the writing you do in education courses will encourage you to reflect on your own attitudes, beliefs, and experiences and how they inform your thoughts about teaching and learning. In an introductory course, for example, you may be asked to write an essay in which you discuss your own education in the context of a theory that you are studying. As a field observer or student teacher, you may be asked to keep a journal or notes in which you reflect on teacher-student interactions, student-student interactions, diversity issues, and student progress. These reflections might then serve as the basis for an essay in which you connect your experiences to course content.

Curriculum designs and lesson plans

In some courses, especially those focused on teaching methods, you will be asked to design individual lessons or units in a particular content area. In an early childhood education course, for example, you might be asked to read one or more children's books and write a plan for a class activity that is related to the reading. In a science methods course, you might be asked to design a unit about plant biology. In a methods course for special education, you might be asked to design an individualized education plan for a specific student. For any of these courses, you might also be asked to integrate technology into your curriculum design.

Reviews of instructional materials

In a review of materials, you assess the value of a set of instructional materials for classroom use. For example, you might be asked to look at several textbooks or software applications and explain which would be most useful in a particular classroom setting.

Case studies

Some education courses require students to conduct and write case studies. Case studies may involve observation and analysis of an individual student, a teacher, or classroom interactions. The goal of a case study may be to determine how the process of teaching or learning takes place or how an event can illuminate something about learning or classroom dynamics.

Research papers

In some education courses, you might be assigned papers that focus on broader educational issues or problems and that require you to conduct research and then formulate your own ideas about the topic. In a course about the history of education, you might be asked to research the evolution of literacy in the United States. In a developmental psychology course, you might be asked to research how students learn mathematics.

Self-evaluations

As a teacher candidate, you will be asked to evaluate your own teaching and learning. The format of the self-evaluation will vary depending on whether you are evaluating yourself as a learner or as a teacher. Sample questions of self-evaluation as a teacher may include the following:

- What were the strengths and weaknesses of your lesson or unit plan?
- How did your lesson further student learning?
- What have you learned about yourself and your students from teaching this class?
- How can you improve your teaching?

Portfolios

Most teacher education programs require you to assemble a teaching portfolio before you graduate. The purpose of the portfolio is to provide information about your teaching experience and your teaching philosophy. The contents of portfolios vary, but common documents include a statement of teaching philosophy, a statement of professional goals, a résumé, evaluations, and sample course materials. Education departments at some institutions will require you to assemble an electronic portfolio as well as a print version.

D5-c Know the questions educators ask.

Educators ask questions that are practical, theoretical, and self-reflective. Practical questions tend to focus on classroom and curriculum issues such as student progress and implementation of new approaches. Theoretical questions focus on how students should be educated and on the intellectual, political, and social contexts of learning. Self-reflective questions allow for discussion of the teacher's own role in the educational process. Any of the following questions could form the basis for a paper in an education course.

- How does this school's language arts curriculum prepare students to be information-literate?
- What are the effects of the use of standardized tests in economically disadvantaged districts in comparison with more affluent districts?
- How do my perceptions of my own education influence the way I approach teaching?

D5-d Understand the kinds of evidence educators use.

Educators and education students rely on evidence that is both quantitative (statistics, survey results, test scores) and qualitative (case studies, observation, personal experience). The following are some examples of evidence used in different situations.

- If you are writing a research paper that compares different approaches to social studies education, you might rely on quantitative evidence such as the results of standardized tests from different school districts.
- For a paper on child development, you might use a combination of personal observation and evidence from published case studies.
- If you are keeping a journal of your student teaching experiences, your evidence would come from your experiences in the classroom and from the changes in your attitudes over time.
- If you are creating a lesson plan, you will focus on your teaching objectives and explain how your plan will achieve those objectives.

D5-e Become familiar with writing conventions in education.

Educators agree on several conventions when they write.

- The personal pronoun *I* is commonly used in reflective writing. It is sometimes used to communicate observations and recommendations.

- Research papers and case studies are generally written in the third person (*he, she, it, they*) and in a formal, objective tone.

- Educators have a specialized vocabulary that includes terms such as *pedagogy* (teaching principles and methods), *practice* (actual teaching), *curriculum* (the written lesson plans followed by a class or school), *assessment* (the determination of whether students or teachers are successful), *achievement tests* (tests that measure what students have learned), and *NCLB* (the No Child Left Behind Act). You will likely use such terms in your writing.

Because the field of education draws on various disciplines, including psychology, history, and sociology, it is important to be aware of writing conventions in those disciplines as well. (See D7 and D10.)

D5-f Use the APA or CMS (*Chicago*) system in writing in education.

Writers in education typically use the style guidelines of the American Psychological Association (APA) or *The Chicago Manual of Style* (CMS) for formatting their paper, for citing sources in the text of their paper, and for listing sources at the end. The APA system is set forth in the *Publication Manual of the American Psychological Association*, 6th ed. (Washington, DC: APA, 2010). CMS style is found in *The Chicago Manual of Style*, 16th ed. (Chicago: University of Chicago Press, 2010). (For more details, see the documentation sections in your handbook.) In education courses, instructors will usually indicate which style they prefer.

D5-g Sample student paper: Reflective essay

In some education courses, you may be asked to write reflective essays in which you describe and analyze your own attitudes, beliefs, and experiences. Some reflective essays focus solely on personal observations while others integrate ideas from other sources as well.

The following reflective essay was written for a service learning course in which students explored issues of diversity, power, and opportunity in school settings. The writer, Onnalee Gibson, used a variety of professional sources to inform her own ideas about her experiences working with an eleventh-grade student. She formatted her paper and cited and listed her sources following the guidelines of the American Psychological Association (APA).

The header consists of a shortened title in all capital letters at the left margin and the page number at the right margin; on the title page only, the shortened title is preceded by the words "Running head" and a colon.

Running head: SERVICE LEARNING: ERIC   1

Full title, writer's name, and school halfway down the page.

A Reflection on Service Learning:

Working with Eric

Onnalee L. Gibson

Michigan State University

An author's note lists specific information about the course or department and can provide acknowledgments and contact information.

Author Note

This paper was prepared for Teacher Education 250, taught by Professor Carter. The author wishes to thank the guidance staff of Waverly High School for advice and assistance.

Marginal annotations indicate APA-style formatting and effective writing.

SERVICE LEARNING: ERIC   2

A Reflection on Service Learning:

Working with Eric

The first time I saw the beautiful yet simple architecture of Waverly
High School, I was enchanted. I remember driving by while exploring my
new surroundings as a transfer student to Michigan State University and
marveling at the long front wall of reflective windows, the shapely bushes,
and the general cleanliness of the school grounds. When I was assigned
to do a service learning project in a local school district, I hoped for the
opportunity to find out what it would be like to work at a school like
Waverly—a school where the attention to its students' needs was evident
from the outside in.

Waverly High School, which currently enrolls about 1,100 students
in grades 9 through 12 and has a teaching staff of 63, is extremely diverse
in several ways. Economically, students range from poverty level to
affluent. Numerous ethnic and racial groups are represented. And in terms
of achievement, the student body boasts an assortment of talents and
abilities.

The school provides a curriculum that strives to meet the needs of
each student and uses a unique grade reporting system that itemizes each
aspect of a student's grade. The system allows both teachers and parents
to see where academic achievement and academic problems surface. Unlike
most schools, which evaluate students on subjects in one number or letter
grade, Waverly has a report card that lists individual grades for tests,
homework, exams, papers, projects, participation, community service, and
attendance. Thus, if a student is doing every homework assignment and is
still failing tests, this breakdown of the grades may effectively highlight
how the student can be helped.

It was this unique way of evaluating students that led to my first
meeting with Eric Johnson, an 11th grader to whom I was assigned as a
tutor. Eric is an African American male who grew up in a nuclear middle-
class family in a Lansing suburb. Teachers noticed over time that Eric's
grades were dropping, yet his attendance, participation, and motivation
were above average. Surprisingly, Eric himself was the one who asked for
a tutor to help him raise his grades. What initially struck me about Eric
was the level of responsibility he seemed to take for his own academic

*Reflective essays
may include
descriptive
passages.*

*Background
information about
the school sets
the scene for
Gibson's personal
experiences.*

*Transition leads
from background
information about
the school to
Gibson's personal
experiences.*

SERVICE LEARNING: ERIC   3

Journal entries are considered personal communication and are cited in the text but not included in the reference list.

achievement. At the time I wrote in my journal (January 31, 2006), "He appears to be a good student. He is trying his best to succeed in school. *He* came to *me* for help and realizes the need for a tutor."

While tutoring Eric, I paid attention to the way he talked about his classes and to the types of assignments he was being asked to complete. My impression was that Waverly High School was fostering student success by doing more than just placing posters in the hallways. Waverly's curriculum encourages analytical thinking, requires group and individual projects that depend on creativity and research, and includes open-ended writing assignments designed to give students opportunities to form their own conclusions. I found this reality both difficult and inspiring; I had not expected an 11th grader's homework to be so challenging. I once said so to Eric, and he responded with a smile: "Yeah. My teachers say it's going to help us when we get to college to already know how to do some of these things."

Personal observations lead to broader insights.

What was surprising to me was the faculty's collective assumption that high school was not the end of a student's career. The fact that teachers talk with students about what will be expected *when* (not *if*) they go to college is significant. That kind of positive language, which I heard many times at Waverly, most certainly affects students' sense of themselves as achievers. In this case, Eric was not preoccupied with worrying about whether he wanted to go to college or would be accepted; rather, he mentally prepared himself for the time when he would actually enroll.

Gibson analyzes her evidence to draw a broader conclusion.

This section bridges academic theory and personal experience.

According to education researcher Jean Anyon (1981), "Students from higher social class backgrounds may be exposed to legal, medical, or managerial knowledge . . . while those of the working classes may be offered a more 'practical' curriculum" (p. 5). I do not see this gravitation toward social reproduction holding true for most students at Waverly High School. Waverly's student body is a mix of social classes, yet the school's philosophy is to push each of its students to consider college. Through its curriculum, its guidance department literature, and its opportunities for career field trips, Waverly is opening doors for all of its students. In Eric's case, I also observed the beginnings of a break in social reproduction. From the start of our tutoring sessions, Eric frequently mentioned that neither of his parents went to college (O. Gibson, journal entry, March 14, 2006). This

SERVICE LEARNING: ERIC   4

made me wonder how his parents talk to him about college. Is the desire
to go to college something they have instilled in him? Have they given
him the message that if he works hard and goes to college he will be
successful? If that is the case, then Eric's parents are attempting to break
the cycle with their children—and they have the good fortune to live in a
school district that supports their desires. In contrast to the idea that
most people have nothing more than social reproduction to thank for their
socioeconomic status (Bowles & Gintis, 1976), Eric seems to believe that
hard work and a college education are keys to his success.

> Source is cited in APA in-text citation style.

    Another key to Eric's success will be the resources he enjoys as
a student at Waverly. Abundance of or lack of resources can play an
important part in students' opportunities to learn and succeed. Because
nearly half of all school funding comes from local property taxes (D. Carter,
class lecture, April 4, 2006), areas with smaller populations or low property
values do not have the tax base to fund schools well. As a result, one
education finance expert has argued, some children receive substandard
education (Parrish, 2002). Waverly does not appear to have serious
financial or funding issues. Each student has access to current textbooks,
up-to-date computer labs, a well-stocked library, a full art and music
curriculum, and numerous extracurricular activities. While countless schools
are in desperate need of a better-equipped library, Waverly's library has a
rich collection of books, magazines and journals, computer stations, and
spaces in which to use all of these materials. It is a very user-friendly
library. This has shown me what the power of funding can do for a school.
Part of Waverly's (and its students') success results from the ample
resources spent on staff and curriculum materials. Adequate school funding
is one of the factors that drive school and student success.

> Class lecture (personal communication) is cited in the text only, not in the reference list.

> Gibson considers the larger implications of her personal observations.

    Aside from funding, placement policies determine school and student
success. A major concern of both educators and critics of education policies
is that schools will place students into special education programs
unnecessarily. Too often students who do not need special education are
coded for special ed—even when they have a learning issue that can be
handled with a good teacher in a mainstream class (D. Carter, class lecture,
April 6, 2006). At Waverly High School, teachers and counselors are not so
quick to shuffle Eric into special ed. I agree with several of Eric's teachers

SERVICE LEARNING: ERIC   5

who feel that he may have a mild learning disability. I began to feel this
way when Eric and I moved from working in a private tutoring space to
working in the library. It was clear to me that he had difficulty paying
attention in a public setting. On February 9, I wrote in my journal:

> Eric was extremely distracted. He couldn't pay attention to what I
> was asking, and he couldn't keep his eyes on his work. There were
> other students in the library today, and he kept eavesdropping on
> their conversations and shaking his head when they said things he
> did not agree with. This is how he must behave in the classroom; he
> is easily distracted but he wants to work hard. I see that it is not
> so much that he needs a tutor because he can't understand what his
> teachers are telling him; it is more that he needs the one-on-one
> attention in a confined room free of distractions.

Even though Eric showed signs of distraction, I never felt as
if he should be coded for special education. I am pleased that the
administration and learning specialists did not decide to place Eric in a
special education track. Eric is exceedingly intelligent and shows promise
in every academic area. He seems to be able to succeed by identifying
problems on his own and seeking resources to help him solve those
problems. He is a motivated and talented student who simply seems like
a typical adolescent.

I came away from my service learning project with an even stronger
conviction about the importance of quality education for a student's
success. Unlike the high school I attended, Waverly pays close attention
to each child and thinks about how to get all its students to succeed
at their own level. Jean Patrice, an administrator, told me, "You have
to be able to reach a student where *they* are instead of making them
come to you. If you don't, you'll lose them" (personal communication,
April 10, 2006), expressing her desire to see all students get something
out of their educational experience. This feeling is common among
members of Waverly's faculty. With such a positive view of student
potential, it is no wonder that 97% of Waverly High School graduates go
on to a four-year university (Patrice, 2006). I have no doubt that Eric
Johnson will attend college and that he will succeed there.

As I look toward my teaching future, I know there is plenty that I

A quotation longer than forty words is indented without quotation marks.

SERVICE LEARNING: ERIC   6

have left to learn. Teaching is so much more than getting up in front of a
class, reiterating facts, and requiring students to learn a certain amount of
material by the end of the year. Teaching is about getting students—one
by one—to realize and act on their potential. This course and this service
learning experience have made me realize that we should never have a
trial-and-error attitude about any student's opportunities and educational
quality.

Conclusion raises
questions for
further reflection.

SERVICE LEARNING: ERIC   7

References

List of references, in APA style, begins on a new page.

Anyon, J. (1981). Social class and school knowledge. *Curriculum Inquiry, 11*(1), 5.

List is alphabetized by authors' last names.

Bowles, S., & Gintis, H. (1976). *Schooling in capitalist America: Educational reform and contradictions of economic life.* New York, NY: Basic Books.

Double-spacing is used throughout.

Parrish, T. (2002). Racial disparities in identification, funding, and provision of special education. In D. Losen & G. Orfield (Eds.), *Racial inequity in special education.* Cambridge, MA: Civil Rights Project and Harvard Education Press.

D6 Writing in engineering

Engineers use the language of mathematics and the methods of science along with the experiences of society to design machines, tools, processes, and systems that will solve problems and accomplish tasks safely and efficiently. There are many different types of engineers: mechanical, chemical, electrical, civil, geological, environmental, and aerospace, to name a few. Each type of engineer addresses problems and tasks in a particular part of the physical world.

Writing plays a major role in the work of engineers, who write reports and recommendations based on their research and their design ideas. Engineers write technical reports addressed to manufacturers or the companies or agencies that hire them. Engineers also communicate their solutions to clients in their own organizations.

As a student of engineering, you will be challenged to devise solutions to real-world problems. Most of your assignments will be open-ended questions that will involve finding or proposing solutions to design challenges; you will be required to compose rationales for your solutions in writing. In laboratory experiments, you will maintain a lab notebook and write reports about your hands-on research. Because engineers usually work in teams, some writing assignments will involve working with other students to give you practice with collaboration.

D6-a Determine your audience and their needs in engineering.

Engineers usually write for readers who have a definite interest in what they have to say. Research and design in engineering never take place in isolation; these activities occur in universities, private industry, and government.

Sometimes your readers will be other engineers and decision makers working in your team or in other groups in your organization; they will expect you to provide a high level of technical detail and to use specialized vocabulary. They need to be able to replicate your work and confirm the results. Sometimes your audience will be a corporate client outside your organization in industry or government. Or your audience might be public-policy decision makers or the general public. Some of these audiences might not have your level of technical expertise, so your writing must be accessible and clear, with a minimum of technical language and jargon. For example, if you are writing a proposal to win a contract for your company or to receive funding for a project, your proposal will have to be written appropriately for an audience consisting of both specialists and nonspecialists.

When you write in engineering courses, keep in mind that you are learning to write for readers who probably have not done the study, research, or design work that you have done. When writing a report, for example, you will write for a reader who was not present in the laboratory or in the field. Even though your professor is in the laboratory with you, always describe your research and experimentation process carefully and thoroughly as if he or she is not familiar with your process. Add spreadsheets, drawings, plates, or illustrations to help your readers visualize your findings.

D6-b   Recognize the forms of writing in engineering.

When you take courses in engineering, you may be asked to write any of the following:

- project notebooks
- laboratory reports
- technical reports
- proposals
- progress reports

Project notebooks

A project notebook is like a personal journal in which you record your work in progress. It is a log in which you can write your observations and data from the experimentation and design processes or brainstorm and explore explanations or interpretations of the data. You might describe the materials you use and the procedures you follow or draw sketches of your design and, later, its construction. A project notebook can be useful as you work through mathematical analysis of your data and your designs and as you pose questions and plan solutions to problems. It can also provide the space in which you make note of tests that work and those that do not. You can write reflections on articles you read, notes from meetings you attend, and logistics for projects you are working on. You might also record your instructor's and peers' comments and critiques.

Make your project notebook as complete and as neat as possible; sign and date entries daily. Remember that your notebook will be useful in your later research, design, and writing. If your notebook is part of an ongoing project that someone else will continue after you, then formality, thoroughness, and neatness will be critical. Notebooks are traditionally kept on paper, but you may keep one electronically to make it easier to record, update, and read. As you move into professional practice, these notebooks will become part of any project's formal records.

Laboratory reports

Engineers present the procedures, materials, and results of their experiments in laboratory reports. These reports are essential to the development of the discipline, as it is through these reports that new knowledge is recorded and communicated to researchers, teachers, and students. Laboratory reports for some assignments may have particular requirements. Generally, the laboratory reports you are assigned will follow the organization used in laboratory reports written by engineers working in industry and government.

Your report will need to accomplish the following:

- establish the main question or problem under investigation and provide some background
- state the objective of the laboratory work (to measure, to verify, to compare, and so on) and the exact methods and procedures step-by-step
- describe and comment on your results, explain what they mean, put any unexpected results in context, and compare your results with established knowledge in the discipline
- place your results in the context of your stated purpose; note patterns apparent in the results, implications for future consideration, and any questions that remain unanswered
- tell your reader if you achieved the predicted or anticipated results; account for any differences if possible

The structure of your laboratory report will function as "instructions" for anyone who wants to replicate your experiment, verify your results, or use your work as a foundation for his or her own research.

You can use the same method and structure to record and report on engineering design projects.

Technical reports

A technical report describes the structure and functions of a design. If the report's purpose is to investigate the failure of a design, tool, or machine, then it is a *forensic report*. The audience for a technical or design report is usually other engineers or a similar audience of experts; it can also be decision makers, regulators, and the courts.

A technical report usually has the following structure:

- executive summary, a one-page concise statement of the most important points in the report
- introduction
- purpose and goals
- methods
- data and findings
- recommendations and action items
- conclusion
- appendices if necessary

Use tables, charts, spreadsheets, maps, figures, and illustrations in the body of your report to present your data and findings or in appendices to support your conclusions. Your recommendations and conclusion should interpret your data, discuss any limitations or boundaries of your work, and suggest action items for this project or other, related projects. Document your work by citing your references in the style recommended by your instructor or the organization for which you are writing.

Proposals

Engineers write project proposals to seek funding from academic and government sources or to describe a project to potential clients. "Selling" a customer on a project is thus an important function of an engineer's job. Many proposals are written with cross-disciplinary teams including sales, marketing, production, and legal departments. A proposal for a client may include a price quote or estimate, also called a "bid."

For your classes, you may write proposals for laboratory projects or to suggest solutions for a hypothetical client (usually your professor) who has given you a technical problem or design problem. Prepare your proposals with sufficient research, appropriate graphics, careful organization, and neat presentation to assist your readers and show them that you are credible.

To make it easy for your readers to say yes to your proposal, give them clear, sufficient information about the project. Begin with an introduction that includes a brief project description and lays out the cost, completion date, and rate of return on investment. In the body of the proposal, provide the following:

- background and rationale for the project, describing the need to be met or the problem to be solved
- how the project will be accomplished
- expected outcomes

- materials and methods
- method of evaluation that will be used to determine that the objectives have been achieved
- timeline (sometimes presented in a Gantt chart, a graphical representation of the overlapping deadlines and milestones for all aspects of the project)
- budget, including deadlines and a list of items that must be funded

You can assume that your readers are receiving other proposals, so you might also provide a résumé or a section describing your skills and experiences that qualify you for the project.

Progress reports

Once a proposal is accepted and a project is under way, an engineer must write progress reports regularly to inform the client of the work accomplished. A progress report can be in the form of a business letter or a memo. It describes any milestones that have been achieved or tasks that have been completed. In engineering classes, your progress reports will be written to your professor to document your accomplishments and to describe the work still to be completed.

In your progress report, you might provide the following:

- a brief project description as a reminder of the scope of the project
- a summary of progress with a list of the tasks that have been completed
- a list of any problems that have arisen and solutions implemented or suggested
- any necessary alterations in deadlines or the budget
- a description of work remaining before the next progress report

Engineers frequently use spreadsheets to present data and provide a "snapshot" of the project at various stages. Spreadsheets can be converted into slides for PowerPoint presentations along with images of the work. Complete project reports will assure your readers that you are reliable, punctual, and in control of progress.

D6-c Know the questions engineers ask.

Engineers explore questions related to designing, repairing, and improving aspects of the physical world. Wherever people require a safer, faster, more effective, more efficient, more comfortable, or less expensive way to accomplish a task, engineers investigate and suggest solutions. The tasks might be related to transportation, to the construction of buildings and bridges, to the design of electrical grids and other city infrastructure, or to the invention of appliances and tools in the home or in the workplace.

Engineers explore questions such as these:

- An aging bridge in an area with heavy traffic must be replaced as soon as possible. What is the best design for a new bridge that can support a heavy payload but can also be built in a short period of time?

- Can a liquid laundry detergent be invented that will dissolve more quickly in water and flow more efficiently through the hoses of a new high-efficiency washing machine?

- What material would be best for resurfacing a parking lot in an area that often floods when it rains? What are the properties of different materials that might be used for this construction project?

- Two aerospace companies have proposed different configurations for the wings of a new fighter plane. Which of the two wing designs will allow the aircraft to achieve the highest possible speed with the lowest possible vibration at the most affordable cost?

- Is it possible to invent electronic devices that can be powered wirelessly rather than with batteries or electrical power?

- Understanding that customers want more environmentally friendly equipment for the home, a manufacturer of lawn mowers asks, Is it possible to construct a new kind of engine, similar to the engines in hybrid cars, that would burn fuel more efficiently and more cleanly than current engines?

D6-d Understand the kinds of evidence engineers use.

Engineers use particular kinds of evidence:

- data from laboratory reports published by other engineers
- observations and measurements of apparatus and processes inside the laboratory
- observations and measurements from building models of proposed projects
- observations and measurements from computer simulations and models
- observations and measurements made in real-world settings

Engineers often begin the design process with computer simulations and analysis. Then they verify the simulated results with models and laboratory experiments. This process saves money for engineering firms and their clients. For example, car companies use multiple computer simulations of car crashes before they crash-test a real car. In your classes, your projects may be "pen and paper" designs: You design and test the project on the computer or with manual calculations but do not actually build the project.

Data in engineering are quantitative; they can be counted. Depending on the nature of the problem or experiment, some data can be qualitative, described without numbers. When a structure fails or displays flaws, forensic engineers perform physical tests and sometimes collect and analyze witness testimony as they seek the causes of the problem.

For example, after a passenger airplane exploded in midair in 1996, engineers spent months reconstructing the aircraft to locate the cause. They discovered that structural problems had resulted in small vibrations. Over a long period of time, the vibrations had caused two electrical wires located near a fuel tank to rub against each other. Eventually the insulation of one of the wires had rubbed away, and the electrical current in the wire caused a spark that ignited vapors from the fuel tank. The engineers arrived at this conclusion only after painstakingly examining numerous components, sometimes in microscopic detail, ruling out many of them, focusing on the relevant ones, and ultimately performing tests in the laboratory to replicate the effects of vibrations on the wires.

D6-e Become familiar with writing conventions in engineering.

Engineers agree on several conventions when they write.

- Engineers often work in teams on research and laboratory projects. In your classes, you will often collaborate with other students. Collaboration requires that team members delegate and accept responsibility, report to one another, share ideas, listen to one another, negotiate differences, and compromise on solutions. Usually one person on the team will be in charge of combining the individually written sections of a report into a single document. Some team members may not be engineers or engineering students. Developing relationships with nonengineering and nonscience students and professionals is essential to effective work and communication in engineering.

- Each type of writing should include standard sections. For example, a laboratory report is not complete if it does not include a section that interprets results.

- Engineers must be brief and clear. When describing a process or an apparatus you used, you will need to write exactly what you did and what resulted. You must present the order of the steps you followed in logical sequence.

- Engineers try to avoid ambiguous pronoun use so that readers will know exactly what a pronoun refers to. Instead of writing *This confirms the original results*, an engineer should write *This new set of data confirms the original results*.

- Engineers use headings and subheadings in their reports and proposals. Engineering reports can be long and detailed, and headings mark the important categories of information and help readers follow the organization. Engineers also divide their reports into clear parts with combinations of numbers and letters denoting major sections and their subsections.

- Engineering is a visual field. Readers expect writers to provide diagrams, illustrations, charts, tables, and graphs. Graphics should support the data and other information in a report; they should be easy to understand, with clear labels and captions.

- Engineers use verb tenses deliberately. They use past tense for laboratory reports (*These results demonstrated*). They use future tense in proposals (*This design will require*). They use both present tense and past tense in progress reports (*The design phase is on schedule* or *The foundation was poured during week 3*).

- Engineers usually use third-person pronouns (*he, she, it, they* rather than *I, me, we*). They use the active voice where possible because it is more direct and concise. For instance, instead of writing *The viability of the instrument was demonstrated by the results*, they write *The results demonstrated the viability of the instrument*.

D6-f   Use the CMS (*Chicago*), IEEE, or USGS system in writing in engineering.

Writers in different fields of engineering use different styles to cite sources in their papers and to list sources at the ends of their papers. Civil engineers, chemical engineers, industrial engineers, and mechanical engineers usually use the name-year system of *The Chicago Manual of Style*, 16th ed. (Chicago: University of Chicago Press, 2010).

Electrical engineers, computer engineers, and mechanical engineers use the *IEEE Citation Reference* (2009), published by the Institute of Electrical and Electronics Engineers.

Engineers and scientists in geology usually use *Suggestions to Authors of the Reports of the United States Geological Survey*, 7th ed. (Washington: GPO, 1991).

When you begin a project in an engineering class, check with your instructor about which style is required for your assignment.

D6-g Sample student paper: Proposal

A proposal recommends a solution to a design or technical problem posed by a client. A typical proposal includes details about how the project will be completed, the required materials and methods of construction, and the expected costs. It often includes alternatives for comparison. The following proposal was written in a junior-level geology engineering course. The student, Alice O'Bryan, explores the options that a fictional company called Ajax might consider for providing proper drainage for a planned park. O'Bryan presents descriptions of several alternatives, including costs, benefits, and overall effectiveness. She used the United States Geological Survey (USGS) guidelines to format her paper and to cite and list her sources.

O'Bryan 1

Full title, writer's
name, course, and
date, centered
halfway down the
page.

Site Stabilization Plan for Erosion Control

Alice O'Bryan

GLY 341

May 5, XXXX

Marginal annotations indicate USGS-style formatting and effective writing.

O'Bryan 2

CONTENTS

The contents page lists all the major headings and subheadings; it can also list minor subheadings, as shown here. The indentation of headings in the contents indicates the hierarchy and organization of the paper.

O'Bryan 3

A USGS proposal often begins with an executive summary that briefly provides background, findings, and recommendations.

EXECUTIVE SUMMARY

Ajax is seeking to develop a 44-acre parcel of land into a recreational park and has requested proposals for erosion control. This proposal recommends a system of terraces and a grassed waterway culminating in a 1-acre constructed lake. While this is not the least expensive method of erosion control, it will be effective at preventing erosion and also will meet Ajax's goals for an aesthetically pleasing park that can attract human visitors as well as aquatic life and wildlife. Two less desirable plans are a system of terraces with a riprapped waterway and a buried pipeline. Both plans are less expensive, but both have drawbacks and do not meet all of Ajax's goals.

The recommended proposal (proposal A) will create a series of 13 vegetative terraces that flow into a grassed waterway approximately 1,200 feet long. The waterway will culminate in a 1-acre lake that will collect the drainage and provide a recreational fishing hole. This proposal has the advantage of not disrupting the open land and in fact enhancing it with planted vegetation along the terraces and waterway and with a lake that can attract wildlife and that can be used for recreational purposes. The cost of this proposal is as follows:

- Terraces: $15,034
- Grassed waterway: $4,000
- 1-acre lake: $18,000-60,000
- Total: $37,034-79,034

Additional costs will be incurred for recovery of the soil if more surface is disturbed than just the terrace and waterway construction areas. (See the summary of costs at the end of the proposal.)

The proposal for terraces and a riprapped waterway (proposal B) includes a riprapped channel that would disrupt the parklike atmosphere and that may not prevent off-site erosion. Its costs are as follows:

- Terraces: $15,034
- Riprapped waterway: $6,000
- Total: $21,034

The buried pipeline (proposal C) is the least desirable option because it is hard to maintain, requires an unattractive retaining wall, and is not suited for the soil type in this area. Its costs are as follows:

O'Bryan 4

- Buried pipeline: $6,000
- Gabion retaining wall: $25,000-50,000
- Total: $31,000-56,000

ANALYSIS OF PROPOSALS
PROPOSAL A: TERRACES AND GRASSED WATERWAY

Nonstructural and preventive erosion control provided by proposal A is the best choice for Ajax because the land is to be developed into a park. It is not the least expensive method, but it is likely to be most effective at meeting all the goals of the project. This proposal recommends a system of 7 terraces, each pair spaced 120 feet apart in the clayey silt soil, and 6 terraces, each pair spaced 150 feet apart in the silty clay soil. These terraces would have a 0.60% channel gradient, which would direct the water into a grassed waterway culminating in a 1-acre lake. A lake of this size is reasonable on a site of 44 acres and is more cost-effective than a smaller lake or a pond, which requires more specialized equipment to construct. The site is well suited for a lake because of its gently sloping topography. While a well-built lake can be expensive, Ajax can save money by using the excavated soil to build the terraces.

PROPOSAL B: TERRACES AND RIPRAPPED WATERWAY

Proposal B includes the same terraces as in proposal A, but the terraces flow into a riprapped channel going through the site and leading water beyond the boundaries of the property. A filter material must underlay the entire area that the riprap will cover (Minnesota Department of Transportation, 2005). Geotextile is the best material for this purpose. On top of this will be a 6-inch layer of granular filter material of uniform thickness over the prepared foundation. With geotextile, the foundation surface must be smooth and free of stones or other debris, and the fabric must not be torn during application. The riprap rocks should be placed from the bottom of the waterway to the top to achieve a uniform size distribution, with the smallest percent of void space possible. When completed, the riprap should not be less than 95% of the specified thickness.

PROPOSAL C: BURIED PIPELINE

A buried pipeline is the least optimal choice for the site. Methods

O'Bryan provides an analysis of three proposals, giving an overview of how each proposal would be implemented and recommending one.

First- and second-level headings are centered in all capital letters.

O'Bryan uses USGS style for citing sources in the text.

O'Bryan 5

of erosion control that are constructed aboveground are preferred because it is much easier to perform maintenance on them. There is no room for error in the design and construction of a buried pipeline. Also, in the site area, clay makes up a large percentage of the soil; the shrink-swell potential of the soil could later damage the pipes. Pipelines are also just as expensive as riprap. For this method, a retaining wall would be constructed of gabion baskets, which are more flexible than concrete and allow for the possibility of establishing vegetation in the spaces. As with the riprap plan, an erosion control blanket is required under the gabion to prevent scouring. There are several drawbacks to the use of gabions. As Lynn Merill (2004) writes, quoting engineer Mark North, "'Gabions may not be appropriate for use in high-traffic areas' where people coming in contact with them run the risk of 'snagging their clothes on the wire.'" In addition, gabions can be very expensive.

GUIDELINES FOR CONSTRUCTION[1]

Geotextile material.—Geotextile material should be "woven, nonwoven, or knit fabric of polymeric filaments or yarns such as polypropylene, polyethylene, polyester, or polyamide formed into a stable network such that the filaments/yarns retain their relative position to each other" (Minnesota Department of Transportation, 2005, p. 907). If the geotextile is being used as an earth reinforcement or under riprap, all sewn seams on the fabric must meet strength requirements.

Erosion control blankets.—Erosion control blankets are designed to be used until vegetation can be established. There are nine different categories of blankets based on use longevity and flow velocity; use longevity ranges from 6-8 weeks through permanent. The category chosen should be specific to the method of construction and to the site. For example, if gabions are built and the flow velocity is calculated to be less than 6.5 ft/s, a category 6 erosion control blanket should be used. The blanket should be laid out parallel to the direction of flow, and adjacent blanket edges should overlap by at least 4 inches and should be stapled.

---

[1]All guidelines are based on Minnesota Department of Transportation, 2005, and Beasley and others, 1984, unless stated otherwise.

O'Bryan provides guidelines that should be followed for any of the three proposals. She uses a footnote to give the sources of her guidelines.

In USGS style, minor subheadings are indented and italicized, followed by a period and a dash.

O'Bryan uses a footnote for a general point related to the entire section.

O'Bryan 6

At the top of the slope, the blanket should be buried in a check slot, which should be backfilled and compacted. Within the channel, the blanket should be stapled every foot.

Silt fences.—No silt should be washed off-site, and the soil must be seeded if it is to be bare for more than 45 days. It is expected that silt fences will be required at some point during construction of any of the proposed plans. It is acceptable to use the standard machine-sliced silt fencing during site grading to keep sediment from moving. Each post of the silt fence should be secured by a minimum of five gun staples 1 inch long.

Excavation.—During excavation, a well-drained condition must be maintained through planned drainage facilities. Topsoil should be stockpiled and covered. If blasting is required, it must be conducted so that materials will not be thrown out of the area and will be easily recoverable. Excavations must have a secure uniformity in grade; if excavations fall below final grade, they must be done with the provision that they are subject to change.

Pipe installation.—Pipes should be installed to collect and discharge water infiltrating into the soil or accumulated in a subcut or to cut off or intercept groundwater flow. The pipes should be constructed of nonperforated threadless copper (TP) pipe. Minimum trench width should be the diameter of the pipe plus two times the diameter. All rocks within the trench should be removed. A fine filter aggregate layer of one pipe diameter should be laid in the bottom of the trench. If perforated pipe is used, it must be wrapped in geotextile. Pipes that will discharge at a constructed gabion wall should be installed so that small movements in the wall will not cause the pipes to separate.

Reseeding.—The purpose of reseeding the area is not just to beautify the landscape. Reseeding is also an effective erosion control method. The application of seed must be conducted with as much rigor and attention to detail as any construction project on the site will be carried out. The establishment of permanent vegetation requires soil tilling, liming, fertilizing, seeding, sodding, mulching, and any other work required to ensure that the plants survive to maturity. Proper planting times must be observed; until the time for seeding has arrived, previously mentioned methods of erosion control must be used. The recommended temporary seeding mixture is mixture number 130; its seeding date varies because this seed has 40% of both winter wheat and oats. The optimal time for planting winter wheat is Aug. 1-Oct. 1, and for oats it is May 1-Aug. 1. Other seed mixture numbers have different planting seasons, as shown in table 1.

If rills or gullies have formed anywhere on the site, they should be filled in prior to seeding and compacted so that they are approximately the same density as the surrounding soil. The seed should be applied according to the seed application rate for its mixture number (see table 2). Hydroseeding is prohibited when wind speeds exceed 15 mph. The traditional seed mixes (numbers 100-280) should be applied through hydroseeding; native mixes, because of the shape of the seed, require a native seed drill. In hydroseeding, seed must be uniformly distributed; otherwise the area must be reseeded. The permanent seed mixture can be applied to an area that is covered with a temporary seed mixture without additional tillage or site preparation. The water-to-straw-bale ratio with tackifier for mulch is 100 gallons to every 50-pound bale.

PROPOSAL A: DETAILS AND GENERAL SPECIFICATIONS

Seeded terraces and waterway.—On this site, there will be 7 sets of terraces 120 feet apart in the clayey silt soil and 6 sets of terraces 150 feet apart in the silty clay soil. The terraces will have a 0.60% gradient. They will begin at elevation 560 feet and will be 600 feet long, increasing by

Table 1. Planting seasons for seed

[From Minnesota Department of Transportation, 2005, table 2575-1, p. 712]

Seed mixture number	Spring	Fall
100	—	Aug. 1-Oct. 1
110	May 1-Aug. 1	—
150, 190	Apr. 1-July 20	July 20-Oct. 20
240, 250, 260, 270	Apr. 1-June 1	July 20-Sept. 20
280	Apr. 1-Sept. 1	—
310, 325, 328, 330, 340, 350	Apr. 15-July 20	Sept. 20-Oct. 20

Margin notes:

Tables are referred to in the text and are placed as close as possible to their text reference.

O'Bryan gives specific details about her recommended proposal.

Table number and title appear above the table. A headnote, in brackets, gives source information; it also can explain abbreviations or symbols.

O'Bryan 8

Table 2. Seed application rates

[From Minnesota Department of Transportation, 2005, table 2575-2, p. 716]

Seed mixture number	Application rate (lb/acre)
100, 110	100
159	40
190	60
240	75
250	70
260	100
270	120
280	50
310	82
325	84
328	88
330, 340, 350	84.5

28.5 feet at each terrace until they reach 1,000 feet in length at elevation 480 feet. Work should start at the base of the area and proceed upward. The terraces will flow into a larger grassed waterway approximately 1,200 feet long that intersects the site.

In USGS style, most numbers are expressed as numerals.

The terraces will be grassed with a native harvest. The waterway will be lined with something comparable to C350 riprap replacement and will also be seeded with a native harvest. The native harvest should consist of seed harvests from stands within 25 miles of the area. Approximately 70% of the mixture should consist of big bluestem and/or Indian grass, though 50% would be acceptable. There should be at least five species of native grasses and 3% (by mass) of native forbs. Since this is to be a recreational area, it will be best not to use a variety of grass that needs seasonal burning unless the park can be closed without financial repercussions and without the fire damaging any infrastructure erected at a later time. The application of herbicides seasonally (spring or summer) is acceptable though not encouraged, as runoff could harm fish and wildlife.

O'Bryan 9

Erosion barrier.—The developer may not disturb more than 14,400 ft^2 at a time in the clayey silt soil or more than 22,500 ft^2 at a time in the silty clay soil without erecting an erosion barrier such as a silt fence on the downslope side. The bare soil above the work area should be stabilized by rocks and mulch at the end of each workday. The developer should create and maintain a covered stockpile of topsoil. If soil is going to be left bare for more than 45 days, it must be seeded. Idle areas should be seeded as soon as possible after grading or within 7 days. The seed should be mixture number 130, consisting of 40% oats, 40% winter wheat, 10% rye grass, and 10% alfalfa, annual. Compacted soils in the area should be deep-tilled to a depth of 18-24 inches to allow for deep root penetration. Six or more inches of organic compost should be laid on top of this and tilled into the top 10 inches of soil.

Lake.—Although a collection system for the runoff water was not a requirement for this proposal, a lake has several advantages and is not prohibitively expensive. It will collect drainage from the constructed waterway, it will attract wildlife to the area and enhance the appeal to visitors, and it can serve as a recreational fishing hole.

Other vegetation.—Revegetation should occur at the end of the major construction phase and should focus not only on establishing grasses in the area but also on planting other forms of vegetation. Some of the options for native plants that are readily available from nurseries are outlined in the "Shoreline Stabilization Handbook" (Northwest Regional Planning Commission, 2004). They include trees, shrubs, herbaceous plants, ferns, and vines. It is preferred that these be native to the area, such as Kentucky bluegrass, and not European or Asian in origin. While the European and Asian grasses have traditionally been used in American landscaping, they tend to have much smaller rooting zones and are not suitable for effective erosion control; they also require more effort to grow in this site soil. Native grasses would not have these problems and would be less expensive to maintain. Shrubs such as sumac, gray dogwood, wild rose, fragrant sumac, and hazelnut are also preferable because they have a dense, low-spreading growth pattern and are attractive.

Proposals usually provide itemized costs for the client.

Cost estimates.—The basic construction of Proposal A will cost Ajax $37,034-79,034. Additional costs of approximately $608,000 would provide

O'Bryan 10

for recovery of the runoff water and enhance the overall appearance and appeal of the area.

DIMENSIONS

Disturbed area	216,283.5 yd^2
Total area	333,330 yd^2
Undisturbed area	117,046.5 yd^2

BASIC COSTS

Terraces	$	15,034.00
Grassed waterway		4,000.00
1-acre lake		18,000.00-60,000.00
TOTAL BASIC COSTS		$37,034.00-79,034.00

ADDITIONAL COSTS (OPTIONAL)

Hydroseeding, tackifier not required	$175,570.00
Hydroseeding, tackifier required	432,567.00
TOTAL ADDITIONAL COSTS	$608,137.00

CONCLUSION

While not the lowest-cost method of erosion control, proposal A meets all the goals of the project and creates an aesthetically pleasing and natural park atmosphere. The constructed appearance of the heavier erosion control options such as riprap and gabions would not mesh well with natural foliage. Such constructions also would not allow for aquatic life, one of the stated goals of the project. Heavy vegetation with the more aesthetic option of terraces is the correct choice in this situation. Native grasses not only will facilitate slope stabilization because of their deep rooting zones but also will attract birds and other wildlife, which would in turn draw wildlife enthusiasts into the park.

A good model for the proposed park is the Rachel Carson National Wildlife Refuge in Maine. While the type of land that is being protected in Maine is different from the land found on the Kentucky site, the Maine park combines the elements Ajax is seeking in its new park: a wildlife refuge, full of native plants, and a recreational area. The Maine park has trails throughout so that visitors have many different views of the beauty of the site. It also offers fishing and hunting and appeals to many different demographics. Ajax should consider this park as an ideal model.

In her conclusion, O'Bryan states again why she recommends proposal A. She ends with a paragraph that speaks plainly to connect with her readers.

The writer uses USGS style to list the sources she consulted in preparing her proposal.

REFERENCES

Beasley, R.P., Gregory, J.M., and McCarty, T.R., 1984, Erosion and sediment pollution control (2d ed.): Ames, Iowa, Iowa State University Press, 354 p.

Merill, L., 2004, Multitalented and versatile—gabions in stormwater management and erosion control: Erosion Control, v. 11, no. 3, http://www.erosioncontrol.com/may-june-2004/gabions-cages -erosion.aspx.

Metropolitan Council, July 2001, Soil erosion control—vegetative methods, *in* Minnesota urban small sites BMP manual: St. Paul, Minn., Metropolitan Council Environmental Services, http://www .metrocouncil.org/environment/Watershed/BMP/CH3_RPPSoilVeget .pdf.

Minnesota Department of Transportation, 2005, Standard specifications for construction: St. Paul, Minn., Minnesota Department of Transportation, http://www.dot.state.mn.us/pre-letting/spec/2005 /2557-2582.pdf.

Northwest Regional Planning Commission, 2004, The shoreline stabilization handbook for Lake Champlain and other inland lakes: St. Albans, Vt., Northwest Regional Planning Commission, http://nsgd.gso.uri.edu /lcsg/lcsgh04001.pdf.

U.S. Fish and Wildlife Service, 2008, Rachel Carson National Wildlife Refuge: Wells, Maine, U.S. Fish and Wildlife Service, http://www.fws .gov/northeast/rachelcarson.

D7 Writing in history

Historians analyze the information available to them to develop theories about past events, experiences, ideas, and movements. Depending on their interests, historians may consider a variety of issues and sources related to economics, politics, social issues, science, the military, gender, the family, or popular culture.

Historians do not simply record what happened at a particular time; rather, they attempt to explain *why* or *how* events occurred and to place those events in a larger context. For example, a historian writing about women in the British military during World War II would not simply describe the positions women held in the armed forces; through an analysis of the available information, the historian might develop a theory about why women were authorized to hold certain jobs and not others and how changes to women's roles affected the evolution of the women's rights movement in the decades that followed.

D7-a Determine your audience and their needs in history.

Historians write for diverse audiences. History scholars research and write books, articles, textbooks, Web sites, and film scripts for peers, teachers, and students. They also write for the general public, nonspecialists who are interested in history and may subscribe to history magazines or make frequent trips to museums. Amateur historians, often called "local historians," do genealogical or community research for a specific audience.

When you write in history, keep in mind that your audience appreciates an author who is knowledgeable and has done thorough research. Use multiple sources and cite your sources fully to assure your readers that your sources are credible. Because primary sources offer important evidence, include photos, maps, letters, or facsimiles. For example, if you are writing a newsletter article about a slave auction that occurred during the 1850s, you might add a picture of the poster that was used to advertise that auction.

D7-b Recognize the forms of writing in history.

Writing in history combines narrative (a description of what happened) and interpretation (an analysis of why events occurred). Historians ask questions that do not have obvious answers and analyze a variety of sources to draw conclusions.

When you take courses in history, you may be asked to write any of the following kinds of documents:

- critical essays
- book reviews
- research papers
- historiographic essays

Critical essays

For some assignments, you will be asked to write a short, critical essay in which you look at a document or group of documents — or perhaps a historical argument written by a scholar. For example, if you were studying the US decision to send troops to Vietnam, you might be asked to analyze one or more of John F. Kennedy's speeches and put forth a theory about why Kennedy chose to authorize the initial troop deployments. In the same course, you might be asked to read a journal article by a scholar analyzing Kennedy's decision and assess the way that scholar uses evidence to support his or her conclusion.

Book reviews

Because historians view their own work as part of an ongoing scholarly conversation, they value the serious discussion of the work of other scholars in the field. In some courses, you may be asked to write a book review analyzing the logic and accuracy of a scholarly work or of several works on the same topic. When you write a book review, you will have to make judgments about how much background information to provide about the book so that your readers will be able to understand and appreciate your critique.

Research papers

When you write a research paper in any course, you are expected to pose a question and examine the available evidence to find an answer to that question. In history courses, a research paper will generally focus on *why* and *how* questions that can be answered using a combination of sources. If you were studying the Vietnam War, you might ask how the rhetoric of the Cold War shaped John F. Kennedy's early Vietnam policy. To answer this question, you might look at government documents from the Kennedy administration, press coverage of Kennedy's foreign policy, Kennedy's own writings, and interviews with those who were involved in policymaking. If you were interested in the role of women in the military during World War II, you might ask why the British government supported the expansion of women's roles in ways that the US government did not.

Historiographic essays

Historiography is the study by historians of how history is written. When you write a historiographic essay, you think about the methods by which other historians have drawn their conclusions. If you were writing a historiographic essay about how the Cold War affected John F. Kennedy's policies, you would analyze how other historians have answered this question. What assumptions or biases influenced their choice and interpretation of sources? What methods shaped their work?

D7-c Know the questions historians ask.

Historians generally ask *how* and *why* questions. Other, more basic questions such as *What happened?* and *Who was involved?* will contribute answers to inform the broader, more controversial questions. Historians choose their questions by considering their own interests, the relevance to the ongoing discussions among scholars, and the availability of sources on the topic. The answer to any one of the following questions could form the basis of a thesis for a history paper.

- What role did nationalism play in the breakup of Yugoslavia in the early 1990s?
- Why did the US Congress decide to grant women the vote?
- How did the Salem witch trials (1692–93) differ from the Salzburg witch trials (1675–90)?
- Why did the Roman Empire collapse?

D7-d Understand the kinds of evidence historians use.

As investigators of the past, historians rely on both primary sources and secondary sources. Primary sources are materials from the historical period being studied—government documents, numerical data, speeches, diaries, letters, and maps. Secondary sources are materials produced after the historical period that interpret or synthesize historical events. The same source can function as either a primary or a secondary source depending on what you are writing about. For example, a newspaper article about Slobodan Milosevic's decision to defend himself during his war crimes trial would be a secondary source in an essay about why Milosevic made this decision. The same article, however, would be a primary source in an essay about newspaper coverage of Milosevic's war crimes trial.

Following are some of the ways historians use evidence.

- For a research paper about the role of women in the British military during World War II, you might find evidence in women's diaries and letters. If you were interested in how the government decided to create women's military services, you could consult records of parliamentary debates or correspondence between military and government leaders. You could also find numerous books by other scholars with information on the topic.

- For a research paper about attitudes toward Prohibition in different parts of the United States, you might consult regional newspapers or correspondence between politicians and their constituents. You might also find numerical data on liquor sales and Prohibition violations to support a hypothesis about regional attitudes.

- For a review of several books about the causes of the Tiananmen Square massacre, your evidence would come from the books themselves as well as other respected sources on the topic.

D7-e Become familiar with writing conventions in history.

No matter what topic they are writing about, historians agree on some general conventions.

- Historians value counterargument. To draw a conclusion about why or how something happened, historians must weigh conflicting theories and interpretations carefully and judiciously. In an essay answering the question of why the US Congress passed the Nineteenth Amendment, you might conclude that politicians truly believed that women should have the right to vote. But you would also need to account for the failure of the same legislation several years earlier. Did politicians change their minds? Or were other factors at work?

- Historians conduct research. Historians, like detectives or forensic specialists, look for explanations by assessing the available evidence rather than relying on assumptions or personal opinions. They look for multiple sources of evidence to confirm their theories, and they avoid value judgments.

- Historians write in the past tense when they are focusing on past events, ideas, and movements. They use the present tense (*Goodman's book reveals new evidence*) or present perfect tense (*Olson has vividly depicted the political scene*) when talking about the contents of another writer's work.

- Historians credit the scholarship of others. Historians are aware that they are joining an existing scholarly conversation, and they place great importance on citing the ideas of other scholars.

D7-f Use the CMS (*Chicago*) system in writing in history.

Writers in history typically use the style guidelines of *The Chicago Manual of Style* (CMS) for formatting their papers, for citing sources in the text of their paper and in endnotes, and for listing sources in a bibliography at the end. CMS style is set forth in *The Chicago Manual of Style*, 16th ed. (Chicago: University of Chicago Press, 2010). (For more details, see the CMS documentation sections in your handbook.)

D7-g Sample student paper: Research essay

A history research paper generally focuses on a *how* or a *why* question, and it answers this question with an analysis of available sources. The student paper beginning on the next page was written for a course on the history of the industrial revolution in the United States. The student, Jenna Benjamin, used the style guidelines of *The Chicago Manual of Style* (CMS) to format her paper and to cite and list her sources.

Title page consists of a descriptive title and the writer's name in the center of the page and the course number, instructor, and date at the bottom of the page.

Wage Slavery or True Independence?
Women Workers in the Lowell, Massachusetts,
Textile Mills, 1820-1850

Jenna Benjamin

American History 200, Section 4
Professor Jones
May 22, XXXX

Marginal annotations indicate CMS-style formatting and effective writing.

In 1813, New England merchant Francis Lowell introduced a new type of textile mill to Massachusetts that would have a permanent impact on family and village life. Over the next three decades, the transformation of home production to factory production of textiles would require a substantial labor force and would lead to the unprecedented hiring of thousands of women. The entrance of young women into the workforce sparked a passionate debate about whether factory work exploited young women and adversely affected society. The young women who worked in the mills received low pay for hard work and had little free time.[1] Were these women victims of the factory system? What was the long-term impact of their experiences? An analysis of the evidence reveals that rather than being exploited, these women workers shaped their experience for their own purposes and actively expanded the opportunities for women.

In the late eighteenth century, great changes in the production of textiles were taking place in England, with a transition from home production to factories using machines and employing children to do most of the work. Conditions in the factories were very bad, and stories of dark and dangerous mills reinforced Americans' prejudices against industrialization.[2] Meanwhile, New Englanders still spun yarn at home and some also wove their own cloth, mostly for their own families. Much of this work was done by women. A spinning wheel was a possession of almost every household.[3] But in the first two decades of the nineteenth century, a slow shift took place in New England from home to factory production.

Some American merchants, like Samuel Slater and Francis Cabot Lowell, began to envision an American textile industry. The first mills they built in the United States were in rural villages and employed whole families, not just children. Since the textile mills hired whole families who already lived in the villages, family and village life was not greatly altered.[4]

A dramatic change in textile production, however, came from a new machine, the power loom, and a new mechanized mill, built first in Waltham, Massachusetts, in 1813 by Francis Lowell and a small group of wealthy Boston merchants.[5] Waltham was not a village with a textile mill in it; it became a "mill town" in which the factory dominated the economic

---

Page header contains the writer's name followed by the page number. Since the title page is counted in the numbering, the first text page is numbered 2.

Introduction frames a debatable issue.

Research questions focus the essay.

Statement of thesis.

Section provides background about the historical period.

Historians write in the past tense when describing past events.

life of a rapidly growing city. Most significantly, the workers in Lowell's mill were not local families but individuals who came from great distances to live and work in the new mill town. When Lowell died in 1817, his business partners spread the new factory system to other places, notably a town on the Merrimack and Concord Rivers twenty-seven miles from Boston; in honor of their friend, they named the town Lowell. It soon became the biggest mill town in the nation, with more than a dozen large integrated mills using mechanical looms.[6]

The growth of Lowell between 1821 and 1840 was unprecedented.[7] A rapidly developing textile industry like the one at Lowell needed more and more people to work the machines in the factories. The mill owners, aware of the negative view of English mill towns, decided to create a community where workers would live in solid, clean housing rather than slums. For their workers, they looked to a large group of people whose labor was not absolutely necessary to the New England farm economy— hundreds (later thousands) of young women who lived on the farms but who could be persuaded to come to Lowell and work in the mills.[8]

Several factors in the social and economic history of New England made this group of workers available. Population growth and scarcity of land to pass down to younger generations of sons caused many New England farmers to send their sons to work on neighboring farms or as apprentices to craftsmen in towns or villages.[9] In addition, the position of women (wives and, especially, daughters) in the family was an inferior one. Adult, property-holding males were citizens with full civil rights, but the same was not true for women *of any age*. Wives had no legal rights, and daughters had no independence. Daughters were bound by social conventions to obey their fathers and rarely were able to earn money of their own. Even travel away from home was unusual. Although the family could not have functioned without the labor of wives and daughters at field work, food preparation, cleaning, washing, and so on, women gained no independent income or freedom as a result. For some young women, their subordinate position in family and society gave them an incentive to embrace the opportunities offered by mill work. Unlike the limited occupation of teaching, which was poorly paid and lasted for only a few months a year, the new mill work was steady, and it paid well.[10]

Note numbers in text refer to endnotes at the end of the paper.

Topic sentence signals a transition to a specific discussion of the women workers.

Benjamin 4

Hiring young women, of course, met strong resistance from fathers who saw their role as protecting their daughters and preparing them for marriage.[11] To confront this resistance, the mill owners created boardinghouses around the mills where groups of girls—ranging in age from fifteen to mid-twenties—lived and took their meals under the care of a housekeeper, usually an older woman. Strict boardinghouse rules were laid down by each company (see fig. 1). Moreover, the girls would

A primary source (a document) provides concrete evidence and adds historical interest.

REGULATIONS

FOR THE
BOARDING HOUSES
OF THE
MIDDLESEX COMPANY.

THE tenants of the Boarding Houses are not to board, or permit any part of their houses to be occupied by any person except those in the employ of the Company.

They will be considered answerable for any improper conduct in their houses, and are not to permit their boarders to have company at unseasonable hours.

The doors must be closed at ten o'clock in the evening, and no one admitted after that time without some reasonable excuse.

The keepers of the Boarding Houses must give an account of the number, names, and employment of their boarders, when required; and report the names of such as are guilty of any improper conduct, or are not in the regular habit of attending public worship.

The buildings and yards about them must be kept clean and in good order, and if they are injured otherwise than from ordinary use, all necessary repairs will be made, and charged to the occupant.

It is indispensable that all persons in the employ of the Middlesex Company should be vaccinated who have not been, as also the families with whom they board; which will be done at the expense of the Company.

SAMUEL LAWRENCE, Agent.

JOEL TAYLOR, PRINTER, Daily Courier Office.

Fig. 1. Each mill company established strict rules for the boardinghouses where its women workers lived. (American Textile History Museum, Lowell, Massachusetts.)

A caption below the writer's visual evidence gives the figure number, a brief description, and information about the source.

(*Source:* Reprinted by permission of the American Textile History Museum, Lowell, Massachusetts.)

never grow into a permanent working class, as it was expected that they would return to their homes for visits and after a year or two would go back to their villages permanently.[12] The mill owners did not advertise for help. They sent recruiters into the countryside to assure parents that their daughters would live under strict supervision in the boardinghouses and at work and that their behavior would be monitored. The owners' efforts were successful: over the years, thousands of young women took the long trip by stagecoach or wagon from their rural homes to mill towns like Lowell.[13]

Besides having to adjust to living in a city in a strange house with a dozen or more other girls, the young women had to get used to the rigorous rules and long hours at the mills.[14] Mill work was an opportunity, but it also was hard work. The girls worked an average of twelve hours a day. The mills operated six days a week, so the only day off was Sunday, part of which was usually spent at church. Thus free time was confined to two or three hours in the evening and to Sunday afternoon.[15] For many, however, this was still more leisure (and more freedom) than they would have had at home.

Despite a workday that took up fourteen hours, including time spent traveling to and from their houses for meals, most of the young women did not find the work very strenuous or particularly dangerous. As the mill owners had promised, Lowell did not resemble the grimy, packed mill towns of England.[16] Still, the work was tedious and confining, with the girls doing the same operation over and over again under the watchful eye of the overseer.[17]

The young women earned an average of three to four dollars a week, from which their board of $1.25 a week was deducted. At that time, no other jobs open to women paid as well.[18] Three or four dollars a week was enough to pay board, send badly needed money home, and still have enough left over for new clothes once in a while. Many women mill workers even established savings accounts, and some eventually left Lowell with several hundred dollars, something they never could have done at home.[19]

Even though their free time was very limited, the young women engaged in a variety of activities. In the evenings, they wrote letters home, entertained visitors (though there was little privacy), repaired their

---

Benjamin introduces evidence that appears to contradict her thesis (counterargument).

Benjamin develops a response to the counterargument, with strong evidence for her thesis.

Details about the beneficial effects on the young mill workers come from primary and secondary sources.

Benjamin 6

clothing, and talked about friends and relatives and also about conditions in the mills. They could go out to the shops, especially clothing shops. The mill girls at Lowell prided themselves on a wardrobe that, at least on Sunday, was not inferior to that of the wives of prosperous citizens.[20] In addition, they attended evening courses that enabled them to extend their education beyond their few years of schooling. They also attended lectures and read novels and essays. So strong was the girls' interest in reading that many mills put up signs warning "No reading in the mills."[21] Some young women even began writing. Determined to challenge the idea that mill girls were mindless drones of the factory and lacked the refinement to ultimately be good wives, about seventy-five mill girls and women contributed in the 1840s to publications featuring stories and essays by the workers themselves.[22]

Benjamin paraphrases information from a secondary source, a late-nineteenth-century book.

The best known of these publications was the *Lowell Offering*. The *Offering* avoided sensitive issues about working conditions, but the women controlled the content of the publication and wrote on subjects (family, courtship, fashion, morality, nature) that interested them.[23] A few of the *Offering* writers even went on to literary careers, not the kind of future that most people expected of factory workers. Charles Dickens toured the mills in 1842 and later said of the girls' writing: "Of the merits of the *Lowell Offering*, as a literary production, I will only observe . . . that it will compare advantageously with a great many English annuals."[24]

Direct quotation provides evidence from the period.

Though the *Offering* was a sign that something unusual was happening in this factory town, the women still worked in an industry that caused them hardship. By the 1830s, tensions in the mills had begun to rise as the companies became more interested in profits and less concerned about their role as protectors of their young workers. Factory owners, observing a decline in the price of their cloth and an increase in unsold inventories, decided to lower their workers' wages.[25] When the reduction was announced in February 1834, the women workers circulated petitions among themselves pledging to stop work (or "turn out") if wages were lowered.[26] When the leader of the petition drive at one mill was fired, many of the women left work and marched to the other mills to call out their workers. It is estimated that one-sixth of all women mill workers walked out as a result. The strikers wrote another petition stating that "we will not go back into the mills to work until our wages are continued . . . as they have been."[27]

Although the "turn out" was brief and did not achieve its purpose, it demonstrated that the women workers did not accept the owners' view that they were minors under the owners' benevolent care. The sense of independence gained by factory work and cash wages led them to reject the idea that they were mere factory hands. Petitions referred to their "unquestionable rights" and to "the spirit of our patriotic ancestors, who preferred privation to bondage." One petition ended, "We are free, we would remain in possession of what kind providence has bestowed upon us, and remain *daughters of free men still*."[28] This language indicates that the women did not think of themselves as laborers complaining about low wages. They were free citizens of a republic and deserved respect as such. Many young women left the mills and went home when mill work came to seem more like "slavery" than independence (a comparison that appeared in the petitions). In 1836, another effort to lower wages led to an even larger "turn out."[29] The willingness of these young women to challenge the authority of the mill owners is a sign that their new lives had given them a feeling of personal strength and solidarity with one another.[30]

Economic recession in the late 1830s and early 1840s led to the layoff of hundreds more women workers. In the 1840s and 1850s, the mill owners tried to maintain profits by increasing the workload and abandoning paternalism toward their workers. To save money, the companies stopped building boardinghouses.[31] The look of Lowell changed as well. Mill buildings took up more of the green space that had been part of the original town plan. By 1850, Lowell did indeed look something like an English mill town.

As conditions in the mills and in the city declined, young New England women were replaced by young Irish immigrants escaping the famine and the poor living conditions in Ireland. Slowly, Lowell became just another industrial city. It was dirty and overcrowded, and its mills were beginning to look run-down.[32]

By 1850, an era had passed. But from the 1820s to the 1840s, the majority of the textile workers were young women who helped make possible the industrialization of New England at the same time as they expanded

---

Benjamin analyzes the quotation to show how it supports the paragraph's main point.

Strong evidence supports the paper's thesis.

Concluding paragraph opens with a brief restatement of part of the thesis.

Benjamin 8

their own opportunities. These early mill workers became models for later women reformers and radicals who raised the banner for equal rights for women in more and more areas of life. The independent mill girls of the 1830s and 1840s resisted pressures from their employers, gained both freedom and maturity by living and working on their own, and showed an intense desire for independence and learning.[33] Great fortunes were made from the textile mills of that era, but within those mills a generation of young women gained something even more precious: a sense of self-respect.

Conclusion considers the broader implications of the thesis.

Benjamin 9

Notes

    1. Caroline F. Ware, *The Early New England Cotton Manufacture* (Boston: Houghton Mifflin, 1931), 4-8; Barbara M. Tucker, *Samuel Slater and the Origins of the American Textile Industry, 1790-1860* (Ithaca, NY: Cornell University Press, 1984), 38-41.

    2. Tucker, *Samuel Slater*, 33-40.

    3. Thomas Dublin, *Women at Work: The Transformation of Work and Community in Lowell, Massachusetts, 1826-1860* (New York: Columbia University Press, 1979), 14; Adrienne D. Hood, "The Gender Division of Labor in the Production of Textiles in Eighteenth-Century Rural Pennsylvania," *Journal of Social History* 27, no. 3 (1994), "Spinning as Women's Work" section, Academic OneFile (A15324645).

    4. Tucker, *Samuel Slater*, 79, 85, 99-100, 111; Barbara M. Tucker, "The Family and Industrial Discipline in Ante-Bellum New England," *Labor History* 21, no. 1 (1979): 56-60.

    5. Robert F. Dalzell, *Enterprising Elite: The Boston Associates and the World They Made* (Cambridge, MA: Harvard University Press, 1987), 26-30; Tucker, *Samuel Slater*, 111-16.

    6. Tucker, *Samuel Slater*, 116-17.

    7. Dublin, *Women at Work*, 19-21, 133-35.

    8. Ibid., 26, 76; Benita Eisler, ed., *The "Lowell Offering": Writings by New England Mill Women, 1840-1845* (Philadelphia: Lippincott, 1977), 15-16.

    9. Christopher Clark, "The Household Economy: Market Exchange and the Rise of Capitalism in the Connecticut Valley, 1800-1860," *Journal of Social History* 13, no. 2 (1979): 175-76, http://www.jstor.org/stable /3787339; Gail Fowler Mohanty, "Handloom Outwork and Outwork Weaving in Rural Rhode Island, 1810-1821," *American Studies* 30, no. 2 (1989): 42-43, 48-49.

    10. Eisler, *"Lowell Offering,"* 16, 193; Clark, "Household Economy," 178-79; Dalzell, *Enterprising Elite*, 33.

    11. On the influence of patriarchy, see Tucker, *Samuel Slater*, 25-26; Harriet H. Robinson, *Loom and Spindle; Or, Life among the Early Mill Girls* (1898), reprinted in *Women of Lowell* (New York: Arno Press, 1974), 194; Barbara Welter, "The Cult of True Womanhood," *American Quarterly* 18, no. 2, pt. 1 (1966): 151, 170-71.

Benjamin 12

Bibliography

Bartlett, Elisha. *A Vindication of the Character and Condition of the Females Employed in the Lowell Mills.* 1841. Reprinted in *Women of Lowell.* New York: Arno Press, 1974.

A Citizen of Lowell. *Corporations and Operatives: Being an Exposition of the Condition [of] Factory Operatives and a Review of the "Vindication," by Elisha Bartlett, MD.* 1843. Reprinted in *Women of Lowell.* New York: Arno Press, 1974.

Clark, Christopher. "The Household Economy: Market Exchange and the Rise of Capitalism in the Connecticut Valley, 1800-1860." *Journal of Social History* 13, no. 2 (1979): 169-89. http://www.jstor.org/stable /3787339.

Dalzell, Robert F. *Enterprising Elite: The Boston Associates and the World They Made.* Cambridge, MA: Harvard University Press, 1987.

Dublin, Thomas. *Women at Work: The Transformation of Work and Community in Lowell, Massachusetts, 1826-1860.* New York: Columbia University Press, 1979.

Eisler, Benita, ed. *The "Lowell Offering": Writings by New England Mill Women, 1840-1845.* Philadelphia: Lippincott, 1977.

"Factory Rules from the Handbook to Lowell, 1848." Illinois Labor History Society. Center for Law and Computers, Chicago-Kent School of Law. Accessed May 12, 2006. http://www.kentlaw.edu/ilhs/lowell.html.

Hood, Adrienne D. "The Gender Division of Labor in the Production of Textiles in Eighteenth-Century Rural Pennsylvania." *Journal of Social History* 27, no. 3 (1994). Academic OneFile (A15324645).

Larcom, Lucy. "Among Lowell Mill-Girls: A Reminiscence." 1881. Reprinted in *Women of Lowell.* New York: Arno Press, 1974.

Mohanty, Gail Fowler. "Handloom Outwork and Outwork Weaving in Rural Rhode Island, 1810-1821." *American Studies* 30, no. 2 (1989): 41-68.

Robinson, Harriet H. *Loom and Spindle; Or, Life among the Early Mill Girls.* 1898. Reprinted in *Women of Lowell.* New York: Arno Press, 1974.

Sins of Our Mothers. Boston: PBS Video, 1988. Videocassette.

Stearns, Bertha Monica. "Early Factory Magazines in New England: The *Lowell Offering* and Its Contemporaries." *Journal of Economic and Business History* (1930): 685-705.

Bibliography begins on a new page and includes all the sources cited in the paper.

Online article with a stable URL.

Entries are listed alphabetically by authors' last names or by title for works with no author.

First line of each entry is at the left margin; subsequent lines are indented ½".

Entries are single-spaced, with double-spacing between entries. (Some instructors may prefer double-spacing throughout.)

D8 Writing in music

Musicians and musicologists — those who study, analyze, and interpret music — write about music for themselves or for larger audiences. Your instructor might ask you to keep a journal to record your impressions and ideas about concerts you attend. If you are a music student, you might write personal reflections about works that you are preparing for performance. Other kinds of writing are intended to inform or educate general audiences. They include reviews of performances and press releases that are published in newspapers, blogs, or other publications. More specialized publications are scholarly journals and concert program notes.

If you are a student learning how to write about music, you will need to train yourself to listen actively rather than passively. Passive listening means just enjoying a performance or recording. This kind of listening is certainly a valid way to hear music, but to write about music you must become more aware of what you are hearing. You must intentionally listen for certain qualities in the music. Active listening also involves learning about the background of a composer or musician to deepen your understanding of the music. As an active listener, you can observe how the audience responds during a performance, and you can analyze and critique the performance as you listen. To help you become a more active listener, your instructor might take your class on field trips to concerts so you can experience a variety of performances. You might attend a classical symphony concert, a chamber music performance, a recital showcasing the talents of a single performer, or a concert by a rock band or a jazz ensemble.

D8-a Determine your audience and their needs in music.

Audiences for music writers include professional musicians, music historians, and researchers, teachers, and students. They read scholarly or teaching journals to learn about new analyses or interpretations of musical compositions and about methods that other musicians, researchers, or teachers are using. Other audiences may include members of the general public, who read reviews of performances in newspapers or on Web sites to help them decide whether to attend concerts. Serious concertgoers read reviews after they attend a performance as a way of helping them think more about their experience at the concert. Audiences attending performances read the printed programs to learn about the biographies of composers and the histories of pieces they will hear. Some readers are in businesses, government agencies, or nonprofit organizations that fund musicians and arts groups. They read grant proposals written by researchers, musicians, teachers, and even students who are seeking funds to support their study or practice of music.

Readers in the field of music want to know the writer's opinion, but they expect the writing to contain more than just statements of personal taste. If the piece of writing is a music review, readers want the writer to evaluate the performance with specific details and examples to justify the writer's opinion. Because the discipline of music is a diverse field with a very long history, understanding one composer, work, or performer requires making connections to others in the field. All readers expect writers about music to make references to other composers, styles, or musicians.

D8-b Recognize the forms of writing in music.

When you take courses in music, you may be asked to write any of the following:

- response papers
- program notes
- press releases
- concert reviews
- journal articles
- grant proposals

Response papers

A response paper is your personal reflection on a piece of music, a composer, a performance, or your own progress as a musician. Your instructor may ask you to write the paper as a brief assignment or as part of a journal that you keep during the course. The purpose of personal response is to brainstorm some initial ideas or to reflect on a work you are studying or a concert you attended. These writing activities will help you generate topics for larger, more formal projects. To help you focus your attention on particular elements of a performance, your instructor may provide questions you can use in forming your response. Your instructor might assign a response paper after you attend a concert and then later require a concert review using your response paper as a starting point. Thus a response paper can help you move from your immediate reactions to a more objective piece of writing. To be sure that your responses are useful for later assignments, make them detailed and thorough. Avoid simply writing that you like or dislike a particular work or performer. Instead, provide details that illustrate exactly why you have that particular reaction.

Program notes

When people attend a formal concert or a recital, they are usually given a program that lists the pieces they will hear and describes those pieces so they can understand and appreciate the music they will hear. Those descriptions are called *program notes*. A program note usually includes a biographical profile of the composer, background information about the composer's historical period, some mention of the first performance of the piece with a list or survey of major performances, and a description of the piece. The description will guide audience members through the performance, describing what they can expect to hear in each section of the piece. One kind of program note is a profile of each performer, describing the performer's major accomplishments and listing schools attended and major past performances. It may also give a brief discography, a listing of recordings that the performer has made professionally. Writing program notes will require you to do some research so you can provide the information readers expect to enhance their enjoyment and understanding of the performance. Think of program notes as small research papers that teach your readers about the music they are going to listen to.

Press releases

A press release is a brief document of no more than 250 words announcing an upcoming musical event to the general public. It is written by the event's organizers and distributed locally for publication in newspapers, in magazines, and on Web sites and as announcements on radio and television. Begin a press release with a one- or two-sentence statement giving the most important information about the event: what it is, who the main performers will be, and the time, date, and location of the event. Your press release can continue with a description of the composers and performers who will be featured. The press release should conclude with any other relevant information such as cost, parking, and a Web site or phone number where readers can get more information.

Concert reviews

Concert reviews might be the most popular kind of writing about music. The reviewer attends a concert, listens actively and intently, and tells readers about the experience. When you write a concert review, begin by engaging your audience with one or more sentences that capture the quality and mood of the entire performance. Tell readers what composers and works were featured and who the performers were. Then write about each part of the concert. Briefly describe what was played and how it was played, stating your opinions about the music and the performers, with examples to illustrate your opinions. You might also integrate historical information about the composer, the piece of music, or the performers. Vivid words and active sentences will give readers a sense of how it felt to attend the performance.

Journal articles

Musicologists research and write about the history and literature of music, and they analyze works of music. They publish their interpretations in scholarly journals and present their work at professional conferences. You may be assigned a paper that involves research and musical analysis. A typical assignment might ask you to explain how a composition reflects its historical period or to trace trends in music in a time period or region. You might explore larger issues such as music in mass media or how technology has changed music. Your assignment might ask you to focus on a relatively unknown composer, performer, or work. If you are writing a journal article about the teaching of music, you might write a how-to paper that proposes an improved way to do something — how to rehearse a high school band more effectively, how to teach jazz improvisation, or how to start a school chamber music festival, for example. A paper of that type would involve reading articles, interviewing teachers and administrators, and using personal observations and experiences.

Grant proposals

Musicians and music teachers often apply for funding to support their projects. They might request money to purchase new equipment for their schools, to organize a summer workshop or camp, to travel to a library for research, or to attend a summer academy or workshop for intense study with well-known teachers. Whether you write a grant proposal on a form provided by the funding agency or draft your own, it typically includes several sections:

- an introduction that briefly describes the project and covers basic details about when, where, and how you expect the project to be achieved
- an outcomes section describing all the objectives you expect to attain with your project
- an itemized list of anticipated expenses

- a timeline section providing a schedule for completion, including deadlines for specific tasks
- a list of qualifications—the personal skills and experience that will enable you to complete the project
- a résumé

D8-c Know the questions musicians and musicologists ask.

Writers about music ask questions that guide them toward analysis and interpretation. The following are some questions that would lead to topics for research papers in music.

- In what ways do the symphonies of Brahms show the influence of earlier classical composers as well as the qualities of the Romantic period?
- How did rock and roll develop from earlier forms of music?
- How did changes in US society and mass media in the 1950s and 1960s influence the development of country music?
- What techniques of music composition and instrumentation has Beirut used to create his unique eastern European Gypsy–inspired brand of indie rock?
- What elements of electro-pop and folk does Ellie Goulding use most effectively in her hit single "Halcyon"?
- What challenges do symphony orchestras in the United States encounter, what are the causes of those challenges, and what are some effective strategies that cities have developed or could develop to build and sustain orchestras?

D8-d Understand the kinds of evidence musicians and musicologists use.

Musicians and musicologists use primary and secondary sources for evidence. A primary source is a music composition that the writer is analyzing or a concert or recording that the writer is reviewing. Secondary sources are books, articles, and Web sites about composers, musicians, or music.

The following are examples of the ways you might use evidence when you write about music.

- For program notes, you would use secondary sources for biographical material about the performer and historical information about the work of music to be performed. You might interview some of the performers (primary sources); for an original work, you might interview the composer, if possible.

- For a research paper tracing the development of Creole music in southern Louisiana, your primary sources could be songs representing different styles of Creole music and stages in the evolution of the music. Secondary sources would be books and other materials about the history of southern society and culture.

- For a review of a performance of Handel's *Messiah*, you would use specific moments from the concert itself as evidence to illustrate your opinions. You might mention how the conductor and the soloists interpreted particular parts of the piece and describe how sections of the orchestra and chorus performed. You might also note performers or moments from the performance that stood out because of their strengths or weaknesses.

D8-e Become familiar with writing conventions in music.

Musicians and musicologists agree on several conventions when they write.

- Musical compositions are known and categorized by detailed or specialized titles. For example, Beethoven's fifth symphony is Symphony no. 5 in C Minor, op. 67 (*op.* is the abbreviation for *opus*, or "work").

- Musicians and musicologists use a specialized vocabulary from music theory and history. Often that vocabulary includes words in Italian, German, or French. For example, movements of a symphony are known by their technical terms, such as the *adagio* section or the *allegro* movement.

- In reflective writing, the first-person pronoun *I* is acceptable. In a music review, it should be used sparingly so the review remains fair and analytical and does not seem to be merely a statement of personal taste. The first person can be used in grant proposals but not in press releases, program notes, or research papers in music.

- Writers use past tense to describe past events such as a composer's life or a performance. They use present tense when reviewing a recording or analyzing a work of music (for example, *In Nickel Creek's new song, the mandolin plays variations on an old folk tune*).

- Music writers use the active voice and active verbs to keep their writing lively and engaging.

D8-f   Use the MLA system in writing in music.

Writers in music typically use the style guidelines of the Modern Language Association (MLA) to format a paper, to document sources within the paper, and to cite sources at the end of the paper. Those guidelines are set forth in the *MLA Handbook*, 8th edition (MLA, 2016). (For more details, see the MLA documentation sections in your handbook.)

In addition, specific information about writing in music can be found in D. Kern Holoman, *Writing about Music: A Style Sheet*, 2nd ed. (U of California P, 2008), and Jonathan Bellman, *A Short Guide to Writing about Music*, 2nd ed. (Longman, 2006).

D8-g   Sample student paper: Concert review

A typical assignment in music courses is a review of a performance or a recording. Reviews appear in newspapers, in magazines, and on Web sites. The following student paper was written in a writing course for music majors and other students interested in music. The student, Tom Houston, attended a local concert for this assignment. He used the style guidelines in the *MLA Handbook* to format his paper and to cite and list his sources.

Tom Houston

Dr. Belland

MUS 291 W

27 February XXXX

Concert Review: Cincinnati Symphony Orchestra

The Cincinnati Symphony Orchestra performed a stunning concert
Saturday evening, February 23, 2008. Those who came, filling Music Hall
to almost two-thirds capacity, were immersed in what became a soul-
searching musical experience provided by Maestro John Adams. The
program selections and the exquisite performances offered the audience
an opportunity to expand their appreciation for contemporary music.

Opening this energetic program was *Tod und Verklärung* ("Death and
Transfiguration"), a tone poem by Richard Strauss. Following the Strauss,
Adams led the orchestra in *On the Transmigration of Souls* and, after the
intermission, *The Dharma at Big Sur*, both composed by Adams.

Strauss wrote *Tod und Verklärung*, a lively musical stampede, when he
was just twenty-five years old. This seems to be a relatively young age to
tackle such a profoundly heavy subject. In his preconcert talk, Adams
observed that at the time Strauss was "a bit overwhelmed at his own
orchestral virtuosity." Very effective in the introduction of this tone poem
is the motif played by the timpani suggesting the faltering heartbeat of a
dying elderly man. Then the music grows to a galloping romp—a very
young Strauss's concept of the old man's entrance into Glory Land. At least
this is the generally accepted interpretation. Listening carefully, one can
hear partway through the Glory Land section the faltering heart still
beating. Strauss might be giving us pre-death hallucinations followed by a
slightly subdued entrance into heaven.

The orchestra under Adams gave an intense interpretation of this
Strauss masterpiece. The gentle, soft voice usually brought to this orchestra
by music director Paavo Järvi would have added a welcome intensified
dramatic contrast to what was a rendition with merely adequate drama
under Adams's baton.

It is strange to think of the Strauss piece as whimsical. It is a
heavyweight probe into heavyweight matter. However, in his preconcert
talk to the early concertgoers, Adams said that he added it to the program

Houston begins
with the time and
place of the concert
and then gives his
overall evaluation
of the performance.

Houston provides
context by listing
the pieces on the
program.

This section vividly
describes the
history and sound
of the Strauss
composition.

Houston evaluates
how the orchestra
performed the
piece, giving
supporting
details from the
performance.

Marginal annotations indicate MLA-style formatting and effective writing.

as "whimsy" but that it might not have been the most effective selection because it added more weight to an already heavy program. The truth of this comment became apparent during Adams's own *On the Transmigration of Souls*.

> Transition contrasts the first work on the program with the next work to be discussed.

As the program notes by Richard E. Rodda indicate, *Transmigration* was originally written for and performed by the New York Philharmonic Orchestra in honor of the victims of the September 11, 2001, terrorist attacks. Adding to the orchestra the voices of the May Festival Chorus, the Cincinnati Children's Choir, and a prerecorded soundtrack, Adams transformed Music Hall into a cathedral. Adams's music avoids evoking the terrible scenes seen so many times, using as the text the simple, heartrending statements of both victims and their loved ones. Each poignant word was sung exquisitely, every phrase clearly understood through the appropriate musical dissonance of the orchestra.

> Houston provides background, description, and an opinion about the performance of the second piece.

The depth of the significance of this work cannot be overstated. Adams captured this event not only through the souls of the victims but also through the souls of the surviving loved ones and the souls of all whose lives were forever changed that morning. The performance began with Adams standing motionless in a silent hall, and it ended with him standing motionless in a silent hall. It seemed almost a sacrilege to clap, but that is all an audience can do. It was like clapping after Communion. Soon Robert Porco, director of the May Festival Chorus, and Robyn Lana, director of the Cincinnati Children's Choir, appeared with Adams to accept a well-deserved tribute from the audience. This seemed to make the extended applause more appropriate and a welcome emotional release.

> Houston uses vivid description to give readers a sense of what it was like to attend the concert.

Following the intermission, violinist Leila Josefowicz appeared with the orchestra to perform Adams's *The Dharma at Big Sur*. This is quintessential Adams at his compositional best. The entire work sounds improvisational, especially the solo violin. The instrument, made especially for Josefowicz, is a six-string electric violin with a very wide range, so different from a traditional violin that the performer is required to learn new technique to play it. The music, moving beyond traditional Western tones, employs quarter, or in-between, tones, which slide up or down, giving a sound that is strange to Western, classically trained ears.

> Houston provides background about an instrument and music that might be unfamiliar to readers.

Houston 3

Josefowicz's enduring energy and technique, the controlled orchestral dissonance and extraordinarily equipped percussion section, and the leprechaunesque gyrations of Adams gave the audience an exciting listening and viewing experience.

We Cincinnatians are traditionally a conservative people, preferring an orchestra to have a traditionally "full" or lush sound, but Adams composes on the leading crest of the wave of minimalism, a contemporary, spare sound that can make an audience uncomfortable. The concert Saturday night moved the Cincinnati audience a step or two forward.

Houston supports his opinion about the final piece with vivid details.

The conclusion summarizes the general impact of the performance on the audience.

Works cited
list begins on a
new page and is
formatted in MLA
style.

Works Cited

Adams, John. Preconcert talk. Cincinnati Symphony Orchestra, Music Hall,
    Cincinnati, 23 Feb. 2008.

Cincinnati Symphony Orchestra. Conducted by John Adams, Music Hall,
    Cincinnati, 23 Feb. 2008. Performance.

Rodda, Richard E. "John Adams: *On the Transmigration of Souls*." Cincinnati
    Symphony Orchestra, 23 Feb. 2008. Program notes.

D9 Writing in nursing

Writing is an important tool in the education of nursing students as well as in the everyday workplaces of the profession. For students learning to become nurses, writing about specific nursing theories and practices, medical cases, and client experiences helps them better understand concepts and skills through research and analytical thinking.

For professional nurses, writing is a crucial means of communication with colleagues in the health care profession, communication that can improve the quality of care for patients, or *clients*, as they are increasingly called. Nurses write charts about their clients (a practice called *charting*), staff memos, patient education booklets, and policies for health care facilities. They may also contribute research articles to journals in the field or craft arguments to attempt to persuade decision makers to change or adopt a particular health care policy.

To write effectively in nursing, you need to support your claims with accurate client observations and current, researched evidence.

D9-a Determine your audience and their needs in nursing.

Nurses write for health care providers such as other nurses, patients or clients, and the staff and administrators of institutions such as clinics and hospitals. Health care providers read documents that inform them about a client's history and needs and a nurse's recommended interventions. Patients or clients read documents to learn about their health care options, home care needs, and nutrition and lifestyle choices. Administrators and staff read instructions, procedures, guidelines, reports, proposals, and policy recommendations that will enable them to make decisions and perform their functions effectively.

Your readers will expect your writing to be grounded in data, with a client's chart information and lab results clearly presented in an objective tone. You should describe your observations of a client's physical and emotional condition directly and thoroughly. You may present those observations using the first-person pronoun *I* or *we*, but be as objective as possible. Confidentiality and sensitivity to a client's background and diversity are essential.

Clients often feel anxious about their medical conditions, and many clients may not be familiar with medical terminology. When you write for clients, respect their right to understand their own medical documents. Write in plain language that is direct and easy to understand, using a minimum of technical terminology and defining such terms when it is necessary to use them. When you write for health care professionals, be precise and use relevant specialized medical terminology.

D9-b   Recognize the forms of writing in nursing.

Students in nursing school are asked to write many different kinds of papers. You might be required to write some of the following types of documents:

- statements of philosophy
- nursing practice papers
- case studies
- research papers
- literature reviews
- experiential or reflective narratives
- position papers

Statements of philosophy

To help you articulate why you want to become a nurse, your instructor may ask you to write your personal philosophy of nursing at the beginning of your professional schooling. This assignment is an opportunity to explain what principles you value, what experiences have shaped your career path, how you plan to put your principles into practice, and perhaps what specialization you are interested in pursuing.

Nursing practice papers

Assignments that ask you to apply your growing knowledge about medicine and care practices can take different forms: a nursing care plan, a concept map, or a nursing process paper. For these practice papers, you provide

- a detailed client history and a nursing diagnosis of the client's health problems
- the interventions you recommend for the client
- your rationales for the interventions
- expected outcomes for the client
- actual, observed outcomes

A concept map is an important technique that students can use to understand how to approach client care or how to sort through possible solutions to a problem. Students create a diagram that shows the connections between the possible diagnoses, the client and medical research data that could support each diagnosis, and the plans for client care that follow from each diagnosis.

Case studies

When you are asked to do a case study, you are given detailed information about a hypothetical client's health issue and are instructed to analyze the data. Case studies help you develop a global view of the many elements that make up a client's health problems and shape the health care decisions you make for the client. In a case study, you might

- interpret laboratory results
- evaluate data from a chart that a nurse on the previous shift has completed
- prioritize the client's medical needs
- determine the necessary guidelines for carrying out any required procedures (such as wound care)
- consider, with sensitivity, how the client's personal history, including language and cultural background, might inform how you interact with the client, answer questions, and respond to his or her needs

Research papers

A research paper assignment calls on you to research and report on a topic relevant to the nursing field—perhaps a particular disease, such as Alzheimer's, or an issue that challenges medical professionals, such as maintaining quality care when the downsizing of nursing staffs leads to longer, more fatiguing shifts. Typically, you are required to use as sources as many as twenty-five scholarly articles published in peer-reviewed journals in medical fields. (Peer-reviewed journals publish manuscripts only after they have been carefully reviewed anonymously by experts in the field.)

In some cases, you will be asked to formulate a research question (such as *Is the use of animal-assisted therapy effective in managing behavioral problems of clients with Alzheimer's?*) and come to a conclusion based on a review of recently published research. In other cases, you may be expected to synthesize information from a number of published articles to answer questions about a nursing practice, such as medication administration, or about a disorder, such as muscular dystrophy.

Literature reviews

Review assignments ask you to read and synthesize published work on a nursing topic. As a nursing student you will read many scholarly articles about medical conditions and nursing practices, so it is important to understand and stay current with the latest advances in the field. In a literature review, you summarize the arguments or findings of one or more journal articles or of a larger body of recent scholarship on a topic. In some cases, you may be asked more specifically to analyze the works critically, evaluating whether the findings seem justified by the data. Such an assignment may be called a *critical review*.

Experiential or reflective narratives

Some of the writing you do as a nursing student will be reflective. To begin to understand what clients are experiencing because of an illness, you might write a personal narrative about what happened to you while caring for a client or what happened to your client as he or she coped with an illness. For example, one student wrote about the increasing sense of isolation and hopelessness that an elderly woman suffered because of her late-stage glaucoma.

Position papers

In a position paper, you take a stance on a controversial issue in the field, such as whether the government should prohibit junk food commercials during children's television programming. You must support your argument with evidence from published research and show the evidence and reasoning that may support an opposing position. A good position paper makes clear why the issue is controversial and important to debate.

D9-c Know the questions nurses ask.

Nursing students ask questions in their writing that help them effectively care for clients. You might ask questions such as the following to understand the needs of clients.

- What information should you collect each day from a client with a particular condition?
- Do the data in the client's chart indicate a normal or an abnormal status of his or her condition?

- What interventions should you take based on the diagnosis of the client's condition? Why are those interventions necessary?
- How do you care for a surgical patient with chronic pain?

D9-d Understand the kinds of evidence nurses use.

When you are writing a paper in nursing, sometimes your evidence will be quantitative (such as lab results or a client's vital signs), and sometimes it will be qualitative (such as your observations and descriptions of a client's appearance or state of mind). The following are examples of the kinds of evidence you might use:

- a client's lab test results
- data from a nurse's client chart
- research findings in a journal article
- direct observation of a client's physical or mental state

Because clients can have multiple medical problems that need to be prioritized for treatment, nurses use evidence to support more than one nursing diagnosis.

D9-e Become familiar with writing conventions in nursing.

Nurses agree on some conventions when they write.

- Nurses increasingly refer to the people in their care as "clients," not "patients."
- Evaluations and conclusions must be based on accurate and detailed information (*At the time of his diagnosis, the client had experienced a 20-lb weight loss in the previous 6 months. His CBC showed a WBC count of 32, an H & H of 13/38, and a platelet count of 34,000*).
- The first-person pronoun *I* is acceptable in reflective papers about your own experience, but you should use an objective voice in the third person for research papers, reviews, case studies, position papers, and papers describing nursing practices (*Postoperative findings: External fixation devices extend from the proximal tibia and fibular shafts of the left foot*).
- Nurses often use the passive voice in describing procedures or recording their observations (*Inflammation was observed at the site of the incision*).

- The identity of clients whose cases are discussed in writing must remain confidential (nurses often make up initials to denote a client's name).

- Direct quotation of sources is rare; instead, nurses paraphrase to demonstrate their understanding of the source material and to convey information economically.

- The APA (American Psychological Association) system of headings and subheadings helps readers see the hierarchy of sections in a paper.

D9-f Use the APA system in writing in nursing.

Writers in nursing typically use the style guidelines of the American Psychological Association (APA) for formatting their paper, for citing sources in the text of their paper, and for listing sources at the end. The APA system is set forth in the *Publication Manual of the American Psychological Association*, 6th ed. (Washington, DC: APA, 2010). (For more details, see the APA documentation sections in your handbook.)

D9-g Sample student paper: Nursing practice paper

If you are asked to write a nursing practice paper, you will need to provide a detailed client history, a nursing diagnosis of the client's health problems, the interventions you recommend to care for the client and your rationales for those interventions, and the expected and actual outcomes for your client. The following student paper was written for a nursing course that focused on clinical experience. The writer, Julie Riss, used the style guidelines of the American Psychological Association (APA) to format her paper and to cite and list her sources.

Running head: ALL AND HTN IN ONE CLIENT

1

The header consists of a shortened title in all capital letters at the left margin and the page number at the right margin; on the title page only, the shortened title is preceded by the words "Running head" and a colon.

Acute Lymphoblastic Leukemia and Hypertension in One Client:

A Nursing Practice Paper

Julie Riss

George Mason University

Full title, writer's name, and school halfway down the page.

An author's note lists specific information about the course or department and can provide acknowledgments and contact information.

Author Note

This paper was prepared for Nursing 451, taught by Professor Durham. The author wishes to thank the nursing staff of Milltown General Hospital for help in understanding client care and diagnosis.

Marginal annotations indicate APA-style formatting and effective writing.

Full title, repeated.

Headings and subheadings, in APA style, mark the sections of the report and help readers follow the organization.

Riss begins by summarizing the client's history using information from his chart and her interview.

Riss respects the client's privacy by using only his initials in her paper.

Riss describes her detailed assessment of the client, using appropriate medical terminology.

Acute Lymphoblastic Leukemia and Hypertension in One Client:

A Nursing Practice Paper

Historical and Physical Assessment

Physical History

E.B. is a 16-year-old white male 5'10" tall weighing 190 lb. He was admitted to the hospital on April 14, 2006, due to decreased platelets and a need for a PRBC transfusion. He was diagnosed in October 2005 with T-cell acute lymphoblastic leukemia (ALL), after a 2-week period of decreased energy, decreased oral intake, easy bruising, and petechia. The client had experienced a 20-lb weight loss in the previous 6 months. At the time of diagnosis, his CBC showed a WBC count of 32, an H & H of 13/38, and a platelet count of 34,000. His initial chest X-ray showed an anterior mediastinal mass. Echocardiogram showed a structurally normal heart. He began induction chemotherapy on October 12, 2005, receiving vincristine, 6-mercaptopurine, doxorubicin, intrathecal methotrexate, and then high-dose methotrexate per protocol. He was diagnosed with hypertension (HTN) due to systolic blood pressure readings consistently ranging between 130s and 150s and was started on nifedipine. E.B. has a history of mild ADHD, migraines, and deep vein thrombosis (DVT). He has tolerated the induction and consolidation phases of chemotherapy well and is now in the maintenance phase, in which he receives a daily dose of mercaptopurine, weekly doses of methotrexate, and intermittent doses of steroids.

Psychosocial History

There is a possibility of a depressive episode a year previously when he would not attend school. He got into serious trouble and was sent to a shelter for 1 month. He currently lives with his mother, father, and 14-year-old sister.

Family History

Paternal: prostate cancer and hypertension in grandfather

Maternal: breast cancer and heart disease

Current Assessment

Client's physical exam reveals him to be alert and oriented to person, place, and time. He communicates, though not readily. His speech and vision are intact. He has an equal grip bilaterally and can move all extremities, though he is generally weak. Capillary refill is less than 2 s. His peripheral pulses are strong and equal, and he is positive for posterior tibial and dorsalis pedis bilaterally. His lungs are clear to auscultation, his respiratory rate is 16, and his oxygen saturation is 99% on room air. He has positive bowel sounds in all quadrants, and his abdomen is soft, round, and nontender. He is on a regular diet, but his appetite has been poor. Client is voiding appropriately and his urine is clear and yellow. He appears pale and is unkempt. His skin is warm, dry, and intact. He has alopecia as a result of chemotherapy. His mediport site has no redness or inflammation. He appears somber and is slow to comply with nursing instructions.

Assessment uses a neutral tone.

Medical Diagnosis #1: Acute Lymphoblastic Leukemia

Leukemia is a neoplastic disease that involves the blood-forming tissues of the bone marrow, spleen, and lymph nodes. In leukemia the ratio of red to white blood cells is reversed. There are approximately 2,500 cases of acute lymphoblastic leukemia (ALL) per year in the United States, and it is the most common type of leukemia in children—it accounts for 75%-80% of childhood leukemias. The peak age of onset is 4 years, and it affects whites more often than blacks and males more often than females. Risk factors include Down syndrome or genetic disorders; exposures to ionizing radiation and certain chemicals such as benzene; human T-cell leukemia/lymphoma virus-1; and treatment for certain cancers.

APA allows extra space above headings when it improves readability.

ALL causes an abnormal proliferation of lymphoblasts in the bone marrow, lymph nodes, and spleen. As the lymphoblasts proliferate, they suppress the other hematopoietic elements in the marrow. The leukemic cells do not function as mature cells and so do not work as they should in the immune and inflammatory processes. Because the growth of red blood cells and platelets is suppressed, the signs and symptoms of the disease are infections, bleeding, pallor, bone pain, weight loss, sore throat, fatigue, night sweats, and weakness. Treatment involves chemotherapy, bone marrow transplant, or stem cell transplant (LeMone & Burke, 2004).

Riss paraphrases the source and uses an APA-style in-text citation.

D9-g Writing in nursing

Medical Diagnosis #2: Hypertension

Primary hypertension in adolescence is a condition in which the blood pressure is persistently elevated to the 95th to 99th percentile for age, sex, and weight (Hockenberry, 2003). It must be elevated on three separate occasions for diagnosis to be made. Approximately 50 million people in the United States suffer from hypertension. It most often affects middle-aged and older adults and is more prevalent in black adults than in whites and Hispanics. In blacks the prevalence between males and females is equal, but in whites and Hispanics more males than females are affected. Risk factors include family history, age, race, mineral intake, obesity, insulin resistance, excess alcohol consumption, smoking, and stress. Hypertension results from sustained increases in blood volume and peripheral resistance. The increased blood volume causes an increase in cardiac output, which causes systemic arteries to vasoconstrict. This increased vascular resistance causes hypertension. Hypertension accelerates the rate of atherosclerosis, increasing the risk factor for heart disease and stroke. The workload of the heart is increased, causing ventricular hypertrophy, which increases risk for heart disease, dysrhythmias, and heart failure. Early hypertension usually exhibits no symptoms. The elevations in blood pressure are temporary at first but then progress to being permanent. A headache in the back of the head when awakening may be the only symptom. Other symptoms include blurred vision, nausea and vomiting, and nocturia. Treatment involves medications such as ACE inhibitors, diuretics, beta-adrenergic blockers, calcium channel blockers, and vasodilators as well as changes in diet, such as decreased sodium intake. An increase in physical activity is essential to aid in weight loss and to reduce stress (LeMone & Burke, 2004).

Chart Review

Active Orders

Vital signs q4h

Fall precautions

OOB as tolerated

Oximetry monitoring—continuous

Riss demonstrates her understanding of the medical condition.

ALL AND HTN IN ONE CLIENT · 5

CBC with manual differential daily in am

Regular diet

Weight—daily

Strict intake and output monitoring

Type and cross match

PRBCs—2 units

Platelets—1 unit

Discharge after CBC results posttransfusion shown to MD

Rationale for Orders

Vital signs are monitored every four hours per unit standard. In addition, the client's hypertension is an indication for close monitoring of blood pressure. He has generalized weakness, so fall precautions should be implemented. Though he is weak, ambulation is important, especially considering the client's history of DVT. A regular diet is ordered—I'm not sure why the client is not on a low-sodium diet, given his hypertension. Intake and output monitoring is standard on the unit. His hematological status needs to be carefully monitored due to his anemia and thrombocytopenia; therefore he has a CBC with manual differential done each morning. In addition, his hematological status is checked posttransfusion to see if the blood and platelets he receives increase his RBC and platelet counts. Transfused platelets survive in the body approximately 1-3 days, and the peak effect is achieved about 2 hr posttransfusion. Though platelets normally do not have to be cross-matched for blood group or type, children who receive multiple transfusions may become sensitized to a platelet group other than their own. Therefore, platelets are cross-matched with the donor's blood components. Blood and platelet transfusions may result in hemolytic, febrile, or allergic reactions, so the client is carefully monitored during the transfusion. Hospital protocol requires a set of baseline vital signs prior to transfusion vital signs. After the blood and platelets have been given, the physician is apprised of CBC results to be sure that the client's thrombocytopenia has resolved before he is discharged.

Riss uses specialized medical terminology.

Riss shows how physiology, prescribed treatments, and nursing practices are related.

ALL AND HTN IN ONE CLIENT   6

Pharmacological Interventions and Goals

Medications and Effects

ondansetron hydrochloride (Zofran) 8 mg PO PRN	serotonin receptor antagonist, antiemetic—prevention of nausea and vomiting associated with chemotherapy
famotidine (Pepcid) 10 mg PO ac	H2 receptor antagonist, antiulcer agent—prevention of heartburn
nifedipine (Procardia) 30 mg PO bid	calcium channel blocker, antihypertensive—prevention of hypertension
enoxaparin sodium (Lovenox) 60 mg SQ bid	low-molecular-weight heparin derivative, anticoagulant—prevention of DVT
mercaptopurine (Purinethol) 100 mg PO qhs	antimetabolite, antineoplastic— treatment of ALL
PRBCs—2 units leukoreduced, irradiated[a]	to increase RBC count
platelets—1 unit[a]	to treat thrombocytopenia

[a]Because these products are dispensed by pharmacy, they are considered a pharmacological intervention, even though technically not medications.

Laboratory Tests and Significance

Complete Blood Count (CBC)[a]

Result name	Result	Abnormal	Normal range
WBC	3.0	*	4.5-13.0
RBC	3.73	*	4.20-5.40
Hgb	11.5		11.1-15.7
Hct	32.4	*	34.0-46.0
MCV	86.8		78.0-95.0
MCH	30.7		26.0-32.0
MCHC	35.4		32.0-36.0
RDW	14.6		11.5-15.5
Platelet	98	*	140-400
MPV	8.3		7.4-10.4

[a]*Rationale:* Client's ALL diagnosis and treatment necessitate frequent monitoring of his hematological status. WBC count, RBC, and hematocrit are decreased due to chemotherapy. The platelet count is low.

Margin notes:

Short tables, like those in this paper, are placed within the text. A longer table can be placed on a separate page.

Riss presents data in several tables for easy reference.

ALL AND HTN IN ONE CLIENT   7

Type and Cross-Match[a]

Result name	Result
ABORH	APOS
ANTIBODY SCR INTERP	NEGATIVE

[a]*Rationale:* To determine client's blood type and to screen for antibodies.

Vital Signs Before, During, and After Blood Transfusion[a]

Vital signs	Time	BP	Pulse	Resp	Temp (oral)
Pre	1705	113/74	92	18	98.7
15 min	1720	118/74	104	12	98.3
30 min	1735	121/74	96	16	99.3
45 min	1750	129/76	101	16	99.3
Post	1805	108/59	99	15	98.9

[a]*Rationale:* To monitor for reaction.

Nursing Diagnosis #1:
Injury, Risk for, Related to Decreased Platelet
Count and Administration of Lovenox

Desired Outcome: Client will remain free of injury.

Interventions

Monitor vital signs q4h

Assess for manifestations of bleeding such as

- Skin and mucous membranes for petechiae, ecchymoses, and hematoma formation
- Gums and nasal membranes for bleeding
- Overt or occult blood in stool or urine
- Neurologic changes

Provide sponge to clean gums and teeth

Apply pressure to puncture sites for 3-5 min

Avoid invasive procedures when possible

Administer stool softeners as prescribed

Implement fall precautions

Monitor lab values for platelets

Administer platelets as prescribed

Measurable Outcomes

Mediport site will remain intact with no signs of bleeding.

Riss prioritizes her diagnoses and recommended interventions and gives a detailed description and rationales for each.

ALL AND HTN IN ONE CLIENT   8

Urine and stool will remain free of blood.

Lab values for anticoagulant therapy will remain in desired range.

Platelet count will remain in normal range.

Client Teaching

Instruct client to avoid forcefully blowing nose, straining to have a bowel
movement, and forceful coughing or sneezing, all of which increase
the risk for external and internal bleeding

Discharge Planning

Instruct client to monitor for signs of decreased platelet count such as easy
bruising, petechiae, or inappropriate bleeding

Nursing Diagnosis #2:

Infection, Risk for, Related to Depressed Body Defenses

Desired Outcome: Client will remain free of infection.

Interventions

Screen all visitors and staff for signs of infection to minimize exposure to
infectious agents

Use aseptic technique for all procedures

Monitor temperature to detect possible infection

Evaluate client for potential sites of infection: needle punctures, mucosal
ulcerations

Provide nutritionally complete meals to support the body's natural
defenses

Monitor lab values for CBC

Administer G-CSF if prescribed

Measurable Outcomes

Mediport site will remain free of erythema, purulent drainage, odor, and
edema.

Client will remain afebrile.

Client Teaching

Instruct client and caregivers in correct hand-washing technique

Discharge Planning

Instruct client and caregivers to avoid live attenuated virus
vaccines

Instruct client to avoid large crowds

*Riss uses specific
examples.*

ALL AND HTN IN ONE CLIENT   9

Nursing Diagnosis #3:
Noncompliance, Related to HTN, as Evidenced by Lack of
Consistent Medication Regimen and Adherence to Dietary Plan

Desired Outcome: Client will follow treatment plan.

Interventions

Inquire about reasons for noncompliance

Listen openly and without judgment

Evaluate knowledge of HTN, its long-term effects, and treatment

Arrange for nutritional consult with dietitian

Measurable Outcomes

Client will take medication as prescribed.

Client's systolic blood pressure will remain in normal range.

Client Teaching

Instruct on medication regimen: appropriate administration and potential
     adverse effects

Provide information on hypertension and its treatment

Discharge Planning

Provide prescriptions

Nursing Diagnosis #4:
Health Maintenance, Ineffective, Related to
Unhealthy Lifestyle and Behaviors

Desired Outcome: Client will make changes in lifestyle.

Interventions

Assist in identifying behaviors that contribute to hypertension

Assist in developing a realistic health maintenance plan including modifying
     risk factors such as exercise, diet, and stress

Help client and family identify strengths and weaknesses in maintaining
     health

Measurable Outcomes

Client will verbalize ways to control his hypertension.

Client will identify methods to relieve stress.

Discharge Planning

Provide information on possible exercise programs

D9-g Writing in nursing

Analysis

Riss summarizes the client's conditions, treatments, and consequences for nursing and discusses client education in psychological and social contexts.

In the case of E.B., there are two separate disease processes at work—ALL and HTN. The ALL is the most immediately pressing of the two and is indirectly responsible for the client's current hospitalization. The chemotherapy treatment for his leukemia has caused thrombocytopenia. This condition places him at high risk for hemorrhage. The anticoagulant therapy for DVT increases this risk even further, not only because it may cause bleeding complications, but because in itself it may cause thrombocytopenia. Therefore, it is imperative to raise his platelet count as quickly as possible. Surprisingly, there were no lab tests ordered to determine his PT and INR, both of which are monitored when a client is on anticoagulant therapy. As his CBC demonstrates, not only is his platelet count low, but his red blood cells are decreased. That is why his physician ordered a transfusion of both PRBCs and platelets.

In terms of E.B.'s diagnosis of HTN, he has a positive family history, which is a major risk factor for developing the disease. Excess weight is also a risk factor, and the client has a history of obesity as well. Because exercise is an important factor in managing the excess weight and stress associated with the disease, his leukemia and the chemotherapy treatments aimed at curing E.B.'s leukemia actually negatively affect his ability to manage the hypertension: He is often too weak and fatigued to participate in much physical activity. Additionally, the steroids have resulted in added weight gain, increasing instead of decreasing the problem. To date, the client has failed to maintain a favorable diet regimen.

E.B.'s family circumstances must be taken into consideration when managing his treatment. Though he resides with both parents, there is some question as to the support and consistency of care he receives. He often appears very unkempt and is at times noncompliant with his hypertension medication. Due to his parents' inability to care for a central venous line (CVL) at home, he has a mediport that can be accessed as needed but requires care. On a positive note, the father is aware of their limitations and tries to work with the staff to make sure that E.B.'s ALL is managed appropriately.

ALL AND HTN IN ONE CLIENT   11

References

Hockenberry, M. (2003). *Wong's nursing care of infants and children.*

St. Louis, MO: Mosby.

LeMone, P., & Burke, K. (2004). *Medical surgical nursing: Critical thinking in*

client care. Upper Saddle River, NJ: Pearson Education.

Riss provides a reference list for sources she cited in her paper. The list is formatted in APA style.

D10 Writing in psychology

Psychologists write with various purposes in mind. They frequently publish articles about their research or present their work at professional conferences. They write proposals to convince funding agencies to award grants for their research. Sometimes psychologists write to influence the opinions held by the public or by decision makers in government, lending their expertise to discussions on issues such as the effects of racism, the challenges of aging, or children's mental health. Psychologists may write analyses for newspaper and magazine opinion pages as well as policy recommendations and advocacy statements.

D10-a Determine your audience and their needs in psychology.

Psychologists write for researchers, psychotherapists, teachers, students, clients, and sometimes members of the government or business community and the general public. Researchers or clinical psychologists may read to find out the results of an experiment, the analysis of new data, or information supporting or critiquing a theory. This information may be useful to readers in developing new research projects or providing services to their clients. Students read to learn about major concepts in the field. Researchers, teachers, and students expect data and findings to be communicated thoroughly in words and in graphics such as diagrams, tables, charts, and graphs. People working in government or academic settings may need information and support for decisions about funding proposed research projects.

In all cases, your readers will expect your writing to be completely objective and to present information as clearly as possible. When you are writing in psychology, you should make thorough use of others' research in the field to demonstrate your credibility. Readers are interested more in empirical data that can be presented quantitatively than in statements from experts. Qualitative information in the form of direct observations and statements from research subjects can help readers understand your conclusions or recommendations.

Your readers will appreciate your precise use of words and a scientific stance with an objective tone. When writing for clients of psychiatric or psychotherapy services, use straightforward language that respects the clients and their right to understand their conditions and needs. Such clients will also expect confidentiality and respect for diversity.

D10-b Recognize the forms of writing in psychology.

When you take courses in psychology, you may be asked to write any of the following:

- literature reviews
- research papers
- theoretical papers
- poster presentations

Literature reviews

You will likely write review papers early in your course work. In a review paper, you report on and evaluate the research that has been published in the field about a particular topic. A literature review does not merely summarize researchers' findings but argues a position with evidence that you assemble from the empirical (that is, experiment-based) studies that you review.

Sometimes a literature review stands alone as a paper, such as a survey of findings from research performed in the past century on what causes loss of memory in old age. In some cases, you will be asked to write a critical review, in which you will analyze the methods and interpretations of data in one or more journal articles. More often you will write a literature review as an introduction to a larger piece of writing, such as a report of your own empirical study. In that case, the literature review surveys previously published findings relevant to the question that your study investigates.

Research papers

When instructors refer to *research papers*, they may have different assignments in mind. A research paper might present your synthesis of many sources of information about, say, emotional responses to music. Your purpose would be to demonstrate your understanding of research findings and the ongoing debates emerging from researchers' investigations.

A research paper might also be a report on the results of an experiment you've conducted and on your interpretation of those results; in this case, your research paper would be an empirical study. A research paper might also relate your interpretations to what others in the field have concluded from their own experiments. Like other scientists, psychologists publish research papers in journals after the papers have undergone rigorous and impartial review by other psychologists (called *peer review*) to make sure that the scientific process used by the researchers is sound.

Whether published in a journal or written for a college course, research papers based on original experiments have the following standard elements:

- the question you set out to research and why your question is important
- a review of research relevant to your question
- your hypotheses (tentative, plausible answers to the research question that your experiment will test) and your predictions that follow from the hypotheses
- the method you used to conduct your experiment
- the results from the experiment
- your analysis of those results

Writers of research reports also use tables and figures to present experimental data in easy-to-grasp visual form.

Theoretical papers

Psychologists often write theoretical papers in which they propose their own theories or extend existing theories about a research problem in the field. For example, in one journal article, a psychologist argues that the field needs to combine attachment theory and social network theory to understand child and adolescent development.

If you are asked to write a theoretical paper for a course, you will be expected to support the theory you propose by pointing to evidence and counterevidence from the literature in the field, to compare your theory with other theories, and possibly to suggest experiments that could test your theory.

Poster presentations

At professional gatherings such as annual conventions, psychologists have the opportunity to present their work in the form of a poster rather than as a formal talk. Conference attendees approach presenters in an exhibit area to talk about the presenters' research, which the posters concisely summarize. A poster typically features an introduction to the project, the method, information about the research or the subjects of an experiment, the results, and the presenter's conclusions.

Poster presentations also feature graphs and tables since it is important to convey information to conference attendees quickly and concisely as they walk through the exhibit area. An effective poster presentation will encourage the audience to ask questions and carry on an informal conversation with the presenter.

Your instructor may ask you to create a poster presentation about an experiment you or other researchers have conducted both to help you understand complex concepts and to practice your communication skills.

NOTE: Some presenters use presentation software to create a slide show that they can click through for a small audience or project on a screen for a larger group. Presenters generally include the same kinds of information in slide presentations as they do in poster presentations.

D10-c Know the questions psychologists ask.

Psychologists generally investigate human behavior and perceptions. Their questions range widely across the different specializations that make up the field, such as animal cognition, personality, social interactions, and infant development, to name a few. The following are questions that specialists in psychology might ask.

- What personality characteristics might affect employees' personal use of work computers?
- When adult learners return to school, what is the impact on their families and working lives?
- Do variations in cerebral blood flow in different areas of the brain predict variations in performance of different imagery tasks?

D10-d Understand the kinds of evidence psychologists use.

To back up their conclusions, psychologists look for evidence in case studies and the results of experiments. They do not use expert opinion as evidence; direct quotations of what other psychologists have written are rare in psychology papers. Instead, papers focus on data (the results of experiments) and on the analysis of the results that the writer has collected.

Depending on their specialization, psychologists may ask questions that require quantitative or qualitative evidence. Quantitative evidence involves numerical measurement; qualitative evidence involves examples and illustrations.

- Quantitative evidence might be facts and statistics: *Regional cerebral blood flow in a total of 26 areas predicted performance, and 20 of these areas predicted performance only in a single task. In a study on what motivates adolescents to quit smoking, 44.7% of the participants reported that they wanted to quit because their parents wanted them to.* Or it might be results of original experiments: *Fraudulent excuse scores were correlated with cheating scores (r = .37, n = 211, p < .0001).*

- Qualitative evidence might be descriptions of interviews or statements of the researcher's observations: *Many of the respondents believed that girls' tendency either to address indirectly or to avoid conflict was supported by adults, who expected them to be* ladylike; *when asked to define this term, they used such descriptors as "mature" and "calm."*

D10-e Become familiar with writing conventions in psychology.

Psychologists use straightforward and concise language and depend on special terms to explain their findings.

- Specialized vocabulary may include terms such as *methods, results, double-blind study, social identity perspective,* and *nonverbal emotions.*

- Often researchers use specific, technical definitions of terms that nonspecialists use differently. For example, if a psychologist asks whether adults with eating disorders are "depressed," the term refers to a specific mental disorder, not to a general mood of sadness.

- When reporting conclusions, writers in psychology use the past tense (*Berkowitz found*) or the present perfect tense (*Berkowitz has found*). When discussing results, they use the present tense (*The results confirm*). They avoid using subjective expressions like *I think* and *I feel.*

D10-f Use the APA system in writing in psychology.

Writers in psychology typically use the style guidelines of the American Psychological Association (APA) for formatting their papers, for citing sources in the text of their papers, and for listing sources at the end. The APA system is set forth in the *Publication Manual of the American Psychological Association*, 6th ed. (Washington, DC: APA, 2010). (For more details, see the APA documentation sections in your handbook.)

D10-g Sample student paper: Literature review (excerpt)

A psychology literature review assignment usually asks you both to survey published research on a topic in the field and to argue your own position with evidence that you assemble from your survey. The student paper excerpted beginning on the next page was written for a second-year developmental psychology course. The student, Valerie Charat, used the style guidelines of the American Psychological Association (APA) to format her paper and to cite and list her sources.

The header consists of a shortened title in all capital letters at the left margin and the page number at the right margin; on the title page only, the shortened title is preceded by the words "Running head" and a colon.

Running head: ADHD IN BOYS VS. GIRLS   1

Full title, writer's name, and school halfway down the page.

Always out of Their Seats (and Fighting):
Why Are Boys Diagnosed With ADHD More Often Than Girls?
Valerie Charat
Harvard University

An author's note lists specific information about the course or department and can provide acknowledgments and contact information.

Author Note
This paper was prepared for Psychology 1806, taught by Professor Korfine.

Marginal annotations indicate APA-style formatting and effective writing.

ADHD IN BOYS VS. GIRLS   2

Abstract

Until the early 1990s, most research on attention deficit hyperactivity disorder (ADHD) focused on boys and did not explore possible gender differences. Recent studies have suggested that gender differences do exist and are caused by personality differences between boys and girls, by gender bias in referring teachers and clinicians, or by the diagnostic procedures themselves. But the most likely reason is that ADHD is often comorbid—that is, it coexists with other behavior disorders that are not diagnosed properly and that do exhibit gender differences. This paper first considers studies of gender differences only in ADHD and then looks at studies of gender differences when ADHD occurs with comorbid disorders. Future research must focus more specifically on how gender differences are influenced by factors such as referrals, family history, and comorbid conditions.

Keywords: ADHD, hyperactivity, attention deficit, gender differences, comorbid conditions

Abstract, a 100-to-150-word overview of the paper, appears on a separate page.

D10-g Writing in psychology

Always out of Their Seats (and Fighting):

Why Are Boys Diagnosed With ADHD More Often Than Girls?

Attention deficit hyperactivity disorder (ADHD) is a commonly diagnosed disorder in children that affects social, academic, or occupational functioning. As the name suggests, its hallmark characteristics are hyperactivity and lack of attention as well as impulsive behavior. For decades, studies have focused on the causes, expression, prevalence, and outcome of the disorder, but until recently very little research investigated gender differences. In fact, until the early 1990s most research focused exclusively on boys (Brown, Madan-Swain, & Baldwin, 1991), perhaps because many more boys than girls are diagnosed with ADHD. Researchers have speculated on the possible explanations for the disparity, citing reasons such as true sex differences in the manifestation of the disorder's symptoms, gender biases in those who refer children to clinicians, and possibly even the diagnostic procedures themselves (Gaub & Carlson, 1997). But the most persuasive reason is that ADHD is often a comorbid condition—that is, it coexists with other behavior disorders that are not diagnosed properly and that do exhibit gender differences.

It has been suggested that in the United States children are often misdiagnosed as having ADHD when they actually suffer from a behavior disorder such as conduct disorder (CD) or a combination of ADHD and another behavior disorder (Disney, Elkins, McGue, & Iancono, 1999; Lilienfeld & Waldman, 1990). Conduct disorder is characterized by negative and criminal behavior in children and is highly correlated with adult diagnoses of antisocial personality disorder (ASPD). This paper first considers research that has dealt only with gender difference in the occurrence of ADHD and then looks at research that has studied the condition along with other behavior disorders.

Gender Differences in Studies of ADHD

Most of the research on ADHD has lacked a comparative component. Throughout the 1970s and 1980s, most research focused only on boys. If girls were included, it was often in such low numbers that gender-based comparisons were unwarranted (Gaub & Carlson, 1997). One of the least debated differences is the dissimilarity in male and female prevalence

---

Full title, repeated.

Charat gives abbreviations in parentheses the first time she uses common psychology terms.

Introduction provides background to the topic and establishes why a literature review on ADHD is necessary.

Thesis states what Charat will argue by describing and analyzing the sources she has reviewed.

Charat uses APA style to cite her sources. Two sources in one parenthetical citation are separated with a semicolon.

Headings, centered, divide the paper into two main sections.

ADHD IN BOYS VS. GIRLS   4

rates. Some studies have claimed a 3:1 ratio of boys with ADHD to girls
with ADHD (American Psychiatric Association, 1987), while others have
cited ratios as high as 9:1 (Brown et al., 1991). The differences in
prevalence have been attributed to a variety of causes, one of which is
that girls may have more internalized symptoms and may be overlooked in
ADHD diagnoses (Brown et al., 1991).

> Charat summarizes key research findings about the paper's central question.

    A study conducted by Breen (1989) sought to test the differences
in cognition, behavior, and academic functioning for boys and girls. Past
research had indicated that boys with ADHD showed more aggressive
behavior while girls showed more learning problems, but the results were
often conflicting. To clarify the existing information, Breen conducted a
study on 39 children aged 6 to 11, from a group of children referred to a
pediatric psychology clinic. All subjects were white, with varying
socioeconomic status. He broke the subjects into three groups: boys with
ADHD, girls with ADHD, and a control group of girls without any psychiatric
or family history of behavioral or emotional problems. Each group was
given a battery of tests to assess cognitive functioning. All children were
also observed in a playroom while they worked math problems, and all were
coded for a variety of behaviors including fidgeting, vocalizing, being out
of their seats, and so on.

> A signal phrase names the author and gives the date of the source in parentheses.

> Charat examines an important study in detail. She summarizes experimental methods used by researchers.

    The results showed that while both groups with ADHD performed
nearly equally across most measures, ADHD boys were generally viewed as
more deviant than normal girls. Girls with ADHD were closer behaviorally to
girls in the control group than to ADHD boys. This finding indicates that it
may be difficult to distinguish girls with ADHD from girls without the
disorder based solely on behavior. This conclusion was corroborated by the
later finding (Brown et al., 1991) that girls with ADHD are often not
clinically referred unless they demonstrate a more severe form of the
disorder than boys do. A contradictory finding (Breen, 1989) was that
ADHD boys and girls displayed rates of disruptive behavior that were not
significantly different from each other, although Breen did not indicate
what forms the disruptive behavior took and whether the girls were less
aggressive than the boys. But as Brown et al. (1991) later pointed out, it
was easier to differentiate ADHD in externalized behaviors—aggression,
inattention, and overactivity—than in internalized behaviors—depression,

> Charat uses the specialized language of the field.

> Source first mentioned on page 3. In subsequent citations, for a source with three to five authors "et al." is used after the first author's name in the text and in parentheses.

D10-g

anxiety, and withdrawal. It is striking, however, that the distinction in Breen's study was clearer not between boys and girls but between girls with and girls without ADHD. Breen concluded that differences between boys and girls with the disorder do not seem significant.

A few drawbacks to Breen's study include a lack of screening for comorbid conduct disorders, which were no doubt present in some of the subjects. The small sample size could have hindered the results, with only 13 subjects in each group. Another limitation is the small cross section: All subjects were white and clinically referred. Therefore, the findings cannot be generalized to a nonclinical, racially diverse population. Finally, the lack of male controls is surprising, given the usual trend to overrepresent boys when studying ADHD. A reasonable comparison would have been between girls with ADHD and boys in a control group to see if the girls' range of antisocial behavior was beyond that of control boys.

Another study (Maughan, Pickles, Hagell, Rutter, & Yule, 1996) investigated the association between reading problems and antisocial behavior. The researchers cited a connection that had previously been made (Hinshaw, 1992, as cited in Maughan et al., 1996) between antisocial behavior and underachievement in early childhood, while aggression and antisocial behavior became salient in later years. Maughan et al. looked specifically at reading because research has shown that children who develop reading problems have higher rates of behavioral problems even before they learn to read (Jorm, Share, Matthews, & Mclean, 1986). It had also been shown that reading problems can affect behavioral development (Pianta & Caldwell, 1992, as cited in Maughan et al., 1996). However, since most studies had been done with boys, the researchers also compared gender differences.

Subjects were selected from a previously conducted study in a population of children who were 10 years old in 1970. The majority were British-born Caucasians of low socioeconomic status. The analysis used two subsamples, one with poor reading scores, the other a randomly sampled control group with average IQ and no reading difficulties. Poor readers were rated as either "backward" or "retarded." The subjects in the backward group were 28 months below average in reading level for their age and IQ. At age 10, children had received psychometric testing, and the study

---

Margin notes:

Charat analyzes the study's shortcomings.

Topic sentence states paragraph's main point.

An indirect source (work quoted in another source) is indicated with the words "as cited in."

An ampersand separates the authors' names in parentheses.

Charat describes the study's methods in detail.

ADHD IN BOYS VS. GIRLS   6

accounted for parental occupation, the child's government benefits status,
and the ranking of the child's state school in terms of economic adversity.
There were follow-ups at ages 14, 17, and early 20s.

Poor readers demonstrated high rates of behavior problems by age 10.
About 40% of the girls and almost 50% of the boys in the retarded reading
group exhibited antisocial behavior at age 10. Interestingly, reading-
retarded girls showed high rates of conduct problems, while the boys did
not. Also, among girls there were much higher rates of antisocial behavior
in the lowest socioeconomic category than in slightly higher socioeconomic
categories. In boys, the differences were not as pronounced. For boys, poor
performance in school was the only predictor of antisocial behavior, while
for girls poor school performance and reading level were predictors.
This finding suggests that for boys, learning difficulties do not increase
the risk of behavior problems, while for girls they do. Inattentiveness and
overactivity were also related to reading problems and were highly related
to antisocial behavior. When inattentiveness and overactivity were factored
in, there were no direct links between reading difficulties and antisocial
behavior. This absent connection means that reading problems do not
cause antisocial behavior. It is when they cannot pay attention or sit long
enough to read that both boys and girls exhibit elevated rates of antisocial
behavior.

By age 14, girls still showed a significant correlation between
reading problems and antisocial behavior, while boys showed no
association. In early adulthood (ages 17 and early 20s), criminality, alcohol
problems, aggression, and personality disorders were found in low rates
in girls. In the sample of girls interviewed in their 20s, 1.9% had juvenile
offense records and 5.4% had records of adult crime. In boys, poor readers
did not show any significant rates of antisocial personality disorders.

The study had several drawbacks. Subject responses at follow-up
periods were not uniformly gathered, and the lack of analysis of female
juvenile offenders made it harder to understand the results in terms of
gender differences and antisocial behavior. The sample consisted only of
inner-city children of low socioeconomic status because they had higher
rates of reading difficulty than other children. But because economic
adversity was found to be a predictor for poor conduct in girls, this group

In APA style,
the numbers
10 and above
are expressed
in numerals;
percentages are
expressed in
numbers with a
percent symbol.

After presenting
the study's findings,
Charat analyzes the
study's weaknesses.

ADHD IN BOYS VS. GIRLS   7

of subjects may have contained a disproportionate number of female
subjects with more severe antisocial behavior.

Charat speculates
on possible
explanations for the
results of the study.

    Of particular interest was that for girls but not for boys, reading
level and low socioeconomic status predicted antisocial behavior. However,
when the children were followed into adulthood, the females who had
originally displayed antisocial behavior did not show elevated rates of
juvenile offenses or adult crime. Perhaps the results indicate that girls
with antisocial and hyperactive behavior in childhood are different from
boys in that they are responding to passing learning impairments rather
than permanent personality problems. Or girls may have continued to have
ADHD, but with internalized rather than externalized symptoms. Another
possibility is that the girls had more severe forms of ADHD because of
sampling bias for socioeconomic status but that they eventually grew out
of the disorder in adolescence while the boys did not.

    Another study (Brown et al., 1991) looked specifically at the
cognitive and academic performance of children with ADHD and compared
internalizing versus externalizing features of the disorder across genders.
As in Breen (1989), Brown et al. (1991) found there were few gender
differences on measures of attention, concentration, and distractibility.
However, some significant differences were found. Parent and teacher
ratings of internalizing and externalizing characteristics described
boys as more aggressive and girls as more unpopular. Girls were also
more commonly held back one or two grades, a finding the researchers
interpreted as evidence of female academic difficulties and possible
neurological disorders or impairments. This would correlate with the
findings of Maughan et al. (1996) of an association between reading
impairment and antisocial behaviors in ADHD girls. However, the data must

If a source is cited
in the text of the
paragraph, only
the authors' names
are given when the
source is cited later
in the text of the
same paragraph.
(The date is required
in all parenthetical
citations.)

also be regarded cautiously. Brown et al. did not use a control group and
thus did not have a standard by which to measure the differences. Any
implication of a neurological impairment in females with ADHD should be
viewed skeptically. The historical perception of women as the weaker or
more defective sex should make any researcher reluctant to postulate . . .

**[Charat continues to describe and analyze researchers' studies and
findings.]**

ADHD IN BOYS VS. GIRLS   11

Conclusion

Although the studies presented here are filled with flaws and contradictory findings, they have a unifying thread. Through direct findings or indirect lack of information, all suggest that the higher rate of male diagnoses of ADHD does not necessarily mean that the disorder actually occurs in boys more often than in girls. Although boys are more commonly diagnosed, this phenomenon could reflect a long-standing history of misperceptions. Since hyperactive and inattentive boys are also often aggressive and disruptive, girls who do not demonstrate similar behaviors may be overlooked.

It is important to reevaluate the way boys and girls are observed and understood when attention and hyperactivity are being assessed. Males and females may display different behaviors, and parents and teachers may interpret their behaviors differently. But when rated by trained researchers, boys and girls identified as having ADHD are rated similarly. However, it is easier to identify externalizing, aggressive behavior than it is to identify internalizing behavior, and this difference may be one of the main factors at the root of the perceived gender differences in the prevalence of ADHD. There is not enough concrete evidence to rule out the possibility that a gender difference does exist, regardless of the fact that boys and girls seem to show equal rates and degrees of symptoms. Until more studies look at population samples, exclude conduct disorders, and take into account possible differences in the ways the symptoms are manifested, it is impossible to conclude that gender differences are the result of social and clinical biases and stereotypes. Further research on genetics and familial rates of the disorder are also necessary to help clarify the relationship between adult antisocial personality disorder and ADHD. Also, until a clear distinction is made between conduct disorder and ADHD, not only in the text of the *DSM-IV* but also in the minds of laypeople and clinicians, it will be difficult to separate children with comorbid disorder and those without it and to assess gender differences as well.

Conclusion presents a synthesis of the paper's points.

Charat raises questions about the research she reviews but adopts a balanced tone in summarizing the sources.

Charat suggests areas for future research.

Conclusion affirms the necessity of continuing investigation.

ADHD IN BOYS VS. GIRLS   12

References

American Psychiatric Association. (1987). *Diagnostic and statistical manual of mental disorders* (3rd ed., rev.). Washington, DC: Author.

American Psychiatric Association. (1994). *Diagnostic and statistical manual of mental disorders* (4th ed.). Washington, DC: Author.

Breen, M. J. (1989). Cognitive and behavioral differences in AdHD boys and girls. *Journal of Child Psychology and Psychiatry, 30,* 711-716. doi:10.1111/j.1469-7610.1989.tb00783.x

Breen, M. J., & Altepeter, T. S. (1990). Situational variability in boys and girls identified as ADHD. *Journal of Clinical Psychology, 46,* 486-490.

Brown, R. T., Madan-Swain, A., & Baldwin, K. (1991). Gender differences in a clinic-referred sample of attention-deficit-disordered children. *Child Psychiatry and Human Development, 22,* 111-127.

Disney, E. R., Elkins, J. J., McGue, M., & Iancono, W. G. (1999). Effects of ADHD, conduct disorder, and gender on substance use and abuse in adolescence. *American Journal of Psychiatry, 156,* 1515-1521.

Faraone, S. V., Biederman, J., Chen, W. J., Milberger, S., Warburton, R., & Tsuang, M. T. (1995). Genetic heterogeneity in attention-deficit hyperactivity disorder (ADHD): Gender, psychiatric comorbidity, and maternal ADHD. *Journal of Abnormal Psychology, 104,* 334-345.

Gaub, M., & Carlson, C. L. (1997). Gender differences in ADHD: A meta-analysis and critical review. *Journal of the American Academy of Child and Adolescent Psychiatry, 36,* 1036-1045.

Jorm, A. F., Share, D. L., Matthews, R., & Mclean, R. (1986). Behaviour problems in specific reading retarded and general reading backward children: A longitudinal study. *Journal of Child Psychology and Psychiatry, 27,* 33-43. doi:10.1111/j.1469-7610.1986.tb00619.x

Lahey, B. B., Piacentini, J. C., McBurnett, K., Stone, P., Hartdagen, S., & Hynd, G. (1988). Psychopathology in the parents of children with conduct disorder and hyperactivity. *Journal of the American Academy of Child and Adolescent Psychiatry, 27,* 163-170.

Lilienfeld, S. O., & Waldman, I. D. (1990). The relation between childhood attention-deficit hyperactivity disorder and adult antisocial behavior reexamined: The problem of heterogeneity. *Clinical Psychology Review, 10,* 699-725.

List of references begins on a new page. The first line of an entry is at the left margin; subsequent lines indent ½".

If an online source has a DOI (digital object identifier), no URL is given.

A work with up to seven authors lists all authors' names. A work with more than seven authors lists the first six followed by three ellipsis dots and the last author's name.

List is alphabetized by authors' last names. All authors' names are inverted; an ampersand separates the last two authors.

ADHD IN BOYS VS. GIRLS   13

Maughan, B., Pickles, A., Hagell, A., Rutter, M., & Yule, W. (1996).
    Reading problems and antisocial behavior: Developmental trends in
    comorbidity. *Journal of Child Psychology and Psychiatry, 37,* 405-418.
    doi:10.1111/j.1469-7610.1996.tb01421.x

Oltmanns, T. F., & Emery, R. E. (1998). Psychological disorders of
    childhood. In *Abnormal psychology* (2nd ed., pp. 572-607). Upper
    Saddle River, NJ: Prentice Hall.

Sprock, J., Blashfield, R. K., & Smith, B. (1990). Gender weighting of
    DSM-III-R personality disorder criteria. *American Journal of
    Psychiatry, 147,* 586-590.

Index

This is the index for Tab D only. For the handbook's main index, see the I (Index) tab.

This is the index for Tab D only. For the
handbook's main index, see the I (Index) tab.

This is the index for Tab D only. For the handbook's main index, see the I (Index) tab.

This is the index for Tab D only. For the
handbook's main index, see the I (Index) tab.

This is the index for Tab D only. For the
handbook's main index, see the I (Index) tab.

Revision Symbols

Letter-number codes refer to sections of this book.

abbr	faulty abbreviation **P9**		p	error in punctuation
adj	misuse of adjective **G4**		ʌ	comma **P1**
add	add needed word **S2**		no ,	no comma **P2**
adv	misuse of adverb **G4**		;	semicolon **P3**
agr	faulty agreement **G1, G3-a**		:	colon **P3**
appr	inappropriate language **W4**		ʋ	apostrophe **P4**
art	article **M2**		" "	quotation marks **P5**
awk	awkward		. ?	period, question mark **P6**
cap	capital letter **P8**		!	exclamation point **P6**
case	error in case **G3-c, G3-d**		— ( )	dash, parentheses **P6**
cliché	cliché **W5-e**		[ ] . . .	brackets, ellipsis mark **P6**
coh	coherence **C5-d**		/	slash **P6**
coord	faulty coordination **S6-c**		pass	ineffective passive **W3**
cs	comma splice **G6**		pn agr	pronoun agreement **G3-a**
dev	inadequate development **C5-b**		proof	proofreading problem **C3-d**
dm	dangling modifier **S3-e**		ref	error in pronoun reference **G3-b**
-ed	error in -*ed* ending **G2-d**		run-on	run-on sentence **G6**
emph	emphasis **S6**		-s	error in -*s* ending **G2-c**
ESL	ESL grammar **M1, M2, M3, M4, M5**		sexist	sexist language **W4-f**
exact	inexact language **W5**		shift	distracting shift **S4**
frag	sentence fragment **G5**		sl	slang **W4-d**
fs	fused sentence **G6**		sp	misspelled word **P7**
gl/us	see glossary of usage **W1**		sub	faulty subordination **S6-d**
hyph	error in use of hyphen **P7**		sv agr	subject-verb agreement **G1, G2-c**
idiom	idiom **W5-d**		t	error in verb tense **G2-f**
inc	incomplete construction **S2**		trans	transition needed **C5-d**
irreg	error in irregular verb **G2-a**		usage	see glossary of usage **W1**
ital	italics **P10**		v	voice **W3**
jarg	jargon **W4-a**		var	sentence variety **S6-b, S6-c, S7**
lc	lowercase letter **P8**		vb	verb error **G2**
mix	mixed construction **S5**		w	wordy **W2**
mm	misplaced modifier **S3-b**		//	faulty parallelism **S1**
mood	error in mood **G2-g**		^	insert
nonst	nonstandard usage **W4-c**		×	obvious error
num	error in use of number **P9**		#	insert space
om	omitted word **S2**		⌣	close up space
¶	new paragraph **C5**			

Detailed Menu